Group Processes

FRONTIERS OF SOCIAL PSYCHOLOGY

Series Editors:
Arie W. Kruglanski, *University of Maryland at College Park*
Joseph P. Forgas, *University of New South Wales*

Frontiers of Social Psychology is a series of domain-specific handbooks. Each volume provides readers with an overview of the most recent theoretical, methodological, and practical developments in a substantive area of social psychology, in greater depth than is possible in general social psychology handbooks. The editors and contributors are all internationally renowned scholars whose work is at the cutting edge of research.

Scholarly, yet accessible, the volumes in the *Frontiers* series are an essential resource for senior undergraduates, postgraduates, researchers, and practitioners and are suitable as texts in advanced courses in specific subareas of social psychology.

Published Titles

Forthcoming Titles

For continually updated information about published and forthcoming titles in the Frontiers of Social Psychology series, please visit:
www.psypress.com/frontiers

Group Processes

Edited by

John M. Levine

LONDON AND NEW YORK

First published 2013 by Routledge part of the Taylor and Francis Group

2 Park Square, Milton Park, Abingdon, Oxon OX14 4RN
711 Third Avenue, New York, NY 10017, USA

Routledge is an imprint of the Taylor & Francis Group, an informa business

First issued in paperback 2017

Library of Congress Cataloging in Publication Data
Group processes / edited by John M. Levine
p. cm. — (Frontiers of social psychology ; 18)
1. Social groups. 2. Group identity. 3. Intergroup relations. I. Levine, John M.
HM716.G762 2012
305—dc23
2012005623

ISBN: 978-1-84872-872-1 (hbk)
ISBN: 978-1-138-10909-4 (pbk)

Typeset in New Caledonia
by EvS Communication Networx, Inc.

To Vernon L. Allen

whose love of social psychology

remains an inspiration

Contents

About the Editor

John M. Levine received his PhD in Psychology from the University of Wisconsin. He is Professor of Psychology and Senior Scientist at the Learning Research and Development Center at the University of Pittsburgh. Dr. Levine has served as Associate Editor of the *Journal of Research in Personality*, both Associate Editor and Editor of the *Journal of Experimental Social Psychology*, and Executive Committe Chair of the Society of Experimental Social Psychology. He is a Fellow of several professional societies, including the Society for Personality and Social Psychology, the Society of Experimental Social Psychology, and the Association for Psychological Science. Dr. Levine has published extensively on such topics as majority and minority influence, reaction to deviance and disloyalty, group socialization, and innovation in work teams. He is an Honorary Professor of Psychology at the University of Kent, UK, and was co-recipient of the Joseph E. McGrath Award for Lifetime Achievement in the Study of Groups from the Interdisciplinary Network for Group Research.

Contributors

Dominic Abrams
Centre for the Study of Group
  Processes
University of Kent
Canterbury, UK

Hamit Coskun
Department of Psychology
Abant Izzet Baysal University
Bolu, Turkey

John F. Dovidio
Department of Psychology
Yale University
New Haven, CT, USA

Samuel L. Gaertner
Department of Psychology
University of Delaware
Newark, DE, USA

Brian C. Gunia
Carey Business School
Johns Hopkins University
Baltimore, MD, USA

Michael A. Hogg
School of Behavioral and Organiza-
  tional Sciences
Claremont Graduate University
Claremont, CA, USA

Tatsuya Kameda
Department of Behavioral Science
Hokkaido University
Sapporo, Japan

Janice R. Kelly
Department of Psychological
  Sciences
Purdue University
West Lafayette, IN, USA

Norbert L. Kerr
Department of Psychology
Michigan State University
East Lansing, MI, USA

John M. Levine
Department of Psychology
University of Pittsburgh
Pittsburgh, PA, USA

Rachael Martinez
Department of Psychology
Loyola University Chicago
Chicago, IL, USA

Richard L. Moreland
Department of Psychology
University of Pittsburgh
Pittsburgh, PA, USA

Bernard A. Nijstad
Department of Human Resource
  Management & Organizational
  Behaviour
University of Groningen
Groningen, The Netherlands

Paul B. Paulus
Department of Psychology
University of Texas at Arlington
Arlington, TX, USA

Radmila Prislin
Department of Psychology
San Diego State University
San Diego, CA, USA

Jennifer R. Spoor
School of Management
La Trobe University
Victoria, Australia

MaryBeth Talbot
Department of Psychology
Loyola University Chicago
Chicago, IL, USA

Erin L. Thomas
Department of Psychology
Yale University
New Haven, CT, USA

Leigh L. Thompson
Kellogg School of Management
Northwestern University
Evanston, IL, USA

R. Scott Tindale
Department of Psychology
Loyola University Chicago
Chicago, IL, USA

Tom R. Tyler
Yale Law School
Yale University
New Haven, CT, USA

Mark Van Vugt
Department of Social and Organiza-
  tional Psychology
VU University Amsterdam
Amsterdam, The Netherlands

Jiunwen Wang
Kellogg School of Management
Northwestern University
Evanston, IL, USA

Group Processes
Introduction and Overview

JOHN M. LEVINE

In order to understand human behavior, it is essential to understand the critical role that groups play in people's lives. Most of us belong to a range of formal and informal groups, including families, work teams, friendship cliques, social clubs, and so on. Not only do we spend a great deal of time in these groups, but they also connect us to larger social aggregates (e.g., political parties, business organizations, religious denominations) that influence our lives in important ways. Groups vary on several dimensions, including size, composition, goals, norms, status systems, and degree of member interaction and interdependence. These factors, in turn, affect both the amount and type of influence that groups exert on their members. In some cases, this influence is easy to observe, as when members of a basketball team execute a coordinated series of plays designed to score a goal. In other cases, influence is more difficult to observe, as when a teenager talking to his parents uses a slang expression that is popular among his friends. In both cases, though, group influence is at work.

Why do groups have the impact that they do? There are two answers to this question, one focusing on distal (very distal) causes and the other focusing on proximal causes. In regard to distal causes, a good case can be made that human propensities to seek, maintain, and value group memberships are rooted in evolution (e.g., Baumeister & Leary, 1995; Caporael & Baron, 1997; Van Vugt & Kameda, this volume). According to this analysis, group memberships were highly adaptive for our early ancestors (e.g., by facilitating reproduction, child rearing, hunting, and defense), and therefore a predisposition toward group living was strongly selected for during the evolution of our species. This line of argument is bolstered by the absence of any evidence that *homo sapiens* ever lived outside groups and by the apparent universality of group living in modern and primitive human societies. This analysis, then, assumes that we are pre-wired to seek and maintain group memberships, which in turn necessitates subordinating personal interests to collective interests. In regard to proximal causes, several motivational states have been posited to underlie group participation (e.g., Forsyth, 2010; Mackie & Goethals, 1987). In addition to survival needs, these include psychological needs (e.g., avoiding isolation, exerting power), informational needs (e.g., understanding one's environment, evaluating one's abilities and opinions), and self-esteem needs (e.g., having a positive social identity). Although some or all of these needs may have evolutionary roots, an emphasis on proximal causes is valuable in highlighting contemporary situational determinants of group participation. Of course, groups do not always satisfy all of the needs of their members. Nonetheless, it is a rare person who chooses to avoid groups altogether and live as a recluse.

GROUP PROCESSES IN SOCIAL PSYCHOLOGY

In light of the importance of groups in human affairs, it is not surprising that social psychologists have long been interested in group processes. This interest was evident when social psychology was first emerging as an empirical science at the end of the nineteenth century. Many of the early core principles of the discipline, including sympathy, imitation, suggestion, the crowd, and the group mind, concerned the impact of groups on their members (Allport, 1954). In addition, according to Allport, the dominant methodology in social psychology, namely experimentation, had its origins in the study of groups. He noted that, "The first experimental problem—indeed the only problem for the first three decades of experimental research—was formulated as follows: *What change in an individual's normal solitary performance occurs when other people are present?*" (p. 46).[1]

Subsequent historical accounts of social psychology have continued to emphasize the importance of group processes. For example, in discussing landmark projects that stimulated the development of experimental social psychology, Jones (1985) pointed to two classic lines of group research—Sherif's (1936) studies of group influence and Lewin, Lippitt, and White's (1939) studies of leadership atmosphere. And in discussing central research areas in the discipline, Jones gave prominence to interdependence and group dynamics. More recently, Ross, Lepper, and Ward (2010) also accorded a central place to groups. They identified intragroup and intergroup processes as a basic content area in social psychology and group influence as a central theme of the field.

Of course, as with virtually all topics in the discipline, interest in group processes has varied over the years (see Levine & Moreland, 2012). For example, during the 1940s, 1950s, and early 1960s, group research played a very prominent role in social psychology, as reflected by the fact that reviews of social psychology in the 1950–1959 *Annual Review of Psychology* were titled, "Social Psychology and Group Processes." This state of affairs did not last, however. In the late 1960s and early 1970s, work on groups within social psychology (at least in North America) suffered what McGrath (1997) labeled a "system crash," for which various explanations have been offered (see McGrath, 1984; Steiner, 1974, 1986; Zander, 1979).

How has group research fared since the system crash? In addition to many narrative reviews of changes in group research over the years, several quantitative analyses have been published (e.g., Abrams & Hogg, 1998; Moreland, Hogg, & Hains, 1994; Randsley de Moura, Leader, Pelletier, & Abrams, 2008; Sanna & Parks, 1997; Wittenbaum & Moreland, 2008). These reviews differ on many dimensions, including the journals sampled, the years covered, the criteria for defining group research, and so on. It is therefore not surprising that different reviewers often reached different conclusions about trends in group research. In spite of this disagreement, two general conclusions about group research since the system crash seem warranted. First, the overall state of contemporary work on groups is much healthier than it was in the late 1960s and early 1970s. Second, most of the growth in the last 40 years has involved intergroup, rather than intragroup, processes.

Notwithstanding the fact that research on intragroup processes currently occupies a less central place in social psychology than it once did, much interesting and important work is being done. Within the last decade, this work has been summarized in several major volumes, some covering the entire field of social psychology, including Kruglanski and Higgins's (2007) *Social Psychology: Handbook of Basic Principles* and Fiske, Gilbert, and Lindzey's (2010) *Handbook of Social Psychology*, and others focusing specifically on groups, including Hogg and Tindale's (2001) *Blackwell Handbook of Social Psychology: Group Processes* and Levine and Hogg's (2010) *Encyclopedia of Group Processes and Intergroup Relations*. In addition, several textbooks dealing with groups have appeared, including Stangor's (2004) *Social Groups in Action and Interaction*, Levine and Moreland's (2006) *Small Groups: Key Readings*, and Forsyth's (2010) *Group Dynamics*.

THE CURRENT VOLUME

While the volumes cited above contain a great deal of useful information about group processes, none provides a succinct yet comprehensive overview of classic and contemporary work on group processes, written by leading researchers and targeted toward upper undergraduate and graduate students as well as scholars who desire a "state of the art" picture of the field. The current volume was designed to fill this niche.

Criteria Used in Selecting Topics

The literature on groups is vast and encompasses work by investigators from several disciplines, including social and organizational psychology, sociology, anthropology, communication, economics, and political science. In keeping with the goals of the *Frontiers of Social Psychology*, this volume emphasizes research done by social psychologists, although work from other disciplines, most notably organizational psychology, is mentioned where relevant. In addition, most of the chapters focus on small groups (containing at least three but seldom more than 10 members). Major exceptions are the chapter on negotiation, which emphasizes dyadic interactions (though embedded in groups and organizations) and the chapter on intergroup relations, which often deals with social categories (e.g., race, gender). Still other chapters, including those on composition and diversity, social dilemmas, justice, and leadership, discuss principles relevant to organizations as well as small groups.

Many criteria for defining "groups" have been suggested over the years (e.g., member interdependence, interaction, and shared identity; group norms, roles, and status systems). However, no consensus exists regarding which criterion is best, and a persuasive case can be made that, rather than attempting to draw a hard-and-fast line between "groups" and "nongroups," it is more productive to view "groupness" as a dimension along which social aggregates can vary (McGrath, 1984; Moreland, 1987). According to this view, groupness varies continuously with the level of social integration among a set of people. Contemporary group researchers expend little energy wrangling about definitional issues, instead emphasizing those aspects of groups that reflect their research concerns and theoretical orientations. This eclecticism in defining groups is evident in the chapters in this volume.

Given the size and diversity of the groups literature in social psychology, choosing topics for inclusion was a challenging task. Those selected include classic topics that continue to elicit theoretical and empirical attention (e.g., majority and minority influence, decision making, performance) as well as newer topics that are likely to be important in the future (e.g., affective processes, creativity, evolution). With one major exception, the chapters focus on intragroup processes, that is, how people feel and think about and behave toward others who belong to the *same* group. The exception is the chapter on intergroup relations. Given that most of the growth in group research over the last 40 years has involved intergroup processes, this topic clearly deserves coverage in a volume on group processes. Although most of the work on intergroup processes deals with people's feelings, thoughts, and behaviors regarding others who belong to a *different* group, the line between intergroup and intragroup processes is not always clear. For example, relations within groups are sometimes influenced by real or imagined relations between groups. The chapter on social identity illustrates the utility of considering how intergroup processes can affect intragroup processes.

Overview of Chapters

The volume contains 13 chapters. Chapters 1 and 2 (Composition and Diversity; Affective Processes) deal with how group members' stable characteristics and temporary states influence group processes and outcomes. Chapters 2–6 (Negotiation; Social Dilemmas; Justice; Majority and Minority Influence) examine how groups manage conflict elicited by members' divergent interests or viewpoints. Chapters 7–10 (Decision Making; Performance; Creativity; Leadership) focus on group members' cooperative efforts to achieve collective goals, such as reaching consensus, creating a tangible product, or developing novel ideas. Chapters 11 and 12 (Social Identity and Groups; Evolution and Groups) differ from previous chapters in an important way. Rather then focusing on a particular group phenomenon or process, they present overarching theoretical frameworks that are relevant to a wide array of phenomena and processes. Finally, Chapter 13 (Intergroup Relations) discusses how members of one group react toward members of other groups.

In Chapter 1, Richard Moreland discusses an important aspect of work group composition, namely members' diversity on such dimensions as personality, ability, demographic characteristics (e.g., race, sex), and tenure in the group. In general, diversity has negative effects on group processes, such as trust, communication, and cohesion, and inconsistent effects (sometimes positive, sometimes negative) on group performance. In seeking to clarify how diversity operates, Moreland reviews work on the conceptualization and measurement of diversity, as well as factors that mediate and moderate its impact on group processes and performance. In this context, he devotes substantial attention to the categorization-elaboration model of diversity effects. Moreland concludes by suggesting directions for future research on diversity, including more longitudinal studies, more work on the interactional behaviors of members of diverse groups, and more attention to the relative importance of actual vs. perceived diversity.

Chapter 2 by Janice Kelly and Jennifer Spoor focuses on largely neglected dimension of group composition—members' affective states. After discussing various affective states that group members and groups as a whole may experience, the authors identify several functions that affect can play in groups, including facilitating communication and enhancing the development of group bonds. Kelly and Spoor then discuss mechanisms by which affect is regulated in groups, some active (e.g., intentional affective induction, affective impression management) and others passive (e.g., emotional contagion). Next the authors review research on how the affective composition of a group can influence group creativity and decision making, with particular attention to the impact of a leader's affective state. They conclude by highlighting the dynamic and reciprocal relationship between the group's affective composition, on the one hand, and its processes and performance, on the other.

In Chapter 3, Leigh Thompson, Jiunwen Wang, and Brian Gunia analyze negotiation processes and outcomes in terms of five systems, or levels.[2] Work at the intrapersonal level emphasizes negotiators' perceptions and inner experiences, focusing on topics such as power and affect. Research at the interpersonal level deals with dyadic negotiation, highlighting such processes as improvisation and mutual trust. Work at the group level takes into account social dynamics beyond the dyad, for example social and group identity, relational and collective identity, and individual–individual vs. group–group negotiation. Research at the organizational level focuses on how negotiators are influenced by larger social networks, examining topics such as choice of a negotiation partner and the impact of reputation. Finally, work at the virtual level deals with how the interaction medium that negotiators use (e.g., face-to-face, email) affects their behaviors and outcomes.

Chapter 4 by Norbert Kerr extends the theme of conflict resolution to social dilemmas, which involve conflict between personal and collective interests in domains such as resource conservation and the provision of public goods. Social dilemmas force group members to choose between competing and cooperating in situations where (a) individual competition provides higher personal payoffs regardless of others' choices but (b) universal competition provides lower collective (and personal) payoffs than universal cooperation. Kerr discusses four lines of social dilemma research that are receiving increasing attention. The first involves fuzzy social dilemmas, in which ambiguity exists about aspects of the situation, such as the size of the resource pool, the size of the group, or others' likely cooperation levels. The second concerns sanctioning systems, or rewards/punishments provided outside the system to encourage cooperation and discourage competition within it. The third involves selective play environments and partner choice, in which participants in social dilemmas have some degree of control over their range of behaviors and interpersonal relationships. Finally, the fourth concerns the frames (or interpretations) that participants place on dilemmas and the degree to which these frames can be primed.

In Chapter 5, Tom Tyler discusses socially-shared justice rules that guide how people apportion resources, make decisions, and treat one another in group settings. These rules function to reduce conflict associated with the distribution of intangible (e.g., respect) as well as tangible (e.g., money) resources. Tyler presents theoretical and empirical work on three kinds of justice. Distributive justice concerns the allocation of tangible resources among group members and the rules used to decide who should get what (e.g., the equity rule specifying that resources should match contributions). Procedural justice concerns the perceived fairness of the decision making process (e.g., opportunity for participation) as well as the overall quality of the treatment that people receive from others (e.g., dignity and respect). And retributive justice concerns the ways in which norm violators (deviants) are treated by other group members. Tyler makes a strong case that, in resource allocation and dispute resolution, people are more concerned with procedural justice than with distributive or retributive justice.

Chapter 6 by John Levine and Radmila Prislin shifts the focus from conflict regarding interests to conflict regarding viewpoints, specifically the validity of competing perceptions or opinions. The authors restrict their attention to settings in which there is little if any interaction among group members, no explicit pressure to arrive at a joint decision, and disagreement between a numerical majority and a numerical minority. Moreover, they focus on cases in which individual members' perceptual or opinion change is the major dependent variable. Levine and Prislin first discuss early work on majority influence, or conformity, including Solomon Asch's classic studies and subsequent research based on the distinction between informational and normative influence. In this context, they review research on the effects of social support, majority size, and public vs. private conformity. The authors then turn to later work on both majority and minority influence stimulated by Serge Moscovich's view of minorities as the engine of social change and majorities as the guardians of the status quo. Here they discuss Moscovich's analysis of social influence, as well as other theorists' perspectives on how majority and minority sources influence recipients' cognitive activity. After reviewing work on the role of social identity in majority and minority influence, Levine and Prislin discuss recent research on factional conflict in interacting groups.

Group life, of course, involves more than conflict reduction aimed at reconciling divergent interests and viewpoints. In addition, group members cooperate to achieve common goals of various kinds. In Chapter 7, Scott Tindale, MaryBeth Talbot, and Rachael Martinez review research on group decision making, focusing on the basic motivational and information processing systems that lead groups to make both good and bad decisions. A major premise of their analysis is that task-relevant cognitions that are shared among group members have a stronger impact on collective decisions than do unshared cognitions. Tindale and his colleagues first discuss work on how distributions of initial member preferences are combined into collective decisions, examining the impact of the group task (e.g., choosing between discrete alternatives vs. making ratings) and the degree of interaction among group members. The authors then discuss research on socially shared cognition, including shared information and shared task representations. Finally, they review work on shared motivation in decision-making groups.

Chapter 8 by Bernard Nijstad deals with group performance on relatively simple tasks in laboratory environments as well as more complex tasks in organizational contexts. Nijstad organizes his review in terms of the two factors that determine whether a group's actual performance reaches its potential performance (defined by the abilities of its members)—members' motivation to work hard and the degree of coordination among their contributions. In regard to motivation, Nijstad reviews work on social facilitation and inhibition, social loafing and free riding, and social compensation and the Köhler effect. In regard to coordination, he discusses research on group members' understanding of their task and their group, focusing on how transactive memory systems and shared mental models influence group performance. Nijstad concludes by addressing the neglected question of how group members' motivation affects the extent to which they coordinate their contributions to achieve joint goals.

In Chapter 9, Paul Paulus and Hamit Coskun focus on a particular aspect of group performance, namely group creativity, which they define as the generation or development of novel ideas or products that have some degree of utility or acceptance. The authors argue that group creativity depends on three key factors—social processes (e.g., social comparison), motivational processes (e.g., group norms and goals), and cognitive processes (e.g., excitation of semantic networks, semantic clustering of ideas within categories). In addition, they identify conditions that are critical for producing synergy in creative groups, including effective means of tapping members' cognitive resources and procedures for overcoming social loafing and production blocking. They also discuss the impact of group diversity on creativity, the relationship between idea generation and idea exploitation, the utility of training as a way to increase creativity, and differences between creativity in laboratory and real-world groups.

Not all group members have an equal impact on collective performance. In particular, people who occupy leadership roles typically exert disproportionate influence because of their power to organize and direct group activities. Leadership is the focus of Chapter 10 by Michael Hogg. After reviewing definitional issues surrounding the construct of leadership, Hogg discusses several theoretical explanations of leadership acquisition, effectiveness, and endorsement. These include the notions that leaders have special personality traits, behave in ways that match the demands of the current situation, develop exchange relationships with followers, inspire followers to adopt a vision that extends beyond their narrow self-interest, exhibit characteristics that match followers' schema of effective leaders, and behave in ways (e.g., embody group norms) that cause followers to view them as prototypic of the group.

In Chapter 11, Dominic Abrams summarizes the social identity approach, which assumes that both intragroup and intergroup behavior depend on the value and meaning that people derive from their group memberships. According to this perspective, people are highly sensitive to their social (intergroup) context, develop prototypes that differentiate the ingroup from outgroups, and often view and evaluate themselves and others in terms of group membership rather than unique personal qualities. After discussing conceptual and measurement issues regarding social identity and motives that underlie identification with a group (self-esteem, meaning, distinctiveness), Abrams reviews research applying social identity principles to group phenomena and processes. These include cohesion and commitment, leadership, social influence, collective mobilization, and reaction to deviance and dissent.

Chapter 12 by Mark Van Vugt and Tatsuya Kameda presents an evolutionary analysis of behavior in groups based on the assumption that group living was an adaptive response to the survival challenges faced by ancestral humans. According to this analysis, as a result of their evolutionary history, modern humans have innate tendencies to exhibit certain behaviors in group situations. After providing an introduction to evolutionary psychology as it relates to group processes, Van Vugt and Kameda discuss various methodological approaches that have been used to study groups from an evolutionary perspective. The authors then discuss six key adaptive challenges that early humans faced in groups (i.e., coordination, social exchange, status regulation, cohesion, collective decision making, intergroup relations) and the psychological mechanisms that evolved to deal with these challenges. In so doing, they review evidence illustrating the utility of evolutionary theory for clarifying a range of group processes and phenomena, including leadership and followership, cooperation norms, status signaling, social identity, decision rules, and intergroup aggression.

Finally, in Chapter 13, John Dovidio, Samuel Gaertner, and Erin Thomas review research on intergroup relations. The authors first discuss how three critical process—social categorization, social identity, and group competition—influence perceptions, feelings, and behaviors between members of different groups. They then examine the experiences of targets of intergroup bias and discrimination, focusing on such questions as how targets deal with their disadvantaged status and when targets fail to recognize unfair treatment and actively endorse the status quo. Next Dovidio and his colleagues review work on the cognitions, feelings, and behaviors that occur when members of different groups interact with one another. Finally, the authors discuss techniques for improving intergroup relations, with a special focus on the advantages and disadvantages of various forms of contact between members of different groups.

NOTES

1   Allport (1954) claimed that Triplett (1898) conducted the first experimental study in social psychology and provided the first evidence of social facilitation. Although widely accepted, this claim has been challenged (see Haines & Vaughan, 1979; Kravitz & Martin, 1986; Prislin & Crano, 2012; Stroebe, 2012).
2   This chapter was reprinted from the *Annual Review of Psychology* (2010. 61: 491–515).

REFERENCES

Abrams, D., & Hogg, M. A. (1998). Prospects for research in group processes and intergroup relations. *Group Processes & Intergroup Relations, 1*, 7–20.

Allport, G. W. (1954). The historical background of modern social psychology. In G. Lindzey (Ed.), *Handbook of social psychology* (Vol. 1, pp. 3–56). Reading, MA: Addison-Wesley.

Baumeister, R. F., & Leary, M. R. (1995). The need to belong: Desire for interpersonal attachments as a fundamental human motivation. *Psychological Bulletin, 117*, 497–529.

Caporael, L. R., & Baron, R. M. (1997). Groups as the mind's natural environment. In J. A. Simpson & D. T. Kenrick (Eds.), *Evolutionary social psychology* (pp. 317–344). Hillsdale, NJ: Erlbaum.

Fiske, S. T., Gilbert, D. T., & Lindzey, G. (2010). *Handbook of social psychology* (5th ed.). Hoboken, NJ: Wiley.

Forsyth, D. R. (2010). *Group dynamics* (5th ed.). Belmont, CA: Wadsworth/Cengage.

Haines, H., & Vaughan, G. M. (1979). Was 1898 a "great date" in the history of experimental social psychology. *Journal of the History of Behavioral Sciences, 15*, 323–332.

Hogg, M. A., & Tindale, R. S. (Eds.). (2001). *Blackwell handbook of social psychology: Group processes*. Malden, MA: Blackwell.

Jones, E. E. (1985). Major developments in social psychology during the past five decades. In G. Lindzey & E. Aronson (Eds.), *The handbook of social psychology* (3rd ed., Vol. 1, pp. 47–107). New York, NY: Random House.

Kravitz, D. A., & Martin, R. (1986). Ringelmann rediscovered: The original article. *Journal of Personality and Social Psychology, 50*, 936–941.

Kruglanski, A. E., & Higgins, E. T. (Eds.). (2007). *Social psychology: Handbook of basic principles* (2nd ed.). New York, NY: Guilford.

Levine, J. M., & Hogg, M. A. (Eds.). (2010). *Encyclopedia of group processes and intergroup relations*. Thousand Oaks, CA: Sage.

Levine, J. M., & Moreland, R. L. (Eds.). (2006). *Small groups.* New York, NY: Psychology Press.

Levine, J. M., & Moreland, R. L. (2012). A history of small group research. In A. W. Kruglanski & W. Stroebe (Eds.), *Handbook of the history of social psychology* (pp. 383–405). New York, NY: Psychology Press.

Lewin, K., Lippitt, R., & White, R. K. (1939). Patterns of aggressive behavior in experimentally created social climates. *Journal of Social Psychology, 10,* 271–301.

Mackie, D. M., & Goethals, G. R. (1987). Individual and group goals. In C. Hendrick (Ed.), *Review of personality and social psychology: Group processes* (Vol. 8, pp. 144–166). Newbury Park, CA: Sage.

McGrath, J. E. (1984). *Groups: Interaction and performance.* Englewood Cliffs, NJ: Prentice-Hall.

McGrath, J. E. (1997). Small group research, that once and future field: An interpretation of the past with an eye to the future. *Group Dynamics: Theory, Research, and Practice, 1,* 7–27.

Moreland, R. L. (1987). The formation of small groups. In C. Hendrick (Ed.), *Review of personality and social psychology: Group processes* (Vol. 8, pp. 80–110). Newbury Park, CA: Sage.

Moreland, R. L., Hogg, M. A., & Hains, S. (1994). Back to the future: Social psychological research on groups. *Journal of Experimental Social Psychology, 30,* 527–555.

Prislin, R., & Crano, W. D. (2012). A history of social influence research. In A. W. Kruglanski & W. Stroebe (Eds.), *Handbook of the history of social psychology* (pp. 321–339). New York, NY: Psychology Press.

Randsley de Moura, G. , Leader, T., Pelletier, J., & Abrams, D. (2008). Prospects for group processes and intergroup relations research: A review of 70 years' progress. *Group Processes & Intergroup Relations, 11,* 575–596.

Ross, L., Lepper, M., & Ward, A. (2010). History of social psychology: Insights, challenges, and contributions to theory and application. In S. T. Fiske, D. T. Gilbert, & G. Lindzey (Eds.), *Handbook of social psychology* (5th ed., Vol. 1, pp. 3–50). Hoboken, NJ: John Wiley.

Sanna, L. J., & Parks, C. D. (1997). Group research trends in social and organizational psychology: Whatever happened to intragroup research? *Psychological Science, 8,* 261–267.

Sherif, M. (1936). *The psychology of social norms.* New York, NY: Harper.

Stangor, C. (2004). *Social groups in action and interaction.* New York, NY: Psychology Press.

Steiner, I. D. (1974). Whatever happened to the group in social psychology? *Journal of Experimental Social Psychology, 10,* 94–108.

Steiner, I. D. (1986). Paradigms and groups. In L. Berkowitz (Ed.), *Advances in experimental social psychology* (Vol. 19, pp. 251–289). Orlando, FL: Academic Press.

Stroebe, W. (2012). The truth about Triplett (1898), but nobody seems to care. *Perspectives on Psychological Science, 7,* 54–57.

Triplett, N. (1898). The dynamogenic factors in pacemaking and competition. *American Journal of Psychology, 9,* 507–533.

Wittenbaum, G. M., & Moreland, R. L. (2008). Small-group research in social psychology: Topics and trends over time. *Social and Personality Psychology Compass, 2,* 187–203.

Zander, A. (1979). The study of group behavior during four decades. *Journal of Applied Behavioral Sciences, 15,* 272–282.

1

Composition and Diversity

RICHARD L. MORELAND

An important aspect of every group is its composition—the number and types of people who belong. Several reviews of research on group composition have appeared over the years, but for present purposes, a paper by Moreland and Levine (1992) seems especially useful.

In that paper, Moreland and Levine argued that all research on group composition can be organized along three broad dimensions. First, different characteristics of group members can be studied. Some researchers study the size of a group, noting the simple presence or absence of members. Other researchers study the kinds of people who belong to a group, focusing on their demographic characteristics (e.g., age, race or ethnicity, gender), abilities (e.g., knowledge, skills), opinions (e.g., beliefs, values), or personalities (e.g., traits, motives, neuroses).

Second, the characteristics of group members can be measured in different ways. Some researchers use measures of central tendency, such as the mean level of a characteristic among group members (for continuous qualities) or the proportion of group members who possess a characteristic (for categorical qualities). Other researchers use measures of variability and thus assess the level of diversity in a group, or compare groups that are heterogeneous with those that are homogeneous. And a few researchers measure special configurations of characteristics in groups. Kanter (1977), for example, studied the problems that can arise in groups containing token members, and some researchers (e.g., Felps, Mitchell, & Byington, 2006) have recently become interested in whether and how one "bad apple" can affect a group.

Finally, different analytical perspectives can be taken toward group composition. Some researchers have viewed group composition as the *consequence* of certain social and/or psychological processes. Sociologists, for example, have focused on the impact of various external factors, such as shared memberships in social networks, or participation in common activities, that bring people into contact (Feld, 1982; McPherson, Popielarz, & Drobnic, 1992; Ruef, 2002). In contrast, psychologists have focused on the impact of various internal factors, such as commitment, that can lead people to enter or leave certain groups and groups to accept or reject certain people (Moreland & Levine, 1982; Schneider, 1987). Other researchers have viewed group composition as a *context* that moderates the operation of various psychological processes. Zajonc and Markus (1975), for example, argued that the intellectual development of a child is shaped by the "intellectual environment" of his or her family, as reflected in the average mental ability of all family members. Most researchers, however, have viewed the composition of groups as a *cause* for other phenomena, such as group structure, dynamics, and performance. Barrick, Stewart, Neubert, and Mount (1998), for example, measured both the abilities and personalities of work group members in various ways (the minimum, maximum, and mean score and the variance in scores), and then used those measures to predict several group outcomes (cohesion, viability, and performance).

A GENERIC MODEL OF GROUP COMPOSITION EFFECTS

This last analytical perspective was the main focus of Moreland and Levine's (1992) paper. One drawback of the research they reviewed was that researchers tended to focus on just one or two individual characteristics, ignoring theory and research on other characteristics, even when they were likely to display similar effects. Moreland and Levine (see also Moreland, Levine, & Wingert, 1996) thus developed a "generic" model of group composition effects that would be applicable to any member characteristic. That model is shown in Figure 1.1.

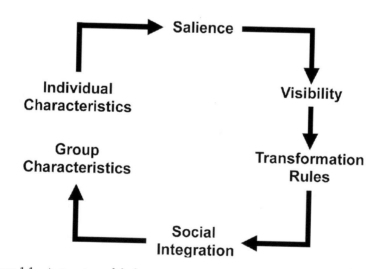

Figure 1.1   A generic model of group composition effects (Moreland & Levine, 1992).

The figure describes the transformation of individual into group character-istics, a complex process in which several variables play a part. The first of these is *salience*, which varies from one individual characteristic to another. Salience determines which characteristics (among all of those that group members pos-sess) are likely to be transformed. Certain characteristics, such as gender or race, are naturally more salient than others, and thus will produce stronger composi-tion effects, at least until group members have interacted enough to discover the other characteristics (e.g., abilities, opinions, personalities) that they possess (cf. Harrison, Price, Gavin, & Florey, 2002). Another factor that can affect the salience of a characteristic is its distribution within a group. Several theorists, especially Mullen (1987), have argued that a characteristic attracts more atten-tion as its variance increases. For example, gender becomes more salient as the proportions of males and females in a group diverge (Kanter, 1977). This sug-gests that more heterogeneous groups will display stronger composition effects. Finally, a characteristic can become salient when it seems relevant to group members' outcomes or lends meaning to their experiences (Oakes, 1987; Van Knippenberg, De Dreu, & Homan, 2004). What can make a characteristic rele-vant or meaningful? The answer depends on situational factors (e.g., the type of task on which a group is working) that direct group members' attention toward particular characteristics and on personal beliefs among group members about which characteristics are most relevant to a given situation. This suggests that when a situation is highly structured, so that its meaning is clear to everyone in a group, or the group's members come from similar backgrounds and thus interpret the situation in similar ways, a narrower range of composition effects will occur and those effects will be stronger.

When an individual characteristic is salient, composition effects involving that characteristic will occur. Every member of a group is likely to possess some level of the characteristic, but everyone may not contribute equally to any com-position effects. *Visibility,* or the extent to which someone's characteristics are noticed by other group members (Marwell, 1963), is an important variable. Vis-ibility varies from one member of a group to another and several factors could influence a person's visibility. For example, people who participate more often in group activities should have more impact on a group, because their charac-teristics are more visible to other members. And visibility should be correlated with status. For example, Schein (1983) claimed that groups often reflect the characteristics of their founders, and leaders' characteristics may have more impact than those of followers on their groups (see Haythorn, 1968). Seniority could increase a person's impact as well, because someone who has been in a group longer will be more familiar to its members. Finally, situational factors, such as the kinds of tasks a group performs and the relationships between its members and outsiders, could affect visibility. When a work group participates in an outdoor team-building exercise, for example, someone who has military experience may gain visibility because he or she possesses (or is believed to pos-sess) relevant skills. And when a local sports team needs new uniforms or equip-ment, someone who has a wealthy relative, or a friend who works for a company that manufactures sports products, may gain visibility as well.

Finally, how do individual characteristics actually combine to affect a group? That is, what rules govern the transformation of individual into group characteristics? Two rules have been identified, although others may exist. According to the *additive rule*, the effects of individual members on a group are independent. This rule implies that a person will affect every group to which he or she belongs in the same way. The additive rule thus reflects a rather mechanistic view of groups. According to the *interactive rule*, however, the effects of individual members on a group are (to some extent) interdependent. This rule implies that a person will affect every group to which he or she belongs differently, depending on who else belongs. The interactive rule thus reflects a more organismic view of groups. When the interactive rule is operating, the transformation of individual into group characteristics is more complex and can thus be difficult to understand or predict (Larson, 2010). The special "chemistry" that occasionally occurs in groups can be interpreted as evidence of interactive composition effects.

When are additive versus interactive transformation rules likely to operate? A group's level of *social integration* is the key factor. Moreland (1987) described social integration in terms of the environmental, behavioral, affective, and cognitive bonds that bind group members together. The more group members think, feel, and act like a single person, the more socially integrated they become. Composition effects that involve the additive transformation rule require little or no social integration, and so such effects are very common. Considerable social integration may be required for composition effects that involve the interactive transformation rule, however, so those effects are much less common.

DIVERSITY IN GROUPS

The main focus of this chapter is diversity and its effects on groups. In recent years, there has been a great surge in diversity research, primarily among organizational psychologists, who want to help managers cope with groups that contain an ever-greater variety of workers (see Friedman & DiTomaso, 1996). Many reviews of research on diversity have been published, covering literally hundreds of studies. (Some recent examples include Bowers, Pharmer, & Salas, 2000; Horwitz and Horwitz, 2007; Jackson, Joshi, & Erhardt, 2003; Jehn, Greer, & Rupert, 2008; Joshi & Roh, 2009; Mannix & Neale, 2005; Van Knippenberg & Schippers, 2007; Webber & Donahue, 2001; Williams & O'Reilly, 1998.)[1] More reviews are likely to appear, because the problems of work group diversity are far from being solved.

Reviews of research on diversity's effects vary widely in the amount and type of research that they cover and the ways in which that research is analyzed (e.g., narrative reviews vs. meta-analyses). Yet there is considerable consistency in the conclusions reviewers have reached. For example, they often agree that whereas diversity has negative effects on group processes (e.g., trust and cooperation, conflict, communication, and cohesion), its effects on group performance are ambiguous. Those effects have been described as "weak" and "inconsistent," among other things. This is not to say that one cannot locate specific studies that reveal positive effects (e.g., Bantel & Jackson, 1989; Hambrick, Cho, & Chen, 1996; Hoffman & Maier, 1961; McLeod, Lobel, & Cox, 1996) or negative effects (e.g., Ancona & Caldwell, 1992; Zenger & Lawrence, 1989) of diversity on group performance. Rather, the problem is that *both* kinds of studies are readily found, along with many studies that reveal no effects at all of diversity on group performance.

So, should research on the performance effects of group diversity be abandoned as a lost cause? Apparently not, because social scientists who study those effects have continued their work, focusing on ways in which it might be improved. Some have suggested that researchers take greater care in conceptualizing and/or measuring diversity. Harrison and Klein (2007), for example, argued that diversity can be viewed in several ways, including separation (different personal characteristics keep people from developing close relationships), variety (different personal characteristics create multiple group configurations), and disparity (different personal characteristics endow some people with greater status than others). Each of these views suggests different ways in which diversity should be measured. The problem with research on diversity, according to Harrison and Klein, is that few researchers specify which view they are taking, which can lead them to measure diversity the wrong way. Other analyses of conceptualization and/or measurement issues in diversity research can also be found (e.g., Bunderson & Sutcliffe, 2002; Humphrey, Hollenbeck, Meyer, & Ilgen, 2007; Shaw, 2004).

Further suggestions for improving research on diversity and group performance have been made as well. For example, another general conclusion reached by many reviewers is that more work is needed on the *mediators* that link diversity to group outcomes. Those mediators are believed to be social processes associated with theories of interpersonal attraction, intergroup relations, and group problem solving.

Regarding interpersonal attraction, diversity is assumed to make group members seem less similar to one another, leading them to like one another less (Berscheid & Walster, 1978; Byrne, 1971). Regarding intergroup relations, diversity is assumed to make the social categorization of others (and the self) more likely in a group (see Tajfel & Turner, 1979; Turner, Hogg, Oakes, Reicher, & Wetherell, 1987), producing ingroup/outgroup biases involving the subgroups created through such categorization (see Wilder, 1986, for an extensive analysis of the consequences of social categorization for groups). To the extent that processes involving similarity/attraction and social categorization actually occur, conflict is likely to arise, damaging a group's performance (De Dreu & Weingart, 2003). But diversity can be associated with helpful processes as well. Regarding group problem solving, for example, diversity is assumed to increase the likelihood that each group member will have a different perspective toward, and information about, the group's task(s). Insofar as each member shares what he or she believes or knows with the rest of the group, and they attend to and accept what was shared, the whole group can develop a broader and deeper understanding of its task(s), making it easier to perform well (see Hinsz, Tindale, & Vollrath, 1997; Larson & Christensen, 1993). Unfortunately, many researchers who study the effects of diversity on group performance simply *assume* that similarity/attraction, social categorization, or group problem solving processes have occurred, without actually measuring them. As a result, too little is known about whether such processes indeed link diversity to group performance, and if so, then exactly how strong those links are and whether other possible links (associated with different social processes, reflecting other theories) exist as well (see Chatman & Flynn, 2001; Milliken & Martins, 1996).

Finally, another general conclusion reached by many reviewers of research on how diversity affects group performance is that potential *moderators* of those effects should be explored. What variables, in other words, can strengthen or weaken diversity's performance effects or perhaps even change such effects from negative to positive (or vice versa)? Many potential moderators have been suggested, though not all of them have yet been studied, and studies of the same moderator by different researchers sometimes yield different results. These moderators can be divided roughly into three categories: characteristics of group members (diversity has different effects on performance, depending on what kinds of people belong to a group), characteristics of the group itself (diversity has different effects on performance in some kinds of groups than in others), and characteristics of the social context in which a group operates (diversity has different effects on performance in different contexts).

Regarding the characteristics of group members, a few researchers have investigated how diversity affects the performance of groups whose members possess certain personality traits, such as openness to experience (Homan et al., 2008), need for cognition (Kearney, Gebert, & Voelpel, 2009), or need for closure (Kruglanski, Shah, Pierro, & Mannotti, 2002). Kearney and his colleagues, for example, found that when group members have a stronger need for cognition, diversity in age and educational background have more positive effects on group performance, perhaps because task-relevant information is processed more thoroughly. Other researchers have studied group members' values, beliefs, and attitudes regarding diversity (e.g., Cramton & Hinds, 2005; Homan, Van Knippenberg, Van Kleef, & De Dreu, 2007; Van Knippenberg & Haslam, 2003; see also Hopkins & Hopkins, 2002; Van Knippenberg & Schippers, 2007). For example, Homan and her colleagues found that a "faultline" actually had positive effects on performance when group members believed that diversity could be helpful. And several researchers have found that the negative effects of diversity on group performance are weaker when group members have a stronger social identity or are otherwise inclined to cooperate with one another (e.g., Chatman, Polzer, Barsade, & Neale, 1998; Jehn & Bezrukova, 2010; Kearney et al., 2009; Roberge & Van Dick, 2009; Van der Vegt & Bunderson, 2005; see also Rink & Ellemers, 2009). Van der Vegt and Bunderson found, for example, that expertise diversity had more positive effects on group learning behaviors and on group performance when members identified more strongly with their groups. Finally, a few reviewers (see Mannix & Neale, 2005), have argued that different kinds of diversity have different performance effects—diversity that involves "surface" characteristics, such as gender or race, (cf. Harrison, Price, & Bell, 1998) has negative effects on group performance, whereas diversity involving "deep" characteristics, such as opinions or personalities, has positive effects. Other reviewers (e.g., Van Knippenberg et al., 2004), however, have argued that the effects of diversity on group performance have little to do with whether surface- or deep-level member characteristics are involved.

Regarding group characteristics, many researchers have found that longevity (how long a group's members have worked together) can moderate the effects of diversity on group performance (see Chatman & Flynn, 2001; Harrison, Price, & Bell, 1998; Harrison et al., 2002; Pelled, Eisenhardt, & Xin, 1999; Watson, Kumar, & Michaelsen, 1993; Zellmer-Bruhn, Maloney, Bhappu, & Salvador, 2008). For example, Harrison and his colleagues found (in both of their studies) that the effects on group performance of diversity in members' "surface" characteristics weaken over time, whereas the effects of diversity in their "deep" characteristics strengthen. This probably occurs because time allows group members to learn more about one another, so that the obvious qualities that drew their attention initially become less salient, to be replaced by the more subtle qualities that members have only recently discovered in one another. Several researchers have also found that any negative effects of diversity on group performance that occur at first are likely to weaken as time passes. Perhaps the members of diverse groups simply learn over time to cope with whatever problems diversity poses for them. Time may also strengthen the cohesion of such groups, thereby buffering them from diversity's negative effects.

Many other researchers have investigated whether and how task factors moderate the effects of diversity on group performance. Such factors include complexity/difficulty (Horwitz & Horwitz, 2007; Jehn, Northcraft, & Neale, 1999; see also Bowers et al., 2000); process and outcome interdependence (Horwitz & Horwitz, 2007; Jehn et al., 1999; Schippers, Den Hartog, Koopman, & Wienk, 2003; Timmerman, 2000); routineness (Pelled et al., 1999); autonomy (Molleman, 2005); and where a task fits into Steiner's (1972) well-known task typology (see Larson, 2010; Moreland et al., 1996). Bowers and his colleagues, for example, found in a meta-analysis that diversity had more positive effects on performance when groups performed more difficult tasks. And in an archival analysis of the composition and performance of professional basketball and baseball teams, Timmerman found that the negative effects of players' age and race diversity were stronger in basketball than in baseball, perhaps because basketball has greater group coordination requirements. Similarly, Schippers and her colleagues found that diversity had more positive effects when groups performed tasks under conditions of greater outcome interdependence. Another area of diversity research in which task characteristics might also play a role involves studies comparing the performance effects of diversity in different types of work groups (e.g., service, manufacturing, technology), whose tasks can differ in a variety of ways (see Bell, 2007; Horwitz & Horwitz, 2007; Joshi & Roh, 2009; Stewart, 2006). Stewart, for example, found that diversity had positive effects on the performance of project teams, but negative effects on the performance of production and management teams. These effects were weak, however, and neither Bell nor Horwitz and Horwitz found any changes in the performance effects of diversity across groups of different types.

Another group characteristic that has been studied by diversity researchers is reflection. How often does a group pause, during or after its task performance, to discuss how well things have been going, analyze why things turned out the way they did, and consider how to make things go better in the future? Many people claim that reflection improves group performance, and although the evidence for that claim is weak (Moreland, 2010), there is some evidence that reflection can moderate the effects of diversity on group performance (Borrill et al., 2000; De Dreu, 2007; Fay, Borrill, Amir, Haward, & West, 2006). De Dreu, for example, found that diversity had more positive effects on performance when groups reflected more often. Maybe reflection allows a group to discover more about its members, so that whatever task-relevant information they have can be identified and used.

A few other group characteristics are also worth noting as possible moderators of the effects of diversity on group performance. One of these is "interpersonal congruence," or the degree to which the rest of a group agrees with each member about who he or she really is. Swann, Polzer, Seyle, and Ko (2004) have argued that diversity can strengthen such congruence in a group, because it provides more opportunities for members to "verify" their self-concepts. As a result, members feel more accepted and are thus more motivated to contribute to the group, thereby improving its performance. Indeed, Polzer, Milton, and Swann (2002) found that when interpersonal congruence was high, diversity had positive effects on group performance, whereas its effects were negative when interpersonal congruence was low. Another characteristic of groups that could moderate the effects of diversity on performance is leadership. Kearney and Gebert (2009), for example, found that transformational leadership can improve the effects of several kinds of diversity on group performance. In their study, diversity in the nationalities and the educational levels of group members were unrelated to group performance, and diversity in members' ages had negative performance effects, when transformational leadership was low. But when transformational leadership was high, diversity in nationalities and educational levels had positive effects on group performance, which was unrelated to diversity in members' ages. Finally, one type of diversity in a group could modify the effects of another type of diversity on the group's performance. The effects of gender diversity on a group's performance, for example, might depend on whether there is also racial diversity in that group. Some researchers have found relationships of this kind. Jehn et al. (1999), for example, found that informational diversity (differences in task perspectives and knowledge) had more positive effects on the performance of groups with less social category diversity (differences in race, gender, or ethnicity) or less value diversity (differences in beliefs about what a group's goals should be). And Pelled et al. (1999) found that several social processes (task conflict, emotional conflict) that are associated with group performance were affected by interactions among different kinds of member diversity (race, gender, age, tenure, and functional background).

Finally, regarding social context characteristics, several reviewers have noted that the effects of diversity on group performance are often different in laboratory versus field studies (see Bell, 2007; Devine & Phillips, 2001; Halfhill, Sundstrom, Lahner, Calderone, & Nielsen, 2005; Joshi & Roh, 2009; Williams & O'Reilly, 1998). In particular, the performance benefits of diversity are often stronger in the laboratory. This is odd, because (for example) the groups studied by laboratory researchers are all newly formed; there is little time for group members to become familiar with one another; the tasks are generally novel; group members are not strongly motivated to perform those tasks well, and so on. All of this seems likely to weaken, not strengthen, the positive effects of diversity on group performance. A more careful analysis of laboratory and field studies is needed, one that identifies the key differences between these research settings and then considers how and why each difference might moderate the performance effects of diversity in groups.

There has also been considerable interest in how the organization surrounding a work group might moderate the effects of diversity on performance. For example, diversity seems to have weaker effects on the performance of groups embedded in organizations that are more diverse (see Joshi & Roh, 2009; Milliken & Martins, 1996; Van Knippenberg & Schippers, 2007). When the organization in which a work group operates is diverse, that might make diversity in the group seem less important, and could also provide group members with more experience at dealing with others different from themselves. Consider, for example, an interesting study by Westphal and Milliken (2000). They found, in corporate boards of directors, that minority members were more influential if they had already played a minority role on other boards, or if the majority members of their board had already played a minority role themselves on other boards. And to illustrate more generally how social contexts (past or present) can shape diversity's effects, the researchers found that minority board members were more influential when they had social network ties to majority board members, either directly or indirectly (e.g., through common memberships on other boards). Finally, because so many organizations have been struggling in recent years to avoid and/or solve problems associated with diversity among workers, there has been considerable interest in the development of special training programs or interventions that could be helpful in that regard. These efforts are often successful—research has often shown that organizations with more positive "diversity climates" experience fewer problems related to group diversity and can solve such problems more readily (see Hopkins & Hopkins, 2002).

THE CEM MODEL OF DIVERSITY EFFECTS

There is no reason, of course, why the mediators and moderators of diversity's effects on group performance have to be studied separately from one another, and indeed, a few plucky researchers have studied them together. Much of this work can be traced to a paper by Van Knippenberg et al. (2004), in which a categorization-elaboration model (CEM) of diversity effects was proposed. In that model, social category diversity (e.g., differences among group members in race, gender, ethnicity) and informational diversity (e.g., differences among group members in their perspectives toward and knowledge about a task) are *both* viewed as potentially valuable for group performance, because each can lead to greater information elaboration (the exchange, analysis, and integration of information about a group's tasks). But social category diversity can also be dangerous, because unless a group's members share a strong, inclusive social identity ("we all belong to the same group"), subgroup identities ("I am a Black group member") may become more salient, creating ingroup/outgroup biases among members of different subgroups, which can weaken group cohesion and produce relational conflict. All of these consequences can harm a group's performance. Groups thus perform best when social category and informational diversity are high and members identify primarily with the group as a whole, rather than with any subgroups.[2]

In terms of mediators and moderators, information elaboration is the primary mediator in the CEM, responsible for any benefits that diversity may have for group performance. A variety of moderators are also included in the model. Some of them involve information processing (e.g., How capable and motivated are group members? Does the task impose a heavy cognitive load and require innovative solutions for problems?). Other moderators involve the salience of the social categories to which group members can be assigned (e.g., How good are the comparative and normative fit of those categories to what is happening in the group? How cognitively accessible are those categories to group members?).

The CEM has stimulated many interesting studies of diversity and performance in groups (e.g., Homan et al., 2008; Kooij de Bode, Van Knippenberg, & Van Ginkel, 2008; Van Dick, Van Knippenberg, Hagele, Guilliame, & Brodbeck, 2008; Van Ginkel & Van Knippenberg, 2008; Van Knippenberg & Haslam, 2003; see also Kearney & Gebert, 2009). An especially compelling example of such work is a study by Homan et al. (2007). These researchers began by forming small work groups, each containing both men and women. To put all these groups at risk for the problems that diversity can create, a strong "faultline" was created in each group. This was accomplished by first testing participants for various personality traits and then providing them with false feedback showing that overall, their personalities were either masculine or feminine in nature. Male participants received feedback indicating that they had masculine personalities, whereas female participants received feedback indicating that they had feminine personalities. Thus, gender and personality type were made to correlate perfectly, creating a strong faultline (Lau & Murnighan, 1998).

Next, everyone was given information about the task that their group would perform—a survival exercise in which group members would pretend that they had been travelling on an airplane that had just crashed (see Johnson & Johnson, 1982). Several items had supposedly been salvaged from the crash site, and the group would have to discuss these and then rank them in terms of their survival value. Every group (as a group) had access to information about all of the items, which could (if considered carefully) yield wise decisions about their survival value. But in some groups, every member was given the same information, whereas in other groups, some of the information was given only to certain members. This created two distinct levels of informational diversity. Finally, beliefs about the value of group diversity were manipulated as well. In some groups, members were told about (bogus) research showing that mixed-gender groups usually perform better than same-gender groups at decision-making tasks. In other groups, however, members were told about research that supported the opposite conclusion.

Group performance was assessed by comparing each group's ranking of the items with the (actual) ranking of an expert at desert survival. Information elaboration was assessed by coding the verbal behavior of group members, as revealed by videotapes made of the groups while they discussed the items. Several interesting results emerged from analyses of these data. First, in terms of group performance, informational diversity had no effects, but there was an effect of diversity beliefs—groups performed better when members believed that mixed-gender groups were better at decision making. There was also an interaction between informational diversity and diversity beliefs, one consistent with the CEM. When information diversity was high, groups performed better if their members believed that mixed-gender groups were better than same-gender groups at decision making. But when informational diversity was low, diversity beliefs had no effect on group performance. The same kind of interaction was found for information elaboration, again consistent with the CEM. Finally, a special mediation analysis revealed that the effects of informational diversity on group performance were due entirely to the changes in information elaboration that diversity produced. This was, of course, consistent with the CEM as well.

FUTURE DIVERSITY RESEARCH

It seems likely that the CEM will continue to generate intriguing research on how, when, and why diversity affects group performance. But other issues seem interesting as well and thus (in my opinion) deserve more research attention too. Some of these issues are largely methodological in nature. For example, more researchers should examine the actual behavior of group members in groups with different types and levels of diversity. This would provide more opportunities to analyze the mediators and moderators of whatever effects diversity has on group performance. It might also lead to unexpected, valuable discoveries about the experience of diversity, such as how group members cope with it (see Ely & Thomas, 2001).

It would also be helpful to do more longitudinal research on how diversity affects group performance. As noted earlier, time seems to change some of diversity's performance effects, causing (for example) "surface-level" member characteristics to have less impact and "deep-level" member characteristics to have more impact. But time could produce other changes as well. In fact, the importance of time does not seem to be fully appreciated by most diversity researchers. The fact is that *the composition of a group is always changing*, even when the faces of group members remain the same. This means that diversity (and maybe its effects on group performance) is always changing too. Some changes in group composition are obvious, as when newcomers enter a group or old-timers leave it. Other changes are more subtle, as when modifications occur in the abilities, opinions, or personalities of group members.

I have been interested in the experiences of newcomers for many years now (Moreland, 1985), so let me focus on them for a moment. The entry of newcomers into groups could have many implications for diversity (and its effects on performance), yet few of these have been investigated. Imagine, for example, a newcomer who differs from current group members and thus increases the level of diversity in the group. How did that person gain entry—was he or she asked to join by members of the group, and if so, then did everyone favor that person's entry, or did some oppose it? If the person was not asked to join, then was the group somehow forced by outsiders to allow him or her to enter (Heilman, 1996)? In either case, how easy was the newcomer's socialization? Was that process difficult, creating many problems? Maybe it took the group a while to realize that the newcomer differed from everyone else, and if so, then was that the newcomer's fault? Did the newcomer try to conceal how different he or she was (see Clair, Beatty, & MacLean, 2005)? When socialization problems arose, which members of the group had to solve them? Had they faced such problems before, with other newcomers (cf. Ziller, 1965), or were those problems unprecedented? Similar questions arise when more than one newcomer enters a group at the same time. And what if multiple newcomers are similar to one another, perhaps more similar than they are to the group's current members (see Li & Hambrick, 2005)? The answers to these and other questions could well affect a group's reactions to any new member(s), and thus (by extension) shape the impact of those members on the group's performance.

Aside from more longitudinal research and research in which group members' behavior is assessed, it would also be helpful to explore possible curvilinear effects of diversity on group performance (Jackson et al., 2003). It is unclear how many researchers check their data for such effects, and if they do not check, then they might reach the wrong conclusions. For example, imagine that the relationship between diversity and group performance is actually U-shaped, as some research has shown (e.g., Gibson & Vermeulen, 2003). In that research, groups performed best when diversity was either low or high, rather than moderate. Or the relationship between diversity and group performance could actually be shaped like an inverted U, as other research has shown (e.g., Dahlin, Weingart, & Hinds, 2005; Thatcher, Jehn, & Zanutto, 2003). In that research, groups performed best when diversity was moderate, rather than either low or high. In both cases, a researcher who looked only for linear relationships in the data would have failed to find them, which might lead to the mistaken conclusion that diversity has no effects at all on group performance. Similar dangers could arise if the effects of diversity on group performance were curvilinear in other ways (imagine a "threshold" relationship, where the performance effects of diversity change when diversity reaches a critical level), or if curvilinear relationships between diversity and group performance were contingent on other variables (Van der Vegt & Bunderson, 2005).

Two other issues are worth noting. Both are more substantive than methodological, though they do have methodological implications. The first issue is whether the actual or the perceived diversity of a group has more impact on its performance. Several reviewers have argued for the importance of subjective diversity (e.g., Harrison & Klein, 2007; Zellmer-Bruhn et al., 2008), and some analyses of how group members monitor and interpret one another's characteristics have appeared (e.g., Bodenhausen, 2010). Those who emphasize subjective diversity also point to studies (e.g., Jehn & Bezrukova, 2010; Pearsall, Ellis, & Evans, 2008) where faultlines had no impact on a group's performance until they were activated by calling group members' attention to them. Such studies are interesting, but how generalizable are their results? Are differences among group members *never* important unless they are recognized? And what if the members of a group *mistakenly* believed that they differ from one another? Would those beliefs affect the group's performance? If so, then how long would it take group members to realize the truth, and once that happened, would any performance effects of their earlier beliefs simply disappear?

Other aspects of perceived diversity might also be interesting to study. Do memories about what a group's members used to be like (before some people left and/or others changed) have any effects on performance? And what about beliefs regarding impending differences among group members? Finally, how might outsiders' perceptions of a group's diversity affect its performance? Such questions all seem interesting, and the potential importance of subjective diversity is clear. But there is a danger that too much attention to subjective diversity could lead researchers to stop studying the effects of diversity in actual groups and focus instead on people's beliefs or memories about diversity's effects in hypothetical groups (see, for example, Van Oudenhoven-Van der Zee, Paulus, Vos, & Parthasarathy, 2009). In my opinion, much could be lost if that happened (see Moreland, Fetterman, Flagg, & Swanenburg, 2010).

Finally, another issue that deserves more research attention is how people try to manage the effects of diversity on the performance of their groups (see Williams & O'Reilly, 1998). Two general approaches can be taken toward such management. One approach is to limit how much diversity occurs at all. In groups that can control their own membership, diversity is actually rare (see McPherson, Smith-Lovin, & Cook, 2001; Milliken & Martins, 1996; Ruef, 2002). And in groups that lack such control, internal activities are often reorganized in ways that create smaller, more homogeneous subgroups (see Schofield & Sagar, 1977).

This suggests that more research is needed on such issues as why, how, and when groups attempt to avoid diversity. As for why diversity is avoided, the answer (given all the research reviewed earlier) probably involves the clear risks of diversity for group processes and its unclear benefits for group performance.

As for how diversity is avoided, several explanations have been offered, but an especially convincing one can be found in Moreland and Levine's (1982) model of group socialization. In that model, membership in a group is viewed as reciprocal and dynamic—reciprocal because both the individual and the group can influence each other and dynamic because the basic nature of the relationship changes over time. The theory describes and explains such changes in terms of three basic processes: evaluation, commitment, and role transition. Evaluation involves judgments made by both the individual and the group about the general rewardingness of their own and alternative relationships. When such judgments are positive, feelings of mutual commitment arise. Those feelings can change over time, rising or falling and occasionally reaching certain decision criteria. When decision criteria are reached by both parties, role transitions occur. These transitions change the nature of the relationship between the individual and the group. Evaluations then continue, though often along different dimensions than before, producing further changes in commitment and possibly other role transitions. In this way, the individual passes through the group, experiencing several phases of membership, separated by various role transitions.

This model suggests three general reasons (see Moreland & Levine, 2003) why diversity is rare in groups, at least when everyone involved can make their own decisions about membership. First, people seldom enter a group whose members differ from themselves, because neither they nor the group are committed enough for entry to occur. Second, if differences among group members arise, then efforts are often made by the group to restore homogeneity—new members are socialized and marginal members resocialized to think and act more like full group members. Finally, people who persist in differing from others do not stay in a group long, because neither they nor the group are committed enough to prevent exit from occurring.

Little is known about the third issue that I raised earlier, namely when groups will attempt to avoid diversity. One factor that is probably important, however, is how diversity has affected group members (both individually and collectively) in the past. Insofar as those effects were more negative than positive, diversity is more likely to be avoided. Another factor that may be important is how diversity is currently affecting other groups and individuals that are known to group members. Again, diversity is more likely to be avoided insofar as those effects are more negative than positive. Finally, expectations about the future might also affect group members' attempts to avoid diversity. Insofar as those expectations are more negative than positive, for themselves and/or for the group, group members may avoid diversity so that whatever resources are needed for solving the problems associated with diversity will remain available, rather than being used to solve other kinds of problems instead.

As they try to manage the effects of diversity on the performance of their groups, a second general approach that people can take (other than avoiding diversity altogether) involves efforts to strengthen the positive effects of diversity and to avoid, weaken or eliminate its negative effects. As noted earlier, several researchers have explored such efforts in large organizations, studying "diversity climates" and the development, implementation, and effectiveness of various diversity training programs and interventions. But comparable research on (less formal) attempts by small groups to manage diversity's effects is harder to find. One interesting exception is a paper by Clair et al. (2005) on how group members who possess a stigmatizing quality decide whether to conceal that quality from other members, or to reveal it (and how to reveal it), hoping to work through any problems that arise as a result. This paper seems relevant because one way to manage diversity is to hide some of the differences among group members, draw members' attention away from them, or portray them as unimportant. Another interesting exception is a paper by Ely and Thomas (2001), who reported a qualitative study of reactions to racial differences among the members of work groups in several large organizations. Three different perspectives on diversity were observed, namely integration and learning, access and legitimacy, and discrimination and fairness. These perspectives shaped how people expressed and managed racial tensions, whether racial minorities felt respected, and how people interpreted racial identity at work. They also determined how well work groups and their members functioned. Integration and learning was the most helpful of the three perspectives in that regard.

DIVERSITY AND OTHER GROUP PHENOMENA

One could argue, I think, that people who study diversity in groups have not taken sufficient advantage of theory and research on other group phenomena that might be relevant to diversity's performance effects. Consider, for example, work on such topics as group cohesion (especially Hogg's 1993 analysis, derived from self-categorization theory); inclusion/exclusion (Levine & Kerr, 2007; Williams, 2007), minority influence (Prislin & Christensen, 2005), reactions to deviance (Levine, 1989), implicit task coordination (Wittenbaum, Vaughan, & Stasser, 1998), socially shared cognition (Mesmer-Magnus & DeChurch, 2010), and how groups are viewed by insiders and outsiders (see work on essentialism, agency, and entitativity, as reviewed by Hamilton, 2007). Diversity is presumably related to many other aspects of groups, but those relationships have not been fully explored.

It is certainly heartening to see so much recent work on diversity, because for many years now, group composition has been a relatively neglected topic area in the world of small groups. Yet diversity is just one aspect of group composition, an area that includes a wide variety of fascinating phenomena. A strong interest in diversity need not be a narrow interest as well—my hope is that those who study diversity will also develop interests in other aspects of group composition.

NOTES

1   Two lines of research relevant to diversity will not be discussed in this chapter. Research on relational demography (see Riordan, 2000) examines the effects on

an individual of being (more versus less) different from other members of a group. Such research has consistently shown that the more different someone is from the rest of a group, the more negative consequences (e.g., less commitment, more turn-over) that person is likely to suffer. Because the unit of analysis in such research is the individual rather than the group, I will not discuss it further. Research on "faultlines" (see Lau & Murnighan, 1998, 2005) acknowledges the fact that group members possess multiple characteristics by considering whether differences among group members are correlated or not (see Eurich-Fulcer & Schofield, 1995). For example, consider two small work groups (A & B). Each group contains four members, two White and two Black, who also differ in their regional backgrounds (North versus South). In one group (A), regional differences are uncorrelated with race (e.g., one White and one Black worker are from the North), but in the other group (B) these differences are perfectly correlated with race (e.g., both White workers are from the North). Lau and Murnighan would argue that racial differences should be more problematic for Group A than for Group B. Because the results of studies testing such ideas are inconsistent and often difficult to interpret (see Molleman, 2005; Pearsall, Ellis, & Evans, 2008; Thatcher, Jehn, & Zanutto, 2003), no further discussion of faultlines will be offered either.

2   Alternatively, group members could view diversity as a critical aspect of their shared social identity ("We are a rainbow"), so that focusing on subgroups does not necessarily weaken the salience of the larger group in which they are found (see Rink & Ellemers, 2009).

REFERENCES

Ancona, D., & Caldwell, D. (1992). Demography and design: Predictors of new product team performance. *Organization Science, 3*, 321–341.

Bantel, K., & Jackson, S. (1989). Top management and innovations in banking: Does the composition of the team make a difference? *Strategic Management Journal, 10*, 107–124.

Barrick, M. R., Stewart, G. L., Neubert, M. J., & Mount, M. K. (1998). Relating member ability and personality to work-team processes and team effectiveness. *Journal of Applied Psychology, 83*, 377–391.

Bell, S. T. (2007). Deep-level composition variables as predictors of team performance: A meta-analysis. *Journal of Applied Psychology, 92*, 595-615.

Berscheid, E., & Walster, H. (1978). *Interpersonal attraction*. Reading, MA: Addison-Wesley.

Bodenhausen, G. V. (2010). Diversity in the person, diversity in the group: Challenges of identity complexity for social perception and social interaction. *European Journal of Social Psychology, 40*, 1–16.

Borrill, C. S., Carletta, J., Carter, A. J., Dawson, J. F., Garrod, S., Rees, A., ... West, M. A. (2000). *The effectiveness of health care teams in the National Health Service*. Birmingham, UK: Action Centre for Health Service Organization Research.

Bowers, C., Pharmer, J. A., & Salas, E. (2000). When member homogeneity is needed in work teams: A meta-analysis. *Small Group Research, 31*, 305–327.

Bunderson, J. S., & Sutcliffe, K. M. (2002). Comparing alternative conceptualizations of functional diversity in management teams: Process and performance effects. *Academy of Management Journal, 45*, 875–893.

Byrne, D. (1971). *The attraction paradigm*. New York, NY: Academic Press.

Chatman, J. A., & Flynn, F. J. (2001). The influence of demographic heterogeneity on the emergence and consequences of cooperative norms in work teams. *Academy of Management Journal, 44,* 956–974.

Chatman, J. A., Polzer, J. T., Barsade, S., & Neale, M. A. (1998). Being different, yet feeling similar: The influence of demographic composition and organizational culture on work processes and outcomes. *Administrative Science Quarterly, 43,* 749–780.

Clair, J. A., Beatty, J. E., & MacLean, T. L. (2005). Out of sight, but not out of mind: Managing invisible social identities in the workplace. *Academy of Management Review, 30,* 78–95.

Cramton, C. D., & Hinds, P. J. (2005). Subgroup dynamics in internationally distributed teams: Ethnocentrism or cross-national learning? In B. Staw & R. M. Kramer (Eds.), *Research in organizational behavior* (Vol. 26, pp. 231–263). Oxford, UK: Elsevier Science.

Dahlin, K. B., Weingart, L. R., & Hinds, P. J. (2005). Team diversity and information use. *Academy of Management Journal, 48,* 1107–1123.

De Dreu, C. K. W. (2007). Cooperative outcome interdependence, task reflexivity, and team effectiveness: A motivated information processing perspective. *Journal of Applied Psychology, 92,* 628–638.

De Dreu, C. K. W., & Weingart, L. R. (2003). Task versus relationship conflict, team performance, and team member satisfaction: A meta-analysis. *Journal of Applied Psychology, 88,* 741–749.

Devine, D. J., & Phillips, J. L. (2001). Do smarter teams do better? A meta-analysis of cognitive ability and team performance. *Small Group Research, 32,* 507–532.

Ely, R. J., & Thomas, D. A. (2001). Cultural diversity at work: The effects of diversity perspectives on work group processes and outcomes. *Administrative Science Quarterly, 46,* 229–273.

Eurich-Fulcer, R., & Schofield, J. W. (1995). Correlated versus uncorrelated social categorizations: The effect on intergroup bias. *Personality and Social Psychology Bulletin, 2,* 149–159.

Fay, D., Borrill, C. S., Amir, Z., Haward, R., & West, M. A. (2006). Getting the most out of multidisciplinary teams: A multi-sample study of team innovation in health care. *Journal of Occupational and Organizational Psychology, 79,* 553–567.

Feld, S. L. (1982). Social structural determinants of similarity among associates. *American Sociological Review, 47,* 797–801.

Felps, W., Mitchell, T. R., & Byington, E. (2006). How, when, and why bad apples spoil the barrel: Negative group members and dysfunctional groups. In B. M. Staw (Ed.), *Research in organizational behavior* (Vol. 27, pp. 175–222). Oxford, UK: Elsevier Press.

Friedman, J., & DiTomaso, N. (1996). Myths about diversity: What managers need to know about changes in the U.S. labor force. *California Management Review, 38,* 54–77.

Gibson, C., & Vermeulen, F. (2003). A healthy divide: Subgroups as a stimulus for team learning behavior. *Administrative Science Quarterly, 48,* 207–239.

Halfhill, T., Sundstrom, E., Lahner, J., Calderone, W., & Nielsen, T. M. (2005). Group personality composition and group effectiveness: An integrative review of empirical research. *Small Group Research, 36,* 83–105.

Hambrick, D., Cho, T., & Chen, M. (1996). The influence of top management team heterogeneity on firms' competitive moves. *Administrative Science Quarterly, 41,* 659–684.

Hamilton, D. L. (2007). Understanding the complexities of group perception: Broadening the domain. *European Journal of Social Psychology, 37,* 1077–1101.

Harrison, D. A., & Klein, K. J. (2007). What's the difference? Diversity constructs as separation, variety, or disparity in organizations. *Academy of Management Review, 32,* 1199–1228.

Harrison, D. A., Price, K. H., & Bell, M. P. (1998). Beyond relational demography: Time and the effects of surface- and deep-level diversity on work group cohesion. *Academy of Management Journal, 41,* 96–107.

Harrison, D. A., Price, K. H., Gavin, J. H., & Florey, A. T. (2002). Time, teams, and performance: Changing effects of surface- and deep-level diversity on group functioning. *Academy of Management Journal, 45,* 1029–1045.

Haythorn, W. W. (1968). The composition of groups: A review of the literature. *Acta Psychologica, 28,* 97–128.

Heilman, M. E. (1996). Affirmative action's contradictory consequences. *Journal of Social Issues, 52,* 105–109.

Hinsz, V. B., Tindale, R. S., & Vollrath, D. A. (1997). The emerging conceptualization of groups as information processors. *Psychological Bulletin, 121,* 43–64.

Hoffman, L., & Maier, N. R. F. (1961). Quality and acceptance of problem solutions by members of homogeneous and heterogeneous groups. *Journal of Abnormal and Social Psychology, 62,* 401–407.

Hogg, M. A. (1993). Group cohesiveness: A critical review and some new directions. In W. Stroebe & M. Hewstone (Eds.), *European review of social psychology* (Vol. 4, pp. 85–111). Chichester, UK: Wiley.

Homan, A. C., Hollenbeck, J. R., Humphrey, S. E., Van Knippenberg, D., Ilgen, D. R., & Van Kleef, G. A. (2008). Facing differences with an open mind: Openness to experience, salience of intragroup differences, and performance in diverse work groups. *Academy of Management Journal, 51,* 1204–1222.

Homan, A. C., Van Knippenberg, D., Van Kleef, G. A., & De Dreu, C. K. W. (2007). Bridging faultlines by valuing diversity: Diversity beliefs, information elaboration, and performance in diverse work groups. *Journal of Applied Psychology, 92,* 1189–1199.

Hopkins, W. E., & Hopkins, S. A. (2002). Effects of cultural recomposition on group interaction process. *Academy of Management Review, 27,* 541–553.

Horwitz, S. K., & Horwitz, I. B. (2007). The effects of team diversity on team outcomes: A meta-analytic review of team demography. *Journal of Management, 33,* 987–1015.

Humphrey, S. E., Hollenbeck, J. R., Meyer, C. J., & Ilgen, D. R. (2007). Trait configurations in self-managed teams: A conceptual examination of the use of seeding for maximizing and minimizing trait variance in teams. *Journal of Applied Psychology, 92,* 885–892.

Jackson, S. E., Joshi, A., & Erhardt, N. L. (2003). Recent research in team and organizational diversity: SWOT analysis and implications. *Journal of Management, 29,* 801–830.

Jehn, K. A., & Bezrukova, K. (2010). The faultline activation process and the effects of activated faultlines on coalition formation, conflict, and group outcomes. *Organizational Behavior and Human Decision Processes, 112,* 24–42.

Jehn, K. A., Greer, L. L., & Rupert, J. (2008). Diversity, conflict, and their consequences. In A. P. Brief (Ed.), *Diversity at work* (pp. 127–174). Cambridge, UK: Cambridge University Press.

Jehn, K. A., Northcraft, G. B., & Neale, M. A. (1999). Why differences make a difference: A field study of diversity, conflict, and performance in work groups. *Administrative Science Quarterly, 44,* 741–763.

Johnson, D. W., & Johnson, F. P. (1982). *Joining together: Group theory and group skills* (2nd ed.). Englewood Cliffs, NJ: Prentice-Hall.

Joshi, A., & Roh, H. (2009). The role of context in work-team diversity research: A meta-analytic review. *Academy of Management Journal, 52,* 599–627.

Kanter, R. M. (1977). Some effects of proportions on group life: Skewed sex ratios and responses to token women. *American Journal of Sociology, 82,* 965–990.

Kearney, E., & Gebert, D. (2009). Managing diversity and enhancing team outcomes: The promise of transformational leadership. *Journal of Applied Psychology, 94,* 77–89.

Kearney, E., Gebert, D., & Voelpel, S. C. (2009). When and how diversity benefits teams: The importance of team members' need for cognition. *Academy of Management Journal, 52,* 581–598.

Kooij de Bode, H. J. M., Van Knippenberg, D., & Van Ginkel, W. (2008). Ethnic diversity and distributed information in group decision making: The importance of information elaboration. *Group Dynamics: Theory, Research, and Practice, 12,* 307–320.

Kruglanski, A. W., Shah, J. Y., Pierro, A., & Mannotti, L. (2002). When similarity breeds content: Need for closure and the allure of homogeneous and self-resembling groups. *Journal of Personality and Social Psychology, 83,* 648–662.

Larson, J. R. (2010). *In search of synergy in small group performance.* New York, NY: Psychology Press.

Larson, L. R., & Christensen, C. (1993). Groups as problem-solving units: Toward a new meaning of social cognition. *British Journal of Social Psychology, 32,* 5–30.

Lau, D., & Murnighan, J. K. (1998). Demographic diversity and faultlines: The compositional dynamics of organizational groups. *Academy of Management Review, 23,* 325–340.

Lau, D., & Murnighan, J. K. (2005). Interactions within groups and subgroups: The dynamic effects of demographic faultlines. *Academy of Management Journal, 48,* 645–659.

Levine, J. M. (1989). Reaction to opinion deviance in small groups. In P. Paulus (Ed.), *Psychology of group influence* (2nd ed., pp. 187–231). Hillsdale, NJ: Erlbaum.

Levine, J. M., & Kerr, N. L. (2007). Inclusion and exclusion: Implications for group processes. In A. E. Kruglanski & E. T. Higgins (Eds.), *Social psychology: Handbook of basic principles* (2nd ed., pp. 759–784). New York, NY: Guilford.

Li, J., & Hambrick, D. C. (2005). Factional groups: A new vantage on demographic faultlines, conflict, and disintegration in work teams. *Academy of Management Journal, 48,* 794–813.

Mannix, E. A., & Neale, M. A. (2005). What differences make a difference? The promise and reality of diverse teams in organizations. *Psychological Science in the Public Interest, 6,* 31–55.

Marwell, G. (1963). Visibility in small groups. *Journal of Social Psychology, 61,* 311–325.

McLeod, P., Lobel, S., & Cox, T. (1996). Ethnic diversity and creativity in small groups. *Small Group Research, 27,* 248–264.

McPherson, J. M., Popielarz, P. A., & Drobnic, S. (1992). Social networks and organizational dynamics. *American Sociological Review, 57,* 153–170.

McPherson, J. M., Smith-Lovin, L., & Cook, J. M. (2001). Birds of a feather: Homophily in social networks. *Annual Review of Sociology, 27,* 415–444.

Mesmer-Magnus, J. R., & DeChurch, L. A. (2010). Information sharing and team per- formance: A meta-analysis. *Journal of Applied Psychology, 94,* 535–546.

Milliken, F. J., & Martins, L. L. (1996). Searching for common threads: Understanding the multiple effects of diversity in organizational groups. *Academy of Management Review, 21,* 402–433.

Molleman, E. (2005). Diversity in demographic characteristics, abilities, and personal- ity traits: Do faultlines affect team functioning? *Group Decision and Negotiation, 14,* 173–193.

Moreland, R. L. (1985). Social categorization and the assimilation of "new" group mem- bers. *Journal of Personality and Social Psychology, 85,* 1173–1190.

Moreland, R. L. (1987). The formation of small groups. In C. Hendrick (Ed.), *Review of personality and social psychology* (Vol. 8, pp. 80–110). Newbury Park, CA: Sage.

Moreland, R. L. (2010). Group reflexivity and performance. In S. R. Thye & E. J. Lawler (Eds.), *Advances in group processes: Group processes* (Vol. 27, pp. 63–95). Bingley, UK: Emerald Press.

Moreland, R. L., Fetterman, J. D., Flagg, J. J., & Swanenburg, K. L. (2010). Behavioral assessment practices among social psychologists who study small groups. In C. R. Agnew, D. E. Carlston, W. G. Graziano, & J. R. Kelly (Eds.), *Then a miracle occurs: Focusing on behavior in social psychological theory and research* (pp. 28–53). New York, NY: Oxford University Press.

Moreland, R. L., & Levine, J. M. (1982). Socialization in small groups: Temporal changes in individual-group relations. In L. Berkowitz (Ed.), *Advances in experi- mental social psychology* (Vol. 15, pp. 137–192). New York, NY: Academic Press.

Moreland, R. L., & Levine, J. M. (1992). The composition of small groups. In E. Lawler, B. Markovsky, C. Ridgeway, & H. Walker (Eds.), *Advances in group processes* (Vol. 9, pp. 237–280). Greenwich, CT: JAI Press.

Moreland, R. L., & Levine, J. M. (2003). Group composition: Exploring the similarities and differences among group members. In M. A. Hogg & J. Cooper (Eds.), *Sage handbook of social psychology* (pp. 367–380). London, UK: Sage.

Moreland, R. L., Levine, J. M., & Wingert, M. L. (1996). Creating the ideal group: Com- position effects at work. In E. H. Witte & J. H. Davis (Eds.), *Understanding group behavior* (Vol. 2, pp. 11–35). Hillsdale, NJ: Erlbaum.

Mullen, B. (1987). Self-attention theory: The effects of group composition on the indi- vidual. In B. Mullen & G. R. Goethals (Eds.), *Theories of group behavior* (pp. 125–146). New York, NY: Springer-Verlag.

Oakes, P. J. (1987). The salience of social categories. In J. C. Turner, M. A. Hogg, P. J. Oakes, S. D. Reicher, & M. S. Wetherell (Eds.), *Rediscovering the social group: A self-categorization theory* (pp. 117–141). Oxford, UK: Basil Blackwell.

Pearsall, M. J., Ellis, A. P., & Evans, J. M. (2008). Unlocking the effects of gender fault- lines on team creativity: Is activation the key? *Journal of Applied Psychology, 93,* 225–234.

Pelled, C. H., Eisenhardt, K. M., & Xin, K. R. (1999). Exploring the black box: An analysis of work group diversity, conflict, and performance. *Administrative Science Quarterly, 44,* 1–28.

Polzer, J. T., Milton, L. P., & Swann, W. B. J. (2002). Capitalizing on diversity: Inter- personal congruence in small work groups. *Administrative Science Quarterly, 47,* 296–324.

Prislin, R., & Christensen, P. N. (2005). Social change in the aftermath of successful minority influence. In W. Stroebe & M. Hewstone (Eds.), *European review of social psychology* (Vol. 16, pp. 43–73). Hove, UK: Psychology Press.

Rink, F., & Ellemers, N. (2009). Managing diversity in work groups: How identity processes affect diverse work groups. In M. Barreto, M. K. Ryan, & M. T. Schmitt (Eds.), *The glass ceiling in the 21st century: Understanding barriers to gender equality* (pp. 281–303). Washington, DC: American Psychological Association.

Riordan, C. M. (2000). Relational demography within groups: Past developments, contradictions, and new directions. *Research in Personnel and Human Resource Management, 19,* 131–174.

Roberge, M. E., & Van Dick, R. (2009). Recognizing the benefits of diversity: When and how does diversity increase group performance? *Human Resource Management Review, 20,* 295–308.

Ruef, M. (2002). A structural event approach to the analysis of group composition. *Social Networks, 24,* 135–160.

Schneider, B. (1987). The people make the place. *Personnel Psychology, 40,* 437–453.

Schein, E. H. (1983). The role of the founder in creating organizational culture. *Organizational Dynamics, 7,* 13–28.

Schippers, M. C., Den Hartog, D. N., Koopman, P. L., & Wienk, J. A. (2003). Diversity and team outcomes: The moderating effects of outcome interdependence and group longevity and the mediating effect of reflexivity. *Journal of Organizational Behavior, 24,* 779–802.

Schofield, J. W., & Sagar, A. (1977). Peer interaction patterns in an integrated middle school. *Sociometry, 40,* 130–138.

Shaw, B. J. (2004). The development and analysis of a measure of group faultlines. *Organizational Research Methods, 7,* 66–100.

Steiner, I. D. (1972). *Group process and productivity.* New York, NY: Academic Press.

Stewart, G. L. (2006). A meta-analytic review of relationships between team design features and team performance. *Journal of Management, 32,* 29–54.

Swann, W. B., Polzer, J. T., Seyle, D. C., & Ko, S. J. (2004). Finding value in diversity: Verification of personal and social self-views in diverse groups. *Academy of Management Review, 29,* 9–27.

Tajfel, H., & Turner, J. (1979). An integrative theory of intergroup conflict. In W. G. Austin & S. Worchel (Eds.), *The social psychology of intergroup relations* (pp. 33–47). Monterey, CA: Brooks/Cole.

Thatcher, S. M., Jehn, K. A., & Zanutto, E. (2003). Cracks in diversity research: The effects of diversity faultlines on conflict and performance. *Group Decision and Negotiation, 12,* 217–241.

Timmerman, T. A. (2000). Racial diversity, age diversity, interdependence, and team performance. *Small Group Research, 31,* 592–606.

Turner, J. C., Hogg, M. A., Oakes, P. J., Reicher, S. D., & Wetherell, M. S. (Eds.). (1987). *Rediscovering the social group: A self-categorization theory.* Oxford, UK: Basil Blackwell.

Van der Vegt, G. S., & Bunderson, J. S. (2005). Learning and performance in multidisciplinary teams: The importance of collective team identification. *Academy of Management Journal, 48,* 532–547.

Van Dick, R., Van Knippenberg, D., Hagele, S., Guilliame, Y. R. F., & Brodbeck, F. C. (2008). Group diversity and group identification: The moderating role of diversity beliefs. *Human Relations, 61,* 1463–1492.

Van Ginkel & Van Knippenberg, D. (2008). Group information elaboration and group decision making: The role of shared task representations. *Organizational Behavior and Human Decision Processes, 105,* 82–97.

Van Knippenberg, D., De Dreu, C. K. W., & Homan, A. C. (2004). Work group diversity and group performance: An integrative model and research agenda. *Journal of Applied Psychology, 89,* 1008–1022.

Van Knippenberg, D., & Haslam, S. A. (2003). Realizing the diversity dividend: Exploring the subtle interplay between identity, ideology, and reality. In S. A. Haslam, D. Van Knippenberg, M. Platow, & N. Ellemers (Eds.), *Social identity at work: Developing theory for organizational practice* (pp. 61–77). New York, NY: Psychology Press.

Van Knippenberg, D., & Schippers, M. C. (2007). Work group diversity. *Annual Review of Psychology, 58,* 515–541.

Van Oudenhoven-Van der Zee, K., Paulus, P., Vos, M., & Parthasarathy, N. (2009). The impact of group composition and attitudes towards diversity on anticipated outcomes of diversity in groups. *Group Processes & Intergroup Relations, 12,* 257–280.

Watson, W., Kumar, K., & Michaelsen, L. (1993). Cultural diversity's impact on interaction process and performance: Comparing homogeneous and diverse task groups. *Academy of Management Journal, 36,* 590–602.

Webber, S. S., & Donahue, L. M. (2001). Impact of highly and less job-related diversity on work group cohesion and performance: A meta-analysis. *Journal of Management, 27,* 141–162.

Westphal, J. D., & Milliken, L. P. (2000). How experience and network ties affect the influence of demographic minorities on corporate boards. *Administrative Science Quarterly, 45,* 366–398.

Wilder, D. A. (1986). Social categorization: Implications for creation and reduction of intergroup bias. In L. Berkowitz (Ed.), *Advances in experimental social psychology* (Vol. 19, pp. 291–355). Orlando, FL: Academic Press.

Williams, K. D. (2007). Ostracism. *Annual Review of Psychology, 58,* 425–452.

Williams, K., & O'Reilly, C. A. (1998). Demography and diversity in organizations: A review of 40 years of research. In B. Staw & L. L. Cummings (Eds.), *Research in organizational behavior* (Vol. 20, pp. 77–140). Oxford, UK: Elsevier Science.

Wittenbaum, G. M., Vaughan, S. I., & Stasser, G. (1998). Coordination in task-performing groups. In R. S. Tindale, J. Edwards, E. J. Posavac, F. B. Bryant, & Y. Suarez-Balcazar (Eds.), *Social psychological applications to social issues: Applications of theory and research on groups* (pp. 177–204). New York, NY: Plenum Press.

Zajonc, R. B., & Markus, G. N. (1975). Birth order and intellectual development. *Psychological Review, 82,* 74–88.

Zellmer-Bruhn, M. E., Maloney, M. M., Bhappu, A. D., & Salvador, R. (2008). When and how do differences matter? An explanation of perceived similarity in teams. *Organizational Behavior and Human Decision Processes, 107,* 41–59.

Zenger, T. R., & Lawrence, B. S. (1989). Organizational demography: The differential effects of age and tenure distributions on technical communication. *Academy of Management Journal, 32,* 353–376.

Ziller, R. C. (1965). Toward a theory of open and closed groups. *Psychological Bulletin, 64,* 164–182.

2

Affective Processes

JANICE R. KELLY and JENNIFER R. SPOOR

The study of small groups has been part of experimental social psychology almost from its inception (Jones, 1998). Across this history, small groups researchers have primarily focused on the task activities of the groups they study, which was evidenced in some of the earliest studies on small groups. For example, Triplett (1898), who is often credited with conducting the first experiment in social psychology (and by extension, small groups), was concerned with demonstrating that working in groups enhanced individual performance. Lewin, Lippitt, and White's (1939) classic studies also examined group productivity, but focused on the consequences of different leadership styles. Finally, Marjorie Shaw's (1932) research comparing group and individual problem solving initiated an extensive inquiry into the factors that facilitate and inhibit group productivity. There were, however, some notable exceptions to the focus on task issues. LeBon (1895/1960) drew on the notion of a "mob mind" in describing the behavior of people in crowds, certainly not an aspect of task performance. Bales (1950) emphasized the importance of both task activities and social-emotional activities to group problem solving. Affective or emotional issues were central to a number of theories of group development, such as Tuckman's (1965) "storming" stage of group development. However, beginning in the 1960s, small group researchers began to turn away from affective processes even more strongly, as the cognitive revolution began to shape the field of social psychology.

Despite this strong focus on task processes, a number of recent developments within other fields of psychology heralded the emergence of interest in affective processes and the social-emotional side of small groups. First, social and cognitive psychologists have repeatedly demonstrated that affect has a profound impact on individuals' memory, cognition, and behavior (Forgas, 1992).

For example, Forgas (1995) argued that when one is not aware of the source of one's affective state, affect infuses one's thoughts and judgments. Second, following from interest in the role of affect in individual responses has been the realization that affect is social in nature (Parkinson, 1996; Wallbott & Scherer, 1986), and in order to be fully understood it must be examined in an interactive context. Third, organizational psychology has experienced its own affective revolution (Brief & Weiss, 2002; Elfenbein, 2008; Weiss & Brief, 2001; Zerbe & Hartel, 2005), with a correspondent focus on affective influences on team behavior (Levine & Moreland, 1990). Finally, there has been a growing interest in group-level emotions as they occur as a function of intergroup relations (Iyer & Leach, 2008; Smith & Mackie, 2008).

As a result of these converging lines of interest, small group researchers have also become more interested in the causes, processes, and consequences of affect in small groups (Barsade & Gibson, 1998; Kelly & Barsade, 2001; Kelly & Spoor, 2006; Spoor & Kelly, 2004). The purpose of this chapter is to review this growing area of research. We first review the variety of affective experiences that groups and group members may experience. We then argue that affect in groups serves important group functions (George, 2002; Spoor & Kelly, 2004). Furthermore, we argue that in order to serve these functions, groups have developed a number of mechanisms to regulate and maintain affective states, and we review the literature on those mechanisms. Finally, we examine the outcomes of those regulatory processes in terms of their effects on group performance and interaction.

AFFECTIVE EXPERIENCES IN GROUPS

Just as individuals may experience a variety of affective states, group members, and perhaps the group as a whole, may also experience a variety of affective states. We are using the term "affect" as an umbrella term to cover a variety of possible affective or evaluative experiences that groups or their members might experience. For example, individuals may experience both less intense, diffuse moods (Forgas, 1992) and more intense, targeted emotions (Frijda, 1994). Individuals also possess affective dispositions, or characteristic ways of affectively responding to the environment (Lazarus, 1991). Individuals who come together in a group setting may experience all of those different types of affect, and the compositional effects that occur may influence other affective and non-affective processes in those groups (Kelly & Barsade, 2001).

Some researchers have posited group-level analogs for some of these individual level affective experiences. For example, George (1996) suggested that some groups develop a shared level of dispositional affect among members—a group affective tone—that leads members to experience consistent or homogeneous affective reactions to various events. Not all groups develop a group affective tone, but George suggests that group members who work together over time experience a number of forces that encourage such convergence. Specifically, she suggests that attraction-selection-attrition processes encourage those with like affective dispositions to come together and subsequently to remain together as a group. Further, group members who experience common outcomes also tend to experience similar emotional consequences of those outcomes, again encouraging the development of similar affective states.

Kelly and Barsade (2001) argued that a group level mood can arise through a combination of top-down components, such as emotion expression norms or the affective context in which the group is operating, and bottom-up compositional components arising from the affective characteristics of the individuals who comprise the group. Interestingly, mood is a characteristic of a group that can be reliably recognized by both group members and by outside observers (Barsade, 2002; Bartel & Saavedra, 2000).

Finally, Barsade and Gibson (1998) suggested that groups are often subject to strong forces, such as successes or failures, which may create strong emotional group level experiences. These sorts of emotional experiences may arise in intergroup contexts (Mackie, Maitner, & Smith, 2009), and intergroup interaction is theorized to give rise to group level emotions such as pride or guilt.

Small group researchers have posited several constructs and processes that are affective in nature. "Group cohesiveness" (Mullen & Copper, 1994; Hogg, 1992) refers to the total sum of forces that bond members together, including affective forces such as positive regard for fellow group members either as individuals or as people who share a common group identity. The related construct of "group rapport" (Tickle-Degnen & Rosenthal, 1987) is defined as a combination of positivity (mutual liking and friendliness), mutual attentiveness, and coordination that can occur in groups. "Primitive emotional contagion" (Hatfield, Cacioppo, & Rapson, 1994) refers to the automatic spread of emotions from person to person. Interestingly, all of these constructs are thought to occur at the group level, or at least via group interaction, which gives some credence to the notion that other affective constructs, such as moods and emotions, can occur at the group level as well. Given the existence of group affective experiences, we turn to the question of what functions these experiences might serve for the group.

FUNCTIONS OF AFFECT IN GROUPS

Affect is thought to be functional for groups by helping to coordinate group activities (Spoor & Kelly, 2004), via the communication and sharing of affective states. Spoor and Kelly suggested that affect can facilitate group activity by improving intragroup communication and encouraging group bonding.

Affect and Communication

Spoor and Kelly (2004) suggested that one critical function of affect in groups is to facilitate communication by helping group members evaluate their environment. Negative affect serves a particularly important communication function, as it is theorized to signal to individuals that there are potential problems in the environment (Larsen, 2000; Tice & Bratslavsky, 2000). For groups, negative affect might signal problems that originate from either within or outside the group. For example, negative affect might indicate dissatisfaction with the group's current performance. Thus, negative affect might encourage group members to more systematically and critically evaluate information and potential outcomes (Kelly, 2001). Consistent with this possibility, prior research has shown that individuals in negative moods often tend to engage in more systematic and elaborate processing of information than do those in positive moods (Schwarz, Bless, & Bohner, 1991), and negative affect has also been shown to increase the likelihood that group members will exchange and discuss critical information (Kooij-de Bode, van Knippenberg, & van Ginkel, 2010). Negative affect might also suggest that current decision alternatives are inadequate, thus prompting group members to generate additional solutions. Consistent with this reasoning, some research has found that negative affect can prompt better performance on idea generation tasks for both individuals (George & Zhou, 2002) and groups (Jones & Kelly, 2009).

Positive affect also serves important communication functions for groups. Positive affect might communicate that group members are expected to cooperate and work together, and positive affect might facilitate smooth interactions. Consequently, positive moods might lead to more satisfaction among group members. Positive affect can also signal that the group has performed well on the task at hand. For example, the link between cohesion and perceived task performance can be bi-directional, such that groups that are more cohesive tend to recall that they performed better (Mullen & Copper, 1994). There is also research showing that people believe that positive emotion displays in groups indicate better group performance (Magee & Tiedens, 2006). Additionally, whereas negative moods may signal dangers in the environment, positive affect may free groups to explore and broaden their perspective on the environment. Thus, group members in positive moods might be able to build on each others' contributions in creativity tasks or elaborate on new information in decision-making groups (e.g., Bramesfeld & Gasper, 2008).

In addition to a communication role, negative affect might also provide important information about the intergroup structure. Negative affect can signal dissatisfaction with a group's current status and serve as an important instigator of collective action to change the status quo (e.g., Walker & Smith, 2002). Negative affect can also indicate that the distribution of group outcomes is unfair, over and above the fairness of individual outcomes. For example, fraternal deprivation (i.e., perceiving that the ingroup's outcomes are unfair relative to the outgroup) is associated with intergroup prejudice, whereas personal deprivation (i.e., perceiving that individual outcomes are unfair) is not (Walker & Smith, 2002). High status groups might also be affected by negative affect. For example, collective guilt is an aversive experience typically experienced by members of high status and advantaged groups. Collective guilt signals dissatisfaction with the ingroup's outcomes and can prompt high status groups to act on behalf of low status groups (Iyer & Leach, 2008; Mallett, Huntsinger, Sinclair, & Swim, 2008).

Affect can communicate information about the intragroup structure as well by serving to reinforce roles and status differences in the group (Houser & Lovaglia, 2002; Keltner & Haidt, 2001; Tiedens, 2000). Research on status and emotional expression indicates that high and low status group members are expected to display and experience different emotions. High status individuals are expected to experience positive emotions, whereas low status individuals are expected to experience negative emotions. Dominant and subordinate group members are also expected to have different emotional responses to negative outcomes. Dominant group members are expected to experience anger, whereas subordinate group members are expected to experience sadness or guilt (Tiedens, 2000, 2001; Tiedens, Ellsworth, & Mesquita, 2000). The emotional states of high status group members might be particularly influential on group interaction. In research on affective convergence, some studies suggest that low status group members are more likely to "catch" the emotions of high status group members than vice versa (Anderson, Keltner, & John, 2003). This does not occur in every case (Hsee, Hatfield, Carlson, & Chemtob, 1990; Spoor & Kelly, 2009), and sometimes high power induces greater interpersonal sensitivity and empathy (Schmid Mast, Jonas, & Hall, 2009). Spoor and Kelly (2009) suggested that the conflicting findings across studies might reflect differences in the legitimacy of the status differential.

High status group members might also have a wider range of acceptable emotions. High power individuals have more freedom to act and emit their dominant responses (Galinsky, Gruenfeld, & Magee, 2003). High power and high status group members may also be in a position to ignore or disregard the emotions of members low in status and power. Thus, differences in the range of acceptable emotional expression might serve as a reminder of the intragroup status structure. It is also important to note that emotional expressions and status have a cyclical and mutually influential relationship (Tiedens, 2000). That is, status dictates which emotional expressions are appropriate, and emotional expressions signify status levels.

Affect and Group Bonding

Spoor and Kelly (2004) argued that a second crucial function of affect in groups is to facilitate the development of group bonds. Affect in groups encourages group members to "get along" and maintain solidarity, which may occur through group cohesion, rapport, and group identification. It is not surprising, then, that cohesion is the most widely studied group affective construct (Kelly & Barsade, 2001). Group cohesion is multidimensional and comprises interpersonal attraction, group pride, and task commitment (Mullen & Copper, 1994). Group cohesion is both an outcome of and a contributor to positive group interaction and processes (Levine & Moreland, 1990), and cohesion is positively linked to group performance (Mullen & Copper, 1994). For example, groups that are more cohesive tend to perform better and have more satisfactory interactions. Cohesion can also encourage group members to increase their effort on behalf of the group and increase their willingness to compensate for a low performing group member (Karau & Williams, 1997). Taken to extremes, cohesion might be a detriment to performance (e.g., groupthink; Janis, 1972), though such extreme outcomes only reinforce the value of group cohesion in promoting group member bonds.

The role of cohesion in group bonding is also demonstrated in the longevity of cohesive groups, as members are more likely to stick with highly cohesive groups than with groups low in cohesion (Forsyth, 1999; Mobley, Griffeth, Hand, & Meglino, 1979). In this respect, group cohesion is similar to the construct of group identification in the intergroup literature. Measures of group identification typically assess ingroup ties, positive affect toward the group, centrality, or some combination of these constructs (Cameron, 2004). Compared to members with low identification, highly identified members are more likely to stick with their group even during negative situations, are more likely to defend the group, and are more likely to conform to group norms (e.g., Jetten, Branscombe, Spears, & McKimmie, 2003). Low identifiers tend to be more instrumental, only standing by their group during good times and when membership has individual benefits.

A concept similar to group cohesion is rapport, which also has positive affective underpinnings (Tickle-Degnen & Rosenthal, 1987). Group rapport consists of mutual attention and involvement, coordination among members, and positive affect. The positive affect component can be measured via affiliative nonverbal behaviors, such as mimicry. Individuals with an affiliation motive are more likely to nonconsciously mimic an interaction partner, compared to individuals with other motives such as accuracy (Lakin & Chartrand, 2003). Lakin, Jefferis, Cheng, and Chartrand (2003) also demonstrated that nonconscious mimicry was directly related to rapport and positive affect.

It is clear that certain kinds of affect facilitate important group functions (George, 2002; Spoor & Kelly, 2004). We suggest, then, that groups have in consequence developed a number of mechanisms to regulate and maintain useful affective states. In fact, George (2002) has recently argued that affect regulation, broadly defined, should be considered a fundamental group process. We turn now to a discussion of the mechanisms involved in affect regulation in groups.

AFFECT REGULATION IN GROUPS

Processes important to the regulation of affect in groups have been specified by George (2002), Kelly and Barsade (2001), and Kelly and Spoor (2006). In discussing these mechanisms, all of these authors agree that some of these regulatory processes are more active (i.e., explicit, intentional, and conscious), whereas others are more passive (i.e., implicit, unintentional, and nonconscious).

Active Processes of Affect Regulation

Some mechanisms of affect regulation may involve relatively intentional and deliberate attempts to induce or alter affective states in group members (Kelly

& Barsade, 2001). That people can intentionally and consciously influence the moods of others has been demonstrated repeatedly in the large literature on mood induction (Isen & Baron, 1991). Mood induction can also occur without others' awareness, and, in fact, outcomes are often altered if the source of the mood induction is known (Schwarz & Clore, 1983).

Intentional affect induction is central to the literature on effective leadership (Ashkanasy & Tse, 2000; Bass & Avolio, 1994; George, 2000). For example, George (2000) argued that a leader's ability to manage subordinates' moods and emotions (i.e., the leader's emotional intelligence) is central to effective leadership, and Ashforth and Humphrey (1995) argued that this skill is essential in transformational leadership. More specifically, transformational leaders provide challenging goals and instill a sense of optimism in followers that they can achieve those goals (Bass & Avolio, 1994; McColl-Kennedy & Anderson, 2002). Transformational leaders serve as models of these emotions.

Affective impression management (i.e., efforts to convince others that one is experiencing a particular affect) may also lead group members to change their emotional expression. Affective impression management is likely to be motivated by social comparison processes (Gump & Kulik, 1997; Sullins, 1991). From this perspective, group members use environmental cues to determine an appropriate evaluative response to situations, and they use emotional expressions to convey these evaluations to fellow group members. These facial expressions then become a source of social comparison within the group. Group members may also adjust their emotional expressions to be line with their expectations regarding other group members' emotions. Consistent with this possibility, Huntsinger, Lun, Sinclair, and Clore (2009) found that participants' moods became more negative when expecting to interact with a negative mood person, whereas participants' moods became more positive when expecting to interact with someone in a positive mood. Thus, people may neutralize their positive facial expressions (and perhaps actively increase negative expressions) when interacting with a sad or anxious person, but also ramp up their positive emotional expressions when interacting with a cheerful person. Moreover, this affective impression management may subsequently alter group members' actual emotional experiences as a result of facial feedback.

Conscious regulation of affective expressions may also occur because of implicit or explicit rules for the appropriate display of emotion in a particular context. Hochschild (1983) introduced the term "emotional labor" to refer to the regulation of feelings and their expression at work and the exchange of such regulation for wages. Hochschild also argued that norms for appropriate emotional display (i.e., emotion norms) are particularly prevalent in service occupations that involve interactions between workers and customers (e.g., flight attendants), though emotion norms arise in any organization that involves interpersonal interaction (Ashforth & Humphrey, 1995). However, the degree to which these norms are made explicit to employees can vary. For example, Rafaeli and Sutton (1989) argued that some emotion display norms are fairly explicit, such as instructions to bank tellers to smile and act friendly. Other norms may be more subtly transmitted, such as through modeling of the desired emotion display.

Kelly and Barsade (2001) argued that small groups, including teams, may also develop norms for the appropriate display of emotions. They suggested that, because of their unique histories, groups may develop idiosyncratic, or local, norms that regulate members' emotional expression either in addition to or instead of norms that occur in the wider organizational context. For example, Stokes (1983) found that therapy groups often developed explicit norms for the open display of emotions, because of the assumption that such a display is beneficial to the therapeutic process.

Research by Kelly and Spoor (2007) suggests another impetus for explicit affect regulation in groups. These researchers asked participants to report on their naïve theories (i.e., lay perceptions) concerning the function of positive and negative affect in various types of groups (e.g., creativity groups, sport teams, decision-making groups). They found evidence for consistency in these theories across participants, as well as differentiation in the perceived function of affect across group types. For example, participants reported that they believed that positive affect would enhance creative processes in creativity groups, but might distract group members from the task in decision-making groups. Kelly and Spoor further showed that participants' naïve theories biased their perceptions of group processes. For example, participants perceived more active task behavior in group members who were described as friends in a negative mood rather than strangers in a negative mood. Presumably, these naïve theories might also motivate group members to regulate their own and their fellow group members' affective states so that they are in an optimal affective state for performance on any particular task.

Passive Processes of Affect Regulation

The processes described in this section generally occur automatically and without conscious intentions on the part of group members. Perhaps the most widely studied passive process is emotional contagion, whereby the moods and emotions of one individual are transferred to nearby individuals (Hatfield et al., 1994). Emotional contagion is facilitated by the mimicry and synchronization of group members' nonverbal and emotional behaviors. Although mimicry can be intentional (Bavelas, Black, Lemery, & Mullett, 1987), a growing number of studies have demonstrated that it often occurs in a relatively automatic and nonconscious fashion (Chartrand & Bargh, 1999; Chartrand & Dalton, 2009). Facial feedback from emotional mimicry is thought to be the underlying mechanism for the transfer of emotions from individual to individual. Although primarily studied in individuals who are exposed to emotional stimuli, there is recent evidence that emotional contagion occurs within interacting groups as well (Barsade, 2002; Bartel & Saavedra, 2000; Spoor & Kelly, 2009; Totterdell, 2000).

Emotional contagion may be supported by other mechanisms. For example, McGrath and Kelly's (1986) Social Entrainment Model suggests that temporal rhythms of social behavior between two or more individuals, including expressive behavior, may become synchronized. This behavioral entrainment, or interaction synchrony (Bernieri, Reznick, & Rosenthal, 1988), may produce or reinforce emotional mimicry.

Affect regulation may also arise from group compositional effects shaped by attraction, selection, and attrition (George, 2002), such that group members self-select into groups in which members are similar on various personality dimensions, including dispositional positive and negative affect (and group members also self-select out of dissimilar groups). Thus, groups tend to form around individuals with similar levels of either positive or negative affect, and the net result is that the group's composition leads to a group affective tone (George, 1989).

Consequences of Affect Regulation

We end this section with a final note on possible consequences of affect regulation in groups. There is evidence that certain forms of affect regulation at the individual level, such as deliberate suppression of an emotional state, can lead to performance decrements (Richards & Gross, 2000). It is possible that similar regulation may lead to performance decrements at the group level, at least for the more intentional forms of affect regulation. There is some evidence for this consequence. Spoor and Kelly (2003) induced either positive or negative mood in group members and crossed that manipulation with information that either positive or negative mood was most effective for performance on the type of task that members were about to engage in. Performance decrements were found in the two conditions in which the induced mood and the effective mood were at odds with one another, suggesting that regulation interfered with performance in those conditions. In another study, Jones and Kelly (2008) asked dyads to either suppress or express their negative emotions while trying to sort a series of negatively evocative pictures. Dyads made more errors in the suppression condition relative to the expression condition and a no information control condition. These results suggest that affect regulation may indeed affect group performance.

AFFECT AND GROUP PERFORMANCE

Understanding the affective composition of groups, how that composition comes to be, and how that composition influences other group processes should remain a central area of investigation for researchers interested in affect in small groups. In particular, many interesting questions remain about the impact of affect on group performance.

The number of published studies that explicitly address the influence of affect on group performance is relatively small, but growing. There are a number of studies that address the effect of group members' mood states on group creativity, the effect of members' mood states on group decision making, and the effect of a leader's mood state on group performance. Below we discuss each of these lines of work, as well as research concerning more general performance outcomes.

Affect and Group Creativity

Research from as far back as the early 1980s has shown that positive mood enhances individual level creativity (Isen, 1984), although the relationship is stronger under some conditions than others (Baas, de Dreu, & Nijstad, 2008; Davis, 2009). More recently, Fredrickson's (2001) broaden-and-build theory of positive affect suggests that positive mood increases creativity by encouraging greater cognitive flexibility, broadening behavioral repertoires, and increasing psychological resilience.

The broaden-and-build theory also has been applied to understand the effects of mood on group creativity (Grawitch, Munz, & Kramer, 2003). Based on this theory, Grawitch and colleagues found that group members working on a creative production task (designing a lunar hotel) who were in positive moods tended to be more creative, more efficient, and perceived group processes in a more positive light than did group members who were in neutral moods. In another study using a brainstorming task, Grawitch, Munz, Elliot, and Mathis (2003) again found positive moods to be beneficial to creative performance.

However, other researchers have suggested that negative moods may be beneficial to creative group performance, at least under some circumstances (George & Zhou, 2002; George & Zhou, 2007; Jones & Kelly, 2009). For example, Jones and Kelly (2009) had three-person groups generate advertising slogans for a travel agency. Groups whose members were in negative moods generated more creative slogans relative to individuals in negative moods, whereas groups and individuals in positive moods performed similarly. Furthermore, creative ideas tended to come later in the brainstorming session for groups whose members were in negative moods than in groups whose members were in positive moods. The investigators suggested that positive moods may signal satisfaction with performance at a relatively early point in the interaction, whereas negative moods may signal lack of satisfaction and so lead members to persist longer on the task.

More research is needed to clarify these contradictory results regarding affect and group creativity. Additionally, it would be interesting to investigate how positive and negative moods in groups are related to creativity over time. Another interesting avenue of research is to examine how heterogeneity of moods in groups affects creativity. For example, Tiedens (2000) suggested that heterogeneity of moods in groups may be related to greater creativity, but there is no empirical evidence for this possibility.

Affect and Group Decision Making

It is not surprising that several researchers have examined the influence of mood on group decision making, given the importance of this task type to group activities. Furthermore, many of these researchers have focused on affective influences on information processing in groups. For example, Kelly and Spoor (2006; Kelly, 2001) proposed that, just as mood can affect how individuals process information (Forgas, 2002), so members' moods may affect how a group discusses and processes information, which may subsequently affect group performance. Individual level research suggests that sad individuals often process information in a bottom-up and relatively systematic manner, whereas happy individuals often process information in a top-down and relatively heuristic manner (Forgas, 1992; Schwarz et al., 1991). Applied to the group level, group discussions among members who are in negative moods should be characterized by greater exchange of critical information, longer discussion times, and more systematic processing of arguments, whereas group discussions among members who are in positive moods should be characterized by less exchange of critical information, shorter discussion times, and more heuristic processing.

Support for this hypothesized pattern of results comes from a number of studies. For example, Kooij-de Bode et al. (2010) found that higher group levels of negative affectivity stimulated a greater exchange of information and led to higher quality decisions on a distributed information sharing task compared to lower group negativity. Kelly (2003) also found evidence for greater exchange of unshared information for negative mood (compared to positive mood) participants working on a hidden profiles task, which led to higher quality decisions. In addition, Forgas (1990) found evidence for more systematic processing of information among groups whose members were in negative (as opposed to positive) moods. Specifically, group discussions tended to attenuate evaluative biases when group members were in negative moods, whereas evaluative biases were accentuated when group members were in positive moods. Consistent with these findings, El Hajje (1997) found that group members in negative moods who were discussing choice dilemmas processed arguments more centrally (systematically) and thus showed more group polarization compared to happy and neutral group members.

In contrast to these results, a recent study by Bramesfeld and Gasper (2008) found that group members in positive moods used more effective decision making strategies than members in negative moods. In particular, positive mood group members who were solving a hidden profile problem exchanged more unshared information than did negative mood members. Bramesfeld and Gasper interpreted their results within a broaden-and-build framework, arguing that positive mood members were more likely to focus on information broadly and help other members overcome initial decision preferences during discussion. A similar perspective was taken in research examining knowledge transfer between group members (Levin, Kurtzberg, Phillips, & Lount, 2010). Levin et al. found that positive feelings (elation or happiness) increased group members' ability to receive and act on new information obtained from fellow members, especially compared to the negative feelings of frustration and anger. An important additional finding was that knowledge transfer was enhanced when the interaction partners were in the same affective state (i.e., congruence), regardless of valence.

Bramesfeld and Gasper (2008) also found that the anticipation of group interaction affected how people in negative and positive moods processed information. People in negative moods tended to become distracted at the prospect of group interaction, whereas people in positive moods tended to become more focused. This is consistent with Park and Hinsz's (2006) argument that groups trigger both an approach motivation and positive moods because of associations of groups with rewards, such as "strength and safety in numbers."

Affect, Leaders, and Performance

A large body of work exists concerning the effect of a leader's affect on group processes (see Hogg, this volume). An emerging view is that the management of followers' emotions is an essential and important skill in effective leadership (Humphrey, 2002; McColl-Kennedy & Anderson, 2002; Pescolido, 2002). For example, Pescolido argued that leaders emerge in times of uncertainty and that the emergent leader's specific role is to manage the emotions of fellow group members by determining the emotional response that would be beneficial for the group and then modeling that response. The leader's emotion is transferred to other group members, and the shared emotional experience that results serves to increase group solidarity. McColl-Kennedy and Anderson (2002) also argued that emotional management is essential to leadership, such that effective transformational leaders must be able to instill optimism in their followers, so that followers feel confident in the face of challenges that the leader specifies.

Positive emotions figure centrally in many studies of effective leadership, and a number of studies have shown that leader positive emotions influence both followers' emotional states and group performance. For example, Johnson (2009) found that when leaders were in positive moods, followers' moods were more positive (presumably because of contagion processes). Similarly, Sy, Côté, and Saavedra (2005) found that when leaders were in a positive mood, followers' moods were also more positive, and the groups experienced a more positive group affective tone. Leader positive mood is also linked to charisma (Johnson, 2009) and transformational leadership (McColl-Kennedy & Anderson, 2002), both of which can increase subordinates' positive affect and facilitate effective performance. For example, Erez, Misangyi, Johnson, and LePine (2008) found that a leader's charisma was positively associated with followers' positive affect and negatively associated with followers' negative affect. In a subsequent lab study, the leader's positive expressions and energetic behavior mediated the relationship. Finally, Bono, Foldes, Vinson, and Muros (2007) found that employees with transformational bosses experienced more positive emotions during interaction with customers and fellow employees.

Leader positive affect has also been clearly linked to group and team performance. For example, groups whose leader was in a positive mood experienced enhanced group processes, including better coordination and efficiency (Sy et al., 2005). George (1995) found that external supervisors rated a work group's performance more favorably when the mood of the group leader was also positive. More recently, Johnson (2009) found that followers performed better when leaders were in positive rather than negative moods. The positive net effect of positive mood leaders could partly derive from the status and role expectations discussed earlier in this chapter, such that positive mood leaders are more effective because their emotions are consistent with their role expectations, freeing the group to perform rather than attend to role incongruities and affect regulation. Consistent with this possibility, studies of leaders' emotional displays (Gaddis, Connelly, & Mumford, 2004; Lewis, 2000; Newcombe & Ashkanasy, 2002) have found that leaders who displayed negative emotions were evaluated less positively than leaders who displayed positive emotions. It is also likely that compared to negative mood leaders, positive mood leaders are more likely to praise and use positive terms when interacting with group members, which is likely to increase group members' motivation to perform well.

It is important to note that group performance may not always benefit from a leader's positive emotions. As discussed above, negative emotions in groups may communicate important information about the environment and task at hand, and a leader's emotions may be a particularly important source of task-relevant information (Van Kleef, 2009; Van Kleef et al., 2009). Consistent with this notion, Van Kleef et al. (2009) found that teams high in epistemic motivation (i.e., desire to have an accurate understanding of situations) performed better when their leader expressed anger rather than happiness when providing performance feedback. This effect was mediated by team members' inferences regarding their performance, suggesting that members were using the leader's negative emotions as a source of performance information.

Other Performance Outcomes

Researchers have also investigated the role of affect in group performance on tasks that do not fit neatly into the task types reviewed above. For example, Jordan, Lawrence, and Troth (2006) assembled student teams to develop a workshop presentation. Teams whose members had high levels of negative mood, assessed via the PANAS, received lower performance ratings (on presentation delivery and argumentation) from external observers. This effect was partially mediated by group cohesion (a negative relationship), task conflict (a positive relationship), and process conflict (a negative relationship).

A few studies have examined the consequences of affect on group performance in intact groups. In initial research on group affective tone in sales teams, George (1990) found that positive group affective tone was associated with reduced absenteeism and increased prosocial behaviors toward customers. In addition, subsequent research has shown that positive group affective tone predicts lower absenteeism over time (Mason & Griffin, 2003). Finally, in an examination of professional cricket teams, Totterdell (2000) found that both the average of team members' moods as well as the player's own mood were positively correlated with the players' subjective ratings of their performance and objective indices (e.g., batting average).

Mood has also been found to affect the behavior of participants engaged in social dilemmas. For example, Hertel, Neuhof, Theuer, and Kerr (2000) found evidence that participants in positive, as opposed to negative, moods engaged in behavior that was more reflective of heuristic processing. Specifically, participants in positive moods tended to imitate their partner's behavior in the context of a Chicken dilemma game. In contrast, participants in negative moods demonstrated more rational strategies reflective of deeper information processing. Sanna, Parks, and Chang (2003) provided evidence across a series of studies that mood interacts with competitive vs. cooperative goals to affect responding in social dilemma tasks. Specifically, negative moods led to more competitive responding when competitive goals were salient, whereas negative moods led to more cooperative responding when cooperative goals were salient. These findings are consistent with evidence that negative moods lead to more systematic processing of information.

Finally, as suggested previously, affect can influence important group processes related to performance, such as the ability to coordinate group members' efforts. For example, Bartel and Saavedra (2000) examined affect and group processes in a diverse sample of organizational work groups. Convergence in members' moods occurred across a variety of mood categories, but was particularly strong for moods characterized by unpleasantness. Convergence in mood was also significantly and positively associated with membership stability, as well as with task and social interdependence. Barsade (2002) also found evidence for the relationship between mood convergence and positive group processes. Specifically, she found that contagion of positive mood was associated with improved group cooperation, decreased conflict, and greater perceived group performance. Finally, specific negative emotions may also negatively impact group processes. For example, Shaw and Duffy (2000) found that group envy (perceiving that you lack the superior qualities of another group member) led to negative group processes, such as increased social loafing and diminished group potency.

Future Directions

It is important to note that the effects of affect do not end with its impact on group performance. The influences of affect on group process and performance are dynamic, with performance outcomes affecting subsequent affective states of group members, the emotional history of the group, and the motivation of group members on subsequent tasks. This dynamic nature of affect is explicitly analyzed in some theories, such as those involving transformational leadership and the leader's ability to manage members' emotions of optimism and frustration over time (McColl-Kennedy & Anderson, 2002). The dynamic nature of affect in groups is present or implied in most theoretical and conceptual discussions of affect in groups (e.g., Kelly & Barsade, 2001; Kelly & Spoor, 2006), but there continues to be a dearth of studies actually examining affective processes over time. However, the long-term and ongoing interactions of most "real world" groups and teams will require that future investigations of group performance be informed by the dynamic nature of affective and performance processes.

CONCLUSION

In this chapter, we argued that affective processes are a central component of group functioning. Affective states permeate our experiences as group members, because of the emotions that we carry into the group and because of our interactions with other members. Group processes are influenced by the flow of emotions from member to member and are shaped by those emotional processes. Furthermore, emotional and group processes influence the performance of individual group members and the group as a whole. The goal of this chapter was to provide a comprehensive summary of the state of current knowledge on emotional processes in small groups and of the roles that moods and emotions play in group process and group performance. We hope that it will serve to increase the research attention focused on this important topic.

REFERENCES

Anderson, C., Keltner, D., & John, O. P. (2003). Emotional convergence between people over time. *Journal of Personality and Social Psychology, 84*(5), 1054–1068.

Ashforth, B. E., & Humphrey, R. H. (1995). Emotions in the workplace: A reappraisal. *Human Relations, 48*(2), 97–125.

Ashkanasy, N. M., & Tse, B. (2000). Transformational leadership as management of emotion: A conceptual review. In N. M. Ashkanasy, C. Hartel & W. Zerbe (Eds.), *Emotions in the workplace: Developments in the study of the managed heart* (pp. 221–235). Westport, CT: Quorum Books.

Baas, M., De Dreu. C. K. W., & Nijstad, B. A. (2008). A meta-analysis of 25 years of mood-creativity research: Hedonic tone, activation, or regulatory focus? *Psychological Bulletin, 134*, 779–806.

Bales, R. F. (1950). *Interaction process analysis: A method for the study of small groups.* Reading, MA: Addison-Wesley.

Barsade, S. G. (2002). The ripple effect: Emotional contagion and its influence on group behavior. *Administrative Science Quarterly, 47*(4), 644–675.

Barsade, S. G., & Gibson, D. E. (1998). Group emotion: A view from top and bottom. In D. H. Gruenfeld, B. Mannix, & M. Neale (Eds.), *Research on managing groups and teams* (pp. 81–102). Stamford, CT: JAI Press.

Bartel, C., & Saavedra, R. (2000). The collective construction of work group moods. *Administrative Science Quarterly, 45*, 802–836.

Bass, B. M., & Avolio, B. J. (1994). *Improving organizational effectiveness through transformational leadership.* Thousand Oaks, CA: Sage.

Bavelas, J. B., Black, A., Lemery, C. R., & Mullett, J. (1987). Motor mimicry as primitive empathy. In N. Eisenberg & J. Strayer (Eds.), *Empathy and its development* (pp. 317–338). New York, NY: Cambridge University Press.

Bernieri, F. J., Reznick, J. S., & Rosenthal, R. (1988). Synchrony, pseudosynchrony, and dissynchrony: Measuring the entrainment process in mother-infant dyads. *Journal of Personality and Social Psychology, 54*, 243–253.

Bono, J. E., Foldes, H. J., Vinson, G., & Muros, J. P. (2007). Workplace emotions: The role of supervision and leadership. *Journal of Applied Psychology, 92*, 1357–1367.

Bramesfeld, K. D., & Gasper, K. (2008). Happily putting the pieces together: A test of two explanations for the effects of mood on group-level information processing. *British Journal of Social Psychology, 47*, 285–309.

Brief, A. P., & Weiss, H. M. (2002). Organizational behavior: Affect in the workplace. *Annual Review of Psychology, 53*, 279–307.

Cameron, J. E. (2004). A three-factor model of social identity. *Self and Identity, 3*(3), 239–262.

Chartrand, T. L., & Bargh, J. A. (1999). The chameleon effect: The perception-behavior link and social interaction. *Journal of Personality and Social Psychology, 76*, 893–910.

Chartrand, T. L., & Dalton, A. N. (2009). Mimicry: Its ubiquity, importance, and functionality. In E. Morsella, J. Bargh, & P. M. Gollwitzer (Ed.), *Oxford handbook of human action* (pp. 458–483). New York, NY: Oxford University Press.

Davis, M. A. (2009). Understanding the relationship between mood and creativity: A meta-analysis. *Organizational Behavior and Human Decision Processes, 108*, 25–38.

Elfenbein, H. A. (2008). Emotion in organizations: A review and theoretical integration. In J. P. Walsh & A. P. Brief (Eds.), *The Academy of Management annals* (Vol. 1, pp. 315–386). New York, NY: Lawrence Erlbaum Associates Inc.

El-Hajje, R. A. (1997). The effect of mood on group decision-making. *Dissertation Abstracts International: Section B: The Sciences and Engineering, 57*, 5976.

Erez, A., Misangyi, V. F., Johnson, D. E., & LePine, M. A. (2008). Stirring the hearts of followers: Charismatic leadership as the transferal of affect. *Journal of Applied Psychology, 93*, 602–615.

Forgas, J. P. (1990). Affective influences on individual and group judgments. *European Journal of Social Psychology, 20*, 441–453.

Forgas, J. P. (1992). Affect in social judgments and decisions: A multiprocess model. In H. Zanna (Ed.), *Advances in experimental social psychology* (Vol. 25, pp. 227–275). New York: Academic Press.

Forgas, J. P. (1995). Emotion in social judgments: Review and a new affect infusion model (AIM). *Psychological Bulletin, 117*, 39–66.

Forgas, J. P. (2002). Feeling and doing: Affective influences on interpersonal behavior. *Psychological Inquiry, 13*, 1–28.

Forsyth, D. R. (1999). *Group dynamics* (3rd ed.). Belmont, CA: Wadsworth.

Fredrickson, B. L. (2001). The role of positive emotions in positive psychology: The broaden-and-build theory of positive emotions. *American Psychologist, 56*, 218–226.

Frijda, N. H. (1994). Varieties of affect: Emotions and episodes, moods, and sentiments. In P. Ekman & R. J. Davidson (Eds.), *The nature of emotion: Fundamental questions*. Oxford, UK: Oxford University Press.

Gaddis, B., Connelly, S., & Mumford, M. D. (2004). Failure feedback as an affective event: Influences of leader affect on subordinate attitudes and performance. *The Leadership Quarterly, 15*, 663–686.

Galinsky, A. D., Gruenfeld, D. H., & Magee, J. C. (2003). From power to action. *Journal of Personality and Social Psychology, 85*(3), 453–466.

George, J. M. (1989). Mood and absence. *Journal of Applied Psychology, 74*(2), 317–324.

George, J. M. (1990). Personality, affect, and behavior in groups. *Journal of Applied Psychology, 75,* 107–116.

George, J. M. (1995). Leader positive mood and group performance: The case of customer service. *Journal of Applied Social Psychology, 25,* 778–794.

George, J. M. (1996). Group affective tone. In M. A. West (Ed.), *Handbook of work group psychology* (pp. 77–93). Chichester, UK: Wiley.

George, J. M. (2000). Emotions and leadership: The role of emotional intelligence. *Human Relations, 53*(8), 1027–1055.

George, J. M. (2002). Affect regulation in groups and teams. In R. G. Lord, R. J. Klimoski & R. Kanfer (Eds.), *Emotions in the workplace: Understanding the structure and role of emotions in organizational behavior* (pp. 183–217). San Francisco, CA: Jossey-Bass.

George, J. M., & Zhou, J. (2002). Understanding when bad moods foster creativity and good ones don't: The role of context and clarity of feelings. *Journal of Applied Psychology, 87,* 687–697.

George, J. M., & Zhou, J. (2007). Dual tuning in a supportive context: Joint contributions of position mood, negative mood, and supervisory behavior to employee creativity. *Academy of Management Journal, 50,* 605–622.

Grawitch, M. J., Munz, D. C., Elliot, E. K., & Mathis, A. (2003). Promoting creativity in temporary problem-solving groups: The effects of positive mood and autonomy in problem definition on idea-generating performance. *Group Dynamics: Theory, Research and Practice, 7,* 200–213.

Grawitch, M. J., Munz, D. C., & Kramer, T. J. (2003). Effects of member mood states on creative performance in temporary workgroups. *Group Dynamics: Theory, Research and Practice, 71,* 41–54.

Gump, B. B., & Kulik, J. A. (1997). Stress, affiliation, and emotional contagion. *Journal of Personality and Social Psychology, 72,* 305–319.

Hatfield, E., Cacioppo, J., & Rapson, R. L. (1994). *Emotional contagion.* New York, NY: Cambridge University Press.

Hertel, G., Neuhof, J., Theuer, T., & Kerr, N. L. (2000). Mood effects on cooperation in small groups: Does positive mood simply lead to more cooperation? *Cognition and Emotion, 14,* 441–472.

Hochschild, A. R. (1983). *The managed heart: Commercialization of human feelings.* Berkeley, CA: University of California Press.

Hogg, M. A. (1992). *The social psychology of group cohesiveness: From attraction to social identity.* New York, NY: Harvester Wheatsheaf.

Houser, J. A., & Lovaglia, M. J. (2002). Status, emotion, and the development of solidarity in stratified task groups. In S. R. Thye & E. J. Lawler (Eds.), *Group cohesion, trust, and solidarity: Advances in group processes* (Vol. 19, pp. 109–137). Amsterdam, The Netherlands: Elsevier Science Ltd.

Hsee, C. K., Hatfield, E., Carlson, J. F., & Chemtob, C. (1990). The effect of power on susceptibility to emotional contagion. *Cognition and Emotion, 4,* 327–340.

Humphrey, R. H. (2002). The many faces of emotional leadership. *The Leadership Quarterly, 13,* 493–504.

Huntsinger, J. R., Lun, J., Sinclair, S., & Clore, G. (2009). Contagion without contact: Anticipatory mood matching in response to affiliative motivation. *Personality and Social Psychology Bulletin, 35*(7), 909–922.

Isen, A. M. (1984). Toward understanding the role of affect in cognition. In J. R. S.

Wyer & T. Srull (Eds.), *Handbook of social cognition* (pp. 170–236). Hillsdale, NJ: Lawrence Erlbaum Associates.

Isen, A. M., & Baron, R. A. (1991). Positive affect as a factor in organizational behavior. In B. M. Staw & L. L. Cummings (Eds.), *Research in organizational behavior* (pp. 1–53). Greenwich, CT: JAI Press.

Iyer, A., & Leach, C. W. (2008). Emotion in inter-group relations. *European Review of Social Psychology, 19,* 86–124.

Janis, I. L. (1972). *Victims of groupthink: A psychological study of foreign-policy decisions and fiascoes.* Oxford, UK: Houghton Mifflin.

Jetten, J., Branscombe, N. R., Spears, R., & McKimmie, B. M. (2003). Predicting the paths of peripherals: The interaction of identification and future possibilities. *Personality and Social Psychology Bulletin, 29,* 130–140.

Johnson, S. K. (2009). Do you feel what I feel? Mood contagion and leadership outcomes. *The Leadership Quarterly, 20,* 814–827.

Jones, E. E. (1998). Major developments in five decades of social psychology. In D. T. Gilbert, S. T. Fiske, Susan, & G. Lindzey (Eds.), *The Handbook of Social Psychology* (4th ed., pp. 3–57). New York, NY: McGraw-Hill.

Jones, E. E., & Kelly, J. R. (2008, May). *Turn that frown upside down: Suppressing negative emotions hurts performance.* Paper presented at the annual meeting of the Midwestern Psychological Association, Chicago, IL.

Jones, E. E., & Kelly, J. R. (2009). No pain, no gains: Negative mood leads to process gains in idea generation groups. *Group Dynamics: Theory, Research, and Practice, 13,* 75–88.

Jordan, P. J., Lawrence, S. A., and Troth, A. C. (2006). Examining the impact of emotional intelligence on team processes and team performance. *Journal of Management and Organization, 12,* 131–145.

Karau, S. J., & Williams, K. D. (1997). The effects of group cohesiveness on social loafing and social compensation. *Group Dynamics: Theory, Research, and Practice, 1,* 156–168.

Kelly, J. R. (2001). Mood and emotion in groups. In M. A. Hogg & R. S. Tindale (Eds.), *The Blackwell handbook of social psychology* (Vol. 3, pp. 164–181). Oxford, UK: Blackwell.

Kelly, J. R. (2003, May). *Group mood and group decision making.* Invited talk presented at the meeting of the Midwestern Psychological Association, Chicago, IL.

Kelly, J. R., & Barsade, S. G. (2001). Mood and emotions in small groups and work teams. *Organizational Behavior and Human Decision Processes, 86,* 99–130.

Kelly, J. R., & Spoor, J. R. (2006). Affective influences in groups. In J. P. Forgas (Ed.), *Affect in social thinking and behavior* (pp. 311–325). New York, NY: Psychology Press.

Kelly, J. R., & Spoor, J. R. (2007). Naïve theories of the effects of mood in groups: A preliminary investigation. *Group Processes and Intergroup Relations, 10,* 203–222.

Keltner, D., & Haidt, J. (2001). Social functions of emotions. In T. J. Mayne & G. A. Bonanno (Eds.), *Emotions: Currrent issues and future directions: Emotions and social behavior* (pp. 192–213). New York, NY: Guilford Press.

Kooij-de Bode, H. J. M., van Knippenberg, D., & van Ginkel, W. P. (2010). Good effects of bad feelings: Negative affectivity and group decision-making. *British Journal of Management, 21*(2), 375–392.

Lakin, J. L., & Chartrand, T. L. (2003). Using nonconscious behavioral mimicry to create affiliation and rapport. *Psychological Science, 14*(4), 334–339.

Lakin, J. L., Jefferis, V. E., Cheng, C. M., & Chartrand, T. L. (2003). The chameleon effect as social glue: Evidence for the evolutionary significance of nonconscious mimicry. *Journal of Nonverbal Behavior, 27,* 145–162.

Larsen, R. J. (2000). Toward a science of mood regulation. *Psychological Inquiry, 11*(3), 129–141.

Lazarus, R. S. (1991). *Emotion and adaptation.* New York, NY: Oxford University Press.

LeBon, G. (1895/1960). *The crowd: A study of the popular mind.* New York, NY: Viking Press.

Levine, J. M., & Moreland, R. L. (1990). Progress in small group research. *Annual Review of Psychology, 41,* 585–634.

Levin, D. Z., Kurtzberg, T. R., Phillips, K. W., & Lount, R. B., Jr. (2010). The role of affect in knowledge transfer. *Group Dynamics: Theory, Research, and Practice, 14,* 123–142.

Lewin, K., Lippitt, R., & White, R. (1939). Patterns of aggressive behavior in experimentally created "social climates." *Journal of Social Psychology, 10,* 271–299.

Lewis, K. M. (2000). When leaders display emotion: How followers respond to negative emotional expression of male and female leaders. *Journal of Organizational Behavior, 21,* 221–234.

Mackie, D. M., Maitner, A. T., & Smith, E. R. (2009). Inter group emotions theory. In T. D. Nelson (Ed.), *Handbook of prejudice, stereotyping, and discrimination* (pp. 285–307). New York, NY: Psychology Press.

Magee, J. C., & Tiedens, L. Z. (2006). Emotional ties that bind: The roles of valence and consistency of group emotion in inferences of cohesiveness and common fate. *Personality and Social Psychology Bulletin, 32,* 1703–1715.

Mallett, R. K., Huntsinger, J. R., Sinclair, S., & Swim, J. K. (2008). Seeing through their eyes: When majority group members take collective action on behalf of an outgroup. *Group Processes & Intergroup Relations, 11,* 451–470.

Mason, C. M., & Griffin, M. A. (2003). Group absenteeism and positive affective tone: A longitudinal study. *Journal of Organizational Behavior, 24,* 667–687.

McColl-Kennedy, J. R., & Anderson, R. D. (2002). Impact of leadership style and emotions on subordinate performance. *The Leadership Quarterly, 13,* 545–559.

McGrath, J. E., & Kelly, J. R. (1986). *Time and human interaction: Toward a social psychology of time.* New York, NY: Guilford Press.

Mobley, W. H., Griffeth, R. W., Hand, H. H., & Meglino, B. M. (1979). Review and conceptual analysis of the employee turnover process. *Psychological Bulletin, 86*(3), 493–522.

Mullen, B., & Copper, C. (1994). The relation between group cohesiveness and performance: An integration. *Psychological Bulletin, 115,* 210–227.

Newcombe, M. J., & Ashkanasy, N. M. (2002). The role of affect and affective congruence in perceptions of leaders: An experimental study. *Leadership Quarterly, 13,* 601–614.

Park, E. S., & Hinsz, V. B. (2006). Strength and safety in numbers: A theoretical perspective on group influences on approach and avoidance motivation. *Motivation and Emotion, 30,* 135–142.

Parkinson, R. (1996). Emotions are social. *British Journal of Psychology, 87,* 663–683.

Pescolido, A. T. (2002). Emergent leaders as managers of group emotion. *The Leadership Quarterly, 13,* 583–599.

Rafaeli, A., & Sutton, R. I. (1989). The expression of emotion in organizational life. In L.

L. Cummings & B. M. Staw (Eds.), *Research in organizational behavior* (pp. 1–42). Greenwich, CT: JAI Press.

Richards, J. M., & Gross, J. J. (2000). Emotion regulation and memory: The cognitive costs of keeping one's cool. *Journal of Personality and Social Psychology, 79,* 410–424.

Sanna, L. J., Parks, C. D., & Chang, E. C. (2003). Mixed-motive conflict in social dilemmas: Mood as input to competitive and cooperative goals. *Group Dynamics: Theory, Research, and Practice, 7,* 26–40.

Schmid Mast, M., Jonas, K., & Hall, J. A. (2009). Give a person power and he or she will show interpersonal sensitivity: The phenomenon and its why and when. *Journal of Personality and Social Psychology, 97*(5), 835–850.

Schwarz, N., Bless, H., & Bohner, G. (1991). Mood and persuasion: Affective states influence the processing of persuasive communications. In M. P. Zanna (Ed.), *Advances in experimental social psychology* (Vol. 24, pp. 161–199). San Diego, CA: Academic Press.

Schwarz, N., & Clore, G. L. (1983). Mood, misattribution, and judgments of well-being: Informative and directive functions of affective states. *Journal of Personality and Social Psychology, 45*(3), 512–523.

Shaw, M. E. (1932). A comparison of individuals and small groups in the rational solution of complex problems. *American Journal of Psychology, 44,* 491–504.

Shaw, M. K., & Duffy, J. D. (2000). The Salieri Syndrome: Consequences of envy in groups. *Small Group Research, 31*(3), 3–23.

Smith, E. R., & Mackie, D. M. (2008). Intergroup emotions. In M. Lewis, J. M. Haviland-Jones, & L. F. Barrett (Eds.), *Handbook of emotions* (3rd ed., pp. 428–439). New York, NY: Guilford Press.

Spoor, J. R., & Kelly, J. R. (2003, February). *Situational norms and group mood: Implications for task performance.* Paper presented at the meeting of the Society for Personality and Social Psychology, Los Angeles, CA.

Spoor, J. R., & Kelly, J. R. (2004). The evolutionary significance of affect in groups: Communication and group bonding. *Group Processes and Intergroup Relations, 7,* 398–416.

Spoor, J. R., & Kelly, J. R. (2009). Mood convergence in dyads: Effects of valence and leadership. *Social Influence, 4*(4), 282–297.

Stokes, J. P. (1983). Components of group cohesion: Intermember attraction, instrumental values, and risk taking. *Small Group Behavior, 14,* 163–173.

Sullins, E. S. (1991). Emotional contagion revisited: Effects of social comparison and expressive style on mood convergence. *Personality and Social Psychology Bulletin, 17*(2), 166–174.

Sy, T., Côté, S., & Saavedra, R. (2005). The contagious leader: Impact of the leader's mood on the group of group members, group affective tone, and group processes. *Journal of Applied Psychology, 90,* 295–305.

Tice, D. M., & Bratslavsky, E. (2000). Giving in to feel good: The place of emotion regulation in the context of general self-control. *Psychological Inquiry, 11*(3), 149–159.

Tickle-Degnen, L., & Rosenthal, R. (1987). Group rapport and nonverbal behavior. In C. Hendrick (Ed.), *Group processes and intergroup relations* (Vol. 9, pp. 113–136). Thousand Oaks, CA: Sage.

Tiedens, L. Z. (2000). Powerful emotions: The vicious cycle of social status positions and emotions. In N. M. Ashkanasy, C. E. Härtel, & W. J. Zerbe (Eds.), *Emotions in the workplace: Research, theory, and practice* (pp. 72–81). Westport, CT: Quorum Books/Greenwood.

Tiedens, L. Z. (2001). Anger and advancement versus sadness and subjugation: The effect of negative emotion expressions on social status conferral. *Journal of Personality and Social Psychology, 80*(1), 86–94.

Tiedens, L. Z., Ellsworth, P. C., & Mesquita, B. (2000). Stereotypes about sentiments and status: Emotional expectations for high- and low-status group members. *Personality and Social Psychology Bulletin, 26*(5), 560–574.

Totterdell, P. (2000). Catching moods and hitting runs: Mood linkage and subjective performance in professional sport teams. *Journal of Applied Psychology, 85,* 848–859.

Triplett, N. (1898). The dynamogenic factors in pace-making and competition. *American Journal of Psychology, 9,* 507–533.

Tuckman, B. W. (1965). Developmental sequences in small groups. *Psychological Bulletin, 63,* 384–399.

Van Kleef, G. A. (2009). How emotions regulate social life: The emotions as social information (EASI) model. *Current Directions in Psychological Science , 18,* 184–188.

Van Kleef, G. A., Homan, A. C., Beersma, B., Van Knippenberg, D., Van Knippenberg, B., & Damen, F. (2009). Seering sentiment or cold calculation? The effects of leader emotional displays on team performance depend on follower epistemic motivation. *Academy of Management Journal, 52*(3), 562–580.

Walker, I., & Smith, H. L. (2002). *Relative deprivation: Specification, development, and integration* (pp. 1–9). New York, NY: Cambridge University Press.

Wallbott, H. G., & Scherer, K. R. (1986). The antecedents of emotional experiences. In K. R. Scherer, H. G. Wallbott, & A. B. Summerfield (Eds.), Experiencing emotion: A cross-cultural study (pp. 69–97). Cambridge, UK: Cambridge University Press.

Weiss, H. M., & Brief, A. P. (2001). Affect at work: An historical perspective. In R. L. Payne & C. L. Cooper (Eds.), *The psychology of work: Theoretically based empirical research.* Hillsdale, NJ: Lawrence Erlbaum.

Zerbe, W., & Hartel, C. E. J. (2005). *Research on emotion in organizations: The effect of affect in organizational settings.* Oxford, UK: Elsevier.

3

Negotiation

LEIGH L. THOMPSON, JIUNWEN WANG,
and BRIAN C. GUNIA

A nytime people cannot achieve their goals without the cooperation of others, they are negotiating. By this definition, negotiation is a ubiquitous social activity. Research on negotiation has been influenced by a wide variety of fields, including mathematics, management, organizational behavior, social psychology, cognitive psychology, economics, communication studies, sociology, and political science. The products of this multidisciplinary approach have been intense theoretical development and an impressive body of empirical findings.

Negotiation research has undergone several phases, characterized by different paradigms of thought. For example, during the 1980s, negotiation research was heavily influenced by game theory and behavioral decision theory. During the 1990s, negotiation research was strongly influenced by social psychology. At the turn of the millennium, negotiation research has become decidedly cognitive in flavor. Each generation of research has provided scholars with a new vantage point from which to examine the complex dance of negotiation.

One of the most important theoretical distinctions in negotiation scholarship is the one defining normative and descriptive research (Raiffa, 1982). Normative research, largely derived from game theory, economics, and mathematics, proposes optimal models of the negotiation problem and prescribes what people would do if they were wise and all-knowing (cf. Luce & Raiffa, 1957; Nash, 1951). In this review, we focus on descriptive research, which recognizes that negotiators do not always behave in a game-theoretic, optimal fashion. The way negotiators actually behave usually departs significantly from normative, economic models (but not necessarily from behavioral economic models; Camerer, 2003). For example, whereas normative models predict that people will/

should almost always defect in a prisoner's dilemma or social dilemma, actual defection rates are dramatically lower than 100% (Camerer, 2003; Komorita & Parks, 1995). Moreover, normative models of negotiation dictate that parties should reach Pareto-optimal settlements, defined as agreements that cannot be improved upon without hurting one or both of the parties' outcomes. However, very few negotiators reach Pareto-optimal outcomes on a regular basis (Thompson, 2009; Thompson & Hastie, 1990).

Our focus is limited to descriptive research influenced by social psychology and its close cousin, organizational behavior—both of which have strongly influenced negotiation research since 1980. We focus on empirical studies that examine the individual negotiator within one or more of five systems—intrapersonal, interpersonal, group, organizational, and virtual. We use these systems as a guide for organizing our review. Within each system, we focus on two overarching themes: integrative negotiation and distributive negotiation, described further below.

The Intrapersonal, Interpersonal, Group, Organizational, and Virtual Systems

We use the term "intrapersonal system" to signify the ways that negotiation behavior and outcomes depend upon the perceptions and inner experiences of the negotiator. For example, the intrapersonal system might include research on how an individual's sense of power influences his or her negotiation behavior, satisfaction, and outcomes. The interpersonal system refers to the ways that negotiators' behavior and outcomes depend upon the presence of the other party or parties—negotiations in the context of others, and the dyadic aspects of negotiation behavior. Investigations of how a negotiator's mood influences the other party's behavior and the ultimate negotiation outcome exemplify this system. The group system encompasses social dynamics that extend beyond a single dyad—for example, group identity, cultural identity, coalitions, and conformity. The organizational system represents a higher level of analysis and examines the negotiator as embedded in a larger network or marketplace. For example, some studies at this level investigate how negotiators choose optimal counterparties in a marketplace of negotiators. Finally, the virtual system focuses on how negotiators' medium of interaction—such as face-to-face, phone, or email—affects the nature and quality of negotiation processes and outcomes. Several studies have investigated whether negotiators are more likely to discover mutual value when negotiating face-to-face or via computer (cf. Morris, Nadler, Kurtzberg, & Thompson, 2002; Naquin & Paulson, 2003; Purdy, Nye, & Balakrishnan, 2000).

Integrative and Distributive Negotiation

Whereas the independent variables or causal factors underlying negotiation have been highly eclectic and strongly influenced by the contemporary theoretical milieu, the dependent variables under investigation have remained consistent across several decades. The main reason for this consistency is the influence of economics on negotiation research. Within negotiation research, the two dependent variables that appear in virtually every published study of negotiation are negotiation processes and outcomes.

Negotiation processes include negotiators' behaviors, cognitions, emotions, and motivations. For example, much social psychological research has focused on negotiator satisfaction and the perceived relationship between the parties (see Curhan, Elfenbein, & Xu, 2006, for a review). Negotiation outcomes include the integrative and distributive features of the agreement. By "integrative," we mean the extent to which the negotiated outcome satisfies the interests of both parties in a way that implies the outcome cannot be improved upon without hurting one or more of the parties involved (i.e., Pareto optimality; Pareto, 1935). A classic example of Pareto optimality is the story of the two sisters who quarreled bitterly over a single orange (Fisher & Ury, 1981). The sisters resolved the dispute by cutting the orange in half, such that each sister received exactly 50%. Later, the sisters discovered that one only needed the juice whereas the other only needed the rind; unfortunately they had failed to realize this during the negotiation itself. Cutting the orange in half was not an integrative outcome, because another feasible solution would have simultaneously improved both sisters' outcomes—one sister could have received all of the juice and the other all of the rind. This solution would have fully maximized both parties' interests. The fact that another feasible solution would have been better for both parties suggests that the actual outcome was suboptimal or Pareto inefficient, as opposed to integrative.

The distributive aspect of negotiation refers to how negotiators divide or apportion scarce resources among themselves. For example, in the classic ultimatum game (Güth, Schmittberger, & Schwarze, 1982; Ochs & Roth, 1989), one person ("player 1") receives a fixed amount of money (say $100) to divide with another person. Player 1 proposes a split of the $100; if player 2 agrees, the proposed split takes effect. If player 2 rejects the proposal, each party gets $0. The split that Player 1 proposes can be perceived to be fair or acceptable to player 2, leading player 2 to accept the offer. In this case, the distributive aspect of the negotiation is the proportion of the original $100 that each negotiator receives.

Recently, the initial focus on the economic outcomes of negotiation has widened to include investigations of subjective outcomes. Whereas rational behavior in negotiation is usually equated with the maximization of economic gain, joint or individual, some have argued that it is equally appropriate to consider social-psychological outcomes, such as the quality of the relationship, the degree of trust between parties, each negotiator's satisfaction, and each person's willingness to negotiate with the other in the future. In an attempt to measure subjective concerns, Curhan and his colleagues surveyed people on what they value in negotiation (Curhan et al., 2006). Four distinct considerations emerged: feelings about instrumental outcomes (i.e., how much money they made), feelings about themselves (e.g., how competent they were in the negotiation), feelings about the process (e.g., whether the conversation was constructive) and feelings about the relationship (i.e., whether the negotiation preserved or strengthened it).

INTRAPERSONAL LEVEL

Negotiation research at the intrapersonal level of analysis clearly recognizes the multiparty nature of negotiation, but it emphasizes how the inner experience of the negotiator impacts negotiation processes and outcomes, and vice-versa. We focus on three interrelated intrapersonal constructs that have received significant research attention in recent years—power, gender, and affect. Many studies of power, gender, and affect in negotiations follow from research stimulated by the work of Steele (Steele & Aronson, 1995), Banaji (Blair & Banaji, 1996), Greenwald (Greenwald, Draine, & Abrams, 1996), Bargh (Bargh & Pietromonaco, 1982), and others on the behavioral effects of unconscious priming. This research examines how subtle, below-threshold activation of concepts influences above-threshold behaviors. In negotiations, above-threshold behaviors substantially impact negotiation processes and outcomes, which may unconsciously activate other cognitions and behaviors.

Power

Power refers to an individual's relative ability to alter other people's outcomes (Keltner, Gruenfeld, & Anderson, 2003). Several studies examine psychological power as a state, operationalized through priming, but others examine power as a trait or individual difference. Although negotiators may have several sources of structural power (French & Raven, 1959), the most commonly investigated source of power is the negotiator's best alternative to a negotiated agreement (BATNA; Fisher & Ury, 1981).

A negotiator's BATNA has become the primary indicator of a negotiator's relative power in negotiation. The BATNA concept was formally introduced by Fisher and Ury in 1981; however, the concept actually traces back to the social exchange theory of Thibaut and Kelley (1959). Exchange theory cites rewards (borrowed from psychology) and resources (borrowed from economics) as the foundation of interpersonal exchanges. Rewards refer to the benefits a person enjoys from participating in a relationship (Thibaut & Kelley, 1959), whereas resources are any commodities, material or symbolic, that can be transmitted through interpersonal behavior (Foa & Foa, 1975) and give one person the capacity to reward another (Emerson, 1972). Satisfaction with an exchange relationship is derived in part from the evaluation of the outcomes available in a relationship. Outcomes are equal to the rewards obtained from a relationship minus the costs incurred.

People in social exchanges compare the outcomes of the current exchange with the outcomes they could achieve in an alternative exchange—these alternative outcomes are operationalized as the "comparison level of alternatives," or CLalt. When the CLalt exceeds the outcomes available in a current relationship, the person is more likely to leave the relationship. The concept of CLalt is parallel to BATNA. When one's BATNA is better than an agreement one can reach with a particular negotiation counterpart, one should choose to not agree and exercise the BATNA instead.

Negotiators' BATNAs are strongly related to their reservation point (RP). RPs are the quantification of a negotiator's BATNA (Raiffa, 1982). According to Raiffa (1982), a negotiator's RP is the point at which a negotiator is indifferent between reaching a deal with party A or walking away from the table and exercising his/her BATNA. For a seller, prices exceeding reservation points are acceptable; for a buyer, prices less than reservation points are acceptable. RPs are generally operationalized as the value attached to a negotiator's BATNA, plus or minus the value of any idiosyncratic preferences they attach to reaching agreement versus exercising the BATNA.

Just as BATNA traces to Thibaut and Kelley's (1959) earlier concept of CLalt, reservation price traces to Walton and McKersie's (1965) concept of resistance point, described in their book *A Behavioral Theory of Labor Relations*. Resistance point is a negotiator's subjectively determined bottom line—the point at which negotiators are indifferent between reaching agreement and walking away, in the midst of the negotiation. Walton and McKersie (1965) postulated that negotiators who had more attractive resistance points were in a more powerful position because they could simply offer the other party just enough to meet their resistance point and claim the rest (the surplus) for themselves. Although the concept of reservation price has largely displaced the concept of resistance point in recent academic research, resistance points provided an important theoretical step toward specifying the concept of bargaining zone. Bargaining zone is basically the overlap between two negotiators' RPs—the buyer's RP minus the seller's RP. If this number is positive, a zone of possible agreement (ZOPA) is said to exist; if it is negative, no ZOPA exists.

Research studying the effects of power have documented that there is a strong, causal relationship between the attractiveness of a negotiator's BATNA and the negotiator's ability to claim resources in a given negotiation (Galinsky & Mussweiler, 2001; Magee, Galinsky, & Gruenfeld, 2007; Mussweiler & Strack, 1999). Negotiators with attractive BATNAs are considered "powerful"; these negotiators are decidedly more assertive in negotiations. For example, powerful people move first, both by initiating negotiations and by making the first offer (Magee et al., 2007). When power is primed (by instructing people to write about a time when they felt powerful or to perform a word-completion task involving words about power), these individuals often make the first offer in negotiations. If the concept of BATNA is a measure of structural power, then chronic tendencies to dominate others in social relationships reflect personal power. Both structural and personal power can improve negotiators' outcomes by leading them to make the first offer (Galinsky & Mussweiler, 2001; Magee et al., 2007; Mussweiler & Strack, 1999).

Although having power may increase a negotiator's propensity to make a first offer, this may depend on the nature of the negotiation. Specifically, it is reasonable to assume that if both negotiators have attractive BATNAs, their motivation to reach mutual agreement is not as high as that of two negotiators with very poor alternatives. Thus, the effects of one's power in a negotiation may depend on the size of the bargaining zone. Given that BATNAs establish the minimum level of benefits one would receive, irrespective of what occurs in the negotiation, their influence quickly diminishes once benefits equivalent to the BATNA value have been attained.

In one study, strong BATNAs improved negotiators' outcomes more when the bargaining zone was small rather than large (Kim & Fragale, 2005). When the bargaining zone was large, power tended to derive more from a negotiator's contribution to the negotiation. In this case, contribution refers to the benefits that a negotiator contributes beyond the value of the counterparty's BATNA. For instance, if the counterparty is selling a house and has a BATNA (e.g., another buyer offering $200K for the house) and the negotiator offers $210K for the house, the difference, or $10K, is the contribution.

Once an offer equaled the value of one's BATNA in Kim and Fragale's research, outcomes depended more on the extent to which the counterparty could contribute value beyond the BATNA. Contributions thus exerted an important influence on negotiation outcomes, especially as the potential agreement became more valuable (relative to negotiators' BATNAs).

Gender

Power is manifested and expressed by negotiators in many ways. For example, power can depend upon structural factors (e.g., BATNA) or on personal characteristics. A negotiator's structural power can change when environmental conditions change, but personal power is, for the most part, fixed. For example, a negotiator who is selling her house and has an attractive offer from a very motivated buyer has a lot of structural power; however, if the buyer suddenly withdraws the offer on the house (perhaps due to a failed home inspection), the negotiator's power plummets. Conversely, a negotiator who is a vice president of a major company and has a lot of personal charm also holds high power, which is more resilient to temporary fluctuations of the market (except in the case of losing her job!). One important source of personal power is gender.

To exert influence in a negotiation, gender must be activated or made salient (Kray & Thompson, 2005). In a series of investigations modeled after Steele and Aronson (1995), Kray, Thompson, and Galinsky (2001) did just this. Specifically, they investigated whether the mere activation of gender (and its accompanying stereotypes) impacts negotiation performance. The prevailing stereotype is that women are less assertive and agentic than men. Because many people see negotiation as a situation requiring assertive and agentic behavior, stereotypically female traits may seem inconsistent with negotiation once the connection is made salient. For these reasons, the mere mention of negotiation might create an internal conflict within women: On one hand, they may believe that performing well requires them to engage in counterstereotypical behaviors. On the other hand, they may believe that others expect them to behave in an accommodating, nonassertive fashion.

Kray et al. (2001) hypothesized that the mention of gender might operate much like stereotype threat (Steele & Aronson, 1995). Gender salience might thus operate like a low-power state, preventing women from acting assertively. In their study, women did, in fact, get worse outcomes than did men in mixed-gender negotiations, when an implicit gender stereotype was subtly activated. However, it was reasoned that explicit activation of the gender stereotype may allow women to counteract it. As predicted, explicitly activated gender stereotypes led to a stereotype-reactance effect, in which women actually outperformed men by claiming more resources (presumably in an attempt to defy the stereotype). Women effectively said, "Well, unassertive behavior and accommodation may be the cultural stereotype of women, but it is surely not me!"

In another series of studies, Kray and colleagues (Kray, Reb, Galinsky, & Thompson, 2004) reasoned that negotiation, like other social activities, can be construed as either a masculine or feminine activity. The masculine construal of negotiation involves agency and assertiveness. It is also possible to construe successful negotiation as understanding human behavior, perceiving nonverbal cues, and building trust. Arguably, these skills are more consistent with the classic female stereotype. Indeed, women outperformed men when traditionally feminine traits were linked with negotiation success, and each gender outperformed the other when the other gender was linked with negotiation ineffectiveness (Kray et al., 2001).

The implications of stereotype activation may also depend on whether negotiators have high or low power (Kray et al., 2004). Specifically, activation of an explicit male stereotype led to negotiated outcomes that favored the high-power negotiator, whereas activation of an explicit female stereotype led to more integrative, win-win outcomes that were beneficial for both parties, much like the sisters who discovered the juice-and-rind tradeoff.

Other studies (Small, Gelfand, Babcock, & Gettman, 2007) examine gender differences in the willingness to initiate negotiation (Babcock, Gelfand, Small, & Stayhn, 2006; Bowles, Babcock, & Lai, 2007; but see Gerhart & Rynes, 1991), tracing these differences to power differences. Because women traditionally have less power than do men in U.S. society (Eagly & Wood, 1982), they initiate negotiations less often; however, this difference is attributable to the fact that situations framed as "negotiation" conflict with politeness norms that prevail in low-power groups (Babcock et al., 2006). Consistent with this reasoning and the links between gender and power, framing negotiations as opportunities to "ask" eliminated gender differences in negotiation initiation, as did priming psychological power (Kray et al., 2001). Along similar lines, Bowles et al. (2007) traced differences in the initiation of negotiation behavior to observers' reactions. Both male and female observers penalized female job candidates for initiating negotiations. Consistent with Small et al.'s (2007) politeness argument, participants rated women who initiated negotiations as less nice and more demanding.

Moreover, women were less likely than were men to initiate negotiations with a male (but not a female) evaluator.

Another stream of gender research examines what happens when women do, in fact, initiate negotiation. Although gender differences in actual negotiation behavior have received exhaustive research attention (e.g., Deal, 2000; Gerhart & Rynes, 1991; Major, Vanderslice, & McFarlin, 1984; Stevens, Bavetta, & Gist, 1993; Watson, 1994), recent meta-analyses (Stuhlmacher & Walters, 1999; Walters, Stuhlmacher, & Meyer, 1998) characterize such differences as modest and context dependent. According to these meta-analyses, women negotiate slightly more cooperatively than do men, but situational factors such as relative power of the negotiator, integrative potential of the task, and mode of communication often override this effect. In addition, other individual differences (i.e., social motives) explain cooperation in negotiation more readily than gender does. For example, negotiators with a prosocial motive behave more cooperatively (and achieve better outcomes) than do those with an egoistic motive (De Dreu, Weingart, & Kwon, 2000). Gender differences seem to explain relatively little variance by comparison, and it is possible that the variance they do explain reflects underlying gender differences in social motives.

There are behavioral implications of gender-dependent power. For example, does maintaining steady eye contact have different power implications for male and female negotiators (Swaab & Swaab, 2009)? When negotiators made eye contact (and when visual access was possible), agreement quality was maximized for women but minimized for men (Swaab & Swaab, 2009). Apparently, women and men had different affective experiences during negotiation. When men made eye contact, perceived power differences were exacerbated, creating a sense of discomfort that undermined agreement quality.

Affect

Forgas's (1995) affect infusion model considers the impact of mood on cognitive processing, identifying two overarching conditions under which mood is likely to affect information processing. The first condition is when situations require cognition about difficult, peripheral subjects; the second is when situations require judgment of obscure, atypical subjects (Forgas 1995). According to the affect infusion model, the adoption of information processing style also depends on a combination of factors such as the novelty, complexity, and salience of the task, and the personality, motivation, affective state, and cognitive capacity of the person involved in the judgment process.

The implication for negotiation processes and outcomes is that feeling good or feeling bad should have important consequences for negotiator cognition and strategies (Lanzetta, 1989). In one study, positive mood generated superior individual outcomes in negotiations with integrative potential characterized by cooperative negotiation strategies (Forgas, 1998). In another study, positive mood decreased evasive and equivocal communications, especially in high-conflict negotiations (Forgas & Cromer, 2004).

One line of research qualifies these findings by demonstrating that the impact of affect depends on power. For example, agreement quality was better predicted by the chronic, positive affect of high-power negotiators than that of low-power negotiators (Anderson & Thompson, 2004). Apparently, the more powerful negotiator's emotions were more influential than the less powerful negotiator's emotions. Furthermore, trait-positive affect, combined with high structural power (i.e., a strong BATNA), helped negotiation dyads reach more integrative agreements without harming either negotiator's individual outcomes (Anderson & Thompson, 2004). Recently, investigations of negative affect such as anger expressions have also been examined (Sinaceur & Tiedens, 2006). Anger expressions produced concessions from negotiators with a poor BATNA, presumably because the angry negotiator communicated "toughness." This finding contrasts somewhat with earlier investigations in which feelings of high anger and low compassion produced lower joint outcomes, but not lower individual outcomes (Allred, Mallozzi, Matsui, & Raia, 1997). Similarly, when negotiators expressed positive affect, negative affect, or neutral affect in a take-it-or-leave-it ultimatum, positive-affect negotiators were most likely to have their ultimatum accepted. Negative-affect negotiators were the least successful (Kopelman, Rosette, & Thompson, 2000).

Other research examined the relationship between economic outcomes, negotiator behavior, and satisfaction (an affective response to negotiation). For example, a negotiator's focus on RP or aspirations influences feelings of success in a negotiation (Thompson, 1995). Negotiators with low RPs felt more successful than did those with high RPs, even though their final settlements were identical. Furthermore, negotiators with low aspirations felt more successful than did negotiators with high aspirations, even though the final settlement was identical. Aspirations influenced negotiators' perceptions of success more than did RPs. In general, aspirations, relative to RPs, exerted a more powerful influence on the demands people made to others in negotiations and how successful they felt about negotiated outcomes.

Along similar lines, negotiators might feel dissatisfied when the counterparty accepts their first offer (Galinsky, Seiden, Kim, & Medvec, 2002). Apparently, when the counterparty immediately accepts one's first offer, a counterfactual thought process is produced (e.g., "Oh no, I should have asked for more!"). This counterfactual thought process results in dissatisfaction, even when negotiators' outcomes were objectively superior to agreements reached later in negotiations. Thoughts about how much better they could have done overwhelmed negotiators' objective outcomes. These findings are consistent with studies demonstrating that negotiators' satisfaction depends heavily on the comparison value on which they focus attention: Negotiators who focused on their target price consistently achieved better outcomes but were less satisfied than those who focused on their BATNA (Galinsky, Mussweiler, & Medvec, 2002). Yet, focusing on the target price during a negotiation and the BATNA after a negotiation allowed negotiators to achieve superior outcomes without the accompanying dissatisfaction.

An array of negative cognitions and emotions confront negotiators who fail to reach deals (O'Connor & Arnold, 2001). For example, negotiators who failed to reach agreement (i.e., impasse) found themselves caught in a distributive spiral such that they interpreted their performance as unsuccessful, experienced negative emotions, and developed negative perceptions of their counterpart and the process. Moreover, they were less willing to work with their counterpart in the future, planned to share less information and behave less cooperatively, and lost faith in negotiation as an effective means of managing conflicts (O'Connor & Arnold, 2001).

INTERPERSONAL LEVEL

Economic and Social Psychological Foundations

Traditionally, negotiation at the interpersonal level has been viewed via the lens of mixed-motive interaction. The concept of mixed-motive interaction was first introduced by economist Thomas Schelling (1960) to refer to situations where two or more parties face a conflict between two motives: cooperation (the integrative aspects of negotiation) and competition (the distributive aspects). In negotiations, individuals must cooperate to avoid impasse and reach mutual agreement, but compete to gain sufficient resources for themselves. Two-person bargaining is thus a classic example of a mixed-motive interaction. Indeed, Lax and Sebenius (1986a) emphasize that all negotiators must balance the "twin tasks" of negotiation: creating value and claiming value.

The interpersonal system in negotiation was also richly stimulated by basic research in the areas of emotional contagion, mimicry, and behavioral synchrony (Chartrand & Bargh, 1999). One finding in these areas, for example, is that people tend to engage in face rubbing, foot shaking, and smiling more in the presence of someone who engages in that behavior (Chartrand & Bargh, 1999). Another is that behavioral mimicry increases liking and rapport between interaction partners (Tiedens & Fragale, 2003). Beyond behavioral mimicry, more complex interpersonal mimicry such as mood contagion (see Neumann & Strack, 2000) and dominance complementarity (see Tiedens & Fragale, 2003) have also been documented. Mood contagion effects demonstrate that people easily assume the moods of others. Dominance complementarity findings demonstrate that people respond to others' dominant behavior with a submissive stance, and vice versa. Furthermore, they demonstrate that when one party complements dominant behavior with submissive behavior, this facilitates interpersonal liking (Tiedens & Fragale, 2003).

Interpersonal Effects of Emotions in Negotiation

Emotions influence negotiations at the interpersonal as well as intrapersonal level. In fact, research on emotions in negotiation bridges the intrapersonal and interpersonal level. Two specific emotions, anger and happiness, have received particular attention from negotiation researchers (Van Kleef, De Dreu, & Manstead, 2004a). Participants in one study received information about the emotional state (anger, happiness, or none) of their opponent (Van Kleef et al., 2004a). Consistent with the research noted above, participants conceded more to an angry opponent than to a happy one. Apparently, people used emotion information to infer the other's limit (i.e., their RP), and they adjusted their demands accordingly. However, this effect was absent when the other party made large concessions. Angry communications (unlike happy ones) induced fear and thereby mitigated the effect of the opponent's experienced emotion. Negotiators were especially influenced by their opponent's emotions when they were motivated to consider them (Van Kleef, De Dreu, & Manstead, 2004b).

The processes and mediators behind the interpersonal effects of emotions may be influenced by the extent to which individuals are motivated to process information systematically and deeply (De Dreu & Carnevale, 2003; Van Kleef et al., 2004b). For instance, participants in one study (Van Kleef et al., 2004b) received information about the opponent's emotion (anger, happiness, or none). Those in the angry condition received a message saying "this offer makes me really angry," whereas those in the happy condition received a message saying "I am happy with this offer." As predicted, negotiators conceded more to an angry opponent than to a happy one, but only when they had low (rather than high) need for cognitive closure—a measure of their chronic motivation to process information systematically. Also, participants were only affected by the other's emotion under low rather than high time pressure, because time pressure reduced their capacity for information processing. Finally, negotiators were only influenced by their opponent's emotions when they had low (rather than high) power, presumably because high-power negotiators had less need and were less motivated to process this information. These results support the motivated information-processing model, which argues that negotiators are only affected by their opponent's emotions if they are motivated to consider them.

Interpersonal Improvisation in Negotiation

Other research has utilized a more qualitative approach to unpack interpersonal processes in negotiations. Beyond the focus on economic outcomes in negotiations, negotiators may sometimes also be focused on relationship processes and outcomes (McGinn & Keros, 2002).

Specifically, McGinn and Keros (2002) highlight the improvisation and the logic of exchange in socially embedded transactions. Socially embedded transactions take into account the fact that negotiators can have deep social ties or share mutual social ties with one another. This is in contrast to the arm's length transaction between individuals, in which individuals share little familiarity or affect and no prolonged past or expected future ties (Granovetter, 1973; Podolny & Baron, 1997; Uzzi, 1997).

By improvisation, McGinn and Keros (2002) conjecture that most people at the outset of a negotiation do not construe it as such. This is because, whereas arm's length transactions are often guided by a logic of profit maximization, embedded transactions (such as between friends) go beyond the focus on outcomes alone; they tend to focus on rules of friendships as opposed to rules of the market.

In a qualitative fashion, McGinn and Keros (2002) used a sense-making lens to illuminate microprocesses underlying socially embedded transactions, investigating how social networks affect the logic of exchange governing the transaction. Transcript analysis of two-party negotiations revealed that most pairs of negotiators quickly coordinated a shared logic of exchange and improvised in accord with its implied rules throughout their interaction. The improvisation took the form of opening up, working together, or haggling. Negotiators used three dynamic processes—trust testing, process clarification, and emotional punctuation—when they had difficulty moving the interaction toward a coherent, mutually agreed-upon pattern. Social embeddedness, or the extent to which an individual shares other social connections with another individual (Granovetter, 1973), eases coordination within negotiation (McGinn & Keros, 2002).

Subjective Value in Negotiation

As noted above, negotiators have noneconomic, relational concerns as well as economic ones. Besides their concern with economic gains, negotiators are also concerned about their feelings about the self, the negotiation process, and the relationship (Curhan et al., 2006). Moreover, the "subjective value" accrued from these components of negotiation have long-lasting impact (Curhan et al., 2006). For example, the subjective value that actual managers derived from job offer negotiations predicted their subsequent job attitudes and turnover intentions better than the economic value they achieved: Subjective value measured at the outset of a negotiation predicted managers' job satisfaction and likelihood of quitting a full one year later. Curiously, negotiators' economic outcomes (i.e., their actual salaries) did not predict satisfaction or turnover. Arguably, the subjective value gained from a negotiation may have more long-lasting impact than the actual economic gains from the negotiation.

However, one potentially important consideration is whether subjective value conflicts with economic value in negotiations. To examine this, negotiators who held relational goals were compared with negotiators who held economic goals. If relational goals hindered economic gain, then it would be reasonable to expect negotiators to underperform relative to economically motivated negotiators (Curhan, Neale, Ross, & Rosencranz-Engelmann, 2008). Indeed, negotiators in egalitarian organizations reached less-efficient (i.e., worse) economic outcomes but had higher relational capital than did those who negotiated in hierarchical organizations. By directly pitting economic gain against relational considerations, this study showed how the structure of one's environment (egalitarian versus hierarchical) can influence one's own goals and therefore negotiation outcomes.

Trust and Tactics

Mutual trust is an essential ingredient in effective organizations (see Dirks & Ferrin, 2001) and negotiations (Kimmel, Pruitt, Magenau, Konar-Goldband, & Carnevale, 1980). Trust, defined as the intention to accept vulnerability based upon positive expectations of the counterpart's behavior and intentions (Rousseau, Sitkin, Burt, & Camerer, 1998), allows negotiators to exchange the information necessary for integrative agreements. Distrusting negotiators are reluctant to share information or ask questions, believing that their counterparts will take advantage of shared information and respond to their questions dishonestly. Conversely, trusting negotiators believe their counterparts will use information to identify integrative agreements. They also tend to believe information that the counterpart shares, accepting it as sincere and accurate (Parks, Henager, Scamahorn, 1996). As a result, trusting negotiators exchange more information about preferences and priorities and achieve more integrative outcomes (Butler 1995; Kimmel et al., 1980; Pruitt & Kimmel, 1977; Weingart, Bennet, & Brett, 1993).

Despite the importance of trust, violations of trust are common (see Elangovan & Shapiro, 1998, for a review), jeopardizing the integrativeness of negotiation outcomes. Given the mixed-motive nature of negotiation, it is tempting for negotiators to use deception to maximize their personal gain. Yet, deception is likely to compromise trust. Thus, an important question is when people will lie in negotiations. People tend to lie when the lures of temptation and uncertainty align with powerless and anonymous victims (Tenbrunsel & Diekmann, 2007). The more negotiators stand to gain economically, the more likely they are to lie (Bazerman, Tenbrunsel, & Wade-Benzoni, 1998). Moreover, the more uncertainty negotiators have about material factors, the more likely they are to lie. Of course, liars often garner a reputation as such, making it more difficult for them to win counterparts' trust in the future (Glick & Croson, 2001).

Given that negotiators may sometimes resort to deceptive tactics in negotiations, another important consideration is how interpersonal trust broken by deceptive behavior can be restored. One theory holds that broken trust can never be fully restored, even if the trust breaker performs a series of consistently trustworthy actions (Schweitzer, Hershey, & Bradlow, 2006), such as fulfilled promises, apologies, and consistently reliable behavior. A promise to change behavior can significantly speed the trust recovery process, but prior deception harms the effectiveness of a promise in accelerating trust recovery. Another perspective holds that apologies can effectively restore trust when the trust violation concerns a matter of competence, but not when it concerns a matter of integrity (Kim, Ferrin, Cooper, & Dirks, 2004).

In a given negotiation, tactics such as threats, bluffs, and disclaimers can affect negotiators' relationships and the grounds for their trust. For example, a buyer-seller simulation with two negotiation periods examined the behavioral and attitudinal consequences of threats, bluffs, and disclaimers (Shapiro & Bies, 1994). Some negotiators received a threat stated as a disclaimer, whereas others did not. Changes in negotiators' evaluations of their partner and negotiation outcomes were examined after some were led to believe their partner had stated a false threat (a bluff). Negotiators who used threats were perceived as more powerful, but they were also perceived as less cooperative and achieved lower integrative agreements than those who did not use threats.

Relationships and Negotiations

Perhaps the most straightforward question one could investigate about the interpersonal aspects of negotiation is whether people involved in a relationship can fashion integrative agreements better than strangers can. Kelley (1982) studied how couples negotiate problems of interdependence. Yet, the first study that truly examined how people in relationships, versus strangers, negotiate was Fry, Firestone, and Williams' (1983) study of dating couples. Paradoxically, strangers were more likely to reach win-win (mutually beneficial agreements) than were dating couples, although the effect did not reach conventional levels of significance. The authors' reasoning was that couples (and perhaps friends) are uncomfortable asserting their own needs and therefore are more willing to settle for sub-optimal agreements.

The orientation that friends bring to a negotiation seems to dictate the outcomes they achieve. Pairs of friends who are similar in communal orientation are most likely to capitalize on joint interests (Thompson & DeHarpport, 1998). However, when friends are dissimilar in communal orientation, their ability to identify compatible issues declines precipitously. Friends who are high in communal orientation are more likely to allocate resources equally than are friends low in communal orientation. The existence of friendships also has significant implications for one's negotiation outcomes (Seidel, Polzer, & Stewart, 2000). Seidel and colleagues analyzed more than 3000 actual salary negotiations and found that having friends in high places within the relevant organization improved salary negotiation outcomes.

Whereas the studies reviewed above tend to focus on economic outcomes, negotiations also involve symbolic resources such as identity and legitimacy. Glynn (2000) studied identity and legitimacy during a musicians' strike at the Atlanta Symphony Orchestra. Glynn analyzed the musicians and administrators as competing parties vying for the legitimacy to define the core identity of the orchestra. Embedded within the multilayered negotiation, Glynn reports, "were conflicts over status and power and, implicitly, control over the resources that would confer such status and power" (p. 291). This study illustrates that relationships not only influence negotiations, but negotiations can reconstitute and reshape relationships.

GROUP LEVEL

The group system focuses on how group dynamics influence negotiation processes and outcomes. In this section, we selectively focus on four major streams of research at the group level: social and group identity, relational and collective identity, group culture, and teams and the discontinuity effect. Some of this research uses paradigms derived from game theory (e.g., social dilemmas), but we include it in this review because it speaks directly to descriptive negotiation research.

Social and Group Identity

According to the group identity perspective, which is part of a larger social identity tradition (e.g., Tajfel, Billig, Bundy, & Flament, 1971), the stronger an individual's group identity, the less sharply he or she distinguishes between self-interest and collective interest. For negotiation, this implies that distributive (personal gains) are less focal than integrative (mutual gains) for negotiators who consider counterparts members of their group. This conjecture has been examined most directly in the social dilemma literature, which examines situations where individual and collective interest are largely opposed.

There are two perspectives concerning choice in a social dilemma situation. From a purely economic point of view, the rational choice is to defect because it yields greater outcomes. Of course, if everyone defects, then the collective welfare of the group suffers. The social psychological viewpoint is that defection is undesirable and people are best served when everyone puts self-interest aside and chooses to maximize group interests. Kramer and Brewer (1984) pioneered the study of group identity in social dilemma and negotiation research. By emphasizing the common fate among group members and the salience of a superordinate group identity, they showed that the degree of cooperation in social dilemmas increases (Brewer & Kramer, 1986; Kramer & Brewer, 1984). Another way of inducing group identity is to extend the length of time a person expects to be part of a group. In one study (Mannix & Loewenstein, 1993), people who expected to be part of a group for a long time were more concerned with the welfare of the group than were people who anticipated a fleeting interaction. Moreover, negotiators who perceived that other group members would leave cooperated less than did those who expected the group to remain intact (Mannix & Loewenstein, 1993).

These studies suggest that making group identity salient tends to activate different negotiation processes, producing different outcomes. Yet, the importance of group identity in mixed-motive interactions such as negotiation has not gone unchallenged. Kerr and Kaufman-Gilliland (1994) examined the impact of social identity on cooperation in social dilemmas. In a carefully constructed set of studies, they found strong support for the idea that it is negotiators' verbal promises that increase cooperation in social dilemmas, not simply the extent to which negotiators feel identified with their group.

Relational and Collective Identity

Recently, work on identity has moved from the extent to which individuals feel they are a part of their group to the nature of the identity. For example, Markus and Kitayama (1991) focused on whether people hold independent or interdependent identities, or self-construals. A person who holds an independent self-construal defines himself or herself in terms of the attributes, preferences, and traits that make him or her unique and autonomous. In contrast, a person with an interdependent self-construal is more likely to define himself or herself in terms of his or her social and group relationships (Gardner, Gabriel, & Lee, 1999; Markus & Kitayama, 1991). In a one-on-one, dispute-negotiation context, Seeley, Gardner, and Thompson (2007) primed independent versus interdependent self-construals and found that negotiators with interdependent self-construals were more generous than were independent negotiators. However, this effect completely reversed in a team-on-team context, such that teams with independent self-construals (i.e., highly defined by their own attributes) were more generous than teams with interdependent self-construals (i.e., defined with reference to the other team). All of these effects held primarily for high-power negotiators. The implication is that interdependent self-construals seem to evoke a benevolent use of power in dyadic contexts but a more exploitative use of power in intergroup contexts.

Very little research has examined the possibility of reverse causality between negotiation and social identity—that the negotiation process itself could influence people's identity. Thompson (1993) examined how negotiation affects intergroup relations. People who negotiated with an out-group member developed more favorable evaluations of the out-group, whereas people who negotiated with an in-group member were more likely to show in-group favoritism. However, when the negotiation situation dictated that negotiators could not reach a mutually beneficial agreement, the positive effects of interpersonal negotiation disappeared. Thus, negotiation with out-group members improves intergroup relations in negotiations with integrative potential. Furthermore, outcomes are comparable regardless of the counterpart's group membership. Whereas individuals expecting to negotiate with out-group members thought they would obtain lower outcomes than those expecting to negotiate with in-group members, the value of the actual outcomes achieved did not differ.

Culture

One important aspect of group identity is culture, or the distinctive characteristics of a particular social group (Lytle, Brett, Barsness, Tinsley, & Janssens, 1995). Culture is manifest in a group's values, beliefs, norms, and behavioral patterns. An underlying feature of Western cultures is the use of formal logic and avoidance of contradiction (Nisbett, Peng, Choi, & Norenzayan, 2001). In contrast, in non-Western cultures, cognition is characterized by a holistic system of thought. Individuals view themselves as embedded and interdependent with a larger social context. They also tend to focus their cognitive attention on relationships and context (Peng & Nisbett, 1999).

One result of this difference in systems of thought is that negotiators from different cultures make more or less use of emotional appeals. Emotional appeals are relatively inconsistent with formal logic. Thus, negotiators from non-Western cultures tend to make more emotional appeals than do U.S. negotiators (Drake, 1995).For instance, Taiwanese negotiators used more normative statements referring to social roles and relationships than did U.S. negotiators (Drake, 1995). Conversely, U.S. negotiators used more statements emphasizing logic and reasoning than did Taiwanese negotiators.

Another important cultural difference between Western negotiators and non-Western negotiators is the motivation that they bring to the negotiating table. Motivation is the focused and persistent energy that drives cognition and behavior (Mook, 2000). Motivation impacts how negotiators approach negotiations and evaluate outcomes. In Western cultures, negotiators tend to judge negotiation outcomes by the joint profit that accrues and the value that they themselves claim (Lax & Sebenius, 1986b; Neale & Bazerman, 1992). However, in non-Western cultures, negotiators may care more about relational capital— the mutual trust, knowledge, and commitment that can accrue from negotiating—more than economic outcomes (Gelfand, Major, Raver, Nishii, & O'Brien, 2006).

For example, Japanese negotiators place a high value on relational capital: They prefer and even insist on negotiating with people with whom they have a relationship or social network, even if it means forgoing potential economic benefits (Graham & Sano, 1989; Yamagishi & Yamagishi, 1994). Indian managers, on the other hand, may assume lower relational capital in the form of mutual trust than do American managers, and negotiations may serve to reaffirm their assumptions (Gunia, Brett, Nandkeolyar, & Kamdar, 2011). In two studies, Indian managers' lower level of trust led to low joint gains relative to the gains of American managers.

Culture also has important effects on how individuals perceive causality. Psychological research has demonstrated that members of Western cultures tend to make the fundamental attribution error more often than do members of non-Western cultures (Nisbett et al., 2001; Peng & Nisbett, 1999). That is, they underestimate the impact of situational factors and overestimate the impact of others' dispositional factors in causing events (Ross, 1977). The result for negotiation is that U.S. negotiators tend to make dispositional attributions for their counterpart's behaviors and discount potential situational attributions (Morris, Larrick, & Su, 1999). Dispositional attributions for negative behaviors lead to negative consequences in negotiations. Specifically, dispositional attributions led to competitive perceptions of the situation and counterpart, resulting in a preference for adversarial instead of collaborative procedures.

Groups and the Discontinuity Effect

A central question in group research is whether "two heads are better than one" (Insko et al., 1987, 1988, 1990; Schopler et al., 1991, 1993). This question was first addressed using a simple prisoner's dilemma game in which negotiators were offered a cooperative (trusting) choice or a defecting (self-interested, exploitive) choice. Overwhelmingly, one-on-one negotiators made more cooperative choices than did group-on-group negotiators, under identical payoffs. Insko et al. (1987) coined the term "discontinuity effect" to describe the empirical finding that one-on-one negotiation behavior cannot be simply extrapolated to group-on-group negotiation behavior. Schopler and Insko (1992) argued that the discontinuity effect was driven by group members' fear of being exploited by the out-group as well as their greed for additional payoffs.

Thompson, Peterson, and Brodt (1996) examined the discontinuity effect in a markedly different negotiation paradigm, in which parties' interests were not completely opposed and a mutually attractive, optimal outcome existed but was not apparent to negotiators. This paradigm was similar to the sisters-and-orange parable in the introduction. In terms of integrative outcomes, group-on-group configurations produced more integrative agreements than did solo-on-solo or solo-on-group. In terms of distributive outcomes, groups earned more than solos. The authors reasoned that in such a negotiation, information processing is paramount; indeed, groups asked more relevant questions, shared more information, and formed more accurate judgments than did solos (see also Peterson & Thompson, 1997). The group-on-group configuration apparently allowed negotiators to seek and process more of the relevant information.

Morgan and Tindale (2002) attempted to resolve the disparate findings between Insko et al. (1987) and Thompson et al. (1996). Morgan and Tindale's insight was that the disparate-appearing findings were based upon dramatically different negotiation tasks: Insko and colleagues used a prisoner's dilemma task, whereas Thompson and colleagues used an integrative bargaining task; the tasks differ in many important ways (see Thompson, 2009, for a review of the differences). In Morgan and Tindale's (2002) study, negotiators were allowed to reach an agreement on either a cooperative or competitive integrative bargaining task in one of three formats (group versus group, group versus single, or one-on-one). Next, negotiators were asked to choose between maintaining the agreed-upon settlement or defecting within a prisoner's dilemma payoff structure. Groups continued to show the discontinuity effect, such that they opted to defect. This was true even when they had performed better than the solo negotiator with whom they had just negotiated. Groups shared motives for defection that differ depending upon the nature of the task and opponent (Morgan & Tindale, 2002).

ORGANIZATIONAL LEVEL

The organizational system represents a higher level of analysis than the previous levels; it examines the negotiator as embedded in a larger network or marketplace. This level of analysis is crucial because in organizations and in markets, dyads rarely operate in isolation from their social context. Instead, each negotiator typically participates in multiple dyadic relationships, and these dyadic relationships aggregate to form a complex social structure that surrounds each dyad and influences trust, expectations, and interpersonal perceptions.

Heider (1958) documented that two people can be connected by a third party, who strengthens or disturbs the relationship among the two. Contemporary sociologists have also documented how dyadic relationships and interpersonal behavior may be influenced by the overall network structure in which the dyad is embedded (e.g., Burt & Knez, 1996; Coleman, 1990; Granovetter, 1985). Despite these foundations, relatively little research has examined how negotiation dyads operate within their larger social context. In this section, we review three streams of negotiation research at the organizational level. The first two examine how interpersonal connections (choosing negotiation partners and reputations) influence negotiation processes. The third looks at how organizational or institutional forces impact negotiations.

Choice of Negotiation Partner

A critical issue facing employees and employers, buyers and suppliers, and joint venture partners is whom to select as a negotiation partner. The vast majority of studies in the existing negotiation literature have simply assigned negotiation partners (Tenbrunsel, Wade-Benzoni, Moag, & Bazerman, 1999). One of the earliest studies that examined this problem of search and deliberation in partner choice was Sondak and Bazerman's (1989) study of matching in quasi-markets. In this paradigm, a large market of buyers and sellers was created and negotiators were told to partner with whomever they pleased, to make a deal. The main finding was that substantial economic suboptimality exists as the result of selection mismatches. People may choose to negotiate with their friends, even though the integrative potential of negotiating with a stranger may be higher (see also Northcraft, Preston, Neale, Kim, & Thomas-Hunt, 1998). Similarly, when people had the option to choose their friend as negotiation partner in a simulated housing market, they often stopped searching and reached a deal with the friend—overlooking other, potentially fruitful negotiation relationships. Ultimately, this led to market inefficiencies (Tenbrunsel et al., 1999).

Reputation and Negotiation Through Time

One consideration that influences the integrative and distributive outcomes negotiators achieve in organizational systems is their reputation. Much sociological and macro organizational research has documented the importance of reputation in markets (e.g., Raub & Weesie, 1990). In one investigation (Glick & Croson, 2001), the impact of reputations among management students in a semester-long negotiation course was examined. Students rated one another on the basis of firsthand experience, from least cooperative to the most cooperative. Four reputational profiles emerged: the "liar-manipulator" (who will do anything to gain advantage), "tough-but-honest" (very tough negotiator who makes few concessions but will not lie), "nice-and-reasonable" (makes concessions), and "cream puff" (makes concessions and is conciliatory regardless of what the other does). Once reputations spread through the market, behavior changed. People acted much tougher when dealing with perceived liar-manipulators, for example. Furthermore, people used tough or manipulative tactics in a defensive fashion with liar-manipulators and tough-but-honest negotiators, but used them in an opportunistic fashion with cream puffs (Glick & Croson, 2001).

Other research examined how reputation is related to history of negotiation behavior, also in an MBA class (Anderson & Shirako, 2008). The development of reputations was tracked among individuals who engaged in multiple negotiation tasks across several weeks. Reputations were only mildly related to the actual history of behavior. However, the link between reputation and behavior was much stronger for some individuals than others. The link was strongest for those who were well known and received the most social attention. In contrast, behavior had little impact on the reputations of lesser-known individuals.

Another, similar perspective suggests that dyadic negotiation is not an isolated event, but rather influences subsequent dyadic negotiations (O'Connor, Arnold, & Burris, 2005). Specifically, the quality of the deals negotiators reached at any point in time were strongly influenced by their previous bargaining experiences. Negotiators who reached an impasse in a prior negotiation were more likely either to impasse in their next negotiation or to reach deals of low joint value relative to those who had reached an initial agreement. Notably, the impact of past performance on subsequent deals was just as strong for negotiators who changed partners on the second occasion. These results highlight the role of bargaining history as a predictor of negotiation behavior. Moreover, they suggest that, at least in some cases, negotiations should be conceptualized as interrelated exchanges rather than discrete incidents.

Organizations also impact negotiations via institutional forces. One controversial perspective argues that organizations or institutions may serve as barriers to negotiations (Wade-Benzoni et al., 2002). Specifically, normative factors (obligations, operating procedures), cognitive factors (cultural values, cognitive frameworks), and regulatory factors (regulations and laws) may impede negotiations. For example, organizations with cultures emphasizing strict adherence to procedure may discourage negotiation by explicitly prohibiting it (normative factor) or by preventing employees from even perceiving it as a viable alternative (cognitive factor). The value-laden lens that organizationally embedded actors bring may also lead to impasse or prevent people from reaching economically efficient outcomes.

VIRTUAL LEVEL

Given the ubiquity of computer-mediated communication technology in business communications, consumer transactions, and interpersonal relationships, virtual negotiation is currently a fertile ground for research (Nadler & Shestowsky, 2006).

A straightforward question one might ask is whether negotiation is best conducted face-to-face or via computer-mediated communication technology. Answers to this question are surprisingly mixed (see Nadler & Shestowsky, 2006, for a review). In some cases, negotiators who interact via computer-mediated technology are less likely to reach integrative outcomes than are negotiators who interact face-to-face (Arunachalam & Dilla, 1995; Barefoot & Strickland, 1982) or via paper and pencil (Griffith & Northcraft, 1994). On the other hand, some studies report no reliable effect of communication medium (Morris et al., 2002; Naquin & Paulson, 2003; Purdy et al., 2000).

With regard to confidence and satisfaction, parties who negotiate face-to-face feel more confident in their performance and satisfied with their negotiation outcome than do those who negotiate via computer (Naquin & Paulson, 2003; Purdy et al., 2000; Thompson & Coovert, 2003). Moreover, compared to parties who negotiate face-to-face, parties who negotiate via email desire less future interaction with their counterpart (Naquin & Paulson, 2003). Despite these differences in subjective outcomes, studies that examined the emotional content of messages in email and face-to-face negotiations found no differences between the two mediums (Morris et al., 2002).

Moderators and Mediators

Though the effects of information technology on interpersonal outcomes in negotiation may currently seem inconclusive, some studies have identified important mediators that may help to explain the effects of technology on negotiation in the future. For instance, negotiators behave more honestly when negotiating face-to-face than via writing (Valley, Moag, & Bazerman, 1998). The communication medium in which bargaining takes place also affects the efficiency and distribution of outcomes (Valley et al., 1998). Face-to-face communication may facilitate more truth-telling and trust than communication via writing, thus influencing negotiation outcomes.

However, negotiators may sometimes behave less cooperatively when they have visual access to one another than when they do not (Carnevale & Isen, 1986; Carnevale, Pruitt, & Seilheimer, 1981). In one investigation, researchers examined the influence of positive affect and visual access on the process and outcome of negotiation in an integrative bargaining task (Carnevale & Isen, 1986). Only when negotiators were face-to-face and not in a positive affective state were there heavy use of contentious tactics, reduced tradeoffs, and few integrative solutions. In other words, when negotiators had visual access and were potentially experiencing negative affect, they were more likely to use contentious tactics.

Other research has examined contexts in which email negotiations may fail or succeed. For instance, Moore, Kurtzberg, Thompson, and Morris (1999) proposed that there were "long" and "short" routes to success in electronically mediated negotiations. A long route to success would involve many of the aspects of deliberate cognitive processing; a short route would involve more heuristic, superficial processing of information (Fiske, 1988; Sloman, 2002).

To understand why email negotiations often fail, another study (Moore et al., 1999) examined two distinct elements of negotiators' relationships: shared membership in a social group and mutual self-disclosure. Some participants negotiated with a member of an out-group (a student at a competitor university), whereas others negotiated with a member of an in-group (a student at the same university). In addition, some negotiators exchanged personal information with their counterparts, such as their hometown and hobbies, whereas others did not. When neither common in-group status nor a personalized relationship existed between negotiators, email negotiations were more likely to end in impasse. These results were attributable to the positive influence of mutual self-disclosure and common group membership on negotiation processes and rapport between negotiators, especially in a relatively impersonal context like email.

CONCLUSION

Our review has focused on a subset of research findings that have strongly impacted the study and practice of negotiation. The research findings span several decades, but the investigations meaningfully build upon one another because the key criteria by which scholars evaluate the quality of negotiation has remained essentially unchanged since the dawn of negotiation research. Modern negotiation research has greatly benefitted from its economic roots, which have provided rigorous methods by which to measure the mutual value created by two or more parties, each motivated to pursue their own interests. The robust empirical fact that most negotiators fail to fully maximize their own gains (as well as mutual gains) when seated at the bargaining table has greatly fueled the fires of negotiation research.

Our focus on intrapersonal, interpersonal, group, organizational and virtual systems has allowed us to examine the wide lens through which the apparently simple task of negotiation may be meaningfully studied. The intrapersonal system provides the most close-up view of negotiation, taking us into the mind and heart of the negotiator, who is either anticipating or engaging in a negotiation. The interpersonal system is particularly meaningful in negotiation research because the dyadic process allows us to examine the presence or absence of interpersonal phenomena such as behavioral synchrony and mutual gaze, which cannot be reduced to the intrapersonal level. The group and organizational systems have been influenced by rich social psychological, as well as sociological and organizational, traditions. Negotiation research, like the universe, appears to be expanding rather than contracting. Indeed, the virtual level has allowed globally dispersed researchers themselves to collaborate while investigating negotiation at a virtual level. Rather than reporting to a physical laboratory, today's research participants often negotiate via computer with people they will never meet.

It is curious how some research topics within the domain of social and organizational psychology sustain themselves over time, whereas others are mere flashes in the pan. Negotiation and bargaining research, by nearly any standard, has withstood the test of time. There are several reasons for its longevity. First, the multidisciplinary nature of negotiation has brought scholars together, especially from social psychology and organizational behavior and also from game theory and economics. These multidisciplinary collaborations have created a rich network of negotiation scholars that lead to shared volumes, conferences, and even jobs and research positions, thereby ensuring the longevity of the field. Nearly every business school offers a course in negotiation that many MBA students take, requiring a cadre of trained faculty members. The faculties often receive their training in PhD programs or in postdoctoral programs that focus primarily on negotiation. Graduate students are attracted to such positions and develop research ideas that are relevant to the broad array of negotiation theory.

A second factor that has contributed to the continued popularity of negotiation research is the fact that it is considered an essential business, if not a life, skill. The demand for negotiation skills spurs the development of negotiation books, courses, seminars, cases, and teaching materials that require theoretical rigor and background. The existence of a normative theory by which to evaluate the performance of negotiators provides a foundation for meaningful research and theory. The existence of descriptive theory provides meaningful insights into negotiations as they typically unfold.

If there is a downside to negotiation research it might be that negotiation has done more taking than giving, meaning that often the negotiation scholarship is essentially about social or organizational phenomena that could frankly be studied as easily in other contexts. For example, one might study behavioral synchrony or mirroring in negotiation, but it is equally plausible to study these same phenomena in other contexts, like small, collaborative teams or job interviews. Similarly, more than two decades of research have focused on extending Kahneman, Slovic, and Tversky's (1982) research on judgment biases (e.g., framing, anchoring, overconfidence) to two-party negotiations (for a review, see Neale & Bazerman, 1994). Despite this prodigious borrowing, our review suggests that negotiation research has yielded many insights of its own and is poised to yield many more in the future.

REFERENCES

Allred KG, Mallozzi JS, Matsui F, & Raia CP. (1997). The influence of anger and compassion on negotiation performance. *Organ. Behav. Hum. Decis. Process.* 70(3), 175–87.

Anderson C, & Shirako A. (2008). Are individuals' reputations related to their history of behavior? *J. Personal. Soc. Psychol.* 94(2), 320–33.

Anderson C, & Thompson LL. (2004). Affect from the top down: how powerful individuals' positive affect shapes negotiations. *Organ. Behav. Hum. Decis. Process.* 95(2), 125–39.

Arunachalam V, & Dilla WN. (1995). Judgment accuracy and outcomes in negotiation— a causal-modeling analysis of decision-aiding effects. *Organ. Behav. Hum. Decis. Process.* 61(3), 289–304.

Babcock L, Gelfand M, Small D, & Stayhn H. (2006). Gender differences in the propensity to initiate negotiations. In D De Cremer, M Zeelenberg, & JK Murnighan (Eds.), *Social Psychology and Economics* (pp. 239–62). Mahwah, NJ: Erlbaum.

Barefoot JC, & Strickland LH. (1982). Conflict and dominance in television-mediated interactions. *Hum. Relat.* 35(7), 559–66.

Bargh JA, & Pietromonaco P. (1982). Automatic information processing and social perception: the influence of trait information presented outside of conscious awareness on impression formation. *J. Personal. Soc. Psychol.* 43(3), 437–49.

Bazerman MH, Tenbrunsel AE, & Wade-Benzoni K. (1998). Negotiating with yourself and losing: making decisions with competing internal preferences. *Acad. Manag. Rev.* 23(2), 225–41.

Blair IV, & Banaji MR. (1996). Automatic and controlled processes in stereotype priming. *J. Personal. Soc. Psychol.* 70(6), 1142–63.

Bowles HR, Babcock L, & Lai L. (2007). Social incentives for gender differences in the propensity to initiate negotiations: Sometimes it does hurt to ask. *Organ. Behav. Hum. Decis. Process.* 103(1), 84–103.

Brewer MB, & Kramer RM. (1986). Choice behavior in social dilemmas: effects of social identity, group size, and decision framing. *J. Personal. Soc. Psychol.* 50(3), 543–49.

Butler JK. (1995). Behaviors, trust, and goal achievement in a win-win negotiating role play. *Group Organ. Manag.* 20(4), 486–501.

Burt RS, & Knez M. (1996). A further note on the network structure of trust: reply to Krackhardt. *Rationality Soc.* 8(1), 117–20.

Camerer C. (2003). *Behavioral Game Theory: Experiments in Strategic Interaction.* New York, NY: Russell Sage Found. Princeton, NJ: Princeton University Press.

Carnevale PJD, & Isen AM. (1986). The influence of positive affect and visual access on the discovery of integrative solutions in bilateral negotiation. *Organ. Behav. Hum. Decis. Process.* 37(1), 1–13.

Carnevale PJD, Pruitt DG, & Seilheimer SD. (1981). Looking and competing: accountability and visual access in integrative bargaining. *J. Personal. Soc. Psychol.* 40(1), 111–20.

Chartrand TL, & Bargh JA. (1999). The Chameleon effect: the perception-behavior link and social interaction. *J. Personal. Soc. Psychol.* 76(6), 893–910.

Coleman JS. (1990). *Foundations of Social Theory.* Cambridge, MA: Harvard University Press.

Curhan JR, Elfenbein HA, & Xu H. (2006). What do people value when they negotiate? Mapping the domain of subjective value in negotiation. *J. Personal. Soc. Psychol.* 91(3), 493–512.

Curhan JR, Neale MA, Ross L, & Rosencranz-Engelmann J. (2008). Relational accommodation in negotiation: effects of egalitarianism and gender on economic efficiency and relational capital. *Organ. Behav. Hum. Decis. Process.* 107(2), 192–205.

Deal JJ. (2000). Gender differences in the intentional use of information in competitive negotiations. *Small Group Res.* 31(6), 702–23.

De Dreu CKW, & Carnevale PJ. (2003). Motivational bases of information processing and strategy in conflict and negotiation. In MP Zanna (Ed.), *Advances in Experimental Social Psychology* (Vol. 35, pp. 235–91). New York, NY: Academic Press.

De Dreu CKW, Weingart LR, & Kwon S. (2000). Influence of social motives on integrative negotiation: a meta-analytic review and test of two theories. *J. Personal. Soc. Psychol.* 78(5), 889–905.

Dirks KT, & Ferrin DL. (2001). The role of trust in organizational settings. *Organ. Sci.* 12(4), 450–67.

Drake LE. (1995). Negotiation styles in intercultural communication. *Int. J. Confl. Manag.* 6(1), 72–90.

Eagly AH, & Wood W. (1982). Inferred sex differences in status as a determinant of gender stereotypes about social influence. *J. Personal. Soc. Psychol.* 43(5), 915–28.

Elangovan AR, & Shapiro DI. (1998). Betrayal of trust in organizations. *Acad. Manag. Rev.* 23(3), 547–66.

Emerson RM. (1972). Exchange theory: Part II. Exchange relations in networks. In J Berger, M Zelditch, & B Anderson (Eds.), *Sociological Theories in Progress* (Vol. 2, pp. 58–87). Boston, MA: Houghton Mifflin.

Fisher R, & Ury W. (1981). *Getting to Yes: Negotiating Agreement Without Giving In.* Boston, MA: Houghton Mifflin.

Fiske ST. (1988). Compare and contrast: Brewer's dual-process model and Fiske et al.'s continuum model. In TK Srull & RS Wyer (Eds.), *Advances in Social Cognition: Vol. 1. A Dual Model of Impression Formation* (pp. 65–76). Hillsdale, NJ: Erlbaum.

Foa UG, & Foa EB. (1975). *Resource Theory of Social Exchange.* Morristown, NJ: General Learning Press.

Forgas JP. (1995). Mood and judgment: The affect infusion model (AIM). *Psychological Bulletin, 117,* 39–66.

Forgas JP. (1998). On feeling good and getting your way. *J. Personal. Soc. Psychol.* 74(3), 565–77.

Forgas JP, & Cromer M. (2004). On being sad and evasive: affective influences on verbal communication strategies in conflict situations. *J. Exp. Soc. Psychol.* 40(4), 511–18.

French JRP, & Raven B. (1959). The bases of social power. In D Cartwright (Ed.), *Studies in Social Power* (pp. 150–67). Ann Arbor, MI: Inst. Soc. Res.

Fry WR, Firestone IJ, & Williams DL. (1983). Negotiating process and outcome of stranger dyads and dating couples. Do lovers lose? *Basic Appl. Soc. Psychol.* 4, 1–16.

Galinsky AD, & Mussweiler T. (2001). First offers as anchors: the role of perspective-taking and negotiator focus. *J. Personal. Soc. Psychol.* 81(4), 657–69.

Galinsky AD, Mussweiler T, & Medvec VH. (2002). Disconnecting outcomes and evaluations: the role of negotiator focus. *J. Personal. Soc. Psychol.* 83(5), 1131–40.

Galinsky AD, Seiden VL, Kim PH, & Medvec VH. (2002). The dissatisfaction of having your first offer accepted: the role of counterfactual thinking in negotiations. *Personal. Soc. Psychol. Bull.* 28(2), 271–83.

Gardner WL, Gabriel S, & Lee AY. (1999). "I" value freedom, but "we" value relationships: self-construal priming mirrors cultural differences in judgment. *Psychol. Sci.* 10(4), 321–26.

Gelfand MJ, Major VS, Raver J, Nishii L, & O'Brien KM. (2006). Negotiating relationally: the dynamics of the relational self in negotiations. *Acad. Manag. Rev.* 31(2), 427–51.

Gerhart B, & Rynes S. (1991). Determinants and consequences of salary negotiations by male and female MBA graduates. *J. Appl. Psychol.* 76(2), 256–62.

Glick S, & Croson R. (2001). Reputation in negotiations. In S Hoch & H Kunreuther (Eds.), *Wharton on Making Decisions* (pp. 177–86). New York, NY: Wiley.

Glynn MA. (2000). When cymbals become symbols: conflict over organizational identity within a symphony orchestra. *Organ. Sci.* 11(3), 285–99.

Graham JL, & Sano Y. (1989). *Smart Bargaining.* New York, NY: Harper Business

Granovetter M. (1973). The strength of weak ties. *Am. J. Sociol.* 78:1360–80.

Granovetter M. (1985). Economic action and social structure: the problem of embeddedness. *Am. J. Sociol.* 91(3), 481–510.

Greenwald AG, Draine SC, & Abrams RL. (1996). Three cognitive markers of unconscious semantic activation. *Science* 273(5282), 1699–702.

Griffith TL, & Northcraft GB. (1994). Distinguishing between the forest and the trees: media, features, and methodology in electronic communication research. *Organ. Sci.* 5(2), 272–85.

Gunia BC, Brett JM, Nandkeolyar A, & Kamdar D. (2011). Paying a price: culture, trust, and negotiation consequences. *Journal of Applied Psychology, 96(4),* 774-89.

Güth W, Schmittberger R, & Schwarze B. (1982). An experimental analysis of ultimatum bargaining. *J. Econ. Behav. Organ.* 3(4), 367–88.

Heider F. (1958). *The Psychology of Interpersonal Relations.* New York, NY: Wiley.

Insko CA, Hoyle RH, Pinkley RL, Hong GY, Slim RM, Dalton, B., … Schopler, J. (1988). Individual-group discontinuity: the role of a consensus rule. *Journal of Experimental Social Psychology, 24(6),* 505–19.

Insko CA, Pinkley RL, Hoyle RH, Dalton B, Hong GY, Slim, R. M., … Thibaut, J. (1987). Individual versus group discontinuity: the role of intergroup contact. *J. Exp. Soc. Psychol.* 23(3), 250–67.

Insko CA, Schopler J, Hoyle RH, Dardis GJ, & Graetz KA. (1990). Individual-group discontinuity as a function of fear and greed. *J. Personal. Soc. Psychol.* 58(1), 68–79.

Kahneman D, Slovic P, & Tversky A. (1982). *Judgment Under Uncertainty: Heuristics and Biases.* London UK: Cambridge University Press.

Kelley HH. (1982). *Personal Relationships: Their Structure and Processes.* Hillsdale, NJ: Erlbaum.

Keltner D, Gruenfeld DH, & Anderson C. (2003). Power, approach, and inhibition. *Psychol. Rev.* 110(2), 265–84.

Kerr NL, & Kaufman-Gilliland CM. (1994). Communication, commitment, and cooperation in social dilemmas. *J. Personal. Soc. Psychol.* 66(3), 513–29.

Kim PH, Ferrin DL, Cooper CD, & Dirks KT. (2004). Removing the shadow of suspicion: The effects of apology versus denial for repairing competence- versus integrity-based trust violations. *J. Appl. Psychol.* 89(1), 104–18.

Kim PH, & Fragale AR. (2005). Choosing the path to bargaining power: an empirical comparison of BATNAs and contributions in negotiation. *J. Appl. Psychol.* 90(2), 373–81.

Kimmel MJ, Pruitt DG, Magenau JM, Konar-Goldband E, & Carnevale PJD. (1980). Effects of trust, aspiration, and gender on negotiation tactics. *J. Personal. Soc. Psychol.* 38, 9–22.

Komorita SS, & Parks CD. (1995). Interpersonal relations: mixed-motive interaction. *Annu. Rev. Psychol.* 46, 183–207.

Kopelman S, Rosette AS, & Thompson LL. (2000). The three faces of Eve: strategic displays of positive, negative, and neutral emotions in negotiations. *Organ. Behav. Hum. Decis. Process.* 99, 81–101.

Kramer RM, & Brewer MB. (1984). Effects of group identity on resource use in a simulated commons dilemma. *J. Personal. Soc. Psychol.* 46(5), 1044–57.

Kray LJ, Reb J, Galinsky AD, & Thompson LL. (2004). Stereotype reactance at the bargaining table: the effect of stereotype activation and power on claiming and creating value. *Personal. Soc. Psychol. Bull.* 30(4), 399–411.

Kray LJ, & Thompson LL. (2005). Gender stereotypes and negotiation performance: an examination of theory and research. *Res. Organ. Behav.* 26, 103–82.

Kray LJ, Thompson LL, & Galinsky A. (2001). Battle of the sexes: gender stereotype confirmation and reactance in negotiations. *J. Personal. Soc. Psychol.* 80(6), 942–58.

Lanzetta JT. (1989). Expectations of cooperation and competition and their effects on observers' vicarious emotional responses. *J. Personal. Soc. Psychol.* 56, 543–54.

Lax DA, & Sebenius JK. (1986a). Interests: The measure of negotiation. *Negotiation J. Process Dispute Settlement* 2(1), 73–92.

Lax DA, & Sebenius JK. (1986b). *The Manager as Negotiator, Bargaining for Cooperative and Competitive Gain.* New York, NY: Free Press.

Luce RD, & Raiffa H. (1957). *Games and Decisions: Introduction and Critical Survey.* New York, NY: Wiley.

Lytle A, Brett JM, Barsness Z, Tinsley CH, & Janssens M. (1995). A paradigm for confirmatory cross-cultural research in organizational behavior. In LL Cummings & BM Staw (Eds.), *Research in Organizational Behavior* (Vol. 17, pp. 167–214). Greenwich, CT: JAI.

Magee JC, Galinsky AD, & Gruenfeld DH. (2007). Power, propensity to negotiate, and moving first in competitive interactions. *Personal. Soc. Psychol. Bull.* 33(2), 200–12.

Major B, Vanderslice V, & McFarlin DB. (1984). Effects of pay expected on pay received: the confirmatory nature of initial expectations. *J. Appl. Soc. Psychol.* 14(5), 399–412.

Mannix EA, & Loewenstein GF. (1993). Managerial time horizons and interfirm mobility: an experimental investigation. *Organ. Behav. Hum. Decis. Process.* 56(2), 266–84.

Markus HR, & Kitayama S. (1991). Culture and the self: implications for cognition, emotion, and motivation. *Psychol. Rev.* 98(2), 224–53.

McGinn KL, & Keros AT. (2002). Improvisation and the logic of exchange in socially embedded transactions. *Adm. Sci. Q.* 47(3), 442–73.

Mook J. (2000). *Motivation.* New York, NY: Prentice Hall.

Moore DA, Kurtzberg TR, Thompson LL, & Morris MW. (1999). Long and short routes to success in electronically mediated negotiations: group affiliations and good vibrations. *Organ. Behav. Hum. Decis. Process.* 77(1), 22–43.

Morgan PM, & Tindale RS. (2002). Group vs individual performance in mixed-motive situations: exploring an inconsistency. *Organ. Behav. Hum. Decis. Process.* 87(1), 44–65.

Morris M, Nadler J, Kurtzberg T, & Thompson LL. (2002). Schmooze or lose: social friction and lubrication in e-mail negotiations. *Group Dyn. Theory Res. Pract.* 6(1), 89–100.

Morris MW, Larrick RP, & Su SK. (1999). Misperceiving negotiation counterparts: when situationally determined bargaining behaviors are attributed to personality traits. *J. Personal. Soc. Psychol.* 77(1), 52–67.

Mussweiler T, & Strack F. (1999). Comparing is believing: a selective accessibility model of judgmental anchoring. In W Stroebe & M Hewstone (Eds.), *European Review of Social Psychology* (Vol. 10, pp. 135–68). Chichester, UK: Wiley.

Nadler J, & Shestowsky D. (2006). Negotiation, information technology, and the problem of the faceless other. In LL Thompson (Ed.), *Negotiation Theory and Research* (pp. 145–72). New York, NY: Psychology Press.

Naquin CE, & Paulson GD. (2003). Online bargaining and interpersonal trust. *J. Appl. Psychol.* 88(1), 113–20.

Nash J. (1951). Non-cooperative games. *Ann. Math.* 54(2), 286–95.

Neale MA, & Bazerman MH. (1992). Negotiator cognition and rationality: a behavioral decision-theory perspective. *Organ. Behav. Hum. Decis. Process.* 51(2), 157–75.

Neale MA, & Bazerman MH. (1994). *Negotiating Rationally*. New York, NY: Free Press.

Neumann R, & Strack F. (2000). "Mood contagion": the automatic transfer of mood between persons. *J. Personal. Soc. Psychol.* 79(2), 211–23.

Nisbett RE, Peng KP, Choi I, & Norenzayan A. (2001). Culture and systems of thought: holistic versus analytic cognition. *Psychol. Rev.* 108(2), 291–310.

Northcraft GB, Preston JN, Neale MA, Kim P, & Thomas-Hunt M. (1998). Non-linear preference functions and negotiated outcomes. *Organ. Behav. Hum. Decis. Process.* 73, 54–75.

Ochs J, & Roth AE. (1989). An experimental study of sequential bargaining. *Am. Econ. Rev.* 79, 355–84.

O'Connor KM, & Arnold JA. (2001). Distributive spirals: negotiation impasses and the moderating role of disputant self-efficacy. *Organ. Behav. Hum. Decis. Process.* 84(1), 148–76.

O'Connor KM, Arnold JA, & Burris ER. (2005). Negotiators' bargaining histories and their effects on future negotiation performance. *J. Appl. Psychol.* 90(2), 350–62.

Pareto V. (1935). *The Mind and Society: A Treatise on General Sociology*. New York, NY: Harcourt Brace.

Parks CD, Henager RF, & Scamahorn SD. (1996). Trust and messages of intent in social dilemmas. *J. Confl. Resolut.* 40, 134–51.

Peng KP, & Nisbett RE. (1999). Culture, dialectics, and reasoning about contradiction. *Am. Psychol.* 54(9), 741–54.

Peterson E, & Thompson LL. (1997). Negotiation teamwork: the impact of information distribution and accountability on performance depends on the relationship among team members. *Organ. Behav. Hum. Decis. Process.* 72(3), 364–83.

Podolny JM, & Baron JN. (1997). Resources and relationships: social networks and mobility in the workplace. *Am. Sociol. Rev.* 62, 673–93.

Pruitt DG, & Kimmel MJ. (1977). Twenty years of experimental gaming: critique, synthesis, and suggestions for the future. *Annu. Rev. Psychol.* 28, 363–92.

Purdy JM, Nye P, & Balakrishnan PV. (2000). The impact of communication media on negotiation outcomes. *Int. J. Confl. Manag.* 11(2), 162–87.

Raiffa H. (1982). *The Art and Science of Negotiation*. Cambridge, MA: Harvard University Press.

Raub W, & Weesie J. (1990). Reputation and efficiency in social interactions: an example of network effects. *Am. J. Sociol.* 96(3), 626–54.

Ross LD. (1977). The intuitive psychologist and his shortcomings: distortions in the attribution process. In *Advances in Experimental Social Psychology*, ed. L Berkowitz, 10:173–220. New York, NY: Academic.

Rousseau DM, Sitkin SB, Burt RS, & Camerer C. (1998). Not so different after all: a cross-discipline view of trust. *Acad. Manag. Rev.* 23(3), 393–404.

Schelling TC. (1960). *The Strategy of Conflict*. Cambridge, MA: Harvard University Press.

Schopler J, & Insko CA. (1992). The discontinuity effect in interpersonal and intergroup relations: generality and mediation. *Eur. Rev. Soc. Psychol.* 3, 121–51.

Schopler J, Insko CA, Graetz KA, Drigotas S, Smith VA, & Dahl K. (1993). Individual-group discontinuity: further evidence for mediation by fear and greed. *Personal. Soc. Psychol. Bull.* 19(4), 419–31.

Schopler J, Insko CA, Graetz KA, Drigotas SM, & Smith VA. (1991). The generality of the individual-group discontinuity effect: variations in positivity-negativity of outcomes, players' relative power, and magnitude of outcomes. *Personal. Soc. Psychol. Bull.* 17(6), 612–24.

Schweitzer ME, Hershey JC, & Bradlow ET. (2006). Promises and lies: restoring violated trust. *Organ. Behav. Hum. Decis. Process.* 101(1), 1–19.

Seeley E, Gardner W, & Thompson L. (2007). The role of the self-concept and social context in determining the behavior of power-holders: self-construal in intergroup vs. dyadic dispute resolution negotiations. *J. Personal. Soc. Psychol.* 93(4), 614–31.

Seidel ML, Polzer JT, & Stewart KJ. (2000). Having friends in high places: effects of social networks on discrimination in salary negotiations. *Adm. Sci. Q.* 45, 1–24.

Shapiro DL, Bies RJ. (1994). Threats, bluffs, and disclaimers in negotiations. *Organ. Behav. Hum. Decis. Process.* 60(1), 14–35.

Sinaceur M, & Tiedens LZ. (2006). Get mad and get more than even: when and why anger expression is effective in negotiations. *J. Exp. Soc. Psychol.* 42(3), 314–22.

Sloman SA. (2002). Two systems of reasoning. In T Gilovich, D Griffin, & D Kahneman (Eds.), *Heuristics and Biases: The Psychology of Intuitive Judgment* (pp. 379–96). London, UK: Cambridge University Press.

Small DA, Gelfand M, Babcock L, & Gettman H. (2007). Who goes to the bargaining table? The influence of gender and framing on the initiation of negotiation. *J. Personal. Soc. Psychol.* 93(4), 600–13.

Sondak H, & Bazerman MH. (1989). Matching and negotiation processes in quasi-markets. *Organ. Behav. Hum. Decis. Process.* 44(2), 261–80.

Steele CM, & Aronson J. (1995). Stereotype threat and the intellectual test: performance of African-Americans. *J. Personal. Soc. Psychol.* 69(5), 797–811.

Stevens CK, Bavetta AG, & Gist ME. (1993). Gender differences in the acquisition of salary negotiation skills: the role of goals, self-efficacy, and perceived control. *J. Appl. Psychol.* 78(5), 723–35.

Stuhlmacher AF, & Walters AE. (1999). Gender differences in negotiation outcome: a meta-analysis. *Pers. Psychol.* 52(3), 653–77.

Swaab RI, & Swaab DF. (2009). Sex differences in the effects of visual contact and eye contact in negotiations. *J. Exp. Soc. Psychol.* 45(1), 129–36.

Tajfel H, Billig MG, Bundy RP, & Flament C. (1971). Social categorization and intergroup behavior. *Eur. J. Soc. Psychol.* 1(2), 149–77.

Tenbrunsel AE, Wade-Benzoni KA, Moag J, & Bazerman MH. (1999). The negotiation matching process: relationships and partner selection. *Organ. Behav. Hum. Decis. Process.* 80(3), 252–83.

Tenbrunsel AE, & Diekmann K. (2007). When you are tempted to deceive. *Negotiation* 1, 9–11.

Thibaut JW, & Kelley HH. (1959). *The Social Psychology of Groups.* New York, NY: Wiley.

Thompson L. (1993). The impact of negotiation on intergroup relations. *J. Exp. Soc. Psychol.* 29(4), 304–25.

Thompson L. (1995). The impact of minimum goals and aspirations on judgments of success in negotiations. *Group Decis. Negotiation* 4, 513–24.

Thompson L, Peterson E, & Brodt SE. (1996). Team negotiation: an examination of integrative and distributive bargaining. *J. Personal. Soc. Psychol.* 70(1), 66–78

Thompson LF, & Coovert MD. (2003). Teamwork online: the effects of computer conferencing on perceived confusion, satisfaction, and postdiscussion accuracy. *Group Dyn. Theory Res. Pract.* 7(2), 135–51.

Thompson LL. (2009). *The Mind and Heart of the Negotiator* (4th ed.). Upper Saddle River, NJ: Prentice Hall.

Thompson LL, & DeHarpport T. (1998). Relationships, good incompatibility, and communal orientation in negotiations. *Basic Appl. Soc. Psychol.* 20(1), 33–44.

Thompson LL, & Hastie R. (1990). Social perception in negotiation. *Organ. Behav. Hum. Decis. Process.* 47(1), 98–123.

Tiedens LZ, & Fragale AR. (2003). Power moves: complementarity in dominant and submissive nonverbal behavior. *J. Personal. Soc. Psychol.* 84(3), 558–68.

Uzzi B. (1997). Social structure and competition in interfirm networks: the paradox of embeddedness. *Adm. Sci. Q.* 42, 35–67.

Valley KL, Moag J, & Bazerman MH. (1998). "A matter of trust": Effects of communication on the efficiency and distribution of outcomes. *J. Econ. Behav. Organ.* 34(2), 211–38.

van Kleef GA, De Dreu CKW, & Manstead ASR. (2004a). The interpersonal effects of anger and happiness in negotiations. *J. Personal. Soc. Psychol.* 86(1), 57–76.

Van Kleef GA, De Dreu CKW, & Manstead ASR. (2004b). The interpersonal effects of emotions in negotiations: a motivated information processing approach. *J. Personal. Soc. Psychol.* 87(4), 510–28.

Wade-Benzoni KA, Hoffman AJ, Thompson LL, Moore DA, Gillespie JJ, & Bazerman MH. (2002). Barriers to resolution in ideologically based negotiations: the role of values and institutions. *Acad. Manag. Rev.* 27(1), 41–57.

Walters AE, Stuhlmacher AF, & Meyer LL. (1998). Gender and negotiator competitiveness: a meta-analysis. *Organ. Behav. Hum. Decis. Process.* 76(1), 1–29.

Walton RE, & McKersie RB. (1965). *A Behavioral Theory of Labor Negotiations: An Analysis of a Social Interaction System.* New York, NY: McGraw-Hill.

Watson C. (1994). Gender versus power as a predictor of negotiation behavior and outcomes. *Negotiation J.* 10(2), 117–27.

Weingart LR, Bennet RJ, & Brett JM. (1993). The impact of consideration of issues and motivational orientation on group negotiation process and outcome. *J. Appl. Psychol.* 78, 504–17.

Yamagishi T, & Yamagishi M. (1994). Trust and commitment in the United States and Japan. *Motiv. Emot.* 18(2), 129–66.

4

Social Dilemmas

NORBERT L. KERR

*I*ntragroup cooperation, broadly conceived, is pervasive in small group contexts. The coordination of effort in task groups, the search for consensus in decision making groups, the search for mutually beneficial integrative solutions in negotiations, the give and take between leaders and followers, and many other topics considered in this volume involve choices between relatively more and less cooperative behavior. But cooperation is the focal concern in research on social dilemmas, a class of high interdependence situations that highlight the conflict between personal and collective interests. In a social dilemma, the personal rewards for competitive (usually termed *defecting*) choices are higher than for a cooperative choice, regardless of what choices others in the group make. In that narrow sense, it is personally rational to compete in social dilemmas. However, the collective and personal rewards of universal cooperation are higher than those for universal defection. So, if everyone in the group makes the "rational," defecting choice, they're all worse off than if they made the "irrational," cooperative choice. In a social dilemma, a personally rational choice is collectively irrational. These dilemmas arise frequently in social life, in problems of resource conservation (Hardin's, 1968, classic *tragedy of the commons* is a well known example), providing public goods (e.g., public radio in the US, which all, including non contributors can use), and economics (e.g., trade protectionism as defection vs. open markets as cooperation).

After several decades of research on prisoner's dilemma games (PDG; e.g., Pruitt & Kimmel, 1977), a simple 2-person social dilemma, social psychological interest in the more general N-person prisoner's dilemma (NPD), or social dilemma, began about 30 years ago, stimulated by Dawes' (1980) and Messick and Brewer's (1983) influential papers. Since then, research interest has grown steadily and rapidly (a PsycINFO search of the phrase "social dilemmas" produced 68 references in the 1980s, 162 in the 1990s, and 1044 after 2000).

The purpose of this chapter is not to comprehensively review the social dilemma literature, an unfeasible task given the vastness of the field. Fortunately, there are a number of reviews available (Agrawal, 2002; Bogaert, Boone, & Declerck, 2008; Komorita & Parks, 1996; Kollock, 1998; Kopelman, Weber, & Messick, 2002; Kerr & Park, 2001; Ledyard, 1995; Weber, Kopelman, & Messick, 2004). Rather, given this volume's title and objectives, my purpose is to describe some of the groundbreaking work going on "at the frontier" of social dilemma inquiry. This sampling of cutting edge work is admittedly selective and idiosyncratic. Moreover, we will not really know for decades which of the frontiers now being explored will actually yield the most useful scientific knowledge. So perhaps it is more accurate to say that the chapter will focus on four broad topics that strike this observer as exciting—1) fuzzy social dilemmas, 2) sanctioning systems, 3) selective play environments and partner choice, and 4) subtle determinants of dilemma perception and behavior. Some other cutting-edge topics that could have as easily been featured in the chapter (and probably would have been, with a different author) will be noted at the end of the chapter.

Some scholars (Messick & Brewer, 1983; Nemeth, 1972) have suggested that early prisoner's dilemma research lost steam when it became too focused on small experimental variations within an already narrow paradigm. One theme that characterizes all of the topics I consider here is that they all illustrate a movement away from narrower to broader conceptual, paradigmatic, and methodological approaches to the study of social dilemmas. For each topic, I will begin by providing some background on the topic, laying out some of the foundational research upon which the newer work at the frontier is based. I will then describe some lines of ground-breaking research within the topic.

FUZZY SOCIAL DILEMMAS

Foundational Research

The prototypical prisoners/social dilemma study involves a well specified task or game with little or no uncertainty about game parameters (e.g., size of the group, options available to players, the interdependencies among players, value of outcomes). In real-world dilemmas, on the other hand, there is often much more ambiguity about both the environment and the people facing the dilemma—such dilemmas might generically be termed *fuzzy dilemmas* (Heckathorn, 1998). The effects of moving from well-specified to fuzzy dilemmas have been an object of considerable research attention.

The most thoroughly studied problem has been the effect of resource/environmental uncertainty, usually examined within a resource-dilemma paradigm where cooperation consists of taking or harvesting less than one might, and where collective overharvesting can lead to the collapse of the resource pool (e.g., if total harvests are greater than the size of the resource pool, no one gets anything). Uncertainty is typically manipulated by letting the size of the resource pool vary. For example, five persons might be allowed to harvest from a pool of 500 points (no environmental uncertainty) vs. one in which the pool could take on any value between 250–750 points (high uncertainty). In the latter case, the group members have to make their harvest decisions before learning the actual size of the pool. The usual finding is that mean harvest sizes (i.e., competitive behaviors) increase with environmental uncertainty. The best supported explanation for this effect is that optimism about likely environments tends to increase with environmental uncertainty (e.g., if the value could range from 250–750, one might assume, optimistically, that it will be somewhat greater than the expected value of 500; see several of the chapters in Suleiman, Budescu, Fischer, & Messick, 2004, for a thorough review of this uncertainty research).

More recent work on fuzzy dilemmas has examined the moderating role of environmental uncertainty and the effects of other kinds of uncertainty. Particularly interesting in the latter regard has been the work by Van Lange and his colleagues on *negative noise*.

Research at the Frontier

Environmental Uncertainty as a Moderating Variable   Not only does environmental uncertainty have a direct and negative effect on cooperation, it also seems to moderate the effects of a number of other variables. An early example is Wit and Wilke's (1998) finding that high social uncertainty (i.e., the range of likely levels of cooperation by others) undermined cooperation only when environmental uncertainty was high. A productive program of research by de Kwaadsteniet, van Dijk, and their colleagues has demonstrated several additional such moderating effects. The basic idea behind these studies is that even when group members cannot communicate, whenever possible they will rely on shared rules to tacitly coordinate their harvesting behavior (e.g., allow those with higher status priority to the resource; de Kwaadsteniet & van Dijk, 2010). Under conditions of low environmental uncertainty (i.e., the size of the resource pool is fixed or has small variability), that rule is usually an equality rule (i.e., each group member will take his/her equal share of the known available pool). However, when environmental uncertainty is high, such coordination is more difficult (since it is unclear just what an equal share should be). De Kwaadsteniet, van Dijk, Wit, and De Cremer (2006) show, for example, that personal dispositions to cooperate (SVOs) have little effect on harvesting when environmental uncertainty is low, with most group members following the equal-harvest rule, but that SVOs show their usual effects when uncertainty is high (i.e., prosocials harvest less than proselves). If we have to justify our harvests to others, we are even more likely to follow the shared and defensible equal-division rule if it is possible to do so (i.e., low environmental uncertainty), but when it is difficult to do so (i.e., high environmental uncertainty), the more easily justified course seems to be to simply harvest less (de Kwaadsteniet, van Dijk, Wit, De Cremer, & de Rooij, 2007). This in turn suggests that uncooperative behavior (e.g., taking more than an equal share) can be more easily seen as counternormative under conditions of low uncertainty. Thus, the more one takes, the more angry and blaming other group members are likely to be. However, under high uncertainty, where large harvests are less easily classified as rule violations, group members are less likely to react with anger to larger harvests.

Other Types of Uncertainty   At least four other types of uncertainty have been examined in social dilemmas. One arises for step-level public goods, where a minimum total level of contributions (the "provision point," PP) is required to provide a public good. Here, higher uncertainty can be achieved via a larger range of possible provision points. Both when group members make their contribution decisions simultaneously (Wit & Wilke, 1998) or sequentially (Au, 2004), increasing provision point uncertainty reduced cooperative behavior. A second is social uncertainty—the range of likely levels of cooperation by others. Here, contributions to a public good tend to be reduced when social uncertainty is high (Sabater-Grande & Georgantzis, 2002; Wit & Wilke, 1998; although see van Dijk, de Kwaadsteniet, & De Cremer, 2009, Exp. 3). A third type of uncertainty is outcome uncertainty, which has been examined via the range of possible values of the public good in a step-level game. As long as every possible value was more valuable than the provision point—i.e., the average group member never risked a loss as long as the public good was obtained— then outcome uncertainty appears to have little or no effect on cooperation (van Dijk, Wilke, Wilke, & Metman, 1999; McCarter, Rockmann, & Northcraft, 2010). However, if the outcome uncertainty is great enough that actual losses are possible, the resulting loss aversion seems to undermine willingness to contribute toward providing the public good (McCarter et al., 2010). A fourth and final type of uncertainty is uncertainty about the size of the group. Here, the effect of group-size uncertainty depends on game features—group size uncertainty seems to enhance cooperation in a common pool resource (CPR) dilemma (Au & Ngai, 2003; de Kwaadsteniet, van Dijk, Wit, & De Cremer, 2008), but to reduce it in a step-level public good game (Au, 2004). These findings highlight the importance of not assuming that the relationships observed in one kind of social dilemma will always generalize to another—one can get very different results with different dilemmas (see Abele, Stasser, & Chartier, 2010).

Negative Noise   An interesting twist on interacting under conditions of uncertainty is provided by the recent program of research undertaken by Van Lange and his colleagues on the effects of "noise" in social dilemma settings. In these studies, noise is a disconnect between what one party does or intends and what the other party experiences. For example, in a relationship, one party may intend to act cooperatively (e.g., get home in time for the special dinner the other has prepared), but fail to do so for reasons quite independent of his/her intent (e.g., get caught in a traffic jam). Van Lange and his colleagues rightly point out that in actual, real-world situations of interdependence, such disconnects clearly occur and may even be commonplace. In such cases, partners have to interpret whether apparently uncooperative behavior should be attributed to the other's unwillingness/disinclination to cooperate or to other non-dispositional factors (with less relevance to the ongoing interaction).

Some of the results of this work are unsurprising—e.g., negative noise undermines cooperation (relative to interactions that are not saddled with such unidirectional uncertainty; e.g., Van Lange, Ouwerkerk, & Tazelaar, 2002; Tazelaar, Van Lange, & Ouwerkerk, 2004). However, the negative effects of negative noise are not insurmountable. Several conditions are sufficient to neutralize or mitigate these effects. One is the opportunity to communicate (Tazelaar et al., 2004). As many a late spouse has discovered, it helps when one can explain that one's apparently uncooperative act has another, more benign explanation. Another is an empathic concern for one's partner (Rumble, Van Lange, & Parks, 2010). One is more likely to give one's partner the "benefit of the doubt" under conditions of uncertainty if one is more inclined to look at things from the partner's perspective. Finally, it appears that those who are dispositionally more inclined to be cooperative in the first place (e.g., those with pro-social social value orientations; e.g., Van Lange, 1999), are relatively more sensitive to the effects of noise (Brucks & Van Lange, 2007). Less cooperative, proself individuals are not as reactive and retaliatory for occasional uncooperative acts with ambiguous causes than those who both are inclined to perform and expect more cooperative behavior. These studies have also linked the adverse effects of noise to malignant attributions about one's partner under noisy conditions—e.g., that the partner is less trustworthy (Klapwijk & Van Lange, 2009), has a non-benign intent (Tazelaar et al., 2004), or that the partner simply does not care about jointly shared resources (Brucks & Van Lange, 2008).

Another interesting finding is that the presence/absence of negative noise may moderate the effects of other variables. It is widely accepted that a tit-for-tat strategy is a particularly effective way to encourage cooperation in other group members (e.g., Axelrod, 1984), but the evidence for this has come from the study of "noiseless" environments, i.e., situations in which one could safely assume that every apparent act of defection was intentional. However, in a more realistic, noisy environment, it seems that relatively more forgiving and generous strategies are more effective than strict reciprocity—a smidgen of generosity softens the risks of an "eye for an eye" (viz., of getting trapped in a cycle of joint defection) in noisy situations where one may inadvertently appear more uncooperative than one really is (Klapwijk & Van Lange, 2009, 2010).

SANCTIONING SYSTEMS

Foundational Research

In his seminal paper on public goods, Garrett Hardin (1968) despaired of groups' abilities to avoid the tragedy of the commons except via "mutual coercion, mutually agreed upon." Thus, from the beginning, one potentially important structural solution to social dilemmas has been the imposition of tangible incentives or punishments outside of the dilemma itself (e.g., mandatory taxation to provide public goods; fines for uncooperative behavior). Few early studies included any possibility for the imposition of sanctions. A few, more recent studies demonstrated that cooperation could be boosted and/or defection deterred by sanctioning systems, whether they were imposed by an external agent (e.g., Rapoport & Au, 2001; Wit & Wilke, 1990), by group members on one another (e.g., Caldwell, 1976; Eek, Loukopoulos, Fujii, & Gärling, 2002; Fehr & Gächter, 2002; McCusker & Carnevale, 1995; Yamagishi, 1986, 1992), or by a group leader (e.g., Van Vugt & De Cremer, 1999). More recent work at the frontier has explored a variety of questions stemming from this foundational research: Exactly why do such sanctioning systems work?; do they sometimes fail or even do harm (i.e., lead to less cooperation)?; can intangible, social sanctions be as effective as tangible ones and, if so, which are most effective and why?

Research at the Frontier

Why Do Sanctions Work?   The answer to this question would seem to be obvious—sanctions alter the incentive structure and people will naturally respond. But there are at least two routes through which sanctioning systems could work—(1) self-interest/greed makes cooperation relatively more personally attractive under sanctioning systems and (2) if one presumes that others are similarly affected, one is less fearful of exploitative choices by others when sanctions are in place. However there seems to be more to sanctioning than such rational recalculations of risks and benefits. For example, Fehr and his colleagues (e.g., Fehr & Fischbacher, 2004a) note that options to punish defectors in their studies are just as popular when one can never play again with the defector as when one can. That is, even when it is costly to punish and any improvement in the punished player's future behavior can be of no benefit to the punisher, many players still seize a punishment option. In fact, even "third parties" who are not playing the game themselves will—although at a somewhat reduced rate—incur costs to punish uncooperative parties, especially if the defector is exploitative (i.e., defects when his/her partner cooperates; Fehr & Fischbacher, 2004b). Both results suggest that the motives for punishing and responding to punishment extend beyond enhancing one's own game payoffs.

Another cue to the roots of sanctioning's effectiveness is that punishing behavior may be mediated by moral emotions (e.g., anger; Gächter & Fehr, 1999; de Kwaadsteniet, van Dijk, Wit, & De Cremer, 2010; O'Gorman, Wilson, & Miller, 2005)—punishment is to some extent the result of anger and also may communicate such anger. Still another cue is that the degree of punishment is tied more closely to the defector's relative level of defection (relative to the level of cooperation of the punisher and/or the group as a whole) than to his or her absolute level of defection (e.g., Fehr & Fischbacher, 2004b; Masclet, Noussair, Tucker, & Villeval, 2003), suggesting that punishment is most likely when group members are violating group norms. Finally, it is those most inclined to view the social dilemma choice as a moral one, those with pro-social orientations (Liebrand, Jansen, Rijken, & Suhre, 1986), who are most sensitive to being sanctioned, particularly with sanctions that emphasize both rewards for cooperation and punishments for defection (Folmer & Van Lange, 2007).

These varied threads of evidence have led several scholars (e.g., Fehr & Fischbacher, 2004a; Mulder, 2009) to conclude that when sanctioning systems work, they do so not only because of their direct impact on incentives and expectations of others' behavior, but also because they increase group members' moral concerns. In other words, sanctioning systems increase potential defectors' awareness that certain behavior is counternormative and their concerns about not violating local or general (e.g., reciprocity, equal outcomes) social norms, and with the social and intrapsychic costs that of violating these norms.

When and Why Do Sanctioning Systems Fail?
There appear to be several ways that sanctioning systems can and do fail. One familiar way is via overjustification effects (e.g., Deci & Ryan, 1985)—external incentives can sometimes undermine internal attributions for behavior (e.g., the intrinsic goal of behaving cooperatively) and hence the willingness to perform this behavior absent those incentives. The introduction of sanctioning systems also may suggest to group members that others lack sufficient internal motivation to cooperate (e.g., high concern for the collective welfare, a disinclination to exploit others). This in turn may undermine one's trust in the cooperativeness of others and, in the absence of the sanctions, one's own willingness to cooperate (Chen, Pillutla, & Yao, 2009; Mulder, van Dijk, Wilke, & De Cremer, 2005; Mulder, van Dijk, De Cremer, & Wilke, 2006). Whereas sanctioning systems can increase moral concerns, it is important that they are seen as retributive measures—that the sanctioned behaviors are in some sense immoral and that the sanctions exist to punish bad and reward good behavior (Mulder, 2009). All else being equal, relatively more severe sanctions are more likely to convey this message, particularly if one has some trust in the authorities that impose the sanctions and as long as the sanction is not viewed as excessive (Mulder, Verboon, & De Cremer, 2009). And, all else being equal, punishments are more likely to convey this message than are rewards (Mulder, 2008); reward systems are more likely to be used to promote voluntary rules, whereas punishment systems tend to be reserved for enforcing obligatory rules.

Sanctioning systems also can be seen as compensatory measures—as a means of compensating "exploited" parties for the costs incurred as a result of others' uncooperative behavior. When this happens, they can undermine defectors' moral concerns and hence backfire. For example, Gneezy and Rustichini (2000) found that imposing a fine on parents for picking up their children late from day care actually increased the incidence of late pickups. Here, the fines suggested to parents that they were compensating the day care for their lateness, and this perception undermined their sense that late pickups was "bad" behavior (i.e., violated a rule or norm; also see Tenbrunsel & Messick, 1999).

The Use of Social Sanctioning Systems

The foregoing research linking sanctioning systems to group members' concerns with the moral implications of their behavior strongly suggests that it is not just the tangible costs and rewards inherent in such systems that give them their power. In addition, sanctioning systems can tell group members what behaviors are expected and approved of. If so, sanctioning systems that simply tell group members that others disapprove of certain behavior (e.g., defection in a social dilemma) may be sufficient to deter that behavior. This has been nicely demonstrated in several studies. For example, Masclet et al. (2003) found that giving group members an option to send "disapproval points" (without any material consequences) to others was sufficient to increase contributions to a public good, nearly as much as an option to send material punishments. Likewise, Carpenter, Daniere, and Takahashi (2004) found that cooperation rates were boosted simply by giving group members an option of sending iconic unhappy faces to fellow members (for similar findings with other emotional cues of disapproval, see Kerr, 2009, and Wubben, De Cremer, & van Dijk, 2008, 2009). Even subtle cues that imply that others might be observing, and hence are capable of approving or disapproving, seem sufficient to boost cooperation (e.g., Burnham & Hare, 2007; Mifune, Hashimoto, & Yamagishi, 2010; Rigdon, Ishii, Watabe, & Kitayama, 2009). For example, Kurzban (2001) found that brief eye contact between male participants prior to allocation decisions boosted cooperativeness in a social dilemma. Even more dramatically, Haley and Fessler (2005) found that, relative to a neutral screensaver, a screensaver image resembling a pair of eyes boosted contributions in an ultimatum game.

The psychological processes underlying such effects are not well understood. Some researchers (e.g., Hardy & Van Vugt, 2006; Mifune et al., 2010) suggest that actual or potential evaluation arouses concerns for one's reputation in the group. Others (e.g., Haley & Fessler, 2005) suggest that rather automatic, evolved perceptual/judgmental modules are the proximal trigger of more cooperative behavior. Still others (e.g., Leary & Baumeister, 2000; Levine & Kerr, 2007) suggest that the key motive is to preserve positive relationships within one's group. This latter perspective assumes that group members are very sensitive to cues that suggest that they might be excluded and alter their behavior (e.g., conform to implied or familiar behavioral norms) to forestall any such exclusion. Consistent with this view, giving group members the possibility of excluding or ostracizing fellow group members reliably boosts cooperative behavior (Cinyabuguma, Page, & Putterman, 2005; Kerr, 1999; Kerr et al., 2009; Masclet, 2003; Ouwerkerk, Kerr, Gallucci, & Van Lange, 2005; Maier-Rigaud, Martinsson, & Staffiero, 2010).

SELECTIVE PLAY ENVIRONMENTS
AND PARTNER CHOICE

Foundational Research

The prototypical early prisoner's/social dilemma study used a *forced play* paradigm where the interdependence structure, behavioral options, and game players were fixed and immutable. Besides being an obviously unrealistic model of most real social dilemmas, such a paradigm also precluded many interesting and feasible routes to solving dilemmas (see Hayashi & Yamagishi, 1998). Simulation and experimental studies of behavior using any of several *selective play* protocols have suggested that it may be easier to achieve higher and more sustainable levels of mutual cooperation than previously realized. Such studies have permitted greater variability in the range of choices and interpersonal relationships available to the players (Gallucci, Van Lange, & Ouwerkerk, 2004). For example:

- Some studies have offered players an *exit option*, permitting them to simply withdraw from the game (e.g., Orbell & Dawes, 1993), or to exit and play with a randomly- (e.g., Schuessler, 1989) or self-selected (e.g., Hayashi & Yamagishi, 1998) new partner. Generally speaking, higher levels of cooperation are achieved with than without such options, particularly for players who are inclined to be cooperative, trusting of others, and unwilling to remain in an exploitative relationship (see Yamagishi & Hayashi, 1996; Hayashi & Yamagishi, 1998; and Gallucci et al., 2004, for reviews).
- A few studies have examined the effect of being able to adjust one's level of interdependence with others—i.e., to seek a relatively more or less interdependent relationship. When both players in dyadic games have this option, very high levels of mutual cooperation can be achieved (Yamagishi, Kanazawa, Mashima, & Terat, 2005). When one player has the option and the other plays a consistent strategy, the option is sensibly used (i.e., the one player increases interdependence for highly cooperative others and decreases interdependence for highly uncooperative others; Van Lange & Visser, 1999). On the other hand, when the other player follows a reciprocal (i.e., tit-for-tat) strategy, more cooperative players seek higher interdependence, but more competitive players seek reduced interdependence (Van Lange & Visser, 1999).
- Still other studies have given players a less restricted set of behavioral options. A nice illustration of this type of study is Kurzban, McCabe, Smith, and Wilson (2001, Exp. 1) who found that giving players a chance to either increment or decrement posted intended levels of cooperation undermined cooperation, relative to a condition where players were only able to *increase* their posted intention. If only the lowest intended contribution were posted for all to see, this "increase only" option could even prompt steadily increasing cooperation (Kurzban et al., 2001, Exp.

2), in line with a *minimum reciprocity rule* (Sugden, 1984), which pre-scribes that one cooperates at or slightly above the least cooperative group member.

More recent research at the frontier has 1) expanded the range and variety of selective-play options and 2) begun to explore what besides one's partner's known cooperativeness leads one (rightly or wrongly) to prefer (or avoid) that person in a social dilemma.

Research at the Frontier

Selective Play Environments   The foundational work reviewed above has tended to make few and narrow departures from a simple forced-choice paradigm and then explore empirically what difference they make in behavior. A rather different approach is that of evolutionary game theorists (e.g., Hofbauer & Sigmund, 1998; Nowak, 2006) who consider many varieties of selective play—for example, does it matter if one can withdraw from interaction?; what if interaction and/or reproduction is restricted only to some others?; what if such restrictions are based on spatial proximity?; what if one's past behavior establishes a reputation that can guide others' willingness to cooperate or affiliate in the future? This approach tends to be less concerned about predicting individual behavior under particular conditions and more concerned with the relative rewardingness (and hence, fitness) of alternative behavioral strategies in large populations that interact across long periods of time. The primary methods of inquiry are simulations and formal theory development.

My goal here is not to try to review or even summarize the burgeoning and complex literature applying evolutionary game theory to the analysis of human cooperation. Since most of the work is done by evolutionary and mathematical biologists, its details are well beyond the scope of this chapter (and this author's competence). I would, though, like to offer a couple of illustrations of how such work illuminates our understanding of behavior in social dilemmas.

We saw above that allowing group members to decline to play or to move to another partner generally increased the level of cooperation in social dilemmas. Hauert, Traulsen, Brandt, Nowak, and Sigmund (2007) went well beyond this conclusion by showing that the option to withdraw from the interdependent relationship may be vital for the success of punishment as a deterrent to defec-tion. If participation in the social dilemma is compulsory, then under reason-able assumptions (e.g., a basic social dilemma structure, imitation of successful strategies, some possibility of mutation from one strategy to another) defectors will come to dominate the population, even if some people are willing to bear the cost of punishing such defectors. But if there is an option of not playing the social dilemma—an option that has a moderate rewardingness—a strategy of cooperating plus punishing noncooperators will come to be the dominant strategy.

As noted earlier, if all members of a population must play a social dilemma, defection evolves and dominates. This remains true when one assumes occasional mutations, resulting in offspring that are somewhat more or somewhat less cooperative than their parents. Killingback, Bieri, and Flatt (2006) reported that this situation changes drastically if the population is divided into subsets (i.e., groups), the game is played not among everyone in the population but within these subgroups only, and there is some small but real chance of dispersal (i.e., movement between groups). Under these assumptions, group members using strategies that maximize cooperation quickly evolve. Others (see Nowak, Tarnita, & Antal, 2010, for an overview) have shown that many other variations on this subgrouping or clustering theme have similar effects, whether the clustering is based on physical proximity, on social networks, some common phenotype, or as in Killingback et al. (2006), on simple grouping of the population into subgroups.

Analyses like these are beginning to appear in the psychological literature (also see Van Vugt & Kameda, this volume). An excellent example is Kameda, Tsukasaki, Hastie, and Berg (2011), who note that the benefits of group collaboration usually show diminishing returns with group size. This is contrary to the usual presumption of social dilemmas, whereby the benefits of cooperation accumulate linearly with the number of cooperators. In both simulations and a lab experiment, Kameda et al. show that if just a few cooperators could produce a big benefit a stable population composed of both cooperators and defectors would evolve. Hence, they show how cooperation can evolve in groups without any special incentives (e.g., special pride in being a cooperator; a valuable reputation for being a cooperator; greater fitness for one's subgroup relative to other subgroups).

Choosing Partners   One interesting selective-play variation is letting group members choose their fellow members. Clearly one would seek social dilemma partners who are trustworthy and avoid or abandon partners who are not. This might be determined through actual experience with the partner, but mistakes in partner selection could be a rather costly. It would be quite useful if there were some means of recognizing trustworthy partners prior to interaction using cues that are observable, reliable, and hard-to-fake (such as some aspect of physical appearance or an involuntary emotional expression; Frank, 1988). These speculations give rise to several related questions: Can people reliably distinguish between more and less cooperative partners based on initial encounters? What cues do they use to make such judgments? What is the actual diagnosticity of such cues?

An early study by Frank, Gilovich, and Regan (1993) demonstrated that a 30-min. "get to know you" session enabled their participants to estimate others' subsequent choices in a simple prisoner's dilemma game at a better than chance level. Qualitatively similar results were reported by Brown, Palameta, and Moore (2003), who showed that opportunities to observe target persons in a variety of contexts (e.g., telling a children's story; describing one's likes and dislikes) was sufficient for the observers to give higher ratings on cooperation-relevant traits (e.g., helpful) to those targets who self-identified themselves as more altruistic.

These early studies suggested that potential partners might well provide cues to their future quality as partners, even when they are not actually functioning as partners—we humans seem to have some ability to recognize good interaction partners. However, they did not reveal just what those cues might be—they could be any of several nonverbal cues, verbal content cues, or some mix of the two. Subsequent studies help narrow the range of possibilities. For example, at least some of the diagnostic cues seem to be contained in nonverbal or appearance behavior. Shelley et al. (2010; Exp. 2) found that naïve judges whose only information about a group of targets was gained through watching a silent videotape of the targets describing the events of the prior day correctly judged that targets with prosocial orientations would use more cooperative strategies in making self/other allocations than would targets with proself orientations.[1] To narrow the range even further, at least some of the diagnostic cues appear to be available from still photographs.[2] Verplaetse, Vanneste, and Braeckman (2007) found that naïve judges could, based only on seeing still photographs, correctly classify both cooperators and defectors in a PDG at rates significantly above chance, but only if the photos were taken at the moment the targets were actually deciding what to do in the PDG (not in a pregame neutral photo or a practice round photo; cf. Brown et al., 2003, Exp. 2). Likewise, Shelley, Page, Rives, Yeagley, and Kuhlman (2010, Exp. 3) found no relationship between the actual cooperativeness of people (assessed via social value orientations) and judge's expected cooperativeness of those same people when only a still photo with a neutral expression was available to judges. These studies suggest that there may be little useful diagnostic information available in flat, neutral, or nonexpressive depictions of potential partners. But the story is very different when some emotional expression is possible. When judges are shown photos of people posing a smile (either with [Exp. 5] or without [Exp. 4] poses of other emotions), they can (to some degree, at least) correctly distinguish between more vs. less cooperative people (Shelley et al., 2010).

All this suggests 1) that we rely upon others' emotional expressions to assess their fitness as cooperation partners (the perceptual link) and 2) that at least some aspects of others' emotional expressiveness are reliably linked to their actual or likely level of cooperation (the behavioral link). There is growing evidence for both links, particularly when it comes to positive emotional expressions. For the perceptual link, people perceive those who smile, particularly those whose smiles are genuine (Duchenne smiles), to be more trustworthy and concerned about others (Brown et al., 2003, Exp. 3; Krumhuber et al., 2007). People are also more willing to act cooperatively towards such smiling partners in games that require trust (Scharlemann, Eckel, Kacelnik, & Wilson, 2001; Krumhuber et al., 2007). Recall that the most useful cues for partner quality should be expressed involuntarily (Frank, 1988), because voluntarily controlled cues are more easily faked and could thus be misleading. In their analysis of silent video clips, Brown et al. (2003) found that judgments of a target's concern for others were reliably associated with a number of such involuntary cues (e.g., Duchenne smiles, brief smiles, a "concern furrow" at the brow), but not with several voluntary ones (e.g., eyebrow flashes and raises, open smiles).

For the behavioral link (between emotional expression and cooperation), there is also growing evidence. All the involuntary facial cues that Brown et al.'s (2003) judges relied upon were also reliably associated with the targets' self-reported levels of altruistic behavior. And the frequency of Duchenne smiles displayed in an interaction between two friends who had to split their experimental earnings was reliably associated with their expressed willingness to extend help to others (Mehu, Grammer, & Dunbar, 2007). In unpublished studies by Carnevale (1977) and Mills (1978) [cited by Shelley et al., 2010], silent videotapes of people describing emotionally charged experiences were judged as relatively more positive for more cooperative people and relatively more negative (angry and sad) for less cooperative people. All of these studies suggest it may be the general positivity of one's facial and nonverbal expressions that signals a more cooperative person (see Schug, Matsumoto, Horita, Yamagishi, & Bonnet, 2010, for a competing interpretation).

Despite the null results reported above for neutral, still pictures, there are also growing indications that physical attractiveness might provide a useful cue for partner selection, at least for male partners. In an early study, Mulford, Orbell, Shatto, and Stockard (1998) found that there was an association between how attractive one perceived a potential partner and how willing one was to play a prisoner's dilemma with that partner. These effects were not moderated by the sex of the judge or the sex of the potential partner. So people seem to think that attractive partners are cooperative partners. Ironically, the actual cooperation data suggest otherwise. Whether attractiveness is indexed by subjective judgments by independent judges (Takahashi, Yamagishi, Tanida, Kiyonari, & Kanazawa, 2006) or by symmetry in body (Zaatari & Trivers, 2007) or face (Sanchez-Pages & Turiegano, 2010), more attractive/symmetric men are in fact *less* cooperative than their less attractive/symmetric brothers. And neither attractiveness (Takahashi et al., 2006) nor symmetry (Zaatari & Trivers, 2007) among females is reliably linked to their willingness to cooperate. This full pattern of results has been interpreted in evolutionary terms (e.g., see Zaatari & Trivers, 2007; Takahashi et al., 2006)—more genetically desirable (i.e., more attractive, symmetric) males may not be as dependent on cooperation to attract mates or to gain other resources (e.g., they can use aggression more effectively). This line of argument implicates other potential indicators of male reproductive or survival fitness, such as testosterone levels. There are some intriguing hints that early exposure to testosterone in utero and resulting observable morphological markers (e.g., 2D:4D ratio; masculinized facial features) are linked to cooperativeness, but the findings are preliminary and inconsistent (cf. Millet & Dewitte, 2006, 2009; Sanchez-Pages & Turiegano, 2010; Pound, Penton-Voak, & Surridge, 2009).

SUBTLE DETERMINANTS OF DILEMMA PERCEPTION AND BEHAVIOR: PRIMING/FRAMING

Foundational Research

The traditional analysis of social dilemmas is an economic, rational-choice, expected-utility one—people can be expected to respond to the objective payoffs available in the situation, or at least to the subjective values that they attach to the possible outcomes. This approach suggests that situational features that do not materially alter the dilemma's incentives should not affect behavior choices. Nevertheless, much early social dilemma research showed that framing a dilemma with a fixed incentive structure in different ways could alter levels of cooperation. For example, framing a problem so that it looks as though a cooperative choice rewards others resulted in more cooperation than a functionally identical framing that looks as though a defecting choice punishes others (Komorita, 1987; Fehr & Gächter, 2000; cf. Kerr & Kaufman-Gilliland, 1997). A fairly large literature has examined framing functionally the same dilemma in public-good terms (where one must decide how much to give toward a shared resource) vs. resource-dilemma terms (where one must decide how much to take from a shared resource). More often than not, cooperation rates have been higher in the latter, "take" framing, but there are many exceptions and complications to such a simple summary (see DeDreu & McCusker, 1997; Tenbrunsel & Northcraft, 2010; and Weber et al., 2004, for reviews).

An appealing alternative to the traditional, rational choice perspective is Weber, Kopelman, and Messick's (2004) appropriateness framework. The latter suggests that behavioral choices are often governed by one's assessment of just what is the most appropriate way to behave in the given situation—by how one answers the question, "what does a person like me do in a situation like this?". From the appropriateness perspective, apparently superficial aspects of the situation—for example, how it is framed or described—can determine how the situation is construed and hence what rules or norms one might follow (Tenbrunsel & Northcraft, 2010). Even the label used to describe a social dilemma can lead to very different construals and behavior. For example, Batson and Moran (1999) found that characterizing a simple prisoner's dilemma game as a "business transaction" resulted in less cooperation than when it was described as a "social exchange". Similarly, Cronk (2007) showed that giving a trust game an extra label (this is an *osatua* game) that was associated among his participants (Maasii men) with need-based giving resulted in giving less and returning less in a trust game than occurred with without such a label. Such associations need not be longstanding—Cronk and Wasielewski (2008) found that having American undergraduates read a brief description of the Maasii culture and the osatua concept led them to exhibit the same framing effects as the Maasii tribesmen who grew up with the concept.

Such findings raise several interesting questions that have gained increasing research attention—for example, can such framing effects be primed?; if so, what are the concepts that effectively prime higher levels of cooperation?; and when and how do such primes work?

Research at the Frontier

If, as the Weber et al. model suggests, the particular construal one puts on a dilemma ("what kind of situation is this and how are people like me supposed to behave in it?") guides one's behavior, then making a particular construal cognitively accessible—e.g., by priming it—should guide how one construes the situation. This was demonstrated early on using fairly heavy-handed primes by Elliott, Hayward, and Canon (1998). Participants first read a set of news briefings that extolled either an entrepreneurial business strategy (i.e., emphasizing autonomy and individual achievement) or a cooperative business strategy (i.e., emphasizing teamwork and group achievement). They were also asked to provide examples of and arguments in favor of their primed strategy. In a second, ostensibly unrelated experiment, Elliott et al. found greater cooperation in a public goods game for those primed with the cooperative strategy. Other studies have shown that far more subtle primes produce similar effects. For example, Hertel and Fiedler (1994) found that priming the positive connotations of cooperation and the negative connotations of competition in an ostensive memory test increased cooperation in a social dilemma (also see Hertel & Fiedler, 1998; Utz, Van Lange, Green, Waldzus, & Bovina, 2005). Subsequent work has shown similar effects for priming or activating business concepts (Kay, Wheeler, Bargh, & Ross, 2004), interdependence/independence (Utz, 2004b), morality (Utz et al., 2005), legality (Callan, Kay, Olson, Brar, & Whitefield, 2010), and broad/high-level vs. narrow/low-level construal mind-sets (Sanna, Chang, Parks, & Kennedy, 2009).

Kay and Ross (2003) provided nice evidence that such priming effects may indeed be mediated by group members' construals of the game. After reading cooperative or competitive words in a scrambled sentence task, participants were shown a generic prisoner's dilemma game and asked to rate how appropriate each of several alternative names would be for the game. Those primed with competition construed the game as one for which competitive behavior was appropriate (e.g., preferred *The Wall Street Game* as a label) and were themselves less willing to be cooperative. Those primed with cooperation construed the game as a more cooperative (e.g., preferred *The Team Game* as a label) and were also more willing to cooperate. The priming effects on behavior were also stronger after participants had already named the game (and settled on a construal) than when they had not yet done so.

Recent work has shown that such priming effects in social dilemmas depend upon aspects of the person being primed and aspects of the dilemma, and such moderation effects have shed considerable light on the underlying psychological processes. For example, priming effects are more pronounced when the dilemma itself is more ambiguous and lacks clear normative demands (Kay et al., 2004), that is, where the context does not already provide a compelling construal. Likewise, priming effects are more pronounced when one does not already have a chronically available construal. Smeesters, Wheeler, and Kay (2009, Exp. 1) found that people with a strong, consistent social value orientation (SVO; regardless of whether it was pro-social or proself) were not affected by primes of religiosity (toward more prosocial behavior) or business (toward less prosocial behavior) in a dictator game, but those with weaker, inconsistent SVOs were. Smeesters, Wheeler, et al. (2009, Exp. 2) also argued that priming the self-concept tends also to prime a set of construals of how one usually acts in various situations. In support of this idea, they also found less sensitivity to religious or business primes on prosocial behavior among those whose self concept had been previously primed.

Whether priming a concept will lead to cooperation vs. competition will depend upon the preexisting associations the target of the priming has. So, for example, people with pro-social orientations think that being smart or competent implies one would act cooperatively (as they themselves act), whereas people with proself orientations believe that anyone who is smart would act competitively (as they tend to act; Van Lange & Kuhlman, 1994). Thus priming competence should tend to increase competitiveness for proselfs but increase cooperativeness for prosocials, which was the pattern Utz, Ouwerkerk, and Van Lange (2004) observed. Likewise, subtly activating the self (by circling first-person pronouns in a text) led to more cooperation among prosocials but to less cooperation among proselves (Utz, 2004a). Likewise, the cooperation-inhibiting effect of priming legal concepts was limited to those who already saw the world in competitive, zero-sum terms (Callan et al., 2010).

Most of the priming results we have been reviewing are fairly straightforward—priming competition or concepts associated with competition increases competitive behavior. But Smeesters, Wheeler, and Kay (2009) suggested that there is a second interesting route for primes—they can color our perception of the other people with whom we may interact. So, for example, priming unkindness could both make a person construe the situation as one where unkind, proself behavior is appropriate and make the person see his/her interaction partner as more unkind. In this example, either kind of priming would be expected to reduce prosocial behavior. But, they suggest, which kind of priming is likely to occur depends upon how focused the person is on others—being focused outward, on others, would tend to engage the second, perceptual route. Smeesters, Yzerbyt, Corneille, and Warlop (2009) present the results of some experiments that were nicely consistent with this theoretical argument.

CONCLUDING THOUGHTS

The four topics we have been considering are only some of those we might have discussed. For example, with but a few exceptions, the first few decades of social dilemma research was conducted in western cultures, predominantly the U.S. and western Europe. Today, there is increasing interest in discovering more about how culture shapes responses to social dilemmas (e.g., Buchan et al., 2009; Yamagishi & Suzuki, 2010). In addition, the growing use of biopsychological and neuroscience methods to analyze behavior has also been reflected in the social dilemma area (e.g., Fehr, 2009; Hein & Singer, 2010). And all the questions that can be posed for individual behavior within social dilemmas—and a few that cannot—may also be examined when groups rather than individuals are the "players" (e.g., Bornstein, 2003; Wildschut & Insko, 2007). Very interesting work is also being done on the way in which key perceptions are formed, such as whether others are trustworthy (e.g., Kramer & Cook, 2004; Yamagishi, 2001) or a particular distribution of outcomes is fair (e.g., van Dijk, Wit, Wilke, & de Kwaadsteniet, 2010). And good progress continues to be made in many traditional areas of social dilemma inquiry (e.g., social value orientations, Bogaert et al., 2008, Van Lange & Joireman, 2010; the efficacy of cooperative action, Yu, Au, & Chan, 2009).

The scientific study of social dilemmas continues to expand and flourish. Most exciting, I think, is the truly multidisciplinary nature of this work. If one attends a social dilemma conference or simply starts browsing through the literature, one will encounter investigators from the natural sciences (e.g., biologists, ethologists, zoologists, ecologists), from the social sciences (e.g., social and organizational psychologists, sociologists, economists, political scientists), and from many applied areas (e.g., environmentalists, engineers, conservationists, regulators, policy advisors). Besides this disciplinary diversity one will also see considerable methodological diversity. In social psychology, laboratory experiments continue to predominate, but one will also encounter simulations, ethnographic studies, field experiments, opinion and resource use surveys, archival analyses, observations of natural behavior, and comparisons across cultures and species. Such a diversity of conceptual and methodological approaches offers the promise and, increasingly, the payoff of converging evidence. The mysteries of human cooperation are not fully explored, but if the activity at the frontiers of our knowledge is any indication, we are well on the way to understanding the core mysteries—when and why we put common interest ahead of self interest.

NOTES

1   It is well established that social value orientations are reliably predictive of cooperative behavior in social dilemma and other mixed motive settings (e.g., Balliet, Parks, & Joireman, 2009).

2   A series of studies by Yamagishi, Tanida, Mashima, Shimoma, and Kanazawa (2003) indirectly bolster this argument. When shown pictures of former cooperators and defectors in prisoners dilemma games and subsequently asked to identify those shown and not shown, participants were better able to recognize former defectors than former cooperators. Interestingly, the false alarm rate was also higher for former defectors than cooperators. Clearly, there is something in even simple facial images of less cooperative others that makes them distinctive and memorable.

REFERENCES

Abele, S., Stasser, G., & Chartier, C. (2010). Conflict and coordination in the provision of public goods: A conceptual analysis of continuous and step-level games. *Personality and Social Psychology Review, 14*, 385–401.

Agrawal, A. (2002). Common resources and institutional sustainability. In E. Ostrom, T. Dietz, N. Dolsak, P. C. Stem, S. Stonich, & E. U. Weber (Eds.), *The drama of the commons* (pp. 41–86). Washington, DC: National Academy Press.

Au, W. (2004). Criticality and environmental uncertainty in step-level public goods dilemmas. *Group Dynamics: Theory, Research, and Practice, 8*(1), 40–61.

Au, W. T., & Ngai, M. Y. (2003). Effects of group size uncertainty and protocol of play in a common pool resource dilemma. *Group Processes & Intergroup Relations, 6*(3), 265–283.

Axelrod, R. (1984). *The evolution of cooperation.* New York, NY: Basic Books.

Balliet, D., Parks, C., & Joireman, J. (2009). Social value orientation and cooperation in social dilemmas: A meta-analysis. *Group Processes & Intergroup Relations, 12*(4), 533–547.

Batson, C. D., & Moran, T. (1999). Empathy-induced altruism in a prisoner's dilemma. *European Journal of Social Psychology, 29*(7), 909–924.

Bogaert, S., Boone, C., & Declerck, C. (2008). Social value orientation and cooperation in social dilemmas: A review and conceptual model. *British Journal of Social Psychology, 47*, 453–480.

Bornstein, G. (2003). Intergroup conflict: Individual, group, and collective interests. *Personality and Social Psychology Review, 7*(2), 129–145.

Brown, W. M., Palameta, B., & Moore, C. (2003). Are there nonverbal cues to commitment? An exploratory study using the zero-acquaintance video presentation paradigm. *Evolutionary Psychology, 1*, 42–69.

Brucks, W. M., & Van Lange, P. A. M. (2007). When prosocials act like proselfs in a commons dilemma. *Personality and Social Psychology Bulletin, 33*(5), 750–758.

Brucks, W. M., & Van Lange, P. A. M. (2008). No control, no drive: How noise may undermine conservation behavior in a commons dilemma. *European Journal of Social Psychology, 38*(5), 810–822.

Buchan, N. R., Grimalda, G., Wilson, R., Brewer, M., Fatas, E., & Foddy, M. (2009). Globalization and human cooperation. *PNAS Proceedings of the National Academy of Sciences, 106*(11), 4138–4142.

Burnham, T. C., & Hare, B. (2007). Engineering human cooperation: Does involuntary neural activation increase public goods contributions? *Human Nature, 18*, 88–108.

Caldwell, M. D. (1976). Communication and sex effects in a five-person prisoner's dilemma game. *Journal of Personality and Social Psychology, 33*(3), 273–280.

Callan, M. J., Kay, A. C., Olson, J. M., Brar, N., & Whitefield, N. (2010). The effects of priming legal concepts on perceived trust and competitiveness, self-interested attitudes, and competitive behavior. *Journal of Experimental Social Psychology, 46*(2), 325–335.

Carnevale, P. (1977). *Cooperators, competitors and individualists encode nonverbal affect.* Paper presented at the Eastern Psychological Association Convention, Boston, MA.

Carpenter, J. P., Daniere, A. G., & Takahashi, L. M. (2004). Cooperation, trust, and social capital in southeast Asian urban slums. *Journal of Economic Behavior & Organization, 55*(4), 505–531.

Chen, X-P., Pillutla, M., & Yao, X. (2009). Unintended consequences of cooperation inducing and maintaining mechanisms in public goods dilemmas: Sanctions and moral appeals. *Group Processes & Intergroup Relations*, 12(2), 241–255.

Cinyabuguma, M., Page, T., & Putterman, L., 2005. Cooperation under the threat of expulsion in a public goods experiment. *Journal of Public Economics*, 89, 1421–1435.

Cronk, L. (2007): The influence of cultural framing on play in the trust game: A Maasai example. *Evolution and Human Behavior, 28*, 352–358.

Cronk, L., & Wasielewski, H. (2008). An unfamiliar social norm rapidly produces framing effects in an economic game. *Journal of Evolutionary Psychology, 6*(4), 283–308.

Dawes, R. M. (1980). Social dilemmas. *Annual Review of Psychology, 31*, 169–193.

Deci, E., & Ryan, R. M., (1985). *Intrinsic motivation and self-determination in human behavior.* New York, NY: Plenum Press.

De Dreu, C. K. W., & McCusker, C. (1997). Gain–loss frames and cooperation in two-person social dilemmas: A transformational analysis. *Journal of Personality and Social Psychology, 72*(5), 1093–1106.

de Kwaadsteniet, E. W., & van Dijk, E. (2010). Social status as a cue for tacit coordination. *Journal of Experimental Social Psychology, 46*(3), 515–524.

de Kwaadsteniet, E. W., van Dijk, E., Wit, A., & De Cremer, D. (2006). Social dilemmas as strong versus weak situations: Social value orientations and tacit coordination under resource size uncertainty. *Journal of Experimental Social Psychology, 42*(4), 509–516.

de Kwaadsteniet, E. W., van Dijk, E., Wit, A., De Cremer, D., & de Rooij, M. (2007). Justifying decisions in social dilemmas: Justification pressures and tacit coordination under environmental uncertainty. *Personality and Social Psychology Bulletin*, 33(12), 1648–1660.

de Kwaadsteniet, E. W., van Dijk, E., Wit, A., & De Cremer, D. (2008). How many of us are there?: Group size uncertainty and social value orientations in common resource dilemmas. *Group Processes & Intergroup Relations*, 11(3), 387–399.

de Kwaadsteniet, E. W., van Dijk, E., Wit, A., & De Cremer, D. (2010). Anger and retribution after collective overuse: The role of blaming and environmental uncertainty in social dilemmas. *Personality and Social Psychology Bulletin*, 36(1), 59–70.

Elliott, C. S., Hayward, D. M., & Canon, S. (1998). Institutional framing: Some experimental evidence. *Journal of Economic Behavior and Organization*, 35(4), 455–464.

Eek, D., Loukopoulos, P., Fujii, S., & Gärling, T. (2002). Spill-over effects of intermittent costs for defection in social dilemmas. *European Journal of Social Psychology*, 32(6), 801–813.

Fehr, E. (2009). *Social preferences and the brain.* San Diego, CA: Elsevier Academic Press.

Fehr, E., & Fischbacher, U. (2004a). Social norms and human cooperation. *Trends in Cognitive Science, 8*(4), 185–190.

Fehr, E., & Fischbacher, U. (2004b). Third-party punishment and social norms. *Evolution and Human Behavior, 25*, 63–87.

Fehr, E., Gächter, S. (2000). *Do incentive contracts crowd out voluntary cooperation?* Working Paper No. 34, Institute for Empirical Research in Economics, University of Zurich, Switzerland.

Fehr, E., & Gächter, S. (2002). Altruistic punishment in humans. *Nature, 415*(6868), 137–140.

Folmer, C. P. R., & Van Lange, P. A. M. (2007). Why promises and threats need each other. *European Journal of Social Psychology, 37*, 1016–1031.

Frank, R. H. (1988). *Passions within reason: The strategic role of the emotions.* New York, NY: W. W. Norton & Co.

Frank, R. H., Gilovich, T., & Regan, D. T. (1993). The evolution of one-shot cooperation: An experiment. *Ethology & Sociobiology, 14*(4), 247–256.

Gächter, S., & Fehr, E. (1999). Collective action as a social exchange. *Journal of Economic Behavior and Organization, 39*, 341–369.

Gallucci, M., Van Lange, P. A. M., & Ouwerkerk, J. W. (2004). Freedom of movement: A strategic analysis of social dilemmas with the option to move. In R. Suleiman, D. V. Budescu, I. Fischer & D. M. Messick (Eds.), *Contemporary psychological research on social dilemmas* (pp. 180–208). New York, NY: Cambridge University Press.

Gneezy, U., & Rustichini, A. (2000). A fine is a price. *Journal of Legal Studies, 29*(1), 1–17.

Haley, K. J., & Fessler, D. M. T. (2005). Nobody's watching? Subtle cues affect generosity in an anonymous economic game. *Evolution and Human Behavior, 26*(3), 245–256.

Hardin, G. (1968). The tragedy of the commons. *Science, 162*, 1243–1248.

Hardy, C. L., & Van Vugt, M. (2006). Nice guys finish first: The competitive altruism hypothesis. *Personality and Social Psychology Bulletin, 32*(10), 1402–1413.

Hauert, C., Traulsen, A., Brandt, H., Nowak, M. A., & Sigmund, K. (2007). Via freedom to coercion: The emergence of costly punishment. *Science, 316*, 1905–1907.

Hayashi, N., & Yamagishi, T. (1998). Selective play: Choosing partners in an uncertain world. *Personality and Social Psychology Review, 2*(4), 276–289.

Heckathorn, D. (1998). *Social cooperation in fuzzy dilemmas: Technological versus valuational uncertainty.* Paper presented at the annual meeting of the American Sociological Association, San Francisco, CA.

Hein, G., & Singer, T. (2010). Neuroscience meets social psychology: An integrative approach to human empathy and prosocial behavior. In M. Mikulincer & P. R. Shaver (Eds.), *Prosocial motives, emotions, and behavior: The better angels of our nature* (pp. 109–125). Washington, DC: American Psychological Association.

Hertel, G., & Fiedler, K. (1994). Affective and cognitive influences in a social dilemma game. *European Journal of Social Psychology, 24*(1), 131–145.

Hertel, G., & Fiedler, K. (1998). Fair and dependent versus egoistic and free: Effects of semantic and evaluative priming on the "ring measure of social values". *European Journal of Social Psychology, 28*(1), 49–70.

Hofbauer, J., & Sigmund, K. (1998). *Evolutionary games and population dynamics.* Cambridge, UK: Cambridge University Press.

Kameda, T., Tsukasaki, T., Hastie, R., & Berg, N. (2011). Democracy under uncertainty: The "wisdom of crowds" and the free-rider problem in group decision making. *Psychological Review, 118*, 76–96.

Kay, A. C., & Ross, L. (2003). The perceptual push: The interplay of implicit cues and explicit situational construals on behavioral intentions in the prisoner's dilemma. *Journal of Experimental Social Psychology, 39*(6), 634–643.

Kay, A. C., Wheeler, S. C., Bargh, J. A., & Ross, L. (2004). Material priming: The influence of mundane physical objects on situational construal and competitive behavioral choice. *Organizational Behavior and Human Decision Processes, 95*(1), 83–96.

Kerr, N. L. (1999). Anonymity and social control in social dilemmas. In M. Foddy et al. (Eds.), *Resolving social dilemmas* (pp. 103–119). Philadelphia, PA: Psychology Press.

Kerr, N. L. (2009). Affective feedback as a means of social control in social dilemmas. Paper presented at the 13th International Conference on Social Dilemmas (ICSD2009), Kyoto, Japan, August 20–24, 2009.

Kerr, N. L., & Kaufman-Gilliland, C. (1997). Rationalizing defection in social dilemmas. *Journal of Experimental Social Psychology, 33*, 211–230.

Kerr, N. L., & Park, E. (2001). Group performance in collaborative and social dilemma tasks: Progress and prospects. In M. Hogg & S. Tindale (Eds.), *Blackwell handbook of social psychology: Vol. 4. Groups.* Malden, MA: Blackwell.

Kerr, N. L., Rumble, A. C., Park, E. S., Parks, C. D., Ouwerkerk, J. W., Gallucci, M., & Van Lange, P. A. M. (2009). "One bad apple spoils the whole barrel": Social exclusion as a remedy for the One Bad Apple Effect. *Journal of Experimental Social Psychology, 45*(4), 603–613.

Killingback, T., Bieri, J., & Flatt, T. (2006). Evolution in group structured populations can resolve the tragedy of the commons. *Proceedings of the Royal Society B, 273*, 1477–1481.

Klapwijk, A., & Van Lange, P. A. M. (2009). Promoting cooperation and trust in "noisy" situations: The power of generosity. *Journal of Personality and Social Psychology, 96*(1), 83–103.

Klapwijk, A., & Van Lange, P. A. M. (2010). *The greater power of generosity.* Unpublished manuscript, Free University of Amsterdam, The Netherlands.

Kollock, P. (1998). Social dilemmas: The anatomy of cooperation. *Annual Review of Sociology, 24*, 183–214.

Komorita, S. S. (1987). Cooperative choice in decomposed social dilemmas. *Personality and Social Psychology Bulletin, 13*, 53–63.

Komorita, S. S., & Parks, C. D. (1996). *Social dilemmas.* Boulder, CO: Westview Press.

Kopelman, S.. Weber, J. M., & Messick, D. M. (2002). Factors influencing cooperation in commons dilemmas: A review of experimental psychological research. In E. Ostrom, T. Dietz, N. Dolsak, P. C. Stern, S. Stonich, & E. U. Weber (Eds.), *The drama of the commons* (pp. 113–156). Washington, DC: National Academy Press.

Kramer, R. M., & Cook, K. S. (2004). *Trust and distrust in organizations: Dilemmas and approaches.* New York, NY: Russell Sage Foundation.

Krumhuber, E., Manstead, A. S. R., Cosker, D., Marshall, D., Rosin, P. L., & Kappas, A. (2007). Facial dynamics as indicators of trustworthiness and cooperative behavior. *Emotion, 7*(4), 730–735.

Kurzban, R. (2001). The social psychophysics of cooperation: Nonverbal communication in a public goods game. *Journal of Nonverbal Behavior, 25*(4), 241–259.

Kurzban, R., McCabe, K., Smith, V. L., & Wilson, B. J. (2001). Incremental commitment and reciprocity in a real-time public goods game. *Personality and Social Psychology Bulletin, 27*(12), 1662–1673.

Leary, M. R., & Baumeister, R. F. (2000). The nature and function of self-esteem: Sociometer theory. In M. P. Zanna (Ed.), *Advances in experimental social psychology* (Vol. 32, pp. 1–62). San Diego, CA: Academic Press.

Ledyard, J. O. (1995). Public goods: A survey of experimental research. In J. H. Kagel & A. E. Roth (Eds.), *The handbook of experimental economics* (pp. 111–194). Princeton, NJ: Princeton University Press.

Levine, J. M., & Kerr, N. L. (2007). Inclusion and exclusion: Implications for group processes. In A. E. Kruglanski and E. T. Higgins (Eds.), *Social psychology: Handbook of basic principles* (2nd ed., pp. 759–784). New York, NY: Guilford.

Liebrand, W. B. G., Jansen, R. W. T. L., Rijken, V. M., & Suhre, C. J. M. (1986). Might over morality: Social values and the perception of other players in experimental games. *Journal of Experimental Social Psychology, 22*, 203–215.

Maier-Rigaud, F. P., Martinsson, P., & Staffiero, G. (2010). Ostracism and the provision of a public good: Experimental evidence. *Journal of Economic Behavior and Organization, 73*(3), 387–395.

Masclet, D. (2003). Ostracism in work teams: A public goods experiment. *International Journal of Manpower, 24*(7), 867–887.

Masclet, D., Noussair, C., Tucker, S., & Villeval, M.-C. (2003). Monetary and non-monetary punishment in the VCM. *American Economic Review, 93*, 366–380.

McCarter, M. W., Rockmann, K. W., & Northcraft, G. B. (2010). Is it even worth it? The effect of loss prospects in the outcome distribution of a public goods dilemma. *Organizational Behavior and Human Decision Processes, 111*(1), 1–12.

McCusker, C., & Carnevale, P. J. (1995). Framing in resource dilemmas: Loss aversion and the moderating effects of sanctions. *Organizational Behavior and Human Decision Processes, 61*(2), 190–201.

Mehu, M., Grammer, K., & Dunbar, R. I. M. (2007). Smiles when sharing. *Evolution and Human Behavior, 28*, 415–422.

Messick, D. M., & Brewer, M. B. (1983). Solving social dilemmas: A review. In L. Wheeler & P. Shaver (Eds.), *Annual review of personality and social psychology* (Vol. 3). Beverly Hills, CA: Sage.

Mifune, N., Hashimoto, H., & Yamagishi, T. (2010). Altruism toward in-group members as a reputation mechanism. *Evolution and Human Behavior, 31*(2), 109–117.

Millet, K., & Dewitte, S. (2006). Second to fourth digit ratio and cooperative behavior. *Biological Psychology, 71*, 111–115.

Millet, K., & Dewitte, S. (2009). The presence of aggression cues inverts the relation between digit ratio (2D:4D) and prosocial behaviour in a dictator game. *British Journal of Psychology, 100*(1), 151–162.

Mills, J. A. (1978). *Social motivations and encoding and decoding of nonverbal affect.* Unpublished undergraduate thesis, University of Delaware, DE.

Mulder, L. B. (2008). The difference between punishments and rewards in fostering moral concerns in social decision making. *Journal of Experimental Social Psychology, 44*(6), 1436–1443.

Mulder, L. B. (2009). The two-fold influence of sanctions on moral concerns. In D. De Cremer (Ed.), *Psychological perspectives on ethical behavior and decision making* (pp. 169–180). Charlotte, NC: Information Age Publishing.

Mulder, L. B., van Dijk, E., De Cremer, D., & Wilke, H. A. M. (2006). Undermining trust and cooperation: The paradox of sanctioning systems in social dilemmas. *Journal of Experimental Social Psychology, 42*(2), 147–162.

Mulder, L. B., van Dijk, E., Wilke, H. A. M., & De Cremer, D. (2005). The effect of feedback on support for a sanctioning system in a social dilemma: The difference between installing and maintaining the sanction. *Journal of Economic Psychology, 26*(3), 443–458.

Mulder, L. B., Verboon, P., & De Cremer, D. (2009). Sanctions and moral judgments: The moderating effect of sanction severity and trust in authorities. *European Journal of Social Psychology, 39*(2), 255–269.

Mulford, M., Orbell, J., Shatto, C., & Stockard, J. (1998). Physical attractiveness, opportunity, and success in everyday exchange. *American Journal of Sociology, 103*(6), 1565–1592.

Nemeth, C. (1972). A critical analysis of research utilizing the prisoner's dilemma paradigm for the study of bargaining. In L. Berkowitz (Ed.), *Advances in experimental social psychology* (Vol. 6, pp. 203–234). New York, NY: Academic Press.

Nowak, M. A. (2006). *Evolutionary dynamics.* Cambridge, MA: Harvard University Press.

Nowak, M. A., Tarnita, C. E., & Antal, T. (2010). Evolutionary dynamics in structured populations. *Philosophical Transactions of the Royal Society B, 365,* 19–30.

O'Gorman, R., Wilson, D. S., & Miller, R. R. (2005). Altruistic punishing and helping differ in sensitivity to relatedness, friendship, and future interactions. *Evolution and Human Behavior, 26*(5), 375–387.

Orbell, J. M., & Dawes, R. M. (1993). Social welfare, cooperators' advantage, and the option of not playing the game. *American Sociological Review, 58*(6), 787–800.

Ouwerkerk, J. W., Kerr, N. L., Gallucci, M., & Van Lange, P. A. M. (2005). Avoiding the social death penalty: Ostracism and cooperation in social dilemmas. In K. D. Williams, J. P. Forgas, & W. von Hippel (Eds.), *The social outcast: Ostracism, social exclusion, rejection, and bullying.* New York, NY: The Psychology Press.

Pound, N., Penton-Voak, I. S., & Surridge, A. K. (2009). Testosterone responses to competition in men are related to facial masculinity. *Proceedings of the Royal Society B, 276,* 153–159.

Pruitt, D. G., & Kimmel, M. J. (1977). Twenty years of experimental gaming: Critique, synthesis, and suggestions for the future. *Annual Review of Psychology, 28,* 363–392.

Rapoport, A., & Au, W. T. (2001). Penalty in common pool resource dilemmas under uncertainty. *Organizational Behavior and Human Decision Processes, 85*(1), 135–165.

Rigdon, M., Ishii, K., Watabe, M., & Kitayama, S. (2009). Minimal social cues in the dictator game. *Journal of Economic Psychology, 30*(3), 358–367.

Rumble, A. C., Van Lange, P. A. M., & Parks, C. D. (2010). The benefits of empathy: When empathy may sustain cooperation in social dilemmas. *European Journal of Social Psychology, 40,* 856–866.

Sabater-Grande, G., & Georgantzis, N. (2002). Accounting for risk aversion in repeated prisoners' dilemma games: An experimental test. *Journal of Economic Behavior and Organization, 48,* 37–50.

Sanchez-Pages, S., & Turiegano, E. (2010). Testosterone, facial symmetry and cooperation in the prisoners' dilemma. *Physiology & Behavior, 99*(3), 355–361.

Sanna, L. J., Chang, E. C., Parks, C. D., & Kennedy, L. A. (2009). Construing collective concerns: Increasing cooperation by broadening construals in social dilemmas. *Psychological Science, 20*(11), 1319–1321.

Scharlemann, J. P. W., Eckel, C. C., Kacelnik, A., & Wilson, R. K. (2001). The value of a smile: Game theory with a human face. *Journal of Economic Psychology, 22,* 617–640.

Schuessler, R. (1989). Exit threats and cooperation under anonymity. *Journal of Conflict Resolution, 33*(4), 728–749.

Schug, J., Matsumoto, D., Horita, Y., Yamagishi, T., & Bonnet, K. (2010). Emotional expressivity as a signal of cooperation. *Evolution and Human Behavior, 31*(2), 87–94.

Shelley, G. P., Page, M., Rives, P., Yeagley, E., & Kuhlman, D. M. (2010). Nonverbal communication and detection of individual differences in social value orientation. In R. M. Kramer, A. E. Tenbrunsel, & M. H. Bazerman (Eds.), *Social decision making: Social dilemmas, social values, and ethical judgments* (pp. 147–170). New York, NY: Routledge.

Smeesters, D., Wheeler, S. C., & Kay, A. C. (2009). The role of interpersonal perceptions in the prime-to-behavior pathway. *Journal of Personality and Social Psychology, 96*(2), 395–414.

Smeesters, D., Yzerbyt, V. Y., Corneille, O., & Warlop, L. (2009). When do primes prime? The moderating role of the self-concept in individuals' susceptibility to priming effects on social behavior. *Journal of Experimental Social Psychology, 45*(1), 211–216.

Sugden, R. (1984). Reciprocity: The supply of public goods through voluntary contributions. *Economics Journal, 94,* 772–787.

Suleiman, R., Budescu, D. V., Fischer, I., & Messick, D. M. (2004). *Contemporary psychological research on social dilemmas* (pp. 315–331). New York, NY: Cambridge University Press.

Takahashi, C., Yamagishi, T., Tanida, S., Kiyonari, T., & Kanazawa, S. (2006). Attractiveness and cooperation in social exchange. *Evolutionary Psychology, 4,* 315–329.

Tazelaar, M. J. A., Van Lange, P. A. M., & Ouwerkerk, J. W. (2004). How to cope with "noise" in social dilemmas: The benefits of communication. *Journal of Personality and Social Psychology, 87*(6), 845–859.

Tenbrunsel, A. E., & Messick, D. M. (1999). Sanctioning systems, decision frames, and cooperation. *Administrative Science Quarterly, 44*(4), 684–707.

Tenbrunsel, A. E., & Northcraft, G. (2010). In the eye of the beholder: Payoff structures and decision frames in social dilemmas. In R. M. Kramer, A. E. Tenbrunsel, & M. H. Bazerman (Eds.), *Social decision making: Social dilemmas, social values, and ethical judgments* (pp. 95–116). New York, NY: Routledge.

Utz, S. (2004a). Self-activation is a two-edged sword: The effects of I primes on cooperation. *Journal of Experimental Social Psychology, 40*(6), 769–776.

Utz, S. (2004b). Self-construal and cooperation: Is the interdependent self more cooperative than the independent self? *Self and Identity, 3*(3), 177–190.

Utz, S., Ouwerkerk, J. W., & Van Lange, P. A. M. (2004). What is smart in a social dilemma? Differential effects of priming competence on cooperation. *European Journal of Social Psychology, 34*(3), 317–332.

Utz, S., Van Lange, P. A. M., Green, E., Waldzus, S., & Bovina, I. (2005). Mary honest always friendly and is: Can scrambled sentences enhance prosocial motivation? *Representative Research in Social Psychology, 28,* 59–70.

van Dijk, E., de Kwaadsteniet, E. W., & De Cremer, D. (2009). Tacit coordination in social dilemmas: The importance of having a common understanding. *Journal of Personality and Social Psychology, 96*(3), 665–678.

van Dijk, E., Wilke, H., Wilke, M., & Metman, L. (1999). What information do we use in social dilemmas? Environmental uncertainty and the employment of coordination rules. *Journal of Experimental Social Psychology, 35*(2), 109–135.

van Dijk, E., Wit, A. P., Wilke, H. A. M., & de Kwaadsteniet, E. W. (2010). On the importance of equality in social dilemmas. In R. M. Kramer, A. E. Tenbrunsel, & M. H. Bazerman (Eds.), *Social decision making: Social dilemmas, social values, and ethical judgments* (pp. 47–69). New York, NY: Routledge.

Van Lange, P. A. M. (1999). The pursuit of joint outcomes and equality in outcomes:

An integrative model of social value orientation. *Journal of Personality and Social Psychology, 77*, 337–349.

Van Lange, P. A. M., & Joireman, J. A. (2010). Social and temporal orientations in social dilemmas. In R. M. Kramer, A. E. Tenbrunsel, & M. H. Bazerman (Eds.), *Social decision making: Social dilemmas, social values, and ethical judgments* (pp. 71–94). New York, NY: Routledge.

Van Lange, P. A. M., & Kuhlman, D. M. (1994). Social value orientations and impressions of partner's honesty and intelligence: A test of the might versus morality effect. *Journal of Personality and Social Psychology, 67*(1), 126–141.

Van Lange, P. A. M., Ouwerkerk, J. W., & Tazelaar, M. J. A. (2002). How to overcome the detrimental effects of noise in social interaction: The benefits of generosity. *Journal of Personality and Social Psychology, 82*(5), 768–780.

Van Lange, P. A. M., & Visser, K. (1999). Locomotion in social dilemmas: How people adapt to cooperative, tit-for-tat, and noncooperative partners. *Journal of Personality and Social Psychology, 77*(4), 762–773.

Van Vugt, M., & De Cremer, D. (1999). Leadership in social dilemmas: The effects of group identification on collective actions to provide public goods. *Journal of Personality and Social Psychology, 76*(4), 587–599.

Verplaetse, J., Vanneste, S., & Braeckman, J. (2007). You can judge a book by its cover: The sequel. A kernel of truth in predictive cheating detection. *Evolution and Human Behavior, 28*(4), 260–271.

Weber, J. M., Kopelman, S., & Messick, D. M. (2004). A conceptual review of decision making in social dilemmas: Applying a logic of appropriateness. *Personality and Social Psychology Review, 8*(3), 281–307.

Wildschut, T., & Insko, C. A. (2007). Explanations of interindividual—intergroup discontinuity: A review of the evidence. *European Review of Social Psychology, 18*, 175–211.

Wit, A., & Wilke, H. A. (1990). The presentation of rewards and punishments in a simulated social dilemma. *Social Behaviour, 5*(4), 231–245.

Wit, A., & Wilke, H. (1998). Public good provision under environmental social uncertainty. *European Journal of Social Psychology, 28*(2), 249–256.

Wubben, M. J. J., De Cremer, D., & van Dijk, E. (2008). When emotions of others affect decisions in public good dilemmas: An instrumental view. *European Journal of Social Psychology, 38*(5), 823–835.

Wubben, M. J. J., De Cremer, D., & van Dijk, E. (2009). How emotion communication guides reciprocity: Establishing cooperation through disappointment and anger. *Journal of Experimental Social Psychology, 45*(4), 987–990.

Yamagishi, T. (1986). The provision of a sanctioning system as a public good. *Journal of Personality and Social Psychology, 51*(1), 110–116.

Yamagishi, T. (1992). Group size and the provision of a sanctioning system in a social dilemma. In W. B. G. Liebrand, D. M. Messick, & H. A. M. Wilke (Eds.), *Social dilemmas: Theoretical issues and research findings* (pp. 267–287). Elmsford, NY: Pergamon Press.

Yamagishi, T. (2001). Trust as a form of social intelligence. In K. S. Cook (Ed.), *Trust in society* (pp. 121–147). New York, NY: Russell Sage Foundation.

Yamagishi, T., & Hayashi, N. (1996). Selective play: Social embeddedness of social dilemmas. In W. Liebrand & D. Messick (Eds.), *Frontiers of social dilemma research* (pp. 363–384). Berlin, Germany: Springer-Verlag.

Yamagishi, T., Kanazawa, S., Mashima, R., & Terai, S. (2005). Separating trust from cooperation in a dynamic relationship: Prisoner's dilemma with variable dependence. *Rationality and Society, 17*(3), 275–308.

Yamagishi, T., & Suzuki, N. (2010). An institutional approach to culture. In M. Schaller, A. Norenzayan, S. J. Heine, T. Yamagishi, & T. Kameda (Eds.), *Evolution, culture, and the human mind* (pp. 185–203). New York, NY: Psychology Press.

Yamagishi, T., Tanida, S., Mashima, R., Shimoma, E., & Kanazawa, S. (2003). You can judge a book by its cover: Evidence that cheaters may look different from cooperators. *Evolution and Human Behavior, 24*(4), 290–301.

Yu, C., Au, W., & Chan, K. K. (2009). Efficacy = endowment × efficiency: Revisiting efficacy and endowment effects in a public goods dilemma. *Journal of Personality and Social Psychology, 96*(1), 155–169.

Zaatari, D., & Trivers, R. (2007). Fluctuating asymmetry and behavior in the ultimatum game in Jamaica. *Evolution and Human Behavior, 28*(4), 223–227.

5

Justice

TOM R. TYLER

Justice is a social judgment. It is created by groups to manage social interactions by preventing conflict and promoting cooperation. As such "justice" involves a set of socially shared rules whose function is to facilitate people's efforts to more efficiently and effectively achieve mutually beneficial goals. Rules of social justice define what is reasonable in group settings, both in terms of how to divide resources and how to make decisions and behave when dealing with others. By so doing justice makes social life more viable. This is true with principles of distributive justice, which indicate who should receive what; with principles of procedural justice, which define how groups should make decisions; and with principles of retributive justice, which indicate how norm violators should be treated.

PERSPECTIVES ON JUSTICE

Relative Deprivation

The idea of scientifically studying justice first became central in the social sciences after World War II with the development of the concept of relative deprivation. Relative deprivation is the suggestion that people's satisfaction or dissatisfaction with outcomes is based upon a comparison of those outcomes to some reference standard. It became a key idea within all of the social sciences (Merton & Kitt, 1950) in the years following the publication of the multivolume series *The American Soldier* (Stouffer, Suchman, DeVinney, Star, & Williams, 1949) and had an enormous impact upon people's general thinking about such key social issues as why people are satisfied or dissatisfied and what leads to engagement in collective actions such as joining labor unions or

111

political organizations to produce social change or rioting to protest disadvantaged conditions.

Although highly influential, relative deprivation theory was not initially a "true" justice theory because it did not argue that comparisons were necessarily shaped by principles of justice, entitlement or "deservingness." Instead, it focused upon when people make comparisons and with whom. The importance of temporal comparisons is reflected in work on collective unrest (Gurr, 1970), while work on social comparisons has become a literature of its own (Masters & Smith, 1987; Olson, Herman, & Zanna, 1986).

The connection of comparison issues to justice emerges as a central theme in later discussions of relative deprivation. The work of Crosby in particular made deservingness a key antecedent of how people respond to outcome discrepancies (Crosby, 1976, 1982). Her work makes a determination about what is appropriate, reasonable, and just as one filter through which people react to individual or group-based outcome discrepancies. In other words, she argues that people only get upset when they feel deprived of something they deserve to receive. Crosby's model is more complex and includes other moderating conditions such as feasibility of attainment and legitimacy that people also consider when reacting to outcome discrepancies. It suggests that people do not necessarily view discrepancies as unjust. It is only when a discrepancy is regarded as being undeserved, for example because it is not due to some reasonable criterion for outcome difference, that people feel anger.

Distributive Justice

Theories of distributive justice supply the missing link connecting feelings to justice because they tie people's reactions to models specifying what people think is fair (Walster, Walster, & Berscheid, 1978). The models do so by arguing that people compare their outcomes to standards of what is a deserved outcome (Walster et al., 1978). In contrast to the relative deprivation literature, in the distributive justice literature there are clear principles for explaining how people decide what they deserve. For example, in work settings they apply the principle of equity. Distributive justice both argues for the importance of the fairness of the allocation of desirable outcomes across people and provides a model for determining what people will think is fair.

People express the greatest satisfaction when they receive a fair distribution, in comparison to receiving more or less in absolute terms, and they are sensitive to being given "too much" or "too little." They incur material losses to pressure others to distribute resources via principles of justice. And they leave situations they view as characterized by the unfair distribution of resources to move to situations where resource distribution is fairer but in which they receive fewer rewards.

As might be expected, those who receive less than they feel they deserve are found to be angry and to engage in a variety of behaviors in reaction, ranging from working less to rioting. Justice researchers have studied many instances in which people have received less than they deserve and have shown that this leads to a strong negative emotional reaction and to efforts to seek restitution. Among disadvantaged groups, complex psychological dynamics are unleashed because the disadvantaged often lack the power to compel justice and must therefore find ways to manage their feelings of unfairness. But the underlying premise that getting too little is psychologically distressing is widely confirmed.

Interestingly, and less intuitively, those who get too much are also found to be unhappy and to engage in efforts to either restore distributive justice by mechanisms such as working harder or giving resources away, or, if those solutions are not practical, by leaving the situation. Giving resources away is especially important because it suggests that the desire to act fairly can influence the advantaged to take actions on behalf of others. It also reflects "true" justice in the sense that the reactions of those who get too little can be explained by either justice or self-interest, while the reactions of those who get too much (i.e. giving resources away) can only be explained by a belief in acting justly.

Principles of Distributive Justice   Walster and others present equity as a general principle of distributive justice. The core of this general argument is linking the concept of distributive justice to judgments of equity, a distributive principle by which people's rewards match their effort or contributions.

Deutsch (1985) supported the argument that distributive justice is important, but suggested that it need not be defined in terms of equity. Instead, he noted, there are many standards of distributive justice. In earlier work, Deutsch (1975) presented three core principles of distributive justice: equity, equality, and need. Equality involves giving everyone similar outcomes, while equity and need differentiate among people either in terms of their productivity or their needs.

Deutsch (1982) suggested that the use of each principle promotes different social goals: equity leads to productivity, equality to social harmony, and need to social welfare. Hence, the principles used depend upon the goals of the interaction. And, Deutsch suggested, the nature of the relationship between people shapes which goals they will seek and, consequently, which principles they will consider appropriate. Deutsch drew upon research concerning the fundamental dimensions of interpersonal relations and defined four key dimensions: cooperative-competitive; equal-unequal power; task-social orientation; and formal vs. informal relations. He argued that the nature of the interdependence between people shapes the importance that they place upon different principles of distributive justice. For example, equal relationships tend to use equality to divide resources.

Barrett-Howard and Tyler (1986) found support for Deutsch's argument and confirmed that both people's degree of concern with distributive justice and their use of particular principles of justice varied depending upon the nature of their interdependence. And, as Deutsch hypothesized, such variations were linked to the fact that people in different types of social settings were pursuing different goals. For example, those who wanted to build social harmony emphasized equality, while those concerned with maximizing social welfare focused upon need.

Are Distributive Justice Principles Distinct From Self-Interest?

Studies typically find that people seek a balance between self-interest and a justice principle in allocation situations. Although influenced by what is in their personal self interest, people distinguish justice from self interest and typically do not simply act in their own interest. A core aspect of shared social rules is that they do not reflect the self-interest of any single individual in the group. Rather, they are a collective effort to define reasonable principles for social interaction that balance the interests of different people in the group. John Rawls captured this quality of justice rules when he talked about the idea of rules developed "behind the veil of ignorance." People try to make rules, he argued, without referencing their own situation. We would, for example, decide if we should reward people for having skills of a particular type without knowing if we would have those skills ourselves (Rawls, 1971).

Of course, in reality people cannot separate their personal attributes and status from their thoughts, feelings, and preferences, so justice rules are a compromise between the interests of various people and groups. However, the core argument is the same—justice principles are shared group assessments of what is reasonable as a compromise among competing self-interests within a given type of situation. As a consequence, distributive justice rules have an ability to help people make consensual allocation decisions, but that ability is diminished to the degree that self-interest motivates justice judgments. If everyone defines justice in terms of their own self-interest, principles of justice will not be able to facilitate agreements across individuals.

The core underlying assumption of justice theories is that people want to cooperate with others but want to find ways to reach stable principles for cooperation that neither put them at a disadvantage by giving them too few outcomes relative to others or produce unstable interactions by giving them too much and leading to anger among others. Justice principles should allow people to exchange resources with others over time in long-term relationships that are beneficial to all parties.

For justice rules to be effective as guides for social coordination, three things must be true. First, there must be consensus about what the principles of justice are. Second, people must be willing to follow those justice rules in the sense that they accept them as guides concerning appropriate compromises with others. Third, people must be willing to enforce these justice rules when others do not follow them. If others try to take "too much" or even "too little," people should be upset and take some form of action. We can first examine these ideas in the context of distributive justice. Rules of justice that pertain to the appropriate distribution of resources between people are referred to as *rules of distributive justice*. These rules tell us what a person is entitled to, or "deserves," under particular social conditions.

Consensus is the first important idea underlying the social utility of justice rules. Justice is a social judgment. Unlike a table, a chair, or another person, there is no physical reality to justice. The concept of justice is created by people in a group to facilitate their interaction, and it only effectively fulfills that function when its meaning is shared among the members of a group. Justice is like a word in a language. A language spoken by one person has no communicative value—the meaning of words must be shared.

The principles of distributive justice are complex, and, as noted above, no single principle is used by people to define distributive justice in all types of settings (Deutsch, 1975). It is interesting therefore that evidence from studies conducted in the United States suggests that within a given context, there is a general social consensus about what principles govern. For example, in the United States people generally agree that work settings should be governed by equity, social settings by equality, and social welfare settings by need (Tyler, 1984).

This consensus is crucial, because without it justice cannot effectively coordinate action. Although there are many possible justice principles (Reis, 1987), research suggests that equity, equality, and need are the three core principles most widely used, at least in the United States (Deutsch, 1985). Of course, it is not necessary that people within all societies agree about principles of distributive justice. Just as everyone in the world need not speak the same language, the only issue is whether people who interact have a shared social framework within which to coordinate their actions. Hence, cross-cultural studies show that different societies have different rules of distributive fairness within particular arenas but that within those societies people tend to agree about a common rule (Tyler, Boeckmann, Smith, & Huo, 1997). This is one of the reasons that cross-cultural interactions are often difficult—people have to first work to establish what the rules are going to be.

Evidence further suggests that people are willing to defer to the principles of distributive justice. In particular, they are most satisfied with outcomes if they think that the outcomes they are receiving are fair. A typical example of this finding is the study by Pritchard, Dunnette, and Jorgenson (1972), in which students were paid a given amount of money to perform a task. However, they were then told that the wage was fair, unfairly high, or unfairly low. Those who thought they were being fairly paid were the most likely to express satisfaction, whereas those who were over- or underpaid were less satisfied.

Other studies have shown that people adjust their effort to reestablish justice. For example, if people are told they are overpaid, they work harder (Walster et al., 1978). This can involve higher levels of output and/or working longer hours. Whatever actions are taken, however, they are motivated by the desire to reestablish justice. Conversely, the amount that employees steal from their workplace has been shown to be linked to their judgments about pay unfairness, with workers stealing more to restore justice if they feel more underpaid. Finally, studies have suggested that people will leave situations in which they feel unfairly overpaid to go to situations in which they are paid less but feel that their pay is more fair (Schmitt & Marwell, 1972).

These findings all suggest that people accept the core principles of distributive justice. Of course, we need to recognize that in many of the experimental studies people are explicitly told that their allocations are fair or unfair. It is important therefore that there is also nonexperimental research to indicate that in field settings people's naturally occurring evaluations of the justice or injustice of their outcomes in groups shape their behavior within those groups, as well as their likelihood of leaving or staying (Tyler et al., 1997).

Finally, recent research has suggested that people will forgo personally beneficial outcomes in an effort to enforce adherence to fairness rules by others (Henrich et al., 2006). As an example, Gurerk, Irlenbusch, and Rockenbach (2006) gave people the opportunity to participate in a setting in which they could enforce cooperative rules at a personal cost. They showed that many people chose this setting, and when they were in it, they were willing to forgo personal gains to punish those people who deviated from cooperative choices. In other words, people were willing to pay costs to enforce fairness rules by punishing those who violated those rules. Recent research on such "altruistic" punishment suggests that personally rewarding neural processes are activated when people engage in behavior designed to protect group rules, suggesting that people's motivation to protect group rules may reflect fundamental human cognitive and emotional processes (Fehr & Gintis, 2007).

Another example of people's willingness to enforce rules of distributive justice is their willingness to support the redistribution of resources to make that distribution fairer for others. One example is a study by Montada and Schneider (1989), who demonstrated that West Germans were willing to redistribute resources to East Germans when they viewed themselves as unfairly advantaged. This is one of many examples showing that people who feel that they are unfairly advantaged are willing to voluntarily redistribute resources to benefit those whom they view as having too little. People also change their level of active effort on behalf of groups, working harder or slacking off when involved in collective efforts, again in response to justice judgments (Tyler & Blader, 2000). In either case, people incur personal losses to uphold principles of distributive justice.

Does justice work as intended? If it does, then relationships characterized by distributive fairness will be more stable and long lasting. This is the finding of studies of long-term interpersonal relationships. Those relationships in which the parties experience their interactions as consistent with distributive fairness are more satisfying and last longer (Sprecher, 2001; Ybema, Kuijer, Buunk, DeJong, & Sanderman, 2001). For example, people who date are more likely to marry, and, when married, their marriages last longer. Therefore, justice norms have the effect of facilitating satisfying and stable long-term social interactions.

Problems With Distributive Justice   Studies suggest that people may have difficulty using distributive justice principles in social interactions when the principles involved require evaluations that rank people by contribution or need. Equality is a simple rule that requires minimal evaluations, so it is often used as an allocation heuristic in social settings. However, other principles, for example equity and need, require people to evaluate the particular abilities or deficits of those involved in interactions, and this can be difficult to do. Research shows that people tend to exaggerate their claims for desirable resources, for example by suggesting that they make important contributions to successful projects for which there will be rewards. As a consequence, it is often hard to allocate limited resources in ways that lead all persons to receive an outcome that they feel matches their contribution to a collective project.

People may also differ in the weights that they assign to different principles of distributive justice. Since most allocations in social settings involve tradeoffs between principles of distributive justice, people have to weigh equality vs. equity, equity vs. need, etc. This is an additional situation in which self-serving biases can be involved, since people's weighting of principles of justice can be influenced by how these principles will affect their outcomes. For example, the highly skilled often emphasize equity; those without skills focus on need or equality.

Walster et al. (1978) made the important point that people are motivated to view justice from a self-interested perspective, but that the degree to which they do so depends upon social conditions. Walster et al. argued that one such condition is the degree to which there are societal authorities telling people what is right in some social setting. One role for authorities is to articulate rules about fairness, thereby facilitating the general willingness of everyone in an allocation setting to accept a given standard for making the allocation. Ambiguity produced by the absence of authorities therefore encourages self-serving views.

Similarly, recent research makes clear that people are less likely to be self-serving when the resources being divided are not amenable to a self-serving allocation. For example, when taking cookies from a plate people take equal amounts because they take one cookie. But, when presented with a more ambiguous resource, for example a bowl of jelly beans, people are more likely to take more than an equal share. Again, ambiguity encourages self-serving behavior.

Such ambiguity makes it hard to use distributive justice as a principle in many group settings. People would be happy if they received what they feel they deserve, but in many cases there are not enough resources to meet people's exaggerated feelings of entitlement. So, it is hard in practice to manage conflicts using this form of justice.

In several thoughtful articles about justice, Leventhal (e.g., 1976, 1980) articulated some of these problems and proposed an expanded justice focus including procedural, as well as distributive, justice. In an article titled, "What should be done with equity theory?", Leventhal (1980) noted several problems with equity theory besides those already outlined. The one that has been most important is that distributive justice is only about outcomes, not the procedures that give rise to them. Leventhal suggested that both types of justice should be considered.

The theoretical arguments of Leventhal became impactful when they were combined with the research program of Thibaut and Walker (1975), who studied procedural justice in the framework of trial procedures for dispute resolution. This research program had a tremendous influence upon the field of justice, providing a set of researchable questions and a methodology for addressing procedural justice questions. Research on justice moved away from distributive justice toward procedural justice, a focus that remains today.

Procedural Justice

Procedural justice is the study of people's subjective evaluations of the justice of processes—whether they are fair or unfair, ethical or unethical, and otherwise accord with people's standards of fair processes for social interaction and decision making. People are quite capable of distinguishing procedural justice from assessments of the fairness of outcomes (*distributive justice*).

In most nontrivial decision making situations, some type of process is needed for gathering relevant evidence, deciding upon and implementing decision rules, and managing the interpersonal processes of gaining acceptance for resource allocations and resolving conflicts. Leventhal (1980) identified seven such structural elements of a procedure: selection of agents for decision making; establishment of ground rules; mechanisms for information gathering; the decision making structure; ways to safeguard procedures to ensure integrity; appeal mechanisms; and change mechanisms. Work on procedural justice focuses on understanding the fairness of the processes associated with these features.

Studies show that people's choices among allocation procedures are influenced by their evaluations of the relative fairness of these procedures, as well as by the favorability and fairness of their outcomes; that people's satisfaction with and willingness to accept allocations and dispute resolution decisions depend upon the fairness of the procedures used to make them; and that people's rule following behavior and cooperation with others are shaped by the procedural fairness of groups, organizations, and societies.

Procedural justice judgments have been the focus of a great deal of research attention by psychologists because they have been found to be a key influence on a wide variety of important group attitudes and behaviors (Lind & Tyler, 1988; Tyler, 2000). Procedural justice has been especially important in studies of decision acceptance and rule following.

One reason that people might comply with rules and authorities is that they anticipate rewards for cooperating and/or fear sanctions from the group for not cooperating. Such instrumental motivations can be effective in motivating compliance in a wide variety of social settings. An alternative reason that people might comply is that they are motivated by their sense of justice to accept what they feel is fair, even if it is not what they want. A key question is whether justice is effective in resolving conflicts and disagreements when people cannot have everything that they want. To the degree that people defer to others because allocation decisions are seen as fair, justice is an important factor in creating and maintaining social harmony. Research suggests that social justice can act as a mechanism for resolving social conflicts and that procedural justice is especially central in such situations.

Thibaut and Walker (1975) conducted the first experiments designed to show the impact of procedural justice. Their studies demonstrated that people's assessments of the fairness of third-party decision-making procedures predicted their satisfaction with the outcomes they received. This finding has been widely confirmed in many subsequent laboratory and field studies of procedural justice, which show that when third-party decisions are fairly made people are more willing to voluntarily accept them. What is striking is that such procedural justice effects are widely found in studies of real disputes in everyday settings involving actual disputants and have an especially important role in shaping adherence to agreements over time.

Beyond the acceptance of decisions, procedural justice also shapes the perceived legitimacy of the authorities and institutions with which people deal, and through such attitudes, their willingness to defer to those authorities and institutions. Studies of the perceived legitimacy of authorities suggest that people decide how much to defer to authorities and to their decisions primarily by assessing the fairness of their decision-making procedures (Tyler, 2006).

Using fair decision-making procedures is the key to developing, maintaining, and enhancing the legitimacy of rules and authorities and gaining voluntary compliance to social rules. Beyond issues of rule following, studies of procedural justice indicate that it plays an important role in motivating commitment to organizations. As a consequence, procedural justice is important in encouraging productivity and extra-role behavior in work organizations (Tyler & Blader, 2000). Procedural justice is a key antecedent of a wide variety of desirable cooperative behaviors in groups, organizations, and societies.

The Psychology of Procedural Justice   The work of Thibaut and Walker (1975) was also important because it articulated a psychological model that explained why people cared about procedural justice. That model, like the models of equity already outlined, linked justice concerns to issues of control over outcomes. It suggested that people value procedural justice because they want to have "voice" (i.e., the opportunity to present evidence to the decision maker). This evidence allows the decision maker to make decisions that best reflect equity (i.e., the merits of different arguments). So, in a real sense, procedural justice leads to distributive justice.

While subsequent research has strongly supported the usefulness of a focus upon procedural justice, it has not supported the social exchange voice focus in the original work. Instead, it has supported Leventhal's broader procedural justice model. In addition to describing the elements that all procedures need to have, Leventhal (1980) identified six principles for evaluating the procedural justice of a procedure. Those principles were: consistency; bias-suppression; accuracy; correctability; representativeness; and ethicality. Of these, representativeness is the element reflecting participation and voice.

Later studies indicate that people care about all of Leventhal's six procedural principles (Tyler, 1988). This suggests that they care about more than their ability to control their outcomes. People care about voice even when they cannot influence decisions, as long as they feel their arguments are being listened to and considered (Tyler and Lind, 1992), suggesting that their motivations for speaking involve more than the desire to shape decisions. Later studies suggest that people value their relationships with other people and groups. As a consequence they care how they are treated because it reflects upon the quality of their relationships to others and, through that, their status with others and in groups, which in turn shapes both sense of self and feelings of self-worth and self-esteem.

The influence of concern about connections to people and groups is reflected in how people define procedural justice (Lind and Tyler, 1988), how they decide whether to accept third party decisions (Tyler and Lind, 1992), and how they decide whether and how much to cooperate with others in groups, organizations, and societies (Tyler and Blader, 2000). This argument leads to suggestions that justice is important because it conveys social messages about inclusion/exclusion, standing within groups, and respect from others.

Retributive Justice

As noted above, groups create procedures, authorities, and institutions to make decisions. Those decisions are then formulated into rules and in many cases laws, all of which reflect the principles of justice that have been outlined. Society then becomes invested in enforcing those rules, both, as has been noted, through the private efforts of people to punish rule breakers and through the role of the state as an enforcer of standards, norms, and rules.

A core feature of all organized groups is that they create rules and enforce those rules by punishing those who break them. While societies differ widely in what their rules are and in how they punish those who transgress them, punishment for rule breaking is central to the maintenance of social order and is found in all societies (Vidmar & Miller, 1980). The nature of these punishments and when they are enacted is the central focus of the study of retributive justice, which involves the principles defining appropriate punishments for wrongdoing (Carlsmith & Darley, 2008; Darley & Pittman, 2003).

It is a general characteristic of social relationships and organized groups that formal or informal rules develop that define appropriate conduct. When such rules are violated, people feel the need to punish rule violators, and this motivation does not only involve those personally harmed by wrongdoing. Other members of the community also act to defend group rules, even when they are not personally involved in a dispute or personally affected by the injustice. Studies of retributive justice demonstrate that people are motivated to punish those who break rules and will incur personal costs to uphold social rules even when they are not the victims of the rule breaking behavior (Carlsmith, Darley, & Robinson, 2002).

Why is it so important to punish wrongdoing? As has been outlined, rules are needed to enable cooperative behavior. For people to effectively live together, they need rules that define appropriate conduct in social settings. For example, there are rules that define justice in social exchange. One such rule is that people need to be honest in representing themselves to others. Such rules enable trust, which facilitates exchange. For example, when someone is buying food, they trust authorities to uphold health standards for production, so they do not need to visit the farm themselves. This facilitates exchange, but it will only work if those rules are enforced. If people break rules, the rules are affirmed when they are punished for that behavior. Similarly, taking advantage of someone undermines the status of the victim, and society wants that status to be reestablished. Hence, the use of justice as a facilitator of cooperation and social coordination requires that the principles of society be defended.

An initial element in reacting to rule breaking is an effort to restore the prior material balance between people. The simplest way to do so is to right the wrong by compensating the victim(s) for harm done. When people react to rule breaking which is judged to be unintentional or without malice, and where it is possible to do so, people often endorse such an approach to righting wrongs. Such compensation can be understood in the distributive justice framework already outlined.

When people are viewed as having deliberately broken rules, either intentionally or because of negligence, their victims and society more generally feel that some type of punishment beyond compensating victims is appropriate (Darley & Pittman, 2003), and in such situations retributive justice departs from the principles of distributive justice. If someone hits a person, the victim does not just hit the offender back, he or she hits the offender harder reflecting an additional punishment for rule breaking. These reactions reflect the judgment that wrongdoing is intentional and reflects a motivated disrespect for social rules, not something that is accidental or unintended.

Studies exploring the nature of the motivation to punish often link punishment to issues of deterrence and incapacitation by arguing that people punish to prevent future wrongdoing. Other studies suggest that the desire for revenge is a key issue. Recent studies suggest that, on the contrary, people's primary reason for punishing is to uphold societal values. Rule breaking is viewed as a threat to those values, and appropriate punishment restores them (Carlsmith, Darley, & Robinson, 2002). Evidence supports the suggestion that people are motivated to punish when they view wrongdoing as undercutting a groups' moral and social values and that they choose the type and severity of punishment to restore an appropriate moral balance. A consequence is that those people whose actions and demeanor show a defiance of or disrespect for society, social values, and/or the social status of their victims are both more likely to be punished and more likely to be punished severely.

Summary

The different kinds of justice outlined above are united by the ubiquitous finding that people are very sensitive to issues of justice and injustice in their dealings with other people in social settings. In fact, such justice-based judgments are found to be key drivers of a wide variety of reactions, including attitudes, emotions, and behaviors. Rawls (1971) famously argued that "justice is the first virtue of social institutions," and the findings of psychological research on justice strongly support the parallel suggestion that people view justice as a pivotal factor shaping their relationships with one another. Hence, while people might react to their experiences in social settings simply in terms of personal self-interest, they do not. Instead, they react to their sense of what is just.

Further, when groups, organizations, or societies are seeking to organize themselves, they become centrally preoccupied with issues of justice. Justice shapes views about whether authorities and institutions are legitimate. Legitimacy in turn influences their ability to call upon group members for voluntary cooperation and support. This argument is summarized by the assumption that people in social settings use the presence or absence of justice as a key heuristic for managing their decisions about whether and in what ways to engage with others (Van den Bos & Lind, 2002).

This argument brings the various types of justice together by suggesting that all are socially created and transmitted mechanisms for managing problems of cooperation and coordination in groups, organizations, and societies. Principles of justice and the development of supportive values facilitate people's efforts to control their motivation to pursue short-term self-interest, a motivation that may well have a biological basis but that nonetheless is an inferior way to approach interactions with others. Put simply, social motivations function to overcome biological tendencies (Campbell, 1975).

PRE-EMINENCE OF PROCEDURAL JUSTICE

Studies of justice in resource allocation and dispute resolution indicate that people focus less upon issues of distributive and retributive justice than they do upon two other issues: the procedures used to make allocation decisions and their interpersonal treatment within those procedures. These two issues have been collectively referred to as procedural justice. Relevant findings emerged both from studies that looked at the weight placed upon these different factors (Alexander & Ruderman, 1987; Tyler & Caine, 1981) and from studies that looked at what people talk about when asked to describe situations in which they feel that injustice has occurred (Messick, Bloom, Boldizar, & Samuelson, 1985; Mikula, Petri, & Tanzer, 1990). In the latter type of study, people are especially likely to mention instances of poor interpersonal treatment (i.e., the lack of courtesy and dignified treatment that they experienced from others). In both of these types of studies, the minimal role played by actual outcome distributions in experiences of injustice was striking.

Huo (2002) used a different approach to addressing this issue but reached a similar conclusion. She created a framework in which participants were asked about what should be given to or withheld from a disliked group (e.g., Nazis, terrorists). Three issues were considered: monetary resources, procedural protections, and/or treatment with fairness and respect. Her results indicated that participants considered denial of interpersonal treatment with dignity and respect the most serious denial, while the denial of monetary resources was the least serious. Denial of procedural protections was intermediate. These findings are consistent with those already presented in that they suggest that people view procedural issues as more important than outcomes, with the quality of interpersonal treatment being especially central to the connection between people.

The conclusion of these studies comparing people's focus on different forms of justice is that people are most strongly affected by issues of procedural justice. Hence, the original focus of theories of relative deprivation and distributive justice upon the allocation of outcomes seems misplaced. It does not mirror the type of justice concerns that preoccupy people in social settings. Because it is central to people's concerns about resource allocation and dispute resolution in groups, procedural justice will be the primary focus of the following discussion. Of course, it is important not to forget outcomes, both because procedures and outcomes often interact (Brockner & Wiesenfeld, 1996) and because outcomes can indirectly shape reactions to injustice (Tyler & Blader, 2000, 2003).

Why is procedural justice so central in social settings? While research suggests that distributive justice rules facilitate stable social interaction, there are problems with using distributive rules as a solution to cooperation and coordination problems. As already noted, people tend to exaggerate their contributions to joint efforts, making it difficult to allocate limited resources. Further, as already noted, there are multiple principles of distributive justice, and no single rule can cover all situations. Hence, there are conflicts among rules. A worker with a sick child invokes the principle of need to justify missing work, whereas a manager invokes equity to argue that the lost productivity should be held against the worker. No single rule is sufficiently complex to handle the problems and issues arising in social interactions.

A second mechanism that groups have for creating stable social interactions is creating authorities and institutions with discretion to make decisions (Messick et al., 1983; Tyler & Degoey, 1995). Authorities have the advantage of being able to adapt to unique or changing situations by deciding to apply different rules or even by changing what the rules are. It is not surprising that one commonly chosen approach that groups adopt to determine "fair" approaches to allocation is to choose an authority and then let that authority exercise discretion. That discretion provides a mechanism through which equity, need, or other similar principles can operate in complex situations (Tyler & Degoey, 1995).

The use of authorities to make discretionary decisions helps make social life more flexible but also raises problems for groups. There have to be mechanisms for determining who will be the authority and for evaluating whether the decisions made by the authority are reasonable and fair. The first issue, establishing an authority, lies at the heart of early work by Lewin on elected leaders (Gold, 1999) and is also central to more recent studies of political leadership. Studies consistently find that people are more likely to defer to leaders who are elected to power using fair procedures. Hence, people are sensitive to how authorities are empowered. The second issue, the fairness of the manner in which authority is exercised, is at the heart of recent procedural justice research (Lind & Tyler, 1988; Tyler, 2000). Research on both issues comes to a strikingly similar conclusion. Authorities are more likely to be deferred to when they are put in office using fair procedures and when they make their decisions using fair procedures.

Defining Procedural Justice

Given the importance of procedural justice, a critical question is how procedural justice is defined. Early work on procedural justice was guided by the influential research program of Thibaut and Walker (1975). They centered their studies on procedures as mechanisms for settling disputes about the allocation of outcomes. In particular, they focused on formal trial procedures that related to decision making processes in legal settings. They proposed that people value procedural justice (operationalized in their research as voice or process control) because it facilitates decision-makers' ability to make equitable judgments. In other words, procedures are valued insofar as they affect the outcomes that are associated with them.

This focus on decision making in allocation contexts is no longer true of procedural justice research. Researchers have increasingly moved their attention away from an exclusive focus on the decision-making function of procedures to include more attention to the interpersonal aspects of procedures. These are important because procedures are used in settings within which people are involved in a social interaction with one another. This is true irrespective of whether the procedure involves bargaining, a market exchange, team interaction among equals, or a third party procedure with a decision-maker, such as mediation or a trial.

In social interactions there is considerable variation in how people treat one another. They can act politely, rudely, respectfully, with hostility, etc. These interpersonal aspects of a procedure—which occur in the context of an interaction whose overt purpose is to make a decision to allocate resources or resolve a conflict—may influence those who are involved. Interpersonal aspects of procedures have been found to be so powerful that some researchers have argued that they might potentially be treated as a separate type of "interactional" justice (Bies & Moag, 1986; Tyler & Bies, 1990). Irrespective of whether the quality of the treatment that people experience via procedures is considered a distinct form of justice (see Blader & Tyler, 2003), justice researchers have increasingly been exploring interpersonal or interactional aspects of procedures—which are reflected in judgments about the quality of one's treatment by others.

Recent discussions of procedural justice recognize four primary elements of procedures that contribute to judgments about their fairness: opportunities for participation, a neutral forum, trustworthy authorities, and treatment with dignity and respect. Blader and Tyler (2003) refer to the first two elements as involving the quality of decision making, while the latter two elements are concerned with the quality of interpersonal treatment.

LEVELS OF JUSTICE

From its inception in the study of relative deprivation, studies of justice and injustice have recognized two levels of analysis: individual and group based. This distinction is reflected in the study of egoistical vs. fraternal deprivation (Runciman, 1966). In addition, building upon the work of Brickman, Folger, Goode, and Schul (1981), researchers have studied societal level distributions, which Brickman labels macrojustice.

A core idea, first articulated in Runciman's (1966) relative deprivation theory, is that people can focus on personal outcomes (egoistic deprivation) or they can be concerned about the outcomes obtained by the groups of which they are members (fraternal deprivation). Subsequent research has suggested that this distinction is important because collective action, such as rioting or, in a more positive vein, the civil rights movement in the United States, is primarily motivated by fraternal deprivation. Egoistical deprivation triggers personal efforts at achievement or, when people see no feasible route toward improvement, self-destructive behaviors such as alcoholism. Hence, the manner in which people interpret their experience is important. If people feel that they are relatively deprived as individuals, they react individually. If they feel relatively deprived due to group membership, their response is collective. And other judgments also matter, for example the perceived feasibility of change.

While most distributive justice research focuses on individual/group level judgments about personal outcomes, it is recognized that people also make judgments about the overall distribution of outcomes in a group or society. This has been referred to as macrojustice (Brickman et al., 1981). Research on macrojustice reveals an interesting inconsistency between levels of justice judgments, with people viewing the macrolevel (i.e., group) distributions that result from microlevel (i.e., individual) principles as unjust. In particular, people strongly endorse rewarding people based upon merit or productivity (the equity principle), but find the overall distribution of resources across society that results to be unfair. People generally want to create a floor below which people cannot sink and sometimes view a lower level of inequality as fairer.

Boeckmann's (1996) dissertation studied levels of justice in the context of retribution. He presented people with scenarios involving wrongdoing varying along two dimensions: the harm was personal or societal and the harm was material or status-linked. He found variations in people's retributive responses linked to both dimensions. In particular, he found that societal harms were viewed as more important to respond to than were personal harms. And, at both levels, status-linked harms were more important to respond to than were material harms. To take an example, spitting on the flag (a non-material harm that relates to identity) was viewed as more serious than despoiling a national park (a material harm).

More recently Wenzel (2004a, 2004b) has integrated these various ideas and argued for a three level model of justice. He argues for distinguishing between individual, group, and inclusive levels of justice. Individual level justice involves personal entitlements. Group level justice involves group entitlements. In the latter case, Wenzel builds upon social identity theory to argue that much of the way that people think about social life is built upon groups, their own and others. Hence, much of justice is about entitlements at the group level. Finally inclusive level justice is about the appropriate distribution of outcomes across all individuals and groups.

THE INTERPLAY OF JUSTICE AND SELF-INTEREST

The studies of justice outlined make clear that justice can motivate people to behave in ways that are not in accord with their sense of their own personal and group interests. For example, the advantaged may give resources to the disadvantaged. On the other hand, such justice motivations are never absolute. Typically people compromise between the motivation to act justly and the desire to act in their self interest.

One of the best illustrations of such compromises is found in the literature on ultimatum games (Güth, Schmittberger, & Schwarze, 1982; Handgraaf, Van Dijk, Wilke, & Vermunt, 2004). In these games, proposers make offers about how to divide some set of resources (for example ten dollars). Responders can either accept or reject this offer. Studies suggest that proposers make, and responders accept, offers somewhere between an equal division and a division favoring the proposer. For example, if ten dollars is to be divided, the successful offers fall between zero and five dollars for the responder (e.g., $4.00). In other words, both parties compromise between self-interest and fairness, with the proposer giving more than he or she would be rationally expected to, and the responder accepting less than an equal division. Further, studies show that responders decline small gains rather than accept "unfairly" low divisions, illustrating that people are willing to incur losses to defend principles of fairness.

Of course, there are other ways to deal with conflicts about justice. Early work on distributive justice pointed to the possibility of motivated social cognition in which people try to restore justice psychologically (Walster et al., 1978). This work first developed the distinction between psychological and behavioral responses to wrongdoing. When someone receives too much or provides too little to others, a conflict is created between his or her behavior and the principles of justice. There are two types of response. One is for outcomes to be reallocated so as to be fair. The victim frequently advocates this response, while the harm doer has mixed feelings—he or she believes in justice but is also benefiting from the unjust situation. Hence, harm doers are motivated to psychologically justify the situation, coming to believe that they deserve the outcomes they have. For example, studies of distributive justice show that people who are "overpaid" find ways to justify their payment by increasing their perception of the difficulty of the task and hence reframing the situation as one in which their pay is reasonable.

The motivation to justify advantage brings harm doers and victims into conflict because the victims want redistribution while the harm doers seek to justify their gains. An important function of social authorities is to lend support to victims, or at least avoid social conflict, by supporting the application of objective standards of fairness, which resolves conflicts, and by discouraging psychological justification, which leads to long-term hostility. More generally, there are a variety of social mechanisms through which the advantaged justify their advantages, with the intention of keeping their advantages without the negative emotions that they might experience from feeling that they are violating principles of justice (Chen & Tyler, 2001; Wakslak, Jost, Tyler, & Chen, 2007).

Recently, Blader (2007) has demonstrated that such motivational judgments occur when the justice of procedures is ambiguous. Using experimental methods, Blader showed that when the nature of a procedure was clear, procedural elements shaped perceived procedural justice. However, when procedures were unclear, justice judgments were influenced by identification with the group and outcome favorability. In other words, nonfairness-related judgments became important in making justice judgments primarily when the justice of the situation was unclear.

THE PSYCHOLOGY OF THE JUSTICE MOTIVE

One of the most important questions raised by the findings that justice matters is why people are motivated to act fairly. Two answers have been proposed.

Instrumental Views of the Psychology of Justice

This perspective was first presented in the literature on distributive justice. In theories of distributive justice, the answer to the question of why people are motivated to act justly is framed in social exchange terms (Thibaut & Kelley, 1959). People are viewed as being concerned with developing effective ways to exchange resources with others, both within particular situations and over time, since such cooperation is generally recognized as being to everyone's advantage. The development of principles of fairness occurs, from this perspective, because it aids in resource exchange.

Shared principles of fairness aid resource exchange because they indicate the distribution of resources that constitutes a reasonable exchange. Having such rules facilitates material exchanges, since there are clear rules for what each person deserves, and each exchange does not have to begin with an effort to define reasonable exchange principles. Such shared principles also facilitate the occurrence of exchanges since they allow people to alleviate their concerns that they are being disadvantaged in exchanges with others (acting like a "sucker") or, conversely, that they are taking advantage of others. People can compare their outcomes to principles of justice to determine if what they are receiving in relationship to others is reasonable and appropriate.

This argument suggests that having principles of distributive fairness is a precursor to effective cooperation and that the ability to develop such shared principles may be a fundamental social skill that has facilitated the evolution of humans into social beings who live in organized societies and cooperate with one another. Recent research has supported this argument by demonstrating that animals that live in group settings, for example monkeys (Brosnan, 2006) and dogs (Range, Horn, Viranyi, & Huber, 2008), also recognize and act in accord with principles of distributive fairness. It is particularly striking that the members of both of these species share with humans the willingness to forego rewards to defend principles of fairness.

Ironically, however, while these arguments support the idea that justice matters, they diminish the social psychological significance of justice findings because they suggest that people's motivation for caring about justice is their own material self interest. Social exchange models, such as that of Rusbult and Van Lange (1996), argue that people in groups have a long-range view of their self-interest, often investing their efforts in groups in anticipation of long-term payoffs. If the principles of distributive justice are accepted as instruments of coordination in the service of self-interest, they show a sophisticated ability on the part of both people and animals to develop coordinating rules and principles. But they do not suggest that people are motivated by intrinsic justice concerns when they act fairly.

An example of the implications of the social exchange argument is provided by discussions of the "scope" of justice. While some writers present the motivation to act justly as a core and universal human motivation (Lerner, 1980, 2003), others argue that it is bounded or limited in scope. The possibility of a scope of justice has important societal implications, since that scope can shift with events so that both individuals and members of groups can be included, or excluded, from the others' moral community. Once outside it, people are no longer accorded the presumption of treatment with dignity and respect for rights that group members in good standing assume they will receive (Nagata, 1993; Opotow, 1990, 1993).

Deutsch (1985) argued that people do not extend their concern about justice to all living things, or even to all people. Rather, their concerns have a clear scope, and outside of that scope people do not act in accord with the principles of distributive fairness. What defines this scope of justice? To Deutsch it is the domain of productive social exchange relationships. In other words, people follow principles of distributive justice with those with whom they see the potential of beneficial social exchanges, rather than feeling some type of intrinsic justice-based motivation to act fairly to everyone. And so those people who are not viewed as candidates for productive social exchange are not treated with justice.

Relational Perspectives on the Psychology of Justice

Subsequent studies have suggested that the instrumental view of justice is incomplete. They have supported the argument that people want the opportunity to present their arguments to the decision maker and thereby have the procedural feature labeled as "voice," as Thibaut and Walker (1975) suggested. However, they have not supported the argument that people simply link voice to decision control and only value the opportunity to address the decision maker when they believe their arguments are shaping the outcome. Studies indicate that people value voice even when they do not believe that their voice leads to decision control.

These findings led to the group-value model (Lind & Tyler, 1988), which focuses on the antecedents of judgments of procedural justice. The group-value model argues that noninstrumental factors influence procedural justice judgments, a prediction confirmed both by the noninstrumental voice effects (Lind, Kanfer, & Earley, 1990; Tyler, 1987) and by demonstrations that people care more about issues of procedural justice when dealing with members of their own group (Tyler, 1999). These include how they are treated and whether their rights are respected. These noninstrumental issues are important because they carry an important social message to people about their status within the group (Lind & Tyler, 1988).

Of course, it is important to note that, like prior models, the group-value model also argues for a scope of justice. In this case that scope is defined by the range of people or groups that are relevant to people's definitions of their status (i.e., to the range of their group). For example, people are less concerned about justice when they are dealing with outsiders than insiders (Smith, Tyler, Huo, Ortiz, & Lind, 1998; Tyler, Lind, Ohbuchi, Sugawara, & Huo, 1998). Further, those people who are less concerned about their status—the quality of their social connections—are generally less influenced by information about justice (De Cremer & Tyler, 2005; Tyler & Lind, 1990). A typical American, for example, is likely to be relatively indifferent to his or her status in Japanese society, so the person is unaffected by variations in treatment by Japanese authorities since that treatment does not communicate information about the person's status in his or her own group.

Recent studies demonstrate that it is possible to prime people so that they are focused upon either instrumental or relational issues. As would be predicted, instrumental priming leads people to focus upon the anticipated outcomes of third-party decisions, reacting to what they are likely to receive. Relational priming, on the other hand, leads people to focus upon the fairness of decision making procedures (Stahl, Vermunt, & Ellemers, 2008). Hence, it is possible for people to adopt either an instrumental or a relational perspective on their social interactions. The degree to which they do so in any given situation depends upon the strength of their identification with the social group within which the interaction occurs. When people identify with the group, they focus more heavily upon relational issues. When they do not identify, they are more instrumental (Huo, Smith, Tyler & Lind, 1996; Smith et al., 1998; Tyler & De Cremer, 2005; Tyler & Degoey, 1995).

CONCLUSION

The findings of justice research are important for several reasons. First, they demonstrate that people's thoughts, feelings and behaviors are determined by their internally held values concerning what is just or fair. These values play an important role in making social life possible because they provide a basis for cooperation among people in groups, organizations, and societies. Second, the findings of justice research provide an important confirmation that the social ties between people are central to their actions in social settings. People in social settings do not act simply as self-interested actors, pursuing individual or group gains and losses. Rather their feelings, thoughts, and behaviors are shaped by their judgments concerning what is appropriate and fair. The demonstration that people are value-based actors provides a clear demonstration of the central role of social motivations in people's actions in groups, communities, organizations, and societies.

A third important implication of justice research concerns procedural justice. It is not obvious that people's engagement in groups would be the result of procedural justice judgments. People could potentially consider a wide variety of aspects of their relationship to their group when they are evaluating the degree to which they want to engage in the group. One thing that we might expect people to consider is reward level—that is, people might consider their salary, the number of resources they are given to manage, and/or the size of their office as key inputs into their judgments about how much to engage themselves in their group. Or, at least, they might consider outcome fairness, as suggested by Thibaut and Walker (1975).

Because an outcome focus is intuitively obvious, the finding that procedural justice is so central to people's thinking is striking. It is especially striking because, of the procedural elements considered, questions of interpersonal treatment consistently emerge as important. In other words, people's focus is upon those aspects of their experience that communicate messages about status, rather than upon those more directly related to issues of decision making. This supports the argument that it is status issues that define people's relationship to groups and procedural justice that provides information about status.

Overall, the literature on justice contributes to a social vision of the person on several levels. First, people care about justice, a socially constructed idea, and view it as the core element of social groups. Second, people think of justice in very relational terms. And, third, studies of how justice influences people's behavior suggests that the key connection between people and groups, communities, organizations, and societies is rooted in their concerns about self and identity. In all of these ways, people show themselves to be fundamentally social animals, concerned about their relationships with others.

REFERENCES

Alexander, S., & Ruderman, A. (1987). The role of procedural and distributive justice in organizational behavior. *Social Justice Research*, 1, 177–198.

Barrett-Howard, E., & Tyler, T. R. (1986). Procedural justice as a criterion in allocation decisions. *Journal of Personality and Social Psychology*, 50, 296–304.

Bies, R. J., & Moag, J. S. (1986). Interactional justice. In R. J. Lewicki, B. M. Sheppard, & M. H. Bazerman (Eds.), *Research on negotiations in organizations* (Vol. 1, pp. 43–55). Greenwich, CT: JAI.

Blader, S. L. (2007). What determines people's fairness judgments? Identification and outcomes influence procedural fairness evaluations under uncertainty. *Journal of Experimental Social Psychology*, 43, 986–994.

Blader, S., & Tyler, T. R. (2003). A four component model of procedural justice: Defining the meaning of a "fair" process. *Personality and Social Psychology Bulletin*, 29(6), 747–758.

Boeckmann, R. J. (1996). *An alternative conceptual framework for offense evaluation: Implications for a social maintenance model of retributive justice.* Unpublished doctoral dissertation. University of California, Berkeley, CA.

Brickman, P., Folger, R., Goode, E., & Schul, Y. (1981). Microjustice and macrojustice. In M. J. Lerner & S. C. Lerner (Eds.), *The justice motive in social behavior.* New York, NY: Plenum.

Brockner, J., & Wiesenfeld, B. M. (1996). An integrative framework for explaining reactions to decisions: Interactive effects of outcomes and procedures. *Psychological Bulletin*, 120, 189–208.

Brosnan, S. F. (2006). Nonhuman species' reactions to inequity and their implications for fairness. *Social Justice Research*, 19(2), 153–185.

Campbell, D. T. (1975). On the conflicts between biological and social evolution and between psychology and moral tradition. *American Psychologist*, 30, 1103–1126.

Carlsmith, K. M., & Darley, J. M. (2008). Psychological aspects of retributive justice. In M. P. Zanna (Ed.), *Advances in Experimental Social Psychology* (Vol. 40, pp. 193–236). San Diego, CA: Elsevier,

Carlsmith, K. M., Darley, J. M., & Robinson, P. (2002). Why do we punish?: Deterrence and just deserts as motives for punishment. *Journal of Personality and Social Psychology*, 83, 284–299.

Chen, E., & Tyler, T. R. (2001). Cloaking power: Legitimizing myths and the psychology of the advantaged. In J. A. Bargh & A. Y. Lee-Chai (Eds.), *The use and abuse of power* (pp. 241–261). Philadelphia, PA: Psychology Press.

Crosby, F. (1976). A model of egoistical relative deprivation. *Psychological Review*, 83, 85–113.

Crosby, F. (1982). *Relative deprivation and working women.* Oxford, UK: Oxford University Press.

Darley, J. M., & Pittman, T. S. (2003). The psychology of compensation and retributive justice. *Personality and Social Psychology Review*, 7, 324–336.

De Cremer, D., & Tyler, T. R. (2005). Managing group behavior: The interplay between procedural justice, sense of self, and cooperation. In M. Zanna (Ed.), *Advances in experimental social psychology* (Vol. 37, pp. 151–218). New York, NY: Academic Press.

Deutsch, M. (1975). Equity, equality, and need: What determines which value will be used as the basis for distributive justice? *Journal of Social Issues*, 31, 137–149.

Deutsch, M. (1982). Interdependence and psychological orientation. In V. J. Delilega & J. Grzelak (Eds.), *Cooperation and helping behavior.* New York, NY: Academic Press.

Deutsch, M. (1985). *Distributive justice.* New Haven, CT: Yale.

Fehr, E., & Gintis, H. (2007). Human motivation and social cooperation. *Annual Review of Sociology, 33,* 43–64.

Gold, M. (1999). *The complete social scientist: A Kurt Lewin reader.* Washington, DC: American Psychological Association.

Gurerk, O., Irlenbusch, B., & Rockenbach, B. (2006). The competitive advantage of sanctioning institutions. *Science, 312,* 108–111.

Gurr, T. (1970). *Why men rebel.* Princeton, NJ: Princeton University Press.

Güth, W., Schmittberger, R., & Schwarze, B. (1982). An experimental analysis of ultimatum games. *Journal of Economic Behaviour and Organization, 3*(4), 367–388.

Handgraaf, M. J. J., Van Dijk, E., Wilke, H. A. M., & Vermunt, R. (2004). Evaluability of outcomes in ultimatum bargaining. *Organizational Behavior and Human Decision Processes, 95,* 97–106.

Henrich, J., McElreath, R., Barr, A., Ensminger, J., Barrett, C., Bolyanatz, A., & Ziker, J. (2006). Costly punishment across human societies. *Science, 312,* 1767–1770.

Huo, Y. J. (2002). Justice and the regulation of social relations: When and why do group members deny claims to social goods? *British Journal of Social Psychology, 41,* 535–562.

Huo, Y. J., Smith, H. J., Tyler, T. R., & Lind, E. A. (1996). Superordinate identification, subgroup identification, and justice concerns: Is separatism the problem, is assimilation the answer? *Psychological Science, 7,* 40–45.

Lerner, M. J. (1980). *The belief in a just world: A fundamental delusion.* New York, NY: Plenum.

Lerner, M. J. (2003). The justice motive: Where social psychologists found it, how they lost it and why they may not find it again. *Personality and Social Psychology Review, 7*(4), 388–399.

Leventhal, G. S. (1976). The distribution of rewards and resources in groups and organizations. In L. Berkowitz and E. Walster (Eds.), *Advances in experimental social psychology* (Vol. 9, pp. 91–131). New York, NY: Academic Press.

Leventhal, G. S. (1980). What should be done with equity theory? New approaches to the study of fairness in social relationships. In K. Gergen, M.Greenberg, & R. Willis (Eds.), *Social exchange* (pp. 27–55). New York, NY: Plenum.

Lind, E. A., Kanfer, R., & Earley, C. (1990). Voice, control, and procedural justice. *Journal of Personality and Social Psychology, 59,* 952–959.

Lind, E. A., & Tyler, T. R. (1988). *The social psychology of procedural justice.* New York, NY: Plenum.

Masters, J. C., & Smith, W. P. (1987). *Social comparison, social justice, and relative deprivation.* Hillsdale, NJ: Erlbaum.

Merton, R. K., & Kitt, A. S. (1950). Contributions to the theory of reference group behavior. In R. K. Merton & P. F. Lazersfeld (Eds.), *Continuities in social research: Studies in the scope and method of "The American Soldier"* (pp. 40–105). Glencoe, IL: Free Press.

Messick, D. M., Bloom, S., Boldizar, J. P., & Samuelson, C. D. (1985). Why we are fairer than others. *Journal of Experimental Social Psychology, 21,* 389–399.

Messick, D. M., Wilke, H., Brewer, M. B., Kramer, R. M., Zemke, P., & Lui, L. (1983).

Individual adaptations and structural changes as solutions to social dilemmas. *Journal of Personality and Social Psychology*, 44, 294–309.

Mikula, G., Petri, B., & Tanzer, N. (1990). What people regard as unjust. *European Journal of Social Psychology*, 22, 133–149.

Montada, L., & Schneider, A. (1989). Justice and emotional reactions to the disadvantages. *Social Justice Research*, 3, 313–334.

Nagata, D. (1993). *Legacy of injustice*. New York, NY: Plenum.

Olson, J. M., Herman, C. P., & Zanna, M. P. (1986). *Relative deprivation and social comparison*. Hillsdale, NJ: Erlbaum.

Opotow, S. (1990). Moral exclusion and injustice. *Journal of Social Issues*, 46, 1–20.

Opotow, S. (1993). Animals and the scope of justice. *Journal of Social Issues*, 49, 71–86.

Pritchard, R. D., Dunnette, M. D., & Jorgenson, D. O. (1972). Effects of perceptions of equity and inequity on worker performance and satisfaction. *Journal of Applied Psychology*, 56, 75–94.

Range, F., Horn, L., Viranyi, Z., & Huber, L. (2008). The absence of reward induces inequity aversion in dogs. *Proceedings of the National Academy of Science*, 106, 340–345.

Rawls, J. (1971). *A theory of justice*. Cambridge, MA: Harvard.

Reis, H. (1987). The nature of the justice motive. In J. C. Masters & W. P. Smith (Eds.), *Social comparison, social justice, and relative deprivation*. Hillsdale, NJ: Erlbaum.

Runciman, W. G. (1966). *Relative deprivation and social justice*. Berkeley, CA: University of California.

Rusbult, C., & Van Lange, P. (1996). Interdependence processes. In E. T. Higgins & A. W. Kruglanski (Eds.), *Social psychology* (pp. 564–596). New York, NY: Guilford.

Schmitt, D. R., & Marwell, G. (1972). Withdrawal and reward allocation as responses to inequity. *Journal of Experimental Social Psychology*, 8, 207–221.

Smith, H. J., Tyler, T. R., Huo, Y. J., Ortiz, D. J., & Lind, E. A. (1998). The self-relevant implications of the group-value model: Group membership, self-worth, and procedural justice. *Journal of Experimental Social Psychology*, 34, 470–493.

Sprecher, S. (2001). Equity and social exchange in dating couples. *Journal of Marriage Family*, 63, 599–613.

Stahl, T., Vermunt, R., & Ellemers, N. (2008). For love or money? How activation of relational versus instrumental concerns affects reactions to decision-making procedures. *Journal of Experimental Social Psychology*, 44, 80–94.

Stouffer, S. A., Suchman, E. A., DeVinney, L.C., Star, S. A., & Williams, R. A., Jr. (1949). *The American Soldier*. Princeton, NJ: Princeton University Press.

Thibaut, J., & Kelley, H. H. (1959). *The social psychology of groups*. New York, NY: Wiley.

Thibaut, J., & Walker, L. (1975). *Procedural justice*. Hillsdale, NJ: Erlbaum.

Tyler, T. R. (1984). Justice in the political arena. In R. Folger (Ed.), *Justice: Emerging psychological perspectives* (pp. 189–225). New York, NY: Plenum.

Tyler, T. R. (1987). Conditions leading to value expressive effects in judgments of procedural justice: A test of four models. *Journal of Personality and Social Psychology*, 52, 333–344.

Tyler, T. R. (1988). What is procedural justice?: Criteria used by citizens to assess the fairness of legal procedures. *Law and Society Review*, 22, 103–135.

Tyler, T. R. (1999). Why people cooperate with organizations: An identity-based perspective. *Research in Organizational Behavior*, 21, 201–246.

Tyler, T. R. (2000). Social justice: Outcome and procedure. *International Journal of Psychology*, 35, 117–125.

Tyler, T. R. (2006). *Why people obey the law*. Princeton, NJ: Princeton University Press.

Tyler, T. R., & Bies, R. (1990). Interpersonal aspects of procedural justice. In J. S. Carroll (Ed.), *Applied social psychology in business settings* (pp. 77–98). Hillsdale, NJ: Erlbaum (pp. 77–98).

Tyler, T. R., & Blader, S. L. (2000). *Cooperation in groups: Procedural justice, social identity, and behavioral engagement*. Philadelphia, PA: Psychology Press.

Tyler, T. R., & Blader, S. (2003). Procedural justice, social identity, and cooperative behavior. *Personality and Social Psychology Review, 7*, 349–361.

Tyler, T. R., Boeckmann, R., Smith, H. J., & Huo, Y. J. (1997). *Social justice in a diverse society*. Denver, CO: Westview.

Tyler, T. R., & Caine, A. (1981). The role of distributional and procedural fairness in the endorsement of formal leaders. *Journal of Personality and Social Psychology, 41*, 642–655.

Tyler, T. R., & De Cremer, D. (2005). Process based leadership: Fair procedures, identification, and the acceptance of change. *Leadership Quarterly, 16*, 529–545.

Tyler, T. R., & Degoey, P. (1995). Collective restraint in a social dilemma situation. *Journal of Personality and Social Psychology, 69*, 482–497.

Tyler, T. R., & Lind, E. A. (1990). Intrinsic versus community-based justice models. *Journal of Social Issues, 46*, 83-94.

Tyler, T. R., & Lind, E. A. (1992). A relational model of authority in groups. In M. Zanna (Ed.), *Advances in experimental social psychology* (Vol. 25, pp. 115–191). New York, NY: Academic Press.

Tyler, T. R., Lind, E. A., Ohbuchi, K., Sugawara, I., & Huo, Y. J. (1998). Conflict with outsiders: Disputing within and across cultural boundaries. *Personality and Social Psychology Bulletin*, 24, 137–146.

Van den Bos, K., & Lind, E. A. (2002). Uncertainty management by means of fairness judgments. In M. P. Zanna (Ed.), *Advances in experimental social psychology* (Vol. 34, pp. 1–60). New York, NY: Academic Press.

Vidmar, N., & Miller, D. T. (1980). The social psychology of punishment. *Law and Society Review*, 14, 565–602.

Wakslak, C. J., Jost, J. T., Tyler, T. R., & Chen, E. (2007). System justification and the alleviation of emotional distress. *Psychological Science, 18*, 267–274.

Walster, E., Walster, G. W., & Berscheid, E. (1978). *Equity: Theory and research*. Boston, MA: Allyn and Bacon.

Wenzel, M. (2004a). A social categorization approach to distributive justice. *European Review of Social Psychology, 15*, 219–257.

Wenzel, M. (2004b). Social identification as a determinant of concerns about individual-, group-, and inclusive-level justice. *Social Psychology Quarterly, 67*, 70–87.

Ybema, J. E., Kuijer, R. G., Buunk, B. P., DeJong, G. M., & Sanderman, R. (2001). Depression and perceptions of inequity among couples facing cancer. *Personality and Social Psychology Bulletin*, 27, 8–13.

6

Majority and Minority Influence

JOHN M. LEVINE AND RADMILA PRISLIN

S ocial influence has played a central role in social psychology since its
inception as a discipline more than 100 years ago (for historical reviews,
see Allport, 1954, and Prislin & Crano, 2012). This role is highlighted
in the classic definition of social psychology as "an attempt to explain how
the thought, feeling, and behavior of individuals are influenced by the actual,
imagined, or implied presence of other human beings" (Allport, 1954, p. 5). And
it is reinforced by the fact that group influence is one of the central themes of
our field (Ross, Lepper, & Ward, 2010).

Given the breadth of Allport's definition, it is not surprising that social influence has been defined and studied in many ways. In differentiating types of
social influence, some reviewers have distinguished between *compliance* and
conformity. Although common psychological processes can underlie both forms
of influence (Cialdini & Goldstein, 2004), they differ in important ways. Compliance occurs when an individual behaviorally acquiesces to an explicit or implicit
request from another person. In some cases, the person making the request has
no formal status or power, as when a salesperson provides an unsolicited gift
with the goal of eliciting reciprocation in the form of a purchase. In other cases,
the requester occupies a position of authority that seems to give him or her the
"right" to demand that people behave in certain ways. Milgram's (1974) famous
research on obedience illustrates the power that authority figures can wield, at
least under certain conditions. In contrast, conformity occurs when a person
changes his or her perceptions, beliefs, or actions in the direction of a perceived
group norm. Besides the fact that compliance is an interpersonal phenomenon
whereas conformity is a group phenomenon, these two forms of influence differ
in other ways (cf. Milgram, 1974). For example, compliance presupposes that
the person making the request desires to exert influence and monitors whether

or not it occurs, whereas conformity can occur without the group desiring to exert influence or monitoring its occurrence. And those who comply with a request usually behave differently than the person making the request, whereas those who conform to a group norm behave similarly to other members.

In this chapter, we focus on influence in group contexts. In so doing, we restrict our attention primarily to cases in which interaction among group members is highly restricted (or absent), there is no explicit pressure to arrive at a joint decision, and individual perceptual or opinion change is the major dependent variable (see Tindale, Talbot, & Martinez, this volume, for work on group decision making). Moreover, we are interested in cases in which the distribution of group members' positions is bimodal and asymmetrical (i.e., only two positions are represented and fewer people hold one position than the other). Thus, we focus on situations in which a numerical minority confronts a numerical majority.[1]

Disagreement between majorities and minorities can be problematical for several reasons. According to Festinger (1950), such disagreement interferes with group members' motives to validate opinions that are not anchored in physical reality and to move toward collective goals. According to social identity researchers (e.g., Marques, Abrams, Paez, & Hogg, 2001), it threatens members' desire to view their group (and therefore themselves) in a favorable light. Two general mechanisms can be used to reduce disagreement between majorities and minorities. One involves position change, in which members of both factions move toward one another (compromise), minority members move toward the majority (conformity, or majority influence), or majority members move toward the minority (innovation, or minority influence). The second involves redefinition of group boundaries, in which majority and/or minority members reject members of the other faction, recruit new group members who are likely to join their faction, or leave the group (Levine & Thompson, 1996).

Social psychological research on majority/minority disagreement has focused primarily on three of these tactics—majority influence, minority influence, and majority rejection of minorities. In the following sections, we review and synthesize theoretical and empirical work on majority and minority influence (for a review of majority rejection of minorities, see Levine & Kerr, 2007). We divide our discussion into (a) early work on majority influence encompassing Asch's (1951, 1952, 1956) classic studies and subsequent research based on the "dependence" perspective (e.g., Festinger, 1950; Deutsch & Gerard, 1955) and (b) later work on both majority and minority influence stimulated by Moscovici's (1976) "conflict" analysis.

MAINTAINING THE STATUS QUO: MAJORITY INFLUENCE

Asch's Studies

Systematic research on majority influence began with Solomon Asch's groundbreaking research (1951, 1952, 1956). In these studies, groups of seven to nine members were asked to make perceptual judgments that involved matching the length of a standard line against three comparison lines. Each group contained one naïve participant who answered next to last and several confederates who gave unanimously incorrect answers on many of the trials. The line-matching task was very easy, as indicated by the fact that control participants (who answered alone with no social pressure) very rarely gave incorrect answers. Nonetheless, Asch (1956) found that approximately one-third of participants' total responses on critical trials involved yielding to the erroneous majority. Although the conformity that Asch found may seem striking, it must be interpreted in the context of his findings that approximately two-thirds of participants' total responses were correct and almost one-fourth of participants never yielded to group pressure. Interestingly, in spite of this mixed picture, Asch's results are often characterized as providing strong and unequivocal evidence that people conform to group pressure (see Friend, Rafferty, & Bramel, 1990). This is ironic, given that Asch did not believe that people invariably go along with others' views and was not surprised to find substantial independence in his studies (see Levine, 1999).

Asch's participants described their group experience as quite unsettling. They reported substantial uncertainty and anxiety at finding themselves in disagreement with several seemingly normal people on a simple perceptual task. In analyzing the reasons why some people consistently conformed to group pressure while others resisted, Asch (1952) identified three forms of yielding and two forms of independence. Among the yielders, most said that, while their perceptions disagreed with those of the majority, they conformed either because they thought the majority was correct or because they did not want to appear different and elicit rejection. A small minority said they conformed because their perceptions of the lines actually agreed with those of the majority. Among the independents, some said they remained completely confident that their perceptions were accurate, while others said that, although their confidence wavered, they felt obligated to report what they saw.

In addition to providing the impetus for scores of subsequent studies on conformity, Asch identified several important moderators of group pressure. These included the sizes of the majority and minority, the minority's response mode (public vs. private), and the characteristics of the perceptual task. For example, Asch found that conformity increased as the number of confederates giving erroneous responses went from one to two to three, but did not increase further even with 15 confederates. Moreover, he discovered that the presence of a single confederate (social supporter) who dissented from the erroneous majority by giving correct answers dramatically reduced conformity. In fact, participants conformed far less when they were opposed by a seven-person majority and had a supporter than when they were opposed by a three-person majority and did not have a supporter. Asch also found that conformity decreased when participants responded privately (rather than publicly) and increased as the perceptual task became more difficult (i.e., as the discrepancy between the standard and comparison lines decreased).

In his later writing, Asch interpreted the conformity he observed as reflecting the essential sociability of human beings. He wrote that this conformity "assures me that the people studied were sensitive to the forces around them, that they responded with feeling; and—if this expression be permitted—that they were human in the good sense of this term … I do not at all take these to be signs of moral blemish. Rather, I would be concerned if they could not respond in these ways" (Asch, 1990, pp. 54-55) (see Levine, 1999, and Prislin & Crano, 2012, for detailed discussions of Asch's views).

Several other explanations for Asch's findings have been proposed. These include Ross, Bierbrauer, and Hoffman's (1976) attributional analysis focusing on minority members' interpretation of the reasons underlying the majority's responses, Baumeister's (1982) self-presentational analysis focusing on minority members' fear of embarrassment, and Abrams, Wetherell, Cochrane, Hogg, and Turner's (1990) self-categorization analysis focusing on the extent to which minority and majority members share a common social identity (see also Mackie & Skelly, 1994). Recently, Hodges and Geyer (2006) proposed a values-pragmatic analysis stipulating that minority members in the Asch situation seek to achieve multiple goals, including truth and social solidarity, by strategically varying their responses (e.g., conforming at some times, resisting at others) in order to maintain a "conversation" with majority members. The most common explanation for Asch's findings, however, emphasizes minority members' cognitive or social dependence on majority members, that is, their desire to give accurate responses on the perceptual stimuli or to avoid rejection by majority members.

Motivational Bases of Conformity: The Dependence Perspective

As noted above, Festinger (1950) argued that social influence in groups serves two important goals—social reality (opinion validation on issues not anchored in physical reality) and group locomotion (movement toward collective goals). This viewpoint presaged similar analyses by several other theorists (e.g., Deutsch & Gerard, 1955; Jones & Gerard, 1967; Kelley, 1952; Thibaut & Strickland, 1956). The most influential was Deutsch and Gerard's distinction between (a) *informational influence*, based on the minority's desire to hold accurate beliefs or opinions coupled with their assumption that the majority can provide valid information and (b) *normative influence*, based on the minority's desire to gain or maintain social approval coupled with their assumption that the majority will reward conformity and punish deviance. In the former case, where people are unsure about the validity of their beliefs and assume that other members are more likely to be correct than they are, they conform in order to reduce uncertainty. In the latter case, where people want to maximize their social outcomes in the group and assume that other members will respond more favorably to conformity than to deviance, they conform in order to win approval and avoid disapproval. In both cases, then, conformity is based on the minority's dependence on the majority.

The distinction between informational and normative influence is quite useful in explaining a number of findings in the conformity literature (see the review by Allen, 1965). Consistent with an informational explanation, majority influence is greater when people are working on a difficult or ambiguous task (e.g., Crutchfield, 1955) and when they have doubts about their task competence (e.g., Hochbaum, 1954). In such cases, people would be expected to feel dependent on others for information about reality. And conformity on difficult tasks is greater when the desire to be accurate is high rather than low (Baron, Vandello, & Brunsman, 1996).

Consistent with a normative explanation, people who deviate from group consensus both expect to receive (e.g., Gerard & Rotter, 1961) and do receive (Levine & Kerr, 2007) more negative evaluations from other group members than do people who conform. In addition, as might be expected if people are concerned about how others evaluate them, conformity is higher when people are under surveillance by other group members (e.g., Deutsch & Gerard, 1955, but see Bond & Smith, 1996) and when they anticipate future interaction with these members (e.g., Lewis, Langan, & Hollander, 1972). Moreover, conformity is higher when people are working for a common goal and hence are interdependent for obtaining rewards than when they are working for individual goals and hence are independent (e.g., Deutsch & Gerard, 1955). One explanation for this finding is that members of common goal groups are more fearful that any deviance on their part will be seen as threatening group goal attainment and hence will be punished. It is worth noting, however, that members of common goal groups conform very little when they believe that such behavior will undermine, rather than advance, group goal attainment (Sakurai, 1975). Finally, people often (though not always) conform more to attractive than to unattractive groups (see Allen, 1965; Turner, 1991). Consistent with a normative interpretation of this effect, people conform to attractive groups when they feel insecure about their acceptance and believe that conformity will increase this acceptance (e.g., Jetten, Hornsey, & Adarves-Yorno, 2006; Walker & Heyns, 1962).

Other research, though not couched in informational/normative terms, is also consistent with the dependence perspective. For example, Allen and Wilder (1980) demonstrated that people who learned that a unanimous group of peers disagreed with their opinions on several statements (e.g., "I would never go out of my way to help another person if it meant giving up some personal pleasure") interpreted key phrases in the statements (e.g., "go out of my way") differently than did control participants who received no majority pressure. Moreover, people who were exposed to the interpretations generated in the majority pressure condition displayed increased conformity. Thus, knowledge of the majority's position can cause minority members to cognitively restructure the stimulus, which in turn may increase their tendency to conform. (It is worth noting that cognitive restructuring can also *follow* conformity; Griffin & Buehler, 1993.) In addition, minority members' attributions for the majority's behavior (Ross, Bierbrauer, & Hoffman, 1976) and their perceptions of majority members' independence (Wilder, 1977, 1978) can affect their tendency to conform. All of this work implicitly assumes that minority members are informationally dependent on the majority and their susceptibility to influence depends on how much weight to give to the majority's judgments.

Social Support   Deutsch and Gerard's (1955) analysis also helps to clarify the psychological mechanisms underlying the power of social support to reduce conformity. As noted earlier, Asch discovered that the presence of one person who dissents from erroneous group consensus by giving correct answers dramatically reduces conformity. Subsequent research by others indicated that the social support effect is quite robust (see Allen, 1975). For example, it works for both objective (e.g., visual perception) and subjective (e.g., opinion) stimuli, and a supporter's ability to reduce conformity continues even after the person leaves the situation, as long as participants continue to judge the same kind of stimuli and the supporter does not explicitly repudiate his or her dissenting position. What accounts for these effects? A major factor is the extent to which social support frees minority members from informational and/or normative dependence on the majority.

In the case of informational pressure, a social supporter can lower minority members' dependence on the majority for information about reality. For example, a supporter who is allegedly competent in judging the experimental stimuli (i.e., has normal vision) is more effective in reducing conformity than is a supporter who is incompetent (i.e., visually handicapped) (Allen & Levine, 1971). Social support can also reduce informational dependence on the majority by preventing cognitive restructuring of the experimental stimulus, which, as Allen and Wilder (1980) demonstrated, can play a key role in producing conformity. In addition to unanimous majority and control conditions, Allen and Wilder included a social support condition in which one person dissented from group consensus by agreeing with participants' opinions on the statements. When the supporter was present, participants' interpretations of the statements were the same as those in the control condition (and different from those in the unanimous majority condition), indicating that the supporter undermined the majority's ability to produce cognitive restructuring.

In the case of normative pressure, a social supporter can lower minority members' dependence on the majority for social approval. This may occur because minority members believe that the supporter will reduce the majority's tendency to punish dissenters. Consistent with this argument, Allen (1975) reported evidence that most people who dissent from group consensus alone expect to be rejected, whereas a much smaller percentage of dissenters who have social support expect rejection. In addition, minority members may assume that the majority will be less likely to attribute their deviance to a personal idiosyncrasy if they have a supporter, which in turn will reduce anger at their behavior (Allen, 1975). However, if minority members believe that the majority is hostile to the supporter for some reason (e.g., because they are prejudiced against his or her racial group), they may be reluctant to accept his or her support and continue to conform at a high level (Boyanowsky & Allen, 1973). This presumably occurs because an alliance with a stigmatized supporter is expected to increase, rather than decrease, punishment from the majority.

Majority Size   Research on social support focuses on the effects of minority size, specifically how one- versus two-person minorities respond to disagreement from a majority. Another important line of conformity research focuses on majority size, specifically how one-person minorities react to disagreement from majorities of different sizes. As noted earlier, Asch discovered that conformity increased until the majority reached three persons and then leveled off. Subsequent research produced a confusing picture, with some studies confirming the existence of a ceiling effect (e.g., Stang, 1976), others indicating increasing conformity as a function of majority size (e.g., Gerard, Wilhelmy, & Conolley, 1968), and still others showing no clear relationship between conformity and majority size (e.g., Goldberg, 1954).

In later analyses, researchers used mathematical models to specify the relationship between majority size and conformity (see Bond & Smith, 1996). For example, Latane and Wolf (1981) used social impact theory to analyze how majority influence is affected by the strength (e.g., status), immediacy (e.g., physical closeness), and number of people holding the majority position. They argued that conformity is related to majority size by a power function. According to their model, conformity increases as majority size increases, but each succeeding majority member produces a smaller increase than the preceding member. Using different assumptions, Tanford and Penrod (1984) argued that conformity is related to majority size by an S-shaped growth (Gompertz) curve. According to their model, the second and third majority members have more impact than the first and total influence eventually reaches some asymptote. In yet another analysis, Mullen (1983) argued that conformity varies positively as a function of the "other-total ratio"—the number of people in the majority faction divided by the total number of people in the minority and majority factions. Mullen's model is unique among the three discussed here in positing a psychological explanation for the relationship between majority size and conformity. He suggested that people become more self-attentive and hence more likely to match salient standards of behavior as the relative size of their subgroup decreases. This interpretation is broadly consistent with an informational explanation of conformity.

A more explicitly informational interpretation was offered by Wilder (1977, 1978), who argued that conformity does not increase with the simple number of people holding a majority position but rather with the number of distinct (i.e., independent) social entities espousing that position. His reasoning resonates with Asch's (1952) position that "Consensus is valid only to the extent to which each individual asserts his own relation to facts and retains his individuality ... the meaning of consensus collapses when individuals act like mirrors that reflect each other" (pp. 494-495). According to Wilder, then, the critical variable in determining conformity is whether the people holding a majority position ostensibly arrived at that position independently. Consistent with this reasoning, Wilder found that conformity varies directly with majority size only if majority members are viewed as independent sources of information about their common position.

This is not to say, of course, that normative pressure cannot produce a positive relationship between majority size and conformity in some contexts. To the extent that minority members are concerned about how they will be evaluated in the group, they are likely to assume that they will receive more rewards/costs for conformity/dissent from larger than from smaller majorities. This should be particularly true if minority members feel they are under surveillance by the majority (if their responses are public rather than private; cf. Raven & Kruglanski, 1970). Consistent with this line of reasoning, Campbell and Fairey (1989) found that, when participants paid close attention to stimuli likely to elicit normative influence (i.e., clearly incorrect majority norms), conformity varied positively with majority size.

Public and Private Conformity   So far, we have restricted our attention to overt, or behavioral, responses to majority pressure. However, majority influence can involve covert responses as well. It is not surprising, then, that researchers have distinguished two forms majority influence—public compliance and private acceptance. If conformity is defined as movement, then public compliance involves overt behavioral change toward the majority's position, whereas private acceptance involves covert attitudinal or perceptual change toward this position. Although Deutsch and Gerard (1955) did not discuss the relationship between informational/normative influence and compliance/acceptance, it has generally been assumed that normative influence produces compliance but not acceptance, whereas informational influence produces both compliance and acceptance. This assumption is consistent with analyses of social influence in dyadic relationships (e.g., Kelman, 1958; Raven & Kruglanski, 1970). However, the relationships between the two types of influence and the two types of conformity are complicated by several factors.

First, thorny methodological problems arise in trying to measure compliance and acceptance (Allen, 1965). An obvious solution involves measuring a person's publicly stated opinion in the presence of majority members at Time 1 and then assessing the same opinion when the person is alone at Time 2. It would be plausible to infer that if the person agreed with the majority at both Time 1 and Time 2, then both compliance and acceptance occurred at Time 1, whereas if the person agreed with the majority at Time 1 but not at Time 2, then only compliance occurred at Time 1. However, private agreement with the majority at Time 2 does not prove that the person also privately agreed at Time 1. Various psychological processes, including dissonance reduction, might have produced agreement between the person's initial public and subsequent private responses. Moreover, when private agreement is absent at Time 2, it may nonetheless have been present at Time 1 but dissipated over time. In some cases, researchers are not interested in distinguishing between compliance and acceptance but rather in assessing only one type of response. In such cases, acceptance is sometimes defined as the amount of "indirect" influence that occurs on issues related, but not identical, to the one on which pressure was exerted.

A second complication is that the binary distinction between compliance and acceptance by no means exhausts the ways in which people might respond to majority pressure (e.g., Allen, 1965; Willis, 1963). For example, Nail (1986) identified eight possible types of influence by crossing pre-exposure private agreement-disagreement, post-exposure public agreement-disagreement, and post-exposure private agreement-disagreement. Among the responses that Nail identified are conversion (pre-exposure private disagreement, post-exposure public agreement, post-exposure private agreement), compliance (pre-exposure private disagreement, post-exposure public agreement, post-exposure private disagreement), independence (pre-exposure private disagreement, post-exposure public disagreement, post-exposure private disagreement), and anticonversion (pre-exposure private agreement, post-exposure public disagreement, post-exposure private disagreement). Subsequently, Nail, MacDonald, and Levy (2000) elaborated Nail's (1986) model by adding a fourth dimension (pre-exposure public agreement-disagreement).

Finally, the assumption that normative influence is associated with compliance alone, whereas informational influence is associated with both compliance and acceptance, has been challenged. One challenge comes from self-categorization theory (e.g., Abrams & Hogg, 1990; Turner, 1991). An important assumption of this theory is that disagreement with others only produces uncertainty when one expects to agree with these others, that is, when they are members of one's ingroup. Another assumption is that others are influential to the extent that their position reflects (is prototypical of) the ingroup norm. And a third assumption is that conformity to an ingroup norm involves both compliance and acceptance. Importantly, self-categorization theory denies the distinction between normative and informational influence, arguing instead that "... the basic influence process is one where the normative position of people categorized as similar to self tends to be subjectively accepted as valid" (Turner, 1991, p. 171). An implication of this viewpoint is that the distinctions between public and private responding and between compliance and acceptance are less relevant for ingroup than ingroup influence (cf. Abrams & Hogg, 1990). Moreover, evidence indicates that people cognitively process messages differently when they come from ingroup versus outgroup members (e.g., Mackie & Queller, 2000; van Knippenberg, 1999).

Traditional conceptualizations of normative/informational influence and compliance/acceptance have also been challenged on other grounds. For example, evidence that normatively motivated influence is not tightly linked to surveillance and can occur in private as well as public settings led Prislin and Wood (2005) to offer a tripartite analysis of the motives underlying social influence. These authors suggested that influence can derive from the desire to be oneself, to maximize rewards and minimize punishments from others, and to have an accurate understanding of reality (cf. Cialdini & Goldstein, 2004). Prislin and

Wood used their motivational typology to analyze the amount and kind of cognitive activity that people engage in when they are exposed to social pressure and the implications of this activity for compliance and acceptance. It is important to note that two or more of these motives may operate at the same time and, in some cases, may affect one another. For example, the motive to hold accurate views may derive from the motive to gain acceptance, because people desiring acceptance may believe that holding accurate views will be rewarded by others. In other words, people may seek to hold such views because of the social (rather than epistemic) benefits of doing so (Levine & Kerr, 2007).

Individual Differences

In discussing determinants of conformity, we have so far ignored the impact of individual differences, that is, enduring personal characteristics that minority members bring into group pressure situations. Two such characteristics have received particular research attention—gender and cultural background.

Whether females differ from males in their responses to majority pressure has been debated for many years. Prior to the early 1980s, the general consensus was that females are more likely to conform. However, during the 1980s, Eagly and her colleagues cast doubt on this simple conclusion. After reviewing many studies, they concluded that, while women were generally more influenceable than men, the size of this effect was small and depended on the research setting (Eagly & Carli, 1981). For example, conformity differences between men and women were rather pronounced when participants were under surveillance by other group members (e.g., Eagly & Chrvala, 1986; Eagly, Wood, & Fishbaugh, 1981), but women were only slightly more influenceable than men in conformity experiments that did not involve surveillance and in attitude change studies. The controversy regarding gender differences in conformity is far from settled, however, as indicated by Bond and Smith's (1996) meta-analysis of 133 studies investigating conformity on Asch's line judgment task. This analysis yielded a robust gender effect indicating higher conformity among women than men.

Within a given society, men and women often learn different ways of responding to social situations, including majority pressure (Eagly, 1978; Eagly & Wood, 1991). In a similar vein, people who grow up in different cultures often learn different ways of responding when they find themselves in a minority opposing a majority. For example, an early study by Berry (1967) found that, when exposed to false group norms on a visual perception task, Temne people from Sierra Leone in Africa conformed more than Eskimo people from Baffin Island in Canada. Berry attributed his results to different child rearing practices in the two cultures—food-accumulating economies, such as that of the Temne, stress conformity in children, whereas hunting and fishing economies, such as that of the Eskimo, stress individualism. More recent evidence was obtained by Bond and Smith (1996) in the meta-analysis mentioned above. They found that people in collectivistic cultures (which emphasize interdependence, cooperation, and social harmony) display higher levels of conformity on Asch's line judgment task than do those in individualistic cultures (which emphasize independence, autonomy, and self-reliance). This may occur because collectivists place more weight on shared goals and care more about others than do individualists.

Not only may conformity vary between societies, it may also vary over time within societies due to political, economic, or other causes. To examine this possibility, Bond and Smith (1996) looked at changes in conformity levels on Asch's line judgment task in the United States from the 1950s to the middle 1990s. They found that conformity generally declined over that time period. How to interpret these results is not clear, however. Were cultural changes the only (or even primary) cause of the reduced conformity? And, if so, which cultural changes were responsible?

Motivational Bases of Nonconformity

In analyzing the normative and informational underpinnings of the social support effect, we touched on some of the motivational factors that influence minority members' resistance to majority pressure. In addition, several other motives may play a role in eliciting nonconformity. One such motive is the desire to produce social change. According to Moscovici (1976), "nomic" minorities, who are convinced that their position is correct, want to gain visibility and social recognition. In order to do so, they confidently and consistently assert their views and try to provoke conflict in the group (see Hollander, 1975; Willis, 1965). A related motive is the desire to help the group achieve its goals and remain true to its values. According to Packer's (2008) normative conflict model, how group members respond to social pressure is determined by their level of identification with group and their perception of the degree of normative conflict within the group. The model stipulates that, when normative conflict is high (because group norms are perceived as undermining group welfare), strongly identified members either challenge these norms or engage in uneasy conformity whereas weakly identified members disengage from the group. In contrast, when normative conflict is low, strongly identified members exhibit loyal conformity whereas weakly identified members engage in either passive nonconformity or strategic conformity.

Nonconformity is not always motivated by a selfless desire to improve the group, however. In many cases, it is motivated by more personal goals. One such goal, highlighted by reactance theory (Brehm & Brehm, 1981), is the desire to restore threatened behavioral freedom. In the context of majority pressure, reactance can stimulate anticonformity, or movement away from the majority's position. Another personal goal is the desire to be liked and accepted by the majority. Because minority members may fear that complete agreement with the majority will be perceived as sycophancy, they may use compromise, or partial conformity, to ingratiate themselves with the majority (Schlenker, 1980). Finally, minority members may be less concerned about how the majority views them than about how they view themselves. In particular, minority members' desire to feel distinctive or unique may cause them to nonconform in one way or another (Hornsey & Jetten, 2004; Imhoff & Erb, 2009).

CHALLENGING THE STATUS QUO: MINORITY INFLUENCE

For all its insights and dramatic demonstrations of the human capacity to conform, the dependence approach to social influence has limited explanatory power. This is because it cannot account for the persistent diversity of opinions within society or for their sometimes dramatic evolution from marginality to orthodoxy. Clearly, these phenomena are difficult, if not impossible, to explain if minorities are always dependent on majorities for information about reality and social acceptance. The first social psychologist to identify the limited scope of the dependence approach for understanding social influence was Serge Moscovici (see Moscovici & Faucheux, 1972). Moscovici's genius was in recognizing that people holding a minority position in a group are not always silenced by pressure to conform but instead sometimes produce social change, or innovation. To engender innovation, according to Moscovici, minority dissent must entail more than passive resistance to prevailing group norms. It must include a well-articulated alternative viewpoint that is actively promoted through engagement and conflict with the majority. In short, it requires minority influence.

Moscovici's Genetic Model and Conversion Theory of Minority Influence

Although he argued that consensus is not the sole outcome of social influence, Moscovici (1976) emphasized that it is precisely the value people place on consensus that arms minorities with the power to exert influence (see Levine, 1989, for a detailed summary and critique of Moscovici's theorizing). By offering a clear alternative to the dominant viewpoint in the group, minorities rupture consensus, calling into question its assumed validity. The resultant conflict is the driving force behind minority influence. To be influential, a minority must engage the majority in a tacit negotiation about the validity of its position. This is a formidable challenge given that minorities are often "pigeonholed, pathologized, deprecated, stigmatized, and dismissed in a countless way" (Moscovici, 1994; p. 239). To counteract being marginalized and ignored, minorities possess but one tool—vigorous advocacy of their position. According to Moscovici's (1976) *genetic model* of social influence, this vigor is conveyed through a behavioral style characterized by investment in the advocated position, autonomy of judgment, consistency over time and modality, and fairness in acknowledging others' positions. Importantly, a minority's behavioral style must not be seen as rigid (i.e., inflexible and dogmatic)—a requirement that forces minorities to walk a fine line in their consistent advocacy for their position (Maass & Clark, 1984; Mugny 1982).

According to Moscovici, the importance of a minority's behavioral style rests in its attributional implications. Consistent and strong advocacy draws attention, making it difficult to dismiss the minority out of hand. Such advocacy also conveys confidence and commitment, especially when the minority persists in its views despite reprisals (Baron & Bellman, 2007). Unable to disregard or silence the minority, the majority experiences both social conflict with the minority and cognitive conflict about the issue under consideration. This socio-cognitive conflict is unpleasant and, under certain conditions, can cause majority members to shift privately to the minority position. Importantly, however, majority members who adopt the minority point of view do not yield publicly, at least at first. Even though each presumably recognizes his or her private change, they do not realize that others have undergone a similar conversion. This pluralistic ignorance (Katz & Allport, 1931) may be resolved eventually through gradual and cautious communication about the newly adopted position. If a sufficient number of majority members publicly acknowledge their private conversion to the minority position, the outcome is social innovation, which institutes a new norm and, *ipso facto*, transforms the initial minority into the majority. In short, minority-induced innovation reconfigures the organization of the group and the relationships among its members.

Moscovici's rich theorizing about the social underpinnings of minority influence was later replaced by an emphasis on cognitive factors. In his *conversion theory*, Moscovici (1980) focused exclusively on cognitive processes underlying minority and majority influence. Reflecting the dual-process theorizing then popular in social psychology (e.g., Chaiken & Trope, 1999), conversion theory postulates different processes of (cognitive) conflict resolution in response to majority and minority advocacy. Disagreement from a majority triggers a comparison process in which the minority's attention is directed toward the social implications of conformity and deviance. The rewards of aligning with the majority cause the minority to exhibit public compliance with majority's position. However, because the minority does not engage in active information processing about the issue under consideration, it does not exhibit private acceptance of the majority's position. By contrast, the majority has little to gain (and often much to lose) from publicly aligning with the minority. Therefore, minority advocacy is unlikely to trigger compliance. Yet, being distinctive, minority advocacy cannot be ignored, and it activates a validation process whereby majority members strive to establish the merit of their position in the context of the minority's alternative. The ensuing cognitive elaboration of the minority's position often leads to acceptance of this position on issues that are related, but not focal, to it. This acceptance introduces additional pressure into a majority member's cognitive system, which over time may produce change on the focal issue. Such change represents conversion, or genuine adoption of the minority's position. According to conversion theory, therefore, change produced by minority advocacy is indirect, delayed, and private.

Conversion theory had a catalytic effect on the field. It inspired numerous empirical tests and spurred much additional theorizing about minority and majority influence, as indicated below. A meta-analytic synthesis of 97 empirical tests revealed that the impact of minority advocacy was most evident on private responses to indirect measures that involved issues tangentially related to the minority's position (Wood, Lundgren, Ouellette, Busceme, & Blackstone, 1994). Minority behavioral style, operationalized as consistency in advocacy, was found to be a significant moderator—minorities that advocated their position consistently were more influential than those that did not do so. On direct measures, both private and public, majority advocacy was substantially stronger than minority advocacy. The pattern of results on (in)direct types of influence on public and private measures suggests that responses to minority advocacy were motivated by concerns that alignment with the minority would have negative identity implications. Identity concerns feature prominently in later theorizing about minority and majority influence (see below).

The Mind-Expanding Effect of Minorities: Divergent-Convergent Thought Model

In addition to changing *what* people think about an issue, majority and minority sources may also affect *how* people think. Nemeth's (1986) *divergent-convergent thought model* postulates differences in the type of thought in response to majority and minority pressure. Given the value people place on agreement with a majority, divergence from a majority is surprising and stressful. When people are under stress, their attention focuses on its source (Easterbrook, 1959). As a result, Nemeth argues, divergence from a majority stimulates thinking about the majority's perspective, which in turn causes adoption of the majority's position. By contrast, divergence from a minority is neither surprising nor stressful. Under (consistent) minority pressure, attention is focused not on the minority's position but rather on the issue under consideration from a broader perspective. Therefore, rather than adopting the minority's position, people exposed to minority disagreement engage in divergent thought characterized by "a greater consideration of other alternatives, ones that were not proposed but would not have been considered without the influence of the minority" (Nemeth, 1986, p. 25). Evidence has documented that the presence of a minority stimulates original solutions to problems (Nemeth & Wachtler, 1983) and complex thinking about the merits of different approaches to problems (Gruenfeld, 1995). Notably, the beneficial effects of a minority are evident irrespective of the correctness of the minority-proposed solution (Schulz-Hardt, Brodbeck, Mojzisch, Kerschreiter, & Frey, 2006). Thus, the positive impact of a minority derives not from its correctness but rather from its liberating effect on thought. By breaking consensus, even incorrect minorities reframe the problem-solving context, thereby stimulating divergent thought. Interestingly, although minorities need not be correct to inspire divergent thought, their dissent must be genuine rather than simulated. Whereas genuine dissent that reflects a minority's own position stimulates divergent thought, simulated (role-played) dissent that reflects devil's advocacy stimulates thought that bolsters the majority position (Nemeth, Brown, & Rogers, 2001).

Thinking About Social Advocacy: Information Processing Approaches

Moscovici's ground-breaking work revitalized the field of social influence, inspiring many other researchers to examine the power of minorities and majorities to exert influence. Much of this research adopted an information processing approach, focusing on the cognitive responses that are elicited by messages attributed to minorities and majorities. This focus on cognitive responses channeled research on social influence in groups toward the persuasion paradigm dominated by dual-mode processing models (e.g., Chaiken & Trope, 1999). These models postulate two prototypical modes of persuasion that fall at the endpoints of a processing effort continuum—one mode characterized by effortful (e.g., systematic) processing of message-relevant information and the other mode characterized by effortless (e.g., heuristic) reliance on readily-available situational cues (such as message form and communicator characteristics). The former mode resembles Moscovici's minority-inspired validation process, whereas the latter mode resembles his majority-inspired comparison process.

Contradicting this position, the *objective consensus approach* postulates systematic processing of majority positions because of their presumed validity ("objective reality") and positive identity implications (Mackie, 1987; De Vries, De Dreu, Gordijn, & Schuurman, 1996). Similarly, the *mere consensus approach* postulates that consensually advocated positions have evaluative implications, with positions being positively valued proportional to the level of support they receive (Erb & Bohner, 2001). Importantly, according to this approach, positively valenced inferences about consensually advocated (majority) positions do not operate merely as heuristic cues. Rather, they bias the processing of message-relevant information, thereby determining the positions that are adopted (Erb & Bohner, 2001). Within this approach, low consensus (minority) positions are deemed risky and are therefore likely to be adopted primarily by risk-inclined individuals (Erb & Bohner, 2010).

The evaluative meaning of consensus is also implicated in the *source-position congruity model* of majority and minority influence (Baker & Petty, 1994). According to this model, positively valued majority positions are expected to be proattitudinal, whereas negatively valued minority positions are expected to be counterattitudinal. When these expectancies are violated by majority sources advocating counterattitudinal positions and minority sources advocating proattitudinal positions, the resultant surprise at the inconsistency, the threat it may pose, or both, motivate a thorough cognitive elaboration of the messages. To the extent that these messages offer compelling arguments, elaboration is favorable, ultimately resulting in the adoption of the advocated position. In contrast, the expected pattern of advocacy (majority sources advocating proattitudinal positions and minority sources advocating counterattitudinal positions) produces little elaboration of the messages. Instead, source information (positive in the case of the majority and negative in the case of the minority) provides a heuristic guide for how to react to the messages.

The information processing approach to social influence has generated a wealth of research and also a great deal of inconsistent findings. For example, some studies have documented systematic processing of majority messages (e.g., Mackie, 1987), others systematic processing of minority messages (e.g., Moscovici, 1980), and still others systematic processing of both majority and minority messages but under different circumstances (e.g., Baker & Petty, 1994; Martin & Hewstone, 2003). Although some authors argue for a single psychological process underlying the effects of both majority and minority sources (Kruglanski & Thompson, 1999), the inconsistency in the findings generated within the prevailing dual-process framework calls for a resolution. The *source-context-elaboration model* (SCEM; Martin & Hewstone, 2008) attempts to reconcile this inconsistency by proposing that messages from both majorities and minorities are processed contingent upon the cognitive-motivational context in which influence occurs. According to Martin and Hewstone (2008, p. 271), "Overall, majorities lead to message processing in a high elaboration context (e.g., high outcome relevance) whereas minorities lead to message processing in intermediate/high elaboration contexts where there is sufficient opportunity for their positive behavioral style to impact upon the majority." Substantial research supports this perspective.

Thinking About Social Advocacy: Social Identity Approaches

As a counterbalance to efforts to explain majority and minority influence in terms of information processing, other research has emphasized the role of social identity. The primary role of group membership in understanding social influence is a core assumption of *self-categorization theory* (Abrams et al., 1990; Turner, 1991). As discussed previously, this theory postulates shared group membership as a condition *sine qua non* for any influence, including that by minority sources. According to this perspective, disparate group membership between sources and targets of influence precludes influence because disagreement with different (outgroup) others is expected and hence does not create uncertainty regarding the validity of one's position. In contrast, disagreement with similar (ingroup) others is unexpected and hence creates uncertainty that must be resolved. Disagreement with an ingroup minority on a dimension that is relevant to the shared identity is typically resolved through recategorization of the minority into a different social category. When, however, recategorization is not possible or an outgroup enters the field of comparison, the ingroup status of the minority provides a basis for acceptance of the minority's advocacy (David & Turner, 2001).

By situating the meaning of social advocacy in group membership, self-categorization theory, and the social identity approach more broadly (Abrams & Hogg, 1990), focus on the motivational complexities that drive reactions to such advocacy. These motives include concerns about uncertainty reduction (Hogg, 2007) and the formation and maintenance of a positive view of the self (Tajfel & Turner, 1986; Wood, Pool, Leck, & Purvis, 1996). For example, Wood and her collaborators demonstrated that, in an attempt to promote a favorable sense of the self, people respond not only to the advocacy of positively-valued reference groups (ingroups) but also to the advocacy of negatively-valued reference groups (outgroups). In the latter case, however, social influence is evident in a distancing from the outgroup and a defensive interpretation of the advocacy that promotes one's positive view of the self (cf. Allen & Wilder, 1980).

Integrating insights of the information processing and social identity approaches, the *leniency contract model* postulates that ingroup minorities exert influence because of the lenient, open-minded evaluation afforded to members of one's group (Crano, 2001). According to this model, the counter-attitudinal nature of minority advocacy precludes its direct acceptance by the majority. Nevertheless, minority advocacy is elaborated in an attempt to understand the unexpected position held by ingroup members. This relatively open-minded elaboration, in turn, can create pressures to accept the minority's viewpoint on measures indirectly related to its appeal. And, over time, such indirect change puts pressure on the focal issue of minority advocacy, which is consequently modified to restore cognitive consistency (Crano & Chen, 1998). The leniency contract model, therefore, accounts for the indirect and delayed nature of minority influence by taking into account identity-based leniency toward ingroup members and the cognitive dynamics that occur in processing minority advocacy (see Crano, 2010, for a fuller description of the model).

Simultaneous consideration of group identity and information processing also characterizes the *conflict elaboration model* (Mugny, Butera, Sanchez-Mazas, & Pérez, 1995; Pérez & Mugny, 1996). This model holds that responses to social advocacy depend on their implications for group identity and the objective vs. subjective nature of standards for their correctness. When responses are socially anchoring by defining group membership in terms of subjective standards (e.g., opinions, attitudes), influence targets publicly yield to ingroup (majority) sources and reject outgroup (minority) sources. In contrast, when responses are socially anchoring in terms of objective standards (e.g., tasks with verifiably correct answers), outgroup (minority) sources that persist in their advocacy force influence targets to carefully examine their message. The result is private and delayed change toward these sources. Indeed, the difference between the subjective tasks typically employed in majority/minority influence studies and the objective tasks that were common in Moscovici's initial studies may account for the seeming inconsistencies in findings about elaboration of minority and majority advocacy (Quiamzade, Mugny, Falomir-Pichastor, & Butera, 2010).

Beyond Individual Thinking: Minority Influence in Interacting Groups

Moscovici's (1976) initial theorizing conceptualized minority influence as the outcome of efforts by small and socially marginalized factions to produce social change. In his book with the telling title of "Social influence and social change," Moscovici (1976) described revolutionary changes in politics, science, art, and fashion as his inspirations for an alternative view of social influence that challenged the then-dominant dependence perspective discussed above. Emphasizing the crucial role of the social conflict, he posited that "in social influence, relations with others take precedence over relations with objects and inter-individual dynamics take precedence over intra-individual dynamics" (Moscovici, 1976, p. 106). Yet, as noted earlier, his initial emphasis on the social underpinnings of minority influence was soon replaced by an emphasis on its cognitive underpinnings.

Why did research on minority influence become "lost in (individual) thought" at the expense of the interpersonal and group phenomena that inspired it? According to Levine and Kaarbo (2001), this shift was likely due to three interrelated reasons. First, although Moscovici's initial theorizing was inspired by observations of social conflict, his empirical studies and subsequent theorizing focused on perceptual and cognitive processes. Thus, Moscovici himself provided a model for subsequent researchers to emphasize intra-individual dynamics at the expense of inter-individual dynamics. Second, it is likely that these researchers also were influenced by the "cognitive revolution" sweeping social psychology at the time (and still dominating it). Clearly, research on social influence in general, and minority influence in particular, has marched in step with the cognitive Zeitgeist. And third, there were (and are) formidable methodological challenges associated with studying minority influence in interacting groups. Assembling groups in the laboratory and recording interactions among members is much more taxing in terms of time and resources than studying individuals' cognitive processes. In a scientific culture that rewards a high rate of research productivity, the professional costs associated with conducting labor-intensive studies of group processes cannot be discounted.

In spite of these inhibitory factors, however, both theoretical and empirical efforts have been made to clarify minority influence in interacting groups. For example, although social psychologists have assumed that successful minorities invariably promote innovation in otherwise conservative groups, this is not always the case. Rather than producing change to a position that is new for the group ("progressive" minorities), they might instead produce change to a position that the group previously held ("reactionary" minorities), block the majority's efforts to produce change to a new group position ("conservative" minorities), or block the majority's efforts to produce change to a previously-held group position ("modernist" minorities) (Levine & Kaarbo, 2001).

Research conducted in decision-making groups has demonstrated that the impact of minorities is not restricted to changing individual members' minds. For example, minorities can influence the scope and the depth of group discussion (Brodbeck, Kerschreiter, Mojzisch, & Schulz-Hardt, 2007; Schulz-Hardt et al., 2006), prevent group polarization (Smith, Tindale, & Dugoni, 1996), and exert more or less influence depending on the verifiability of their position (Smith & Tindale, 2010). Studies conducted in interacting groups that must reach consensus reveal minority influence that is often direct, immediate, and public (Smith et al., 1996). This stands in contrast to the typical findings in studies examining individual-level processing of minority advocacy (Wood et al., 1994). Apparently, the need to reach consensus creates mutual interdependence between minority and majority factions, which enables the minority to exert influence in spite of its inferiority in size. If, in addition, the minority faction can appeal to a symbolic value system that is shared with the majority, it is especially likely to produce direct influence. This occurs because a shared value system serves to validate the minority's position, functioning as a powerful "social proof" (Tindale, Smith, Thomas, Filkins, & Sheffey, 1996).

Minority influence in interacting groups is additionally illustrated by research on newcomers as agents of change in small, task-performing groups (Levine & Choi, 2010). For example, a newcomer's suggestion for changing a group's task strategy is more likely to be adopted if the group is not strongly committed (vs. strongly committed) to its original strategy and if it previously failed (vs. succeeded) on the task (Choi & Levine, 2004). Moreover, a newcomer's suggestion voiced in an assertive, compared to a nonassertive, manner is more likely to be adopted (Hansen & Levine, 2009). And newcomers' task-relevant expertise facilitates their ability to exert influence, especially when they share a social identity with other group members (Kane, Argote, & Levine, 2005). Yet, shared identity may be a double-edged sword. Although it may facilitate the adoption of newcomers' innovative suggestions, it also may be an obstacle to their voicing such suggestions (Phillips, 2003, Study 2; also see Morrison & Miller, 2008). Thus, it is important to examine the effects of social contextual factors on minority influence at every stage of the influence process, including initial voicing of dissent. Finally, newcomer influence extends beyond changing a group's task strategy to affecting the quality of its performance. For example, Choi and Thompson (2005) demonstrated that groups that underwent membership change (replacement of a current member by a new member who had previous experience in another group) performed better on an idea generation task than did groups with stable membership. Taken together, these studies indicate that minorities have the capacity to change not only individuals' judgments and attitudes but also their manifest behavior in group settings, which has long been a neglected area of inquiry (Stroebe, 2010).

The generalizability of laboratory findings on minority influence is documented in rare but valuable studies conducted in organizational settings. These studies reveal that minority dissent in organizational teams leads to creative thought just as it does in the laboratory. Importantly, however, implementation of these novel ideas requires a particular organizational climate. Thus, minority innovation is greater when team members have high rather than low participation in decision making (De Dreu & West, 2001), reflect upon their objectives and strategies for achieving them (De Dreu, 2002), and operate in a safe environment characterized by trust and support (De Dreu, Nijstad, Bechtold, & Baas, 2011).

Just as various aspects of group dynamics affect minority influence so does minority influence affect group dynamics. Successful minorities who transform themselves into majorities change not only their position within the group but also the group as a whole. For example, in the immediate aftermath of such social change, the group is weakened as successful minorities fail to identify with it whereas losing majorities show strong disidentification. This overall decrease in identification is associated with a general increase in hostility, reduced helpfulness, negative expectations for future interactions, and a desire to exit the group (Prislin & Christensen, 2005a). Importantly, whereas successful minorities are unenthusiastic about the group in which they prevail, this lack of enthusiasm does not extend to their newly acquired majority position. They in fact place more emphasis on the benefits associated with numerical supremacy in the group than do their stable counterparts (stable majorities). In particular, successful minorities value power (Christensen, Prislin, & Jacobs, 2009) and are quite willing to exercise it to benefit themselves, especially when feeling uncertain about their newly acquired position (Prislin, Sawicki, & Williams, 2011).

The situation is not always so bleak, however. When successful minorities are assured of their position, they readily identify with the group in which they prevailed (Prislin, Levine, & Christensen, 2006). Moreover, over a period of time, successful minorities gradually increase their identification with the group (Prislin & Christensen, 2005b, Study 2). This latter finding highlights the importance of a temporal perspective in understanding social influence in groups (cf. Levine & Moreland, 1985). People's interpretations of influence attempts and reactions to them evolve over time. For example, successful influence that attracts new followers tends to make expanding minorities (Clark, 2001), but not expanding majorities (Gordijn, De Vries, & De Dreu, 2002), more influential. Successful influence by minorities also feeds back to boost the certainty with which they argue their position and, in turn, their ability to generate cogent arguments in support of that position (Prislin, Boyle, et al., 2011). Thus, when examined over time and in the context of interactive exchanges, influence in groups is revealed as a dynamic and multidirectional process (Mason, Conrey, & Smith, 2007).

SUMMARY

In this chapter, we reviewed theoretical and empirical work, beginning in the 1950s and continuing to the present day, on social influence in groups. We focused on cases in which a numerical minority confronts a numerical majority and discussed the conditions under which (a) minority members move toward the majority (conformity, or majority influence) and (b) majority members move toward the minority (innovation, or minority influence). In most of the studies we reviewed, interaction among group members was quite restricted, members were not under pressure to arrive at a joint decision, and perceptual or attitude change on the part of individual members was the major dependent variable. Our review was divided into two major sections. The first focused on the role of majority influence in maintaining the status quo within a group. The second focused on the role of minority influence in challenging this status quo.

In discussing majority influence, we first presented Asch's (1951, 1952, 1956) classic conformity research and then reviewed subsequent work based on the dependence perspective, which posits that social influence is based on two primary motives—desire to hold accurate beliefs or opinions and desire to gain and maintain social approval (e.g., Deutsch & Gerard, 1955). We then used this distinction between informational and normative influence to explain a wide range of findings in the conformity literature, including the impact of task difficulty, response surveillance, task interdependence, group attractiveness, cognitive restructuring of the stimulus situation, and both minority and majority size. We also discussed the relationship between informational/normative influence and public compliance/private acceptance, as well the impact of individual differences (in gender and culture) on conformity. Finally, we mentioned several group-oriented and self-oriented motives that can stimulate nonconformity (i.e., resistance to majority pressure).

In discussing minority influence, we first examined the ground-breaking theoretical work of Serge Moscovici, which revolutionized research on social influence in groups. After discussing his genetic model and conversion theory, we reviewed subsequent theoretical analyses of minority influence. Although later theorists shared Moscovici's fascination with minority influence, they (like he) sought to provide an integrated analysis that explains majority as well as minority influence. These analyses (which include the divergent-convergent thought model, the objective consensus approach, the mere consensus approach, the source-position congruity model, the source-context-elaboration model, self-categorization theory, the leniency-contract model, and the conflict elaboration model) all conceptualize minority (and majority) influence as an intra-individual (cognitive), rather than an inter-individual (social), process. In the final section of the chapter, we discussed several recent efforts to move beyond this mindset by conceptualizing and studying minority influence in terms of factional conflict in interacting groups. In this context, we reviewed work on minority influence in decision-making groups, newcomer innovation in work teams, and the (not always positive) consequences of minority-induced social change.

Over the years, majority and minority influence have elicited a great deal of research attention from social psychologists. The continuing vitality of these topics is indicated by recent edited volumes devoted in part (e.g., Butera & Levine, 2009; Jetten & Hornsey, 2011) or in full (e.g., Martin & Hewstone, 2010) to them. Although prognostications regarding future research trends are always risky, we believe the critical role that majority and minority influence play in shaping group dynamics will ensure continued interest in these topics.

NOTE

1 Because of this focus, we do not discuss Sherif's (1935) important work on the development of group norms. For a summary, see Prislin and Crano (2012).

REFERENCES

Abrams, D., & Hogg, M. A. (1990). Social identification, self-categorization and social influence. *European Review of Social Psychology, 1*, 195–228.

Abrams, D., Wetherell, M., Cochrane, S., Hogg, M. A., & Turner, J. C. (1990). Knowing what to think by knowing who you are: Self-categorization and the nature of norm formation, conformity and group polarization. *British Journal of Social Psychology, 29*, 97–119.

Allen, V. L. (1965). Situational factors in conformity. In L. Berkowitz (Ed.), *Advances in experimental social psychology* (Vol. 2, pp. 133–175). New York, NY: Academic Press.

Allen, V. L. (1975). Social support for nonconformity. In L. Berkowitz (Ed.), *Advances in experimental social psychology* (Vol. 8, pp. 1–43). New York, NY: Academic Press.

Allen, V. L., & Levine, J. M. (1971). Social support and conformity: The role of independent assessment of reality. *Journal of Experimental Social Psychology, 7*, 48–58.

Allen, V. L., & Wilder, D. A. (1980). Impact of group consensus and social support on stimulus meaning: Mediation of conformity by cognitive restructuring. *Journal of Personality and Social Psychology, 39*, 1116–1124.

Allport, G. W. (1954). The historical background of modern social psychology. In G. Lindzey (Ed.), *Handbook of social psychology* (Vol. 1, pp. 3–56). Reading, MA: Addison-Wesley.

Asch, S. E. (1951). Effects of group pressure upon the modification and distortion of judgments. In H. Guetzkow (Ed.), *Groups, leadership, and men* (pp. 177–190). Pittsburgh, PA: Carnegie.

Asch, S. E. (1952). *Social psychology*. New York, NY: Prentice Hall.

Asch, S. E. (1956). Studies of independence and conformity: I. A minority of one against a unanimous majority. *Psychological Monographs, 70* (Whole No. 416).

Asch, S. E. (1990). Comments on D. T. Campbell's chapter. In I. Rock (Ed.), *The legacy of Solomon Asch: Essays in cognition and social psychology* (pp. 53–55). Hillsdale, NJ: Erlbaum.

Baker, S. M., & Petty, R. E. (1994). Majority and minority influence: Source position imbalance as a determinant of message scrutiny. *Journal of Personality and Social Psychology, 67*, 5–19.

Baron, R. S., & Bellman, S. B. (2007). No guts, no glory: Courage, harassment and minority influence. *European Journal of Social Psychology, 37*, 101–124.

Baron, R. S., Vandello, J. A., & Brunsman, B. (1996). The forgotten variable in conformity research: Impact of task importance on social influence. *Journal of Personality and Social Psychology, 71*, 915–927.

Baumeister, R. F. (1982). A self-presentational view of social phenomena. *Psychological Bulletin, 91*, 3–26.

Berry, J. W. (1967). Independence and conformity in subsistence-level societies. *Journal of Personality and Social Psychology, 7*, 415–418.

Bond, R., & Smith, P. B. (1996). Culture and conformity: A meta-analysis of studies using Asch's (1952b, 1956) line judgment task. *Psychological Bulletin, 119*, 111–137.

Boyanowsky, E. O., & Allen, V. L. (1973). Ingroup norms and self-identity as determinants of discriminatory behavior. *Journal of Personality and Social Psychology, 25*, 408–418.

Brehm, S. S., & Brehm, J. W. (1981). *Psychological reactance: A theory of freedom and control*. New York, NY: Academic Press.

Brodbeck, F., Kerschreiter, R., Mojzisch, A., & Schulz-Hardt, S. (2007). Group decision making under conditions of distributed knowledge: The information asymmetries model. *Academy of Management Review, 32,* 459–479.

Butera, F., & Levine, J. M. (Eds.) (2009). *Coping with minority status: Responses to exclusion and inclusion.* New York, NY: Cambridge University Press.

Campbell, J. D., & Fairey, P. J. (1989). Informational and normative routes to conformity: The effect of faction size as a function of norm extremity and attention to the stimulus. *Journal of Personality and Social Psychology, 57,* 457–468.

Chaiken, S., & Trope, Y. (Eds.) (1999). *Dual process theories in social psychology.* New York, NY: Guilford Press.

Choi, H.-S., & Levine, J. M. (2004). Minority influence in work teams: The impact of newcomers. *Journal of Experimental Social Psychology, 40,* 273–280.

Choi, H.-S., & Thompson, J. M. (2005). Old wine in a new bottle: Impact of membership change on group creativity. *Organizational Behavior and Human Decision Processes, 98,* 121–132.

Christensen, P. N., Prislin, R., & Jacobs, E. (2009). Motives for social influence after social change: Are new majorities power hungry? *Social Influence, 4,* 200–215.

Cialdini, R. B., & Goldstein, N. J. (2004). Social influence: Compliance and conformity. *Annual Review of Psychology, 55,* 591–621.

Clark, R. D. III. (2001). Effects of majority defection and multiple minority sources on minority influence. *Group Dynamics: Theory, Research, and Practice, 5,* 57–62.

Crano, W. D. (2001). Social influence, social identity, and ingroup leniency. In C. K. W. De Dreu & N. K. De Vries (Eds.), *Group consensus and minority influence: Implications for innovation* (pp. 122–159). Oxford, UK: Blackwell.

Crano, W. D. (2010). Majority and minority influence in attitude formation and attitude change: Context/categorization-leniency contract theory. In R. Martin & M. Hewstone (Eds.), *Minority influence and innovation: Antecedents, processes and consequences* (pp. 53–77). New York, NY: Psychology Press.

Crano, W. D., & Chen, X. (1998). The leniency contract and persistence of majority and minority influence. *Journal of Personality and Social Psychology, 74,* 1437–1450.

Crutchfield, R. S. (1955). Conformity and character. *American Psychologist, 10,* 191–198.

David, B., & Turner, J. C. (2001). Majority and minority influence: A single process. In C. K. W. De Dreu, & N. K. De Vries (Eds.), *Group consensus and minority influence: Implications for innovation* (pp. 91–121). Oxford, UK: Blackwell.

De Dreu, C. K. W. (2002). Team innovation and team effectiveness: The importance of minority dissent and reflexivity. *European Journal of Work and Organizational Psychology, 11,* 285–298.

De Dreu, C. K. W., Nijstad, B. A., Bechtold, M. N., & Baas, M. (2011). Group creativity and innovation: A motivated information processing perspective. *Psychology of Aesthetics, Creativity, and the Arts, 5,* 83–89.

De Dreu, C. K. W., & West, M. A. (2001). Minority dissent and team innovation: The importance of participation in decision making. *Journal of Applied Psychology, 86,* 1141–1201.

Deutsch, M., & Gerard, H. B. (1955). A study of normative and informational social influences upon individual judgment. *Journal of Abnormal and Social Psychology, 51,* 629–636.

De Vries, N. K., De Dreu, C. K. W., Gordijn, E., & Schuurman, M. (1996). Majority vs. minority influence: A dual-role interpretation. *European Review of Social Psychology, 7,* 145–172.

Eagly, A. H. (1978). Sex differences in influenceability. *Psychological Bulletin, 85,* 86–116.

Eagly, A. H., & Carli, L. L. (1981). Sex of researchers and sex-typed communications as determinants of sex differences in influenceability: A meta-analysis of social influence studies. *Psychological Bulletin, 90,* 1–20.

Eagly, A. H., & Chrvala, C. (1986). Sex differences in conformity: Status and gender role interpretations. *Psychology of Women Quarterly, 10,* 203–220.

Eagly, A. H., & Wood, W. (1991). Explaining sex differences in social behavior: A meta-analytic perspective. *Personality and Social Psychology Bulletin, 17,* 306–315.

Eagly, A. H., Wood, W., & Fishbaugh, L. (1981). Sex differences in conformity: Surveillance by the group as a determinant of male nonconformity. *Journal of Personality and Social Psychology, 40,* 384–394.

Easterbrook, J. A. (1959). The effect of emotion on cue utilization and the organization of behavior. *Psychological Review, 66,* 183–201.

Erb, H.-P., & Bohner, G. (2001). Mere consensus effects in minority and majority influence. In C. K. W. De Dreu & N. K. De Vries (Eds.), *Group consensus and minority influence: Implications for innovation* (pp. 40–59). Malden, MA: Blackwell.

Erb, H.-P., & Bohner, G. (2010). Consensus as the key: Toward parsimony in explaining majority and minority influence. In R. Martin & M. Hewstone (Eds.), *Minority influence and innovation: Antecedents, processes and consequences* (pp. 79–103). New York, NY: Psychology Press.

Festinger, L. (1950). Informal social communication. *Psychological Review, 57,* 271–282.

Friend, R., Rafferty, Y., & Bramel, D. (1990). A puzzling misinterpretation of the Asch "conformity" study. *European Journal of Social Psychology, 20,* 29–44.

Gerard, H. B., & Rotter, G. S. (1961). Time perspective, consistency of attitude, and social influence. *Journal of Abnormal and Social Psychology, 62,* 565–572.

Gerard, H. B., Wilhelmy, R. A., & Conolley, E. S. (1968). Conformity and group size. *Journal of Personality and Social Psychology, 8,* 79–82.

Goldberg, S. C. (1954). Three situational determinants of conformity to social norms. *Journal of Abnormal and Social Psychology, 49,* 325–329.

Gordijn, E. H., De Vries, N. K., & De Dreu, C. K. W. (2002). Minority influence on focal and related attitudes: Change in size, attributions, and information processing. *Personality and Social Psychology Bulletin, 28,* 1315–1326.

Griffin, D., & Buehler, R. (1993). Role of construal processes in conformity and dissent. *Journal of Personality and Social Psychology, 65,* 657–669.

Gruenfeld, D. H. (1995). Status, ideology, and integrative complexity on the U.S. Supreme Court: Rethinking the politics of decision making. *Journal of Personality and Social Psychology, 68,* 5–20.

Hansen, T., & Levine, J. M. (2009). Newcomers as agents of change: Effects of newcomers' behavioral style and team's performance optimism. *Social Influence, 4,* 46–61.

Hochbaum, G. M. (1954). The relation between group members' self-confidence and their reactions to group pressures to uniformity. *American Sociological Review, 19,* 678–687.

Hodges, B. H., & Geyer, A. L. (2006). A nonconformist account of the Asch experiments: Values, pragmatics, and moral dilemmas. *Personality and Social Psychology Review, 10,* 2–19.

Hogg, M. A. (2007). Uncertainty-identity theory. In M. P. Zanna (Ed.), *Advances in experimental social psychology* (Vol. 39, pp. 69–126), San Diego, CA: Elsevier.

Hollander, E. P. (1975). Independence, conformity, and civil liberties: Some implications from social psychological research. *Journal of Social Issues, 31,* 55–67.

Hornsey, M. J., & Jetten, J. (2004). The individual within the group: Balancing the need to belong with the need to be different. *Personality and Social Psychology Review, 8,* 248–264.

Imhoff, R., & Erb, H.-P. (2009). What motivates nonconformity? Uniqueness seeking blocks majority influence. *Personality and Social Psychology Bulletin, 35,* 309–320.

Jetten, J., & Hornsey, M. J. (Eds.) (2011). *Rebels in groups: Dissent, deviance, difference, and defiance.* Chichester, UK: Wiley-Blackwell.

Jetten, J., Hornsey, M. J., & Adarves-Yorno, I. (2006). When group members admit to being conformist: The role of relative intragroup status in conformity self-reports. *Personality and Social Psychology Bulletin, 32,* 162–173.

Jones, E. E., & Gerard, H. (1967). *Foundations of social psychology.* New York, NY: Wiley.

Kane, A. A., Argote, L., & Levine, J. M. (2005). Knowledge transfer between groups via personnel rotation: Effects of social identity and knowledge quality. *Organizational Behavior and Human Decision Processes, 96,* 56–71.

Katz, D., & Allport, F. H. (1931). *Student attitudes.* Syracuse, NY: Craftsman Press.

Kelley, H. H. (1952). Two functions of reference groups. In G. E. Swanson, T. Newcomb, & E. Hartley (Eds.), *Readings in social psychology* (pp. 410–414). New York, NY: Holt.

Kelman, H. C. (1958). Compliance, identification, and internalization: Three processes of attitude change. *Journal of Conflict Resolution, 2,* 51–60.

Kruglanski, A. W., & Thompson, E. P. (1999). Persuasion via a single route: A view from the unimodel. *Psychological Inquiry, 10,* 83–109.

Latane, B., & Wolf, S. (1981). The social impact of majorities and minorities. *Psychological Review, 88,* 438–453.

Levine, J. M. (1989). Reaction to opinion deviance in small groups. In P. B. Paulus (Ed.), *Psychology of group influence* (2nd ed., pp. 187–231). Hillsdale, NJ: Erlbaum.

Levine, J. M. (1999). Solomon Asch's legacy for group research. *Personality and Social Psychology Review, 3,* 358–364.

Levine, J. M., & Choi, H-S. (2010). Newcomers as change agents: Minority influence in task groups. In R. Martin & M. Hewstone (Eds.), *Minority influence and innovation: Antecedents, processes and consequences* (pp. 229–262). New York, NY: Psychology Press.

Levine, J. M., & Kaarbo, J. (2001). Minority influence in political decision-making. In C. K. W. De Dreu, & N. K. De Vries (Eds.), *Group consensus and minority influence: Implications for innovation* (pp. 229–257). Oxford, UK: Blackwell.

Levine, J. M., & Kerr, N. L. (2007). Inclusion and exclusion: Implications for group processes. In A. W. Kruglanski & E. T. Higgins (Eds.), *Social psychology: Handbook of basic principles* (2nd ed., pp. 759–784). New York, NY: Guilford.

Levine, J. M., & Moreland, R. L. (1985). Innovation and socialization in small groups. In S. Moscovici, G. Mugny, & E. Van Avermaet (Eds.), *Perspectives on minority influence* (pp. 143–169). Cambridge, UK: Cambridge University Press.

Levine, J. M., & Thompson, L. (1996). Conflict in groups. In E. T. Higgins & A. W. Kruglanski (Eds.), *Social psychology: Handbook of basic principles* (pp. 745–776). New York, NY: Guilford Press.

Lewis, S. A., Langan, C. J., & Hollander, E. P. (1972). Expectation of future interaction and the choice of less desirable alternatives in conformity. *Sociometry, 35,* 440–447.

Maass, A., & Clark, R. D. III. (1984). Internalization versus compliance: Differential processes underlying minority influence and conformity. *European Journal of Social Psychology, 13,* 197–215.

Mackie, D. M. (1987). Systematic and nonsystematic processing of majority and minority persuasive communications. *Journal of Personality and Social Psychology, 53,* 41–52.

Mackie, D. M., & Queller, S. (2000). The impact of group membership on persuasion: Revisiting "who says what to whom with what effect?". In D. J. Terry & M. A. Hogg (Eds.), *Attitudes, behavior, and social context: The role of norms and group membership* (pp. 135–155). Mahwah, NJ: Erlbaum.

Mackie, D. M., & Skelly, J. J. (1994). The social cognition analysis of social influence: Contributions to the understanding of persuasion and conformity. In P. G. Devine, D. L. Hamilton, & T. M. Ostrom (Eds.), *Social cognition: Impact on social psychology* (pp. 259–289). San Diego, CA: Academic Press.

Marques, J. M., Abrams, D., Paez, D., & Hogg, M. A. (2001). Social categorization, social identification, and rejection of deviant group members. In M. A. Hogg & R. S. Tindale (Eds.), *Blackwell handbook of social psychology: Group processes* (pp. 400–424). Malden, MA: Blackwell.

Martin, R., & Hewstone, M. (2003). Majority versus minority influence: When, not whether, source status instigates heuristic or systematic processing. *European Journal of Social Psychology, 39,* 585–593.

Martin, R., & Hewstone, M. (2008). Majority versus minority influence, message processing, and attitude change: The source-context-elaboration model. In M. P. Zanna (Ed.), *Advances in experimental social psychology* (Vol. 40, pp. 237–326). San Diego, CA: Elsevier.

Martin, R., & Hewstone, M. (Eds.) (2010). *Minority influence and innovation: Antecedents, processes and consequences.* New York, NY: Psychology Press.

Mason, W. R., Conrey, F. R., & Smith, E. R. (2007). Situating social influence processes: Dynamic, multidirectional flows of influence within social networks. *Personality and Social Psychology Review, 11,* 279–300.

Milgram. S. (1974). *Obedience to authority: An experimental view.* New York, NY: Harper & Row.

Morrison, K. R., & Miller, D. T. (2008). Distinguishing between silent and vocal minorities: Not all deviants feel marginal. *Journal of Personality and Social Psychology, 94,* 871–882.

Moscovici, S. (1976). *Social influence and social change.* London, UK: Academic Press.

Moscovici, S. (1980). Toward a theory of conversion behavior. In L. Berkowitz (Ed.), *Advances in experimental social psychology* (Vol. 13, pp. 209–239). San Diego, CA: Academic Press.

Moscovici, S. (1994). Three concepts: Minority, conflict, and behavioral style. In S. Moscovici, A. Mucchi-Faina, & A. Maass (Eds.), *Minority influence* (pp. 233–251). Chicago, IL: Nelson-Hall.

Moscovici, S., & Faucheux, C. (1972). Social influence, conformity bias, and the study of active minorities. In L Berkowitz (Ed.), *Advances in experimental social psychology* (Vol. 6, pp. 149–202). New York, NY: Academic Press.

Mugny, G. (1982). *The power of minorities.* London, UK: Academic Press.

Mugny, G., Butera, F., Sanchez-Mazas, M., & Pérez, J. A. (1995). Judgments in conflict: The conflict elaboration theory of social influence. In B. Boothe, R. Hirsig, A. Helminger, B. Meier, & R. Volkart (Eds.), *Perception—evaluation—interpretation: Swiss monographs in psychology* (Vol. 3, pp. 160–168). Bern, Switzerland: Huber.

Mullen, B. (1983). Operationalizing the effect of the group on the individual: A self-attention perspective. *Journal of Experimental Social Psychology, 19*, 295–322.

Nail, P. R. (1986). Toward an integration of some models and theories of social response. *Psychological Bulletin, 100*, 190–206.

Nail, P. R., MacDonald, G., & Levy, D. A. (2000). Proposal of a four-dimensional model of social response. *Psychological Bulletin, 126*, 454–470.

Nemeth, C. J. (1986). Differential contributions of majority and minority influence. *Psychological Review, 93*, 23–32.

Nemeth, C., Brown, K., & Rogers, J. (2001). Devil's advocate versus authentic dissent: Stimulating quantity and quality. *European Journal of Social Psychology, 31*, 707–720.

Nemeth, C. J., & Wachtler, J. (1983). Creative problem solving as a result of majority vs. minority influence. *European Journal of Social Psychology, 13*, 45–55.

Packer, D. J. (2008). On being both with us and against us: A normative conflict model of dissent in social groups. *Personality and Social Psychology Review, 12*, 50–72.

Pérez, J. A., & Mugny, G. (1996). The conflict elaboration theory of social influence. In E. H. Witte & J. H. Davis (Eds.), *Understanding group behavior: Small group processes and interpersonal relations* (Vol. 2, pp. 191–210). Mahwah, NJ: Erlbaum.

Phillips, K. W. (2003). The effects of categorically based expectations on minority influence: The importance of congruence. *Personality and Social Psychology Bulletin, 29*, 3–13.

Prislin, R., Boyle, S., Davenport, C., Farley, A., Jacobs, E., Michalak, J., … Xu, Y. (2011). On being influenced while trying to persuade: The feedback effect of persuasion outcomes to the persuader. *Social Psychological and Personality Science, 2*, 51–58.

Prislin, R., & Christensen, P. N. (2005a). Social change in the aftermath of successful minority influence. *European Review of Social Psychology, 16*, 43–73.

Prislin, R., & Christensen, P. N. (2005b). The effects of social change within a group on membership preferences: To leave or not to leave. *Personality and Social Psychology Bulletin, 31*, 595–609.

Prislin, R., & Crano, W. D. (2012). History of social influence research. In A. W. Kruglanski & W. Stroebe (Eds.), *Handbook of the history of social psychology* (pp. 321–339). New York, NY: Psychology Press.

Prislin, R., Levine, J. M., & Christensen, P. N. (2006). When reasons matter: Quality of support affects reactions to increasing and consistent support. *Journal of Experimental Social Psychology, 42*, 593–601.

Prislin, R, Sawicki, V., & Williams, D. K. (2011). New majorities' abuse of power: Effects of perceived control and social support. *Group Processes and Interpersonal Relations, 14*, 489–504.

Prislin, R., & Wood, W. (2005). Social influence in attitudes and attitude change. In D. Albarracin, B. Johnson, & M. P. Zanna (Eds.), *The handbook of attitudes* (pp. 671–705). Mahwah, NJ: Erlbaum.

Quiamzade, A., Mugny, G., Falomir-Pichastor, J. M., & Butera, F. (2010). The complexity of majority and minority influence process. In R. Martin & M. Hewstone (Eds.), *Minority influence and innovation: Antecedents, processes and consequences* (pp. 1–52). New York, NY: Psychology Press.

Raven, B. H., & Kruglanski, A. W. (1970). Conflict and power. In P. Swingle (Ed.), *The structure of conflict* (pp. 69–109). New York, NY: Academic Press.

Ross, L., Bierbrauer, G., & Hoffman, S. (1976). The role of attribution processes in conformity and dissent: Revisiting the Asch situation. *American Psychologist, 31,* 148–157.

Ross, L., Lepper, M., & Ward, A. (2010). History of social psychology: Insights, challenges, and contributions to theory and application. In S. T. Fiske, D. T. Gilbert, & G. Lindzey (Eds.), *Handbook of social psychology* (5th ed., Vol. 1, pp. 3–50). Hoboken, NJ: John Wiley.

Sakurai, M. M. (1975). Small group cohesiveness and detrimental conformity. *Sociometry, 38,* 340–357.

Schlenker, B. R. (1980). *Impression management: The self-concept, social identity, and interpersonal relations.* Monterey, CA: Brooks-Cole.

Schulz-Hardt, S., Brodbeck, F., Mojzisch, A., Kerschreiter, R., & Frey, D. (2006). Group decision making in hidden profile situations: Dissent as a facilitator for decision quality. *Journal of Personality and Social Psychology, 91,* 1080–1093.

Sherif, M. (1935). A study of some social factors in perception. *Archives of Psychology, 27,* (Whole No. 187), 1–60.

Smith, C. M., Tindale, R. S. (2010). Direct and indirect minority influence in groups. In R. Martin & M. Hewstone (Eds.), *Minority influence and innovation: Antecedents, processes and consequences* (pp. 263–284). New York, NY: Psychology Press.

Smith, C. M., Tindale, R. S., & Dugoni, B. L. (1996). Minority and majority influence in freely interacting groups: Qualitative versus quantitative differences. *British Journal of Social Psychology, 35,* 137–149.

Stang, D. J. (1976). Group size effects on conformity. *Journal of Social Psychology, 98,* 175–181.

Stroebe, W. (2010). Majority and minority influence and information processing: A theoretical and methodological analysis. In R. Martin & M. Hewstone (Eds.), *Minority influence and innovation: Antecedents, processes and consequence* (pp. 201–225). New York, NY: Psychology Press.

Tajfel, H., & Turner, J. C. (1986). The social identity theory of intergroup behavior. In S. Worchel & W. G. Austin (Eds.), *Psychology of intergroup relations* (2nd ed., pp. 7–24). Chicago, IL: Nelson Hall.

Tanford, S., & Penrod, S. (1984). Social influence model: A formal integration of research on majority and minority influence processes. *Psychological Bulletin, 95,* 189–225.

Thibaut, J. W., & Strickland, L. H. (1956). Psychological set and social conformity. *Journal of Personality, 25,* 115–129.

Tindale, R. S., Smith, C., Thomas, L. S., Filkins, J., & Sheffey, S. (1996). Shared representations and asymmetric social influence in small groups. In E. H. Witte & J. H. Davis (Eds.), *Understanding group behavior: Consensual action in small groups* (pp. 81–103). Hillsdale, NJ: Erlbaum.

Turner, J. C. (1991). *Social influence.* Pacific Grove, CA: Brooks/Cole.

van Knippenberg, D. (1999). Social identity and persuasion: Reconsidering the role of group membership. In D. Abrams & M. A. Hogg (Eds.), *Social identity and social cognition* (pp. 315–331). Malden, MA: Blackwell.

Walker, E. L., & Heyns, R. W. (1962). *An anatomy for conformity.* Englewood Cliffs, NJ: Prentice-Hall.

Wilder, D. A. (1977). Perception of groups, size of opposition, and social influence. *Journal of Experimental Social Psychology, 13,* 253–268.

Wilder, D. A. (1978). Homogeneity of jurors: The majority's influence depends upon their perceived independence. *Law and Human Behavior, 2,* 363–376.

Willis, R. H. (1963). Two dimensions of conformity-nonconformity. *Sociometry, 26,* 499–513.

Willis, R. H. (1965). Conformity, independence, and anticonformity. *Human Relations, 18,* 373–388.

Wood, W., Lundgren, S., Ouellette, J. A., Busceme, S., & Blackstone, T. (1994). Minority influence: A meta-analytical review of social influence processes. *Psychological Bulletin, 115,* 323–345.

Wood, W., Pool G, J., Leck K., & Purvis, D. (1996). Self-definition, defensive processing, and influence: The normative impact of majority and minority groups. *Journal of Personality and Social Psychology, 71,* 1181–1193.

7

Decision Making

R. SCOTT TINDALE, MARYBETH TALBOT, and RACHAEL MARTINEZ

*I*t has been common wisdom over the years that decisions made by groups will be better (or at least less bad) than decisions made by single individuals. Luckily, this common wisdom tends to be correct (Hill, 1982; Kerr & Tindale, 2004). There is now a very large literature demonstrating the *"Wisdom of Crowds"* (Suroweiki, 2004), or at least the performance advantage of groups over individuals. Thus, the fact that important decisions are often made by groups rather than individuals tends to be good for society and the institutions within which the decisions are made (Davis, 1980). However, there is also evidence that the superiority of groups is not a given (Janis, 1982; Kerr, MacCoun, & Kramer, 1996; Tindale, 1993). In many cases, groups have been shown to make disastrous decisions with deadly consequences (e.g., the Challenger explosion, Bay of Pigs incident, instances of ethnic cleansing, etc.; Forsyth, 2009, Nijstad, 2009; Tindale, Munier, Wasserman, & Smith, 2002). Until recently, the theories used to explain the good decisions and actions of groups have differed from those used to explain the poor decisions and actions. However, recent attempts to identify the basic principles underlying group decision making have begun to show that both good and bad decisions by groups may stem from the same underlying processes (Kerr & Tindale, 2004; Tindale, 2008). These processes, some adapted over many eons of human evolution, have served groups, and their members, well (Kameda & Tindale, 2006; see Van Vugt and Kameda, this volume). However, as human environments have changed, some of these basic processes have led to less than optimal if not disastrous consequences. In situations where the outcomes tend to be negative, these basic processes are not suited to the informational or motivational environment and therefore do not lead to superior performance. Thus, for both good and bad outcomes, the basic group processes remain largely the same, but the environments in which they occur differ in terms of the degree to which such processes are useful.

We have two main goals for this chapter. First, we attempt to provide a selective review of classic and recent theory and research on group decision making. Our main focus will be on recent theories and findings, though how this work developed from and informs earlier approaches will be included. In this context, we will also attempt to show that the quality of group decisions tends to follow from the degree to which basic motivational and information processing systems in groups match the environmental/situational constraints surrounding the decision. Research over the past two decades has emphasized, to a greater degree than earlier work, the motivational and information processing characteristics of groups, and our review will follow that trend. Finally, we will make some prescriptive statements about how and when groups should perform well naturally and what types of interventions or adaptations might be useful for helping groups perform better when their natural tendencies lead them astray.

A major theme of the chapter is "social sharedness" (Kameda, Tindale, & Davis, 2003; Tindale & Kameda, 2000). Social sharedness is the idea that task-relevant cognitions (broadly defined) that the members of a group have in common, or share, exert a greater influence on the group than do similar constructs that are not shared among the members. The cognitions that are shared can vary from preferences for decision alternatives or information about the alternatives to heuristic information processing strategies that the members cannot even articulate. However, the greater the degree of sharedness for a particular task relevant cognition, the greater the likelihood that it will influence the group decision. In general, we will argue that social sharedness is often adaptive and probably evolved as a useful aspect of living in groups (Kameda & Tindale, 2006). However, a shift in context in which the shared cognition is inappropriate to the current situation can lead groups to make poor decisions. We feel that dysfunctional sharedness is the key necessary condition for groupthink (Janis, 1982) and can help to explain how groups make bad decisions even when they have the information necessary to avoid them. One of the key benefits of diversity in groups (see Moreland, this volume) is to prevent dysfunctional sharedness.

Social sharedness works on many different levels and across a variety of domains. Much of the early work in group decision making used member preferences for particular decision alternatives as its basic starting point. We will summarize this work and discuss more recent ideas in this domain. However, much of the recent work on group decision making has focused more broadly on cognition and motivation. Thus, the majority of our discussion will focus on these constructs and how advances in relevant theory and research have changed our perceptions of how groups make decisions in a variety of contexts. Finally, we will attempt to synthesize what we currently know and to point to areas where greater investigative efforts are needed.

COMBINING PREFERENCES

Early work on group decision making tended to focus on the distribution of initial member preferences and how such preferences get combined into a group, or collective, response (Davis, 1969, 1973; Steiner, 1972). This is known as the "combinatorial approach" to group decision making (Davis, 1982). One of the earliest and most influential papers in this tradition proposed that groups should be able to choose the best, or correct, choice alternative if at least one of the members prefers that alternative at the beginning of group discussion (Lorge & Solomon, 1955). This model became known as "truth wins" (Steiner, 1972; Laughlin, 1980) since if "truth" is known by at least one member, it wins out as the group's final response. A number of scholars extended and refined Lorge and Solomon's model by attempting to describe various different ways in which members' preferences could be combined into a group decision (Smoke & Zajonc, 1962; Steiner, 1972). These extensions and refinements culminated in Davis's (1973) social decision scheme (SDS) theory, which provided a framework for modeling different combination processes for different group sizes and member preference distributions.

Group Decision Tasks Involving Choices between Discrete Alternatives

SDS theory assumes that a set of discrete decision alternatives are known by the group members and that each member favors a particular alternative at the beginning of deliberation. It then attempts to describe the group consensus process using a matrix of conditional probabilities mapping different member preference distributions to different consensus choices made by the group. For example, in a six-person group choosing between two decision alternatives (e.g., guilty vs. not guilty in a jury), there are seven ways in which the group members might initially array themselves across the alternatives: 6 guilty and 0 not guilty, 5 guilty and 1 not guilty, ... 0 guilty and 6 not guilty. Given a population of potential group members in which some proportion favors one alternative over the other (e.g., 40% favor guilty and 60% favor not guilty), the likelihood of each initial preference distribution is estimable. The SDS matrix then maps each initial preference distribution to a distribution of group outcomes based on theory or a set of assumptions concerning the consensus process by which members' initial preferences are reconciled.

Table 1 contains two examples of SDS matrices. The "Proportionality" model assumes that the likelihood that a group will choose a particular alternative is proportional to the number of members initially favoring that alternative. This, in essence, equates the probability of the group choosing a particular alternative with the probability in the population of any given individual choosing that alternative. This model is often used as a baseline when comparing group and individual response tendencies, though it does provide a good fit to group decision data in some situations (Davis, 1982). In contrast, the "Majority

TABLE 7.1   Sample Social Decision Scheme Matrices: Proportionality and Majority Wins—Equiprobability Otherwise

Member Distribution		Proportionality		Maj. Wins—Equi. Other	
A	B	A	B	A	B
6	0	1.00	0.00	1.00	0.00
5	1	0.83	0.17	1.00	0.00
4	2	0.67	0.33	1.00	0.00
3	3	0.50	0.50	0.50	0.50
2	4	0.33	0.67	0.00	1.00
1	5	0.17	0.83	0.00	1.00
0	6	0.00	1.00	0.00	1.00

Note: Maj. Wins—Equi. Other. = Majority Wins—Equiprobability Otherwise.

Wins—Equiprobability Otherwise" model combines a main decision scheme (Majority Wins) with a sub-scheme (Equiprobability Otherwise) that holds when no majority exists (the sub-scheme is not necessary with an odd group size with 2 alternatives). This model predicts that the group will choose the alternative favored by a majority virtually all of the time. In cases where no majority exists (in this example, when the two alternatives each are supported by 3 group members), the model predicts that the two alternatives are equally likely (50%) to be chosen. Group decision making in many domains is accurately predicted by simple majority models such as this one (Tindale, Kameda, & Hinsz, 2003). Once the probability of each group member choosing a particular alternative is known, a binomial (or multinomial in cases with more than two decision alternatives) probability distribution can be used to estimate the probability of each preference distribution occurring, and then those probabilities are multiplied by the conditional probabilities in the matrix to predict the overall group decision probabilities (see Davis, 1973, 1982, and Stasser, Kerr, & Davis, 1989, for a more thorough discussion of the basic SDS theory).

Figure 1 shows the implications of the Proportionality and Majority Wins—Equiprobability Otherwise models across different individual preference probabilities. The Proportionality model predicts that group response probabilities will increase linearly as individual response probabilities increase. However, for the Majority Wins–Equiprobability Otherwise model, the decision alternative preferred by the most people is given a boost relative to the individual choice probability. When the likelihood of an individual choosing guilty in this case is less than .50, groups are especially unlikely to choose guilty. However, when the probability of an individual choosing guilty is higher than .50, groups are especially likely to choose guilty. Thus, the preference that is *shared* by the greatest number of group members is advantaged at the group level. Majority models (and plurality models when there are more than two response alternatives) predict this "shared preference," or "faction size," effect, and there is a large body of empirical evidence that supports its existence (see Tindale et al., 2003; Kameda et al., 2003 for reviews).

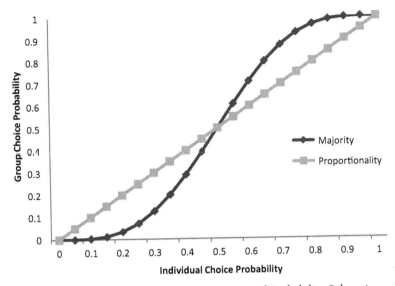

Figure 7.1   Proportionality and Majority Wins—Equal Probability Otherwise model predictions as a function of individual member choice probability

One of the key aspects of majority/plurality processes is that they tend to exacerbate in the group distribution those response tendencies that are prevalent at the individual level. Thus, in situations where the outcome of a decision can be defined as good or bad (or at least better or worse) by some criteria, a majority/plurality process could lead groups to make better decisions than the average individual when individuals tended toward the "good" response alternative. However, exactly the same process could lead groups to make worse decisions than the average individual when individual preferences tended in that direction. Since the basic majority/plurality process pushes the group in the direction initially favored by most of its members, it can lead to either good or poor decisions, depending on how members initially lean.

Fortunately, it appears that majority/plurality processes tend to work quite well in many natural decision settings involving groups (Hastie & Kameda, 2005; Sorkin, Hays, & West, 2001; Sorkin, West, & Robinson, 1998). Hastie and Kameda compared a variety of different ways groups could choose to move forward in an uncertain environment with many different response options. Overall, they found that a simple majority/plurality process (i.e., going with the alternative with the greater degree of support) was more accurate than any other decision rule with similar computational complexity. Majority models even did better than best member models (going with the alternative preferred by the person whose choices have been most accurate in the past) and performed similarly to models that required much greater levels of computation (e.g., weighted averaging models based on past performance). Hastie and Kameda argued that the generally high levels of accuracy combined with the low computational load may explain why majority processes are so pervasive in social aggregates. In a similar vein, Sorkin et al. (2001) developed a signal detection model of group performance and found that optimal group performance based on weighting individual members by their decision accuracy is only marginally better than using a majority/plurality process and that majorities tended to perform very close to optimal levels. Using these same models, Sorkin and his colleagues also showed that simple majorities tend to perform better than "super" majorities (those requiring 60% or 67% member agreement to reach a consensus) (Sorkin et al., 1998). Thus, although majority/plurality processes can both attenuate and exacerbate errors in group decision making, in most natural environments they tend toward the former.

Group Decision Tasks Involving Ratings or Estimations

Majority/plurality models are well defined when decision alternatives are discrete and groups are asked to choose one of the possible alternatives. However, many group decision tasks require groups to reach consensus on a point along a continuum (e.g., amount of money to invest or an estimation of the likelihood of some event) where it is unlikely that members' specific positions will overlap. Thus, majority/plurality models of group choice are not appropriate for groups making ratings or estimations (Stasser & Dietz-Uhler, 2001). Although a variety of models can be (and have been) applied to these types of situations (see Grofman & Owen, 1986; Hinsz, 1999, for examples), we will focus mainly on three that have received a reasonable amount of empirical support.

One of the most basic models of group judgment is a simple arithmetic average. Assuming each group member starts discussion with a well defined preference point, and assuming each member is equally influential, the mean of the initial distribution seems a reasonable compromise. A number of studies have found that a simple averaging model provides a decent approximation of final group outcomes (Graesser, 1982; Gigone & Hastie, 1993), especially when groups are making multiple judgments in a limited timeframe. Interestingly, a simple average of the initial member preferences is also quite accurate in objective terms (Wallsten, Budescu, Erev, & Diederich, 1997). Much like a sample mean tends to better estimate the population mean than does any single estimate, the average of multiple members' judgments will often better reflect the true score (if one exists) than will any of the individual member's estimates. Wallsten et al. have shown that the average of members' judgments tends to become close to asymptotically accurate even with group sizes as small as six.

Another model that has fared well empirically is the median model (Black, 1958; Davis, Au, Hulbet, Chen, & Zaroth, 1997; Crott, Szilvas, & Zuber, 1991; Laughlin, 2011a, 2011b). Quite often, means and medians are quite similar, but medians tend to be less sensitive to outliers. Thus, in cases where median models are accurate representations of the group process, group members with deviant positions tend to exert little if any influence on the final group outcome.

Black's (1958) work on social choice models showed that median positions form equilibria under certain circumstances and thus are likely to be stable group choice outcomes. His Median Voter Theorem posited that when member preference curves are single peaked (i.e., each member has a single best point along the response continuum and a member's evaluation of other points on the continuum are relatively lower as a function of their distance from that best point), the median of the members' initial preferences is the most stable outcome (see Laughlin, 2011b, for a more thorough discussion of social choice models generally). Crott et al. (1991) showed that a median model could explain group polarization and provided a very good fit to group consensus on choice dilemma items. Davis et al. (1997) also found a median model to provide a good fit to damage award judgments by mock civil juries.

Davis (1996) also derived a group consensus model for continuous response dimensions called the Social Judgment Schemes (SJS) model. The model assumes that the amount of influence a particular group member has on the final group response is an inverse exponential function of the sum of the distances from that member's position to all other members' positions. Thus, members who are most similar to other members on the response dimension have greater influence on the final group response than do members whose preferences are less similar to other members overall (see Davis, 1996, and Kameda et al., 2003, for a more formal discussion of the model). The model is similar to a median model in that it under-weights deviant or outlying positions. It differs from a median model in that all group members get at least some influence in the final decision. Research has generally supported its viability in a number of group decision settings (Davis et al., 1997; Ohtsubo, Masuchi, & Nakanishi, 2002; Hulbert, Parks, Chen, Nam, & Davis, 1999) and also demonstrated its similarity to the median model (Davis et al., 1997).

Kameda et al. (2003; see also Tindale & Kameda, 2000) have argued that both the SJS model and the median model are similar to majority/plurality models in that they represent social sharedness at the preference level. On a continuous response dimension, members often will not have exactly the same preference. However, the SJS model explicitly gives more weight to members whose preferences share similar spaces on the dimension, and median models tend to do this as well, though less directly by basically ignoring outliers. Thus, the member preferences that share a relatively narrow region on the response dimension become quite influential, and the greater the degree of sharedness (the more members who all share the same general area of the response dimension) the more likely it is that the group's final response will be located within that region. Much like majority/plurality processes, both SJS and median models predict groups will outperform individuals when most members show a bias toward better or more accurate positions on the continuum. However, if the typical individual is biased toward a less optimal or accurate scale position, these models will exacerbate the bias and lead to group performance decrements (Kerr & Tindale, 2011).

Group Decision Making Without Interaction

The models and research discussed thus far have typically assumed interacting groups in which information and preference exchange tend to lead to median or majority supported outcomes. However, such models can also be used simply as aggregation algorithms without any member interaction at all (Kerr & Tindale, 2011). Quite often, group forecasting involves obtaining individual estimates from many people (usually experts) and then aggregating them statistically is some fashion (Wallsten et al., 1997). There is very little evidence that group discussion adds much in terms of accuracy in many decision situations, and there is some evidence that simple algorithms (e.g., averaging, majority wins) are more accurate and less variable. Group discussion can lead to high status or very talkative members biasing the group response toward their views. Such social processes lead to greater error variance relative to results produced by algorithms. Structured group decision systems (e.g., Delphi Technique, computerized decision support systems) can reduce such error variance and typically show no adverse effects, except reduced member satisfaction (Rohrbaugh, 1979; Adams, Roch, & Ayman, 2005). Recently, a number of studies have shown that group decision making based on market principles can lead to very accurate group decisions (Maciejovsky & Budescu, 2007; Wolfers & Zitzewitz, 2004). Group interaction in such systems involves bidding for shares of particular response alternatives. Members can watch the behavior of others and the relative share prices, but they do not interact in the typical sense of information exchange and negotiation. Such systems have been shown to be quite accurate and are becoming more prevalent in a number of decision environments (Wolfers & Zitzewitz, 2004).

SOCIALLY SHARED COGNITIONS

Shared Information

A major theme and dominant paradigm underlying much of the work on group decision making and performance over the past 25 years had its start with a paper by Stasser and Titus (1985). Using a paradigm called the "hidden profile," Stasser and Titus showed that information that was initially shared by all of the group members was much more likely to be brought up during group discussion and was much more influential in the final group decision than was information held by only one member. By giving all the positive information about an inferior alternative to all members, and dividing the greater amount of positive information about a superior alternative among the group members so that each member only has part of it, Stasser and Titus showed that groups rarely shared enough of the unshared information to allow the group to realize that their initial consensus alternative was not as good as one of the others they could choose. When all of the information was shared by all members, groups easily found the superior alternative. The "shared information" or "common knowledge" effect (Stasser and Titus, 1985; 1987; Gigone and Hastie, 1993), as it came to be called, has been replicated hundreds of times, and the hidden profile paradigm has dominated group decision making research ever since (see Brodbeck, Kerschreiter, Mojzisch, & Shulz-Hardt, 2007, for a review).

Probably the main reason the initial finding had such a profound impact on the field was that different information provided by different group members was seen as one of the key features of group processes that allowed groups to outperform individuals (Vinokur & Burnstein, 1974; Davis, 1969). Although there is now a fair amount of evidence that groups do in fact perform better if their members share their unique information (Winquist & Larson, 1998; Brodbeck et al., 2007), it is also quite clear that groups do not do this naturally in many settings (Stasser, 1999). The fact that shared, as opposed to unshared, information plays a much larger role in most group decision settings definitely changed the way most researchers thought about groups and led to many studies attempting to better understand the phenomenon and discover ways to increase information sharing in groups.

A number of complementary processes have been found to contribute to the shared information effect (see Brodbeck et al., 2007 for a review). One of the most important was proposed by Stasser and Titus (1985, 1987) in their original work. Using a basic binomial probability model, they showed that information that is widely shared has a greater chance of being brought up simply because more members can mention it. In contrast, information that is unique to a single member can only be divulged by that person. Later work also showed that information repetition can be explained in the same way (Larson, Christensen, Abbot, & Franz, 1996; Savadori, Van Swol, & Sniezek, 2001). However, other factors have also been shown to be important. For example, group processing goals affect how much unique information is shared. Groups with an accuracy, or problem solving, goal bring up more unique information (and more information generally) than groups with a consensus, or "closure," goal (Postmes, Spears, & Cihangir, 2001; Stewart & Stasser, 1995). Particularly when groups have consensus motivation, groups reach agreement quickly before all of the information is discussed. When a hidden profile is present, early consensus tends to form around the less optimal alternative (Karau & Kelly, 1992; Kelly & Karau, 1999; Kruglanski & Webster, 1996). Another contributing factor is that group members quite often form initial individual preferences for certain decision alternatives based on the information they have. Once this occurs, it biases the information that they share and prevents preference-inconsistent information from being discussed (Greitemeyer & Schulz-Hardt, 2003; Kerschreiter, Schulz-Hardt, Mojzisch, & Frey, 2008). Recent research has shown that simply knowing other group members' preferences can inhibit information sharing by forcing attention toward preferences rather than the information underlying them (Mojzisch& Schulz-Hardt, 2010). Research also shows that shared information is seen as more important and more valid that unshared information (Wittenbaum, Hubbell, & Zuckerman, 1999).

Most of the current research findings have been nicely encapsulated by Brodbeck et al. (2007) in their Information Asymmetries Model of group decision making. The model categorizes the various conditions that lead to poor information processing in groups into three basic categories. The first category, negotiation focus, encompasses the various issues surrounding initial member preferences. If groups view the decision making task mainly as a negotiation, members negotiating which alternative should be chosen tend to focus on alternatives and not on the information underlying them. Hastie, Penrod, and Pennington (1983) referred to this group process in juries as "verdict driven" (as opposed to "evidence driven"). The second category, discussion bias, encompasses those aspects of group discussion that tend to favor shared vs. unshared information (e.g., items shared by many members are more likely to be discussed). The third category, evaluation bias, encompasses the various positive perceptions associated with shared information (e.g., shared information is more valid, sharing shared information leads to positive evaluations by other group members). All three categories are good descriptions of typical group decision-making and can lead to biased group decisions and inhibit cross-fertilization of ideas and individual member learning (Brodbeck et al., 2007).

A key aspect of the Brodbeck et al. (2007) model is that the various aspects of information processing in typical groups only lead to negative outcomes when information is distributed asymmetrically across group members, as when a hidden profile is present. Although such situations do occur and groups can make disastrous decisions under such circumstances (Janis, 1982; Messick, 2006), they are not typical of most group decision environments. In situations where members have independently gained their information through experience, the shared information they have is probably highly valid and more useful than unique information or beliefs held by only one member. Thus, the fact that members share preferences and information in many group decision contexts is probably adaptive and has generally served human survival well (Hastie & Kameda, 2005; Kameda & Tindale, 2006). In addition, groups are often (but not always) sensitive to cues in the environment that indicate that information is not symmetrically distributed (Brauner, Judd, & Jacquelin, 2001; Stewart & Stasser, 1998). Although minorities often are not very influential in groups, if minority members have at their disposal critical information that others do not have and that implies the initial group consensus may be wrong, other group members will pay attention to them. And, as we will discuss later, minority members who favor superior alternatives in environments where the superiority can be demonstrated can be very persuasive and lead majorities to switch their preferences (Laughlin & Ellis, 1986).

Two other aspects of shared information in group decision making are worth noting. First, not only does bringing up shared information make one seem more informed and intelligent in a group (Wittenbaum et al., 1999), having a greater degree of shared information at one's disposal relative to other group members makes one more influential and more leader-like (Kameda, Ohtsubo, & Takezawa, 1997). Kameda et al. defined such a situation as "cognitive centrality" in that certain members are more central in the group's network of information due to their information having more overlap with information held by other members. Being more "cognitively central" in the group makes such members influential and leads other members to perceive them as leaders. Second, recent research has shown that asymmetric information distribution in groups can also lead to group indecision (Nijstad & Kaps, 2008; Nijstad, 2008). If negative information about decision alternatives is generally shared, whereas more positive information is unequally distributed across group members, groups often find none of the candidates acceptable even when one of the alternatives clearly would be acceptable if all of the information available to the group were considered (Nijstad & Kaps, 2008).

Given the pervasiveness of the shared information effect, a fair amount of research has focused on how to increase the likelihood that all relevant information is brought up during group discussion. One partial remedy is to make sure that groups have a record of all of the information present during group discussion (Sheffey, Tindale, & Scott, 1989; Sawyer, 1997). There is some recent evidence that group support systems can aid in this regard by allowing greater access to such information (Haseman & Ramamurthy, 2004). As noted earlier, groups that share an accuracy, or problem solving, orientation to the decision problem bring up more unique information and perform better than groups with a consensus orientation (Postmes et al., 2001; Stasser & Stewart, 1992; more on this topic will be discussed later under shared group motivation). Setting up a norm of information sharing or having a leader who encourages and stimulates information exchange throughout the process have shown promise in terms of greater information sharing and better performance (Larson, Foster-Fishman, & Franz, 1998). Also, instructing group members to avoid forming initial impressions or preferences, and not allowing such preferences if present to be shared early in the discussion, has also been shown to be helpful (Larson et al., 1998; Mojzisch et al., 2010). Setting up a transactive memory system (Wegner, 1986) where certain group members are responsible for certain types of information also has been shown to help groups process more information (Stasser, Vaughan, & Stewart, 2000). Groups that structure their tasks such that information is exchanged completely before any discussion of preferences or final decisions also tend to perform better (Brodbeck, Kerschreiter, Mojzisch, Frey, & Schulz-Hardt, 2002). The main things that seem to be important are a focus on information rather than preferences, memory aids or reduced information load per group member, and a focus on accuracy over consensus (Brodbeck et al., 2007).

Shared Task Representations and Mental Models

Specific pieces of information (and preferences) are not the only types of cognitions that group members can share (Resnick, Levine, & Teasley, 1991; Tindale & Kameda, 2000). Laughlin (1980, 1999) has argued that one of the reasons that groups are better problem solvers than are individuals is that group members often share a conceptual system that allows them to realize when a proposed solution is correct within that system. This shared conceptual system, or background knowledge, is what allows a minority member with a correct answer to influence a larger incorrect faction to change its preference to the correct alternative. Such situations are well described by SDS models called "Truth Wins" and "Truth Supported Wins" (Laughlin, 1980). Truth Wins predicts that any group that has at least one member with the correct answer will be able to solve the problem correctly (Lorge & Solomon, 1955; Laughlin, 1980). Truth Supported Wins argues that at least two members of the group must have the correct answer in order for the group to solve the problem correctly (Laughlin, 1980). For groups with more than 4 members, both models predict minority influence for minorities with the correct answer. Laughlin and Ellis (1986) proposed that such minority influence processes are likely to occur for demonstrable or "intellective" tasks (those that have a demonstrably correct solution) and that the shared conceptual system is a key component of demonstrability. For "judgmental" tasks (those without a demonstrably correct solution), majority/plurality processes are more likely to occur.

Tindale, Smith, Thomas, Filkins, and Sheffey (1996) argued that the shared conceptual system underlying demonstrability is but one instance of what they referred to as "shared task representations." They defined a shared task representation as "any task/situation relevant concept, norm, perspective, or cognitive process that is shared by most or all of the group members (Tindale et al., 1996, p. 84). "Task/situation relevant" means that the representation must have implications for the choice alternatives involved, and the degree to which a shared representation affects group decision processes and outcomes will vary as a function of its relevance. Its influence will also vary by the degree to which it is shared among the group members—the greater the degree of sharedness (the more members who share it), the greater its influence. If no shared task representation exists, or if multiple conflicting representations are present, groups will tend to follow a symmetric majority/plurality process. However, when a shared task representation does exist, the group decision process will tend to become asymmetric in favor of alternatives that fit within or are supported by the representation. Under such conditions, majorities/pluralities favoring an alternative consistent with the shared representation are more powerful than are identically sized majorities/pluralities favoring alternatives that are not consistent with or supported by the representation. In addition, minorities favoring an alternative consistent with the shared representation can sometimes be more influential than majorities favoring an alternative inconsistent with the shared representation.

Although Laughlin's work (1980; Laughlin & Ellis, 1986) is probably the strongest example of the effects of shared representations, a number of other potent examples exist. For example, much of the work on mock-jury decision making (Davis, 1980; MacCoun & Kerr, 1988; Tindale, Nadler, Krebel, & Davis, 2001) has shown that "not guilty" is an easier verdict to defend than "guilty". In other words, majorities favoring guilty are less successful than are majorities favoring not guilty. In addition, juries that are evenly divided between guilty and not guilty, and even some juries with a sizable minority favoring not guilty, reach a not guilty verdict much of the time (MacCoun & Kerr, 1988; Tindale, Davis, Vollrath, Nagao, & Hinsz, 1990). MacCoun and Kerr showed that this asymmetry toward not guilty only occurs when juries are provided with a "reasonable doubt" verdict criterion. Tindale et al. (1996) argued that the reasonable doubt criterion serves as a shared task representation that tells jurors that they should look for and pay attention to reasonable doubts, and if they exist, they should vote not guilty. More recent research has shown that religion can also work as a shared task representation. Smith, Dykema-Engblade, Walker, Niven, and McGough (2000) showed that minorities against the death penalty were persuasive in altering majority positions on the issue when they framed their arguments in terms of religion ("Thou shalt not kill"), where as other types of arguments were ineffective. The shared religious orientations of the group members provided a context within which religious arguments could be very effective even though they conflicted with the majority's initial preference.

A number of studies have shown that individual decision biases can act as shared task representations, unexpectedly leading groups to perform worse in certain decision situations than comparable single individuals. Tindale (1989) showed that biased feedback meant to induce a conservative (high criterion) promotion strategy in a job situation led minorities favoring the option to not promote an employee to win out over majorities favoring the option to promote. Tindale (1993) also showed that groups will exacerbate typical errors tendencies found at the individual level. Kahneman, Slovic, and Tversky (1982) describe how individuals often violate the rules of probability when making intuitive judgments that involve probabilities. For example, individuals sometimes estimate the likelihood of conjunctive events (e.g., Linda is a feminist and a bank teller) as greater than one or both of the elementary events involved in the conjunction (Linda is a feminist, Linda is a bank teller). Since the conjunction is a subset of the elementary events, such a judgment is inconsistent with the basic laws of probability. Tindale (1993) found that for conjunctive probability judgments where individuals are likely to make such errors, groups made even more errors. In addition, groups were more influenced by members who made errors than they were by members who avoided such errors. However, groups made fewer errors than individuals and did not show the asymmetric influence processes for conjunction problems that were not prone to individual errors.

Multiple studies have produced similar group error tendencies and asymmetric influence processes when comparing groups and individuals on problems where base rate underutilization is prevalent (Argote, Devadas, & Melone, 1990; Augustinova, Oberlé, & Stasser, 2005; Hinsz, Tindale, & Nagao, 2008). For these problems, groups exacerbate the individual tendency to focus on somewhat unreliable case-specific information (e.g., the witness said the car in the hit-and-run accident on a dark night was green but was only correct in color judgments 80% of the time in a simulated test), and tend to ignore or underutilize base rate information (e.g., green cars are quite rare in this city). However, in situations where base rate information seems more valid than individuating information (the witness was correct only 20% of the time in the simulated test), groups are more likely to use it than are individuals (Hinsz et al., 2008). An interesting aspect of these results is that the group members do not realize they share a particular biased approach to the problems and often do not discuss strategies. Consensus simply tends to form more often around those alternatives that are consistent with the bias than alternatives that are not consistent with the bias.

Although realizing that a particular task representation is shared is not necessary for the asymmetric influences processes to emerge, there is evidence that a shared realization that all members share a particular approach or orientation to a problem can increase the likelihood that it is used effectively by the group. Van Ginkel and van Knippenberg (2008), using a hidden profile paradigm, manipulated whether members had an "information sharing" or a "consensus" representation of the task and also whether the task representations were shared or unshared. In addition, some groups knew what the other members' task representations were while other groups had no such shared meta-knowledge. Groups that shared an information sharing representation, and knew that they shared it, performed better than groups that simply shared the representation but did not collectively realize it. In a separate study by van Ginkel, Tindale, and van Knippenberg (2009), the investigators found that group reflexivity (allowing groups to think about and reflect on the task before or during performance: Carter & West, 1998; Schippers & Edmondson, 2006) helped groups to form appropriate shared task representations and also helped them to use task representations that they already shared. It is possible that this type of shared meta-knowledge allowed group members to feel safer in sharing information because they knew that all members were expected to share information. This is consistent with research on trust in groups in which trust and familiarity among group members allow them to share information and defend their positions more effectively (Cronin & Weingart, 2008).

Much of the work demonstrating the effects of shared task representations has involved ad hoc groups in which the shared background knowledge or approach to the task was acquired from members' prior experiences or shared environments. However, groups can create shared structures for defining how the group operates and approaches its task. Such structures are typically referred to as group-level or shared mental models (Rentsch & Hall, 1994; Cannon-Bowers, Salas, & Converse, 1993; Hinsz, 1995). Mental models refer to mental representations of the task and the behaviors associated with performing the task (Rouse & Morris, 1986). At the group level, mental models also involve roles and interdependencies among group members. Cannon-Bowers et al. (1993) differentiated between task models and team models. Task models involve the various steps involved in the task and the resources (e.g., equipment) necessary to accomplish it. Group, or team, models involve the information and skills that members have that are relevant to the task and the ways in which their skills and behaviors must be coordinated in order to move efficiently toward task completion. Team mental models can enhance performance to the degree that the models are accurate and the members all share the same model. Team training on both task and team models tends to improve performance by insuring that all aspects of both models are shared (Weiner, Kanki, & Helmreich, 1993; Helmreich, 1997). Such performance enhancements have been shown for cockpit crews on jetliners and surgery teams in hospitals.

However, sharedness for either the task or group model will only enhance performance to the degree that the model is accurate. Stasser and Augustinova (2008) has shown that distributed decision situations often produce better outcomes if information is simply sent up through the system by each group member without requiring any type of intermediary judgments by others. However, many groups assume that allowing judgments from various members is useful and thus use such a model to guide their behavior. Although aggregate judgments by many actors with different types and amount of information tend to be more accurate than judgments made by single individuals (Kerr & Tindale, 2011), in distributed systems where each member has only one type of information, asking all of the members to make judgments adds noise to the system. In addition, research has shown that it is better for members not to know that others might have the same information that they do because it reduces their feelings of criticality and decreases the likelihood that they will send all of their relevant information forward. Tschan et al. (2009) have shown that critical information easily available to emergency medical teams is often overlooked because each member assumes that someone else would have discovered and presented the information if it was relevant. Thus, intuitive mental models shared by group members can inhibit performance if they are inaccurate in terms of the task or if they lead to decreased information sharing. Once again, although shared mental models often tend to improve group decision making, they can also lead to poor decisions when the model that is shared is inappropriate for the particular decision context.

SHARED MOTIVATIONS IN GROUPS

Motivation in groups has been a topic of interest in social psychology since its earliest days as a field of inquiry (Triplett, 1898). Many studies have focused on how groups affect the amount of effort expended by their members, and both motivation gains and losses have been demonstrated (Williams & Karau, 1991; Kerr & Tindale, 2004; Weber & Hertel, 2007). Motivation has also been an important topic in group, as well as individual, decision making, and until recently the basic motivational assumption was hedonism. Many models of collective decision making use basic game theoretic, or utility maximization, principles to explain how members both choose initial preferences and move toward consensus (Kahn & Rapoport, 1984). Thus, much of the early work on group decision making tended to treat individual group members as players in a utility maximization game (Budescu, Erev, & Zwick, 1999). Game theory approaches are quite prevalent and also quite useful for understanding social behavior (Kameda & Tindale, 2006), but other motives more associated with the group level of analysis have also been found to be important (Tajfel & Turner, 1979;

Levine & Kerr, 2007). In addition, many of these motivations were discovered because social behavior did not follow game theoretic expectations (Tajfel, 1981; Dawes, van de Kragt, & Orbell, 1988).

Probably the most heavily researched of these more recent motives involves social identity (Hogg & Abrams, 1988; Tajfel & Turner, 1979). Since social identity theory is covered in depth in another chapter in this volume (see Abrams), we will focus only on one particular motive derived from the theory—the ingroup bias (Hogg & Abrams, 1988). There is now substantial evidence that when group members think about themselves as a group (and thus share a social identity), they begin to behave in ways that protect the group from harm or enhance its overall welfare. Many of the implications of this bias are positive for the group, but there are situations where it prevents the group from making good decisions. For example, groups are more likely than individuals to lie about preferences and resources in a negotiation setting (Stawiski, Tindale, & Dykema-Engblade, 2009). Probably the most prominent example in which protecting or enhancing the group's welfare leads to less than optimal decisions is the inter-individual-intergroup discontinuity effect (Schopler & Insko, 1992; Wildschut, Pinter, Vevea, Insko, & Schopler, 2003). This effect was initially demonstrated by McCallum et al. (1985) in research comparing individuals to groups playing a prisoner's dilemma game. The prisoner's dilemma game is a mixed motive situation in which the dominant, or individually rational, response is not to cooperate with the other player. However, when both players make the non-cooperative choice, they both do poorly. The only collectively rational choice is for both players to cooperate, which leads to the greatest collective payoff and to moderate positive gains for each player. When two individuals play the game and are allowed to discuss the game before making choices, they end up cooperating more than 80% of the time. However, when two groups play the game and each group must choose between cooperation and non-cooperation, groups quite often choose not to cooperate. Over multiple plays of the game, groups end up locked in the mutual non-cooperation payoff and earn far lower payoffs compared to the inter-individual situation. This effect has been replicated many times using different types of mixed motive game structures and different sized groups (see Wildschut et al., 2003, for a review).

Insko and colleagues (Insko, Schopler, Hoyle, Dardis, & Graetz, 1990) have shown that both fear and greed are important when groups play these types of games. Groups, more than individuals, tend to be fearful of being taken advantage of by the other player. However, even when playing the game against a single individual, groups still are more likely to choose non-cooperation, thinking they can take advantage of the more cooperative individual (Morgan & Tindale, 2002; McGlynn, Harding, & Cottle, 2009). Thus, groups both protect themselves by choosing non-cooperation but also attempt to insure that they do as well or better than the other player. Interestingly, there is little evidence that, in the intergroup context, the effect stems from wanting to hurt the outgroup. Recent studies by Halevy, Bornstein, and Sagiv (2008) show that in games that include a choice that only aids the ingroup and has no effect on the outgroup, groups virtually always choose this option over options that only hurt the out-group or that both aid the ingroup and hurt the outgroup.

Morgan and Tindale (2002) showed that the effect is at least partly due to asymmetries in the influence processes among the group members, much like those found for shared task representations. Prior to making a group choice as to whether to cooperate or not, all group members were asked to privately note their individual preferences. Although preferences for cooperation were slightly lower when playing against a group, most individual members favored coopera-tion regardless of the type of opponent. Thus, most of the groups entered the discussion with majorities favoring cooperation. However, minorities favoring non-cooperation were quite persuasive and won out over cooperative majorities two-thirds of the time. Moreover, majorities favoring non-cooperation virtu-ally never lost to minorities favoring cooperation. Tindale (2008) argued that the shared motivation to protect or enhance the group (the group protection/enhancement norm) acted much like other shared task representations and made the non-cooperative response easier to defend because it was consistent with the shared motivation.

Recent work on shared motivations in decision-making groups has begun to use theories of individual motivations, or goal orientations, to help under-stand how such orientations influence group processes and outcomes (De Dreu, Nijstad, & van Knippenberg, 2008; Molden, Lucas, Topper, & Murnighan, 2009). One theory that has begun to prove useful is Higgins's (1999) regulatory focus theory. Higgins argues that there are two general motivational orientations that people use to guide their behavior. Promotion focus is associated with striv-ing for rewards and gains in the environment and tends to lead to risky behavior. Prevention focus is associated with striving for safety and security concerns and tends to lead to conservative behavior. Levine, Higgins, and Choi (2000) manipu-lated either a gain or loss focus in groups and then observed whether group members would begin to converge on similar task strategies over time. Their results showed that group members' strategies did converge and become more similar over trials of a recognition memory task. In addition, the convergence moved toward more risky strategies for promotion focused groups and toward more conservative strategies for prevention focused groups. Molden et al. (2009) argued that prevention focused groups, as opposed to promotion focused groups, should be more concerned with protecting and securing the group through fol-lowing group norms and obligations to other group members. Thus, in mixed motive situations, members of prevention focused groups should be more likely to donate to the group and view equality of outcomes across group members as more important. Across five studies, this is exactly what they found. Prevention focused groups showed higher contributions to public goods and made more equal allocations in trust and dictator games than did promotion focused groups. These effects were mediated by increased concerns for cooperation and fairness when prevention, as opposed to promotion, focus was initiated.

De Dreu, Nijstad, and van Knippenberg (2008) developed a model of group judgment and decision-making based on the combination of epistemic and social motives. Called the "motivated information processing in groups" model (MIP-G), the model argues that information processing in groups is better understood by incorporating two orthogonal motives; high vs. low epistemic motivation, and pro-social vs. pro-self motivation. Earlier work on negotiation had shown that negotiators who share both high epistemic motivation and a pro-social orientation were better able to find mutually beneficial tradeoffs and reach better integrative agreements as compared to negotiators with any other combination of motives (De Dreu & Carnevale, 2003; De Dreu, 2010). Recent research now shows that the same appears to hold true for groups working cooperatively to solve a problem or make a decision. According to the model, high epistemic motivation involves a goal to be accurate or correct, which should lead to deeper and more thorough information search and analysis (Kruglanski & Webster, 1996). Work on the information sharing effects has consistently demonstrated that instilling a goal of accuracy or defining the task in terms of solving a problem both increase information sharing (Postmes et al., 2001; Stasser & Stewart, 1992). Members who are high in prosocial motivation helps to insure that all types of information held by each member are likely to be disseminated, rather than just information supporting the position held by the member. Recent research showing that members who focus on preferences rather than information impede information sharing is quite consistent with this assertion (Mojzisch & Schulz-Hardt, 2010). The model predicts that group information processing will only approach optimal levels when group members are high on both epistemic motivation and pro-social orientation. This is because that is the only combination that produces both systematic and thorough processing of information in an unbiased manner. Although the model is fairly recent, it does a good job of explaining a number of well replicated findings and has fared well in the few direct attempts to test it (Bechtoldt, De Dreu, Nijstad, & Choi, 2010; De Dreu, 2007).

IMPLICATIONS AND FUTURE DIRECTIONS

One of the main implications of this review is that group decision making theory and research is alive and well. Research from various disciplines and vantage points has both clarified traditional findings and helped to develop new theoretical perspectives. One of the most important new perspectives encompasses the return and expansion of motivational concepts in relation to how groups make decisions. Much of the work in the 1980's and 1990's revolved around the new paradigm (at the time) of groups as information processors (Hinsz, Tindale, & Vollrath, 1997; Larson & Christensen, 1993). Although this work revolutionized our understanding of how groups actually use and share information when trying to reach consensus, motivational issues remained in the background. However, recent reviews (Wittenbaum, Hollingshead, & Botero, 2004) and new theoretical directions (De Dreu, Nijstad, & van Knippenberg, 2008; Halevy et al., 2008) have brought motivation back to its proper and prominent place for understanding group decision making. In addition, this work has begun to reunite research on negotiation and bargaining with work on more cooperatively oriented groups. Group members who start with different ideas based on different information and who attempt to reach consensus may not be all that dissimilar to groups in which conflicts are more resource than idea based (De Dreu, 2010). Finding that the same set of shared motivations leads to both better integrative solutions and better collective decisions should help to develop new theoretical innovations in both topic areas.

Another overarching theme in this review is that most groups follow some very basic processes when trying to reach consensus. These basic processes are typically well suited to collective endeavors, but in some cases can lead to disastrous results. Thus, we do not need different theories to understand how and when groups do well versus poorly (e.g., Janis, 1982). Although "Groupthink" is now embedded in our cultural milieu and will probably remain with us for the foreseeable future, we hope that group decision researchers will no longer feel the need explain poor group decisions as unnatural or reflecting dysfunctional processes (Baron, 2005). In decision making groups, majorities often win, group members conform to salient group norms, shared knowledge is relied upon, shared perspectives or strategies predominate, and shared motives for protection and enhancement produce ingroup favoritism. Such processes often stem from natural adaptations to group life (Kameda & Tindale, 2006; Brewer & Caporael, 2006) and often serve groups well. However, in our current multicultural and mega-informational environment, some of these processes lead to dysfunctional behaviors and less-than-desirable outcomes.

The notion that poor group decision outcomes can flow from quite natural group processes is not to say that such outcomes are foregone conclusions. We now have a fairly good understanding of how groups process information and how appropriate group composition and process interventions can reduce or prevent decision failures. Brodbeck et al. (2007) outlined important aspects of group process and situational contexts that can lead to thorough vs. biased information processing. We now know that diversity of opinion and minority influence can be especially helpful in group settings to insure that members think through cognitively complex issues (Smith & Collings, 2009). Although some social sharedness is necessary to provide common ground, groups can only learn and innovate in situations where at least some unique information is available (Tindale, Stawiski, & Jacobs, 2008). In addition, recent work on motivation in groups demonstrates that groups will often avoid producing poor outcomes for other groups when such options are available (Halevy et al., 2008). And De Dreu et al. (2008) show that groups that strive for accuracy and prosocial outcomes process information more thoroughly and in a less biased fashion. Designing both groups and environments that take into account these informational and motivational attributes should help to avoid many of the pitfalls that natural group processes can engender. This is also where efforts on group decision support systems should be focused. Allowing group members to exchange and integrate large amounts of information in generally safe and trusting environments should be where technology can be most helpful.

Probably the dominant underlying theme of the review revolved around the notion of social sharedness (Tindale & Kameda, 2000). There is now a fair amount of evidence showing that preferences, information, motives, goals, strategies, etc., that are shared among group members tend to have an inordinate influence on group process and outcomes. However, much of the research has tended to focus on only one aspect of sharedness. Very little research has gone into how patterns of sharedness across these aspects of groups interact and influence one another. There is work showing that certain patterns of shared information can create shared preference structures and that shared motives can influence the types of information focused on by group members. However, little has been done to understand how sharedness of different types and potentially at different depths might affect many aspects of group functioning. Recent work by Echterhoff, Higgins, and Levine (2009) has focused on the concept of "shared reality" as a way of understanding the "saying is believing" effect. They posit that shared reality: (a) refers to inner states rather than overt behaviors; (b) involves a common view about a target entity; (c) serves both epistemic and relational goals; and (d) requires experiencing a successful connection to another's inner state (Echterhoff et al., 2009). Although focused on a very different topic domain, these criteria for shared reality may provide guidance toward a more thorough understanding of how the various dimensions of sharedness operate to influence group processes and outcomes. They may also prove useful for studying how groups change and mature overtime, a still understudied area of groups generally, and decision making groups specifically. Groups that share a common reality, due to extended interactions overtime or shared experiences, may reach consensus quite differently than groups composed of less familiar members with fewer shared experiences. Although the recent resurgence of small group research (Moreland, Hogg, & Hains, 1994) has taught us much about group decision processes, we still have much more to learn.

ACKNOWLEDGMENTS

Preparation of the chapter was supported by a grant from the National Science Foundation (BCS-0820344) to the first author.

REFERENCES

Adams, S. J., Roch, S. G., & Ayman, R. (2005). Communication medium and member familiarity: The effects on decision time, accuracy, and satisfaction. *Small Group Research, 36*, 321–353.

Argote, L., Devadas, R., & Melone, N. (1990). The base rate fallacy: Contrasting processes of group and individual judgment. *Organizational Behavior and Human Decision Processes, 46*, 296–310.

Augustinova, M., Oberlé, D., & Stasser, G. (2005). Differential access to information and anticipated group interaction: Impact on individual reasoning. *Journal of Personality and Social Psychology, 88*, 619–631.

Bechtoldt, M. N., De Dreu, C. K. W., Nijstad, B. A., & Choi, H.-S. (2010). Motivated information processing, epistemic social tuning, and group creativity. *Journal of Personality and Social Psychology, 99*, 622–637.

Black, D. (1958). *The theory of committees and elections.* Cambridge, UK: Cambridge University Press.

Brauner, M., Judd, C. M., & Jacquelin, V. (2001). The communication of social stereotypes: The effects of group discussion and information distribution on stereotypic appraisals. *Journal of Personality and Social Psychology, 81*, 463–471.

Brewer, M. B., & Caporael, L. R. (2006). An evolutionary perspective on social identity: Revisiting groups. In M. Schaller, J. A. Simpson, & D. T. Kenrick (Eds.) *Evolution and social psychology* (pp. 143–162). New York, NY: Psychology Press.

Brodbeck, F. C., Kerschreiter, R., Mojzisch, A., Frey, D., & Schulz-Hardt, S. (2002). The dissemination of critical, unshared information in decisionmaking groups: The effects of prediscussion dissent. *European Journal of Social Psychology, 32*, 35–56.

Brodbeck, F. C., Kerschreiter, R., Mojzisch, A., & Schulz-Hardt, S. (2007). Group decision making under conditions of distributed knowledge: The information asymmetries model. *Academy of Management Journal, 32*, 459–479.

Budescu, D. V., Erev, I., & Zwick, R. (Eds.). (1999). *Games and human behavior.* Mahwah, NJ: Lawrence Erlbaum Associates.

Cannon-Bowers, J. A., Salas, E., & Converse, S. A. (1993). Shared mental models in team decision making. In N. J. Castellan, Jr. (Ed.), *Individual and group decision making* (pp. 221–246). Hillsdale, NJ: Erlbaum.

Carter, S. M., & West, M. A. (1998). Team reflection, effectiveness, and mental health in BBC-TV production teams. *Small Group Research, 29*, 583–601.

Cronin, M., & Weingart, L. (2008). The differential effects of trust and respect on team conflict. In K. Behfar & L. Thompson (Eds.) *Conflict in organizational groups: New directions in theory and practice.* Chicago, IL: Northwestern University Press.

Crott, H. W., Szilvas, K., & Zuber, J. A. (1991). Group decision, choice shift, and group polarization in consulting, political and local political scenarios: An experimental investigation. *Organizational Behavior and Human Decision Processes, 49*, 22–41.

Davis, J. H. (1969). *Group performance.* New York, NY: Addison-Wesley.

Davis, J. H. (1973). Group decisions and social interactions: A theory of social decision schemes. *Psychological Review, 80*, 97–125.

Davis, J. H. (1980). Group decisions and procedural justice. In M. Fishbein (Ed.), *Progress in social psychology* (Vol. 1, pp. 157–229). Hillsdale, NJ: Erlbaum.

Davis, J. H. (1982). Social interaction as a combinatorial process in group decision. In H. Brandstatter, J. H. Davis, & G. Stocker-Kreichgauer (Eds.), *Group decision making* (pp. 27–58). London, UK: Academic Press.

Davis, J. H. (1996). Group decision making and quantitative judgments: A consensus model. In E. Witte & J. H. Davis (Eds.), *Understanding group behavior: Consensual action by small groups* (Vol. 1, pp. 35–59). Mahwah, NJ: Lawrence Erlbaum.

Davis, J. H., Au, W., Hulbert, L., Chen, X., & Zarnoth, P. (1997). Effect of group size and procedural influence on consensual judgment of quantity: The example of damage awards on mock civil juries. *Journal of Personality and Social Psychology, 73*, 703–718.

Dawes, R. M., van de Kragt, A. J., & Orbell, J. M. (1988). Not me or thee but we: The importance of group identity in eliciting cooperation in dilemma situations: Experimental manipulations. *Acta Psychologica, 68*, 83–97.

De Dreu, C. K. W. (2007). Cooperative outcome interdependence, task reflexivity, and team effectiveness: A motivated information processing perspective. *Journal of Applied Psychology, 92,* 628–638.

De Dreu, C. K. W. (2010). Social conflict: The emergence and consequences of struggle and negotiation. In S. T. Fiske, D. T. Gilbert, & H. Lindzey (Eds.). *Handbook of social psychology* (5th ed., Vol. 2, pp. 983–1023). New York, NY: Wiley.

De Dreu, C. K. W., & Carnevale, P. J. D. (2003). Motivational bases of information processing and strategy in conflict and negotiation. In M. P. Zanna (Ed.), *Advances in Experimental Social Psychology* (Vol. 35, pp. 235–291). New York, NY: Academic Press.

De Dreu, C. K. W., Nijstad, B. A., & Van Knippenberg, D. (2008). Motivated information processing in group judgment and decision making. *Personality and Social Psychology Review, 12,* 22–49.

Echterhoff, G., Higgins, E. T., & Levine, J. M. (2009). Shared reality: Experiencing commonality with others? Inner states about the world. *Perspectives on Psychological Science, 4,* 496–521.

Forsyth, D. R. (2009). *Group dynamics* (5th ed.). Belmost, CA: Wadsworth, Cengage Learning.

Gigone, D., & Hastie, R. (1993). The common knowledge effect: Information sharing and group judgment. *Journal of Personality and Social Psychology, 65,* 959–974.

Graesser, C. C. (1982). A social averaging theorem for group decision making. In N. H. Anderson (Ed.), *Contributions of information integration theory* (Vol. 2, pp. 1–40). New York, NY: Academic Press.

Greitemeyer, T., & Shulz-Hardt, S. (2003). Preference consistent evaluation of information in the hidden profile paradigm: Beyond group-level explanations for the dominance of shared information in group decisions. *Journal of Personality and Social Psychology, 84,* 322–339.

Grofman, B., & Owen, G. (Eds.) (1986). *Decision research* (Vol. 2). Greenwich, CT: JAI Press.

Halevy, N., Bornstein, G., & Sagiv, L. (2008). "In-group love" and "out-group hate" as motives for individual participation in intergroup conflict: A new game paradigm. *Psychological Science, 19,* 405–411.

Haseman, P. S., & Ramamurthy, K. (2004). Collective memory support and cognitive conflict group decision-making: An experimental investigation. *Decision Support Systems, 36,* 261–281.

Hastie, R., & Kameda, T. (2005). The robust beauty of majority rules in group decisions. *Psychological Review, 112,* 494–508.

Hastie, R., Penrod, S. D., & Pennington, N. (1983). *Inside the jury.* Cambridge, MA: Harvard University Press.

Helmreich, R. L. (1997). Managing human error in aviation. *Scientific American, 276,* 62–67.

Higgins, E. T. (1999). Promotion and prevention as a motivational duality: Implications for evaluative processes. In S. Chaiken & Y. Trope (Eds.), *Dual-process theories in social psychology* (pp. 503–525). New York, NY: Guilford Press.

Hill, G. W. (1982). Group versus individual performance: Are, N + 1 heads better than one? *Psychological Bulletin, 91,* 517–539.

Hinsz, V. B. (1995). Mental models of groups as social systems: Considerations of specification and assessment. *Small Group Research, 26,* 200–233.

Hinsz, V. B. (1999). Group decision making with responses of a quantitative nature:

The theory of social decision schemes for quantities. *Organizational Behavior and Human Decision Processes, 80,* 28–49.

Hinsz, V. B., Tindale, R. S., & Nagao, D. H. (2008). Accentuation of information processes and biases in group judgments integrating base-rate and case-specific information. *Journal of Experimental Social Psychology, 44,* 116–126.

Hinsz, V. B., Tindale, R. S., & Vollrath, D. A. (1997). The emerging conception of groups as information processors. *Psychological Bulletin, 121,* 43–64.

Hogg, M. A., & Abrams, D. (1988). *Social identification: A social psychology of intergroup relations and group processes.* London, UK: Routledge.

Hulbert, L. G., Parks, C. D., Chen, X., Nam, K., & Davis, J. H. (1999). The plaintiff bias in mock civil jury decision making: Consensus requirements, information format and amount of consensus. *Group Processes and Intergroup Relations, 2,* 59–77.

Insko, C. A., Schopler, J., Hoyle, R. H., Dardis, G. J., & Graetz, K. A. (1990). Individual–group discontinuity as a function of fear and greed. *Journal of Personality and Social Psychology, 58,* 68–79.

Janis, I. (1982). *Groupthink* (2nd ed.). Boston, MA: Houghton-Mifflin.

Kahn, J. P., & Rapoport, A. (1984). *Theories of coalition formation.* Hillsdale, NJ: Lawrence Erlbaum.

Kahneman, D., Slovic, P., & Tversky, A. (1982). *Judgment under uncertainty: Heuristics and biases.* New York, NY: Cambridge University Press.

Kameda, T., Ohtsubo, Y., & Takezawa, M. (1997). Centrality in socio-cognitive network and social influence: An illustration in a group decision making context. *Journal of Personality and Social Psychology, 73,* 296–309.

Kameda, T., & Tindale, R. S. (2004). Evolutionary/adaptive thinking as a meta-theory for systematic group research: An extended 'fungus-eater' approach. *Group Processes and Intergroup Relations, 7,* 299–304.

Kameda, T., & Tindale, R. S. (2006). Groups as adaptive devices: Human docility and group aggregation mechanisms in evolutionary context. In M. Schaller, J. A. Simpson, & D. T. Kenrick (Eds.) *Evolution and social psychology* (pp. 317–342). New York, NY: Psychology Press.

Kameda, T., Tindale, R. S., & Davis, J. H. (2003). Cognitions, preferences, and social sharedness: Past, present and future directions in group decision making. In S. L. Schneider & J. Shanteau (Eds.), *Emerging perspectives on judgment and decision research* (pp. 458–485). New York, NY: Cambridge University Press.

Karau, S. J., & Kelly, J. R. (1992). The effects of time scarcity and time abundance on group performance quality and interaction process. *Journal of Experimental Social Psychology, 28,* 542–571.

Kelly, J. R., & Karau, S. J. (1999). Group decision making: The effects of initial preferences and time pressure. *Personality and Social Psychology Bulletin, 255,* 1342–1354.

Kerr, N. L., MacCoun, R. J., & Kramer, G. P. (1996). Bias in judgment: Comparing individuals and groups. *Psychological Review, 103,* 687–719.

Kerr, N. L., & Tindale, R. S. (2004). Small group decision making and performance. *Annual Review of Psychology, 55,* 623–656.

Kerr, N. L., & Tindale, R. S. (2011). Group-based forecasting: A social psychological analysis. *International Journal of Forecasting, 27,* 14–40.

Kerschreiter, R., Schulz-Hardt, S., Mojzisch, A., & Frey, D. (2008). Biased information search in homogeneous groups: Confidence as a moderator of anticipated task requirements. *Personality and Social Psychology Bulletin, 34,* 679–691.

Kruglanski, A. W., & Webster, D. M. (1996). Motivated closing of the mind: "seizing" and "freezing." *Psychological Review, 103,* 263–283.

Larson, J. R., & Christensen, C. (1993). Groups as problem solving units: Toward a new meaning of social cognition. *British Journal of Social Psychology, 32,* 5–30.

Larson, J. R. Jr., Foster-Fishman, P. G., & Franz, T. M. (1998). Leadership style and the discussion of shared and unshared information in decision making groups. *Personality and Social Psychology Bulletin, 24,* 482–495.

Larson, J. R. Jr., Christensen, C., Abbot, A. S., & Franz, T. M. (1996). Diagnosing groups: Charting the flow of information in medical decision making teams. *Journal of Personality and Social Psychology, 71,* 315–330.

Laughlin, P. R. (1980). Social combination processes of cooperative, problem-solving groups on verbal intellective tasks. In M. Fishbein (Ed.), *Progress in social psychology* (Vol. 1, pp. 127–155). Hillsdale, NJ: Lawrence Erlbaum.

Laughlin, P. R. (1999). Collective induction: Twelve postulates. *Organizational Behavior and Human Decision Processes, 80,* 50–69.

Laughlin, P. R. (2011a). Social choice theory, social decision scheme theory, and group decision making. *Group Processes and Intergroup Relations, 14,* 63–80.

Laughlin, P. R. (2011b). *Group problem solving.* Princeton, NJ: Princeton University Press.

Laughlin, P. R., & Ellis, A. L. (1986). Demonstrability and social combination processes on mathematical intellective tasks. *Journal of Experimental Social Psychology, 22,* 177–189.

Levine, J. M., Higgins, E. T., & Choi, H. S. (2000). Development of strategic norms in groups. *Organizational Behavior and Human Decision Processes, 82,* 88–101.

Levine, J. M., & Kerr, N. L. (2007). Inclusion and exclusion: Implications for group processes. In A. E. Kruglanski & E. T. Higgins (Eds.), *Social psychology: Handbook of basic principles* (2nd ed., pp. 759–784). New York, NY: Guilford.

Lorge, I., & Solomon, H. (1955). Two models of group behavior in the solution of eureka-type problems. *Psychometrica, 20,* 139–148.

MacCoun, R., & Kerr, N. L. (1988). Asymmetric influence in mock jury deliberations: Juror's bias for leniency. *Journal of Personality and Social Psychology, 54,* 21–33.

Maciejovsky, B., & Budescu, D. V. (2007). Collective induction without cooperation? Learning and knowledge transfer in cooperative groups and competitive auctions. *Journal of Personality and Social Psychology, 92*(5), 854–870. doi: 10.1037/0022-3514.92.5.854

McCallum, D. M., Harring, K., Gilmore, R., Drenan, S., Chase, J., Insko, C. A., & Thibault, J. (1985). Competition between groups and between individuals. *Journal of Experimental Social Psychology, 21,* 310–320.

McGlynn, R. P., Harding, D. J., & Cottle, J. L. (2009). Individual-group discontinuity in group-individual interactions: Does size matter? *Group Processes and Intergroup Relations, 12,* 129–143.

Messick, D. M. (2006). Ethics in groups: The road to hell. In E. Mannix, M. Neale, & A. Tenbrunsel (Eds.), *Research on managing groups and teams: Ethics in groups* (Vol. 8). Oxford, UK: Elsevier Science Press.

Molden, D. C., Lucas, G. L., Topper, S., & Murnighan, K. (2009). *Motivations for promotion or prevention during social exchange: Effects on cooperation, reciprocity, and altruism.* Symposium address, Annual Meeting of the Society for Personality and Social Psychology, Tampa, FL.

Mojzisch, A., & Schulz-Hardt, S. (2010). Knowing others' preferences degrades the quality of group decisions. *Journal of Personality and Social Psychology, 98,* 794–808.

Moreland, R. L., Hogg, M. A., & Hains, S. C. (1994). Back to the future: Social psychological research on groups. *Journal of Experimental Social Psychology, 30,* 527–555.

Morgan, P. M., & Tindale, R. S. (2002). Group vs. individual performance in mixed motive situations: Exploring an inconsistency. *Organizational Behavior and Human Decision Processes, 87,* 44 65.

Nijstad, B. A. (2009). *Group performance.* New York, NY: Psychology Press.

Nijstad, B. A. (2008). Choosing none of the above: Persistence of negativity after group discussion and group decision refusal. *Group Processes and Intergroup Relations, 11* , 525–538.

Nijstad, B. A., & Kaps, S. C. (2008). Taking the easy way out: Preference diversity, decision strategies, and decision refusal in groups. *Journal of Personality and Social Psychology, 94,* 860–870.

Ohtsubo, Y., Masuchi, A., & Nakanishi, D. (2002). Majority influence processes in group judgment: Test of the social judgment scheme model in a group polarization context. *Group Processes and Intergroup Relations, 5,* 249–261.

Postmes, T., Spears, R., & Cihangir, S. (2001). Quality of decision making and group norms. *Journal of Personality and Social Psychology, 80,* 918–930.

Rentsch, J. R., & Hall, R. J. (1994). Members of great teams think alike: A model of team effectiveness and schema similarity among team members. *Advances in Interdisciplinary Studies of Work Teams, 1,* 223–261.

Resnick, L. B., Levine, J. M., & Teasley, S. D. (Eds.). (1991). *Perspectives on socially shared cognition.* Washington, DC: American Psychological Association.

Rohrbaugh, J. (1979). Improving the quality of group judgment: Social judgment analysis and the Delphi technique. *Organizational Behavior and Human Performance, 24,* 73–92.

Rouse, W. B., & Morris, N. M. (1986). On looking into the black box: Prospects and limits in the search for mental models. *Psychological Bulletin, 100,* 349–363.

Savadori, L., van Swol, L. M., & Sniezek, J. A. (2001). Information sampling and confidence within groups and judge advisor systems. *Communication Research, 28,* 737–771.

Sawyer, J. E. (1997). *Information sharing and integration in multifunctional decision-making groups.* Paper presented at the Society of Judgment and Decision Making Annual Meeting, Philadelphia, PA.

Schopler, J., & Insko, C. A. (1992). The discontinuity effect in interpersonal and intergroup relations: generality and mediation. In W. Stroebe & M. Hewstone (Eds.), *European Review of Social Psychology* (Vol. 3, pp. 122–151). Chichester, UK: John Wiley & Sons.

Schopler, J., Insko, C. A., Graetz, K. A., Drigotas, S. M., Smith, V. A., & Dhal, K. (1993). Individual-group discontinuity: Further evidence for mediation by fear and greed. *Personality and Social Psychological Bulletin, 19,* 419–431.

Sheffey, S., Tindale, R. S., & Scott, L. A. (1989). *Information sharing and group decisionmaking.* Paper presented at the Midwestern Psychological Association Annual Convention, Chicago, IL.

Schippers, M. C., & Edmondson, A. C. (2006, August). *The role of team reflection in team information processing.* Paper presented at the Annual Meeting of the Academy of Management, 2006 Atlanta, GA.

Smith, E. R., & Collings, E. C. (2009). Contextualizing person perception: Distributed social cognition. *Psychological Review, 166,* 343–364.

Smith, C. M., Dykema-Engblade, A., Walker, A., Niven, T. S., & McGough, T. (2000). Asymmetrical social influence in freely interacting groups discussing the death penalty: A shared representations interpretation. *Group Processes and Intergroup Relations, 3,* 387–401.

Smoke, W. H., & Zajonc, R. B. (1962). On the reliability of group judgments and decision. In J. H. Crisswell, H. Solomon, & P. Suppes (Eds.), *Mathematical methods in small group processes* (pp. 322–333). Stanford, CA: Stanford University Press.

Sorkin, R. D., Hays, C., & West R. (2001). Signal detection analysis of group decision making. *Psychological Review, 108,* 183–201.

Sorkin, R. D., West, R., & Robinson, D. E. (1998). Group performance depends on the majority rule. *Psychological Science, 9,* 456–463.

Stasser, G. (1999). A primer of Social Decision Scheme Theory: Models of group influence, competitive model-testing, and prospective modeling. *Organizational Behavior and Human Decision Processes, 80,* 3–20.

Stasser, G., & Augustinova, M. (2008). Social engineering in distributed decisionmaking teams: some implications for leadership at a distance. In S. Weisband (Ed.), *Leadership at a distance* (pp. 151–167). New York, NY: Lawrence Erlbaum Associates.

Stasser, G., Kerr, N. L., & Davis, J. H. (1989). Influence processes and consensus models in decision-making groups. In P. Paulus (Ed.), *Psychology of group influence* (2nd ed., pp. 279–326). Hillsdale, NJ: Lawrence Erlbaum.

Stasser, G., & Dietz-Uhler, B. (2001). Collective choice, judgment, and problem-solving. In M. Hogg & S. Tindale (Eds.) *Blackwell handbook of social psychology: Group processes* (Vol. 4, pp. 31–55). Oxford, UK: Blackwell Publishers.

Stasser, G., & Stewart, D. (1992). Discovery of hidden profiles by decisionmaking groups: Solving a problem versus making a judgment. *Journal of Personality and Social Psychology, 63,* 426–434.

Stasser, G., & Titus, W. (1985). Pooling of unshared information in group decision making: Biased information sampling during discussion. *Journal of Personality and Social Psychology, 48,* 1467–1478.

Stasser, G., & Titus, W. (1987). Effects of information load and percentage of shared information on the dissemination of unshared information during group discussion. *Journal of Personality and Social Psychology, 53,* 81–93.

Stasser, G., Vaughan, S. I., & Stewart, D. D. (2000). Pooling unshared information: The benefits of knowing how access to information is distributed among members. *Organizational Behavior and Human Decision Processes, 82,* 102–116.

Stawiski, S., Tindale, R. S., & Dykema-Engblade, A. (2009). The effects of ethical climate on group and individual level deception in negotiation. *International Journal of Conflict Management, 20,* 287–308.

Steiner, I. (1972). *Group process and productivity.* New York, NY: Academic Press.

Stewart, D. D., & Stasser, G. (1995). Expert role assignment and information sampling during collective recall and decision making. *Journal of Personality and Social Psychology, 69,* 619–628.

Stewart, D. D., & Stasser, G. (1998). The sampling of critical unshared information in decision-making groups: The role of an informed minority. *European Journal of Social Psychology, 23*, 95–113.

Suroweiki, J. (2004). *The wisdom of crowds.* New York, NY: Doubleday.

Tajfel, H. (1981). Social stereotypes and social groups. In J. C. Turner & H. Giles (Eds.), *Intergroup behaviour* (pp. 144–167). Oxford, UK: Blackwell.

Tajfel, H., & Turner, J. C. (1979). An integrative theory of intergroup conflict. In W. G. Austin & S. Worchel (Eds.), *The social psychology of intergroup relations* (pp. 33–47). Monterey, CA: Brooks/Cole.

Tindale, R. S. (1993). Decision errors made by individuals and groups. In N. Castellan, Jr. (Ed.), *Individual and group decision making: Current issues* (pp. 109–124). Hillsdale, NJ: Lawrence Erlbaum Associates.

Tindale, R. S. (2008). *The wisdom (an occasional lack thereof) of groups.* Presidential Address presented at the Midwestern Psychological Association Annual Convention, Chicago, IL.

Tindale, R. S., Davis, J. H., Vollrath, D. A., Nagao, D. H., & Hinsz, V. B. (1990). Asymmetrical social influence in freely interacting groups: A test of three models. *Journal of Personality and Social Psychology, 58*, 438–449.

Tindale, R. S., & Kameda, T. (2000). Social sharedness as a unifying theme for information processing in groups. *Group Processes and Intergroup Relations, 3*, 123–140.

Tindale, R. S., Kameda, T., & Hinsz, V. B. (2003). Group decision making. In J. Cooper & M. Hogg (Eds.), *Sage handbook of social psychology* (pp. 381–403). London, UK: Sage.

Tindale, R. S., Munier, C., Wasserman, M., & Smith, C. M. (2002). Group processes and the Holocaust. In L. Newman & R. Erber (Eds.), *Understanding genocide: The social psychology of the Holocaust* (pp. 143–161). New York, NY: Oxford University Press.

Tindale, R. S., Nadler, J., Krebel, A., & Davis, J. H. (2001). Procedural mechanisms and jury behavior. In M. A. Hogg & R. S. Tindale (Eds.), *Blackwell handbook in social psychology: Group processes* (pp. 574–602). Oxford, UK: Blackwell Publishers.

Tindale, R. S., Smith, C. M., Thomas, L. S., Filkins, J., & Sheffey, S. (1996). Shared representations and asymmetric social influence processes in small groups. In E. Witte & J. Davis (Eds.) *Understanding group behavior: Consensual action by small groups* (Vol. 1, pp. 81–103). Mahwah, NJ: Lawrence Erlbaum Associates.

Tindale, R. S., Stawiski, S., & Jacobs, E. (2008). Shared cognitions and group learning. In V. Sessa & M. London (Eds.), *Work group learning: Understanding, improving, and assessing how groups learn in organizations* (pp. 73–90). New York, NY: Lawrence Erlbaum Associates.

Triplett, N. (1898). The dynamogenic factors in pacemaking and competition. *Journal of Psychology, 9*, 507–533.

Tschan, F., Semmer, N. K., Gurtner, A., Bizzari, L., Spychiger, M., Breuer, M., & Marsch, S. U. (2009). Diagnostic accuracy, explicit reasoning, confirmation bias, and illusory transactive memory: A simulation study of group decision making in medical teams. *Small Group Research, 40*, 271–300.

van Ginkel, W., Tindale, R. S., & van Knippenberg, D. (2009). Team reflexivity, development of shared task representations, and the use of distributed information in group decision making. *Group Dynamics, 13*, 265–280.

van Ginkel, W. P., & van Knippenberg, D. (2008) Group information elaboration and group decision making: The role of shared task representations. *Organizational Behavior and Human Decision Process, 105*, 82–97.

Vinokur, A., & Burnstein, E. (1974). The effects of partially shared persuasive arguments on group induced shifts: A group problem solving approach. *Journal of Personality and Social Psychology, 29*, 305–315.

Wallsten, T. S., Budescu, D. V., Erev, I., & Diederich, A. (1997). Evaluating and combining subjective probability estimates. *Journal of Behavioral Decision Making, 10*, 243–268.

Weber, B., & Hertel, G. (2007). Motivation gains of inferior group members: A meta-analytical review. *Journal of Personality and Social Psychology, 93*(6), 973–993.

Wegner, D. M. (1986). Transactive memory: A contemporary analysis of the group mind. In B. Mullen & G. R. Goethals (Eds.), *Theories of group behavior* (pp. 185–208). New York, NY: Springer Verlag.

Weiner, E. L., Kanki, B., & Helmreich, R. L. (1993). *Cockpit resource management.* San Diego, CA: Academic Press.

Wildschut, T., Pinter, B., Vevea, J. L., Insko, C. A., & Schopler, C. A. (2003). Beyond the group mind: A quantitative review of the interindividual-intergroup discontinuity effect. *Psychological Bulletin, 129*, 698–722.

Williams, K. D., & Karau, S. J. (1991). Social loafing and social compensation: The effects of expectations of coworkers performance. *Journal of Personality and Social Psychology, 61*, 570–581.

Winquist, J. R., & Larson, J. R. (1998). Information pooling: When it impacts group decision making. *Journal of Personality and Social Psychology, 74*, 371–377.

Wittenbaum, G. M., Hollingshead, A. B., & Botero, I. C. (2004). From cooperative to motivated information sharing in groups: Moving beyond the hidden profile paradigm. *Communication monographs, 7*, 286–310.

Wittenbaum, G. M., Hubbell, A. P., & Zuckerman, C. (1999). Mutual enhancement: Toward an understanding of the collective preference for shared information. *Journal of Personality and Social Psychology, 77*, 967–978.

Wolfers, J., & Zitzewitz, E. (2004). Prediction markets. *Journal of Economic Perspectives, 18*(2), 107–126.

8

Performance

BERNARD A. NIJSTAD

INTRODUCTION

*T*here are different reasons why people form, join, or are assigned to groups, but an important one is to perform some task together. For example, students are assigned to groups to write an essay or research report together, teams in companies are formed to improve customer satisfaction, military teams perform operations on enemy territory, and groups of friends decide to organize a party together. Often, these groups are formed because their specific task cannot be accomplished by an individual working alone. At other times the task could in principle be done by individuals, but it is believed that performing it in a group is somehow more effective or efficient (or more fun). For groups of both kinds, the ultimate goal therefore is to perform well, and group performance is a topic that has been studied in social psychology since its beginnings (e.g., Ringelmann, 1913; Triplett, 1898).

In his seminal work on group performance, Ivan Steiner (1972) suggested that groups need two things to perform up to their potential (i.e., the level of performance they can hypothetically reach given their resources): sufficient motivation on the part of members to contribute to the group's performance and an adequate coordination of members' contributions. Reflecting this idea, this chapter is organized into two sections, one focusing on members' motivation and the other focusing on coordination among members. To reduce overlap with other chapters in this volume (e.g., the chapters on decision making, creativity, and leadership), this chapter mainly (but not exclusively) discusses basic research on performance of groups on relatively simple (oftentimes physical) tasks in the first section and more applied research on team performance in organizational or military contexts in the second section. In addition to reviewing classic work on motivation and coordination, the chapter also high-lights several strands of recent work (see Nijstad, 2009, for a more detailed review).

MOTIVATION, EVALUATION, AND GROUP PERFORMANCE

Three Early Studies

The study of the relation between motivation and group performance dates back to the late nineteenth century. One of the first studies was performed by Triplett (1898), who reported experiments on the effects of the presence of other group members on individual performance. He found that adolescents could spin fishing reels more quickly when working in co-acting pairs than when working alone. Triplett's finding that people perform *better* when work-ing in co-action situations has received much attention in the literature on social facilitation (e.g., Bond & Titus, 1983; Zajonc, 1965).

Ringelmann (1913) reported experiments in which he asked individuals and groups of different sizes to pull a rope as hard as they could. He found that group performance was much *worse* than would be expected based on individ-ual performance and that the effectiveness of groups decreased with group size. This inverse relation between group size and performance was later labeled the Ringelmann effect (Ingham, Levinger, Graves, & Peckham, 1974) and has received much attention in the literature on social loafing (e.g., Karau & Wil-liams, 1993; Latané, Williams, & Harkins, 1979).

Finally, Köhler (1926, 1927) asked his participants to lift weights as often as they could alone (using a weight of 41 kg) or in pairs (using an 82 kg weight). He systematically varied the ability of the dyad members and found that, when members were of moderately unequal ability, the dyad performed much *better* than expected (based on the individual abilities of the members). This effect was not found when dyad members were very similar or very dissimilar in ability. This so-called Köhler effect that people working together sometimes perform much better than expected has recently received substantial research attention (for a review, see Weber & Hertel, 2007).

The outcomes of these three classic studies differ dramatically: Triplett and Köhler found that people performed better when working together, whereas Ringelmann found that people performed worse in a group. However, it is clear that these findings are related, and several authors have noted parallels between the relevant studies (e.g., Harkins, 1987; Sanna, 1992; Weber & Hertel, 2007). In all the experiments, the tasks that people performed were fairly simple physi-cal tasks, in which performance largely depended on effort. Furthermore, in all the experiments, evaluation seemingly plays a crucial role (also Harkins & Jackson, 1985). Spinning fishing reels side-by-side implies that each individual's performance can easily be evaluated by comparing it to the co-actor's perfor-mance, and this makes people work harder. Pulling a rope together implies that one's efforts *cannot* be easily monitored or evaluated, and this makes people work less hard (i.e., social loafing). And when two people lift a weight together, it becomes very obvious who is the first to give up, making both people's performance easy to evaluate, and in this situation people work harder. Recent research has shed more light on the relations between evaluation, motivation, and group performance in the context of social facilitation, social loafing, and the Köhler effect.

Social Facilitation and Inhibition (SFI)

Zajonc's Drive Theory   Work on social facilitation and inhibition (SFI) examines how the presence of others (as audience or co-actors) influences the performance of a focal actor. Although Triplett (1898) found that people performed better in the presence of others (social facilitation), it has also been found that the presence of others can negatively impact the focal actor's performance (social inhibition; e.g., Baron, 1986; Zajonc, 1965). SFI has been extensively studied (for example, in 1983, Bond and Titus meta-analyzed 241 relevant studies). Despite its long history of scientific scrutiny, recent years have seen a number of publications reporting new insights regarding this phenomenon.

Theories of SFI address the question of why the presence of others sometimes improves an individual's performance, while at other times it has negative effects. Zajonc (1965, 1980) formulated the first theory to account for this mixed pattern of findings. His drive theory argues that the mere presence of others increases generalized drive or arousal, which enhances the emission of a dominant response. This improves performance on tasks in which the dominant response is correct or appropriate (e.g., in easy or well-learned tasks), but it reduces performance when the dominant response is incorrect or inappropriate (e.g., in difficult or new tasks). This explanation nicely fit the data (positive effects were generally found in easy or well-learned tasks, whereas negative effects were generally found in difficult or new tasks), and subsequent tests of the theory yielded supportive results. For example, Zajonc and Sales (1966) found that the presence of others indeed enhanced the tendency to emit a dominant response.

Later research identified problems with Zajonc's theory, which led to the development of alternative theories. A first problem with Zajonc's theory was that the mere presence of others did not always produce SFI effects. For example, these effects were not found with an inattentive audience or when the behavior of the audience was predictable and could be easily monitored (see e.g., Cottrell, Wack, Sekerak, & Rittle, 1968; Guerin, 1986; Klinger, 1969). This may imply that SFI effects only occur when people assume that the audience evaluates their performance or when it is distracting. A second problem was that the mere presence of others did not always lead to physiological arousal: Bond and Titus's (1983) meta-analysis only found a small effect of others' presence on arousal for difficult tasks and no effect for easy tasks (also see Blascovich, Mendes, Hunter, & Salomon, 1999). Several alternative theories were therefore developed. One of these, Distraction Conflict Theory, has elicited recent work and so deserves to be discussed in more detail.

SFI, Distraction, and Attention

Sanders, Baron and colleagues (e.g., Sanders & Baron, 1975; Sanders, Baron, & Moore, 1978) suggested that SFI results from attentional conflict. Their Distraction Conflict Theory presumes that the presence of an audience or co-actors attracts attention, which is also needed to perform the task. When distraction is hard to ignore and when attending to the distracter and the task at the same time is difficult, an attentional conflict occurs. In turn, this attentional conflict produces arousal and increased drive and effort. As in Zajonc's theory, this leads to facilitation of simple responses and impairment of complex responses. The main difference between Zajonc's drive theory and Distraction Conflict Theory is that, in the latter, the presence of others only has effects when it is distracting and leads to an attentional conflict (i.e., mere presence is not enough).

Distraction Conflict Theory makes several unique predictions that have received support (see Baron, 1986, for an overview). First, the presence of others is indeed distracting (e.g., Baron, Moore, & Sanders, 1978; Strube, Miles, & Finch, 1981). Second, social presence only leads to SFI effects when it attracts people's attention (Huguet, Galvaing, Monteil, & Dumas, 1999; Muller & Butera, 2007; also see Guerin, 1986) and when it leads to an attentional conflict (Groff, Baron, & Moore, 1983). Third, non-social distracters also can produce SFI effects. While it is perhaps obvious that (social or non-social) distraction should produce impairment on difficult tasks (i.e., where one needs one's full attention to perform the task), it is less obvious that distracters should produce facilitation on easy tasks. Yet, this is what the theory predicts, and one mechanism for this effect is overcompensation: Because people are aware that distracters impair performance, they try harder to compensate for the impairment, which in turn facilitates their performance on easy tasks. Sanders and Baron (1975) indeed found that a non-social distracter improved performance on easy tasks and impaired performance on difficult tasks.

More recent studies of the relation between attention and SFI do not assume that an attentional conflict leads to the emission of a dominant response, but rather that distraction causes people to restrict their attentional focus in an attempt to compensate for the distracter (e.g., Huguet et al., 1999; Muller & Butera, 2007). This 'attentional view' argues that performance will benefit for those tasks in which a narrow attentional focus is helpful (mostly simple tasks), but for tasks in which attention to a broader range of cues is necessary performance will deteriorate (mostly difficult tasks). Critical support for this prediction derives from studies in which the dominant response is incorrect but in which the presence of an audience or co-actors nevertheless leads to performance improvements. Examples are the Stroop interference effect (Huguet et al., 1999) and the 'illusory conjunction effect' (Muller & Butera, 2007). In the Stroop task, people have to name the ink color in which a word is printed, and sometimes the color is incongruent with the printed word (e.g., the word *red* printed in green ink). The dominant response is to read the word, which interferes with people's ability to name the color in which it is printed when the word is incongruent with the color. In the illusory conjunction effect, the dominant response is a tendency to think that a target object is present (e.g., "$") when in fact only its primitive characteristics (e.g., "S" and "|") are briefly presented (e.g., 70 ms). In both cases, the tendency to emit the dominant response is *reduced* when distracting others are present, which is inconsistent with Zajonc's drive theory. The improved performance that occurs when distracting others are present presumably occurs because these others cause participants to focus more on the central cues of the task (i.e., ink color in the Stroop task and the primitive characteristics in the illusory conjunction effect).

SFI and Mere Effort   A new perspective on SFI was offered by Harkins (2006; also McFall, Jamieson, & Harkins, 2009). Harkins and colleagues argued that SFI is due to mere *effort*: When people expect that their performance is evaluated, they work harder. Similar to Zajonc's drive theory, this is expected to enhance people's tendency to emit a dominant or pre-potent response. Performance will improve on simple tasks where the pre-potent response is correct or (importantly) when people know that their response is incorrect but they can correct it. However, performance will decline on more difficult tasks where the pre-potent response is incorrect and there is no clear task strategy that leads to the correct response.

Harkins (2006) found support for this line of reasoning for the Remote Associates Test (RAT; Mednick & Mednick, 1967). The RAT requires participants to examine a set of three words (e.g., "elephant," "lapse," "vivid") and find a fourth word that is associated with all of them (e.g., "memory"). Harkins found that evaluation expectations led participants to generate associates for the three stimulus words separately (the pre-potent response). This strategy was successful for easy RAT items, because with easy items the correct solution is strongly associated with at least one of the stimulus words. However, it led participants astray on more difficult RAT items, because the correct answer was a close associate of none of the three stimulus words, and the generation of close associates actually inhibited the generation of the correct answer. Follow-up research examined other tasks, including the Stroop task and the anti-saccade task (McFall et al., 2009). It was shown that participants who expected evaluation did not have a weaker tendency to emit the dominant response. Rather, they performed better because they were faster than participants who were not evaluated to *correct* their initial erroneous response. In sum, these results suggest that mere effort may be responsible for (some) SFI effects.

Conclusion   Hundreds of studies have examined SFI over the course of more than 100 years, and there still are inconsistencies and debates in the literature. Nevertheless, a few conclusions can be drawn. Firstly, the presence of others leads to the expectation that one's performance is evaluated. In turn, this makes people work harder, at least when they believe that working harder will increase their chances of a positive evaluation (e.g., when they believe they are capable of performing well and their efforts will thus pay off; also see Sanna, 1992; Sanna & Shotland, 1990). For example, in co-action situations people will work hard especially when their co-actor is slightly superior, but not when the co-actor is inferior or much better. This occurs because by working hard one may achieve the level of performance of a slightly superior co-actor and thus prevent a negative evaluation (e.g., Muller & Butera, 2007; Seta, 1982; cf. Festinger, 1954). In contrast, when a co-actor is inferior there is no need to work hard, while with a co-actor who is much better one may not be able to achieve the co-actor's level of performance (so there is no point trying). Second, working harder does not always improve performance. In some cases, such as for difficult RAT problems, the relation between effort and performance is absent or even negative (Harkins, 2006). Third, audiences and co-actors can be quite distracting. Consequences of such distraction are that people try to compensate for the distraction by putting in additional effort (e.g., Sanders & Baron, 1975) or that people restrict their attentional scope (Huguet et al., 1999; Muller & Butera, 2007). In any case, distraction makes people less likely to perform well on difficult tasks for which they need their full cognitive capacity.

Motivation Losses and Gains

Introduction   Working in a group sometimes implies that group members' individual inputs can be observed and easily evaluated. At other times, group members contribute to a common group product, and it is difficult or impossible to establish who has exactly contributed what. Rope-pulling, as studied by Ringelmann (1913), is a good example: It is almost impossible to establish who has pulled with what strength. Based on the reasoning put forward above, one would thus expect that the lack of 'evaluability' of individual contributions makes people expend less energy when working in a group as compared to when working alone. That people sometimes reduce their effort in a group context is well established in the literatures on social loafing (Ingham et al., 1974; Latané et al., 1979) and free riding (Kerr, 1983; Kerr & Bruun, 1981, 1983). We briefly summarize these literatures and then discuss recent work showing that people sometimes work harder in the context of a group.

Social Loafing and Free Riding   Ivan Steiner (1972) proposed that groups often fail to realize their potential performance (i.e., the performance they could hypothetically achieve given the resources of their members and the demands of the group task) because of process loss. He identified two sources of process loss—failure of group members to exert maximum effort (motivation loss) and ineffective coordination among group members (coordination loss). In the 1970s and 1980s, much attention was devoted to studying motivation loss in groups, in particular after Ingham et al. (1974) and Latané et al. (1979) showed that motivation loss could indeed be responsible for groups performing poorly.

Research has identified two reasons why group members may work less hard in a group than when alone. The first is social loafing, which occurs when individual contributions cannot be evaluated. For example, Williams, Harkins, and Latané (1981) found that group members worked less hard (they were asked to shout as loudly as they could) when the contributions of individual members could not be monitored. However, people did not show this motivation loss when they believed that each member's contribution was individually identifiable. Harkins and Jackson (1985) found that identifiability per se was not critical, but rather whether individual contributions could be evaluated. They found that social loafing occurred when group members were identifiable but it was hard to evaluate their performance, because different members worked on tasks that were not directly comparable (making comparisons between group members uninformative and reducing evaluability).

The second reason why people work less hard in the context of a group is free riding. This effect is due to group members' belief that their contribution is dispensable (i.e., not needed for the group to perform well). Kerr and Bruun (1983) argued that free-riding effects depend on a combination of member ability and task type (see Steiner, 1972, for a discussion of different task types). They found that low-ability people perceived their contribution to be dispensable and did not work hard (i.e., engaged in free riding) when group performance depended on the performance of the best group member (i.e., in disjunctive tasks), whereas high-ability people tended to free ride when group performance depended on the performance of the worst member (i.e., in conjunctive tasks). Importantly, these effects were found even though every group member's performance was completely identifiable. The free riding effect is therefore not due to people 'hiding in the crowd' (as in social loafing), but rather to people perceiving their efforts to be dispensable.

Social Compensation and the Köhler Effect More recent work has investigated the possibility that people sometimes actually work harder in a group than on their own. As with motivation losses, two types of motivation gains have been distinguished: social compensation and the Köhler effect. Whereas in social compensation it is mainly the high-ability or high-performing members who work harder, in the Köhler effect it is mainly the low-ability or low-performing members who work harder.

Social compensation occurs when (high-ability) members believe the performance of their group is important and at the same time perceive that without their putting in additional effort the group will not succeed (Williams & Karau, 1991). In this situation, members should feel very *in*dispensable, and indeed Williams and Karau found that dyad members worked harder than individuals when these two conditions were met (also see Todd, Seok, Kerr, & Messé, 2006). It should be noted, though, that it is unlikely that high-ability members will continue to work hard forever. Indeed, people generally dislike having to compensate for the lack of ability or motivation of others and may stop putting in extra effort (e.g., they want to avoid exploitation by free-riding fellow group members; see Kerr, 1983) and eventually will probably leave the group to join other groups that are more rewarding (cf. Moreland & Levine, 1982).

As described earlier, evidence for the second type of motivation gain—the Köhler effect—dates from the 1920s, when Köhler (1926, 1927) observed that dyads sometimes performed better than would be expected based on the abilities of individual dyad members (see Witte, 1989, and Stroebe, Diehl, & Abakoumkin, 1996). This was particularly likely when dyad members were moderately dissimilar in ability (also see Messé, Hertel, Kerr, Lount, & Park, 2002). As the task (lifting a bar) mainly depended on effort, moderately dissimilar dyads thus showed evidence of motivation gains.

Hertel, Kerr, and Messé (2000) noted that Köhler made the wrong comparison, because he compared the performance of dyads with the average performance of the individual dyad members. However, lifting a heavy bar together is a conjunctive task, in which the weaker member is decisive: If this person can no longer lift the bar, the stronger member can never compensate for that. This has two implications. First, the motivation gain found by Köhler seems mostly due to the weaker dyad member working harder. Second, the observed motivation gain is even more dramatic than Köhler indicated: When comparing the performance of the dyad with the expected performance of the weaker member, a larger motivation gain effect is found than when comparing it to the average expected performance of both members (the weaker and the stronger combined).

Evidence now clearly indicates that there are two distinct causes of the Köhler motivation gain effect (see Hertel et al., 2000; Weber & Hertel, 2007). The first is that people who work alongside a slightly superior coworker compete with the stronger member and work harder to avoid being the weaker member of the pair. Note that, according to this explanation (which is similar to explanations for social facilitation effects), the Köhler effect should occur in any co-action situation in which the performance of two people might easily be compared (i.e., it is an evaluability effect). Indeed, Lount, Park, Kerr, Messé, and Seok (2008) found that the Köhler effect is more pronounced when the stronger member can evaluate the weaker member's performance. The second mechanism is that the weaker members feel indispensable: They believe that their effort is crucial for the group to perform well, and failure would be entirely their fault. Interestingly, the first mechanism is based on individualistic motives (wanting not to perform worse than the other), whereas the second mechanism is based on social motives (wanting to prevent group failure).

In a recent meta-analysis, Weber and Hertel (2007) found evidence for both mechanisms. Furthermore, they found that the competition effect was especially pronounced for males, whereas the indispensability effect was more pronounced for females (also see Kerr et al., 2007; Nijstad, Van Vianen, Stroebe, & Lodewijkx, 2004; Weber, Wittchen, & Hertel, 2009). This pattern seems in line with the general idea that males are more concerned with competition and status (individualistic motives) while females are more concerned with collective welfare (e.g., Eagly, 1987). It also seems consistent with findings showing that social loafing effects are less pronounced for those people who put high value on the performance of their group (e.g., Everett, Smith, & Williams, 1992; Karau & Williams, 1993, 1997; Zaccaro, 1984). In other words, people are prepared to work hard for their group (and perhaps show motivation gains rather than losses) when they value the performance of their group highly.

Integration

Different authors have argued that many of the findings reported above can be integrated within the framework of Expectancy-Value theory (e.g., Hertel et al., 2000; Karau & Williams, 1993; Nijstad, 2009; Shepperd, 1993; Shepperd & Taylor, 1999). Expectancy-Value theory (Vroom, 1964) argues that motivation is a multiplicative function of expectancy, instrumentality, and value (see Figure 1, top panel). People will exert effort to the degree that (a) they believe that putting in more effort will lead to better performance (expectancy), (b) they believe that performance will be associated with valued outcomes (instrumentality), and (c) they value these outcomes positively. This theory can account for several of the findings in the SFI literature. Being watched by an audience or working alongside a (slightly superior) co-actor implies that performance is instrumental to receiving (self-) praise or criticism, and therefore motivation increases. However, if people doubt whether they can perform well (e.g., have low expectancy or self-efficacy because, for example, the task is difficult; Sanna, 1992), these positive effects on motivation will not occur. Furthermore, task performance will only improve if it is closely and positively related to effort (cf. Harkins, 2006).

In a group situation, the relation between (individual) effort and eventual (individual) outcomes is more complicated (see Figure 8.1, bottom panel). In particular, there are two extra steps—a step from individual performance to

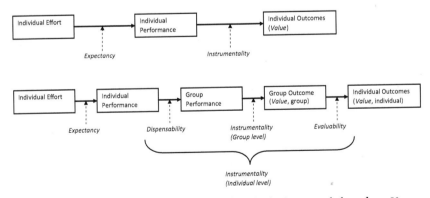

Figure 8.1   Expectancy-value theory for individuals (top panel; based on Vroom, 1964) and group members (bottom panel; based on Karau & Williams, 1993). Taken from Nijstad (2009).

group performance, and a step from group outcome to individual outcome. The first of these (i.e., from individual to group performance) is closely related to (in)dispensability: When people feel that their contribution is dispensable, they perceive no relation between their performance and group performance, and they will consequently let others do the hard work (i.e., they will free-ride). However, sometimes a group situation may lead to feelings of indispensability, which seems to be the case for high-ability members in the social compensation effect and for low-ability members in the Köhler effect.

A second complication is that performing well as a group may not always be associated with individual outcomes, and this may lead to social loafing. Indeed, the social loafing effect occurs when the contributions of individual group members cannot be evaluated, and high group performance seems to have no individual benefits (while contributing to it is unpleasant or effortful). However, this effect (and social loafing) is reduced when people value high group outcomes, which will be the case when they strongly identify with their group, and is, for example, more common for female than for male group members.

COORDINATION AND GROUP PERFORMANCE

Introduction: Coordination, Interdependence, and Teamwork

Group member motivation in many instances is a necessary but not a sufficient condition for groups to perform well. Even in fairly simple tasks, such as pulling a rope during a tug-of-war, coordination also is essential (e.g., group members need to pull in the same direction at the same time). Indeed, coordination losses have been found to contribute to such groups performing poorly, as Steiner (1972) had suggested (e.g., Ingham et al., 1974; Latané et al., 1979). The need for effective coordination is also clearly recognized in the literature on performance of organizational teams. Effective coordination among team members is essential to the degree that members are interdependent, and many definitions of what teams are incorporate interdependence. For example, Cohen and Bailey (1997, p. 241) define teams as follows:

> A team is a collection of individuals who are interdependent in their tasks, who share responsibility for outcomes, who see themselves and are seen by others as an intact social entity embedded in one or more social systems (for example, business unit or the corporation), and who manage their relationships across organizational boundaries.

Two types of interdependence are often distinguished. Task interdependence refers to the degree to which team members need one another to accomplish their tasks, and outcome interdependence refers to the degree to which members depend on one another to obtain valued outcomes (see e.g., Van der Vegt & Van de Vliert, 2002; Wageman, 1995). Task and outcome interdependence do not necessarily co-occur. For example, team members might have to work closely together, but individual members rather than the team as a whole might be evaluated and rewarded. Similarly, a room full of telemarketers may actually have very low task interdependence (they individually try to sell a product), but still may get collective rewards (e.g., depending on how many products were sold by the collective; Van der Vegt & Van de Vliert, 2002). Research has shown that such a mismatch between task and outcome interdependence has detrimental effects on team functioning. This work has shown that congruence between task and outcome interdependence (rather than incongruence) leads to higher levels of job satisfaction and commitment (Van der Vegt, Emans, & Van de Vliert, 2000) and to better performance (Saavedra, Earley, & Van Dyne, 1993; Wageman, 1995).

How to achieve effective coordination among team members has received some attention in recent years. In particular, this research has focused on team members' understanding of their task and their team ('emergent collective cognition'; see DeChurch & Mesmer-Magnus, 2010, for a meta-analysis). Two related lines of inquiry are research on transactive memory systems and work on shared mental models. Both focus on how group members learn to work more effectively together. However, the transactive memory literature emphasizes coordination in a situation in which knowledge and skills are distributed among group members, whereas the shared mental models literature emphasizes the degree to which cognition is shared among group members.

Transactive Memory and Group Performance

A transactive memory system refers to the information and skills possessed by each member of a group combined with a shared awareness of who knows what (Wegner, Giuliano, & Hertel, 1985; see also Liang, Moreland, & Argote, 1995; Wegner, 1986; for a review see Peltokorpi, 2008). Knowing whom to turn to for specific information or skills can greatly benefit group process (e.g., seeking help from the right person), and it may also improve group performance because tasks are assigned to those members who can best perform them (i.e., effective specialization). For example, knowing who knows what (i.e., publicly recognized expertise) has been shown to improve decision quality in decision making groups, because members were better able to share and coordinate their unique informational resources (e.g., Stasser, Stewart, & Wittenbaum, 1995; Stasser, Vaughan, & Stewart, 2000; Stewart & Stasser, 1995; Van Ginkel & Van Knippenberg, 2009). It has also been shown to improve performance because it allowed group members to distribute tasks to the most capable people (Liang et al., 1995). DeChurch and Mesmer-Magnus's (2010) meta-analysis demonstrated that transactive memory systems were positively related to group performance, both when performance was measured objectively and when it was measured subjectively. Further, evidence for such a positive relationship was obtained both in the laboratory, using ad hoc groups, and in the field, using ongoing teams.

A transactive memory system develops during group interaction, and as such is an emergent property of a group (cf. Marks, Mathieu, & Zaccaro, 2001).

Indeed, in their seminal investigation, Liang and colleagues (1995; also Moreland, Argote, & Krishnan, 1998) found that groups whose members were initially trained together later performed better at their task (assembling a radio) than did groups whose members were trained separately and that this occurred because the groups trained together had formed an effective transactive memory system. Lewis (2004) additionally found that face-to-face communication and initially distributed expertise facilitated the formation of a transactive memory system. Finally, trust among group members also facilitates the development of a transactive memory system (Akgun, Byrne, Keskin, Lynn, & Imamoglu, 2005; also Rau, 2005). In short, the opportunity to interact and communicate about one's areas of expertise facilitates the development of a transactive memory.

Because a transactive memory usually develops when group members interact or are trained together, it may be disrupted when members are replaced. Indeed, Lewis, Belliveau, Herndon, and Keller (2007; also Moreland, Argote, & Krishnan, 1996) argued that after member replacement, the group's transactive memory system is no longer accurate: An old member who was responsible for specific knowledge has left the group, and there is a gap in the transactive memory system that a newcomer might not be able to fill. When groups continue to rely on their (no longer accurate) transactive memory after member replacement, performance will suffer. Lewis et al. found evidence for this, but also found that these negative effects of member replacement on group performance could be prevented when members were asked to explicitly reflect on their task. Thus, a mindless application of an outdated transactive memory system seems to have detrimental consequences for group performance.

Shared Mental Models and Group Performance

The related concept of shared mental models was suggested by Cannon-Bowers, Salas, and Converse (1993). Mental models can be defined as "mechanisms whereby humans are able to generate descriptions of system purpose and form, explanations of system functioning and observed system states, and predictions of future system states" (Rouse & Morris, 1986, p. 351). Cannon-Bowers et al. (1993) have applied the idea of mental models to explain why high-performing teams sometimes are able to coordinate their actions smoothly without explicit communication (also Cannon-Bowers & Salas, 1990). They proposed that expert teams develop a compatible (similar) understanding of the key elements of their performance environment (i.e., a shared mental model), which improves their coordination and performance. Although the concepts of transactive memory and shared mental models are clearly related, the literatures on these topics have largely developed separately (DeChurch & Mesmer-Magnus, 2010).

Shared mental models can include organized knowledge about the team itself as well as about the team task (e.g., Mathieu, Heffner, Goodwin, Salas, & Cannon-Bowers, 2000). Task knowledge includes knowledge about equipment, technology, and task procedures and strategies. Team knowledge includes knowledge about team interaction (e.g., roles and responsibilities) and team members' characteristics (e.g., knowledge, skills, and preferences; cf. transactive memory). Of course, these knowledge structures can be accurate, but they can also be inaccurate. Further, all team members might have identical mental models, but team members may also vary in their mental models. Both mental model accuracy and 'sharedness' (or similarity) have been linked to team performance (Edwards, Day, Arthur, & Bell, 2006; Lim & Klein, 2006; Marks, Sabella, Burke, & Zacarro, 2002; Mathieu et al., 2000). For example, Lim and Klein (2006) found that both mental model accuracy and similarity predicted performance of military teams, and Edwards et al. (2006) obtained similar findings for dyads playing a computer game. Also in DeChurch and Mesmer-Magnus's (2010) meta-analysis both similarity and accuracy of mental models was positively associated with team performance. Finally, this meta-analysis found that both mental models related to the task and those related to the team were associated positively with performance.

An important question is how these shared mental models develop. Edwards et al. (2006) considered this question and found that team members' general mental ability predicted the degree to which they formed accurate mental models, and the superior performance of teams high in general mental ability was due to their better mental models. Marks et al. (2002) investigated the effects of cross-training, defined as "an instructional strategy in which each team member is trained in the duties of his or her teammates" (Volpe, Cannon-Bowers, Salas, & Spector, 1996, p. 87). The goal of cross-training is to increase knowledge of other team members' roles and responsibilities and thus enhance coordination among team members. There are several types of cross-training. Blickensderfer, Cannon-Bowers, and Salas (1998) distinguished positional clarification (receiving verbally presented information about teammates' jobs), positional modeling (observing the behaviors of team members performing their jobs), and positional rotation (performing the teammate's job). Marks et al. (2002) found that all three types of cross-training increased the degree to which teams developed shared mental models, which in turn improved their performance. In addition, Marks et al. found some evidence that more in-depth types of cross-training (positional modeling and rotation) were more effective than positional clarification, but the differences were not very large.

Integration

The literatures on transactive memory systems and shared mental models both clarify the effects of cognition on effective coordination and group performance. The main difference is that complementary and unique knowledge is emphasized in the transactive memory literature, while similar and shared knowledge is emphasized in the shared mental models literature (DeChurch & Mesmer-Magnus, 2010; Kozlowski & Ilgen, 2006). Yet, the transactive memory literature also incorporates the notion that the perceptions of expertise differentiation within a team must be shared, and transactive memory systems can thus be seen as one specific form of a shared mental model (i.e., a shared mental model about how knowledge and skills are distributed in the group; Boles, 1999).

It may, however, be the case that transactive memory systems are helpful in slightly different situations than are shared mental models. Transactive memory systems are needed to locate people who have the required knowledge or skills, and this may be important mainly in situations in which formal roles and responsibilities have not clearly been defined. In those situations, informal task specialization may develop, which will (given that it is accurate and the right people perform the right task) help the group to perform well. In contrast, shared mental models may be particularly helpful in situations in which there is (formal) role differentiation. In those situations, group members must coordinate their behaviors to perform optimally as a group, and some (shared) knowledge about how different roles and responsibilities relate to task performance will be helpful. Indeed, studies of transactive memory systems have examined how training people as a group may benefit task performance, allowing for informal task specialization to occur (e.g., Liang et al., 1985), whereas studies of shared mental models have examined cross-training, allowing group members to acquire knowledge of other members' roles in the group (e.g., Marks et al., 2002).

It was noted that membership change may disrupt the effective functioning of a group, because it interferes with the group's transactive memory (e.g., Lewis et al., 2007). However, it is also clear that membership change may sometimes have beneficial effects on group performance, for example because newcomers are sources of creativity and innovation (e.g., Choi & Levine, 2004; Choi & Thompson, 2005; Nemeth & Ormiston, 2007). Also in organizational teams, it has been found that some turnover is actually beneficial (Katz, 1982). As in many areas of life, it thus seems that stability and change both have their advantages and disadvantages, and change is sometimes needed when old routines no longer work. This presents a possible downside of transactive memory systems and shared mental models: Groups may continue to rely on them even when the situation has changed and their mental picture of the group or the task is no longer correct.

CONCLUSIONS

When looking at the last decades of group performance research, two developments stand out. First, much of the work that examines group performance appears in the applied psychology, management, and organizational behavior literature, as well as in social psychology. This trend, already noted by Moreland, Hogg, and Hains (1994) and by Sanna and Parks (1997), has continued in recent decades. A big advantage of this state of affairs is that theories about group performance are tested both in the (social-psychological) laboratory, allowing tests of causal hypotheses, and in the field, ensuring real-world relevance. It is encouraging that findings (e.g., on transactive memory systems and shared mental models) often generalize from the lab to the field.

Second, and perhaps related, recent decades have seen a shift toward studying process gains and effective groups, rather than process losses and ineffective groups. The work on the Köhler motivation gain effect (e.g., Weber & Hertel, 2007) as well as the work on transactive memory systems and shared mental models (DeChurch & Mesmer-Magnus, 2010; Peltokorpi, 2008) are good examples. Another example is the literature on group brainstorming, which has shifted from studying process loss to studying the possibility of high group creativity (Paulus & Nijstad, 2003; Stroebe, Nijstad, & Rietzschel, 2010; see Paulus & Coskun, this volume). Indeed, teamwork is the reality in many organizations, and from an applied perspective the question of how to make groups function effectively is perhaps more relevant than the question why groups are ineffective. The literature on shared mental models, for example, developed with the aim of understanding high-performing teams that operate in a dynamic context (Cannon-Bowers et al., 1993).

This chapter has reviewed two broad areas of research—work on the relationship between motivation and group performance and work on the relationship between coordination and group performance. What was not discussed is the relationship between motivation and coordination. Recently, several authors have argued that group members are not necessarily interested in optimally coordinating their contributions (e.g., De Dreu, Nijstad, & Van Knippenberg, 2008; Wittenbaum, Hollingshead, & Botero, 2004). Members may also be interested in pursuing their own self-interest (e.g., their own career, 'winning' an argument, free riding on the efforts of others) rather than the collective interest of the group, which may interfere with optimal coordination. Therefore, group members need to be motivated to coordinate their activities, and they will do so to the extent that they value collective performance. Potentially useful things, such as transactive memory systems or shared mental models, may not even develop when group members are not motivated to contribute to group success (also Peltokorpi, 2008). One way to achieve such 'pro-social motivation' (De Dreu et al., 2008) is to reward group performance rather than individual performance (also see DeMatteo, Eby, & Sundstrom, 1998; Pearsall, Christian, & Ellis, 2010; Wageman, 1995). Another way is to provide effective leadership (also see Hogg, this volume). For example, transformational leadership is presumed to stimulate followers to move beyond immediate self-interest and strive toward a collective purpose, mission, or vision (e.g., Burns, 1978; Bass, 1985; Bass & Avolio, 1990). It would seem likely that transactive memory systems and shared mental models more readily develop when group members are high on pro-social motivation, which in turn depends on appropriate reward systems and leadership.

There may be another connection between transactive memory systems and motivation. Transactive memory systems emphasize the unique contributions of group members and may therefore lead group members to feel indispensable. This will prevent free riding and may even lead to motivation gains. However, this will happen only to the extent that (a) group members believe their unique knowledge or skills are required for the task and (b) they are motivated to strive for collective outcomes (see also De Dreu et al., 2008). The reciprocal relations between group cognition and motivation thus seem to present a fruitful area for future research.

In closing, group performance research in the last decades seems to lead to less pessimistic conclusions than the work of earlier decades. Groups and teams do not always cause process losses, and process gains are sometimes observed. When group members are motivated to work hard towards collective goals, and when they are given the opportunity to develop a shared and adequate understanding of their task, groups can be very effective.

REFERENCES

Akgun, A. E., Byrne, J. C., Keskin, H., & Lynn, G. S., & Imamoglu, S. Z. (2005). Knowledge networks in new product development projects: A transactive memory perspective. *Information & Management 42*(8), 1105–1120.

Baron, R. S. (1986). Distraction-conflict theory: Progress and problems. In L. Berkowitz (Ed.), *Advances in experimental social psychology* (Vol. 19, pp. 1–40). Ontario, Canada: Elsevier.

Baron, R. S, Moore, D. L., & Sanders, G. S. (1978). Distraction as a source of drive in social facilitation research. *Journal of Personality and Social Psychology, 36*, 816–824.

Bass, B. M. (1985). *Leadership and performance beyond expectations.* New York, NY: Free Press.

Bass, B. M., & Avolio, B. J. (1990). The implications of transactional and transformational leadership for individual, team, and organizational development. In R. W. Woodman & W. A. Passmore (Eds.), *Research in organizational change and development* (Vol. 4, pp. 231–272). Greenwich, CT: JAI Press.

Blascovich, J., Mendes, W. B., Hunter, S. B., & Salomon, K. (1999). Social "facilitation" as a challenge and threat. *Journal of Personality and Social Psychology, 77*, 68–77.

Blickensderfer, E., Cannon-Bowers, J. A., & Salas, E. (1998). Cross training and team performance. In J. A. Cannon-Bowers & E. Salas (Eds.), *Making decisions under stress: Implications for individual and team training* (pp. 299–311). Washington, DC: American Psychological Association.

Boles, T. L. (1999). Themes and variations in shared cognition in organizations. In L. L. Thompson, J. M. Levine, & D. M. Messick (Eds.), *Shared cognition in organizations: The management of knowledge* (pp. 327–348). Mahwah, NJ: Erlbaum.

Bond, C. F., Jr., & Titus, L. J. (1983). Social facilitation: A meta-analysis of 241 studies. *Psychological Bulletin, 94*, 265–292.

Burns, J. M. (1978). *Leadership.* New York, NY: Harper & Row.

Cannon-Bowers, J. A., & Salas, E. (1990). *Cognitive psychology and team training: Shared mental models in complex systems.* Paper presented at the Annual Meeting of the Society of Industrial and Organizational Psychology, Miami, FL.

Cannon-Bowers, J. A., Salas, E., & Converse, S. A. (1993). Shared mental models in expert team decision making. In N. J. Castellan, Jr. (Ed.), *Current issues in individual and group decision making* (pp. 221–246). Hillsdale, NJ: Erlbaum.

Choi, H. S., & Levine, J. M. (2004). Minority influence in work teams: The impact of newcomers. *Journal of Experimental Social Psychology, 40*, 273–280.

Choi, H. S. & Thompson, L. (2005). Old wine in a new bottle: Impact of membership change on group creativity. *Organizational Behavior and Human Decision Processes, 98,* 121–132.

Cohen, S. & Bailey, D. (1997). What makes teams work: Group effectiveness research from the shop floor to the executive suite. *Journal of Management, 23,* 239–290.

Cottrel, N. B., Wack, D. L., Sekerak, G. J., & Rittle, R. H. (1968). Social facilitation of dominant responses by the presence of an audience and the mere presence of others. *Journal of Personality and Social Psychology, 9,* 245–250.

DeChurch, L. A., & Mesmer-Magnus, J. R. (2010). The cognitive underpinnings of effective teamwork: A meta-analysis. *Journal of Applied Psychology, 95,* 32–53.

De Dreu, C. K. W., Nijstad, B. A., & Van Knippenberg, D. (2008). Motivated information processing in group judgment and decision making. *Personality and Social Psychology Review, 12,* 22–49.

DeMatteo, J. S., Eby, L. T., & Sundstrom, E. (1998). Team based rewards: Current empirical evidence and directions for future research. *Research in Organizational Behavior, 20,* 141–183.

Eagly, A. H. (1987). *Sex differences in social behaviour: A social role interpretation.* Hillsdale, NJ: Erlbaum.

Edwards, B. D., Day, E. A., Arthur, W. Jr., & Bell, S. T. (2006). Relationships among team ability composition, team mental models, and team performance. *Journal of Applied Psychology, 91,* 727–736.

Everett, J. J., Smith, R. E., & Williams, K. D. (1992). Effects of team cohesion and identifiability on social loafing in relay swimming performance. *International Journal of Sport Psychology, 23,* 311–324.

Festinger, L. (1954). A theory of social comparison processes. *Human Relations, 7,* 117–140.

Groff, B. D., Baron, R. S., & Moore, D. L. (1983). Distraction, attentional conflict, and drivelike behavior. *Journal of Experimental Social Psychology, 19,* 359–380.

Guerin, B. (1986). Mere presence effects in humans: A review. *Journal of Experimental Social Psychology, 22,* 38–77.

Harkins, S. (1987). Social loafing and social facilitation. *Journal of Experimental Social Psychology, 23,* 1–18.

Harkins, S. G. (2006). Mere effort as the mediator of the evaluation-performance relationship. *Journal of Personality and Social Psychology, 91,* 436–455.

Harkins, S. G., & Jackson, J. M. (1985). The role of evaluation in eliminating social loafing. *Personality and Social Psychology Bulletin, 11,* 457–465.

Hertel, G., Kerr, N. L., & Messé, L. A. (2000). Motivation gains in performance groups: Paradigmatic and theoretical developments on the Köhler effect. *Journal of Personality and Social Psychology, 79,* 580–601.

Huguet, P., Galvaing, M. P., Monteil, J. M., & Dumas, F. (1999). Social presence effects in the Stroop task: Further evidence for an attentional view of social facilitation. *Journal of Personality and Social Psychology, 77,* 1011–1025.

Ingham, A. G., Levinger, G., Graves, J., & Peckham, V. (1974). The Ringelmann effect: Studies of group size and group performance. *Journal of Experimental Social Psychology, 10,* 371–384.

Karau, S. J., & Williams, K. D. (1993). Social loafing: A meta-analytic review and theoretical integration. *Journal of Personality and Social Psychology, 65,* 681–706.

Karau, S. J., & Williams, K. D. (1997). The effects of group cohesiveness on social loafing and social compensation. *Group dynamics: Theory, Research, and Practice, 1,* 156–168.

Katz, R. (1982). The effects of group longevity on project communication and perfor-mance. *Administrative Science Quarterly, 27,* 81–104.

Kerr, N. L. (1983). Motivation losses in small groups: A social dilemma analysis. *Journal of Personality and Social Psychology, 45,* 819–828.

Kerr, N. L., & Bruun, S. E. (1981). Ringelmann revisited: Alternative explanations for the social loafing effect. *Personality and Social Psychology Bulletin, 7,* 224–231.

Kerr, N. L., & Bruun, S. E. (1983). Dispensability of member effort and group motiva-tion losses: Free-rider effects. *Journal of Personality and Social Psychology, 44,* 78–94.

Kerr, N. L., Messé, L. A., Seok, D. H., Sambolec, E. J., Lount, R. B., & Park, E. S. (2007). Psychological mechanisms underlying the Köhler motivation gain. *Person-ality and Social Psychology Bulletin, 33,* 828–841.

Klinger, E. (1969). Feedback effects and social facilitation of vigilance performance: Mere coaction versus potential evaluation. *Psychonomic Science, 14,* 161–162.

Köhler, O. (1926). Kraftleistungen bei Einzel und Gruppenarbeit [Physical performance in individual and group situations]. *Industrielle Psychotechnik, 3,* 274–282.

Köhler, O. (1927). Ueber den Gruppenwirkungsgrad der menschlichen Koerperarbeit und die Bedingungen optimaler Kollektivkraftreaktion [On group efficiency of physical labor and the conditions of optimal collective performance]. *Industrielle Psychotechnik, 4,* 209–226.

Kozlowski, S. W. J., & Ilgen, D. R. (2006). Enhancing the effectiveness of work groups and teams. *Psychological Science in the Public Interest, 7,* 77–124.

Latané, B., Williams, K., & Harkins, S. (1979). Many hands make light the work: The causes and consequences of social loafing. *Journal of Personality and Social Psy-chology, 37,* 822–832.

Lewis, K. (2004). Knowledge and performance in knowledge-worker teams: A longitu-dinal study of transactive memory systems. *Management Science, 50,* 1519–1533.

Lewis, K., Belliveau, M., Herndon, B., & Keller, J. (2007). Group cognition, member-ship change and performance: Investigating the benefits and detriments of col-lective knowledge. *Organizational Behavior and Human Decision Processes, 103,* 159–178.

Lim, B. C., & Klein, K. J. (2006). Team mental models and team performance: A field study of the effects of team mental model similarity and accuracy. *Journal of Orga-nizational Behavior, 27,* 403–418.

Liang, D. W., Moreland, R., & Argote, L. (1995). Group versus individual training and group performance: The mediating role of transactive memory. *Personality and Social Psychology Bulletin, 21,* 384–393.

Lount, R. B., Park, E. S., Kerr, N. L., Messé, L. A., & Seok, D. H. (2008). Evaluation concerns and the Köhler effect: The impact of physical presence on motivation gains. *Small Group Research, 38,* 795–812.

Marks, M. A., Mathieu, J. E., & Zaccaro, S. J. (2001). A temporally based framework and taxonomy of team processes. *Academy of Management Review, 26,* 356–376.

Marks, M. A., Sabella, M. J., Burke, C. S., & Zaccaro, S. J. (2002). The impact of cross-training on team effectiveness. *Journal of Applied Psychology, 87,* 3–13.

Mathieu, J. E., Heffner, T. S., Goodwin, G. F., Salas, E., & Cannon-Bowers, J. A. (2000). The influence of shared mental models on team process and performance. *Journal of Applied Psychology, 85,* 273–283.

McFall, S. R., Jamieson, J. P., & Harkins, S. G. (2009). Testing the mere effort account of the evaluation-performance relationship. *Journal of Personality and Social Psychology, 96*, 135–154.

Mednick, S. A., & Mednick, M. T. (1967). *Examiner's manual: Remote Associates Test.* Boston, MA: Houghton Mifflin.

Messé, L. A., Hertel, G., Kerr, N. L., Lount, R. B., & Park, E. S. (2002). Knowledge of partner's ability as a moderator of group motivation gains: An exploration of the Köhler discrepancy effect. *Journal of Personality and Social Psychology, 82,* 935–946.

Moreland, R. L., Argote, L., & Krishnan, R. (1996). Socially shared cognition at work: Transactive memory and group performance. In J. L. Nye & A. M. Brower (Eds.), *What's social about social cognition? Research on socially shared cognition in small groups* (pp. 57–84). Thousand Oaks, CA: Sage.

Moreland, R. L., Argote, L., & Krishnan, R. (1998). Training people to work in groups. In R. S. Tindale, L. Heath, J. Edwards, E. J. Posavac, F. B. Bryant, Y. Suarez-Balcazar, et al. (Eds.), *Theory and research on small groups* (pp. 37–60). New York, NY: Plenum.

Moreland, R. L., Hogg, M. A., & Hains, S. C. (1994). Back to the future: Social psychological research on groups. *Journal of Experimental Social Psychology, 30,* 527–555.

Moreland, R. L., & Levine, J. M. (1982). Socialization in small groups: Temporal changes in individual-group relations. In L. Berkowitz (Ed.), *Advances in experimental social psychology* (Vol. 15, pp. 137–192). New York, NY: Academic Press.

Muller, D., & Butera, F. (2007). The focusing effect of self-evaluation threat in co-action and social comparison. *Journal of Personality and Social Psychology, 93*, 194–211.

Nemeth, C. J., & Ormiston, M. (2007). Creative idea generation: Harmony versus stimulation. *European Journal of Social Psychology, 37*, 524–535.

Nijstad, B. A. (2009). *Group performance.* Hove, UK: Psychology Press.

Nijstad, B. A., Van Vianen, A. E. M., Stroebe, W., & Lodewijkx, H. F. M. (2004). Persistence in brainstorming: Exploring stop rules in same-sex groups. *Group Processes and Intergroup Relations, 7*, 195–206.

Paulus, P. B., & Nijstad, B. A. (2003). *Group creativity: Innovation through collaboration.* New York, NY: Oxford University Press.

Pearsall, M. J., Christian, M. S., & Ellis, A. P. J. (2010). Motivating interdependent teams: Individual rewards, shared rewards, or something in between? *Journal of Applied Psychology, 95*, 183–191.

Peltokorpi, V. (2008). Transactive memory systems. *Review of General Psychology, 12,* 378–394.

Rau, D. (2005). The influence of relationship conflict and trust on the transactive memory: Performance relation in top management teams. *Small Group Research, 36,* 746–771.

Ringelmann, M. (1913). Recherches sur les moteurs animés: Travail de l'homme. *Annales de l'Insitut National Agronomique, 12*, 1–40.

Rouse, W. B., & Morris, N. M. (1986). On looking into the black box: Prospects and limits in the search for mental models. *Psychological Bulletin, 100*, 349–363.

Saavedra, R. P., Earley, P. C., & Van Dyne, L. (1993). Complex interdependence in task-performing groups. *Journal of Applied Psychology, 78*, 61–72.

Sanders, G. S., & Baron, R. S. (1975). The motivation effects of distraction on task performance. *Journal of Personality and Social Psychology, 32*, 956–963.

Sanders, G. S., Baron, R. S., & Moore, D. L. (1978). Distraction and social comparison as mediators of social facilitation effects. *Journal of Experimental Social Psychology, 14,* 291–303.

Sanna, L. J. (1992). Self-efficacy theory: Implications for social facilitation and social loafing. *Journal of Personality and Social Psychology, 62,* 774–786.

Sanna, L. J., & Parks, C. D. (1997). Group research trends in social and organizational psychology: What happened to intragroup research? *Psychological Science, 8,* 261–267.

Sanna, L. J., & Shotland, R. L. (1990). Valence of anticipated evaluation and social facilitation. *Journal of Experimental Social Psychology, 26,* 82–92.

Seta, J. J. (1982). The impact of comparison processes on coactors' task performance. *Journal of Personality and Social Psychology, 42,* 281–291.

Shepperd, J. A. (1993). Productivity loss in performance groups: A motivation analysis. *Psychological Bulletin, 113,* 67–81.

Shepperd, J. A., & Taylor, K. M. (1999). Social Loafing and expectancy-value theory. *Personality and Social Psychology Bulletin, 25,* 1147–1158.

Stasser, G., Stewart, D. D., & Wittenbaum, G. M. (1995). Expert roles and information exchange during discussion: The importance of knowing who knows what. *Journal of Experimental Social Psychology, 31,* 244–265.

Stasser, G., Vaughan, S. I., & Stewart, D. D. (2000). Pooling unshared information: The benefits of knowing how access to information is distributed among group members. *Organizational Behavior and Human Decision Processes, 82,* 102–116.

Steiner, I. D. (1972). *Group process and productivity.* New York, NY: Academic Press.

Stewart, D. D., & Stasser, G. (1995). Expert role assignment and information sampling during collective recall and decision making. *Journal of Personality and Social Psychology, 69,* 619–628.

Stroebe, W., Diehl, M., & Abakoumkin, G. (1996). Social compensation and the Koehler effect: Toward a theoretical explanation of motivation gains in group productivity. In E. Witte & J. H. Davis (Eds.) *Understanding group behavior* (Vol. 2, pp. 37–65). Mahwah, NJ: Lawrence Erlbaum.

Stroebe, W., Nijstad, B. A., & Rietzschel, E. F. (2010). Beyond productivity loss in brainstorming groups: The evolution of a question. In M. P. Zanna & J. M. Olson (Eds.), *Advances in experimental social psychology* (Vol. 43, pp. 157–203). New York, NY: Academic Press.

Strube, M. J., Miles, M. E., & Finch, W. H. (1981). The social facilitation of a simple task: Field tests of alternative explanations. *Personality and Social Psychology Bulletin, 7,* 701–707.

Todd, A. R., Seok, D., Kerr, N. L., & Messé, L. A. (2006). Social compensation: Fact or social comparison artifact? *Group Processes & Intergroup Relations, 9,* 431–442.

Triplett, N. (1898). The dynamogenic factors in pacemaking and competition. *American Journal of Psychology, 9,* 507–533.

Van der Vegt, G. S., Emans, B. J. M., & Van de Vliert, E. (2000). Affective responses to intragroup interdependence and job complexity. *Journal of Management, 26,* 633–655.

Van der Vegt, G. S. & Van de Vliert, E. (2002). Intragroup interdependence and effectiveness: Review and proposed directions for theory and practice. *Journal of Managerial Psychology, 17,* 50–67.

Van Ginkel, W. P., & Van Knippenberg, D. (2009). Knowledge about the distribution of information and group decision making: When and why does it work? *Organizational Behavior and Human Decision Processes, 108,* 218–229.

Volpe, C. E., Cannon-Bowers, J. A., Salas, E., & Spector, P. (1996). The impact of cross-training on team functioning: An empirical examination. *Human Factors, 38,* 87–100.

Vroom, V. H. (1964). *Work and motivation.* New York, NY: Wiley.

Wageman, R. (1995). Interdependence and group effectiveness. *Administrative Science Quarterly, 40,* 145–180.

Weber, B. & Hertel, G. (2007). Motivation gains of inferior members: A meta-analytic review. *Journal of Personality and Social Psychology, 93,* 973–993.

Weber, B., Wittchen, M., & Hertel, G. (2009). Gendered ways to motivation gains in groups. *Sex Roles, 60,* 731–744.

Wegner, D. M. (1986). Transactive memory: A contemporary analysis of the group mind. In B. Mullen & G. R. Goethals (Eds.), *Theories of group behavior* (pp. 185–208). New York, NY: Springer-Verlag.

Wegner, D. M., Giuliano, T., & Hertel, P. T. (1985). Cognitive interdependence in close relationships. In W. J. Ickes (Ed.), *Compatible and incompatible relationships* (pp. 253–276). New York, NY: Springer-Verlag.

Williams, K. D., Harkins, S., & Latané, B. (1981). Identifiability as a deterrent to social loafing: Two cheering experiments. *Journal of Personality and Social Psychology, 40,* 303–311.

Williams, K. D., & Karau, S. J. (1991). Social loafing and social compensation: The effects of expectations of co-worker performance. *Journal of Personality and Social Psychology, 61,* 570–580.

Witte, E. H. (1989). Köhler rediscovered: The anti-Ringelmann effect. *European Journal of Social Psychology, 19,* 147–154.

Wittenbaum, G. W., Hollingshead, A. B., & Botero, I. C. (2004). From cooperative to motivated information sharing in groups: Moving beyond the hidden profile paradigm. *Communication Monographs, 71,* 286–310.

Zaccaro, S. (1984). Social loafing: The role of task attractiveness. *Personality and Social Psychology Bulletin, 10,* 99–106.

Zajonc, R. B. (1965). Social facilitation. *Science, 149,* 269–274.

Zajonc, R. B. (1980). Compresence of group influence. In P. B. Paulus (Ed.), *Psychology of group influence* (pp. 35–60). Hillsdale, NJ: Lawrence Erlbaum.

Zajonc, R. B., & Sales, S. M. (1966). Social facilitation of dominant and subordinate responses. *Journal of Experimental Social Psychology, 2,* 160–168.

9

Creativity

PAUL B. PAULUS and HAMIT COSKUN

For many years there was a strong research interest in creativity as an individual activity (Simonton, 1984, 1999; Sternberg, 2006), emphasizing the impact of such personal factors as developmental experiences and thinking styles. Great discoveries in science were mostly attributed to personal genius (Simonton, 1984, 2004). However, in the past 20 years there has been an increasing awareness of the social dynamics involved in creativity (Amabile, 1983; Dacey & Lennon, 1998; Purser & Montuori, 1999), and there has been a strong interest in innovation in work teams and organizations (Choi & Thompson, 2005; Zhou & Shalley, 2007). This interest has led to increased research on the group creative process (Mannix, Neale, & Goncalo, 2009; Paulus & Nijstad, 2003).

CREATIVE COLLABORATION, GROUP CREATIVITY, AND TEAM INNOVATION

Creativity is typically defined as the generation or development of novel ideas or products that have some degree of utility or acceptance (Amabile, 1983; Woodman, Sawyer, & Griffin, 1993). This definition makes sense since it is certainly more difficult to come up with useful or acceptable ideas or products than those that are simply novel. Famous paintings, symphonies, and theories represent just some of the products that are both novel and have gained acceptance, and televisions and computers are among the many novel products that have been very useful. Much of the group creativity literature has distinguished between the generation of novel ideas and their utility since these may reflect different processes. Often the creative process is seen as involving different phases, such as idea generation, selection of feasible ideas, development of ideas into potentially useful innovations, and finally implementation, engineering, and marketing of the innovation (Parnes, 1975).

Creative collaboration is a term that is often encountered and can be used to encompass a wide variety of creative activities that involve social interaction. In the scholarly literature this term is often used when describing longer-term creative relationships of two or more individuals. Several books have described these types of collaborations among highly creative individuals (Farrell, 2001; John-Steiner, 2000). The term is also often used for educational practices in which students work on joint projects (collaborative learning; pair learning). It is presumed that such experiences have important educational benefits and may enhance innovative learning (Kanev, Kimura, & Orr, 2009).

Much research on collaborative creativity has involved structured task groups in short-term laboratory settings (what we call *group creativity*). Task groups can be defined as collections of three or more individuals working on a common task or goal. Two individuals working together are called a dyad and are often not considered a group (Moreland, 2010). However, many of the same processes that play a role in creative groups also play a role in creative dyads (John-Steiner, 2000), so there is no strong theoretical rationale for excluding pairs of creative collaborators from our discussion.

Collaborative creativity also takes place in organized work teams. Team scholars tend to define teams as two or more individuals who work collaboratively through specific roles toward some shared goal (Salas, Rosen, Burke, & Goodwin, 2009). Most of the research on creativity in teams has involved work teams in organizational settings. The team studies typically involve an assessment of the creative process through surveys of team members and ratings of innovative outcomes by team members and/or supervisors (Hülsheger, Anderson, & Salgado, 2009). Whereas most of the creativity research involving laboratory groups has focused on the ideation phase of creativity, research on teams often focuses on actual implementation of innovations (West, 2003, 2004). For this reason studies of team creativity often use the term *team innovation* to label the process being studied. Since researchers studying laboratory groups and work teams have somewhat different foci, these two areas of research are often viewed as two distinct areas (Paulus & Van der Zee, 2004). However, since teams are groups, there is little justification for ignoring the team literature in a review of group creativity (Moreland & Levine, 2009). So in this review we will take a broad view of the group creative process, taking into account the literatures on group creativity, team innovation, and other types of creative collaborations.

In many studies of group creativity, interacting individuals are compared with the same number of non-interacting individuals, labeled a nominal group. This kind of comparison provides information on the extent to which the group interaction enhances creativity. Many studies using the brainstorming paradigm in which individuals try to generate a large number of ideas as a group have found that such groups actually generate fewer ideas than do nominal groups (Diehl & Stroebe, 1987; Mullen, Johnson, & Salas, 1991). Interestingly, participants in group brainstorming perceive their performance more favorably than do solitary performers (Paulus, Dzindolet, Poletes, & Camacho, 1993; Stroebe, Diehl, & Abakoumkin, 1992). In other words, group members have the perception that group interaction enhanced their performance while in fact it hindered their performance. What does this mean? Should teams not work together on innovation projects, or are these findings limited to the performance of ad hoc groups in a short term setting? Does the illusion of productivity found in laboratory groups explain the positive evaluations often obtained in work teams? That is, are the positive perceptions obtained in work teams simply illusory? We will address these questions below.

In our review we will focus on the group creativity literature and its relevance for a broader theory of group creativity (Nijstad & Stroebe, 2006; Paulus & Brown, 2007; Paulus & Dzindolet, 2008). We will then relate this perspective to the literatures on team innovation and creative collaboration in long-term groups. This will suggest potential avenues for broadening and enriching the research on group creativity.

COGNITIVE, SOCIAL, AND MOTIVATIONAL PROCESSES IN GROUP CREATIVITY

Paulus and his colleagues have developed a model that integrates the cognitive, social, and motivational processes involved in group creativity (Paulus & Brown, 2003, 2007; Paulus & Dzindolet, 2008; see Figure 1). This model, which has roots in an earlier cognitive-motivational model of group task performance (Paulus, 1983), provides a useful framework for organizing much of the literature on group creativity (see Paulus, Dugosh, Dzindolet, Coskun, & Putman, 2002; Paulus, Levine, Brown, Minai, & Doboli, 2010). The model identifies several group, task, and situational variables, which influence group creativity and innovation via their impact on cognitive, motivational, and social processes. Rather than discussing the model in detail, we will first summarize some of the social and motivational processes involved in group creativity and then discuss some of the cognitive processes.

Social and Motivational Processes

A critical social process is the sharing of ideas, which is influenced by some of the same factors that influence other social processes. For example, Paulus and Dzindolet (1993) found that the sharing process is influenced by the natural tendency of individuals to compare their performance with that of others (Festinger, 1954). It is presumed that group brainstormers are attuned both to the rate and the quality of the ideas generated by their fellow group members. There is a tendency in groups for the performance of the brainstormers to converge, or become more similar over time, both in terms of rate and type of ideas (Camacho & Paulus, 1995; Paulus, Larey, & Dzindolet, 2000; Roy, Gauvin, & Limayem, 1996; Ziegler, Diehl, & Zijlstra, 2000). Thus most group brainstormers

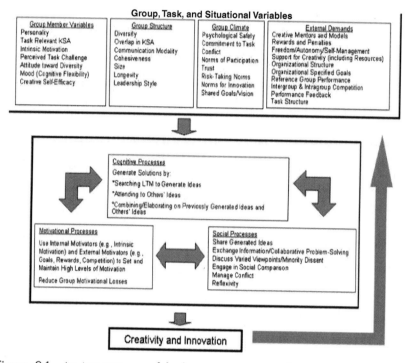

Figure 9.1 An integrative model of group creativity and team innovation (from Paulus & Dzindolet, 2008).

view their performance as fairly comparable to that of their fellow brainstormers. Individual brainstormers do not have such a basis of comparison for their performance. One consequence, mentioned above, is that group brainstormers evaluate their performance more favorably than do individual brainstormers (Paulus et al., 1993; Paulus, Larey, & Ortega, 1995; Stroebe et al., 1992).

Social processes (in particular social comparison) can help to explain production losses in groups (performance deficits in interacting groups relative to nominal groups). The various constraints on the performance of groups, such as production blocking (having to wait one's turn to share ideas) and evaluation apprehension (worrying about how others will evaluate one's contributions) (Diehl & Stroebe, 1987), insure that groups initially perform at a low level. Through the social comparison process, this low performance level may become normative and carry over to subsequent sessions. Further, since in laboratory studies using ad hoc groups there may be little intrinsic or extrinsic incentive for a high level of performance, the low producers in the group may be more influential than the high producers (via downward comparison on the part of high producers; Camacho & Paulus, 1995; Paulus & Dzindolet, 1993).

However, under conditions where there are strong intrinsic or extrinsic incentives, upward comparison on the part of low producers may occur. When participants are provided feedback about their performance relative to others, they are motivated to perform at a higher level, due possibly to enhanced feelings of competition (Coskun, 2000; Lount & Phillips, 2007; Michinov & Primois, 2005; Munkes & Diehl, 2003; Paulus, Larey, Putman, Leggett, & Roland, 1996). Similarly, when participants are told at the beginning of brainstorming about a high performance level of other brainstormers, their performance is significantly enhanced (Coskun, 2000; Paulus & Dzindolet, 1993). The importance of social comparison processes was demonstrated in a study in which individuals were exposed to either 8 or 40 ideas from someone who was presumed to be similar to them in creativity or to either 8 or 40 ideas generated by a computer. Those who thought that the ideas came from a similar person were more influenced by the rate of idea exposure than were those who thought that the ideas came from a computer (Dugosh & Paulus, 2005).

In regard to motivational processes, group norms are important. One might expect that if a group had a strong orientation for individuality or uniqueness, the group would be motivated to generate more unique ideas, especially if creative ideas are the goal. Alternatively, a group with a more collective or group harmony orientation might demonstrate enhanced creativity if that is the group goal or norm since members of such groups might be more likely to behave in accord with that norm. Goncalo and Staw (2006) found results consistent with the individualistic prediction in a study manipulating individualistic and collectivistic orientations and whether group members were instructed to generate creative or practical ideas for a problem solving task. Individualistic groups that were instructed to be creative had more ideas and more novel ideas than did collectivistic groups that were instructed to be creative. When groups were instructed to generate practical ideas, there were no significant differences on these measures between the individualistic and collectivistic groups. Thus, an individualistic norm in groups seems to support the expression and sharing of novel ideas because of a reduced concern about what others might think. Moreover, it appears that group norms influence creative behavior especially when one's identity as a member of the group is very salient (Adarves-Yorno, Postmes, & Haslam, 2007).

When groups are involved in creative activities, there is typically an implicit or explicit goal associated with idea generation. This goal may be to come up with a lot of ideas or very creative ideas or both. The group goal has important implications for the group's performance. One of the most important determinants of performance in groups is perceived efficacy (Baer, Oldham, Jacobsohn, & Hollingshead, 2008), and group goals can have a strong influence on this efficacy (Larey & Paulus, 1995). If group goals are set too high, groups may feel reduced efficacy, and this may inhibit their performance (Latham & Locke, 2009). However, it is important for groups to have a challenging goal, and their performance is most enhanced if they had a role in setting this goal (Haslam, Wegge, & Postmes, 2009).

Very little research has been conducted on how groups deal with different goals (Litchfield, 2008). Quantity of ideas is the major goal in brainstorming research. We know that a quantity goal increases the total number of ideas

(Paulus & Dzindolet, 1993) and that the number of good ideas is positively related to the total number of ideas (Diehl & Stroebe, 1987). Yet no study has directly compared the impact of the four subgoals typically employed in brainstorming studies (generate as many ideas as possible, don't criticize others' ideas, say what comes to mind, build on others' ideas). However, one study found that the "don't criticize" rule may not be critical to brainstorming success since encouraging debate and even criticism did not inhibit creativity on a brainstorming task (Nemeth and Ormiston, 2007).

Cognitive Processes

Two cognitive models of group creativity have recently been proposed. These models share some basic assumptions: The idea sharing process requires group members to search their relevant knowledge or memory for relevant ideas. The sharing of these ideas can stimulate group members to think of additional ideas or areas of knowledge. The mutual exchange process can lead to an increase in the number of ideas generated in the group, the number of categories explored, and the novelty of the ideas.

Semantic Network Model   Paulus and Brown (Brown & Paulus, 2002; Paulus & Brown, 2003, 2007) have suggested that creativity in idea generating groups occurs to the extent that idea sharing stimulates excitation in group members' semantic networks (networks of related ideas or categories). Ideas from one person may stimulate a similar idea in another person if the two people share similar or overlapping associative networks. This is because related concepts or ideas are likely to activate one another (Collins & Loftus, 1975). Consistent with this perspective, Dugosh and Paulus (2005) found that priming college students with ideas that were fairly common in prior brainstorming sessions with similar students resulted in the generation of more ideas and more unique ideas than priming with uncommon ideas. This presumably occurs because common ideas are more likely to be related to the semantic networks of the student participants. Other evidence comes from a series of experiments that manipulated the relationship of dual words in either distant (e.g., apple–eagle) or close (e.g., apple–grapes) associations and that asked participants to come up with more words from these associations prior to the brainstorming session (Coskun, 2009). Consistent with the associative memory perspective, the participants who worked on close associations generated more unique ideas in the subsequent brainstorming session than did those who worked on distant associations.

An important feature of the semantic network model is the accessibility of the categories of ideas relevant to the brainstorming task. Some categories may be relatively unique and unrelated to more common categories. These unique categories may not be accessed unless there is some external stimulus or reminder to do so. Exposing individuals to unique categories does in fact enhance the number of ideas generated from such categories (Dugosh &

Paulus, 2005; Leggett, 1997; Nijstad, Stroebe, & Lodewijkx, 2002). Another important factor in the impact of shared ideas is the degree to which individuals pay attention to these ideas (Coskun & Yilmaz, 2009; Dugosh, Paulus, Roland, & Yang, 2000). Unless participants attend to the ideas, one would not expect any associative impact. The semantic network model has been formalized as a computational model involving a matrix of probabilities of transitions from one category to another. This model has been able to replicate the findings of a number of brainstorming studies (Brown & Paulus, 1996; 2002; Brown, Tumeo, Laroy, & Paulus, 1998; Coskun & Yilmaz, 2009; Paulus et al., 2010)

One of the key predictions of the associative memory model is that individuals are stimulated by exposure to ideas from others. This prediction has been supported in several studies showing that exposing brainstorming individuals to a relatively large number of ideas increases the number of ideas they generate (Dugosh & Paulus, 2005; Dugosh et al., 2000). Moreover, increased exposure to irrelevant ideas or information reduces the number of ideas generated (Dugosh et al., 2000), because this type of material can interfere with semantic associations relevant to the task. For this reason, instructing brainstormers to avoid sharing ideas that are irrelevant to the task enhances idea generation in groups (Putman & Paulus, 2009).

Search for Ideas in Memory Model   Nijstad and Stroebe (2006) have developed an associative memory model of group creativity that provides a detailed analysis of the memory search and idea production processes. This model overlaps somewhat with the Paulus and Brown (2003, 2007) semantic network model but focuses on the generation of specific ideas and the importance of "flow of ideas" rather than the category transition process (Brown et al., 1998). According to Nijstad and Stroebe, a consistent flow of ideas is likely when individuals search within a specific category because of the semantic clustering of ideas within the category. When individuals switch categories, they have to begin a new search, and the generation of ideas should be slower because it inevitably takes time to search one's memory for new categories. Nijstad and Stroebe (2006) argue that idea sharing has a positive effect because it reduces the time needed to develop one's own search cues for new categories. When individuals cannot come up with an idea within a certain period of time, this is experienced as a "failure". This can be a signal to the person that he or she has run out of ideas and needs to stop trying to generate more ideas (Nijstad, Stroebe, & Lodewijkx, 2006). Since groups should be able to generate more total ideas than individuals, groups should persist longer. In a study in which interactive groups were allowed to continue brainstorming until they felt it was a good time to stop, groups indeed brainstormed longer than individuals (Nijstad, Stroebe, & Lodewijkx, 1999). Yet, even with the increased time to brainstorm, interactive groups did not exceed the performance of comparable nominal groups. Nijstad et al. (2006) argued that the enhanced experience of "failure" for individual brainstormers is at least partly responsible for positive perceptions of performance in group brainstorming relative to individual brainstorming.

The Role of Cognitive Stimulation   The two models discussed above have stimulated a number of studies on the cognitive processes involved in group idea generation and provided a basis for predicting synergistic effects of group idea sharing. One of the basic goals of cognitively oriented research has been to determine whether shared ideas can stimulate additional ideas in groups. That would seem to be an obvious outcome. However, when group members are sharing ideas, they have to take turns—only one person can effectively have the floor at a given time. So it is not possible for group members simply to generate a flow of ideas off the tops of their heads. They can express some of their ideas as they occur, but they also have to coordinate turns with the other group members, listen to their ideas, and possibly build on those ideas. While one is listening to ideas from others, one may forget the ideas that one has "on hold," and the semantic associations related to those ideas may dissipate (Diehl & Stroebe, 1987; Nijstad & Stroebe, 2006; Paulus & Brown, 2003, 2007). In fact, Nijstad, Stroebe, and Lodewijkx (2003) found that a critical factor in people's ability to generate ideas in a given period of time is their ability to express ideas as they occur. This is obviously difficult in face-to-face groups. Another limiting factor of idea generation is that it may lead to fixation on a limited range of topics (Baruah & Paulus, 2009; Larey & Paulus, 1999; Ziegler et al., 2000). In group interaction, it is natural to focus on one topic at a time. So when one person shares an idea on a topic, others may generate ideas in the same category. This may lead to the generation of a large number of ideas within a particular category but may limit the range of categories surveyed (Nijstad & Stroebe, 2006; Rietzschel, Nijstad, & Stroebe, 2007; Santanen, Briggs, & De Vreede, 2004).

An alternative for enhancing cognitive stimulation in groups is to use electronic or writing procedures for exchanging ideas (Dennis & Williams, 2003; Heslin, 2009). These procedures can be designed so that individuals can share ideas as they occur without having to wait their turn to present these ideas. Moreover, when one has a temporary halt in one's idea generation process, one can use that as an opportunity to examine ideas that have been shared by others (e.g., in an electronic format or in a stack of shared ideas or posted notes). These procedures allow one to take advantage of the semantic flow of individual ideation and the stimulating effects of periodic exposure to ideas from others. Studies have found that the production losses typically experienced in groups are not observed when electronic brainstorming or brainwriting procedures are used. In fact, these paradigms are the only ones that have produced evidence of synergy in which interacting groups generate more ideas than do nominal groups (De Rosa, Smith, & Hantula, 2007; Paulus & Yang, 2000).

SYNERGY IN CREATIVE GROUPS

As the work on electronic brainstorming and brainwriting suggests, the search for synergy has been a major focus of the research on group task performance and creativity (Larson, 2009). The basic rationale for bringing groups together for creative projects is that such interactions will lead to more and better ideas. Synergy has been assumed in case studies of unusually creative groups (Farrell, 2001; John-Steiner, 2000; Sawyer, 2007; Sutton & Hargadon, 1996). These case studies provide detailed descriptions of these groups and are useful in pointing out potentially critical factors in their success. However, it is not possible to determine with any certainty which of the many factors was indeed critical. Given the intelligence of the people involved in these groups, they may have come up with great ideas or products no matter what the group process was. Similarly, studies of team innovation have found some factors that influence perception of innovation (Hülsheger et al., 2009; West and Richter, 2008), but they have not compared the performance of innovative teams with the performance of non-team controls to determine the extent to which team interaction enhances innovation.

Conditions Required for Synergy

What are the critical conditions for group synergy? First of all, it is important to overcome the factors related to production loss in groups—social loafing, evaluation apprehension, production blocking, and downward comparison. So group members should be held accountable for their individual contributions to the group (Paulus et al., 1996). This can be accomplished by some system that allows the tracking of individual contributions. Group members should feel free to express ideas as they occur without fear of others' criticisms (Diehl & Stroebe, 1987). The interaction process should allow for unconstrained exchange of ideas as in electronic brainstorming and brainwriting. And since group members may move their performance in the direction of low performing members, there should be some incentive for high levels of performance or some sense of competition (Paulus & Dzindolet, 2008). These various procedures can reduce production losses in groups. Second, to attain synergy it is important that the group interaction process allow for an effective tapping of the cognitive resources of each group member. Therefore, the task needs to be structured so that there can be an effective meshing of individual idea generation and processing of shared ideas. Group members need to able to tap shared ideas when they wish, and they may benefit from incubation sessions after a period of idea exposure. The provision of such a session immediately after a shared brainstorming session allows for tapping additional associations stimulated during the sharing period (Dugosh et al., 2000; Paulus & Yang, 2000), and brief breaks during the sharing process can also provide such a benefit (Paulus, Nakui, Putman, & Brown, 2006). Third, it is important for group members to pay careful attention to the shared ideas (Paulus & Brown, 2007). This may be difficult when one is faced with the multiple tasks of generating ideas, attending to ideas of others, and building on those ideas. Asking participants to remember shared ideas appears to be one way to increase attention and idea generation (Dugosh et al., 2000). Finally, synergy should be most likely when the group has diverse areas of expertise related to the problem. This would increase the range of topics or relevant categories of ideas explored and subsequently the number of ideas generated (Baruah & Paulus, 2009; Coskun, 2005; Nijstad & Stroebe, 2006). However, it is also possible that exposure to many categories will lead to superficial tapping of these categories rather than a deeper exploration of the most relevant categories (Nijstad & Stroebe, 2006). One may be more likely to come up with creative ideas if one is primed to focus on a specific subcategory of a problem (Coskun, Paulus, Brown, & Sherwood, 2000; Rietzschel et al., 2007). However, this can be at the expense of generating ideas in other categories. Since the most creative ideas are likely to occur during an in-depth search of a category, it may be important to balance the range of categories explored with the depth of exploration.

Evidence for Synergy

Using the above approaches, a number of studies have found evidence for synergy in creative groups (De Rosa et al., 2007; Dugosh et al., 2000; Dugosh & Paulus, 2005; Paulus & Yang, 2000). More specifically, they have demonstrated that interactive brainstorming groups can generate more ideas than comparable nominal groups. It is important to note that all of these studies used electronic or writing exchange procedures. Another way to minimize the potential negative effects of group interaction while still gaining stimulation is to brainstorm in pairs. Evidence indicates that pairs of face-to-face brainstormers typically show little if any deficit in performance relative to nominal pairs (Diehl & Stroebe, 1987; Mullen et al., 1999). More importantly, one study with a relatively difficult brainstorming task found that interacting pairs outperformed nominal pairs by about 50% (Wilson, Timmel, & Miller, 2004). So keeping face-to-face groups as small as possible is one way to obtain synergy with such groups.

Interestingly, research on electronic brainstorming has found that the synergistic benefits increase with the size of the group (Dennis & Williams, 2003). The beneficial effects of electronic brainstorming on both the number of ideas generated and their rated novelty is most evident when groups have eight or more members (De Rosa et al., 2007). So far there is not a clear explanation for this effect. It could reflect the stimulating effect of the wide range of ideas and categories that result as groups increase in size. It could also reflect increased motivation in that group members may feel more competitive as groups get larger and they see the accumulation of a large number of ideas. These factors may produce increased idea generation in electronic brainstorming groups where production blocking is not an issue.

DIVERSITY AND CREATIVITY

Group members can vary along a wide variety of personal dimensions, including age, gender, race, personality, values, experience, and expertise. At present there is a strong emphasis on promoting diversity in work and educational settings and an assumption that interaction among diverse group members will be beneficial for social relations. Although some studies have demonstrated such benefits (Pettigrew & Tropp, 2008), others have shown that member diversity is often related to negative social relations, consistent with the literatures suggesting a strong bias in favor of those who are similar to oneself or who belong to one's ingroup (Hogg, 2006). It is also often assumed that diversity in work groups will enhance their performance. This is a reasonable assumption given the increased breadth of perspectives and knowledge in diverse groups. However, systematic reviews have not supported this view. In terms of general group performance, some studies have shown increased performance, some have found reduced performance, and others have found no effect (Bowers, Pharmer, & Salas, 2000; Mannix & Neale, 2005 ; Van Knippenberg & Schippers, 2007; Webber & Donahue, 2001).

Several reviews have examined a broad range of factors that might determine whether there are benefits of diversity in groups (see Moreland, this volume). For example, such benefits may depend on the type of diversity (Bowers et al., 2000; Harrison & Klein, 2007; Mannix & Neale, 2005), with benefits somewhat more likely when the diversity involves differences in deep-level or task-relevant information and when the task is difficult. It seems obvious that groups whose members have diverse knowledge needed for a task are more likely to perform this task effectively than are groups that do not have this knowledge. There is some evidence of this from self-report studies of team creativity (Hülsheger et al., 2009), and a few studies have obtained support using objective performance measures. For example, in several brainstorming studies, ethnic and cultural diversity were related to increased quality or range of ideas (McLeod, Lobel, & Cox, 1996; Nakui, Paulus, & Van der Zee, 2011; Watson, Kumar, & Michaelson, 1993). However, thus far there are no compelling studies of the benefits of expertise or knowledge diversity on creativity (Derry, Gernsbacher, & Schunn, 2005; Van Knippenberg & Schippers, 2007).

Part of the problem with knowledge diversity is that people with different areas of expertise may also differ from one another in their values and interests and how they perceive the task (Cronin & Weingart, 2007; Gebert, Boerner, & Kearney, 2006). So a team of interdisciplinary scientists may have a wealth of diverse knowledge to share, but their effective collaboration requires a willingness to learn about each other's areas of expertise and to carefully integrate and align this with one's own. This has been emphasized in the elaboration model of Van Knippenberg and Schippers (2007). In order for diversity to facilitate creativity, group members must be motivated to process information from other members. One factor that facilitates this is having a positive attitude toward diversity (Homan, Van Knippenberg, Van Kleef, & De Dreu, 2007; Mitchell, Nicholas, & Boyle, 2009; Nakui et al., 2011). For example, ethnic diversity in groups was related to enhanced novelty of ideas only when group members had positive attitudes toward diverse groups (Nakui et al., 2011). Two other factors that appear to enhance the benefits of diversity for creativity are a generally supportive social context (Mannix & Neale, 2005) and a longer time working together as a team (Watson et al., 1993).

Another key factor in enhancing the benefits of diversity for creativity may be "common ground," or what Mannix and Neale (2005) term "bridging". That is, it may be important for group members to realize that they have common interests and values (Chatman, Polzer, Barsade, & Neale, 1998; Ely & Roberts, 2008). An analysis of successful real-world collaborative groups indicates that they typically have a common vision and set of values (Farrell, 2001). This provides a strong foundation upon which diverse perspectives can be exchanged without breaking up the group. It may be important to allow a diverse group to first develop common interests and values and a sense of cohesion before it begins serious exchange of diverse perspectives (Van der Zee & Paulus, 2009). Having some common *cognitive* ground may also be helpful. As discussed earlier, exposure to relatively common ideas is more likely to stimulate additional unique ideas than is exposure to unique ideas (Dugosh & Paulus, 2005). Moreover, group members who begin brainstorming with a focus on a common set of categories generate more overall ideas than do those who begin with a focus on different categories (Baruah & Paulus, 2009). Also consistent with the common ground perspective is the fact that moderate levels of diversity seem to be most beneficial for information sharing (Dahlin, Weingart, & Hinds, 2005).

The literature on diversity provides additional evidence on how difficult it is to obtain synergistic benefits from group interaction. As with the research on group brainstorming, simply exchanging complementary perspectives in a group does not insure that the group will be particularly creative. Such creative benefits will only be realized when the social, motivational, and task conditions are optimal for careful and motivated processing of shared ideas, even those that might elicit some negative emotional reactions.

IDEA GENERATION VERSUS EXPLOITATION

Most of the research on creative performance in groups has focused on idea generation, or divergent thinking. However, as noted earlier, the creative process in real-world settings often involves several phases, including problem selection, idea generation, idea evaluation, and idea implementation (Parnes, 1975). (The latter two phases are often discussed together as the exploitation phase.) As suggested by Amabile (1996), these phases are likely to be influenced differently by particular processes. For example, a "low evaluative" setting encouraging the generation of a large number of ideas may be good for producing ideas, but exploitation requires selection of the ideas with the greatest potential and then their effective implementation. This may require a "high evaluative" setting characterized by various judgment, decision, and negotiation processes. There is very little research that has examined the idea generation and exploitation phases independently. Most studies on work team innovation use self-report measures that do not clearly distinguish between these two phases. Only a few studies on group creativity have examined different phases of the creative process. Two studies asked participants to brainstorm and then to select their best ideas (Putman & Paulus, 2009; Rietzschel, Nijstad, & Stroebe, 2006). Both of these studies found that the average originality of the selected ideas was no better than the average originality of all the ideas generated by the individuals or groups. There appears to be a bias toward the more common ideas being selected as the best ideas (Putman & Paulus, 2009). Putman and Paulus (2009) had individuals brainstorm as a group or as individuals prior to evaluating their ideas as a group. As usual, nominal groups generated more ideas (and more novel ideas), and they were subsequently able to select more novel ideas from this larger pool in comparison to the interactive groups. However, this benefit for nominal groups did not occur when they evaluated their ideas as individuals in comparison to interactive groups evaluating ideas as a group (Rietzschel et al., 2006).

FACTORS THAT ENHANCE GROUP CREATIVITY

We have highlighted some of the key processes involved in group creativity and discussed a number of factors that enhance group creativity. Among those that reflect the cognitive aspects of the process are being exposed to a large number of ideas, being exposed to diverse ideas, being aware of unique categories of knowledge, having a shared category focus, engaging in solitary brainstorming sessions after group brainstorming, taking brief breaks during brainstorming, and having minimum exposure to irrelevant information. It also seems beneficial to avoid cognitive overload by having participants focus on idea categories in sequence rather than consider them all at once (Coskun et al., 2000) and by structuring electronic brainstorming so that individuals are exposed to only a limited number of new ideas each time they submit an idea (Santanen et al., 2004). There are also a number of social factors that influence the number of ideas generated. More ideas are generated when groups have high standards or goals and are provided feedback about their performance. One interesting finding is that almost all of these effects have a similar positive effect for individual performers and groups (Paulus & Brown, 2003). Only the shared category focus (Baruah & Paulus, 2009) and the aftereffects assessments (Dugosh et al., 2000; Paulus & Yang, 2000) have shown differential benefits for groups.

Training Group Creativity

The various findings we have summarized suggest that there are a number of ways to increase group creativity. And in fact there are many people making a good living facilitating and training teams for creative work. How effective is such training? There is a literature on training creativity, and the presumption is that creativity can be learned (Runco, 2004; Scott, Leritz, & Mumford, 2004). Amabile and Mueller's (2007) componential theory of creativity suggests that one should be able to train task-relevant skills and creativity-relevant skills, and there is some evidence that such training or related experience does enhance creativity (Nickerson, 1999). Yet according to the componential model, one also needs intrinsic motivation. Studies of team innovation suggest that intrinsic motivation may be very important to creativity (Carmeli & Spreitzer, 2009), but controlled studies of group creativity have not assessed the role of intrinsic motivation and the possibility of training groups to be so motivated.

Of the few studies that have examined training of creative groups, some have found that facilitators who monitor the group interaction can enhance the performance of interacting brainstorming groups to the point that they perform at a level similar to that of nominal groups (Offner, Kramer, & Winter, 1996; Oxley, Dzindolet, & Paulus, 1996). However, what happens when the facilitator goes away? Have the participants acquired any skills that carry over to subsequent group sessions? This issue was examined in a study in which groups were trained for an hour in various aspects of effective brainstorming (being efficient, attentive, taking advantage of diversity, and practicing brainstorming with feedback) (Baruah & Paulus, 2008). It was found that training enhanced the subsequent performance of the groups on a new brainstorming task (both in terms of number of ideas and their originality). If one hour of training can have such an impact, it is reasonable to assume that more extensive training using the right techniques will have an even more positive impact. One important aspect of training may be direct experience with the task in a group setting (Gino, Todorova, Miron-Spektor, & Argote, 2009; Moreland, Argote, & Krishnan, 1996). Such direct experience appears to increase mutual awareness of who knows what and who is good at what (transactive memory). This can be very useful as the group tries to coordinate the various aspects of the task and the creative process.

Providing a Supportive Context for Creativity

Even though a group may be trained in various skills relevant to the task, it is important to have a supportive context for creativity, whether this be in short term settings or in organizations. Most of the suggestions for what this context should entail come from the team innovation literature. According to this literature, it is important to have an environment that allows group members to feel comfortable with one another and to feel free to be creative. Among the factors that contribute to a supportive context for creativity are group cohesion, a low degree of relationship conflict, support for innovation, and a feeling of participative safety (i.e., that one does not have to fear the consequences of one's creative actions) (Hülsheger et al., 2009). One reason these factors may enhance creativity is that they increase the positive mood state of the group members. Evidence indicates that such positive moods, especially if they are at least moderately high in activation level (such as feelings of joy, happiness, or positive excitement) enhance divergent thinking (Baas, De Dreu, & Nijstad, 2008; Davis, 2008; Grawitch, Munz, Elliott, & Mathis, 2003).

Groups should also have a positive disposition toward the creative task. They should have a strong vision or clear commitment to their goals, high standards of performance, and effective communication. Groups are not likely to develop these unless they have effective leadership. It appears that the most effective leadership for such groups (whether this is internal or external to the group) is provided by a transformational leader (Eisenbeiss, Van Knippenberg, & Boerner, 2008; Zaccaro, Heinen, & Shuffler, 2009). Such a leader inspires creativity through inducing a shared vision, having high expectations, showing individual consideration and support, and encouraging followers to take innovative approaches (Bass, 1998). A positive disposition toward the creative task not only helps motivate creative behavior, but the consequent success of the group in creative activities may increase individuals' and the group's skills and sense of efficacy (Baer et al., 2008). Efficacy, or the conviction that one is able to accomplish a particular task, is an important factor in a wide range of performance settings, including creative ones (Bandura, 2000; Henderson, 2004).

CREATIVITY IN LABORATORY AND REAL-WORLD GROUPS: SIMILARITIES AND DIFFERENCES

Although much of our review has focused on group creativity in controlled laboratory settings, there has been a growing recognition of the importance of the creative process both in long-term collaborative groups (John-Steiner, 2000; Kanigel, 1986; Sawyer, 2007; Schrage, 1995) and in work teams embedded in organizations (Bennis & Biederman, 1997; Mannix et al., 2009; Paulus, 2000, 2007; Thompson & Choi, 2006). These latter lines of work on collaborative creativity in real-world settings provide an important context for assessing the theoretically oriented research on group creativity that has dominated social psychology. The experimental literature in turn provides a theoretical basis for understanding the creative process in real-world groups and suggests ways to enhance their effectiveness.

Most of the work on innovation by work teams in organizations has been restricted to outsiders' and team members' perceptions of the innovation process and its outcomes (Hülsheger et al., 2009). This work suggests that job relevant diversity, task and goal interdependence, and team size are all positively related to team innovation. Diversity and team size are assumed to have positive effects because they increase the range of information and knowledge available to the team. Task and goal interdependence are assumed to have positive effects because they insure that group members will attend to one another and increase their motivation for the task. These findings are thus consistent with the importance of both cognitive and motivational factors in group creativity. Research on work teams indicates that additional factors associated with innovation include vision (shared goal commitment), participative safety, support for innovation, task orientation, and communication. Again each of these is consistent with research in group creativity demonstrating the importance of goals, low evaluation apprehension, motivational factors, task focus, and effective exchange of ideas (Paulus & Dzindolet, 2008). Team innovation is also facilitated by cohesion. This has not been found to be an important factor in short-term settings, perhaps because it is difficult to develop strong cohesion in such settings.

Studies of long-term creative collaboration have been primarily restricted to descriptive analyses of groups (e.g., Farrell, 2001; John-Steiner, 2000). In an extensive analysis of collaborative groups, or circles, of authors, poets, artists, psychoanalysts, and activists, Farrell (2001) noted that much of their critical interaction occurred in dyads. Thus, members of these groups gained much social and intellectual support from a specific partner. Analyses of these interactions were particularly interesting in that they highlighted various stages through which these groups moved, namely formation, rebellion against authority, constructing a new vision, creative work, collective action, separation, and reunion. Of course not all creative groups go through these stages, but research on work teams also suggests that time is important (Mohammed, Hamilton, & Lin, 2009). Collaborative groups typically consist of 3 to 5 members, and they begin to work in pairs in the vision stage. This fits with the notion that effective creative groups should stay relatively small. In the creative work stage, group members alternate between working alone, working in pairs, and meeting as a circle. This meshes nicely with the stimulation/incubation perspective of group interaction in brainstorming environments, which suggests the need for individual reflection time after group interaction. It is important to note that when long-term collaborative groups carry out a collective project, the complexity of the process often yields social conflicts and subsequent separation from the circle. So even in these groups, the negative effects of social conflicts are evident.

CONCLUSIONS

We have reviewed the literature on group creativity from the vantage points of the research on temporary groups in controlled experiments, work teams in organizations, and long-term collaborative groups in real-world settings. The work on teams and long-term collaborative groups has provided a rich set of findings about the factors that influence creativity in these settings. The work on laboratory groups has provided detailed cognitive, social, motivational models of the group creative process and tested the impact of various factors that facilitate and inhibit group creativity. Although these three research traditions represent different contexts and use different methodologies and samples, we have found considerable consistency among their results.

It is clear from research on laboratory groups that face-to-face groups have a difficult time being creative. Practically all of the published studies have found that such groups generate fewer ideas and fewer good ideas than do nominal groups. Since the average rated creativity of the ideas generated by interacting groups and individuals is about the same, it appears that simply collecting ideas generated by individuals may be the best way to come up with a high number of good ideas (Reinig, Briggs, & Nunamaker, 2007). However, it has been found that when groups interact by means of writing or computers, the production loss due to group interaction is not observed, and these groups can in fact exhibit both more creative ideas and more novel ideas than nominal groups. Furthermore, a wide range of conditions can enhance group creativity, similar to the many ways in which team innovation can be enhanced (Paulus, Dzindolet, & Kohn, 2011). For example, when face-to-face brainstorming groups are given extended time to generate ideas, their performance improves relative to nominal groups. From this vantage point, one can see the groups and teams literatures are fairly consistent. In short-term settings, groups will likely demonstrate production losses. However, with increased time in the group and extended periods of interaction, groups may become fairly effective. They should become more cohesive, develop transactive memory systems, have more opportunities for deeper processing or elaboration of the shared information, and have multiple opportunities to move between individual and group performance, thereby taking full advantage of individual incubation, or reflection time. Further support for such a congruency perspective comes from the fact that many of the factors that have been found to facilitate group interaction also facilitate team interaction (see also Paulus, Nakui & Putman, 2005). Thus, the positive perceptions of participants and observers of innovation in teams may have some basis in reality.

Of course, full support for this congruency perspective will require additional research both in laboratory and field settings. In the former case, longer-term experimental studies with groups of individuals who work together on meaningful projects are required. These could be done in laboratories by having real-world work groups perform relevant tasks under controlled conditions (e.g., Paulus et al., 1995). This would allow a more precise assessment of the synergistic potential for creative interactions in such groups in comparison to these same individuals performing their tasks in isolation. Alternatively, one could do experimental studies in actual work settings in which manipulations of relevant variables and precise measures of group processes and of performance, and perceptual outcomes are possible. Such studies would enable an examination of consistency between team member performance and perceptions. We do not know of any such studies to date.

An important issue for research on real-world work teams is that many (perhaps most) of their creativity tasks cannot be decomposed to assess nominal group performance. For example, a task that requires high levels of expertise from a chemist, biologist and a mathematician cannot be done by just one of those individuals. This is the major reason for the popularity of multi-disciplinary and interdisciplinary teams in science and engineering. Nonetheless, it would still be of interest to examine this type of situation with a set of tasks varying in the extent to which they are feasible for individuals with differing expertise. For example, a chemist, biologist, and mathematician may all be able to come up individually with creative solutions for a more environmentally sustainable college campus. A number of scholars have noted the difficulties encountered by interdisciplinary teams (Derry et al., 2005) and cross-functional teams (Cronin & Weingart, 2007). One implication of the research on group creativity is that the meetings that take place in real-world teams may not be nearly as productive as the participants assume. By using the insights from group creativity research to make these meetings more effective, we may be able to enhance the innovative potential of these teams.

Although there has been a tremendous growth in research on group creativity over the past 20 years, there is still much to learn about the creative process. Experimental research has provided only a few demonstrations of creative synergy in groups, and most research in work settings has been restricted to verbal reports. There is a need for more research with long-term groups in real-world settings that involves an objective assessment of the creative process. This type of research will be difficult and time consuming, but it is necessary in order to more effectively link the theoretically oriented research from laboratory settings to more realistic groups. Such research can further clarify the importance of such factors as group member diversity, group and intergroup exchange processes, and the other variables outlined in Figure 1. This type of research will also enable us to explore the roles of temporal processes, including turnover, in groups as well as the extent to which the creative process involves the actual combination or integration of shared ideas.

ACKNOWLEDGMENTS

This chapter and related efforts are supported by a collaborative grant BCS 0729305 to the first author from the National Science Foundation, which includes support from the Deputy Director of National Intelligence for Analysis and a collaborative CreativeIT grant 0855825 from the National Science Foundation.

Any opinions, findings, and conclusions or recommendations expressed in this material are those of the authors and do not necessariliy reflect the views of the National Science Foundation.

REFERENCES

Adarves-Yorno, I., Postmes, T., & Haslam, S. A. (2007). Creative innovation or crazy irrelevance? The contribution of group norms and social identity to creative behavior. *Journal of Experimental Social Psychology, 43*, 410–416.

Amabile, T. (1983). The social psychology of creativity: A componential conceptualization. *Journal of Personality and Social Psychology, 45*, 357–376.

Amabile, T. M. (1996). *Creativity in context.* Boulder, CO: Westview Press.

Amabile, T. M., & Mueller, J. S. (2007). Studying creativity, its processes, and its antecedents: An exploration of the componential theory of creativity. In J. Zhou & C. Shalley (Eds.), *Handbook of organizational creativity.* Mahwah, NJ: Lawrence Erlbaum Associates.

Bass, B. M. (1998). *Transformational leadership: Industrial, military, and educational impact.* Mahwah, NJ: Lawrence Erlbaum Associates.

Baas, M., De Dreu, C. K. W., & Nijstad, B. A. (2008). A meta-analysis of 25 years of research on mood and creativity: Hedonic tone, activation, or regulatory focus? *Psychological Bulletin, 134*, 779–806.

Baer, M., Oldham, G. R., Jacobsohn, G. C., & Hollingshead, A. B. (2008). The personality composition of teams and creativity: The moderating role of team creative confidence. *Journal of Creative Behavior, 42*, 255–282.

Bandura, A. (2000). Exercise of human agency through collective efficacy. *Current Directions in Psychological Science, 9,* 75–78.

Baruah, J., & Paulus, P. B. (2008). Effects of training on idea generation in groups. *Small Group Research, 39,* 523–541.

Baruah, J., & Paulus, P. (2009). Enhancing group creativity: The search for synergy. In E. A. Mannix, M. A. Neale, & J. A. Goncalo (Eds.), *Creativity in groups: Research on managing groups and teams* (Vol. 12, pp. 29–56). Bingley, UK: Emerald Group Publishing Limited.

Bennis, W. G., & Biederman, P. W. (1997). *Organizing genius: The secrets of creative collaboration.* Reading, MA: Addison-Wesley.

Bowers, C. A., Pharmer, J. A., & Salas, E. (2000). When member homogeneity is needed in work teams: A meta-analysis. *Small Group Research, 31,* 305–327.

Brown, V. R., & Paulus, P. B. (1996). A simple dynamic model of social factors in group brainstorming. *Small Group Research, 27,* 91–114.

Brown, V. R., & Paulus, P. B. (2002). Making group brainstorming more effective: Recommendations from an associative memory perspective. *Current Directions in Psychological Science,11,* 208–212.

Brown, V., Tumeo, M., Larey, T. S., & Paulus, P. B. (1998). Modeling cognitive interactions during group brainstorming. *Small Group Research, 29,* 495–526.

Camacho, L. M., & Paulus, P. B. (1995). The role of social anxiousness in group brainstorming. *Journal of Personality and Social Psychology, 68,* 1071–1080.

Carmeli, A., & Spreitzer, G. M. (2009). Trust, connectivity, and thriving: Implications for innovative behaviors at work. *Journal of Creative Behavior, 43,* 169–199.

Chatman, J. A., Polzer, J. T., Barsade, S. G., & Neale, M. A. (1998). Being different yet feeling similar: The influence of demographic composition and organizational culture on work processes and outcomes. *Administrative Science Quarterly, 43,* 749–780.

Choi, H-S., & Thompson, L. (2005). Old wine in a new bottle: Impact of membership change on group creativity. *Organizational Behavior and Human Decision Processes, 98,* 121–132.

Collins, A. M. & Loftus, E. F. (1975). A spreading activation theory of semantic processing. *Psychological Review, 82,* 407–428.

Coskun, H. (2000). *The effects of outgroup comparison, social context, intrinsic motivation, and collective identity in brainstorming groups.* Unpublished doctoral dissertation. The University of Texas at Arlington, TX.

Coskun, H. (2005). Cognitive stimulation with convergent and divergent thinking exercising in brainwriting: Incubation, sequence priming, and group context. *Small Group Research, 36,* 466–498.

Coskun, H. (2009). The effects of associative exercises on the idea generation during brainstorming. *Turkish Journal of Psychology, 24,* 45–46.

Coskun, H., Paulus, P. B., Brown, V., & Sherwood, J. J. (2000). Cognitive stimulation and problem presentation in idea generation groups. *Group Dynamics: Theory, Research, and Practice, 4,* 307–329.

Coskun, H., & Yilmaz, O. (2009). A new dynamical model of brainstorming: Linear, nonlinear, continuous (simultaneous), and impulsive (sequential) cases. *Journal of Mathematical Psychology, 53,* 253–264.

Cronin, M. A., & Weingart, L. R. (2007). Representational gaps, information processing, and conflict in functionally diverse teams. *Academy of Management Review, 32,* 761–773.

Dacey, J. S., & Lennon, K. H. (1998). *Understanding creativity: The interplay of biological, psychological, and social factors.* San Francisco, CA: John Wiley & Sons, Inc.

Dahlin, K., Weingart, L., & Hinds, P. (2005). Team diversity and information use. *Academy of Management Journal, 48,* 1107–1123.

Davis, M. A. (2008). Understanding the relationship between mood and creativity: A meta-analysis. *Organizational Behavior and Human Decision Processes, 108,* 25–38.

Dennis, A. R., & Williams, M. L. (2003). Electronic brainstorming: Theory, research, and future directions. In P. B. Paulus & B. A. Nijstad (Eds.), *Group creativity: Innovation through collaboration* (pp. 160–180). New York, NY: Oxford University Press.

De Rosa, D. M., Smith, C. L., & Hantula, D. A. (2007). The medium matters: Mining the long-promised merit of group interaction in creative idea generation tasks in a meta-analysis of the electronic group brainstorming literature. *Computers in Human Behavior, 23,* 1549–1581.

Derry, S. J., Gernsbacher, M. A., & Schunn, C. D. (2005). *Interdisciplinary collaboration: An emerging cognitive science.* Mahwah, NJ: Lawrence Erlbaum.

Diehl, M., & Stroebe, W. (1987). Productivity loss in brainstorming groups: Toward the solution of riddle. *Journal of Personality and Social Psychology, 53,* 497–509.

Dugosh, K. L., & Paulus, P. B. (2005). Cognitive and social comparison processes in brainstorming. *Journal of Experimental Social Psychology, 41,* 313–320.

Dugosh, K. L., Paulus, P. B., Roland, E. J., & Yang, H. (2000). Cognitive stimulation in brainstorming. *Journal of Personality and Social Psychology, 79,* 722–735.

Eisenbeiss, S. A., Van Knippenberg, D., & Boerner, S. (2008). Transformational leadership and team innovation: Integrating team climate principles. *Journal of Applied Psychology, 93,* 1438–1446.

Ely, R. J., & Roberts, L. M. (2008). Putting your own down. In A. Brief (Ed.), *Diversity at work* (pp. 175–201). New York, NY: Cambridge University Press.

Farrell, M. P. (2001). *Collaborative circles: Friendship dynamics & creative work.* Chicago, IL: University of Chicago Press.

Festinger, L. (1954). A theory of social comparison processes. *Human Relations, 7,* 117–140.

Gebert, D., Boerner, S., & Kearney, E. (2006). Cross-functionality and innovation in new product development teams: A dilemmatic structure and its consequences for the management of diversity. *European Journal of Work and Organizational Psychology, 15,* 431–458.

Gino, F., Todorova, G., Miron-Spektor, E., & Argote, L. (2009). When and why prior task experience fosters team creativity. In E. A. Mannix, M. A. Neale, & J. A. Goncalo (Eds.), *Creativity in groups: Research on managing groups and teams* (Vol. 12, pp. 87–110). Bingley, UK: Emerald Group Publishing Limited.

Grawitch, M. J., Munz, D. C., Elliott, E. K., & Mathis, A. (2003). Promoting creativity in temporary problem-solving groups: The effects of positive mood and autonomy in problem definition on idea-generating performance. *Group Dynamics: Theory, Research, and Practice, 7,* 200–213.

Goncalo, J. A., & Staw, B. M. (2006). Individualism-collectivism and group creativity. *Organizational Behavior and Human Decision Processes, 100,* 96–109.

Harrison, D. A., & Klein, K. J. (2007). What's the difference: Diversity constructs as separation, variety, or disparity in organizations. *Academy of Management Review, 32,* 1199–1228.

Haslam, S. A., Wegge, J., & Postmes, T. (2009). Are we on a learning curve or a treadmill? The benefits of participative group goal setting become apparent as tasks become increasingly challenging over time. *European Journal of Social Psychology* 39, 430–446.

Henderson, S. J. (2004). Inventors: The ordinary genius next door. In R. J. Sternberg, E. E. Grigorenko, & J. L. Singer (Eds.), *Creativity: From potential to realization* (pp. 103–126). Washington, DC: American Psychological Association.

Heslin, P. A. (2009). Better than brainstorming? Potential boundary conditions to brainwriting for idea generation in organizations. *Journal of Occupational and Organizational Psychology, 82,* 129–145.

Hogg, M. A. (2006). Social identity theory. In P. J. Burke (Ed.), *Contemporary social psychological theories* (pp. 111–136). Palo Alto, CA: Stanford University Press.

Homan, A. C., Van Knippenberg, D., Van Kleef, G. A., & De Dreu, C. K. W. (2007). Bridging faultlines by valuing diversity: Diversity beliefs, information elaboration, and performance in diverse work groups. *Journal of Applied Psychology, 92,* 1189–1199.

Hülsheger, U. R., Anderson, N., & Salgado, J. F. (2009). Team-level predictors of innovation at work: A comprehensive meta-analysis spanning three decades of research. *Journal of Applied Psychology, 94,* 1128–1145.

John-Steiner, V. (2000). *Creative collaboration.* New York, NY: Oxford University Press.

Kanev, K., Kimura, S., & Orr, T. (2009). A framework for collaborative learning in dynamic group environments. *Journal of Distance Education Technologies, 7,* 58–77.

Kanigel, R. (1986). *Apprentice to genius: The making of a scientific dynasty.* New York, NY: Macmillan.

Latham, G. P. & Locke, E. A. (2009). Science and ethics: What should count as evidence against the use of goal setting? *Academy of Management Perspectives, 23,* 88–91.

Larey, T. S., & Paulus, P. B. (1995). Social comparison and goal setting in brainstorming groups. *Journal of Applied Social Psychology, 26,* 1579–1596.

Larey, T. S., & Paulus, P. B. (1999). Group preference and convergent tendencies in groups: A content analysis of group brainstorming performance. *Creativity Research Journal, 12,* 175–184.

Larson, J. R. (2009). *In search of synergy in small group performance.* New York, NY: Psychology Press.

Leggett, K. L. (1997). *The effectiveness of categorical priming in brainstorming.* Unpublished Master's thesis, University of Texas at Arlington, TX.

Litchfield, R. C. (2008). Brainstorming reconsidered: A goal-based view. *Academy of Management Review, 33,* 649–668.

Lount, R. B., & Phillips, K. W. (2007). Working harder with the out-group: The impact of social category diversity on motivation gains. *Organizational Behavior and Human Decision Processes, 103,* 214–224.

Mannix, E. A., & Neale, M. A. (2005). What difference makes a difference: The promise and reality of diverse groups in organizations. *Psychological Science in the Public Interest, 6,* 31–55.

Mannix, E. A., Neale, M., & Goncalo, J. A. (Eds.). (2009). *Creativity in groups: Research on managing groups and teams* (Vol. 12). Bingley, UK: Emerald Group Publishing Limited.

McLeod, P. L., Lobel, S. A., & Cox, T. H. (1996). Ethnic diversity and creativity in small groups. *Small Group Research, 27,* 248–264.

Michinov, N., & Primois, C. (2005). Improving productivity and creativity in online groups through social comparison process: New evidence for asynchronous electronic brainstorming. *Computers in Human Behavior, 21,* 11–28.

Mitchell, R., Nicholas, S., & Boyle, B. (2009). The role of openness to cognitive diversity and group processes in knowledge creation. *Small Group Research, 40,* 535–554.

Mohammed, A., Hamilton, K., & Lin, A. (2009). The incorporation of time in team research: Past, current, and future. In E. Salas, G. F. Goodwin, & C. S. Burke (Eds.), *In team effectiveness in complex organizations: Cross-disciplinary perspectives and approaches* (pp. 321–348). New York, NY: Routledge.

Moreland, R. L. (2010). Are dyads really groups? *Small Group Research, 41,* 251–267.

Moreland, R. L., Argote, L., & Krishnan, R. (1996). Social shared cognition at work: Transactive memory and group performance. In J. L. Nye & A. M. Brower (Eds.), *What's social about social cognition? Research on socially shared cognition in small groups* (pp. 57–84). Thousand Oaks, CA: Sage Publications.

Moreland, R. L., & Levine, J. M. (2009). Building bridges to improve theory and research on small groups. In E. Salas, G. F. Goodwin, & C. S. Burke (Eds.), *Team effectiveness in complex organizations and systems: Cross-disciplinary perspectives and approaches* (pp. 17–38). New York, NY: Routledge.

Mullen, B., Johnson, C., & Salas, E. (1991). Productivity loss in brainstorming groups: A meta-analytic integration. *Basic and Applied Social Psychology, 12,* 3–24.

Munkes, J., & Diehl, M. (2003). Matching or competition? Performance comparison processes in an idea generation task. *Group Processes and Intergroup Relations, 6,* 305–320.

Nakui, T., Paulus, P. B., & Van der Zee, K. I. (2011). The role of attitudes in reactions to diversity in work groups. *Journal of Applied Social Psychology, 41,* 2327–2351.

Nemeth, C. J., & Ormiston, M. (2007). Creative idea generation: Harmony versus stimulation. *European Journal of Social Psychology, 37,* 524–535.

Nickerson, R. A. (1999). *Enhancing creativity.* In R. J. Sternberg (Ed.), *Handbook of creativity* (pp. 392–430). Cambridge, UK: Cambridge University Press.

Nijstad, B. A., & Stroebe, W. (2006). How the group affects the mind: A cognitive model of idea generation in groups. *Personality and Social Psychology Review, 10,* 186–213.

Nijstad, B. A., Stroebe, W., & Lodewijkx, H. M. F. (1999). Persistence of brainstorming groups: How do people know when to stop? *Journal of Experimental Social Psychology, 35,* 165–185.

Nijstad, B. A., Stroebe, W., & Lodewijkx, H. F. M. (2002). Cognitive stimulation and interference in groups: Exposure effects in an idea generation task. *Journal of Experimental Social Psychology, 38,* 535–544.

Nijstad, B. A., Stroebe, W., & Lodewijkx, H. F. M. (2003). Production blocking and idea generation: Does blocking interfere with cognitive processes? *Journal of Experimental Social Psychology, 39,* 531–548.

Nijstad, B. A., Stroebe, W., & Lodewijkx, H. M. F. (2006). The illusion of group productivity: A reduction of failures explanation. *European Journal of Social Psychology, 36,* 31–48.

Offner, A. K., Kramer, T. J., & Winter, J. P. (1996). The effects of facilitation, recording, and pauses on group brainstorming. *Small Group Research, 27,* 283–298.

Oxley, N. L., Dzindolet, M. T., & Paulus, P. B. (1996). The effects of facilitators on the performance of brainstorming groups. *Journal of Social Behavior and Personality, 11,* 633–646.

Parnes, S. J. (1975). CPSI: A program for balanced growth. *Journal of Creative Behavior, 9,* 23–29.

Paulus, P. B. (1983). Group influence on individual task performance. In P. B. Paulus (Ed.), *Basic group processes* (pp. 97–120). New York, NY: Springer-Verlag.

Paulus, P. B. (2000). Groups, teams, and creativity: The creative potential of idea-generating groups. *Applied Psychology: An International Review, 49,* 237–262.

Paulus, P. B. (2007). Fostering creativity in groups and teams. In J. Zhou & C. E. Shalley (Eds.), *The handbook of organizational creativity* (pp. 159–182). Boca Raton, FL: Taylor & Francis Group.

Paulus, P. D., & Brown, V. (2003). Enhancing ideational creativity in groups: Lessons from research on brainstorming. In P. B. Paulus & B. A. Nijstad (Eds.), *Group creativity: Innovation through collaboration* (pp. 110–136). New York, NY: Oxford University Press.

Paulus, P. B., & Brown, V. R. (2007). Toward more creative and innovative group idea generation: A cognitive-social-motivational perspective of group brainstorming. *Social and Personality Psychology Compass, 1,* 248–265.

Paulus, P. B., Dugosh, K. L., Dzindolet, M. T., Coskun, H., & Putman, V. L. (2002). Social and cognitive influences in group brainstorming: Predicting production gains and losses. *European Review of Social Psychology, 12,* 299–325.

Paulus, P. B., & Dzindolet, M. T. (1993). Social influence processes in group brainstorming. *Journal of Personality and Social Psychology, 64,* 575–586.

Paulus, P. B., & Dzindolet, M. T. (2008). Social influence, creativity and innovation. *Social Influence, 3,* 228–247.

Paulus, P. B., Dzindolet, M. T., & Kohn, N. (2011). Collaborative creativity: Group creativity and team innovation. In M. D. Mumford (Ed.), *Handbook of organizational creativity* (pp. 325–354). New York, NY: Elsevier.

Paulus, P. B., Dzindolet, M. T., Poletes, G., & Camacho, L. M. (1993). Perception of performance in group brainstorming: The illusion of group productivity. *Personality and Social Psychology Bulletin, 19,* 78–89.

Paulus, P. B., Larey, T. S., & Dzindolet, M. T. (2000). Creativity in groups and teams. In M. Turner (Ed.), *Groups at work: Advances in theory and research* (pp. 319–338). Hillsdale, NJ: Erlbaum.

Paulus, P. B., Larey, T. S., & Ortega, A. H. (1995). Performance and perception of brainstormers in an organizational setting. *Basic and Applied Social Psychology, 17,* 249–265.

Paulus, P. B., Larey, T. S., Putman, V. L., Leggett, K. L., & Roland, E. J. (1996). Social influence processes in computer brainstorming. *Basic and Applied Social Psychology, 18,* 3–14.

Paulus, P. B., Levine, D., Brown, V., Minai, A. A., & Doboli, S. (2010). Modeling ideational creativity in groups: Connecting cognitive, neural and computational approaches. *Small Group Research, 41*(6), 688–724.

Paulus, P. B., Nakui, T., & Putman, V. L. (2005) Group brainstorming and teamwork: Some rules for the road to innovation. L. Thompson & H. Choi (Eds.), *Creativity and innovation in organizational teams* (pp. 69–86). Mahwah, NJ: Lawrence Erlbaum.

Paulus, P. B., Nakui, T., Putman, V. L., & Brown, V. R. (2006). Effects of task instructions and brief breaks on brainstorming. *Group Dynamics: Theory, Research, and Practice, 10*(3), 206–219.

Paulus, P. B., & Nijstad, B. A. (Eds.). (2003). *Group creativity: Innovation through collaboration*. New York, NY: Oxford University Press.

Paulus, P. B., & Van der Zee, K. I. (2004). Should there be a romance between teams and groups? *Journal of Occupational and Organizational Psychology, 77,* 475–480.

Paulus, P. B., & Yang, H. (2000). Idea generation in groups: A basis for creativity in organizations. *Organizational Behavior and Human Decision Processes, 82,* 76–87.

Pettigrew, T. F., & Tropp, L. R. (2008). How does intergroup contact reduce prejudice? Meta-analytic tests of three mediators. *European Journal of Social Psychology, 38,* 922–934.

Purser, R., & Montuori, A. (Eds.). (1999). *Social creativity* (Vol. 2). Cresskill, NJ: Hampton Press.

Putman, V. L., & Paulus, P. B. (2009). Brainstorming, brainstorming rules, and decision making. *The Journal of Creative Behavior, 43,* 23–39.

Reinig, B. A., Briggs, R. O., & Nunamaker, J. F. (2007). On the measurement of ideation quality. *Journal of Management Information Systems, 23,* 143–161.

Rietzschel, E. F., Nijstad, B. A., & Stroebe, W. (2006). Productivity is not enough: A comparison of interactive and nominal brainstorming groups on idea generation and selection. *Journal of Experimental Social Psychology, 42,* 244–251.

Rietzschel, E. F., Nijstad, B. A., & Stroebe, W. (2007). Relative accessibility of domain knowledge and creativity: The effects of knowledge activation on the quantity and originality of generated ideas. *Journal of Experimental Social Psychology, 43,* 933–946.

Roy, M. C., Gauvin, S., & Limayem, M. (1996). Electronic brainstorming: The role of feedback on productivity. *Small Group Research, 27,* 215–247.

Runco, M. A. (2004). Everyone has creative potential. In R. J. Sternberg, E. E. Grigorenko, & J. L. Singer (Eds.), *Creativity: From potential to realization* (pp. 21–30). Washington, DC: American Psychological Association.

Salas, E., Rosen, M. A., Burke, C. S., & Goodwin, G. F. (Eds.). (2009). The wisdom of collectivities in organizations: An update of teamwork competencies. In E. Salas, G. F. Goodwin, & C. S. Burke (Eds.), *Team effectiveness in complex organizations: Cross-disciplinary perspectives and approaches* (pp. 39–79). New York, NY: Routledge.

Santanen, E. L., Briggs, R. O., & De Vreede, G. (2004). Causal relationships in creative problem solving: Comparing facilitation interventions for ideation. *Journal of Management Information Systems, 20,* 167–173.

Sawyer, R. K. (2007). *Group genius: The creative power of collaboration*. New York, NY: Basic Books.

Schrage, M. (1995). *No more teams: Mastering the dynamics of creative collaboration*. New York, NY: Currency Doubleday.

Scott, G., Leritz, L. E., & Mumford, M. D. (2004). The effectiveness of creativity training: A quantitative review. *Creativity Research Journal, 16*(4), 361–388.

Simonton, D. K. (1984). *Genius, creativity and leadership*. Cambridge, MA: Harvard University Press.

Simonton, D. K. (1999). *Origins of genius: Darwinian perspectives on creativity*. New York, NY: Oxford University Press.

Simonton, D. K. (2004). *Creativity in science: Chance, logic, genius, and zeitgeist*. New York, NY: Cambridge University Press.

Sternberg, R. (2006). Creating a vision of creativity: The first 25 years. *Psychology of Aesthetics, Creativity, and the Arts, S,* 2–12.

Stroebe, W., Diehl, M., & Abakoumkin, G. (1992). The illusion of group effectivity. *Personality and Social Psychology Bulletin, 18,* 643–650.

Sutton, R. I., & Hargadon, A. (1996). Brainstorming groups in context: Effectiveness in a product design firm. *Administrative Science Quarterly, 41,* 685–718.

Thompson, L. L., & Choi, H. (Eds.). (2006). *Creativity and innovation in organizational teams.* Mahwah, NJ: Lawrence Erlbaum Associates.

Van der Zee, K. I., & Paulus, P. B. (2008). Social psychology and modern organizations: Balancing between innovativeness and comfort. In L. Steg, A. P. Buunk, & T. Rothengatter (Eds.), *Applied social psychology: Understanding and managing social problems* (pp. 271–200). New York, NY: Cambridge University Press.

Van Knippenberg, D., & Schippers, M. C. (2007). Work group diversity. *Annual Review of Psychology, 58,* 515–541.

Watson, W. E., Kumar, K., & Michaelson, L. K. (1993). Cultural diversity's impact on interaction process and performance: Comparing homogeneous and diverse task groups. *Academy of Management Journal, 36,* 590–602.

Webber, S. S., & Donahue, L. M. (2001). Impact of highly and less job-related diversity on work group cohesion and performance: a meta-analysis. *Journal of Management, 27,* 141–162.

West, M. A. (2003). Innovation implementation in work teams. In P. B. Paulus, & B. A. Nijstad (Eds.), *Group creativity: Innovation through collaboration* (pp. 245–276). New York, NY: Oxford University Press.

West, M. A. (2004). *Effective teamwork: Practical lessons from organizational research.* Malden, MA: BPS Blackwell.

West, M. A., & Richter, A. W. (2008). Climates and cultures for innovation and creativity at work. In J. Zhou & C. E. Shalley (Eds.), *Handbook of organizational creativity* (pp. 211–236). New York, NY: Taylor & Francis Group.

Wilson, D. S., Timmel, J. J., & Miller, R. R. (2004). Cognitive cooperation: When the going gets tough, think as a group. *Human Nature, 15,* 225–250.

Woodman, R. W., Sawyer, J. E., & Griffin, R. W. (1993). Toward a theory of organizational creativity. *The Academy of Management Review, 18,* 293–321.

Zaccaro, S. J., Heinen B., & Shuffler, M. (2009). Team leadership and team effectiveness. In E. Salas, G. F. Goodwin, & C. S. Burke (Eds.), *Team effectiveness in complex organizations: Cross-disciplinary perspectives and approaches* (pp. 83–111). New York, NY: Routledge.

Zhou, J., & Shalley, C. E. (2007). *The handbook of organizational creativity.* Boca Raton, FL: Taylor & Francis Group.

Ziegler, R., Diehl, M., & Zijlstra, G. (2000). Idea production in nominal and virtual groups: Does communication improve group brainstorming? *Group Processes and Intergroup Relations, 3,* 141–158.

10

Leadership

MICHAEL A. HOGG

*P*eople are influenced by the groups they belong to, either directly by fellow group members or indirectly by the group's norms. In both cases some individuals play a more influential role than others, occupying a leadership position in influencing individual group members and in defining and promulgating the group's norms. Leadership is very much a group process of social influence (Chemers, 2001; Hogg, 2007a, 2010), yet many perspectives on leadership approach it as an interpersonal influence process or a matter of behavioral styles that to varying degrees reflect leadership personality attributes (for overview see Yukl, 2010).

The scientific study of leadership is enormous and spans many disciplines (e.g., psychology, history, political science, organizational and management sciences). Goethals, Sorenson, and Burns's (2004) *Encyclopedia of leadership* runs to 2,000 pages and has 373 entries by 311 scholars. The popular interest, one might more accurately call it obsession, with leadership and leaders is even greater. Some have even argued that leadership may serve an evolutionary function for the survival of our species (Van Vugt, Hogan, & Kaiser, 2008). In this chapter I focus on what social psychology and the organizational sciences have taught us about leadership—with a particular emphasis on leadership as a group and social influence process. I therefore provide an overview of theory, not a review of empirical studies.

The chapter opens with a discussion of some key themes and trends in leadership research and a discussion of issues revolving about defining leadership. One of the simplest ways to account for effective leadership is to maintain that some people simply have personalities suited to leadership whereas the rest of us do not. In reaction to this perspective, others have argued that all of us have the ability to lead if the situation is right. And still others have argued that it is not personality that is important but what leaders actually do, so we need to be

241

able to classify different leadership behaviors. Knowing something about what leaders do, and about the importance of the situations in which leadership is called for, researchers were able to develop contingency theories of leadership that specified what kinds of leadership behaviors are best suited to what kinds of leadership situations.

A key feature of leadership is that leaders interact with those they lead—their followers. Transactional theories of leadership focus on how effective leadership is a transaction between leaders and followers in which each party provides the other with valued resources. Another key feature of leadership is that leaders are often of most use to a group when it is doing badly or needs to adapt to changed circumstances. To be effective the leader needs to transform the group—such transformational leadership often rests on the leader having or being perceived to have a charismatic leadership personality.

Followers play a key role in leadership—although leaders can use power to bully people into "following," genuine leadership requires followers to believe that the leader is honorable and competent and that his or her ideas are good ideas. Therefore, effective leadership rests to a substantial degree on followers' perceptions and evaluations of the leader and their schemas and stereotypes of leaders and leadership. One thing that people look to their leaders for is reliable information about group norms—what the group stands for and what it means to be, and how one should behave as, a group member. Thus, leadership has an important identity function within and between groups. It is therefore not surprising that leaders who are viewed as "one of us," selflessly acting in the best interests of the group, earn the group's trust and are thus able to be effective innovators.

TRENDS AND THEMES IN LEADERSHIP RESEARCH

Leadership is a quintessentially social psychological phenomenon, involving people interacting with and influencing others in the context of a group. Not surprisingly leadership has been a key focus for social psychologists studying social influence and group processes—particularly during the heyday of small groups research in the 1940s, 1950s and 1960s (e.g., Cartwright & Zander, 1953; Lewin, 1947; see Shaw, 1976).

With the unprecedented growth of social psychology in the 1960s, research specialization separated the study of leadership from the study of influence, with leadership researchers and influence researchers coming to inhabit separate scientific universes. Then, associated with and in response to the early 1970s crisis of confidence in social psychology (e.g., Elms, 1975), social psychologists focused increasing attention on social cognition (e.g., Devine, Hamilton, & Ostrom, 1994) and the study of intergroup relations and identity processes in groups (e.g., Taylor & Brown, 1979; Tajfel, 1984; see Yzerbyt & Demoulin, 2010). Diminishing attention was paid to interactive small group processes including leadership (see Abrams & Hogg, 1998; Moreland, Hogg, & Hains, 1994; Wittenbaum & Moreland, 2008).

Some scholars drew the pessimistic conclusion that social psychology no longer studied small interactive groups (e.g., Steiner, 1974), and others noted that the study of interactive group processes including leadership was alive and well but outside social psychology, in the organizational sciences (e.g., Levine & Moreland, 1990; Sanna & Parks, 1997; Tindale & Anderson, 1998). Regarding leadership these assertions were probably true. Fiedler's (1964, 1967) contingency theory of leadership can in many ways be considered the high-water mark of significant social psychological research on leadership, and Hollander's (1985) handbook chapter on leadership and power the closing parenthesis on that era of leadership research in social psychology.

The study of leadership has of course a natural home in the organizational and management sciences. In the world of work people's career advancement and personal prosperity hinge on securing leadership positions, such as becoming a member of the senior management team and perhaps ultimately the CEO (chief executive officer), and organizational success and societal prosperity rest heavily on effective organizational leadership. While social psychology largely turned its back on leadership, leadership research has thrived and expanded exponentially in the organizational and management sciences.

In recent years, however, social psychology has become markedly more interested in leadership. This is attributable in part to a revival of interest in small interactive group processes (Wittenbaum & Moreland, 2008) and a group perspective on leadership (e.g., Chemers, 1997, 2001). It has also been stimulated by leadership research that focuses on power (e.g., Fiske & Dépret, 1996; see Fiske, 2010), gender (e.g., Eagly & Carli, 2007; Eagly & Karau, 2002; Eagly, Karau, & Makhijani, 1995; see Wood & Eagly, 2010), social cognition and social perception (e.g., Lord & Brown, 2004; Lord, Brown, & Harvey, 2001), and social identity and intergroup relations (e.g., Hogg, 2001; Hogg & Van Knippenberg, 2003; Van Knippenberg & Hogg, 2003). This increasing interest in leadership is evidenced by the publication of several recent social psychology handbook chapters on leadership (e.g., Chemers, 2001; Hogg, 2007a, 2010; Lord, Brown, & Harvey, 2001).

WHAT IS LEADERSHIP

There are as many definitions of leadership as there are theories of or perspectives on leadership. One helpful definition is provided by Chemers, who defines leadership as "a process of social influence through which an individual enlists and mobilizes the aid of others in the attainment of a collective goal" (Chemers, 2001, p. 376). Leadership requires there to be one or more individuals who influence the behavior of other individuals or the group as whole—where there are leaders there must be followers.

Definitions of leadership can be quite broad and inclusive, which begs the question of what is *not* leadership. Typically, leadership as an influence process is distinguished from influence processes that rely on compliance, power, or conformity. Compliance is not leadership—people simply go along behaviorally with a request or suggestion and accede to an idea in order to be liked or to avoid disapproval. In such cases, there is little or no internal acceptance of the idea (e.g., Cialdini & Trost, 1998). The exercise of power is certainly not leadership (Chemers, 2001; Lord, Brown, & Harvey, 2001; Raven, 1993)—people obey orders to avoid punishment. This is ultimately a form of bullying and tyranny based on fear (e.g., Haslam & Reicher, 2005) and often visited on followers by narcissistic leaders (Rosenthal & Pittinsky, 2006). Conformity is not leadership—people behaviorally and somewhat routinely follow norms in order to gain approval, avoid censure, and generally not stick out. Here, the norms are not internally accepted (e.g., Turner, 1991).

In contrast, and providing some more specific criteria than Chemers's (2001) definition, the development and communication of an idea (vision, norm, etc.) that is positively received, freely accepted, internalized, and adhered to by the group certainly is leadership. Leaders play a critical role in defining collective goals—in this respect leadership is more typically a group process than an interpersonal process.

In discussing leadership it is important to distinguish between effective/ineffective leaders and good/bad leaders (e.g., Kellerman, 2004). Effective leaders are successful in setting new goals, whatever they might be, and influencing others to achieve them. Here, the evaluation of leadership is largely an objective matter of fact—how much influence did the leader have in setting new goals and getting these goals accepted and achieved? Most leadership research is concerned with leadership effectiveness. In contrast, evaluating whether a leader is good or bad is a subjective judgment based on one's preferences and values. This might involve evaluating leaders in terms of their behavior (e.g., friendly, overbearing, charismatic), the morality of the means they use to influence others and achieve goals (e.g., persuasion, coercion, democratic decision making), and the nature of the goals that they advocate (e.g., saving the environment, producing a commodity, waging war). "Good" leaders are those who have attributes we applaud, use means we approve of, and set and achieve goals we value.

PERSONALITY ATTRIBUTES AND INDIVIDUAL DIFFERENCES

An intuitively appealing way to explain leadership is in terms of personality—some people have personality attributes that equip them for leadership in almost all situations, whereas others do not. This "great person" perspective on leadership has an illustrious history, going back to Plato and ancient Greece (see Takala, 1998). The view that leadership effectiveness is innate (e.g., Galton, 1892) is generally rejected by most "great person" scholars, who prefer the view that leadership ability is acquired early in life as an enduring constellation of personality attributes that imbue people with charisma and a predisposition to lead (e.g., Carlyle, 1841; House, 1977).

The enduring appeal of personality perspectives on leadership is not surprising. People, including scientists, pay substantial attention to leaders because they have so much influence over us all. Because leaders stand out against the background of the group and are the focus of our attention, we underemphasize the contribution of situational factors to effective leadership and instead attribute it to an underlying personality disposition (cf. Gilbert & Malone, 1995; Haslam, Rothschild, & Ernst, 1998). There is evidence that people do indeed view leadership in this way (e.g., Fiske & Dépret, 1996; Meindl, 1995; Meindl, Ehrlich, & Dukerich, 1985).

Attempts to identify a constellation of personality traits that reliably predict effective leadership have not met with a great deal of success. Early research identified only a handful of weak correlates, among which intelligence and talkativeness were the most reliable. As a result, Stogdill concluded that leadership is not "mere possession of some combination of traits" (Stogdill, 1948, p. 66), and others proclaimed that the search for a leadership personality is simplistic and futile (e.g., Conger & Kanungo, 1998). In addition to the fact that general correlations among traits, and between traits and effective leadership, are low (Stogdill, 1974, reported an average correlation of .30), there is a pervasive debate within social psychology over whether personality is a generative cause of behavior or simply a re-description of behavior (see Rhodewalt, 2008).

Nevertheless, the view that some people are better leaders than others because they have enduring traits that predispose them to lead effectively has re-emerged, as we see below, in a different guise in modern theories of transformational leadership that place an emphasis on charisma (e.g., Avolio & Yammarino, 2003; Bass, 1985; Conger & Kanungo, 1998). Rather than focusing on specific traits, this tradition focuses on the "Big Five" personality dimensions of extraversion/surgency, agreeableness, conscientiousness, emotional stability, and intellect/openness to experience. A meta-analysis by Judge, Bono, Ilies, and Gerhardt (2002) reported a multiple correlation of .58 between these attributes and effective leadership, with extraversion/surgency, intellect/openness to experience, and conscientiousness as the best predictors.

LEADER BEHAVIORS

Predicated on early dissatisfaction with the validity and predictive reliability of personality as the cause of leadership, some researchers took the diametrically opposed view that absolutely anyone can lead effectively if the situation is right. However, research suggests that this is too extreme. For example, Simonton (1980) analyzed 300 military battles and found that, while personal attributes of leaders were significant correlates of leadership effectiveness, situational factors were also quite important.

A more plausible perspective is that effective leadership rests on a match between the attributes of the person and the requirements of a specific leadership situation. Different situations call for different leadership properties, and therefore the most effective leader is the group member who is best equipped to help the group achieve its objectives in a specific situation (Bales, 1950). For example, Carter and Nixon (1949) had pairs of students perform three different tasks—an intellectual task, a clerical task, and a mechanical assembly task. Those who took the lead in the first two tasks rarely led in the mechanical assembly task. Relatedly, Sherif, Harvey, White, Hood, and Sherif (1961; Sherif, 1966) documented in their boys' camp studies that different boys assumed a leadership role when the situation changed from intragroup norm formation to competition between groups.

This perspective, which raised the question of exactly what do leaders do, is associated with some of social psychology's classic leadership research. For example, Lippitt and White (1943) manipulated leadership style (autocratic, democratic, and laissez-faire) and measured the effect on group atmosphere, morale, and effectiveness in clubs for young boys. They found that a democratic leadership style was most effective—it produced a friendly, group-centered, task-oriented atmosphere that was associated with relatively high group productivity and was unaffected by whether the leader was physically present or not.

Another program of research identified two key leadership roles: *task specialist* and *socio-emotional specialist* (Bales, 1950). No single person could occupy both roles simultaneously, and the task-specialist was more likely to be the pre-eminent leader. Task specialists tend to be centrally involved, often by offering opinions and giving directions, in the task-oriented aspects of group life, whereas socio-emotional specialists tend to respond and pay attention to the feelings of other group members.

The Ohio State leadership studies constitute a third research program (e.g., Fleishman, 1973; Stogdill, 1974). A scale for measuring leadership behavior was devised, the *leader behavior description questionnaire* (LBDQ), and a distinction was drawn between *initiating structure* and *consideration*. Leaders high on initiating structure define the group's objectives and organize members' work towards the attainment of these goals: they are task-oriented. Leaders high on consideration are concerned with the welfare of subordinates and seek to promote harmonious relationships in the group: they are relationship-oriented. Unlike Bales (1950), who believed that task-oriented and socio-emotional attributes were inversely related, the Ohio State researchers believed their dimensions to be independent. In other words, a single person could be high on both initiating structure (task-oriented) and consideration (socio-emotional), and such a person would be a particularly effective leader. Research supports this latter view (e.g., Sorrentino & Field, 1986; Stogdill, 1974).

This general distinction between a leadership style that attends to group task performance and one that attends to relationships among group members pervades the leadership literature. For example, it surfaces in Fiedler's (1964) contingency theory of leadership, and in a different guise in leader-member exchange (LMX) theory's emphasis on the quality of the leader's relationship with his or her followers (e.g., Graen & Uhl-Bien, 1995). It is a distinction that transcends culture, though what constitutes task-oriented or socio-emotional leadership behavior may vary between cultures (e.g., Smith, Misumi, Tayeb, Peterson, & Bond, 1989).

CONTINGENCY THEORIES

Contingency theories are a class of theories of leadership that focus on the way in which the effectiveness of particular leadership behaviors or styles is contingent on properties of the situation. Some behaviors or styles are better suited to some situations or tasks than to others. There are many contingency theories, of which the most significant are Fiedler's contingency theory, normative decision theory, and path-goal theory.

Fiedler's Contingency Theory

The contingency theory most familiar to social psychologists is that proposed by Fiedler (1964, 1967). Fiedler, like Bales (1950), distinguished between task-oriented and relationship-oriented leaders. To measure leadership style, Fiedler devised an ingenious least preferred coworker (LPC) scale in which respondents rate their least preferred coworker. Respondents with high LPC scores are relationship-oriented (because they are generous toward a poor-performing coworker); respondents with low LPC score are task oriented (because they are harsh on a poor performer).

Fiedler classified situations in terms of the quality of leader-member relations, the structural clarity of the task, and the power and authority the leader has by virtue of his or her position. Good leader-member relations in conjunction with a clear task and significant position-power furnish maximal "situational control" (making leadership easy), whereas poor leader-member relations, a fuzzy task, and little position-power furnish minimal situational control (making leadership difficult).

Fiedler predicted that task-oriented leaders (low LPC) would be most effective when situational control is low (the group needs a directive leader to focus on getting things done) *and* when it is high (the group is doing just fine so there is little need to worry about morale and relationships), whereas relationship-oriented leaders (high LPC) would be most effective when situational control falls between these extremes. Against a background of some controversy and criticism focused on the personal stability of leadership style and the measurement of situational control (e.g., Peters, Hartke, & Pohlmann, 1985), Fiedler's predictions have generally been supported (see meta-analyses by Strube & Garcia, 1981; Schriesheim, Tepper, & Tetrault, 1994). However, one worrying finding (Kennedy, 1982) is that the 20% or so of leaders who have neither high nor low LPC scores are actually the most effective leaders of all, and their effectiveness is not influenced by situational control. Another limitation of Fiedler's theory is that it is static, in that it does not focus on the dynamic interactions that occur between leaders and followers and among followers.

Normative Decision Theory

Normative decision theory (NDT) is a contingency theory focused on leadership in group decision-making contexts (Vroom & Jago, 1988; Vroom & Yetton,

1973). The theory states that leaders can choose among three decision-making strategies: autocratic (subordinate input is not sought), consultative (input is sought, but the leader retains authority to make the final decision), and group decision-making (leader and subordinates are equal partners in a shared decision-making process). Moreover, the effectiveness of these strategies is contingent on the quality of leader-subordinate relationships (which influences how committed and supportive subordinates are) and on task clarity and structure (which influences the leader's need for subordinate input).

According to the theory, autocratic leadership is most effective when subordinate commitment and support are high and the task is clear and well structured. Consultative leadership is most effective when the task is less clearly structured, because greater subordinate involvement is required. Group-decision making works best when subordinates are not very committed or supportive, because it is necessary to elevate participation and commitment. NDT is reasonably well supported (e.g., Field & House, 1990), in that leaders and managers report better decisions and better subordinate ratings when they follow the prescriptions of the theory. However, (perhaps not surprisingly) there is a tendency for subordinates to prefer fully participative group decision-making even when it is not the most effective strategy.

Path-Goal Theory

Another well-known contingency theory is path-goal theory (PGT: House, 1971; House & Mitchell, 1974). According to PGT, a leader's main function is to motivate followers by clarifying the paths (i.e., behaviors and actions) that will help them attain their goals. There are two types of behaviors available to leaders to do this: *structuring*, where the leader directs task related activities, and *consideration*, where the leader addresses followers' personal and emotional needs. This distinction is captured by the leader behavior description questionnaire (LBDQ) described above.

PGT predicts that structuring will be most effective when followers are unclear about their goals and how to reach them (e.g., when the task is new, difficult, or ambiguous). When tasks are well understood, structuring is less effective and can backfire because followers view the behavior as meddlesome micro-management. Consideration is most effective when the task is boring or uncomfortable, but it can backfire when followers are already engaged and motivated because it is considered distracting and unnecessary.

Empirical support for PGT is mixed, and most scholars agree that tests of the theory are incomplete, overly simplistic, and methodologically flawed (Schriesheim & Neider, 1996). For these reasons, research on PGT tapered off in the early 1980s. Recently, however, House (1996) has re-invigorated the theory by addressing some of these concerns and updating the theory. For example, the interpersonal focus of the original formulation has been expanded to include ways in which a leader can motivate an entire work group rather than just individual followers.

Path-goal theory is a contingency theory because it focuses on the situation-contingent effectiveness of leadership behaviors, but it can also be considered a transactional theory because it focuses on transactions between leaders and followers that enhance motivation and lead to goal attainment.

TRANSACTIONAL LEADERSHIP

Contingency theories are limited because they do not focus on the dynamic interaction between leaders and followers in which both parties provide the mutual support and gratification that allow leaders to lead and encourage followers to follow (Messick, 2005). In contrast, transactional theories treat leadership as an exchange process, similar to contractual relations in economic life that are based on good faith. To get things accomplished, leaders interact with followers to set expectations and goals and provide recognition and rewards for task completion (Burns, 1978). Mutual benefits are exchanged (transacted) between leaders and followers against a background of contingent rewards and punishments that shape cooperation and trust (Bass, 1985). These transactions have an equity dimension (Walster, Walster, & Berscheid, 1978). Because effective leaders play a larger role in steering groups to their goals than do followers, followers reinstate equity by rewarding such leaders with social approval, praise, prestige, and status and power, which are the trappings of effective leadership.

Idiosyncrasy Credit

An early transactional perspective on leadership is Hollander's (1958; Hollander & Julian, 1970) analysis of idiosyncrasy credit. Hollander argues that, to be effective, leaders need the group to allow them to be innovative and to experiment with new ideas and new directions—in other words, to be idiosyncratic. Hollander drew on equity considerations to argue that leaders who conform closely to group norms as they scale the organizational ladder accumulate "idiosyncrasy credits" with the group. When the leader arrives at the top of the organization, followers return these credits (as a resource) to the leader, who can then "spend" them by behaving idiosyncratically (i.e., innovatively). An early study by Merei (1949) supports this analysis. Merei introduced older children who had shown leadership potential into small groups of younger children in a Hungarian nursery and found that the most successful leaders were those who initially complied with existing group practices and who only later introduced minor variations.

Hollander focuses primarily on interpersonal relationships within groups. However, the basic idea that leaders who initially conform to group norms are ultimately allowed to be innovative and, paradoxically, non-normative, has recently been given a more explicitly group-oriented treatment (see below) by the social identity analysis of leadership (Hogg, 2001; Hogg & Van Knippenberg, 2003). Because leaders who conform to group norms are assumed to identify strongly with the group and thus are "one of us," if they behave non-normatively and innovatively they are trusted to be doing so in the best interest of the group (cf. Abrams, Randsley de Moura, Marques, & Hutchison, 2008).

Vertical Dyad Linkage and Leader-Member Exchange Theories

Leader-member transactions are center stage in the vertical dyad linkage (VDL) model of leadership (Danserau, Graen, & Haga, 1975). According to VDL, leaders develop dyadic exchange relationships with different specific subordinates. In these relationships, the subordinate can either be treated as a close and valued 'ingroup' member or as a distant and less valued 'outgroup' member.

In leader-member exchange (LMX) theory (e.g., Graen & Uhl-Bien, 1995; Sparrowe & Liden, 1997), the notion of a dichotomy of ingroup vs. outgroup leader-member relationships has been replaced by a continuum of quality of exchange relationships, ranging from ones based on mutual trust, respect, and obligation (high quality LMX relationships) to ones based on the formal employment contract between leader and subordinate (low quality LMX relationships). According to the theory, effective leadership rests on the development of high quality LMX relationships, which motivate subordinates to internalize the group's and the leader's goals. In low quality relationships, subordinates merely comply with the leader's goals, without internalizing them as their own. However, high quality relationships are labor intensive and so over time leaders tend to develop them with only a small subset of group members and develop low quality relationships with the rest of the group.

There is substantial evidence for the theory. For example, differentiated LMX relationships exist in most organizations. High quality LMX relationships are more likely to develop when the leader and the subordinate have similar attitudes, like one another, and belong to the same socio-demographic groups. Moreover, high quality LMX relationships are associated with better performing and more satisfied workers who are more committed to the organization and less likely to leave (Gerstner & Day, 1997; Graen & Uhl-Bien, 1995; Schriesheim, Castro, & Cogliser, 1999).

One limitation of LMX theory is that it focuses exclusively on dyadic leader-member relations, without locating such relationships within the wider context of shared group membership in which followers' reactions to leaders are influenced by their perceptions of the leader's relations with other group members (Hogg, Martin, Epitropaki, Mankad, Svensson, & Weeden, 2005; Scandura, 1999). Evidence indicates that members who identify strongly with a group (a) prefer a more depersonalized leadership style that treats all members relatively equally as group members and (b) support the leader more when this happens (Hogg et al., 2005).

TRANSFORMATIONAL LEADERSHIP

Transactional theories of leadership represent a perspective on leadership, but transactional leadership is itself a leadership style in which leaders appeal to followers' self-interest. In contrast, transformational leaders inspire followers to adopt a vision that involves more than individual self-interest (Burns, 1978; Judge & Bono, 2000). A third leadership style—laissez-faire leadership, which involves not making choices or taking decisions and not rewarding others or shaping their behavior—has been added to transactional and transformational leadership to complete Avolio's (1999) full-range leadership theory (see Antonakis & House, 2003).

Transformational leadership has three main components: (a) individualized consideration (the leader is sensitive to followers and attempts to raise their aspirations, improve their abilities, and satisfy their needs), (b) intellectual stimulation (the leader challenges and attempts to improve followers' mind-sets and practices), and (c) charismatic/inspiring leadership (the leader provides the energy, reasoning, and sense of urgency that transforms followers) (Avolio & Bass, 1987; Bass, 1985). Transformational (and transactional) leadership are measured by the multifactor leadership questionnaire (MLQ), which has generated an enormous body of findings (e.g., Lowe, Kroeck, & Sivasubramaniam, 1996).

Critics of transformational leadership have argued that little if anything is known about what happens in the heads of followers to transform leader behavior into follower thought and behavior. One possibility is that followers personally identify with the leader and in this way make the leader's vision their own (Shamir, House, & Arthur, 1993). A second possibility is that the behavior of transformational leaders causes followers to identify more strongly with the organization's core values (Dvir, Eden, Avolio, & Shamir, 2002). And a third possibility, derived from the social identity theory of leadership (Hogg, 2001; Hogg & Van Knippenberg, 2003; see below), is that successful transformational leadership causes members to identify with the group and consider the leader to be a prototypical group member whom they can trust to define identity-relevant group norms. When this occurs, members follow and internalize the leader's innovative and transformational ideas.

Charisma and Charismatic Leadership

Charisma plays a pivotal role in transformational leadership. Charismatic people are emotionally expressive, enthusiastic, driven, eloquent, visionary, self-confident, and responsive to others (e.g., House, Spangler, & Woycke, 1991). These attributes allow a leader to be persuasive in convincing others to buy his or her vision for the group and sacrifice personal goals for collective goals. According to Meindl and colleagues, visionary leaders elevate followers' sense of shared identity to produce a collective "heroic motive" that places group goals ahead of personal goals (Meindl et al., 1985; Meindl & Lerner, 1983).

Charismatic leaders should not be mistaken for narcissistic leaders (Rosenthal & Pittinsky, 2006). Narcissistic leaders do not lead so much as intimidate and bully followers. Although they have some attributes of charisma, these are dwarfed by, among other attributes, grandiosity, self-importance, and entitlement (Baumeister, Smart, & Boden, 1996).

Transformational leadership theorists have drawn a distinction between good and bad charisma (e.g., O'Connor, Mumford, Clifton, Gessner, & Connelly, 1995). Good charismatic leaders use "socialized charisma" to improve society—they are transformational heroes (e.g., Gandhi). Bad charismatic leaders use "personalized charisma" to tear down society—they are non-transformational villains (e.g., Hitler). Of course, the problem here is that one person's transformational hero can be another person's villain.

There is another concern about the role of charisma in transformational leadership. Charismatic leadership is a product of the leader's personal characteristics and followers' reactions to these characteristics. In other words, personal characteristics alone do not guarantee charismatic leadership (e.g., Bryman, 1992). However, it is difficult to escape the inference that leader charisma is an enduring personality trait. Charismatic leadership has been linked to the Big Five personality traits of extraversion/surgency, agreeableness, and intellect/openness to experience (e.g., Judge et al., 2002) and to the related construct of visionary leadership, which posits that visionary leaders are special people who can identify attractive goals for a group and mobilize followers to internalize these goals (e.g., Conger & Kanungo, 1998). Critics therefore worry that charismatic leadership recreates some of the problems of earlier personality theories of leadership (see Haslam & Platow, 2001).

An alternative perspective is that followers construct a charismatic personality for their leader. That is, charisma is a consequence, not a cause, of effective leadership. For example, Meindl (1995; Meindl et al., 1985) coined the term *romance of leadership* to describe how people attribute effective leadership to the leader's behavior and overlook the other possible causes. The social identity theory of leadership (e.g., Hogg, 2001; Hogg & Van Knippenberg, 2003—see below) provides a similar analysis. The basic idea here is that social identity processes associated with group identification cause members who identify strongly with their group to view prototypical leaders as influential and attractive, imbue them with trust, and allow them to be innovative. Followers attribute these qualities to the leader's personality, thus constructing a charismatic leadership personality. Empirical studies provide support for the attributional construction of charisma (e.g., Fiske & Dépret, 1996; Meindl et al., 1985) and for the social identity perspective on charisma and leadership (Haslam & Platow, 2001; Platow & Van Knippenberg, 2001).

LEADER PERCEPTIONS AND LEADERSHIP SCHEMAS

Leader Categorization Theory

Leader categorization theory (LCT), also called implicit leadership theory, focuses on people's leadership schemas and the causes and consequences of categorizing someone as a leader (e.g., Lord, Brown, Harvey, & Hall, 2001; Lord, Foti, & DeVader, 1984; Lord, Foti, & Phillips, 1982; Lord & Hall, 2003). It assumes that leadership perceptions significantly impact leader selection decisions and leader endorsement, which in turn affect a leader's power base and ability to influence others.

According to LCT, in making leadership judgments people match characteristics of the leader against the relevant schema they have of effective leadership. Originally, leader schemas were considered to be fixed and relatively general cognitive structures (e.g., Lord, Foti, & DeVader, 1984), but more recently they have been viewed as flexible structures that are regenerated in situ to meet contextual demands (e.g., Lord, Brown, Harvey, & Hall, 2001; Lord & Hall, 2003). In both cases, the better the match between the leader's characteristics and the perceiver's leadership schema, the more favorable is the leadership judgment.

LCT focuses on categories and associated schemas of leadership and leaders (e.g., presidents, CEOs, popes), not on social groups as categories (e.g., nations, corporations, religions). LCT's leader categories are tied to tasks and functions and transcend groups. For example, a CEO schema applies to many companies (e.g., Apple, Toyota, Starbucks), even though each company may have very different group norms and prototypes.

Expectation States and Status Characteristics

Two other theories that focus on leader categorization are expectation states/status characteristics theory and role congruity theory. Both theories describe how the perceived match between a leader's characteristics and abstract conceptions of status and leadership affect leadership judgments and thus the ability to lead effectively.

Expectation states/status characteristics theory (e.g., Berger, Fisek, Norman, & Zelditch, 1977; Berger, Wagner, & Zelditch, 1985; Ridgeway, 2001) argues that the perceived status of group members rests on the extent to which they are considered to have *specific status characteristics* (attributes that make them competent at what the group does) and *diffuse status characteristics* (attributes that are socially valued because they are stereotypical of high status groups in society). According to the theory, influence, and thus leadership, is a function of the extent to which people possess both kinds of characteristics (Ridgeway, 2003).

Role Congruity Theory

Role congruity theory focuses on gender and leadership (Eagly & Karau, 2002; also see Eagly, 2003; Heilman 1983), but is also a more general theory of negative reactions to people who do not fit role expectations (e.g., Eagly & Diekman, 2005). Even in comparatively progressive western democracies where women are relatively well represented in middle-management, they are still underrepresented relative to men in senior management and "elite" leadership positions—there is a "glass ceiling" (Eagly & Carli, 2007; Eagly, Makhijani, & Klonsky, 1992; Eagly et al., 1995). Although women tend to adopt different leadership styles than men, they are usually rated as just as effective leaders as men and are perceived to be slightly more transformational, participative, and engaged in contingent reward behaviors (Eagly, Johannesen-Schmidt, Van Engen, & Vinkenburg, 2002). So, why the glass ceiling?

According to role congruity theory, there is a "gender gap" in leadership because there is greater overlap between general leader schemas and agentic male stereotypes than between leader schemas and communal female stereotypes. Thus, people have more favorable perceptions of male leaders than of female leaders, and it is easier to lead effectively if you are male than female. One implication is that the evaluation of male and female leaders will change if the leadership schema changes or if people's gender stereotypes change. For example research has shown that male leaders are evaluated more favorably than female leaders when the role is defined in more masculine terms and vice versa when the role is defined in less masculine terms (Eagly et al., 1995). So, people with traditional gender stereotypes will endorse a male but not a female leader of a group with instrumental norms and a female but not a male leader of a group with expressive norms (Hogg, Fielding, Johnson, Masser, Russell, & Svensson, 2006).

Another factor than plays a role in the gender leadership gap is a tendency for women to claim authority less effectively than men (though once authority is claimed, men and women are equally effective). According to Bowles and McGinn (2005), obstacles to claiming authority include, in addition to role incongruity, lack of critical management experience, time-consuming family responsibilities, and lack of motivation to engage in self-promotion in the pursuit of top leadership positions. It is possible that the underlying reason for women's reticence to claim authority is stereotype-threat (Steele, Spencer, & Aronson, 2002)—women may fear that stereotypes about women and leadership will be confirmed, and so their motivation to take on leadership roles is diminished. In addition, self-promotion and leadership-claiming are non-female stereotypic behaviors that can be interpreted as "pushy" and can attract negative reactions from group members (Rudman, 1998).

SOCIAL IDENTITY AND LEADERSHIP

Leadership is a group process in which followers play a key role in permitting leaders to lead. In fact, some researchers have turned leadership research on its head to focus on "followership" and how followers can be empowered to create effective leaders (e.g., Kelley, 1992; Riggio, Chaleff, & Lipman-Blumen, 2008; Shamir, Pillai, Bligh, & Uhl-Bien, 2006).

Social Identity Theory of Leadership

An influential perspective on leadership in which leader and follower roles are intertwined is the social identity theory of leadership (Hogg, 2001, 2008; Hogg & Van Knippenberg, 2003; Van Knippenberg & Hogg, 2003—for empirical overviews also see Ellemers, de Gilder, & Haslam, 2004; Van Knippenberg, Van

Knippenberg, De Cremer, & Hogg, 2004). The core assumptions of this theory are that groups provide us with a social identity and our leaders are the most significant and reliable source of information about that identity. Therefore, we look to leaders to learn what the group's attributes are and who we are as group members (see Abrams, this volume).

According to the theory, as group membership becomes more important to self-definition and members identify more strongly with the group, leaders who are perceived to be more group prototypical are more effective than leaders who are perceived to be less group prototypical. Moreover, as prototypicality assumes greater importance, other determinants of effective leadership, such as leadership schemas, become less important (e.g., Hains, Hogg, & Duck, 1997; Hogg, Hains, & Mason, 1998). Thus, prototypical leaders are effective because they embody the group's defining attributes and because they are consensually positively evaluated as group members and therefore have elevated status.

For prototypical leaders, the group is central to self-definition—for example, they behave in group-serving ways, embody group norms, and treat ingroup members fairly. These behaviors confirm their prototypicality and communicate to the group that the leader is "one of us" (e.g., Platow, Hoar, Reid, Harley, & Morrison, 1997; Platow & Van Knippenberg, 2001). Prototypical leaders are therefore given legitimacy (Tyler, 1997; see Platow, Reid, & Andrew, 1998) and trusted to be acting in the best interest of the group (e.g., Brewer, 1981; Hogg, 2007b; Yamagishi & Kiyonari, 2000). This allows prototypical leaders to be innovative by diverging from group norms and steering the group in new directions. In this way, social identity leadership processes may account for Hollander's (1958) idea, discussed above, that to be effective a leader needs initially to conform to group norms to earn "idiosyncrasy credits." The key factor in the social identity analysis is that the leader behaves in ways that build trust based on shared identity and the perception that he or she is totally committed to the group (cf. Abrams et al., 2008).

Prototypical leaders are often invested by the group with charisma, which strengthens their authority and facilitates innovative and transformational leadership. As noted above, the social identity perspective views charisma as an attribution-based social construction (e.g., Haslam & Platow, 2001; Platow & Van Knippenberg, 2001). Prototypical leaders are the focus of attention, and members attribute their positive qualities to stable aspects of their personalities (cf. Gilbert & Malone, 1995; Haslam et al., 1998).

Social identity leadership processes confer on leaders considerable power to maintain their leadership position. Through talk they can manipulate the group prototype in ways that protect or promote their prototypically central position (Hogg & Reid, 2006; also see Fiol, 2002; Reid & Ng, 2000). In fact, effective leaders are often "entrepreneurs of identity" who are adept at manipulating how the group sees itself (Reicher & Hopkins, 1996, 2003). For example, such leaders can highlight prototypical aspects of their behavior and obfuscate non-prototypical aspects, characterize as marginal those members who do not share their prototype of the group, and identify as relevant those outgroups that highlight their own prototypicality.

Trust and the Group-Value Model

Trust is critically important in leadership (Dirks & Ferrin, 2002; Kellerman, 2004), and, as we have seen, one reason to trust leaders is that they are prototypical—they are one of us. Shared group membership is a powerful basis for trust (Brewer, 1981; Hogg, 2007b; Yamagishi & Kiyonari, 2000).

Another basis for trust is the belief that leaders treat group members fairly and with respect. Tyler's group-value model (Lind & Tyler, 1988) and his relational model of authority in groups (Tyler, 1997; Tyler & Lind, 1992) identify fairness and justice perceptions as critical to group life. Because leaders make decisions that have important consequences for members (e.g., promotions, allocation of duties), members are concerned about how fair the leader is in making these decisions. In judging fairness, people focus on both distributive justice (how fair are the outcomes of the leader's decision) and procedural justice (how fair are the procedures that the leader used to make the decision).

Justice and fairness judgments influence reactions to those in authority and thus influence leadership effectiveness (e.g., De Cremer, 2003). Moreover, procedural justice is particularly important. Fair procedures serve a social identity function (Tyler, 2003)—they convey respect for and positive evaluation of followers as group members and thus build member identification that fuels cooperative and compliant behavior. As members identify more strongly with the group, they care more that the leader is procedurally fair and less that the leader is distributively fair (e.g., Brockner, Chen, Mannix, Leung, & Skarlicki, 2000; Lipponen, Koivisto, & Olkkonen, 2005; see Tyler, this volume).

Trust in leadership also plays a significant role in resolving social dilemmas. Social dilemmas are crises of trust that are notoriously difficult to resolve (Dawes & Messick, 2000), but can be ameliorated by accentuating a common social identity that generates trust among group members (e.g., Brewer & Schneider, 1990; De Cremer & Van Vugt, 1999). Leadership can play an important role in this process. An effective leader can transform selfish individual goals into shared group goals by building a sense of common identity, shared fate, interindividual trust, and custodianship of the collective good (e.g., De Cremer & Van Knippenberg, 2003; De Cremer & Van Vugt, 2002; Van Vugt & De Cremer, 1999).

Intergroup Leadership

Almost all group-focused theories of leadership emphasize what happens within a group—they have an intragroup focus. The social identity theory of leadership, with its emphasis on ingroup prototypicality, shared group membership, ingroup trust, and so forth, is no exception. However, the great challenge of leadership is often not to build a common identity and vision for a homogeneous collection of individuals, but rather to transcend and bridge profound divisions within the larger group. For example, how does one effectively lead a nation divided into polarized political parties, ethnic groups, religious factions, and so forth? Leadership therefore often has an intergroup dimension (Hogg, 2009; Hogg, Van Knippenberg, & Rast, 2012; Pittinsky, 2009; Pittinsky & Simon, 2007).

One problem for effective intergroup leadership is that the leader of the overarching group often comes from, or is closely affiliated with, one of the subgroups. In other words, the leader is an ingroup member for some people and an outgroup member for others. In such cases, "outgroup" leaders are viewed as highly unprototypical and thus suffer compromised effectiveness (Duck & Fielding, 1999, 2003). Indeed, one reason why corporate mergers so often fail is that the leader of the "new" organization is viewed by many as a member of the former outgroup (e.g., Terry, Carey, & Callan, 2001; Ullrich & Van Dick, 2007).

So, what is the solution in intergroup leadership situations? One possibility is for the leader to build a common ingroup identity that transcends and ultimately erases subgroup boundaries (Gaertner & Dovidio, 2000; Gaertner, Dovidio, Anastasio, Bachman, & Rust, 1993). However, this can be almost impossible to achieve because of the leader affiliation issues mentioned above and also because the process poses a serious threat to the distinctiveness of the subgroups and the associated identities that members cherish (e.g., Abrams & Hogg, 2010; Dovidio & Gaertner, 2010; Hornsey & Hogg, 2000).

To circumvent this problem, intergroup leaders may be more effective if they strive to balance the superordinate identity of the larger group with the distinctive identities of the various subgroups (e.g., Hornsey & Hogg, 2000). One way to do this is for the leader to construct and embody a *relational intergroup identity* that defines the superordinate group in terms of the mutually beneficial relationships between distinctive and valued subgroups (Hogg, Van Knippenberg, & Rast, 2012).

CLOSING COMMENTS

In this chapter, I have reviewed the main themes, perspectives, and theories in leadership research. Although most leadership research is conducted in the organizational and management sciences, this has not always been so—leadership was once an important focus in social psychology, and there has been a recent revival of interest in this topic by social psychologists. The revival places center-stage the important link between leadership and the social psychology of influence, identity, and group processes. I make no apologies for privileging this social psychological perspective in my account—leadership is quintessentially a social psychological process that lies at the heart of group processes.

There is a great deal still to be learned about leadership. But what we do know is that leadership involves an individual (or set of individuals) forging and communicating a vision for the group that other members internalize as a part of who they are and how they should behave. Effective leaders can transform individual goals and associated individual actions into shared goals and associated coordinated actions. Coercion and the exercise of power to secure compliance or obedience are not leadership. Although personality may not play a significant role in effective leadership, the perception that one is charismatic may help to make one more persuasive. However, it is important that leadership style matches the demands of the leadership situation. Being viewed by the group as "one of us", a prototypical group member who is procedurally fair, builds a sound foundation of trust and loyalty that allows the leader to be innovative.

REFERENCES

Abrams, D., & Hogg, M. A. (1998). Prospects for research in group processes and intergroup relations. *Group Processes and Intergroup Relations, 1,* 7–20.

Abrams, D., & Hogg, M. A. (2010). Social identity and self-categorization. In J. F. Dovidio, M. Hewstone, P. Glick, & V. M. Esses (Eds.), *The Sage handbook of prejudice, stereotyping and discrimination* (pp. 179–193). London, UK: Sage.

Abrams, D., Randsley de Moura, G., Marques, J. M., & Hutchison, P. (2008). Innovation credit: When can leaders oppose their group's norms? *Journal of Personality and Social Psychology, 95,* 662–678.

Antonakis, J., & House, R. J. (2003). An analysis of the full-range leadership theory: The way forward. In B. J. Avolio & F. J. Yammarino (Eds.), *Transformational and charismatic leadership: The road ahead* (pp. 3–33). New York, NY: Elsevier.

Avolio, B. J. (1999). *Full leadership development: Building the vital forces in organizations.* Thousand Oaks, CA: Sage.

Avolio, B. J., & Bass, B. M. (1987). Transformational leadership, charisma and beyond. In J. G. Hunt, B. R. Balaga, H. P. Dachler, & C. A. Schriesheim (Eds.), *Emerging leadership vistas* (pp. 29–50). Elmsford, NY: Pergamon Press.

Avolio, B. J., & Yammarino, F. J. (Eds.). (2003). *Transformational and charismatic leadership: The road ahead.* New York, NY: Elsevier.

Bales, R. F. (1950). *Interaction process analysis: A method for the study of small groups.* Reading, MA: Addison-Wesley.

Bass, B. M. (1985). *Leadership and performance beyond expectations.* New York, NY: Free Press.

Baumeister, R. F., Smart, L., & Boden, J. M. (1996). Relation of threatened egotism to violence and aggression: The dark side of high self-esteem. *Psychological Review, 103,* 5–33.

Berger, J., Fisek, M. H., Norman, R. Z., & Zelditch, M. Jr. (1977). *Status characteristics and social interaction.* New York, NY: Elsevier.

Berger, J., Wagner, D., & Zelditch, M. Jr. (1985). Expectation states theory: Review and assessment. In J. Berger & M. Zelditch Jr (Eds.), *Status, rewards and influence* (pp. 1–72). San Francisco, CA: Jossey-Bass.

Bowles, H. R., & McGinn, K. L. (2005). Claiming authority: Negotiating challenges for women leaders. In D. M. Messick & R. M. Kramer (Eds.), *The psychology of leadership: New perspectives and research* (pp. 191–208). Mahwah, NJ: Erlbaum.

Brewer, M. B. (1981). Ethnocentrism and its role in interpersonal trust. In M. B. Brewer & B. Collins (Eds.), *Scientific inquiry and the social sciences* (pp. 345–360). San Francisco, CA: Jossey-Bass.

Brewer, M. B., & Schneider, S. (1990). Social identity and social dilemmas: A double-edged sword. In D. Abrams & M. A. Hogg (Eds.), *Social identity theory: Constructive and critical advances* (pp. 169–184). London, UK: Harvester Wheatsheaf.

Brockner, J., Chen, Y.-R., Mannix, E. A., Leung, K., & Skarlicki, D. P. (2000). Culture and procedural fairness: When the effects of what you do depend on how you do it. *Administrative Science Quarterly, 45*, 1238–1259.

Bryman, A. (1992). *Charisma and leadership.* London, UK: Sage.

Burns, J. M. (1978). *Leadership.* New York, NY: Harper & Row.

Carlyle, T. (1841). *On heroes, hero-worship, and the heroic.* London, UK: Fraser.

Carter, L. F., & Nixon, M. (1949). An investigation of the relationship between four criteria of leadership ability for three different tasks. *The Journal of Psychology, 27*, 245–261.

Cartwright, D., & Zander, D. (Eds.). (1953). *Group dynamics: Research and theory.* New York, NY: Harper & Row.

Chemers, M. M. (1997). *An integrative theory of leadership.* Mahwah, NJ: Erlbaum.

Chemers, M. M. (2001). Leadership effectiveness: An integrative review. In M. A. Hogg & R. S. Tindale (Eds.), *Blackwell handbook of social psychology: Group processes* (pp. 376–399). Oxford, UK: Blackwell.

Cialdini, R. B., & Trost, M. R. (1998). Social influence: Social norms, conformity, and compliance. In D. Gilbert, S. T. Fiske & G. Lindzey (Eds.), *The handbook of social psychology* (4th ed., Vol. 2, pp. 151–192). New York, NY: McGraw-Hill.

Conger, J. A., & Kanungo, R. N. (1998). *Charismatic leadership in organizations.* Thousand Oaks, CA: Sage.

Danserau, F., Jr., Graen, G., & Haga, W. J. (1975). A vertical dyad linkage approach to leadership within formal organizations: A longitudinal investigation of the role making process. *Organizational Behavior and Human Performance, 13*, 46–78.

Dawes, R. M., & Messick, D. M. (2000). Social dilemmas. *International Journal of Psychology, 35*, 111–116.

De Cremer, D. (2003). A relational perspective on leadership and cooperation: Why it matters to care and be fair. In D. Van Knippenberg & M. A. Hogg (Eds.), *Leadership and power: Identity processes in groups and organizations* (pp. 109–122). London, UK: Sage.

De Cremer, D., & Van Vugt, M. (2002). Intergroup and intragroup aspects of leadership in social dilemmas: A relational model of cooperation. *Journal of Experimental Social Psychology, 38*, 126–136.

De Cremer, D., & Van Knippenberg, D. (2003). Cooperation with leaders in social dilemmas: On the effects of procedural fairness and outcome favorability in structural cooperation. *Organizational Behavior and Human Decision Processes, 91*, 1–11.

De Cremer, D., & Van Vugt, M. (1999). Social identification effects in social dilemmas: A transformation of motives. *European Journal of Social Psychology, 29*, 871–893.

Devine, P. G., Hamilton, D. L., & Ostrom, T. M. (Eds.). (1994). *Social cognition: Impact on social psychology.* San Diego, CA: Academic Press.

Dirks, K. T., & Ferrin, D. L. (2002). Trust in leadership: Meta-analytic findings and implications for research and practice. *Journal of Applied Psychology, 87*, 611–628.

Dovidio, J. F., & Gaertner, S. L. (2010). Intergroup bias. In S. T. Fiske, D. T. Gilbert, & G. Lindzey (Eds.), *Handbook of social psychology* (5th ed., Vol. 2, pp. 1084–1121). New York, NY: Wiley.

Duck, J. M., & Fielding, K. S. (1999). Leaders and subgroups: One of us or one of them? *Group Processes and Intergroup Relations, 2*, 203–230.

Duck, J. M., & Fielding, K. S. (2003). Leaders and their treatment of subgroups: Implications for evaluations of the leader and the superordinate group. *European Journal of Social Psychology, 33*, 387–401.

Dvir, T., Eden, D., Avolio, B. J., & Shamir, B. (2002). Impact of transformational leadership training on follower development and performance: A field experiment. *Academy of Management Journal, 45*, 735–744.

Eagly, A. H. (2003). Few women at the top: How role incongruity produces prejudice and the glass ceiling. In D. Van Knippenberg & M. A. Hogg (Eds.), *Leadership and power: Identity processes in groups and organizations* (pp. 79–93). London, UK: Sage.

Eagly, A. H., & Carli, L. L. (2007). *Through the labyrinth: The truth about how women become leaders.* Boston, MA: Harvard Business School Press.

Eagly, A. H., & Diekman, A. B. (2005). What is the problem? Prejudice as an attitude-in-context. In J. F. Dovidio, P. Glick, & L. Rudman (Eds.). *On the nature of prejudice: Fifty years after Allport* (pp. 19–35). Malden, MA: Blackwell.

Eagly, A. H., Johannesen-Schmidt, M., Van Engen, M. L., & Vinkenburg, C. (2002). Transformational, transactional, and laissez-faire styles: A meta-analysis comparing men and women. *Psychological Bulletin, 129*, 569–591.

Eagly, A. H., & Karau, S. J. (2002). Role congruity theory of prejudice toward female leaders. *Psychological Review, 109*, 573–598.

Eagly, A. H., Karau, S. J., & Makhijani, M. G. (1995). Gender and the effectiveness of leaders: A meta-analysis. *Psychological Bulletin, 117*, 125–145.

Eagly, A. H., Makhijani, M. G., & Klonsky, B. G. (1992). Gender and the evaluation of leaders: A meta-analysis. *Psychological Bulletin, 111*, 3–22.

Ellemers, N., de Gilder, D., & Haslam, S. A. (2004). Motivating individuals and groups at work: A social identity perspective on leadership and group performance. *Academy of Management Review, 29*, 459–478.

Elms, A. C. (1975). The crisis of confidence in social psychology. *American Psychologist, 30*, 967–976.

Fiedler, F. E. (1964). A contingency model of leadership effectiveness. In L. Berkowitz (Ed.), *Advances in experimental social psychology* (Vol. 1, pp. 149–190). New York, NY: Academic Press.

Fiedler, F. E. (1967). *A theory of leadership effectiveness.* New York, NY: McGraw-Hill.

Field, R. H. G., & House, R. J. (1990). A test of the Vroom-Yetton model using manager and subordinate reports. *Journal of Applied Psychology, 75*, 362–366.

Fiol, C. M. (2002). Capitalizing on paradox: The role of language in transforming organizational identities. *Organization Science, 13*, 653–666.

Fiske, S. T. (2010). Interpersonal stratification: Status, power, and subordination. In S. T. Fiske, D. T. Gilbert, & G. Lindzey (Eds.), *Handbook of social psychology* (5th ed., Vol. 2, pp. 941–982). New York, NY: Wiley.

Fiske, S. T., & Dépret, E. (1996). Control, interdependence and power: Understanding social cognition in its social context. *European Review of Social Psychology, 7*, 31–61.

Fleishman, E. A. (1973). Twenty years of consideration and structure. In E. A. Fleishman & J. F. Hunt (Eds.), *Current developments in the study of leadership.* Carbondale, IL: South Illinois University Press.

Gaertner S. L., & Dovidio, J. F. (2000). *Reducing intergroup bias: The common ingroup identity model.* New York, NY: Psychology Press.

Gaertner, S. L., Dovidio, J., Anastasio, P., Bachman, B., & Rust, M. (1993). The common ingroup identity model: Recategorization and the reduction of intergroup bias. *European Review of Social Psychology, 4,* 1–26.

Galton, F. (1892). *Heredity genius: An inquiry into its laws and consequences.* London, UK: Macmillan.

Gerstner, C. R., & Day, D. V. (1997). Meta-analytic review of Leader-Member Exchange Theory: Correlates and construct issues. *Journal of Applied Psychology, 82,* 827–844.

Gilbert, D. T., & Malone, P. S. (1995). The correspondence bias. *Psychological Bulletin, 117,* 21–38.

Goethals, G. R., Sorenson, G. J., & Burns, J. M. (Eds.). (2004). *Encyclopedia of leadership.* Thousand Oaks, CA: Sage.

Graen, G. B., & Uhl-Bien, M. (1995). Relationship-based approach to leadership: Development of leader–member exchange (LMX) theory of leadership over 25 years: Applying a multi-level multi-domain approach. *The Leadership Quarterly, 6,* 219–247.

Hains, S. C., Hogg, M. A., & Duck, J. M. (1997). Self-categorization and leadership: Effects of group prototypicality and leader stereotypicality. *Personality and Social Psychology Bulletin, 23,* 1087–1100.

Haslam, N., Rothschild, L., & Ernst, D. (1998). Essentialist beliefs about social categories. *British Journal of Social Psychology, 39,* 113–127.

Haslam, S. A., & Platow, M. J. (2001). Your wish is our command: The role of shared social identity in translating a leader's vision into followers' action. In M. A. Hogg & D. J. Terry (Eds.), *Social identity processes in organizational contexts* (pp. 213–228). Philadelphia, PA: Psychology Press.

Haslam, S. A., & Reicher, S. D. (2005). The psychology of tyranny. *Scientific American, 16,* 44–51.

Heilman, M. E. (1983). Sex bias in work settings: The lack of fit model. *Research in Organizational Behavior, 5,* 269–298.

Hogg, M. A. (2001). A social identity theory of leadership. *Personality and Social Psychology Review, 5,* 184–200.

Hogg, M. A. (2007a). Social psychology of leadership. In A. W. Kruglanski & E. T. Higgins (Eds.), *Social psychology: Handbook of basic principles* (2nd ed., pp. 716–733). New York, NY: Guilford.

Hogg, M. A. (2007b). Social identity and the group context of trust: Managing risk and building trust through belonging. In M. Siegrist, T. C. Earle, & H. Gutscher (Eds.), *Trust in cooperative risk management: Uncertainty and scepticism in the public mind* (pp. 51–71). London, UK: Earthscan.

Hogg, M. A. (2008). Social identity theory of leadership. In C.L. Hoyt, G. R. Goethals, & D. R. Forsyth (Eds.), *Leadership at the crossroads: Vol. 1. Leadership and psychology* (pp. 62–77). Westport, CT: Praeger.

Hogg, M. A. (2009). From group conflict to social harmony: Leading across diverse and conflicting social identities. In T. Pittinsky (Ed.), *Crossing the divide: Intergroup leadership in a world of difference* (pp. 17–30). Cambridge, MA: Harvard Business Publishing.

Hogg, M. A. (2010). Influence and leadership. In S. T. Fiske, D. T. Gilbert, & G. Lindzey (Eds.), *Handbook of social psychology* (5th ed., Vol. 2, pp. 1166–1207). New York, NY: Wiley.

Hogg, M. A., Fielding, K. S., Johnson, D., Masser, B., Russell, E., & Svensson, A. (2006).

Demographic category membership and leadership in small groups: A social identity analysis. *The Leadership Quarterly, 17*, 335–350.

Hogg, M. A., Hains, S. C., & Mason, I. (1998). Identification and leadership in small groups: Salience, frame of reference, and leader stereotypicality effects on leader evaluations. *Journal of Personality and Social Psychology, 75*, 1248–1263.

Hogg, M. A., Martin, R., Epitropaki, O., Mankad, A., Svensson, A., & Weeden, K. (2005). Effective leadership in salient groups: Revisiting leader-member exchange theory from the perspective of the social identity theory of leadership. *Personality and Social Psychology Bulletin, 31*, 991–1004.

Hogg, M. A., & Reid, S. A. (2006). Social identity, self-categorization, and the communication of group norms. *Communication Theory, 16*, 7–30.

Hogg, M. A., & Van Knippenberg, D. (2003). Social identity and leadership processes in groups. In M. P. Zanna (Ed.), *Advances in experimental social psychology* (Vol. 35, pp. 1–52). San Diego, CA: Academic Press.

Hogg, M. A., Van Knippenberg, D., & Rast, D. E. III. (2012). Intergroup leadership in organizations: Leading across group and organizational boundaries. *Academy of Management Review, 37*, 232–255.

Hollander, E. P. (1958). Conformity, status, and idiosyncrasy credit. *Psychological Review, 65*, 117–127.

Hollander, E. P. (1985). Leadership and power. In G. Lindzey & E. Aronson (Eds.), *Handbook of social psychology* (3rd ed., Vol. 2, pp. 485–537). New York, NY: Random House.

Hollander, E. P., & Julian, J. W. (1970). Studies in leader legitimacy, influence, and innovation. In L. Berkowitz (Ed.), *Advances in experimental social psychology* (Vol. 5, pp. 34–69). New York, NY: Academic Press.

Hornsey, M. J., & Hogg, M. A. (2000). Assimilation and diversity: An integrative model of subgroup relations. *Personality and Social Psychology Review, 4*, 143–156.

House, R. J. (1971). A path-goal theory of leadership effectiveness. *Administrative Science Quarterly, 16*, 321–338.

House, R. J. (1977). A 1976 theory of charismatic leadership. In J. G. Hunt & L. Larson (Eds.), *Leadership: The cutting edge* (pp. 189–207). Carbondale, IL: Southern Illinois University Press.

House, R. J. (1996). Path-goal theory of leadership: Lessons, legacy, and a reformulated theory. *The Leadership Quarterly, 7*, 323–352.

House, R. J., & Mitchell, T. R. (1974). Path-goal theory of leadership. *Journal of Contemporary Business, 3*, 81–98.

House, R. J., Spangler, W. D., & Woycke, J. (1991). Personality and charisma in the US presidency: A psychological theory of leader effectiveness. *Administrative Science Quarterly, 36*, 364–396.

Judge, T. A., & Bono, J. E. (2000). Five-factor model of personality and transformational leadership. *Journal of Applied Psychology, 85*, 751–765.

Judge, T. A., Bono, J. E., Ilies, R., & Gerhardt, M. W. (2002). Personality and leadership: A qualitative and quantitative review. *Journal of Applied Psychology, 87*, 765–780.

Kellerman, B. (2004). *Bad leadership: What it is, how it happens, why it matters.* Cambridge, MA: Harvard Business School Press.

Kelley, R. E. (1992). *The power of followership.* New York, NY: Doubleday.

Kennedy, J. (1982). Middle LPC leaders and the contingency model of leader effectiveness. *Organizational Behavior and Human Performance, 30*, 1–14.

Levine, J. M., & Moreland, R. L. (1990). Progress in small group research. *Annual Review of Psychology, 41,* 585–634.

Lewin, K. (1947). Frontiers in group dynamics. *Human Relations, 1,* 5–42.

Lind, E. A., & Tyler, T. R. (1988). *The social psychology of procedural justice.* New York, NY: Plenum Press.

Lippitt, R., & White, R. (1943). The 'social climate' of children's groups. In R. G. Barker, J. Kounin & H. Wright (Eds.), *Child behavior and development* (pp. 485–508). New York, NY: McGraw-Hill.

Lipponen, J., Koivisto, S., & Olkkonen, M. E. (2005). Procedural justice and status judgements: The moderating role of leader ingroup prototypicality. *Leadership Quarterly, 16,* 517–528.

Lord, R. G., & Brown, D. J. (2004). *Leadership processes and follower identity.* Mahwah, NJ: Erlbaum.

Lord, R. G., Brown, D. J., & Harvey, J. L. (2001). System constraints on leadership perceptions, behavior and influence: An example of connectionist level processes. In M. A. Hogg & R. S. Tindale (Eds.), *Blackwell handbook of social psychology: Group processes* (pp. 283–310). Oxford, UK: Blackwell.

Lord, R. G., Brown, D. J., Harvey, J. L., & Hall, R. J. (2001). Contextual constraints on prototype generation and their multilevel consequences for leadership perceptions. *Leadership Quarterly, 12,* 311–338.

Lord, R. G., Foti, R. J., & DeVader, C. L. (1984). A test of leadership categorization theory: Internal structure, information processing, and leadership perceptions. *Organizational Behavior and Human Performance, 34,* 343–378.

Lord, R. G., Foti, R. J., & Phillips, J. S. (1982). A theory of leadership categorization. In J. G. Hunt, U. Sekaran, & C. Schriesheim (Eds.), *Leadership: Beyond establishment views* (pp. 104–121). Carbondale, IL: Southern Illinois University Press.

Lord, R., & Hall, R. (2003). Identity, leadership categorization, and leadership schema. In D. Van Knippenberg & M. A. Hogg (Eds.) *Leadership and power: Identity processes in groups and organizations* (pp. 48–64). London, UK: Sage.

Lowe, K. B., Kroeck, K. G., & Sivasubramaniam, N. (1996). Effectiveness correlates of transformational and transactional leadership: A meta-analytic review. *The Leadership Quarterly, 7,* 385–425.

Meindl, J. R. (1995). The romance of leadership as a follower-centric theory: A social constructionist approach. *The Leadership Quarterly, 6,* 329–341.

Meindl, J. R., Ehrlich, S. B., & Dukerich, J. M. (1985). The romance of leadership. *Administrative Science Quarterly, 30,* 78-102.

Meindl, J. R., & Lerner, M. (1983). The heroic motive: Some experimental demonstrations. *Journal of Experimental Social Psychology, 19,* 1–20.

Merei, F. (1949). Group leadership and institutionalization. *Human Relations, 2,* 23–39.

Messick, D. M. (2005). On the psychological exchange between leaders and followers. In D. M. Messick & R. M. Kramer (Eds.), *The psychology of leadership: New perspectives and research* (pp. 81–96). Mahwah, NJ: Erlbaum.

Moreland, R. L., Hogg, M. A., & Hains, S. C. (1994). Back to the future: Social psychological research on groups. *Journal of Experimental Social Psychology, 30,* 527–555.

O'Connor, J., Mumford, M. D., Clifton, T. C., Gessner, T. L., & Connelly, M. S. (1995). Charismatic leaders and destructiveness: A historiometric study. *The Leadership Quarterly, 6,* 529–558.

Peters, L. H., Hartke, D. D., & Pohlmann, J. T. (1985). Fiedler's contingency theory of leadership: An application of the meta-analytic procedure of Schmidt and Hunter. *Psychological Bulletin, 97,* 274–285.

Pittinsky, T. (Ed.). (2009). *Crossing the divide: Intergroup leadership in a world of difference.* Cambridge, MA: Harvard Business Publishing.

Pittinsky, T. L., & Simon, S. (2007). Intergroup leadership. *The Leadership Quarterly, 18,* 586–605.

Platow, M. J., Hoar, S., Reid, S. A., Harley, K., & Morrison, D. (1997). Endorsement of distributively fair and unfair leaders in interpersonal and intergroup situations. *European Journal of Social Psychology, 27,* 465–494.

Platow, M. J., Reid, S. A., & Andrew, S. (1998). Leadership endorsement: The role of distributive and procedural behavior in interpersonal and intergroup contexts. *Group Processes and Intergroup Relations, 1,* 35–47.

Platow, M. J., & Van Knippenberg, D. (2001). A social identity analysis of leadership endorsement: The effects of leader ingroup prototypicality and distributive intergroup fairness. *Personality and Social Psychology Bulletin, 27,* 1508–1519.

Raven, B. H. (1993). The bases of power: Origins and recent developments. *Journal of Social Issues, 49,* 227–251.

Reicher, S. D., & Hopkins, N. (1996). Self-category constructions in political rhetoric: An analysis of Thatcher's and Kinnock's speeches concerning the British miners' strike (1984–5). *European Journal of Social Psychology, 26,* 353–371.

Reicher, S., & Hopkins, N. (2003). On the science of the art of leadership. In D. Van Knippenberg & M. A. Hogg (Eds.), *Leadership and power: Identity processes in groups and organizations* (pp. 197–209). London, UK: Sage.

Reid, S. A., & Ng, S. H. (2000). Conversation as a resource for influence: Evidence for prototypical arguments and social identification processes. *European Journal of Social Psychology, 30,* 83–100.

Rhodewalt, F. (Ed.) (2008). *Personality and social behavior.* New York, NY: Psychology Press.

Ridgeway, C. L. (2001). Social status and group structure. In M. A. Hogg & R. S. Tindale (Eds.), *Blackwell handbook of social psychology: Group processes* (pp. 352–375). Oxford, UK: Blackwell.

Ridgeway, C. L. (2003). Status characteristics and leadership. In D. Van Knippenberg & M. A. Hogg (Eds.), *Leadership and power: Identity processes in groups and organizations* (pp. 65–78). London, UK: Sage.

Riggio, R. E., Chaleff, I., & Lipman-Blumen, J. (Eds.). (2008). *The art of followership: How great followers create great leaders and organizations.* San Francisco, CA: Jossey-Bass.

Rosenthal, S. A., & Pittinsky, T. L. (2006). Narcissistic leadership. *The Leadership Quarterly, 17,* 617–633.

Rudman, L. A. (1998). Self-promotion as a risk factor for women: The costs and benefits of counterstereotypical impression management. *Journal of Personality and Social Psychology, 74,* 629–645.

Sanna, L. J., & Parks, C. D. (1997). Group research trends in social and organizational psychology: Whatever happened to intragroup research? *Psychological Science, 8,* 261–267.

Scandura, T. A. (1999). Rethinking leader-member exchange: An organizational justice perspective. *The Leadership Quarterly, 10,* 25–40.

Schriesheim, C. A., Castro, S. L., & Cogliser, C. C. (1999). Leader-member exchange

(LMX) research: A comprehensive review of theory, measurement, and data-analytic practices. *The Leadership Quarterly, 10,* 63–113.

Schriesheim, C. A., & Neider, L. L. (1996). Path-goal leadership theory: The long and winding road. *The Leadership Quarterly, 7,* 317–321.

Schriesheim, C. A., Tepper, B. J., & Tetrault, L. A. (1994). Least preferred co-worker score, situational control, and leadership effectiveness: A meta-analysis of contingency model performance predictions. *Journal of Applied Psychology, 79,* 561–573.

Shamir, B., House, R., & Arthur, M. (1993). The motivational effects of charismatic leadership: A self-concept based theory. *Organization Science, 4(3),* 1–17.

Shamir, B., Pillai, R., Bligh, M. C., & Uhl-Bien, M. (Eds.). (2006). *Follower-centered perspectives on leadership: A tribute to the memory of James R. Meindl.* Greenwich, CT: Information Age Publishing.

Shaw, M. E. (1976). *Group dynamics* (2nd ed.). New York, NY: McGraw-Hill.

Sherif, M. (1966). *In common predicament: Social psychology of intergroup conflict and cooperation.* Boston, MA: Houghton-Mifflin.

Sherif, M., Harvey, O. J., White, B. J., Hood, W., & Sherif, C. (1961). *Intergroup conflict and cooperation: The robbers' cave experiment.* Norman, OK: University of Oklahoma Institute of Intergroup Relations.

Simonton, D. K. (1980). Land battles, generals and armies: Individual and situational determinants of victory and casualties. *Journal of Personality and Social Psychology, 38,* 110–119.

Smith, P. B., Misumi, J., Tayeb, M., Peterson, M., & Bond, M. (1989). On the generality of leadership style measures across cultures. *Journal of Occupational Psychology, 62,* 97–109.

Sorrentino, R. M., & Field, N. (1986). Emergent leadership over time: The functional value of positive motivation. *Journal of Personality and Social Psychology, 50,* 1091–1099.

Sparrowe, R. T., & Liden, R. C. (1997). Process and structure in leader-member exchange. *Academy of Management Review, 22,* 522–552.

Steele, C. M., Spencer, S. J., & Aronson, J. (2002). Contending with group image: The psychology of stereotype and social identity threat. In M. P. Zanna (Ed.), *Advances in experimental social psychology* (Vol. 34, pp. 379–440). San Diego, CA: Academic Press.

Steiner, I. D. (1974). Whatever happened to the group in social psychology? *Journal of Experimental Social Psychology, 10,* 1467–1478.

Stogdill, R. M. (1948). Personal factors associated with leadership: A survey of the literature. *Journal of Psychology, 25,* 35–71.

Stogdill, R. (1974). *Handbook of leadership.* New York, NY: Free Press.

Strube, M. J., & Garcia, J. E. (1981). A meta-analytic investigation of Fiedler's contingency model of leadership effectiveness. *Psychological Bulletin, 90,* 307–321.

Tajfel, H. (Ed.) (1984). *The social dimension: European developments in social psychology.* Cambridge, UK: Cambridge University Press.

Takala, T. (1998). Plato on leadership. *Journal of Business Ethics, 17,* 785–798.

Taylor, D. M., & Brown, R. J. (1979). Towards a more social psychology. *British Journal of Social and Clinical Psychology, 18,* 173–179.

Terry, D. J., Carey, C. J., & Callan, V. J. (2001). Employee adjustment to an organizational merger: An intergroup perspective. *Personality and Social Psychology Bulletin, 27,* 267–280.

Tindale, R. S., & Anderson, E. M. (1998). Small group research and applied social psychology: An introduction. In R. S. Tindale, L. Heath, J. Edwards, E. J. Posavac, F. B. Bryant, Y. Suarez-Balcazar, et al. (Eds.), *Social psychological applications to social issues: Theory and research on small groups* (Vol. 4, pp. 1–8). New York, NY: Plenum Press.

Turner, J. C. (1991). *Social influence.* Buckingham, UK: Open University Press.

Tyler, T. R. (1997). The psychology of legitimacy: A relational perspective on voluntary deference to authorities. *Personality and Social Psychology Review, 1,* 323–345.

Tyler, T. R. (2003). Justice, identity, and leadership. In D. Van Knippenberg & M. A. Hogg (Eds.) *Leadership and power: Identity processes in groups and organizations* (pp. 94–108). London, UK: Sage.

Tyler, T. R., & Lind, E. A. (1992). A relational model of authority in groups. In M. P. Zanna (Ed.), *Advances in experimental social psychology* (Vol. 25, pp. 115–191). New York, NY: Academic Press.

Ullrich, J., & Van Dick, R. (2007). The group psychology of mergers and acquisitions. In C. L. Cooper & S. Finkelstein (Eds.), *Advances in mergers and acquisitions* (Vol. 6, pp. 1–15). Bingley, UK: Emerald.

Van Knippenberg, D., & Hogg, M. A. (2003). A social identity model of leadership in organizations. In R. M. Kramer & B. M. Staw (Eds.), *Research in organizational behavior* (Vol. 25, pp. 243–295). Greenwich, CT: JAI Press.

Van Knippenberg, D., Van Knippenberg, B., De Cremer, D., & Hogg, M. A. (2004). Leadership, self, and identity: A review and research agenda. *The Leadership Quarterly, 15,* 825–856.

Van Vugt, M., & De Cremer, D. (1999). Leadership in social dilemmas: The effects of group identification on collective actions to provide public goods. *Journal of Personality and Social Psychology, 76,* 587–599.

Van Vugt, M., Hogan, R., & Kaiser, R. (2008). Leadership, followership, and evolution: Some lessons from the past. *American Psychologist, 63,* 182–196.

Vroom, V. H., & Jago, A. G. (1988). *The new leadership.* Englewood Cliffs, NJ: Prentice Hall.

Vroom, V. H., & Yetton, P. W. (1973). *Leadership and decision-making.* Pittsburgh, PA: University of Pittsburgh Press.

Walster, E., Walster, G. W., & Berscheid, E. (1978). *Equity theory and research.* Boston, MA: Allyn & Bacon.

Wittenbaum, G. M., & Moreland, R. L. (2008). Small group research in social psychology: Topics and trends over time. *Social and Personalitiy Psychology Compass, 2,* 187–205.

Wood, W., & Eagly, A. H. (2010). Gender. In S. T. Fiske, D. T. Gilbert, & G. Lindzey (Eds.), *Handbook of social psychology* (5th ed., Vol. 1, pp. 629–667). New York, NY: Wiley.

Yamagishi, T., & Kiyonari, T. (2000). The group as the container of generalized reciprocity. *Social Psychology Quarterly, 63,* 116–132.

Yukl, G. (2010). *Leadership in organizations* (7th ed.). Upper Saddle River, NJ: Pearson Education.

Yzerbyt, V., & Demoulin, S. (2010). Intergroup relations. In S. T. Fiske, D. T. Gilbert, & G. Lindzey (Eds.), *Handbook of social psychology* (5th ed., Vol. 2, pp. 1024–1083). New York, NY: Wiley.

11

Social Identity and Groups

DOMINIC ABRAMS

This chapter summarizes the social identity approach to group processes. The social identity approach was developed to provide a metatheoretical framework that, uniquely in social psychology, insisted that researchers should articulate theoretical constructs at the social cognitive, social interactive, intergroup, and societal levels (see Abrams & Hogg, 2004). This metatheory was couched as an alternative, antidote, and rival to extant theories of intra-group and intergroup behavior that were based on interpersonal relationships, costs and rewards, personality, or cognitive biases. Fundamentally, according to the social identity approach, intragroup and intergroup behavior both have to be conceived of as deriving from the value and meaning that a group has for its members within its social context. Because another chapter in this volume (Dovidio, Gaertner, & Thomas) concentrates on intergroup relations, the focus here will be primarily on the nature and structure of social identity and its implications for processes within groups, including cohesiveness and commitment, leadership, influence, and deviance.

A rigorous review of the academic literature over the last 70 years revealed a steady increase in groups research, and between 1997 and 2007, over one third of the papers on groups in social psychology's top eight journals invoked social identity as a key concept (Randsley de Moura, Leader, Pelletier, & Abrams, 2008). Currently (February 2011) results from a Google search on the term "social identity theory" produced 96,700 hits, a 36 per cent increase since March 2009, and a higher number than references to many other influential theories in social psychology (e.g., 83,000 for the "theory of reasoned action", 35,400 for "intergroup contact", 16,800 for "social influence theory", and 47,000 for "cognitive dissonance theory"). An important reason for this enormous influence and reach is that the social identity metatheory embraces sub-theories that deal with both the content and the context of group behavior. That is, the theory concerns the psychology that enables people to relate their group memberships to themselves as individuals and to society at large. Tajfel's (1974, 1981) foundational theorizing generated two different aspects of the theory. Tajfel and Turner's (1979) "social identity theory of intergroup relations" was primarily concerned with the group and identity in the context of conflict and struggle between groups within a larger social structure. Turner's (1985) "social identity theory of the group", ultimately emerging as self-categorization theory (Turner, Hogg, Oakes, Reicher, & Wetherell, 1987), developed a detailed account of the social-cognitive processes that underpin the psychological linkage between the self and a group. These two aspects of the theory provide the basis of a diverse array of more specific explanations for phenomena such as group cohesion, leadership, social influence, and the malleability of the self. Crucially, the overarching metatheory assumes that intergroup relations, intragroup relations, and the self are woven together in such a way that they can have reciprocal influence.

This review summarizes the key concepts of the social identity approach within social identity theory and self-categorization theory. It then considers the types of groups for which social identity is relevant, how social identity has been conceptualized and measured vis-a-vis other aspects of identity and cultural differences, and the motives associated with social identity. The review then examines the role of social identity in group cohesion and commitment, leadership, social influence, collective mobilization, and deviance and dissent.

KEY CONCEPTS OF THE SOCIAL IDENTITY APPROACH

Social Identity Theory and Intergroup Context

Social Identity Theory (SIT) originates from ideas proposed almost two decades before Tajfel and Turner's (1979) classic chapter, namely Bruner's (1957) "new look" in perception and Tajfel's (1959) work on the accentuation principle in categorization. A decade later, Tajfel's (1969) paper on the cognitive aspects of prejudice applied to the phenomenon of stereotyping the principle that people accentuate similarities within and differences between continuous stimuli, once those stimuli have been categorized. Thus, categorization, and not just differences in the actual characteristics of different groups, explains why group members are seen in terms of stereotypes rather than as unique individuals.

A fundamental distinction in the social identity perspective was that between social identity and personal identity. Social identity, "the individual's knowledge that he [sic] belongs to certain social groups together with some emotional and value significance to him of this group membership" (Tajfel, 1972, p. 292), was assumed to be the basis for intragroup and intergroup processes. A clear distinction was made between social and personal identity, which were associated with group/intergroup processes and individual/interpersonal processes, respectively. An important point was that both types of processes could arise in groups but that interpersonal processes, such as attraction or interdependence, could not fully explain the coordinated nature of group processes. Thus, social identity theory claimed to offer an approach that remained psychological but did not reduce the explanation of group processes to purely individual processes or characteristics (see Hogg & Abrams, 1988; Abrams & Hogg, 2004).

The social identity approach, along with Moscovici's approach (e.g., his 1981 theory of social representations), offered a distinctive European contrast to individualistic North American theories that essentially accepted Floyd Allport's (1924) assertion that the psychology of groups could be understood entirely based on understanding the psychology of individuals. Previous approaches had explained intergroup behavior using purely personal characteristics or motives. These included the psychodynamic approach used in Adorno, Frenkel-Brunswik, Levinson, & Sanford's (1950) *The Authoritarian Personality*, explanations of crowd behavior as arising from primitive instincts (Le Bon, 1895); explanations of protest as arising from personal frustration and deprivation (see Crosby, 1976); explanations of stereotypes as arising from faulty cognitive processes (Hamilton & Gifford, 1976); explanations of group opinion extremity as arising from within-group influence (cf. Myers & Lamm, 1976); and explanations of intergroup conflict as arising from conflicting goals and negative interdependence (Sherif & Sherif, 1966).

The social identity approach, in contrast, emphasized the role of the social context and its subjective meaning and the idea that shared meaning, rather than direct interpersonal influence or material interests, is the basis of coherent collective behavior. Moreover, this meaning is channeled through the self-concept, which provides the necessary psychological connection between individuals and society. This combination of an explicit analysis of the role of social context and the mediation of its effects on behavior through identity provided the platform on which the approach could be applied not just to intergroup behavior but also to intragroup processes and behavior. Because the intergroup and intragroup aspects are inextricably linked, this chapter necessarily refers to aspects of both, while focusing primarily on intragroup phenomena.

Through the 1970s, Tajfel and his co-workers focused on demonstrating that social categorization that includes the self provides the basis for discrimination against outgroup members. A key innovation was the use of the minimal group paradigm, in which research participants responded to anonymous others about whom the only salient information was their group membership (own vs. other). In this paradigm, the groups are arbitrarily and temporarily created, with no prior history and no interpersonal connection among the members. Even with no direct route to satisfy self-interest, participants in this paradigm typically assign resources in a way that ensures their own group "wins" over the outgroup. This occurs even when the resources are symbolic rather than real and even when participants' ingroup "loses" in absolute terms. The paradigm demonstrates quite powerfully that people are spontaneously motivated to ensure a relatively positive evaluation of their ingroup, illustrating a transformation from self-evaluation as in individual to self-evaluation as a group member, which can be enhanced by ensuring that one's group attains superiority by receiving more than the outgroup. Whereas most people advocate the principle that all individuals should be treated fairly (Smetana, 2006), once people view themselves in terms of their membership in a social category, even for a very short time and based on trivial, or 'minimal,' criteria, they tend to favor others who share their own group membership over those who do not. The minimal group paradigm continues to provide the baseline condition in much contemporary social identity research (Bourhis, Sachdev, & Gagnon, 1994), in part because it establishes a social identity that has no prior history and no basis in interpersonal relationships.

Tafjel's mission was not merely to explain how cognitive mechanisms can account for social behavior but also to explain how shared categorization, or social identity, is central to the way in which people engage with the wider social structure in which groups are embedded. In combination with the desire to sustain a positive social identity, people's judgments of their ingroup and relevant outgroups are framed by their understanding of their relationship in the context of society as a whole (Tajfel, 1974; Tajfel & Turner, 1979). It was the extension of social identity theory into self-categorization theory (Turner et al., 1987) that made explicit how and why the social identity approach is also central to the psychology of small groups and intragroup processes.

Self-Categorization Theory and Depersonalization

The cognitive bases of social identity were elaborated in self-categorization theory (SCT), which has been used to explain social identity salience and its implications for such phenomena as social influence and group cohesion. According to SCT, influence within groups can be explained using the concept of referent informational influence (Turner, 1985), the idea that norms form within groups because of members' shared understanding of their ingroup's differences from outgroups (rather than mimicry, modeling, direct interpersonal pressure, or other factors). Moreover, group cohesion and solidarity can be explained in terms of shared focus and attraction to a group prototype rather than to specific individuals (Hogg, 1993). These ideas are discussed in more detail later.

One of the more arresting propositions of SCT is that identity itself, specifically the salience of social identity, can change depending on the social context (Oakes, Haslam, & Turner, 1994). Oakes (1987) proposed that the cognitive *accessibility* of particular social categorizations and their *fit* to the current context determine identity salience. A social categorization is more likely to be applied if it is has been used frequently in the past (*chronic accessibility*) and is clearly relevant to the current situation (*situational accessibility*). It will fit the situation better if it maps onto similarities and differences among people's attributes or actions within the situation (*comparative fit*) and if it makes sense of people's behavior there (*normative fit*). Not all of these elements have to be in place for a particular social identity to be salient, however. For example, minimal group experiments create high situational accessibility and high comparative fit, but there is no chronic accessibility or normative fit. The latter elements seem more likely to be important when real groups are involved.

SCT holds that ingroup and outgroup *prototypes* are derived through social comparisons that maximize the *meta-contrast ratio*—intergroup differences relative to intragroup differences. An ingroup prototype, namely the psychological representation of the ingroup, depends on which other groups it is compared with and the dimensions, or attributes, on which the groups are compared. For example vegetarians may view themselves as relatively more or less vegetarian depending on whether they compare with meat eaters or vegans, respectively (cf. White, Schmitt, & Langer, 2006).

The meta-contrast process means that category members sharing a social identity are viewed in terms of their closeness to the group prototype rather than their unique personal qualities. In other words, category members are perceptually *depersonalized*. Just as categorization can result in depersonalized stereotyping of outgroup members, it can also result in category members *self*-stereotyping themselves in terms of ingroup attributes. This idea has been extensively tested and verified. For example, when social identity is salient, higher self-focus results in more intergroup bias and more ascription of ingroup characteristics to the self (Abrams, 1994; Eidelman & Silvia, 2010).

It is important to understand that, unlike deindividuation (Deiner, 1980), self-stereotyping does not represent a loss of humanity or identity, but rather a transition in the meaning of identity from personal to social. For example, women apply gender stereotypes to themselves more when intergender comparisons are salient than when intragender comparisons are salient (Guimond, Chatard, Martinot, Crisp, & Redersdorff, 2006), and children show a similar effect by the age of five (Bennett & Sani, 2008). Self-stereotyping is increased if people already identify strongly with their group and its status or distinctiveness is threatened (Simon & Hamilton, 1994; Spears, Doosje, & Ellemers, 1997).

TYPES OF GROUPS AND SOCIAL IDENTITY

There are various typologies of groups. For example, groups can vary in "entitativity," as defined by their members' shared fate, interdependence, type and level of interaction, and shared goals (Hamilton & Sherman, 1996; McGarty, Yzerbyt, & Spears, 2002). Groups also vary in size, function, and history, which means that some (such as ethnic groups) may be more important than others (such as recreational sports groups) for social identity (Deaux, Reid, Mizrahi, & Ethier, 1995). And Prentice, Miller, and Lightdale (1994) proposed that some groups are more readily characterized in terms of members' categorical features (e.g., gender), or their "common identity," whereas others are more clearly defined by dynamic social interactions among members, or their "common bonds" (e.g., a family or work team) (see also Poole & Hollingshead, 2005).

From the social identity perspective, these differences are less relevant than the principle that a group is primarily a psychological construct that comes into being when, for whatever reason, two or more people share the same social self-definition—the same social identity. This process of social identification can arise for any of the types of group described above. Shared identity based on depersonalized self-categorization means that the individual and group become psychologically interchangeable. Depersonalization underpins commitment and adherence to group norms and explains why people readily assume that ingroup members share their own attributes (Otten, 2002) and internalize the properties of the ingroup as a whole as part of the self (e.g., Wright, Aron, & Tropp, 2002). Self-stereotyping also provides a powerful account of group cohesiveness, commitment, and mobilization, which will be discussed later.

CONCEPTUAL AND MEASUREMENT ISSUES IN SOCIAL IDENTITY

Tajfel defined social identity as including cognitive, emotional, and connotative (value and behavioral intention) components. Space does not permit extended discussion of the various operationalizations and measures of social identity suggested by later researchers (see Abrams & Hogg, 2001, Leach et al., 2008). Instead, a few particularly important contributions will be mentioned.

Recently, researchers have focused on how social identity is implicated in different types of social contexts. For example, Brewer (2001) proposed four types of social identity, or kinds of relationship between the self and a social group: (a) *person-based social identities* involve internalization of properties of groups as part of one's self-concept; (b) *relational social identities* are based on specific relationships that tie one to a specific group (cf. Markus & Kitayama's (1991) "interdependent self"); (c) *group-based social identities* are self-categorized social identities that assign social categories, such as gender, as well as temporary memberships to the self in relevant contexts; and (d) *collective identities* involve engagement in social action to define the image of the group to others. Although these four kinds of social identity are manifested differently, they share the feature that, regardless of whether thoughts, feelings, and behaviors arise in a lone individual or in a mass of people, they involve social identity if the actors perceive themselves and others in terms of shared category or group characteristics. This perception may depend on the task at hand and the wider socio-cultural context.

Attention has also been given to the relative importance of personal and social identity. For example, Sedikides and Gaertner (2001) argued that personal identity has primacy over social identity because personal identity is more stable, enduring, and cognitively accessible. It has also been argued that culture has a substantial impact on whether people accord primacy to individuals or groups. Some have suggested that social identity is more important in collectivistic cultures, such as Japan and China, where people display a high level of conformity to group norms (Bond & Smith, 1996), than in individualistic cultures, such as the United States. However, different types or levels of group membership may come into play in different cultures. For example, collectivistic cultures may be more likely to specify which types of groups are part of a person's social identity (e.g., through traditions of loyalty to the family, the organization, or the nation), whereas in individualistic cultures people may be freer to adopt different group memberships as a way of defining their identity. Ironically then, individualism can be a powerful group norm within Western culture so that people who identify with a group with a norm of individualism behave more individualistically (McAuliffe, Jetten, Hornsey, & Hogg, 2003). This 'independence paradox' (Salvatore & Prentice, 2011) suggests that people who are dispositionally independent can flourish in group contexts that value innovation and eccentricity. In principle, therefore, despite possible cross-cultural or situational differences in the way social identity is manifested, social identification processes are the same across cultures. For example, group identity motivates commitment to organizations to a similar degree in both individualistic and collectivistic cultures (Randsley de Moura, Abrams, Retter, Gunnarsdottir, & Ando, 2009).

It is important to note that the social identity approach is not concerned with *whether* the individual or collective self has primacy but rather *when* a particular level of self-conception is dominant in a particular social context (Abrams & Hogg, 2001; Simon, 2004). Thus, both SIT and SCT view personal and social identity not as stable structures but rather as flexible self-conceptualizations that fit particular social comparative contexts (Abrams & Hogg, 2001). This issue was developed more explicitly in SCT, which describes identity salience as reflecting the functional antagonism between different levels of a hierarchy of self-categorizations. Consistent with this approach, emotions can be distinguished at the individual and group levels. In a study of students' national, university, and political identities, Smith, Seger, and Mackie (2007) showed that group emotions (e.g., feeling pride of the group) are experienced distinctly from individual emotions (e.g., pride from personal success or failure), group emotions are amplified when people identify more strongly with the group, group emotions are socially shared (they arise and dissipate similarly among all group members), and group emotions contribute to regulating intragroup and intergroup attitudes, action tendencies, and behavior (e.g., group members will act in ways to continue group success).

SOCIAL IDENTITY MOTIVES

A central question is why people identify with a group and what motivations follow. Abrams and Hogg (1988) identified three important motives, namely people's needs for self-esteem, meaning/certainty, and distinctiveness. SIT, as articulated by Tajfel and Turner (1979), focused on the basic human motive for self-esteem (Sedikides & Strube, 1997), proposing that people are motivated to attain positive distinctiveness of their ingroup vis-à-vis outgroups because of the positive self-evaluation that is associated with that distinctiveness. Abrams and Hogg (1988) unpacked this "self-esteem hypothesis," which assumes there is a positive correlation between ingroup bias and self-esteem, into two corollaries. The hypothesis implies both that (a) expressing ingroup favoritism should enhance self-esteem and (b) low self-esteem should motivate efforts to find positive ingroup distinctiveness, for example, by expressing ingroup bias. Subsequent research has supported the positive correlation between self-esteem and ingroup bias, and the causal direction from ingroup bias to high self-esteem is better supported than the causal direction from low self-esteem to increased ingroup bias (Rubin & Hewstone, 1998).

Testing these two corollaries appropriately requires attention to a number of technical issues, most importantly whether self-esteem is measured at the relevant level (i.e., collective) and with the right specificity (i.e., relating to the particular group that is being evaluated). One methodologically adequate test of the prediction that ingroup favoritism enhances self-esteem (Houston & Andreopoulou, 2003) measured Greek students' collective self-esteem prior to and following their evaluation of ingroup (Greek) and outgroup (either American or Turkish) students. For both outgroups, evaluative differentiation favoring the ingroup promoted positive collective self-esteem.

Some research has shown that positive self-evaluation (measured through global personal self-esteem) is associated with positive evaluation of novel ingroups in a minimal group situation (Gramzow & Gaertner, 2005), supporting the idea that ingroup evaluations are based on a projection of positivity toward the personal self. However, it is hardly a fair test of Tajfel's hypothesis to contrast personal identity based on an entire life with a collective identity based on (in this instance) a minimal categorization and then to conclude that positive regard for novel ingroups is essentially an extension of personal self-regard. Many novel ingroups are, after all, not minimal but come furnished with rich social evaluative content and reputations.

When real groups are involved, the implications of self-esteem for group identity and vice versa become much richer and more complex. For example, the relationship between self-esteem and intergroup bias is moderated by the extremity of self-esteem, the strength with which people identify with the ingroup, and the situational presence or absence of intergroup threat (Aberson, Healy, & Romero, 2000; Rubin & Hewstone, 1998). For example, Smurda, Wittig, and Gokalp (2006) found that when students read that their university had a bad evaluation relative to an outgroup university, those who identified strongly showed both a decrease in implicit self-esteem and increased ingroup favoritism, which was followed by raised implicit self-esteem. This study highlights the dynamic relationship between group behavior and self-esteem and reinforces the conclusion that this may be highly specific to particular domains of esteem and action (Hunter et al., 2004). Individual differences are also relevant to social identity motives because some people are more sensitive to the esteem-implications of negative group comparisons than are others (Amiot & Hornsey, 2010), though other psychological responses can buffer the self-evaluative consequences of stigma (Major, Quinton, & McCoy, 2002).

Other motives also come into play when social identity is salient. These may include motivation to show ingroup positivity without a matching degree of outgroup negativity and security motives such as need to belong (cf. Baumeister & Leary, 1995). Indeed, along with belonging and control needs (see Williams, 2007); the two themes of meaning and distinctiveness (Abrams & Hogg, 1988) have gained greater currency in recent years. These themes recur in different theories (Brewer, 2007; Heine, Proulx, & Vohs, 2006).

Hogg and Abrams (1993) proposed that a powerful influence on group behavior is psychological uncertainty. Uncertainty-identity theory (Hogg, 2007) posits that an epistemic motive associated with social categorization is the desire to reduce uncertainty. Social categorization enhances certainty by clearly defining the boundaries and norms (prototypes) for group membership and behavior. These prototypes provide the sense that there is a collective consensus about what is valuable, important, and appropriate for the group and its members. When facing uncertainty, people are therefore motivated to be part of a group characterized by a clear prototype.

A range of evidence is consistent with the idea that people who seek certainty also strive to maintain clear boundaries for the ingroup and to promote intragroup uniformity. Indeed, this seems to characterize the high internal cohesiveness, well-defined rules and norms, and authoritarian structures of many extremist groups. For example, terror management research shows that mortality salience (implicitly, uncertainty about one's own longevity) promotes worldview defense (Pyszczynski, Greenberg, & Solomon, 1997). Groups that feel threatened by social uncertainty are also more likely to espouse system justifying beliefs (Jost & Hunyadi, 2002), belief in a just world (Furnham & Procter, 1989), and right-wing authoritarianism (Altemeyer, 1998). In a similar vein, adherence to religions, particularly religions that are highly entitative (viewed as a coherent group based on proximity, similarity, common fate and pregnance; Campbell, 1958) may be especially attractive to people who are feeling uncertain about themselves (Hogg, Adelman, & Blagg, 2010).

One way that group membership confers certainty is by providing group distinctiveness. Brewer's (1991) optimal distinctiveness theory proposes that people are motivated to find a balance between two conflicting needs—for inclusion/sameness within a group and distinctiveness/uniqueness from other groups. Too much of either quality results in a quest to find a better balance. People's sense of their group's distinctiveness is dependent on the social comparative context. For example, when numerical membership information leads people to see their group's distinctiveness as either very high or very low, they compensate by elevating their evaluations of their group (e.g., Pickett & Brewer, 2005). Survey research similarly shows that consumers use distinctive characteristics of particular consumer brands to define their social identity (Berger & Heath, 2008). For example adolescents spend more time and money on musical genres that, objectively, provide intermediate rather than very high or low levels of distinctiveness relative to other genres, consistent with the idea that intermediate distinctiveness produces stronger social identification (Abrams, 2009). These findings suggest that there is a complex interaction between the social context and group identity. The context affords particular possibilities in terms of potential group memberships with differing levels of distinctiveness. People may also have more or less freedom or opportunities to be part of groups that provide distinctiveness, reduce uncertainty, or raise their self-esteem.

GROUP COHESION AND COMMITMENT

An assumption of the social identity perspective is that attraction to others is based on shared category-based similarity. Specifically, the psychological basis for group cohesion is that members have a perception of shared similarity on dimensions that define the group—its prototype. Thus, whereas liking of friends is based on *personal attraction* (traditional interpersonal attraction), feelings toward fellow group members is based on depersonalized *social attraction* to the group prototype (Hogg, 1993). This analysis means that people cooperate with, or support, fellow members because doing so aligns self-interest with group-interest, making members psychologically indistinguishable. Depersonalized social attraction also increases trust and confidence that fellow members will make equal contributions to group welfare (De Cremer & Van Vugt, 1999). There could be many reasons why this occurs, including evolutionary advantages of supporting one's group to secure collective protection, influence, or power (Caporael, 2001). Indeed, it has been suggested that the fact that social categorization generates positive ingroup regard (and cohesiveness), even with groups that are minimal or ad hoc, illustrates potential evolutionary advantages (Gaertner, Iuzzini, Witt, & Orina, 2006). On the other hand, given that different intergroup comparisons can quite readily change the definition of what ingroup one belongs to (e.g., a switch of self-categorization based on a salient ethnic membership to a salient team membership), it seems that social categorization can as easily be a basis for being fickle as being consistent in terms of who one cooperates with. Thus, it could militate against survival of any particular group.

Depersonalized social attraction and group cohesion do not arise in a vacuum. Research in the realistic conflict tradition (e.g., Sherif & Sherif, 1966) demonstrated that conflict between groups can promote solidarity and cohesion within groups. However, the social identity approach holds that, even without direct conflict, contrasts between groups provide part of the basis for distinctive ingroup prototypes to which group members are attracted (Hogg, 1993). Thus, group cohesiveness can arise simply from people's awareness that entitative ingroups and outgroups exist (Gaertner & Schopler, 1998). It has also been argued that specific outgroups are not necessary for ingroup social identity to be meaningful (Abrams, 1992), and Gaertner et al. (2006) have shown, using minimal groups, that positive ingroup regard can flow from intragroup interaction even when there is no explicit outgroup and even among people who do not imagine a potential outgroup. The social identity approach would argue, in contrast, that a comparative context is always present, even if it is implicit ('not us', or the background against which the group is focal). For example, in the context of a minimal group experiment involving three interacting individuals, implicit contrasts for student participants might be non-participants, the experimenters, or faculty members.

Organizational Identity

Groups exist within complex social environments, so that a group may be in conflict with some groups but not others, or may be fighting for higher status with groups above it in the hierarchy or resisting threats from groups below it. Often groups must deal with multiple outgroups, as is the case for many organizations (e.g., there are multiple universities, multiple producers of computers, multiple states within a country, etc.). Research on organizational social identity is therefore important both for its practical value and its contribution to expanding the scope of theory on social identity (e.g., Ashforth & Mael, 1989). The contrast with traditional perspectives that focus on roles, job characteristics, rewards, and satisfaction is striking because the social identity approach emphasizes the psychological representation of the organization (or group within it) as a driver of organizational outcomes (e.g., Haslam, 2004; Hogg & Terry, 2000). Work on organizational social identity demonstrates, for example, that employees' identification with an organization is consistently related to other forms of commitment, such as team and organizational citizenship, loyalty, and turnover (Ellemers, Kortekaas, & Ouwerkerk, 1999; Randsley de Moura et al., 2009).

Tyler and Blader (2003) proposed a Group Engagement Model that focuses on the way that social identity and procedural justice combine to create enduring commitment to organizations. According to this model, characteristics of an organization can affect how strongly members identify with it. People identify more when the organization's status is high and its procedures are seen to be fair. Identification in turn promotes psychological engagement among members such that they express favorable attitudes toward the organization, adopt organizational values, and engage in citizenship behavior to support the organization. For example, in two field studies Blader and Tyler (2009) found that employees' social identity was strongly related to, and mediated the effects of, procedural justice and economic outcomes on extra-role behavior as judged by supervisors. Moreover, Fuller et al. (2006) used data from company records, supervisors' judgments, and subordinates' self reports to show that subordinates' perceptions of the organization's external prestige and the respect accorded to individuals within the organization predicted organizational identification. Prestige, respect and identification also predicted willingness to engage in constructive challenges to organizational policy (see the later discussion of constructive dissent).

Societies contain multiple groups, and these are arranged differently in different countries and cultures. However, the study of social identity in organizations provides a useful way to analyze how identification relates to social structures because organizations are bounded and well-defined. Indeed, one of the challenges for any organization is how to remain a coherent entity. Given that organizations contain many smaller groups, there are perpetual intergroup comparisons that involve conflicting values, roles, objectives, and reward structures. A department or team may foster ingroup identification as a subordinate category within the organization as a whole. Interestingly, the ingroup bias that often results is not incompatible with positive identification with the over-arching organization (Hennessy & West, 1999).

LEADERSHIP

Many theories of leadership have been proposed over the years (see Hogg, this volume). We focus here on the social identity theory of leadership, which proposes that group members who embody group norms better than others are seen as more prototypical, are disproportionately influential, and are more likely to be viewed as leaders (Hogg, 2001; Hogg & van Knippenberg, 2003). According to this view, members are attracted to the prototypical position first and the occupant of that position second. The salience of highly prototypical group members means they are likely to attract dispositional attributions for their actions, fostering an aura of charisma that can enhance their influence and further encourage conformity from other members. In principle, this "virtu-ous circle" promotes ever stronger identification with the group both from the leader, who behaves in a group-serving manner, and from other members, who increasingly trust and respect the leader (e.g., Tyler, 1997). For example, Hains, Hogg, and Duck (1997) showed that when group membership becomes more salient, it is a leader's prototypicality rather than his or her match to the 'good leader' stereotype that determines his or her evaluations.

Other evidence also supports the social identity perspective on leader-ship. For example, van Knippenberg, Lossie, and Wilke (1994) showed that a prototypical ingroup member has more influence over other group members' attitudes than does a non-prototypical member. Moreover, Cicero, Pierro, and van Knippenberg (2007) found that workers in various organizations were most satisfied if they viewed their leader as a more prototypical member. In a simi-lar vein, van Dijk, and De Cremer (2008) found that high but not low iden-tifiers perceived more prototypical leaders to be fairer than less prototypical leaders. And Platow, van Knippenberg, Haslam, van Knippenberg, and Spears (2006) showed that more prototypical leaders were viewed as more charismatic, regardless of their personal characteristics.

Some proponents of the social identity perspective on leadership even go as far to claim that charisma "is not a gift that [leaders] *possess*, and it is certainly not a characteristic of their personality.... Rather ... it is a gift that followers *bestow* on leaders for being representative of 'us'" (Haslam, Reicher, & Platow, 2011, p. 103). Despite such strong claims, it is hard to imagine that some leaders are not more charismatic than others, that personality and possession of rel-evant social or task skills do not play a role, or that some leaders are not better than others at articulating a group's ideals. Indeed, much of Haslam et al.'s dis-cussion of leadership contains excellent examples of skilled leaders who actively promote the group. Successful leaders act as 'entrepreneurs' of identity (Reicher & Hopkins, 2001), defining group boundaries and objectives in creative and vivid ways. Nonetheless, the key point is that the glue that binds leaders to their groups (and vice versa) is members' identification with their group (Van Vugt &

Hart, 2004) and a close match between the leader's attributes and actions, on the one hand, and the group's prototypical attributes, norms, and goals, on the other.

It is worth noting a curious feature of much of the social identity and leadership research. Many of the studies compare leaders who behave one way versus another, but there is relatively little consideration of the possibility that leaders are the same as other members on dimensions other than the influence they exert. In other words, there is not much evidence that leaders who act charismatically, or in leader-like ways, or on behalf of the group, or are highly prototypical, are judged very differently from other members who show similar characteristics. In general, leaders have more power than other group members, but a leader's additional influence and impact may stem from his or her perceived power or formal authority rather than because he or she is inherently different from other group members, an issue that is returned to in the section on deviance.

SOCIAL INFLUENCE

The social identity perspective on social influence places the intergroup comparative context central to the activation and content of group norms. For example, traditional theories of social influence in groups gave a very prominent role to informational and normative influence (Deutsch & Gerard, 1955; see Levine & Prislin, this volume). Rather than assuming there are dual routes to influence, the social identity perspective holds that a single process is at work. Group prototypes define the normative position, and because members are attracted to the prototype they align themselves with it. The social identity explanation of group polarization—the finding that group members converge to a more extreme position than the average of the individual members' positions (Moscovici & Zavalloni, 1969)—is that the ingroup prototype is displaced away from that of contrasting outgroups. It is this ingroup prototype, rather than specific influence from individual group members, that is responsible for the polarized group opinion.

Evidence for the impact of the ingroup prototype in social influence is well documented (Postmes, Haslam, & Swaab, 2005; Turner, 1991). For example, Abrams, Wetherell, Cochrane, Hogg, and Turner (1990) showed that the Asch conformity effect was stronger when the source of influence was ingroup rather than outgroup members and that, when groups were asked to form consensual opinions, the amount of group polarization was dependent on whether the group's social identity was salient. More strikingly, using Sherif's (1936) autokinetic effect paradigm, which shows that a group will develop a norm when judging ambiguous stimuli, Abrams et al. found that naïve participants resisted the norm being established by a set of confederates if these people were labeled as belonging to a different social category.

The important point is that social identity defines who are the legitimate sources of influence as well as what the norm is. Unsurprisingly, subsequent research has shown that people who identify more strongly with an ingroup are more likely to find ingroup members and ingroup norms to be persuasive (Cooper, Kelly, & Weaver, 2001). Similarly, research on attitude-behavior correspondence shows that the impact of subjective norms associated with the ingroup is larger the more a person identifies with the ingroup (Terry & Hogg, 1996). Interestingly, in a study of students' perceptions of campus alcohol consumption, Reid, Cropley, and Hogg (see Hogg & Reid, 2006) found that students who perceived themselves to be prototypical of students in general were accurate in their perceptions of the drinking norm whereas those who did not perceive themselves to be prototypical overestimated the level of alcohol consumption by peers.

Emler and Reicher (2005) highlighted that a crucial role of groups is to provide a medium for members' reputations to be established and sustained. Likewise, Abrams (1994) argued that group members actively self-regulate in terms of group identity and goals and in terms of the way other group members perceive them. That is, in line with Durkheim's (1915) and Simmel's (1955) sociological theorizing, group identity gains its meaning and direction through intragroup processes that are embedded in a wider social context. Thus, being a 'delinquent' may range, depending on the social context, from being someone who occasionally argues with authority to someone who is part of a street gang involved in regular acts of physical violence. Consistent with this idea, zero tolerance crime policies may work, in part, by reducing the threshold of criminality such that less extreme acts are sufficient for would-be criminals to establish a credible reputation with their criminal peers (cf. Dur & van der Weele, 2011).

Haslam, Oakes, Reynolds, and Turner (1999) have shown that discussion in small groups can promote consensus around group stereotypes (in this example the autostereotype of Australians) and that this effect is stronger when social rather than personal identity is salient. However, Postmes, Spears, and Chihangir (2001) have shown that, depending on whether a cohesive group has been formed with a consensus building or a diversity orientation, social identity salience during a subsequent decision making task led members to value either shared or unshared information more highly, respectively (cf. Stasser & Titus, 1985). This highlights that social identity can accommodate diversity of opinion and that the 'prototype' or norm can be defined in terms of the style or goal of the group and not just a specific attitude or action.

A broader point is that groups create a shared reality (see Levine & Higgins, 2001; Tindale, Meisenhelder, Dykema-Engblade, & Hogg, 2001), which is to say that intragroup communication establishes the range and content of evidence, experience, and activity that is relevant for understanding a situation or task. In terms of social identity theory, this means that the group provides a subjective reality in which to define itself by identifying the relevant boundaries and prototypes that make it unique. For example, Postmes, Spears, and Lea (2000) observed that students' computer-mediated communication was clustered into different groups that gradually developed distinctive and homogeneous styles and rules over time. This and other evidence highlights that social identity can emerge from intragroup processes, or be a 'bottom-up' inductive process (Postmes et al., 2005), as well as a "top down" deductive process that affects intragroup interaction and activity. Thus, the point that social identity can be derived from, can influence, and can be expressed through intragroup interaction and does not eliminate individual agency within the group (Abrams, 1992) is gaining increasing currency (Postmes & Jetten, 2006).

COLLECTIVE MOBILIZATION

Shared identity is an important basis on which people support particular social causes. Therefore, the intergroup context and group identification are important determinants that frame the way groups establish a common goal, shared emotion, and norms for action (Kawakami & Dion, 1995). Even in extreme situations such as crowd violence, rather than the crowd being a disorganized, chaotic, and disinhibited mob (as described by deindividuation approaches; cf. Diener, 1980), it often involves a set of people whose shared identity gives them common goals and norms for action (Reicher, Spears, & Postmes, 1995). In addition, collective action is likely to involve shared group-based affect, specifically anger. For example, Leonard, Moons, Mackie, and Smith (2011) found that women's perceptions and action tendencies in response to sex discrimination were affected by awareness of other women's anger, suggesting that self-stereotyping involves emotional as well as descriptive (trait) components.

Collective mobilization inevitably requires intragroup coordination. Contextual features such as anonymity, lack of external accountability, alcohol consumption, and darkness are known to affect behavior within groups. For example, violence targeted at members of an outgroup, such as lynchings, become more extreme when relative group size increases the salience of ingroup/outgroup differences (Leader, Mullen, & Abrams, 2008). A group's capacity to mobilize is also constrained by practical, material, and outcome considerations. These can be sufficient to cause inequality and injustice to prevail for substantial periods of time (e.g., under the oppressive rule of a dictator) before a group can mobilize to change the status quo. Simon et al. (1998) and Simon and Klandermans (2001) view political mobilization as a process that moves from construing shared grievances, to blaming political opponents, to connecting one's group's cause to the values of society as a whole. These transitions are likely to involve the intragroup processes of sharing information, sharing experiences, and interacting with other group members in order to arrive at agreement about the validity and benefits of action.

A variable that has been highlighted as critical is self-efficacy (Kelly & Breinlinger, 1996; van Zomeren, Postmes, & Spears, 2008). For example, Abrams and Randsley de Moura (2002) found that collective efficacy (belief that the group can achieve its goals) predicted students' participation in a rent strike on campus, while Abrams, Hinkle, and Tomlins (1999) showed that personal efficacy was important in residents' plans to leave Hong Kong prior to the

1997 transition from British to Chinese sovereignty. These examples highlight that processes within groups may often be essential to give social identity its meaning, reality, and validity, and to mobilize and coordinate group behavior (see also Abrams, 1992; Postmes et al., 2005).

In the last decade or so, an increasingly important medium for collective mobilization has been the internet. In some ways, internet communication has blurred the distinction between social category membership and face-to-face small group membership. As McGarty, Lala, and Douglas (2010) point out, opinion consensus can be achieved rapidly across geographical, and even linguistic, boundaries through internet news groups, Facebook, and so on. Moreover, far from becoming disengaged or deindividuated when connecting to an internet group, group members may experience depersonalization and subsequent group identification, consistent with Reicher et al.'s (1995) social identity model of deindividuation effects. Those who identify strongly with an opinion group are more likely to become involved in active engagement with its issues, i.e., to become activists who do things to facilitate the group's objectives (McGarty, Bliuc, Thomas, & Bongiorno, 2009). These rapid and dynamic processes suggest that people may often seek to consolidate their opinions and concerns by finding a 'group' that shares those concerns. Such groups may begin with fuzzy boundaries but then become well-defined and distinctive, providing a basis for social identification. In turn, social identity orients action in terms of relevant comparison groups, ingroup prototypes, and norms. However, it is also important that for many groups, an interest in sharing opinions, rather than reaching consensus or mobilizing action, may be most important norm (McGarty et al., 2010).

DEVIANCE AND DISSENT

Not only do groups try to control their collective outcomes by struggling with rival groups, they also try to control the actions of their members. In particular, Schachter's (1951) classic research showed that groups focus their attention on, and respond negatively to, members who do not conform to the group's modal opinion. A large amount of subsequent work has confirmed and extended Schachter's findings regarding reaction to opinion deviates (see Levine & Kerr, 2007, for a review). Over the last 20 years, the role of social identity has become a central point of interest. An important finding from this line of work is that ingroup and outgroup deviants are not treated similarly. Relative to likeable people, unlikeable people are derogated much more if they are ingroup members than if they are outgroup members. However, this so-called "black sheep effect" (Marques & Páez, 1994) also depends on how evaluations of the deviants reflect on evaluators' social identity. According to subjective group dynamics theory (e.g., Marques, Abrams, Páez, & Martinez-Taboada, 1998), deviants from both the ingroup and outgroup attract attention because they potentially affect the subjective validity of ingroup norms. Ingroup deviants pose a special problem because people want to bolster their social identity and the deviant represents a challenge to the value and identity of the ingroup, as well as disrupting the clarity of distinctions between groups. According to the theory, it is by derogating these ingroup deviants that group identity is reinforced. Consistent with this premise, derogation of a group deviant is increased when the members are all perceived as belonging to the same group rather than just as individuals (Marques, Abrams, & Serodio, 2001), and derogation of ingroup deviants results in more positive ingroup stereotypes (Hutchison, Abrams, Gutierrez, & Viki, 2008) and more positive social identity (Marques et al., 1998). In addition, stronger intergroup group differentiation (e.g., ingroup bias) is accompanied by stronger intragroup differentiation between normative and deviant members, even among children as young as eight years of age (Abrams, Rutland, Pelletier, & Ferrell, 2009).

Just as it is important to look at individuals in the context of their group, it is also important to understand the relation of that group to the wider social system. When people encounter a deviant group member, the deviance may involve different types of norms. According to subjective group dynamics theory, people should be relatively unconcerned about departures from *descriptive* group norms, such as a female who has a lower voice than is typical, but they should be highly concerned about departures from *prescriptive* group norms. These latter norms express the group's values and goals, such as upholding a particular ideological position.

A further distinction can be made between generic and oppositional norms (see Abrams 2011). Generic norms are those that both ingroup *and* outgroup members are expected to support, whereas oppositional norms are those that ingroup members are expected to support and outgroup members are expected to oppose (or vice versa). When generic norms are salient, both ingroup and outgroup members who dissent from the norms should be disliked, though this rejection should be stronger for ingroup than outgroup deviants (the black sheep effect). However, when oppositional norms are salient, people are likely to derogate ingroup members who show even the slightest gravitation towards outgroup norms but to favor outgroup members who, relative to other outgroup members, lean toward ingroup norms. This reversal of the usual pattern of intergroup bias when judging deviant group members who contravene oppositional norms has been demonstrated with both children and adults and in the contexts of gender norms, norms about asylum seeking, conditions for overseas students, and disloyalty in groups including corporate bankers, soccer fans, school teams, and even minimal groups (see Randsley de Moura, Abrams, Marques, & Hutchison, 2011).

Evidence shows consistently that group members' reactions to deviants reflect a strategic goal of sustaining positive ingroup identity, and this often depends on a balance of pressures for internal uniformity and resistance to external threats (e.g., Morton, Postmes, & Jetten, 2007). However, the degree of internal threat is also highly relevant. The particular role or status of the deviant within the ingroup can determine the strength of reaction by other members. For example, Pinto, Marques, Levine, and Abrams (2010) showed that the black sheep effect was only strong if the deviant was a full member of the group. If the deviant was a new member or a marginal member, the effect was weaker. In addition, groups advocated different techniques for dealing with ingroup deviants occupying different roles. More specifically, punishment was advocated for full members and education was advocated for new members.

In analyzing reaction to deviance in groups, it is important to consider how dissenters ever manage to influence a group (see Levine & Prislin, this volume). One mechanism for such influence has been termed "loyal dissent" (Packer, 2009; Packer & Chasteen, 2010). Group members who identify strongly with their group seem more willing to show dissent if they believe the group norms are harmful. This might capture the situation of people who rebel to overthrow a corrupt political regime or people who take a moral stand of a more modest kind. Groups do accept criticism more readily from loyal ingroup members than from outgroup members (Hornsey, Grice, Jetten, Paulsen, & Callan, 2007), yet from the group's point of view such dissent can be highly threatening and therefore carries significant risks for the dissenter. There do seem to be circumstances in which dissent is more likely to be tolerated. One, mentioned earlier, is when the dissenter is not a full member of the group (Pinto et al., 2010). Another is when the dissent is an extremist version of the group's norm (Abrams, Marques, Bown, & Henson, 2000).

Social identity theory helps to explain why groups follow leaders into extreme positions through processes such as group polarization and acceptance of extremist pro-norm deviance. However, it is more difficult to explain how leaders can meet a more common challenge, namely to shift away from the group's prototypical position, moderating its ambitions, perhaps to compromise, join coalitions, and even merge with other groups. Many European governments depend on such compromises because they have parliamentary systems that leave no single political party in overall control. It seems that a 'change' agenda may release leaders from the constraints of their prior commitments or promises. Consistent with this idea, Abrams, Randsley de Moura, Hutchison, and Marques (2008) found that, compared with deviant ordinary members and ex-leaders or current leaders, more lenient treatment, or 'innovation credit,' was given to deviant members who were about to assume the role of *new* leader. This may explain why political leaders who are facing re-election (current leaders) may emphasize the fear of instability and disruption from changing the status quo (reinforcing their prototypicality for the group), whereas opponents seeking power (would-be incoming leaders) emphasize the certain advantages of change, aiming to capitalize on their potential innovation credit (Abrams, 2011).

FUTURE DIRECTIONS

While it is sometimes tempting to view all group phenomena through the lens of the social identity approach, it is more useful to treat the social identity approach as complementary to other perspectives. For example, sociological approaches (Deaux & Burke, 2010; Emler & Reicher, 2005) and cognitive motivational approaches (Abrams, 1994; Sassenberg & Woltin, 2008) help to explain how and why people manage their social identities actively and strategically. Research is also increasingly concerned with social identity development, social identity stability and change (Bennett & Sani, 2008), and the way that social identity is embedded in a larger societal structure (Levy & Killen, 2008).

Social identity is relevant for any situation that involves contact, whether real or imagined, between members of different social groups, and thus it is central to finding solutions to intergroup conflict (Dovidio, Eller, & Hewstone, 2011; Wagner, Tropp, Finchilescu, & Tredoux, 2008). It is also relevant for social inclusion and exclusion of individuals who are perceived as belonging to a stigmatized social group, of deviant members within groups, and of entire groups because they are perceived to have different status or different rights than more powerful groups (Abrams & Christian, 2007).

Social identity is amenable to investigation using a wide variety of measures and levels of measurement. For example, it is strongly implicated in everyday discourse (Wetherell & Mohanty, 2010) and communication generally (Reid & Giles, 2005). Some evidence suggests that people physically approach their ingroups more if they essentialize social categories, suggesting social identity is embodied to some extent (Bastian, Loughnan, & Koval, 2011). Apparently, social identity is also detectable at the neuropsychological level (Derks, Inzlicht, & Kang, 2008).

Although social identity was conceived over 50 years ago, it has become more rather than less relevant to the nature of modern society. Tajfel's early experiments surprised researchers by showing how quickly and readily people could adopt a transitory social identity. Whether within a small group, an organization, a country, or across continents, social identification is a psychological process that has increasing power as a result of advances in technology and communication. This transformation in the scope of social identity has been faster than in any previous era. People can now rapidly form social relationships, establish shared goals and aspirations, and forge collective solidarity without the need to be physically near to one another. These changes raise questions about the limits of social identity: How rapidly can a group be created and act as a unit? How easy is it to dissolve or replace social identities? How will people manage multiple competing or conflicting social identities, both simultaneous and sequential? How will small groups protect themselves from members showing loyalty to competing identities and affiliations? How will individuals adapt to the possibility that their loyalty to a group is not reciprocated or that the group itself may disappear? How will processes of group socialization, which typically take time and involve building a set of commitments and relationships, work when groups themselves are created, changed, or abandoned rapidly? These are but a few of the many possible directions for future social identity research.

REFERENCES

Aberson, C. L., Healy, M. R., & Romero, V. L. (2000). Ingroup bias and self-esteem: A meta-analysis. *Personality and Social Psychology Review, 4*, 157–173. doi: 10.1207/S15327957PSPR0402_04

Abrams, D. (1992). Processes of social identification. In G. Breakwell (Ed.). *The social psychology of the self-concept* (pp. 57–100). London, UK: Academic Press/Surrey University Press.

Abrams, D. (1994). Social self-regulation. *Personality and Social Psychology Bulletin, 20*, 473–483. doi: 10.1177/0146167294205004

Abrams, D. (2009). Social identity on a national scale: Optimal distinctiveness and young people's self-expression through musical preference. *Group Processes and Intergroup Relations, 12*, 303–317. doi: 10.1177/1368430209102841

Abrams, D. (2011). Extremism is normal: The roles of deviance and uncertainty in shaping groups and society. In M. A. Hogg & D. L. Blalock (Eds.), *Extremism and the psychology of uncertainty* (pp. 36–54). Chichester, UK: John Wiley & Sons.

Abrams, D., & Christian, J. N. (2007). A relational analysis of social exclusion. In D. Abrams, J. N. Christian, & D. Gordon (Eds.), *Multidisciplinary handbook of social exclusion research* (pp. 211–232). Oxford, UK: Wiley-Blackwell.

Abrams, D., Hinkle, S. W., & Tomlins, M. (1999). Leaving Hong Kong: The roles of attitude, subjective norm, perceived control, social identity and relative deprivation. *International Journal of Intercultural Relations, 23*, 319–338. doi: 10.1016/S0147-1767(98)00041-8

Abrams, D., & Hogg, M. A. (1988). Comments on the motivational status of self-esteem in social identity and intergroup discrimination. *European Journal of Social Psychology, 18*, 317–334. doi: 10.1002/ejsp.2420180403

Abrams, D., & Hogg, M. A. (2001). Collective identity: Group membership and self-conception. In M. A. Hogg & R. S. Tindale (Eds.), *Blackwell handbook of social psychology: Group processes* (pp. 425–460). Oxford, UK: Blackwell.

Abrams, D., & Hogg, M. A. (2004). Metatheory: Lessons from social identity research. *Personality and Social Psychology Review, 8*, 98–106. doi: 10.1207/s15327957pspr0802_2

Abrams, D., Marques, J. M., Bown, N. J., & Henson, M. (2000). Pro-norm and anti-norm deviance within in-groups and out-groups. *Journal of Personality and Social Psychology, 78*, 906–912.

Abrams, D., & Randsley de Moura, G. (2002). The psychology of collective political protest. In V. C. Ottati, R. S. Tindale, J. Edwards, D. O'Connell, E. Posavac, E. Suarez-Balcazar, L., et al. (Eds.), *The social psychology of politics: Social psychological application to social issues* (Vol. 5, pp. 193–214). New York, NY: Plenum Press.

Abrams, D., Randsley de Moura, G., Hutchison, P., & Marques, J. M. (2008). Innovation credit: When can leaders oppose their groups? *Journal of Personality and Social Psychology, 95*, 662–678. doi: 10.1037/0022-3514.95.3.662

Abrams, D., Rutland, A., Pelletier, J., & Ferrell, J. (2009). Group nous and social exclusion: The role of theory of social mind, multiple classification skill and social experience of peer relations within groups. *Child Development, 80*, 224–243. doi: 10.1111/j.1467-8624.2008.01256.x

Abrams, D., Wetherell, M., Cochrane, S., Hogg, M. A., & Turner, J. C. (1990). Knowing what to think by knowing who you are: Self-categorization and the nature of norm formation, conformity and group polarization. *British Journal of Social Psychology, 29,* 97–119.

Adorno, T. W., Frenkel-Brunswik, E., Levinson, D. J., & Sanford, R. N. (1950). *The authoritarian personality.* Oxford, UK: Harpers.

Allport, F. H. (1924). *Social psychology.* Boston, MA: Houghton Mifflin.

Altemeyer, B. (1998). The other "authoritarian personality". In M. Zanna (Ed.), *Advances in experimental social psychology* (Vol. 30, pp. 47–92). Orlando, FL: Academic Press.

Amiot, C. E., & Hornsey, M. J. (2010). Collective self-esteem contingency and its role in predicting intergroup bias. *Self and Identity, 9*(1), 62–86. doi: 10.1080/15298860802605895

Ashforth, B. E., & Mael, F. A. (1989). Social identity theory and the organization. *Academy of Management Review, 14,* 20–39. doi: 10.2307/258189

Baumeister, R. F., & Leary, M. R. (1995). The need to belong: Desire for interpersonal attachments as a fundamental human motivation. *Psychological Bulletin, 117,* 497–529. doi: 10.1037/0033-2909.117.3.497

Bennett, M., & Sani, F. (2008). Children's subjective identification with social groups: A self-stereotyping approach. *Developmental Science, 11,* 69–75.

Berger, J., & Heath, C. (2008). Who drives divergence? Identity-signaling, out-group dissimilarity, and the abandonment of cultural tastes. *Journal of Personality and Social Psychology, 95,* 593–607. doi: 10.1037/0022-3514.95.3.593

Bastian, B., Loughnan, S., & Koval, P. (2011). Essentialist beliefs predict automatic motor responses to social categories. *Group Processes and Intergroup Relations, 14,* 559–567. doi: 10.1177/1368430210385258

Blader, S. L., & Tyler, T. R. (2009). Testing and extending the group engagement model: Linkages between social identity, procedural justice, economic outcomes, and extrarole behaviour. *Journal of Applied Psychology, 94,* 445–464. doi: 10.1037/a0013935

Bond, R., & Smith, P. B. (1996). Culture and conformity: A meta-analysis of studies using Asch's (1952b, 1956) line judgment task. *Psychological Bulletin, 119,* 111–137. doi: 10.1037/0033-2909.119.1.111

Bourhis, R. Y., Sachdev, I., & Gagnon, A. (1994). Intergroup research with the Tajfel matrices: Methodological notes. In M. Zanna & J. Olson (Eds.), *The psychology of prejudice: The Ontario symposium* (Vol. 7, pp. 209–22). Hillsdale, NJ: Erlbaum.

Brewer, M. B. (1991). The social self: On being the same and different at the same time. *Personality and Social Psychology Bulletin, 17,* 475–482. doi: 10.1177/0146167291175001

Brewer, M. B. (2001). The many faces of social identity: Implications for political psychology. *Political Psychology, 22,* 115–125. doi: 10.1111/0162-895X.00229

Brewer, M. B. (2007). The importance of being we: Human nature and intergroup relations. *American Psychologist, 62*(8), 728–738. doi: 10.1037/0003-066X.62.8.728

Bruner, J. S. (1957). On perceptual readiness. *Psychological Review, 64,* 123–152. doi: 10.1037/h0043805

Campbell, D. T. (1958). Common fate, similarity, and other indices of the status of aggregates of persons as social entities. *Behavioral Science, 3,* 14–25.

Caporael, L. R. (2001). Parts and wholes: The evolutionary importance of groups. In C. Sedikides & M. B. Brewer (Eds.), *Individual self, relational self, collective self* (pp. 241–258). Philadelphia, PA: Psychology Press.

Cicero, L., Pierro, A., & van Knippenberg, D. (2007). Leader group prototypicality and job satisfaction: The moderating role of job stress and team identification. *Group Dynamics: Theory, Research and Practice, 11*, 165–175.

Cooper, J., Kelly, A. K., & Weaver, K. (2001). Attitude norms, and social groups. In M. A. Hogg & R. S. Tindall (Eds.), *Blackwell handbook of social psychology* (Vol. 3, pp. 259–282). Oxford, UK: Blackwell. doi: 10.1002/9780470998458.ch11

Crosby, F. (1976). A model of egoistic relative deprivation. *Psychological Review, 83*, 85–113.

Deaux, K., & Burke, P. (2010). Bridging identities. *Social Psychology Quarterly, 73*, 315–320. doi:10.1177/0190272510388996

Deaux, K., Reid, A., Mizrahi, K., & Ethier, K. A. (1995). Parameters of social identity. *Journal of Personality and Social Psychology, 68*, 280–291. doi: 10.1037/0022-3514.68.2.280

De Cremer, D., & Van Vugt, M. (1999). Social identification effects in social dilemmas: A transformation of motives. *European Journal of Social Psychology, 29*, 871–893. doi: 10.1002/(SICI)1099-0992(199911)29:7<871::AID-EJSP962>3.0.CO;2-I

Derks, B., Inzlicht, M., & Kang, S. (2008). The neuroscience of stigma and stereotype threat. *Group Processes and Intergroup Relations, 11*, 163–181. doi: 10.1177/1368430207088036

Deustch, M., & Gerard, H. B. (1955). A study of normative and informational social influences upon individual judgment. *Journal of Abnormal and Social Psychology, 51*, 629–636.

Diener, E. (1980). Deindividuation: The absence of self-awareness and self-regulation in group members. In P. B. Paulus (Ed.), *Psychology of group influence* (pp. 209–242). Hillsdale, NJ: Erlbaum.

Dovidio, J. F., Eller. A., & Hewstone, M. (2011). Improving intergroup relations through direct, extended and other forms of indirect contact. *Group Processes and Intergroup Relations, 14*, 147–160.

Dur, R., & van der Weele, J. (2011). *Status-seeking in criminal subcultures and the double dividend of zero-tolerance.* IZA Discussion Paper Series, No. 5484. Bonn, Germany.

Durkehim, E. (1915). *The elementary forms of religious life.* London, UK: Allen and Unwin.

Eidelman, S., & Silvia, P. J. (2010). Self-focus and stereotyping of the self. *Group Processes and Intergroup Relations, 13*, 263–273. doi: 10.1177/1368430209353631

Ellemers, N., Kortekaas, P., & Ouwerkerk, J. W. (1999). Self-categorisation, commitment to the group and group self-esteem as related but distinct aspects of social identity. *European Journal of Social Psychology, 29*, 371–389. doi: 10.1002/(SICI)1099-0992(199903/05)29:2/3<371::AID-EJSP932>3.0.CO;2-U

Emler, N., & Reicher, S. D. (2005). Delinquency: Causes or consequences of social exclusion? In D. Abrams, M. A. Hogg, & J. M. Marques (Eds.), *The social psychology of inclusion and exclusion* (pp. 211–242). New York, NY: Psychology Press.

Fuller, J. B., Hester, K., Barnett, T., Frey, L., Relyea, C., & Beu, D. (2006). Perceived external prestige and internal respect: New insights into the organisational identification process. *Human Relations, 59*, 815–846. doi: 10.1177/0018726706067148

Furnham, A., & Procter, E. (1989). Belief in a just world: Review and critique of the individual difference literature. *British Journal of Social Psychology, 28*, 365–384.

Gaertner, L., Iuzzini, J., Witt, M. G., & Orina, M. M. (2006). Us without them: Evidence for an intragroup origin of positive in-group regard. *Journal of Personality and Social Psychology, 90*, 426–439. doi: 10.1037/0022-3514.90.3.426

Gaertner, L., & Schopler, J. (1998). Perceived ingroup entitativity and intergroup bias: An interconnection of self and others. *European Journal of Social Psychology, 28,* 963–980.

Gramzow, R. H., & Gaertner, L. (2005). Self-esteem and favoritism toward novel ingroups: The self as an evaluative base. *Journal of Personality and Social Psychology, 88,* 801–815. doi: 10.1037/0022-3514.88.5.801

Guimond, S., Chatard, A., Martinot, D., Crisp, R. J., & Redersdorff, S. (2006). Social comparison, self-stereotyping, and gender differences in self-construals. *Journal of Personality and Social Psychology, 90,* 221–242. doi: 10.1037/0022-3514.90.2.221

Hains, S. C., Hogg, M. A., & Duck, J. (1997). Self-categorization and leadership: Effects of group prototypicality and leader stereotypicality. *Personality and Social Psychology Bulletin, 23,* 1087–1099.

Hamilton, D. L., & Gifford, R. K. (1976). Illusory correlation in interpersonal perception: A cognitive basis of stereotypic judgments. *Journal of Experimental Social Psychology, 12,* 392–407.

Hamilton, D. L., & Sherman, S. J. (1996). Perceiving persons and groups. *Psychological Review, 103,* 336–355. doi: 10.1037/0033-295X.103.2.336

Haslam, S. A. (2004). *Psychology in organisations: The social identity approach* (2nd ed.). London, UK: Sage.

Haslam, S. A., Oakes, P. J., Reynolds, K., J., & Turner, J. C. (1999). Social identity salience and the emergence of stereotype consensus. *Personality and Social Psychology Bulletin, 25,* 809–818.

Haslam, S. A., Reicher, S. D., & Platow, M. J. (2011). *The new psychology of leadership: Identity, influence and power.* New York, NY: Psychology Press.

Heine, S. J., Proulx, T., & Vohs, K. D. (2006). The Meaning Maintenance Model: On the coherence of social motivation. *Personality and Social Psychological Review, 10,* 88–111.

Hennessy, J., & West, M. A. (1999). Intergroup behavior in organizations: A field test of social identity theory. *Small Group Research, 30,* 361–382. doi: 10.1177/104649649903000305

Hogg, M. A. (1993). Group cohesiveness: A critical review and some new directions. In W. Stroebe & M. Hewstone (Eds.), *European review of social psychology* (Vol. 4, pp. 85–111). Chichester, UK: John Wiley.

Hogg, M. A. (2001). A social identity theory of leadership. *Personality and Social Psychology Review, 5,* 184–200.

Hogg, M. A. (2007). Uncertainty-identity theory. In M. P. Zanna (Ed.), *Advances in experimental social psychology* (Vol. 39, pp. 69–126). San Diego, CA: Academic Press.

Hogg, M. A., & Abrams, D. (1988). *Social identifications: A social psychology of intergroup relations and group processes.* London, UK: Routledge.

Hogg, M. A., & Abrams, D. (1993). An uncertainty reduction model of group motivation. In M. A. Hogg & D. Abrams (Eds.), *Group motivation: Social psychological perspectives* (pp. 173–190). London, UK: Harvester Wheatsheaf.

Hogg, M., Adelman, J. R., & Blagg, R. D. (2010). Religion in the face of uncertainty: An uncertainty-identity theory account of religiousness. *Personality and Social Psychology Review, 14,* 72–83. doi: 10.1177/1088868309349692

Hogg, M. A., & Reid, S. A. (2006). Social categorization and human communication: The social identity perceptive and group norms. *Communication Theory, 16,* 7–30. doi: 10.1111/j.1468-2885.2006.00003.x

Hogg, M. A., & Terry, D. J. (2000). Social identity and self-categorization processes in organizational contexts. *Academy of Management Review, 25,* 121–140. doi: 10.2307/259266

Hogg, M. A., & van Knippenberg, D. (2003). Social identity and leadership processes in groups. In M. P. Zanna (Ed.), *Advances in experimental social psychology* (Vol. 35, pp. 1–52). San Diego, CA: Academic Press.

Hornsey, M. J., Grice, T., Jetten, J., Paulsen, N., & Callan, V. (2007). Group directed criticisms and recommendations for change: Why newcomers arouse more resistance than old-timers. *Personality and Social Psychology Bulletin, 33,* 1036–1048. doi: 10.1177/0146167207301029

Houston, D. M., & Andreopoulou, A. (2003). Tests of both corollaries of social identity theory's self-esteem hypothesis in a real group setting. *British Journal of Social Psychology, 42,* 357–370. doi: 10.1348/014466603322438206

Hunter, J. A., Kypri, K., Stokell, N. M., Boyes, M., O'Brien, K. S., & McMenamin, K. A. (2004). Social identity, self-evaluation and in-group bias: The relative importance of particular domains of self-esteem to the in-group. *British Journal of Social Psychology, 43,* 59–81. doi: 10.1348/014466604322915980

Hutchison, P., Abrams, D., Gutierrez, R., & Viki, T. (2008). Getting rid of the bad ones: The relationship between group identification, deviant derogation and identity maintenance. *Journal of Experimental Social Psychology, 44,* 874–881. doi: 10.1016/j.jesp.2007.09.001

Jost, J. T., & Hunyadi, O. (2002). The psychology of system justification and the palliative function of ideology. In W. Stroebe & M. Hewstone (Eds.), *European review of social psychology* (Vol. 13, pp. 111–153). Hove, UK: Psychology Press.

Kawakami, K., & Dion, K. L. (1995). Social identity and affect as determinants of collective action: towards an integration of relative deprivation and social identity theories. *Theory and Psychology, 5,* 551–577. doi: 10.1177/0959354395054005

Kelly, C., & Breinlinger, S. (1996). *The social psychology of collective action: Identity, injustice and gender.* London, UK: Taylor & Francis.

Leach, C. W., van Zomeren, M., Zebel, S., Vliek, M., Pennekamp, S. F., Doosje, B., … Spears, R. (2008). Group-level self-definition and self-investment: A hierarchical (multi-component) model of in-group identification. *Journal of Personality and Social Psychology, 95,* 144–165. doi: 10.1037/0022-3514.95.1.144

Leader, T., Mullen, B, & Abrams, D. (2008). Without mercy: The immediate impact of group size on lynch mob atrocity. *Personality and Social Psychology Bulletin, 33,* 1340–1352.

Le Bon, G. (1895). *The crowd.* London, UK: Unwin.

Leonard, D. J., Moons, W. G., Mackie, D. M., & Smith, E. R. (2011). "We're mad as hell and we're not going to take it anymore": Anger self-stereotyping and collective action. *Group Processes and Intergroup Relations, 14,* 99–111. doi: 10.1177/1368430210373779

Levine, J. M., & Higgins, E. T. (2001). Shared reality and social influence in groups and organizations. In F. Butera & G. Mugny (Eds.), *Social influence in social reality: Promoting individual and social change* (pp. 33–52). Seattle, WA: Hogrefe & Huber.

Levine, J. M., & Kerr, N. L. (2007). Inclusion and exclusion: Implications for group processes. In A. E. Kruglanski & E. T. Higgins (Eds.), *Social psychology: Handbook of basic principles* (2nd ed., pp. 759–784). New York, NY: Guilford.

Levy, S. R., & Killen, M. (Eds.). (2008). *Intergroup attitudes and relations in childhood through adulthood*. Oxford, UK: Oxford University Press.

Major, B., Quinton, W. J., & McCoy, S. K. (2002). Antecedents and consequences of attributions to discrimination: Theoretical and empirical advances. In M. P. Zanna (Ed.), *Advances in experimental social psychology* (Vol. 34, pp. 251–330). San Diego, CA: Academic Press.

Markus, H., & Kitayama, S. (1991). Culture and the self: Implications for cognition, emotion and motivation. *Psychological Review, 98*, 224–253. doi: 10.1037/0033-295X.98.2.224

Marques, J., Abrams, D., Páez, D., & Martinez-Taboada, C. (1998). The role of categorization and in-group norms in judgments of groups and their members. *Journal of Personality and Social Psychology, 75*, 976–988. doi: 10.1037/0022-3514.75.4.976

Marques, J. M., Abrams, D., & Serodio, R. (2001). Being better by being right: Subjective group dynamics and derogation of in-group deviants when generic norms are undermined. *Journal of Personality and Social Psychology, 81*, 436–447. doi: 10.1037/0022-3514.81.3.436

Marques, J. M., & Páez, D. (1994). The black sheep effect: Social categorization, rejection of in-group deviates, and perception of group variability. In W. Stroebe & M. Hewstone (Eds.), *European review of social psychology* (Vol. 5, pp. 37–68). Chichester, UK: John Wiley.

McAuliffe, B. J., Jetten, J., Hornsey, M. J., & Hogg, M. A. (2003). Individualist and collectivist group norms: When it's OK to go your own way. *European Journal of Social Psychology, 33*, 57–70. doi: 10.1002/ejsp.129

McGarty, C., Bliuc, A.-M, Thomas, E. F., & Bongiorno, R. T. (2009). Collective action as the material expression of opinion-based group membership. *Journal of Social Issues, 65*, 839–857.

McGarty, C., Lala, G., & Douglas, K. M. (2010). Opinion-based groups: (Racist) talk and (collective) action on the Internet. In Z. Birchmeier, B. Dietz-Uhler, & G. Stasser (Eds.), *Strategic uses of social technology: An interactive perspective of social psychology* (pp. 145–171). Cambridge, UK: Cambridge University Press.

McGarty, C., Yzerbyt, V. Y., & Spears, R. (Eds.). (2002). *Stereotypes as explanations: The formation of meaningful beliefs about social groups*. Cambridge, UK: Cambridge University Press.

Morton, T. A., Postmes, T., & Jetten, J. (2007). Playing the game: When group success is more important than downgrading deviants. *European Journal of Social Psychology, 37*, 599–616.

Moscovici, S. (1981). On social representations, In J. P. Forgas (Ed.), *Social cognition* (pp. 181–209). New York, NY: Academic Press.

Moscovici, S., & Zavalloni, M. (1969). The group as a polarizer of attitudes. *Journal of Personality and Social Psychology, 12*, 125–135.

Myers, D. G., & Lamm, H. (1976). The group polarization phenomenon. *Psychological Bulletin, 83*, 602–627.

Oakes, P. J. (1987). The salience of social categories. In J. C. Turner, M. A. Hogg, P. J. Oakes, S. D. Reicher, & M. S. Wetherell (Eds.), *Rediscovering the social group: A self-categorization theory* (pp. 117–141). Oxford, UK: Blackwell.

Oakes, P. J., Haslam, S. A., & Turner, J. C. (1994). *Stereotyping and social reality*. Oxford, UK: Blackwell.

Otten, S. (2002). "Me" and "us" or "us" and "them"? The self as heuristic for defining novel ingroups. In W. Stroebe & M. Hewstone (Eds.), *European review of social psychology* (Vol.13, pp. 1–33). Hove, UK: Psychology Press.

Packer, D. J. (2009). Avoiding groupthink: Whereas weakly identified members remain silent, strongly identified members dissent about collective problems. *Psychological Science, 20,* 546–548. doi: 10.1111/j.1467-9280.2009.02333.x

Packer, D. J., & Chasteen, A. L. (2010). Loyal deviance: Testing the normative conflict model of dissent in social groups. *Personality and Social Psychology Bulletin, 36,* 5–18. doi: 10.1177/0146167209350628

Pickett, C. L., & Brewer, M. B. (2005). The role of exclusion in maintaining in-group inclusion. In D. Abrams, M. A. Hogg, & J. M. Marques (Eds.), *The social psychology of inclusion and exclusion* (pp. 89–112). New York, NY: Psychology Press.

Pinto, I., Marques, J. Levine, J. M., & Abrams, D. (2010). Membership status and subjective group dynamics: Who triggers the Black Sheep Effect? *Journal of Personality and Social Psychology, 99,* 107–119. doi:10.1037/a0018187

Platow, M., van Knippenberg, D., Haslam, S. A., van Knippenberg, B., & Spears, R. (2006). A special gift we bestow on you for being representative of us: Considering leader charisma from a self-categorization perspective. *British Journal of Social Psychology, 45,* 303–320.

Poole, M. S., & Hollingshead, A. B. (Eds.). (2005). *Theories of small groups: Interdisciplinary perspectives.* Thousand Oaks, CA: Sage Publications.

Postmes, T., & Jetten, J. (Eds.). (2006). *Individuality and the group: Advances in social identity.* London, UK: Sage.

Postmes, T., Haslam, S. A., & Swaab, R. I. (2005). Social influence in small groups: An interactive model of social identity formation. *European Review of Social Psychology, 16,* 1–42. doi: 10.1080/10463280440000062

Postmes, T., Spears, R., & Chihangir, S. (2001). Quality of decision making and group norms. *Journal of Personality and Social Psychology, 80,* 918–930.

Postmes, T., Spears, R., & Lea, S. (2000). The formation of group norms in computer-mediated communication. *Human Communication Research, 26,* 341–371.

Prentice, D. A., Miller, D., & Lightdale, J. R. (1994). Asymmetries in attachment to groups and to their members: Distinguishing between common-identity and common-bond groups. *Personality and Social Psychology Bulletin, 20,* 484–493. doi: 10.1177/0146167294205005

Pyszczynski, T., Greenberg, J., & Solomon, S. (1997). Why do we need what we need? A terror management perspective on the roots of human social motivation. *Psychological Inquiry, 8,* 1–20. doi: 10.1207/s15327965pli0801_1

Randsley de Moura, G., Abrams, D., Marques, J., & Hutchison, P. (2011). Innovation credit: When and why do group members give their leaders license to deviate from group norms? In J. Jetten & M. J. Hornsey (Eds.), *Rebels in groups: Dissent, deviance, difference and defiance* (pp. 238–258). Chichester, UK: John Wiley and Sons.

Randsley de Moura, G., Abrams, D., Retter, C., Gunnarsdottir, S., & Ando, K. (2009). Identification as an organizational anchor: How identification and job satisfaction combine to predict turnover intention. *European Journal of Social Psychology, 39,* 540–557. doi: 10.1002/ejsp.553

Randsley de Moura, G. R., Leader, T. I., Pelletier, J. P., & Abrams, D. (2008). Prospects for group processes and intergroup relations research: A review of 70 years' progress. *Group Processes and Intergroup Relations, 11,* 575–596. doi: 10.1177/1368430208095406

Reicher, S. D., & Hopkins, N. (2001). *Self and nation: Categorization, contestation and mobilization*. London, UK: Sage.

Reicher, S. D., Spears, R., & Postmes, T. (1995). A social identity model of deindividuation phenomena. *European Review of Social Psychology, 6*, 161–197.

Reid, S. A., & Giles, H. (2005). Intergroup relations: Its linguistic and communicative parameters. *Group Processes and Intergroup Relations, 8*, 211–214. doi: 10.1177/1368430205053938

Rubin, M., & Hewstone, M. (1998). Social identity theory's self-esteem hypothesis: A review and some suggestions for clarification. *Personality and Social Psychology Review, 2*, 40–62. doi: 10.1207/s15327957pspr0201_3

Salvatore, J., & Prentice, D. A. (2011). The independence paradox. In J. Jetten & M. J. Hornsey (Eds.), *Rebels in groups* (pp. 201–218). Oxford, UK: Blackwell Publishing Ltd.

Sassenberg, K., & Woltin, K. (2008). Group-based self-regulation: The effects of regulatory focus. In W. Stroebe & M. Hewstone (Eds.), *European review of social psychology* (Vol. 19, pp. 126–164). New York, NY: Psychology Press.

Schachter, S. (1951). Deviation, rejection and communication. *Journal of Abnormal and Social Psychology, 46*, 190–207.

Sedikides, C., & Gaertner, L. (2001). A homecoming to the individual self: Emotional and motivational primacy. In C. Sedikides & M. B. Brewer (Eds.), *Individual self, relational self, collective self* (pp. 7–25). Philadelphia, PA: Psychology Press.

Sedikides, C., & Strube, M. J. (1997). Self-evaluation: To thine own self be good, to thine own self be sure, to thine own self be true, and to thine own self be better. In M. P. Zanna (Ed.), *Advances in experimental social psychology* (Vol. 29, pp. 209–296). New York, NY: Academic Press.

Sherif, M. (1936). *The psychology of social norms*. New York, NY: Harper.

Sherif, M., & Sherif, C. W. (1966). *Groups in harmony and tension*. New York, NY: Octagon Books.

Simmel, G. (1955). *Conflict and the web of group affiliations*. New York, NY: Free Press.

Simon, B. (2004). *Identity in a modern society: A social psychological perspective*. Oxford, UK: Blackwell.

Simon, B., & Hamilton, D. L. (1994). Self-stereotyping and social context: The effects of relative in-group size and in-group status. *Journal of Personality and Social Psychology, 66*, 699–711. doi: 10.1037/0022-3514.66.4.699

Simon, B., & Klandermans, B. (2001). Politicized collective identity: A social psychological analysis. *American Psychologist, 56*, 319–331. doi: 10.1037/0003-066X.56.4.319

Simon, B., Loewy, M., Sturmer, S., Weber, U., Freytang, P., Habig, C., ... Spahlinger, P. (1998). Collective identification and social movement participation. *Journal of Personality and Social Psychology, 74*, 646–658. doi: 10.1037/0022-3514.74.3.646

Smetana, J. G. (2006). Social-cognitive domain theory: Consistencies and variations in children's moral and social judgments. In M. Killen & J. G. Smetana (Eds.), *Handbook of moral development* (pp. 119–154). Mahwah, NJ: Lawrence Erlbaum Associates.

Smith, E., Seger, C. R., & Mackie, D. M. (2007). Can emotions be truly group level? Evidence regarding four conceptual criteria. *Journal of Personality and Social Psychology, 9*, 431–446. doi: 10.1037/0022-3514.93.3.431

Smurda, J. D., Wittig, M. A., & Gokalp, G. (2006). Effects of threat to a valued social identity on implicit self-esteem and discrimination. *Group Processes and Intergroup Relations, 9*, 181–197. doi: 10.1177/1368430206062076

Spears, R., Doosje, B., & Ellemers, N. (1997). Self-stereotyping in the face of threats to group status and distinctiveness: The role of group identification. *Personality and Social Psychology Bulletin, 23*, 538–553. doi: 10.1177/0146167297235009

Stasser, G., & Titus, W. (1985). Pooling of unshared information in group decision making: Biased information sampling during discussions. *Journal of Personality and Social Psychology, 48*, 1467–1478.

Tajfel, H. (1959). Quantitative judgement in social perception. *British Journal of Psychology, 50*, 16–29.

Tajfel, H. (1969). Cognitive aspects of prejudice. *Journal of Social Issues, 25*, 79–97.

Tajfel, H. (1972). Social categorization. English manuscript of 'La catégorisation sociale'. In S. Moscovici (Ed.), *Introduction à la psychologie sociale* (Vol. 1, pp. 272–302). Paris, France: Larousse.

Tajfel, H. (1974). *Intergroup behaviour, social comparison and social change.* Unpublished Katz-Newcomb lectures, University of Michigan, Ann Arbor, MI.

Tajfel, H. (1981). Social stereotypes and social groups. In J. C. Turner & H. Giles (Eds.), *Intergroup behaviour* (pp. 144–167). Oxford, UK: Blackwell.

Tajfel, H., & Turner, J. C. (1979). An integrative theory of intergroup conflict. In W. G. Austin & S. Worchel (Eds.), *The social psychology of intergroup relations* (pp. 33–47). Monterey, CA: Brooks/Cole. (Reprinted in M. A. Hogg & D. Abrams [2001]. *Intergroup relations.* New York, NY: Psychology Press.)

Terry, D. J., & Hogg, M. A. (1996). Group norms and the attitude-behavior relationship. A role for group identification. *Personality and Social Psychology Bulletin, 22*, 776–793. doi: 10.1177/0146167296228002

Tindale, R. S., Meisenhelder, H. M., Dykema-Engblade, A. A., & Hogg, M. A. (2001). Shared cognition in small groups. In M. A. Hogg, & R. S. Tindale (Eds.), *Blackwell handbook of social psychology: Group processes* (pp. 1–30). Oxford, UK: Blackwell.

Turner, J. C. (1985). Social categorization and the self-concept: A social cognitive theory of group behavior. In E. J. Lawler (Ed.), *Advances in group processes: Theory and research* (Vol. 2, pp. 77–122). Greenwich, CT: JAI Press.

Turner, J. C. (1991). *Social influence.* Milton Keynes, UK: Open University Press.

Turner, J. C., Hogg, M. A., Oakes, P. J., Reicher, S. D., & Wetherell, M. S. (1987). *Rediscovering the social group: A self-categorization theory.* Oxford, UK: Blackwell.

Tyler, T. R. (1997). The psychology of legitimacy: A relational perspective on voluntary deference to authorities. *Personality and Social Psychology Review, 1*, 323–345. doi: 10.1207/s15327957pspr0104_4

Tyler, T. R., & Blader, S. L. (2003). The Group Engagement Model: Procedural justice social identity and cooperative behavior. *Personality and Social Psychology Review, 7*, 349–361. doi: 10.1207/S15327957PSPR0704_07

van Dijk, M., & De Cremer, D. (2008). How leader prototypicality affects followers' status: The role of procedural fairness. *European Journal of Work and Organizational Psychology, 17*, 226–250.

van Knippenberg, D., Lossie, N., & Wilker, H. (1994). Ingroup prototypicality and persuasion. Determinants of heruistic and systematic message processing. *British Journal of Social Psychology, 33*, 289–300.

Van Vugt, M., & Hart, C. (2004). Social identity as social glue: The origins of group loyalty. *Journal of Personality and Social Psychology, 86*, 585–598. doi: 10.1037/0022-3514.86.4.585

van Zomeren, M., Postmes, T., & Spears, R. (2008). Towards an integrative social identity model of collective action: A quantitative research synthesis of three socio-psychological perspectives. *Psychological Bulletin, 134,* 504–535. doi: 10.1037/0033-2909.134.4.504

Wagner, U., Tropp, L. R., Finchilescu, G., & Tredoux, C. (Eds.). (2008). *Improving intergroup relations: Building on the legacy of Thomas F. Pettigrew.* Oxford, UK: Blackwell.

Wetherell, M., & Mohanty, C. T. (2010). *The Sage handbook of identities.* London, UK: Sage.

White, J. B., Schmitt, M. T., & Langer, E. J. (2006). Horizontal hostility: Multiple minority groups and differentiation from the mainstream. *Group Processes and Intergroup Relations, 9,* 339–358. doi: 10.1177/1368430206064638

Williams, K. D. (2007). Ostracism. *Annual Review of Psychology, 58,* 425–452.

Wright, S. C., Aron, A., & Tropp, L. R. (2002). Including others (and groups) in the self: Self-expansion and intergroup relations. In J. P. Forgas & K. D. Williams (Eds.), *The social self: Cognitive, interpersonal, and intergroup perspectives* (pp. 343–363). New York, NY: Psychology Press.

12

Evolution and Groups

MARK VAN VUGT and TATSUYA KAMEDA

Camp 10 Ms. Above the river Plate
Monday July 23rd, 1804.

"A fair morning—sent out a party of 5 men to look to timber for Ores two
other parties to hunt at 11 oClock Sent, G. Drewyer & Peter Crusett ½ Indn.
to the Otteaus Village about 18 ms. West of our Camp, to invite the Chiefs
& principal men of that nation to come & talk with us &. & also the panis if
they Should meet with any of that nation (also on the S. Side of the Plate 30
ms. higher up). (at this season of the year all the Indians in this quarter are in
the Plains hunting the Buffalow from Some Signs Seen by our hunter and the
Prairies being on fire in the derection of the Village induce a belief that the
Nation have returned to get green Corn).

(By William Clark, Co-Captain of the Corps of Discovery
[Nebraska edition of the Lewis & Clark journals
edited by Gary E. Mouton]. All errors are original.)

This quote comes from the journals of William Clark, who together with
Meriwether Lewis, led the expedition of the American West from 1804–
1806. On the orders of President Jefferson, Lewis and Clark organized
an expedition, travelling up the Missouri River to the Rocky Mountains and
westward along possible river routes to the Pacific Ocean. The journal of their
3-year journey (along with a crew of 33 men) through unexplored territories
in the US provides a vivid example of the many challenges that human groups
encounter in natural environments. This list includes problems as diverse as
securing food, finding safe shelters, acquiring knowledge about places, animals and plants, protection against predators and hostile outgroups, developing

peaceful intergroup relationships, transmitting useful information, following orders, and executing leadership and followership.

These are remarkably similar to the challenges that groups have faced throughout human evolutionary history. Extrapolating from anthropological and archaeological data, for at least several hundreds of thousands of years our human ancestors lived in small and closely tied groups—much like the Lewis and Clark band yet including men, women and children—in natural environments. Although we can only speculate about life in ancestral environments, there is little doubt that, throughout human evolution, groups have been key to the success of humans.

Applying evolutionary theory, group living can be viewed as an adaptive strategy that increased the survival and reproductive success of ancestral humans. This strategy was so successful that humans are among the most "groupish" animals on the planet and together with the social insects have achieved ecological dominance (Wilson, Van Vugt, & O'Gorman, 2008). Thus, students of group dynamics would be well served to take seriously the role of human evolution in shaping our group psychology. Viewing group processes through the lens of evolutionary theory also enables group psychologists to work together with biologists, anthropologists, economists, neuroscientists, sociologists, and other behavioural scientists in developing an overarching theoretical framework on group dynamics.

Charles Darwin pioneered this new evolutionary science of groups. In his second book, *The Descent of Man*, Darwin wrote: "With those animals which were benefited by living in close association, the individuals which took the greatest pleasure in society would best escape various dangers, while those that cared least for their comrades, and lived solitary, would perish in greater numbers" (1871, p. 105). Essentially, Darwin provided an evolutionary account for the affiliation motive which is subsequently identified as one of the core human needs (Baumeister & Leary, 1995).

For ancestral humans, evolving in hostile natural environments where dangers were common and resources were scarce, group associations provided safety and comfort. Only as group members could our ancestors acquire reproductively relevant resources such as food and water and defend themselves against hostile animals and antagonistic outgroups. The conceptual implication is that humans have an innate group psychology that regulates their group interactions. This yields a practical implication as well. By applying the tools of evolutionary theory and psychology we have the potential to more fully understand real-world group processes and improve the design of teams and organizations.

Take the example of groupthink, the phenomenon that highly cohesive groups under time pressures and directive leadership engage in poor decision-making (Janis, 1972). From an evolutionary perspective, groupthink can be seen as the outcome of a trade-off between two distinct strategies, getting the right information (accuracy) and keeping group unity (cohesion). Under certain conditions, such as an imminent external threat, it can be functional for all group members to form a united front and adhere to a group decision, regardless of whether the decision is factually correct. This does not necessarily imply that it produces the best outcomes, especially in complex modern environments. The ill-fated invasion of the Falkland Islands and the NASA Challenger disaster suggest that our evolved inclination to strive for group unity may have dire consequences indeed.

In this chapter we first provide a brief introduction to evolutionary psychology and its application to group processes. Second we discuss the diversity of methodological approaches that are used by evolutionary psychologists to find evidence for group-level adaptations. Third we address the various functions of groups in human evolution, and suggest that humans have evolved a host of psychological mechanisms to solve critical challenges in six domains of group life: (a) coordination, (b) social exchange, (c) status, (d) group cohesion, (e) collective decision-making, and (f) intergroup relations. Finally we provide short and selective reviews of the current state of knowledge in evolutionary research on each of these six group challenges. We conclude by addressing some conceptual and practical implications of a new evolutionary science of group dynamics.

APPLYING EVOLUTIONARY THINKING TO GROUP PROCESSES

An evolutionary approach to the study of groups starts with the recognition that the physiological, neurological, and psychological processes involved in producing human group behaviour are products of biological evolution. It follows, therefore, that conceptual insights of evolutionary sciences can, when applied with rigour and care, produce novel discoveries about human group psychology (Caporael, 1997; Van Vugt & Schaller, 2008). Indeed evolutionary inquiries have not only provided deeper explanations for the origins of already-recognized psychological phenomena such as mate preferences and fears and phobias, they also have produced an impressive array of novel theories, hypotheses, and empirical discoveries about the way humans behave in groups and feel about them (Buss, 2005; Kameda & Tindale, 2006).

Evolutionary theory contains three simple premises based on the three core Darwinian principles which together account for every aspect of living matter: (1) variation, (2) selection, and (3) retention. First, there is variation in traits among individuals—to illustrate with an example, some individuals are loners who prefer a solitary existence, whereas others are joiners who prefer to be in groups. Second, some of these trait variants enable their bearers to compete more successfully for reproductive resources—joiners can share resources and defend themselves better and as a result they have a better chance to produce offspring (selection). Third, these traits are heritable such that offspring resemble parents—joiners (or loners) are more likely to have children with joiner (or loner) genes (retention). Repeated over time, this continuing process of variation, selection, and retention produces organisms and species that are well adapted to the environment in which they live: All modern humans are the descendants of individuals who preferred group life over a solitary existence.

An evolutionary psychology approach to group dynamics has the following core assumptions:

(1) Humans Have Social Brains

As a member of the family of primates, humans have evolved as a group living species and therefore it is likely that many of our cognitive adaptations are social psychological. For early humans, group life formed a buffer against perturbations of the natural environment, so there must have been selection for traits facilitating group formation and group interaction. The social brain hypothesis (Dunbar, 2001) posits that humans have evolved large brains in order to make the most of living in large, complex social groupings. In support of the social brain hypothesis, comparative studies have found a positive correlation between the size of the pre-frontal cortex and average group size, comparing humans with other primates and comparing primates with other mammals. Humans come out on top, having both a relatively large pre-frontal cortex and an associated large average group size. From the brain data, the extrapolated group size for humans is around 150 individuals—also known as Dunbar's number—which corresponds roughly to the size of a small community like a neighbourhood or religious community that can be held together through informal social control. One hundred and fifty is also the median number of recipients on people's Christmas card lists according to a UK study (Hill & Dunbar, 2003).

(2) Selection Forces Operate Together

Selection for groupish traits—traits that enable individuals to enjoy and function well in groups, such as sociability—is called social selection, and this should be seen as a complementary selection force to natural selection which reflects adaptations to the physical (natural) environment (Nesse, 2007). Sexual selection is a specific case of social selection, and some group-level traits may be the result of this selection force. Sexually selected traits evolve because they increase the chances of an organism finding a sexual mate or being chosen as a mate. For instance, some conspicuous group behaviours such as public generosity or the display of humour have been interpreted as sexually selected traits because these acts make individuals more attractive to the opposite sex (Griskevicius, Goldstein, Mortensen, Cialdini, & Kenrick, 2006; Iredale, Van Vugt, & Dunbar, 2008; Miller, 2000).

Most selection models assume that social traits have evolved because they benefit the individual possessing that trait—for instance, empathy enables an individual to assess other people's intentions so that the person can protect himself or herself against possible exploitation. Yet recent theorizing suggests that groupish traits may also have been selected because they produce benefits to the group to which the individual belongs, thus producing an indirect pay-off to the individual (Caporael, 1997; Wilson et al., 2008). Perhaps empathy evolved in humans not so much to protect against cheaters but to build up cooperative groups that do better than groups with less empathic members in competing for scarce resources. Darwin was an early proponent of these group selection models and he used group selectionist thinking to account for the evolution of morality:

> A tribe including many members who, from possessing [a high degree of] the spirit of patriotism, fidelity, obedience, courage and sympathy, were always ready to aid one another, and to sacrifice themselves for the common good, would be victorious over most other tribes; and this would be natural selection.
>
> (Darwin, 1871, p. 203).

After some fierce objection against group selection, evolutionary scientists are increasingly considering it a useful framework for examining human group behaviour although there is an ongoing debate about whether group selection operates on genes, culture or perhaps a combination (Richerson & Boyd, 2006; Wilson et al., 2008). Perhaps the lesson is that for each groupish trait one must look at both the individual and group benefits associated with it, and in many cases there may be multi-level selection forces operating in conjunction. For instance, having a sense of humour may have the function to impress members of the opposite sex (a sexually selected trait) but this trait may have evolved originally because of its function in fostering group cohesion (Gervais & Wilson, 2005).

(3) Evolved Psychological Mechanisms

Group-level adaptations come in many different forms, and many contain physiological, neurological, psychological, and behavioural elements. Adaptive group decision-making is activated by a set of evolved psychological mechanisms that are instantiated in the brain. For instance, human language is a biological adaptation enabling humans to transmit information efficiently. Language requires the presence of both physical structures, such as Broca's area, and psychological mechanisms, such as a theory of mind, that enable humans to communicate effectively. Thus, if humans can talk but chimpanzees (one of our closest living relatives) cannot, it is because these two species differ in their evolved physiology and psychology. (Language may be a group-level adaptation that gave early human groups an edge in the competition for reproductively relevant resources.) Similarly, trust in strangers may be triggered by a psychological mechanism telling us to trust individuals who look familiar. This psychological mechanism might be activated by the secretion of a hormone such as oxytocin which plays a role in forming emotional attachments (De Dreu et al., 2010). The key message is that any group behaviour is regulated by both psychological (emotions, cognitions) and neurophysiological (brain activity, hormones, neurotransmitters) mechanisms that evolved through natural selection.

(4) Automatic "If-Then" Decision Rules

Group-level adaptations can be regarded as a set of heuristics or conditional (if-then) decision rules that are activated in appropriate conditions. Because a social group is a complex environment it pays for humans to have a broad repertoire of conditional decision rules to make adaptive choices under a variety of conditions. For instance, a conditional decision rule such as "I will only cooperate if my partner cooperates but otherwise I will defect" enables an individual to maximize his or her outcomes in social exchange situations (Axelrod, 1984). Many of these decision rules are likely to be highly automatic, meaning that they require little conscious deliberation to produce adaptive behaviours in a wide range of situations.

(5) Domain Specificity of Mechanisms

Many groupish traits are likely to be domain-specific decision rules. They exist in the form they do because they solved a particular, recurrent group problem in our ancestral environment, such as understanding how to defend the group or climb the group status hierarchy. The primary aim of an evolutionary psychology approach to group dynamics is to identify, analyse, and understand specific adaptive group problems as well as the psychological mechanisms that have evolved to solve them.

For instance, the phenomenon of social exclusion can be described in many different ways—for example, when does it occur and to whom, and what are the consequences for the victims? An evolutionary psychology approach would additionally focus on the different functions of social exclusion in solving adaptive group problems in ancestral environments. This "adaptationist" analysis suggests at least three evolved functions of social exclusion: (1) excluding individuals who are likely to be non-reciprocators, (2) excluding individuals who behave unpredictably, and (3) excluding individuals who constitute a contagion risk or coalitional threat (Kurzban & Leary, 2001). Each of these functions may have a unique underlying psychology which is triggered by different stimuli and which produces different behaviours that can solve the specific problem. For instance, people show aggression towards a free-rider and behavioural avoidance to a person carrying a disease threat (Kerr & Levine, 2008; Van Vugt & Park, 2009).

(6) Adaptations to Past Environments

A sixth assumption is that evolution through natural selection is a painstakingly slow process spanning many generations. The implication is that our evolved group psychology reflects adaptations to past rather than present environments. Because modern humans live in very different environments from their ancestors, some of our evolved psychological mechanisms may not produce behaviours that are currently adaptive. For instance, most of the interactions in ancestral human groups were probably with close kin, and so we may not have evolved psychological machinery that is fine-tuned to interacting with genetic strangers. An implication is that we are more likely to trust strangers if they elicit kinship cues, such as facial resemblance, co-residence, or other "familiar" cues such as sharing the same surname (Park, Schaller, & Van Vugt, 2008). Thus, it is true that in modern organizations humans still carry around Stone Age brains.

(7) Asking Special Questions

An evolutionary approach to group processes offers a meta-theoretical framework, guided by evolutionary theory, in which a particular group behaviour must be understood at different levels of analysis. From this perspective, it is important to ask four questions about a behaviour, corresponding to (1) its form, (2) its development within individuals, (3) its evolutionary history, and (4) its ultimate functions (Tinbergen, 1963). The first question concerns the proximate causes of a group behaviour, for instance why do people conform to norm X but not to norm Y? Many psychologists are mainly interested in this first level. The second question concerns the developmental (ontogenetic) aspects of a behaviour such as conformity, for instance how do conformity rates vary across the life-time of people, and why is it that adolescents are particularly likely to break societal norms? The third question concerns the evolutionary (phylogenetic) history of a behaviour, for instance do other species also have social norms and are these norms similar or different from those of humans? The answer to this question provides an indication of the origins of a trait (Brosnan, Newton-Fisher, & Van Vugt, 2009). The fourth question concerns the ultimate functions of a behaviour, for instance what might have been the benefits of norm conformity for early humans? The third and fourth question most interest evolutionary-minded group scientists. Ideally one should get answers to each of these questions to draw a complete picture of a particular group behaviour, and this often requires adopting a multi-disciplinary perspective.

(8) Falsifying Evolutionary Theory

Finally, although the theoretical framework we offer is guided by the principles of evolutionary theory, evolutionary-minded group researchers are not seeking to test evolutionary theory per se, because evolution and natural selection are scientific facts. What they are testing are specific predictions derived from hypotheses generated by middle-level evolutionary theories (Buss, 1995). For instance, the theory of indirect reciprocity suggests that individuals cooperate in large groups because doing so benefits their reputations (Nowak, 2006). A hypothesis that follows is that when people's actions are public they will cooperate more. This produces the specific prediction that when people know that they are being watched by another person they become more generous. This prediction has received substantial support in both the laboratory and field (Bateson, Nettle, & Roberts, 2006; Hardy & Van Vugt, 2006). Thus, while evolutionary theory offers a framework that enables researchers to generate new hypotheses and predictions, falsifying them does not cast doubt on the validity of evolutionary theory per se.

METHODOLOGICAL APPROACHES TO STUDYING GROUPS FROM AN EVOLUTIONARY PERSPECTIVE

Evolutionary psychology represents an enormously diverse set of theories, methods, and analytical perspectives (Gangestad & Simpson, 2007; Schaller, Simpson, & Kenrick, 2006; Scher & Rauscher, 2003). This conceptual and methodological diversity results, in part, from the fact that evolutionary psychology attracts contributions from scientists with an unusually diverse range of scholarly backgrounds—not just scholars with different kinds of training within psychology, but scholars from biology, primatology, zoology, anthropology, economics, and various other academic disciplines. In addition, this diversity is a functional response to the high evidentiary standards that are applied to theories and hypotheses in evolutionary psychology (Conway & Schaller, 2002). Truly convincing support for an evolutionary hypothesis about some aspect of group psychology needs not only to document the existence of the predicted psychological phenomenon, but also needs to provide evidence for the alleged evolutionary origins of that phenomenon. The first part is relatively easy. The second part is hard.

It is exceedingly difficult to collect behavioural data in ancestral environments or to empirically track the actual evolution of an alleged psychological adaptation. Instead, evolutionary psychologists must rely on a multitude of other, more indirect sources of evidence to build a nomological network of findings and inter-relate these findings to offer support for an evolutionary hypothesis (Schmitt & Pilcher, 2004).

Evolutionary psychologists frequently begin with general theories—often from the core principles of evolutionary biology—that guide their attention toward potential psychological adaptations. Common theories used by evolutionary psychologists include inclusive fitness theory, parental investment theory, life-history theory, costly signalling theory, and evolutionary game theory. If a hypothesized group adaptation flows directly from a general evolutionary theory, then evolutionary psychologists feel a degree of confidence in the existence of a group-level adaptation. For example, differences in parental investment lead to the hypotheses that men signal their ability to acquire resources to women through public acts of generosity and that women find generous men sexually more attractive (Iredale et al., 2008).

Evolutionary psychologists sometimes apply computer simulations to study the evolution of group processes. In these simulations agents that reflect particular social strategies (such as a cooperative or defective strategy) interact with each other and their fitness outcomes are examined to see if particular patterns emerge over time. For instance, simulation studies show that stable levels of cooperation can evolve in even large groups as long as agents can keep track of the past interactions of other agents (image scoring; Nowak, 2006). Game theory models can be helpful in identifying the conditions under which certain group traits evolve, especially when they are competing with alternative traits. For instance, the Prisoner's Dilemma Game has been used to model the evolution of cooperation. This model makes clear that mutual defection is the unique equilibrium in a one-shot play—which is the outcome most likely to emerge empirically. Only by making additional assumptions, such as repeated play between the same actors, is there an opportunity for the evolution of cooperation—for instance, through Tit-for-Tat (Axelrod, 1984).

Experimental methods of behavioural economics and social psychology are also increasingly used to find evidence for social adaptations. These methods are used to study interactions between players in games such as the Prisoner's Dilemma Game, the Ultimatum Game, the Dictator Game, and the Public Good Game in which players allocate resources. These methods have produced many interesting findings, for instance by identifying the conditions under which players cooperate with each other to defeat a common outgroup (Van Vugt, De Cremer, & Janssen, 2007).

Methods from experimental cognitive psychology are also often used by evolutionary psychologists to find evidence for social adaptations. For instance, relevant experiments have shown that men typically perform better than women on spatial rotation tasks, whereas women typically perform better than men on spatial memory tasks (Silverman & Eals, 1992). One evolutionary interpretation of this result is that ancestral men—the primary hunters—evolved spatial capacities in order to navigate through an unfamiliar terrain and track moving prey. In contrast, ancestral women—the primary gatherers—evolved memory capacities in order to remember fixed locations where fruits and nuts could be collected.

Psychological surveys can also provide evidence for social adaptations by collecting self-report data about people's experiences in real-world groups. For instance, survey evidence reveals that the most important determinant of people's judgments about ideal group members is their trustworthiness, regardless of the type of group or the nature of the group task (Cottrell, Li, & Neuberg, 2007). This suggests that humans have evolved decision rules to interact with people based upon how much trust they elicit (Simpson, 2007).

Additional evidence for hypothesized group adaptations emerges from recent advances in neuroscience. Brain imaging studies, for instance, have the potential to provide data relevant to specific neural structures associated with group-relevant cognition and behaviour (Adolphs, 1999; Duchaine, Cosmides, & Tooby, 2001). For instance, fMRI research has shown that when people experience social exclusion, there is brain activity in a region that is also activated when people experience physical pain, suggesting that these two kinds of "pain" share the same evolutionary background (Eisenberger, Lieberman, & Williams, 2003). Moreover, hormonal research can help identify the hormonal correlates of particular group-level adaptations, such as the connection between status seeking and testosterone (Josephs, Sellers, Newman, & Metha, 2006).

Behaviour genetics studies may be useful in clarifying whether a particular social adaptation has a substantial genetic component. Generally, when a trait has a low heritability (the degree to which children resemble their parents on this trait) it means that the trait is relatively fixed in a population, which suggests a species-typical biological adaptation. For instance, because every human is capable of acquiring it, language is a species typical adaptation with low heritability. In contrast, a high heritability index suggests that there may be important individual differences in a trait. This points to the possibility that there has been selection for different versions of the trait in human evolution. For instance, introversion and extraversion are traits with substantial heritable components, and this suggests that they may reflect different evolutionary strategies—e.g., introversion may be functional in stable groups and extraversion in unstable groups (Nettle, 2006).

Anthropological and ethnographic databases can provide additional evidence for an evolutionary hypothesis, testing the extent to which specific kinds of group-relevant phenomena are universal across human cultures. This kind of evidence is necessary to differentiate between phenomena that are evolutionary adaptations and those that are more recent, culture-specific manifestations (Norenzayan, Schaller, & Heine, 2006). For instance, research on Western and Eastern cultures suggests that whereas the tendency for positive self-regard is universal, the specific way it is expressed differs across cultures (Sedikides, Gaertner, & Toguchi, 2003).

Finally, cross-species evidence is instrumental in testing speculations about the evolutionary history of an alleged social adaptation. Both chimpanzees and humans, for instance, form coalitions to engage in intergroup violence— a finding implying that the underlying psychological mechanisms predate the divergence of chimpanzee and hominid lines from their immediate common ancestor (Brosnan et al., 2009).

When considered together, the findings from these diverse lines of inquiry have produced important insights into the evolutionary bases of group processes. Although no single finding tells a definitive story about the evolutionary significance of any specific group behaviour, together they point to the existence of a number of specialized mechanisms for dealing with the key challenges of group life.

KEY ADAPTIVE PROBLEMS OF GROUP LIFE

What were the key adaptive challenges that early humans faced living in groups, and what mechanisms could have evolved to solve these? Based on the literature, we identify six critical group challenges:

1. coordinating group activities (coordination);
2. exchanging resources (social exchange);
3. negotiating group hierarchies (status);
4. keeping groups together (group cohesion);
5. making collective decisions (collective decision-making); and
6. interacting with members of outgroups (intergroup relations).

This list is neither exhaustive nor mutually exclusive yet it is a good starting point for building an adaptationist framework for analysing group processes.

Furthermore, the list corresponds closely to the core themes of group dynamics identified in textbooks such as Forsyth's *Group Dynamics* (2010).

Each adaptive group challenge contains a subset of different problems that all need to be solved to produce a good outcome. For example, coordinating a group activity, such as moving the group from one location to another, requires identifying an appropriate location to move to, deciding when to move and for how long, assessing which individuals possess the specific leadership expertise for the task, motivating individuals to follow, keeping the group together while on the move, replacing ineffective leaders, and setting up contingency plans (Van Vugt et al., 2008).

None of these adaptive group challenges has been fully analysed using an evolutionary framework. Yet various research programs have contributed to developing such analyses by providing evidence for evolved psychological mechanisms that address a particular group challenge. The promise of an evolutionary science of group dynamics lies in the generativity and productivity of this approach in formulating novel hypotheses and providing supportive empirical evidence. To date not many group-level adaptations have been explored fully in terms of their form, function, phylogeny, and ontogeny. In the remainder of the chapter, we offer an illustrative set of findings of evolutionary inspired research programs for each of these core group challenges.

(1) Coordination

As a nomadic group living species, early humans would have had to solve problems associated with coordinating their activities with other individuals in sometimes very large groups. For instance, when moving they would have had to decide where to move to and when and for how long to stay there. It would have been potentially lethal for them to stay in one place for too long. To solve this would have required specialized mechanisms for identifying situations as requiring coordination, developing rules for how to achieve coordination (e.g., turn-taking, leadership), and then carrying it out.

Leadership and Followership   One evolved mechanism that has recently been identified as facilitating social coordination is leadership and followership. There are multiple indications that leadership might be a social adaptation. Game-theory models show that leadership—where one individual takes the initiative and others follow—is a powerful solution in coordination games. Consider for instance, Pat and James, who are thirsty and must find a water hole. They must stay together as a form of protection, but how do they decide which waterhole to go to? In such cases it is adaptive for one individual to take the initiative to go to a particular water hole, which leaves the other no option but to follow. Coordinating on the same water hole is the equilibrium solution to this game, which suggests at least the possibility that leadership and followership are evolved strategies (Van Vugt, Hogan, & Kaiser, 2008).

An implication is that leadership–followership interaction emerges spontaneously and does not require much brain power to achieve. The emergence of leadership has been documented across many different animal species that face functionally important coordination problems, including teaching in ants, selecting foraging sites in honey bees (the famous waggle dance performed by scout bees), movement in stickleback fish, and peace-keeping in nonhuman primates (King, Johnson, & Van Vugt, 2009). Among human beings, similar kinds of coordination problems also result in the emergence of leader–follower relations. This occurs quickly and spontaneously across many different situations and cultures, suggesting adaptation (Brown, 1991).

Of course, the exact leadership structure varies across situations and cultures, and there is evidence for both highly democratic and highly despotic leadership structures in humans (Bass, 1990). They likely represent different adaptive solutions to different local group conditions—for instance, dictatorial leadership might have emerged initially in response to an immediate external crisis that required quick and decisive action (Van Vugt, 2009).

There is ample evidence that leadership emergence is more likely among individuals with a predisposition to take initiatives, for example, because they have extraverted, assertive, ambitious, energetic, or dominant personalities (Bass, 1990). Because many such traits have a moderately strong heritable component, it suggests that the evolutionary reason why there are individual differences in such traits is because they help individuals solve coordination problems (Nettle, 2006; Van Vugt, 2006).

The underlying evolutionary logic of leadership also yields hypotheses about the psychological mechanisms underlying followership and leader emergence. An evolutionary approach hypothesizes that humans possess specialized mechanisms for identifying people who are most appropriate for solving a given adaptive problem such as warfare or peacekeeping between groups. Recent studies suggest that warfare elicits a masculine leader prototype, whereas peace elicits a feminine leader prototype (Little, Burris, Jones, & Roberts, 2007; Spisak, Dekker, Kruger, & Van Vugt, 2012; Van Vugt & Spisak, 2008; cf. Lord, DeVader, & Alliger, 1986).

Transactive Memory   Another coordination device that may have evolved to support group coordination is a transactive memory system which enhances the capacity of groups to store and quickly access information by dividing cognitive tasks among group members. Cognitive cooperation is common in social insects and one famous example is the waggle dance of the honey bee, a group decision making device for selecting foraging sites (Seeley, 1995). Research on humans also suggests that members working in the same group often specialize in different areas and group members are very quick at recognizing and using each other's expertise (Littlepage, Hollingshead, Drake, & Littlepage, 2008). People who are expert in a particular domain not only have more information on a given topic but they are also the ones who are responsible for storing new information in their area of expertise. A set of experiments showed that teams performed better on a group task to the extent that the team members divided their cognitive tasks more efficiently. Furthermore, members of teams with better transactive memory systems also trusted each other's expertise more (Moreland, Argote & Krishnan, 1996). Not surprising, considering that—especially at more complex cognitive tasks—groups outperform individuals (Wilson, Timmel, & Miller, 2004).

Mimicry and Behavioural Synchrony   Another evolved mechanism for social coordination is mimicry whereby individuals imitate each other in terms of their actions, expressions, or postures. Mimicry is a highly automated process—it is sometimes referred to as the chameleon effect (Bargh & Chartrand, 1999)—and its main function is to smooth coordination between interaction partners. Mimicry is possible in humans because of the evolution of sophisticated cognitive capacities such as theory of mind and empathy that likely emerged late in human evolution (around 50,000 years ago). Research suggests that mimicry and other forms of behavioural synchrony (such as making the same moves while dancing) increases people's liking for each other and their willingness to share: If people are being mimicked they become more generous (Van Baaren, Holland, Kawakami, & van Knippenberg, 2004). Finally, synchrony of emotions, both positive and negative, facilitates group performance.

(2) Social Exchange

Social exchange—cooperation for mutual benefit—is a pervasive and cross-culturally universal feature of human group life. Exchanging vital resources with others is fundamental for any gregarious species, yet humans are unique in being able to establish large-scale cooperation with genetically-unrelated individuals.

Cheater Detection   Evolutionary models suggest that for social exchanges with non-kin members to persist stably, individuals must be able to detect "cheaters" who do not reciprocate resources (Axelrod, 1984; Trivers, 1971). Cosmides (1989) argued that humans have an evolved cognitive mechanism specialized for cheater detection. A brain-imaging study with a patient who had bilateral limbic system damage provided some evidence for this thesis. Using the Wason's four-card selection task paradigm, Stone, Cosmides, Tooby, Kroll, and Knight (2002) showed that, compared to normal controls, the patient's performance was impaired only when the logical reasoning task was framed as detecting violators of social contracts. The performance remained intact when the task was framed as detecting violators of non-contractual rules. This dissociation suggests that cheating (violations of social contracts) may be processed separately from other types of social violations by our brains.

Cooperation Norms   Human collective action is often governed by a norm of "conditional cooperation" (Fehr & Fischbacher, 2004). This norm dictates that an individual should cooperate if other group members cooperate, whereas he or she is allowed to not cooperate if the others defect. Fischbacher, Gächter, and Fehr (2001) examined participant's willingness to contribute in a one-shot public-goods experiment as a function of the average contribution of the other group members. Despite the economic incentives to free-ride (contribute nothing), 50% of the participants matched their contributions with the average contribution of other members. Furthermore, when participants simply observed the interaction of two players in a Prisoner's Dilemma Game, they spent their own endowment to punish players who defected unilaterally but not players who defected bilaterally (Fehr & Fischbacher, 2004). This pattern indicates that the norm of conditional cooperation ("unilateral defection is not acceptable": Axelrod, 1984) is enforced by neutral observers ("third parties").

The evolutionary perspective suggests a novel hypothesis about the psychological mechanisms underlying enforcement of cooperation norms. Given that exchanges of valuable resources occur mainly within ingroups, violation of cooperation norms should be more serious to one's survival if committed by another ingroup member than if committed by an outgroup member. If so, then non-cooperative behaviour by ingroup members should be punished more severely than non-cooperative behaviour by outgroup members. Using the third-party punishment paradigm, Shinada, Yamagishi, and Ohmura (2004) confirmed this prediction. Such selective sanctioning includes not only physical punishment but also social exclusion, collectively denying the violator's access to interpersonal relations in a group. Research reveals that interpersonal exclusion can provoke strong negative emotional responses in the targeted individuals, including intense anger, pain and depression (Eisenberger et al., 2003). People are highly sensitive to interpersonal exclusion because of its adaptive significance (Kerr & Levine, 2008; Van Vugt & Park, 2009).

Distribution Norms   Distribution norms refer to a set of shared beliefs that prescribes how resources should be distributed among group members. Evidence suggests that motives for egalitarian sharing often operate strongly in resource distribution (Fehr & Schmidt, 1999; Kameda, Takezawa, Ohtsubo, & Hastie, 2010). For example, results from numerous one-shot Ultimatum Game experiments indicate that modal offers by a proposer for a responder's share are around 40–50% and that offers in this range are rarely rejected (Camerer, 2003). Although there are some cultural differences, extremely small offers (1–10%) are rarely seen in ultimatum bargaining experiments conducted in a wide range of societies including primordial as well as industrialized ones (Henrich, Boyd, Bowles, Gintis, & Fehr, 2004).

Indeed, egalitarian sharing of hunted meat constitutes a core feature of hunter-gatherer life. Compared to collected resources (e.g., cassava), hunted meat is often the target of communal sharing. Kaplan and Hill (1985) argued that the sharing system functions is a collective risk-reduction device. While acquisition of collected resources is relatively stable and dependable, acquisition of meat is a highly variable, uncertain event. By including many individuals in the sharing group, the variance in meat supply decreases exponentially (Gurven, 2004). Kameda, Takezawa, and Hastie (2003) conducted a series of evolutionary computer simulations to test the robustness of communal sharing as a risk-pooling system. They argued that free-riders who enjoy sharing of meat that other members have acquired but refuse to share their own acquisitions can potentially destroy the egalitarian-sharing system, which is a public good ("social insurance") sustained only by members' cooperation. Surprisingly, the simulation results showed that egalitarian sharing norm can evolve robustly under uncertainty while overcoming the free-rider problem. This implies that our minds are built to be highly sensitive to cues of uncertainty in resource acquisition. Kameda, Takezawa, Tindale, and Smith (2002) showed that such uncertainty cues promoted people's willingness to share with others beyond their personal distributive ideologies.

(3) Status

Our ancestors lived in increasingly large and complex social groups over evolutionary time and as a result there would have been intense competition for scarce resources such as food, water, and sexual mates (Dunbar, 2004). This competition paved the way for the emergence of status hierarchies whereby people's status would determine their access to reproductively relevant resources. To negotiate one's position in the group hierarchy would require specialized mechanisms for assessing one's relative status as well as mechanisms for climbing the group hierarchy and for maintaining a high status position (once obtained).

Status Signalling Humans have likely evolved a set of adaptations to signal their relative status to others. For instance, they display non-verbal signals such as a firm handshake or a poised posture to let others know that they hold a high status position and deserve respect. High status individuals also walk faster (Schmitt & Atzwanger, 1995) and are more likely to tell other people what to do (Forsyth, 2010). When people seek status they speak clearly and loudly, take more initiatives in conversations, and focus attention on their personal achievements. Just like their primate cousins, high status humans have attention holding power, meaning that they are the focus of attention in groups (Keltner, Gruenfeld, & Anderson, 2000). Along with other primates humans also have differentiated behavioural patterns for interacting with other individuals of higher or lower status than they possess. High status competitors are treated with respect, whereas low status competitors are treated in submissive ways (Brosnan et al., 2009).

Status Emotions Humans have also likely evolved a set of specific status-related emotions. When people experience a status gain—for example, winning an award—they tend to feel pride, and when they experience a loss in status—for example, making a stupid remark—they tend to feel shame (Tracy & Robbins, 2004). Similarly people can feel a vicarious sense of pride or shame when the group or team that they identify with experiences a status gain or loss—for example winning or losing a sports competition. Such emotional experiences are likely to be accompanied by hormonal fluctuations in testosterone, a physiological status marker. In a study with chess players, the winners experienced an increase in testosterone whereas the losers experienced a decrease (Mazur, Booth, & Dabbs, 1992).

Self-Esteem   Humans are also likely to have evolved mechanisms for monitoring their status position, and self-esteem may be an internal gauge of an individual's relative status. When people feel valued by their peers their self-esteem goes up, and when they feel devalued or ostracized their self-esteem goes down (Williams, 2009). Self-esteem likely functions as a "sociometer" that monitors people's standing in a group and motivates action when people feel their status is being threatened (Leary, 1999). When people find themselves in a low status position without having the resources to climb the hierarchy, they may become depressed. Depression can be thought of as an adaptive response to avoid status competitions with peers.

From an evolutionary perspective it would be useful to draw a distinction between different forms of self-esteem which reflect different status problems (Kirkpatrick & Ellis, 2004). For example, concerns about one's standing as a potential sexual mate might be quite independent from concerns about being a respected group member or concerns about the standing of one's group (cf. individual vs. collective self-esteem).

Competitive Altruism   It has been suggested that humans are helpful toward each other because by doing so they receive status benefits. This phenomenon is called competitive altruism (Hardy & Van Vugt, 2006; Roberts, 1998). Experimental research suggests that generous individuals receive more status than nongenerous individuals and are preferred as group leaders (Hardy & Van Vugt, 2006). Computer simulations show that when agents can freely interact with each other and each individual gets a status score (an image score)—which indicates whether he or she cooperated or defected in previous interactions—cooperation becomes the norm (Nowak, 2006). Evidence for competitive altruism has been found in several other primate species as well (Brosnan et al., 2009).

Competitive altruism requires psychological mechanisms for monitoring one's relative status and mechanisms for improving it. Research suggests that when people think they are being watched by others (i.e., their status is being assessed), they become more generous (Bateson, 2006; Hardy & Van Vugt, 2006)—even a pair of eyes on the computer screen makes people behave more generously (Haley & Fessler, 2005). In addition, status concerns an increase people's willingness to preserve the environment and engage in bystander helping (Griskevicius et al., 2010). Men become especially generous when they are being observed by an attractive female (Iredale et al., 2008; Van Vugt & Iredale, 2012).

(4) Group Cohesion

No doubt one of the main problems for ancestral human groups was to maintain cohesion (Dunbar, 2004). Cohesion has been defined as "the resultant of all the forces acting on people to remain in their group" (Festinger, 1950). In light of the importance of staying together as a unit in a hostile savannah environment, our ancestors (as well as other social species) had to evolve mechanisms to preserve social cohesion. Furthermore, as human social networks increased in size over the course of human evolution, we would expect these bonding mechanisms to have become increasingly sophisticated. To maintain group cohesion would require specialized mechanisms to recognize oneself and others as belonging to the same group as well as mechanisms to feel emotionally connected with others in increasingly large groups. Here we discuss a few such adaptive mechanisms.

Social Identity Thinking of people who are not necessarily around all the time as belonging to the same group as you requires the capacity for symbolic thought whereby symbols such as language or rituals become markers of shared group membership. A symbolic social identity allowed our ancestors to connect with a large network of individuals who were spread around a particular area, and this may have been quite helpful in sharing resources as well as in competing with other groups. Research shows that human social identity is highly group based and that people spontaneously make us vs. them categorizations (Tajfel & Turner, 1979). Groups with highly identifying members are also more cohesive (Jetten, Spears, & Manstead, 1996).

Preserving group cohesion also requires a sense of group loyalty whereby individuals are prepared to forego attractive alternatives in favour of staying with their current group. A sense of loyalty is deeply ingrained in human psychology. When individuals highly identify with a group, they develop strong feelings of group loyalty which increases the attractiveness of their group membership relative to alternative memberships (Van Vugt & Hart, 2004).

Religion, Music, Dance and Laughter Humans have many specialized behavioural mechanisms for fostering group cohesion, which may have deep evolutionary roots. Religion, for instance, is an effective method to promote cohesion between strangers and mobilize them for joint action on behalf of a group (Atran, 2002). Similarly, dance and music may have ancient roots. According to evolutionary anthropologists dance and music may have evolved as adaptations for connecting large networks of genetic strangers (Dunbar, 2004). Another possible evolved mechanism for fostering group cohesion is laughter. Laughter is a highly automatic and contagious phenomenon that quickly spreads positive emotions through a crowd. It is known to increase endorphine level and promote trust among strangers (Dunbar, Baron, Frangou, Pearce, Van Leeuwen, Stow, Partridge, MacDonald, Barra, & Van Vugt, 2011).

(5) Group Decision Making

Utilizing group members' various cognitive as well as physical resources efficiently by careful coordination is a core feature of group life, supported by the language faculty. Group decision making is a good example of such coordination.

Animal Group Decision Making   Recent evidence in behavioural ecology suggests that "group decision making" is not exclusively human (Conradt & List, 2009). Seeley (1995) provides a review of honey-bee "group decision making." In late spring or early summer when a colony of bees divides to find a new nest, several hundred bees fly out as "scouts" to inspect potential nest sites. Upon returning to the current nest, these scout bees perform waggle dances to advertise any good sites they have discovered and their locations; the duration of the dance depends on the scouts' perception of the site's quality (the better the site, the longer the dance). Because other bees are more likely to visit and inspect the sites advertised by scout bees, high-quality sites receive more subsequent visits and advertisements. Such a positive feedback loop eventually leads to a "group consensus" about the best site.

Although honey-bee "group decision making" may look more like an automated self-organization than a deliberate coordination, the social-aggregation processes (advertising a favourable site through waggle dances to recruit more fellow searchers) are in fact highly coordinated. Even though honey bees do not rely on language or formal voting for aggregation, they can achieve a group-level "consensus" efficiently. And, most importantly, the bees usually can choose the best site, a phenomenon called the "wisdom of the hive" (Seeley, 1995). Evidently, some well-structured social-coordination mechanisms that yield collective wisdom are an outcome of natural selection.

Despotism vs. Democracy   What is the key evolved decisional structure that enables collective wisdom in honey bees and in some other animals? Conradt and Roper (2003) compared two contrasting structures, "despotism" and "democracy", in the animal kingdom (cf. Van Vugt, 2009). Using a stochastic model, they showed that democratic decisions usually yield better fitness outcomes to group members than despotism—even when the despot is the most experienced group member, it pays other members to accept the despot's decision only when group size is small and the difference between their own and the despot's information is large. Conradt and Roper (2003) argued that democratic decisions are more beneficial "primarily because they tend to produce less extreme decisions, rather than because each individual has an influence on the decision per se" (p. 155).

Hastie and Kameda (2005) extended these ideas to human group decision making. Most naturally occurring environments for humans as well as animals are characterized by large statistical uncertainties. These uncertainties affect many key decisions, including choice of foraging/nest sites, choice of travel routes, monitoring of predators, and so on (Kameda & Nakanishi, 2002, 2003). Given that no single individual (despot) can handle these uncertainties alone even though he/she is highly experienced, the more viable and reliable ("less extreme", Conradt & Roper, 2003) decisional structure in the long run is to use groups as an aggregation device. By aggregating members' opinions, random errors in individual perceptions under uncertainty are cancelled collectively, as implied by the law of large numbers in statistics (Surowiecki, 2004). Hastie and

Kameda (2005) compared several decision rules, which differed in computational loads, in terms of their net efficiencies under uncertainty. These included the Best Member ("despotism") rule and the Majority/Plurality ("democracy") rule. Results from both computer simulations and laboratory experiments showed that the Majority/Plurality rule fared quite well, performing at levels comparable to much more computationally-taxing rules. Furthermore, the Majority/Plurality rule outperformed the despotic Best Member rule, even when members were not forced to cooperate for group endeavour and free-riding was possible (Kameda, Tsukasaki, Hastie, & Berg, 2011).

The Robust Beauty of Majority Rules   These results indicate that, despite its computational simplicity, the Majority/Plurality rule can achieve surprisingly high levels of performance. Such observations may explain the popularity of the Majority/Plurality rule across the full spectrum of human groups from hunter-gatherer and tribal societies (Boehm, 1996) to modern industrial democracies (Davis, 1973; Devine, Clayton, Dunford, Seying, & Pryce, 2001; Kerr & Tindale, 2004), as well as the animal cases in which democratic decisions are often more beneficial than despotism (Conradt & List, 2009; Conradt & Roper, 2003). Of course, phylogenetically, humans are quite distantly related to honey-bees and other "lower" species. Yet, the striking similarities in decision styles between the two most social species on the earth suggest that humans and honey-bees have evolved structurally similar group aggregation mechanisms (i.e., utilizing the law of large numbers) to solve similar adaptive problems (e.g., foraging). Dealing with uncertainty is the key challenge underlying the evolution and use of these mechanisms.

(6) Intergroup Relations

A final problem that our ancestors faced was how to deal with members of other groups. As population densities increased in human evolution so did the competition for scarce resources, and early human groups increasingly came into contact with members of rival groups. On the one hand, relations with outgroups provided opportunities for sharing resources such as food, mates, and information. On the other hand, intergroup relations could be a source of tension and conflict over scarce resources. As a consequence, humans likely possess highly specialized mechanisms that enable them to reap the benefits of intergroup relations while avoiding the costs.

Fear of Strangers   As part of this evolved intergroup psychology, humans are relatively suspicious and even fearful of strangers. Fear of strangers is an innate response which is seen among young children. Fear is strongest toward outgroup males presumably because they constituted a considerable physical threat in ancestral times (McDonald, Navarrete, & Van Vugt, 2012). Outgroups not only posed a significant physical threat in ancestral environments but also a disease threat (think of the spread of contagious diseases). Hence, fear of strangers might also serve the function of avoiding pathogens. A recent study showed that ethnocentrism is strongest among women who are in the early stage of pregnancy presumably because they (and their foetus) are most at risk of catching a disease (Navarrete, Fessler, & Eng, 2007).

Intergroup Aggression and Warfare   An adaptive solution to intergroup competition is engaging in organized violence against members of outgroups. Intergroup aggression is common in humans, and it also found in other primates, including chimpanzees (Brosnan et al., 2009). Humans and chimpanzees use coalitional aggression to gain access to reproductively relevant resources such as territories and sexual mates. In both species such coalitions usually consist of males, arguably because males have more to gain from participating in intergroup conflict—what has been dubbed the "male warrior hypothesis" (Van Vugt, 2009). Research on the male warrior hypothesis shows that men are more "tribal" than women: They are more aggressive in intergroup encounters and have a stronger inclination to infrahumanize outgroup members. Men are also more likely to make sacrifices on behalf of their group during intergroup conflict (Van Vugt et al., 2007). Consistent with the male warrior hypothesis, a recent study suggests that physically formidable men have a stronger preference for intergroup aggression and warfare than do less formidable men (Sell, Cosmides, & Tooby, 2009).

Peacemaking and Reconciliation   In past environments intergroup relations also provided opportunities for trading, and so it is likely that humans also evolved mechanisms for engaging in peaceful interactions with outgroups provided that they did not pose a physical or disease threat. For instance, members of high status groups readily offer help to members of low status outgroups when intergroup helping reaffirms the status difference between the groups (dependency vs. autonomy helping: Nadler, 2002). People also tend to be more forgiving of moral transgressions from outgroup members than ingroup members. Finally, even after a lethal intergroup conflict such as the Rwandan genocide, reconciliation efforts between the groups seem to bear fruit (Paluck, 2009). From an evolutionary perspective, we expect that women have a particularly important role in peacekeeping between groups because they are less tribal and possess superior empathic skills (Van Vugt, 2006).

THE PROMISE OF AN EVOLUTIONARY SCIENCE OF GROUP DYNAMICS

An evolutionary approach to group dynamics can be fruitful in at least four different ways. First, an evolutionary perspective can provide a more complete understanding of particular group processes by asking fundamental questions about the functions, origins and evolution of these phenomena. A more complete account inevitably follows from rigorous attempts to establish conceptual linkages between evolutionary processes operating on ancestral populations and psychological processes operating within contemporary groups.

Second, an evolutionary perspective can help overcome biases and blind spots in the study of groups. It strikes us as odd that the social psychological literature on group decision-making often focuses on what is wrong with groups, disregarding the fact that the group is the natural environment for humans (Caporael, 1997; Wilson et al., 2008). Examples include research on groupthink, brainstorming, group polarization, and information sharing. A cursory reading of these literatures all too easily suggests that people are poor collective decision-makers (Wilson et al., 2008). Any such conclusion, however, is inaccurate (or, at the very least, overly simplistic), and we believe that an evolutionary perspective can produce more sophisticated and accurate conclusions about group decision-making (Kameda & Tindale, 2006).

Third, an evolutionary approach is useful in yielding novel hypotheses about traditional group phenomena. For example, Kenrick, Griskevicius, and colleagues have applied evolutionary reasoning to produce a number of new hypotheses about group phenomena such as status, conformity, and social influence that are unlikely to have been stimulated by other theoretical frameworks (Griskevicius et al., 2007; Kenrick, Li, & Butner, 2003; Sundie, Cialdini, Griskevicius, & Kenrick, 2006).

Finally, an evolutionary approach can expand the boundaries of scientific inquiry on group dynamics by suggesting important group phenomena that have previously received little if any attention from group researchers. Laughter, language, gossip, dance, music, sports, culture, and religion are increasingly being understood as group-level adaptations, that is, as manifestations of psychological processes that connect individuals to each other in large and diverse groups, and these insights have benefited from evolutionarily-informed inquiry (Atran & Norenzyan, 2004; Dunbar, 2004; Van Vugt & Schaller, 2008).

In short, an evolutionary perspective reinforces our awareness that group dynamics are fundamental to the study of human nature. Furthermore, it provides a set of conceptual and empirical tools that can be used to understand and describe group processes more completely and accurately.

REFERENCES

Adolphs, R. (1999). Social cognition and the human brain. *Trends in Cognitive Sciences, 3*, 469–479.

Atran, S. (2002). In gods we trust: The evolutionary landscape of religion. Oxford, UK: Oxford University Press.

Atran, S., & Norenzayan, A. (2004). Religion's evolutionary landscape: Counterintuition, commitment, compassion, communion. *Behavioural and Brain Sciences, 27*, 713–777.

Axelrod, R. (1984). *The evolution of cooperation.* New York, NY: Basic Books.

Bargh, J. A., & Chartrand, T. L. (1999). The unbearable automaticity of being. *American Psychologist, 54*, 462–479.

Barkow, J. (2005). *Missing the revolution: Darwinism for social scientists.* Oxford, UK: Oxford University Press.

Bass, B. M. (1990). *Bass and Stogdill's Handbook of leadership: Theory, research, and managerial applications* (3rd ed.). New York, NY: Free Press.

Bateson, M., Nettle, D., & Roberts, G. (2006). Cues of being watched enhance cooperation in a real-world setting. *Biology Letters, 2,* 412–414.

Baumeister, R. F., & Leary, M. (1995). The need to belong: Desire for interpersonal attachments as a fundamental human motivation. *Psychological Bulletin, 117,* 497–529.

Boehm, C. (1996). Emergency decisions, cultural-selection mechanics, and group selection. *Current Anthropology, 37,* 763–793.

Brosnan, S., & De Waal, F. (2003). Monkeys reject unequal pay. *Nature, 425,* 297–299.

Brosnan, S. F., Newton-Fisher, N. E., & Van Vugt, M. (2009). A melding of minds: When primatology meets personality and social psychology. *Personality and Social Psychology Review, 13,* 129–147.

Brown, D. (1991). *Human universals.* Boston, MA: McGraw-Hill.

Buss, D. M. (1995). Evolutionary psychology: A new paradigm for psychological science. *Psychological Inquiry, 6,* 1–30.

Buss, D. M. (2005). *Handbook of evolutionary psychology.* Hoboken, NJ: Wiley.

Camerer, C. (2003). *Behavioural game theory: Experiments in strategic interaction.* Princeton, NJ: Princeton University Press.

Caporeal, L. (1997). The evolution of truly social cognition: The core configurations model. *Personality and Social Psychology Review, 1,* 276–298.

Conradt, L., & List, C. (Eds.). (2009). Theme issue: Group decision making in humans and animals. *Philosophical Transactions of the Royal Society B, 364,* 719–852.

Conradt, L., & Roper, T. J. (2003). Group decision-making in animals. *Nature, 421,* 155–158.

Conway, L. G., III, & Schaller, M. (2002). On the verifiability of evolutionary psychological theories: An analysis of the psychology of scientific persuasion. *Personality and Social Psychology Review, 6,* 152–166.

Cosmides, L. (1989). The logic of social exchange: Has natural selection shaped how humans reason? Studies with the Wason selection task. *Cognition, 31,* 187–276.

Cottrell, C. A., Li, N. P., & Neuberg, S. L. (2007). What do people desire in others? A sociofunctional perspective on the importance of different valued characteristics. *Journal of Personality and Social Psychology, 92,* 208–231.

Darwin, C. (1871). *The descent of man.* London, UK: John Murray.

Davis, J. H. (1973). Group decision and social interaction: A theory of social decision schemes. *Psychological Review, 80,* 97–125.

De Dreu, C. K. W., Greer, L. L., Handgraaf, M. J. J., Shalvi, S., Van Kleef, G. A., Bass, M., ... Feith, S. W. W. (2010). The neuropeptide oxytocin regulates parochial altruism in intergroup conflict among humans. *Science, 328,* 1408–1411.

Devine, D. J., Clayton, L. D., Dunford, B. B., Seying, R., & Pryce, J. (2001). Jury decision making: 45 years of empirical research on deliberating groups. *Psychology, Public Policy, and Law, 7,* 622–727.

Duchaine, B., Cosmides, L., & Tooby, J. (2001). Evolutionary psychology and the brain. *Current Opinion in Neurobiology, 11,* 225–230.

Dunbar, R. I. M. (1993). Coevolution of neocortical size, group size, and language in humans. *Behavioral and Brain Sciences, 16,* 681–735.

Dunbar, R. I. M. (2004). *Grooming, gossip, and the evolution of language.* London, UK: Faber & Faber.

Dunbar, R. I. M., Baron, R., Frangou, A., Pearce, E., Van Leeuwen, E., Stow, J., Partridge, G., MacDonald, I., Barra, V., & van Vugt, M. (2011). Social laughter is correlated with an elevated pain threshold. *Proceedings of the Royal Society-B, 279,* 1161–1167.

Eisenberger, N. I., Lieberman, M. D., & Williams, K. D. (2003). Does rejection hurt: An fMRI study of social exclusion. *Science, 302*, 290–292.

Fehr, E., & Fischbacher, U. (2004). Third party sanctions and social norms. *Evolution and Human Behaviour, 25*, 63–87.

Fehr, E., & Schmidt, K.M. (1999). A theory of fairness, competition, and cooperation. *Quarterly Journal of Economics, 114*, 817–868.

Festinger L. (1950). Informal social communication. *Psychological Review, 57*, 271–282.

Fischbacher, U., Gächter, S., & Fehr, E. (2001). Are people conditionally cooperative? Evidence from a public goods experiment. *Economics Letters, 71*, 397–404.

Forsyth, D. (2010). *Group dynamics*. Belmont, CA: Wadsworth.

Gangestad, S. W., & Simpson, J. A. (2007). *The evolution of mind: Fundamental questions and controversies*. New York, NY: Guilford Press.

Gervais, M., & Wilson, D. S. (2005). The evolution and functions of laughter and humour: A synthetic approach. *Quarterly Review of Biology, 80*, 395–430.1

Griskevicius, V., Goldstein, N. J., Mortensen, C. R., Cialdini, R. B., & Kenrick, D. T. (2006). Going along versus going alone: When fundamental motives facilitate strategic (non)conformity. *Journal of Personality and Social Psychology, 91*, 281–294.

Griskevicius, V., Tybur, J. M., Sundie, J. M., Cialdini, R. B., Miller, G. F., & Kenrick, D. T. (2007). Blatant benevolence and conspicuous consumption: When romantic motives elicit strategic costly signals. *Journal of Personality and Social Psychology, 93*, 85–102.

Gurven, M. (2004). To give or not to give: An evolutionary ecology of human food transfers. *Behavioural and Brain Sciences, 27*, 543–559.

Haley, K., & Fessler, D. (2005). Nobody's watching. *Evolution and Human Behavior, 26*, 245–256.

Hardy, C. L., & Van Vugt, M. (2006). Nice guys finish first: The competitive altruism hypothesis. *Personality and Social Psychology Bulletin, 32*, 1402–1413.

Hastie, R., & Kameda, T. (2005). The robust beauty of majority rules in group decisions. *Psychological Review, 112*, 494–508.

Henrich, J., Boyd, R., Bowles, S., Gintis, H., & Fehr, E. (2004). *Foundations of human sociality: Economic experiments and ethnographic evidence from fifteen small-scale societies*. Oxford, UK: Oxford University Press.

Hill, R. A., & Dunbar, R. I. M. (2003). Social network size in humans. *Human Nature, 14*, 53–72.

Iredale, W., Van Vugt., M., & Dunbar, R. (2008). Showing off in humans: Male generosity as mate signal. *Evolutionary Psychology, 6*, 386–392.

Janis, I. (1972). *Victims of group think*. Boston, MA: Houghton Mifflin.

Jetten, J., Spears, R., & Manstead, A. (1996). Intergroup norms and intergroup discrimination. *Journal of Personality and Social Psychology, 71*, 1222–1233.

Josephs, R. A., Sellers, J. G., Newman, M. L., & Metha, P. (2006). The mismatch effect: When testosterone and status are at odds. *Journal of Personality and Social Psychology, 90*, 999–1013.

Kameda, T., & Nakanishi, D. (2002). Cost-benefit analysis of social/cultural learning in a non-stationary uncertain environment: An evolutionary simulation and an experiment with human subjects. *Evolution and Human Behaviour, 23*, 373–393.

Kameda, T., & Nakanishi, D. (2003). Does social/cultural learning increase human adaptability? Rogers's question revisited. *Evolution and Human Behaviour, 24*, 242–260.

Kameda, T., Takezawa, M., & Hastie, R. (2003). The logic of social sharing: An evolutionary game analysis of adaptive norm development. *Personality and Social Psychology Review, 7*, 2–19.

Kameda, T., Takezawa, M., Ohtsubo, Y., & Hastie, R. (2010). Are our minds fundamentally egalitarian? Adaptive bases of different sociocultural models about distributive justice. In M. Schaller, A. Norenzyan, S. J. Heine, T. Yamagishi, & T. Kameda (Eds.), *Evolution, culture, and the human mind* (pp. 151–163). New York, NY: Psychology Press.

Kameda, T., Takezawa, M., Tindale, R. S., & Smith, C. (2002). Social sharing and risk reduction: Exploring a computational algorithm for the psychology of windfall gains. *Evolution and Human Behaviour, 23*, 11–33.

Kameda, T., & Tindale, R. S. (2006). Groups as adaptive devices: Human docility and group aggregation mechanisms in evolutionary context. In M. Schaller, J. A. Simpson, & D. T. Kenrick (Eds.), *Evolution and social psychology* (pp. 317–341). New York, NY: Psychology Press.

Kameda, T., Tsukasaki, T., Hastie, R., & Berg, N. (2011). Democracy under uncertainty: The wisdom of crowds and the free-rider problem in group decision making. *Psychological Review, 118*, 76–96.

Kaplan, H., & Hill, K. (1985). Food sharing among Ache foragers: Tests of explanatory hypotheses. *Current Anthropology, 26*, 223–246.

Keltner, D., Gruenfeld, D., & Anderson, C. (2000). Power, approach and inhibition. *Psychological Review, 110*, 265–284.

Kenrick, D. T., Li, N. P., & Butner, J. (2003). Dynamical evolutionary psychology: Individual decision-rules and emergent social norms. *Psychological Review, 110*, 3–28.

Kerr, N. L., & Levine, J. (2008). The detection of social exclusion: Evolution and beyond. *Group Dynamics, 12*, 39–52.

Kerr, N. L., & Tindale, R. S. (2004). Group performance and decision making. *Annual Review of Psychology, 55*, 623–655.

King, A., Johnson, D. D. P., & Van Vugt, M. (2009). The origins and evolution of leadership. *Current Biology, 19*, 1591–1682.

Kirkpatrick, L., & Ellis, B. (2004). An evolutionary psychological approach to self-esteem. In M. Brewer and M. Hewstone (Eds.), *Self and social identity* (pp. 52–77). Malden, MA: Blackwell.

Kurzban, R., & Leary, M. R. (2001). Evolutionary origins of stigmatization: The functions of social exclusion. *Psychological Bulletin, 127*, 187–208.

Leary, M. R. (1999). Making sense of self-esteem. *Current Directions in Psychological Science, 8*, 32–35.

Little, A. C., Burris, R., Jones, B., & Roberts, S. C. (2007). Facial appearance affects voting decisions. *Evolution and Human Behavior, 28*, 18–27.

Littlepage, G. E., Hollingshead, A. B., Drake, L. R., & Littlepage, A. M. (2008). Transactive memory and performance in work groups: Specificity, communication, ability differences, and work allocation, *Group Dynamics: Theory, Research, and Practice, 12*, 223–241.

Lord, R. G., DeVader, C. L., & Alliger, G. M. (1986). A meta-analysis of the relation between personality traits and leadership perceptions: An application of validity generalization procedures. *Journal of Applied Psychology, 71*, 402–410.

Maner, J. K., & Mead, N. (2010). The essential tension between leadership and power: When leaders sacrifice group goals for the sake of self-interest. *Journal of Personality and Social Psychology, 99*, 482–497.

Mazur, A., Booth, A., & Dabbs, J. M. (1992). Testosterone and chess competition. *Social Psychology Quarterly, 55*, 70–77.

McDonald, M. M., Navarrete, C. D., & Van Vugt, M. (2012). Evolution and the psychology of intergroup conflict: The Male Warrior Hypothesis. *Philosophical Transactions of the Royal Society-B, 367,* 670–679.

Miller, G. (2000). *The mating mind.* New York, NY: Anchor.

Moreland, R., Argote, L., & Krishnan, R. (1996). Socially shared cognition at work. In J. Nye & A. Brower (Eds.), *What's social about social cognition.* Thousand Oaks, CA: Sage.

Nadler, A. (2002). Intergroup helping relations as power relations. *Journal of Social Issues, 58,* 487–502.

Navarrete, C. D., Fessler, D. M. T., & Eng, S. J. (2007). Elevated ethnocentrism in the first trimester of pregnancy. *Evolution and Human Behavior, 28,* 60–65.

Nesse, R. (2007). Runaway selection for displays of partner value and altruism. *Biological Theory, 2,* 143–155.

Nettle, D. (2006). The evolution of personality variation in humans and other animals. *American Psychologist, 61,* 622–631.

Norenzayan, A., Schaller, M., & Heine, S. J. (2006). Evolution and culture. In M. Schaller, J. A. Simpson, & D. T. Kenrick (Eds.), *Evolution and social psychology* (pp. 343–366). New York, NY: Psychology Press.

Nowak, M. A. (2006). Five rules for the evolution of cooperation. *Science, 314,* 1560–1563.

Park, J., Schaller, M., & Van Vugt, M. (2008). The psychology of human kin recognition: Heuristic cues, erroneous inferences, and their implications. *Review of General Psychology, 12,* 215–235.

Richerson, P. J., & Boyd, R. (2006). *Not by genes alone: How culture transformed human evolution.* Chicago, IL: Chicago University Press.

Roberts, G. (1998). Competitive Altruism: From reciprocity to the handicap principle, *Proceedings of the Royal Society of London: Series B, 265,* 427–431.

Schaller, M., Simpson, J., & Kenrick, D. (2006). *Evolution and social psychology.* Hove, UK: Psychology Press.

Scher, S. J., & Rauscher, F. (2003). *Evolutionary psychology: Alternative approaches.* Boston, MA: Kluwer.

Schmitt, A., & Atzwanger, K. (1995). Walking fast ranking high: A sociobiological perspective on pace. *Ethology and Sociobiology, 16,* 451–462.

Schmitt, D. P., & Pilcher, J. J. (2004). Evaluating evidence of psychological adaptation: How do we know one when we see one? *Psychological Science, 15,* 643–649.

Sedikides, C., Gaertner, L., & Toguchi, Y. (2003). Pancultural self-enhancement. *Journal of Personality and Social Psychology, 84,* 60–79.

Seeley, T. D. (1995). *The wisdom of the hive: The social physiology of honey bee colonies.* Cambridge, MA: Harvard University Press.

Sell, A., Cosmides, L., & Tooby, J. (2009). Human adaptations for the visual assessment of strength and fighting ability from body and face. *Proceedings of the Royal Society-B, 276,* 575–584.

Shinada, M., Yamagishi, T., & Ohmura, Y. (2004). False friends are worse than bitter enemies: "Altruistic" punishment of in-group members. *Evolution and Human Behaviour, 25,* 379–393.

Silverman, I., & Eals, M. (1992). Sex differences in spatial abilities: Evolutionary theory and data. In J. H. Barkow, L. Cosmides, & J. Tooby (Eds.), *The adapted mind: Evolutionary psychology and the generation of culture* (pp. 533–549). New York, NY: Oxford University Press.

Simpson, J. A. (2007). Psychological foundations of trust. *Current Directions in Psychological Science, 16,* 264–268.

Spisak, B., Dekker, P., Kruger, M., & Van Vugt, M. (2012). Warriors and peacekeepers: Testing a biosocial implicit leadership hypothesis of intergroup relations using masculine and feminine faces. *PLoS ONE, 7,* 1–8.

Stone, V. E., Cosmides, L., Tooby, J., Kroll, N., & Knight, R. T. (2002). Selective impairment of reasoning about social exchange in a patient with bilateral limbic system damage. *Proceedings of the National Academy of Sciences, 99,* 11531–11536.

Sundie, J. M., Cialdini, R. B., Griskevicius, V., & Kenrick, D. T. (2006). Evolutionary social influence. In M. Schaller, J. A. Simpson, & D. T. Kenrick (Eds.), *Evolution and social psychology* (pp. 287–316). New York, NY: Psychology Press.

Surowiecki, J. (2004). *The wisdom of crowds: Why the many are smarter than the few and how collective wisdom shapes business, economies, societies and nations.* New York, NY: Doubleday.

Tajfel, H., & Turner, J. (1979). An integrative theory of intergroup conflict. In W. Austin & S. Worchel (Eds.), *The psychology of intergroup relations* (pp. 33–47). Monterey, CA: Brooks/Cole.

Tinbergen, N. (1963). On the aims and methods in ethology. *Zeitschrift for Tierpsychology, 20,* 410–433.

Tracy, J., & Robbins, R. (2004). Show your pride: Evidence for a discrete emotion expression. *Psychological Science, 15,* 194–197.

Trivers, R. L. (1971). The evolution of reciprocal altruism. *Quarterly Review of Biology, 46,* 35–57.

Van Baaren, R. B., Holland, R. W., Kawakami, K., & van Knippenberg, A. (2004). Mimicry and prosocial behavior. *Psychological Science, 15,* 71–74.

Van Vugt, M. (2006). Evolutionary origins of leadership and followership. *Personality and Social Psychology Review, 10,* 354–371.

Van Vugt, M. (2009). Despotism, democracy and the evolutionary dynamics of leadership and followership. *American Psychologist, 64,* 54–56.

Van Vugt, M., De Cremer, D., & Janssen, D. (2007). Gender differences in cooperation and competition: The male warrior hypothesis. *Psychological Science, 18,* 19–23.

Van Vugt, M., & Hart, C. M. (2004). Social identity as social glue: The origins of group loyalty. *Journal of Personality and Social Psychology, 86,* 585–598.

Van Vugt, M., & Iredale, W. (2012). Men behaving nicely: Public goods as peacock tails. *British Journal of Psychology,* doi: 10.1111/j.2044-8295.201102093

Van Vugt, M., Hogan, R., & Kaiser, R. (2008). Leadership, followership, and evolution: Some lessons from the past. *American Psychologist, 63,* 182–196.

Van Vugt, M., Johnson, D., Kaiser, R., & O'Gorman, R. (2008). The mismatch hypothesis: An evolutionary perspective on leadership. In D. Forsyth, A. Goethals, & C. Hoy (Eds.), *Social psychology and leadership.* New York, NY: Praeger.

Van Vugt, M., & Park, J. (2009). Guns, germs, and tribal social identities: Evolutionary perspectives on the social psychology of intergroup relations. *Social and Personality Psychology Compass, 3,* 927–938.

Van Vugt, M., & Schaller, M. (2008). Evolutionary perspectives on group dynamics: An introduction. *Group Dynamics, 12,* 1–6.

Van Vugt, M., & Spisak, B. R. (2008). Sex differences in leadership emergence during competitions within and between groups. *Psychological Science, 19,* 854–858.

Williams, K. D. (2009). Ostracism: A temporal need-threat model. *Advances in Experimental Social Psychology, 41,* 275–314.

Wilson, D. S., Timmel, J., & Miller, R. (2004). Cognitive cooperation: When the going gets tough, think as a group. *Human Nature, 15,* 225–250.

Wilson, D. S., Van Vugt, M., & O'Gorman, R. (2008). Multi-level selection theory and major evolutionary transitions: Implications for psychological science. *Current Directions in Psychological Science, 17,* 6–9.

13

Intergroup Relations

JOHN F. DOVIDIO, SAMUEL L. GAERTNER,
and ERIN L. THOMAS

*T*he term *intergroup relations* refers to the ways in which people perceive, think about, feel about, act towards, and react to others on the basis of different social group memberships. Intergroup relations are based on feelings of collective identity. Taylor and Moghaddam (1994), for example, emphasize that intergroup relations represent "any aspect of human interaction that involves individuals perceiving themselves as members of a social category, or being perceived by others as belonging to a social category" (p. 6). However, we further emphasize that intergroup relations are fundamentally *relational*. That is, understanding intergroup relations requires considering not only the ways in which people with different collective identities think and feel about members of other groups unilaterally. It also requires consideration of how the processes, nature, and outcomes of intergroup *interactions* are shaped by and, in turn, shape the ways in which people think about their own group and view and behave toward other groups in the future.

Seeing people as social group members, rather than as unique individuals, has a profound effect on perception, cognition, affect, and behavior (Tajfel & Turner, 1979). People think and feel differently about others when social identity is salient than when personal identity is salient (Brewer, 1988; Fiske, Lin, & Neuberg, 1999). Moreover, social exchange is systematically different when people view themselves as members of different groups (inter*group* relations) than when they conceive of themselves as individuals (inter*personal* relations). For instance, research on the *interindividual-intergroup discontinuity effect* (Wildschut & Insko, 2007) reveals that groups are more competitive than individuals, in large part because groups are more fearful of each other and display more greed.

This chapter reviews the processes that determine intergroup relations. We first consider the foundational role of social categorization on intergroup perceptions; we then discuss how social identity further influences people's motivations and consequent orientations toward their own and other groups. After that, we explore how functional relations between the groups can exacerbate intergroup bias or improve intergroup relations. Going beyond the orientations of members of one group toward another group and its members, we then consider the experiences of targets of intergroup bias. Next, we review evidence concerning the role of intergroup interaction in exacerbating or ameliorating intergroup bias and tension. We then consider the conditions that promote positive intergroup relations, and we conclude by identifying key issues and future directions for research on intergroup relations.

SOCIAL CATEGORIZATION

Social categorization forms an essential basis for human perception, cognition, and functioning because human survival depends on the ability to make sense of complex environments. In order to do this efficiently, people abstract meaning from their perceptions and develop heuristics to simplify the elements of their surroundings. Categorizing these elements is a fundamental and necessary process for deriving meaning from the world.

Categorization is a universal facet of human thinking and is essential for efficient psychological functioning. The ability to sort objects, events, and people quickly and effectively into meaningful categories is automatic and often based on physical similarity, proximity, or shared fate (Campbell, 1958). The instant an object is categorized, it is assigned the properties of the category as a whole, thus enabling people to make quick decisions about incoming information and eliminating time-consuming and inefficient consideration of the meaning of every stimulus or experience. In turn, categorization relieves cognitive resources, which allows individuals to perform other tasks.

In an often-overwhelming social world, a natural consequence of categorization is the compromise of accuracy for efficiency (Fiske & Taylor, 2007). When people or objects are categorized into groups, differences between group members tend to be minimized when the categorizer forms impressions of or makes decisions about the target (Tajfel, 1969). As a result, members of the same category are regarded as more similar than they actually are and more similar than they were before they were categorized together. Moreover, distinctions between members of different categories tend to be exaggerated. In short, categorization enhances perceptions of similarities within and differences between groups and the magnitude of these distortions increases with the salience of the categorization (Turner, 1985). These differences are even more pronounced for *social* categorization, as within- and between-group distortions are perceived as inherent to the nature of human groups and are generalized to dimensions (e.g., character traits) beyond those that originally differentiated the categories (Allport, 1954).

A core aspect of social categorization is the (de)classification of individuals as members of one's ingroup. Because the self is the nucleus of social perception, categorizing people fundamentally involves a distinction between the group containing the self, the ingroup, and other groups, outgroups. This differentiation process creates a world divided between the "we's" and the "they's" and is composed of four elements: categorization, identification, comparison, and psychological distinctiveness (Tajfel & Turner, 1979). People first put themselves and others into labeled categories. They then associate (i.e., identify) with certain groups (i.e., ingroups) and compare ingroups with other groups to attempt to distinguish themselves from and positively compare themselves to those outgroups. This process results in a number of ingroup/outgroup biases (see Dovidio & Gaertner, 2010).

People favor ingroup over outgroup members, both explicitly and implicitly in evaluations (Otten & Wentura, 1999). People also show a preference for ingroup members who show bias against an outgroup (Castelli, Tomelleri, & Zogmaister, 2008). Consequently, people are more generous and forgiving in their behavioral attributions of ingroup versus outgroup members. Positive behaviors and successful outcomes of ingroup members are more likely to be attributed to stable, internal characteristics, whereas negative behaviors and unsuccessful outcomes are more likely to be ascribed to the dispositions of outgroup members (Hewstone, 1990). The *linguistic intergroup bias* (Maass, Salvi, Arcuri, & Semin, 1989) predicts that individuals will describe positive ingroup and negative outgroup behaviors in abstract terms that implicitly cast the behaviors as generalizable and link them to stable characteristics. By contrast, negative ingroup and positive outgroup behaviors will be described in relatively concrete terms that cast them as situational occurrences. These cognitive and linguistic biases perpetuate social biases and stereotypes, even in the face of disconfirming evidence.

Another factor promoting stereotyping is the systematic bias in how people perceive similarity within groups. In particular, people see members of an outgroup as generally similar to one another (i.e., *outgroup homogeneity effect*) while ingroup members are perceived as more distinctive and individualistic (see Boldry, Gaertner, & Quinn, 2007). As a consequence, people are more likely to generalize the behavior of one outgroup member to other outgroup members and, thus, to the group as a whole. This generalization to the entire outgroup is particularly likely to occur for negative, stereotypic behaviors (Henderson-King & Nisbett, 1996), which may be seen as inherent in the character of the outgroup (Jost & Hamilton, 2005) and personally and socially threatening to the ingroup member. These outgroup generalizations are generally resistant to the disconfirming influence of counter-stereotypic outgroup behaviors.

Finally, categorization has profound effects on individuals' behavioral orientations toward others. Upon social categorization, people exhibit a physical readiness to approach ingroup members and avoid outgroup members (Paladino & Castelli, 2008). Moreover, people are more helpful toward ingroup versus outgroup members (Dovidio et al., 1997), are more cooperative and trustful of ingroup versus outgroup members (Gaertner & Dovidio, 2000; Voci, 2006), exercise more personal restraint when using endangered resources with ingroup versus outgroup members (Kramer & Brewer, 1984), and are more generous in their reward allocations to ingroup versus outgroup members (Mullen, Brown, & Smith, 1992).

In summary, to manage the complexity of their social environment and enhance efficiency, people fundamentally rely on social categories in perceiving others and forming impressions and making judgments about them. However, the distinction, which is made spontaneously, between groups in which one is a member (ingroups) and those for which one is not a member (outgroups) has a profound impact on how others are perceived and evaluated: People automatically evaluate ingroup members more favorably than outgroup members and think in deeper and more differentiated ways about ingroup members. Moreover, people tend to dismiss negative behaviors by ingroup members but accentuate unfavorable actions of outgroup members in the ways they make attributions about, talk about, and make generalizations to other group members. This pattern of preferential treatment promotes intergroup bias, contributing directly to divergent expectations of, perceptions of, and behavior toward ingroup versus outgroup members.

SOCIAL IDENTITY

The degree to which individuals identify with their ingroup moderates how they think about themselves and others. The more strongly individuals identify with the ingroup, the more strongly they see themselves as typical members of the group (Hogg, 2010). This typicality includes ways of thinking and behaving that are specific to and characteristic of the group. Ingroup identification also moderates the extent to which people experience group-based emotions. A strongly-identified individual more strongly considers the group to be part of the self and, thus, is more likely than a weakly-identified individual to experience emotions in response to events that affect individuals in his or her group (Gordijn, Wigboldus, & Yzerbyt, 2001). Group characteristics, in turn, become norms or standards for the individual's behavior and systematically shape his or her motivations. *Social identity theory* (Tajfel & Turner, 1979) and, more recently, *self-categorization theory* (Turner, 1985; Turner, Hogg, Oakes, Reicher, & Wetherell, 1987) explain when and why individuals identify with and behave as members of specific social groups (see Abrams, this volume).

Social identity theory differentiates personal identity, the elements of self-identity derived from individual traits and interpersonal relationships, from social identity, the elements of self-identity derived from social group membership. According to social identity theory, individuals have a repository of personal and social identities available to them, with each identity informing the individual of who he or she is and what the respective identity entails. This perspective suggests that a person defines the self along a continuum that ranges, at one extreme, from the self as a distinct individual with personal motives, goals, and achievements to the self as the embodiment of a social collective or group. When personal identity is salient, the individual relates to others on an interpersonal level, and personality characteristics (e.g., authoritarianism) and personal goals and attitudes primarily guide behaviors. However, when social identity is salient, the behavior between individuals assumes an intergroup quality because each person serves as a representative of his or her respective ingroup. As a consequence, people's behavior is shaped more by their perceptions of group values and interests and by their group positions (Verkuyten & Hagendoorn, 1998).

People often seek an intermediate point between personal and social selves in order to balance their opposing needs to be different from others and to belong and share a sense of similarity with others. *Optimal distinctiveness theory* (Brewer, 1991) proposes that people prefer membership in small groups in order to satisfy their competing motives for differentiation and assimilation. Achieving this balance between motives enhances one's feelings of connection to the group, reduces feelings of uncertainty, and increases group cohesiveness (Hogg, 1996).

Individuals have multiple social identities, however. The specific social context directly impacts which of these many identities is most salient at a given time. Social qualities that make one feel distinctive in a particular context (e.g., being a woman in a group of men) or situations that draw attention to a particular group membership (e.g., a women's rights rally) typically make the corresponding identity salient. Activating different identities, in turn, critically determines how people think and behave. For example, when Asian girls' female identity was made salient, they performed more poorly on a mathematics test (a gender-inconsistent task) than when this identity was not activated. Conversely, when their Asian identity was emphasized, they performed better on the mathematics test than when this group identity was not salient, a result that is consistent with expectations associated with that ethnic identity (Shih, Pittinsky, & Ambady, 1999).

A key premise of social identity theory is that people's context-specific attention to their personal and social identities is driven by their motivation to feel positively about themselves. One way to achieve this end is to join social groups that elicit a positive identity; another is to increase the perceived worthiness of the social groups to which one already belongs. To the extent that people are motivated to regard themselves positively, they will also be motivated to differentiate themselves from outsiders, that is, to see as much difference as possible between their ingroups and those groups to which they do not belong (Tajfel & Turner, 1979).

According to social identity theory, individuals can use one of three different strategies to enhance their social identity (Jetten, Schmitt, Branscombe, & McKimmie, 2005; Tajfel & Turner, 1979): They can leave an existing social group and join one that is more positively valued (i.e., social mobility). Alternatively, their group can seek positive distinctiveness by emphasizing a different basis for social comparison from the one that defines the status relationship—one on which the ingroup appears superior (i.e., social creativity; see Mullen et al., 1992, for a review). Finally, a person's social group can strive to distinguish itself positively through direct opposition with outgroups (i.e., social competition). Thus, the desire to enhance social identity in itself can increase motivations to compete against other groups.

Self-categorization theory, which evolved from social identity theory, emphasizes how categorizing oneself as a member of a group depersonalizes self-perceptions and systematically alters the way in which people relate to members of other groups (Turner et al., 1987; see also Hogg, 2010). Categorizing the self and others into groups produces prototype-based perceptions. Self-categorization leads people to see themselves in terms of the defining properties of the ingroup (i.e., the ingroup prototype) and to view themselves and others in the group as interchangeable exemplars. As a consequence, people experience depersonalized attraction to other ingroup members, become compliant to group norms, and act in accordance with group-based motivations and goals. When individuals are categorized as members of an outgroup, they are seen in strongly homogeneous and stereotypic ways, accentuating differences between the groups. These processes promote ethnocentric motivations, which in turn lead to competitive, discriminatory, and exploitative intergroup relations.

Social identity theory has inspired a number of other theoretical developments in social psychology that further highlight the role of group categorization in motivations to achieve positive distinctiveness and, consequently, in the arousal of intergroup bias and conflict. *Terror management theory* (Greenberg, Landau, Kosloff, & Solomon, 2009) posits that adherence to group values reduces the terror humans experience in response to mortality salience by enhancing individuals' feelings of security and self-esteem and, in turn, providing meaning and organization to life. Arousing mortality concerns (for example, by having people write about death compared to dental pain) magnifies the interindividual-intergroup discontinuity effect, particularly by increasing intergroup aggression (McPherson & Joireman, 2009).

Social dominance theory (Sidanius & Pratto, 1999) proposes that, because of the evolutionary advantage of hierarchical relations, groups are hierarchically organized within societies and are motivated to maintain their higher status and power over other groups. People who more strongly endorse this ideology—those higher in Social Dominance Orientation—believe more strongly that group hierarchies are inevitable and desirable, and they see the world as involving greater zero-sum competition between groups for resources. From the perspective of social dominance theory, most forms of group conflict and oppression are manifestations of this predisposition.

FUNCTIONAL INTERGROUP RELATIONS

Work on social categorization and social identity suggests that these processes alone are sufficient to predispose people to view intergroup relations in competitive terms. However, beyond these strong perceptions of social competitiveness, several theories of functional relations between groups point to actual competition itself as a fundamental cause of intergroup prejudice and conflict.

Realistic group conflict theory (Bobo, 1999; Campbell, 1965; Sherif, 1966), for example, posits that the perception of intergroup resource competition fuels efforts to reduce outgroups' access to resources. In particular, Sherif, Harvey, White, Hood, and Sherif (1961) proposed that when groups are competitively interdependent, the interplay between the actions of each group results in positive outcomes for one group and negative outcomes for the other. Thus, in their respective attempts to obtain favorable outcomes for themselves, the actions of the members of each group are realistically perceived to be calculated efforts to frustrate the goals of the other group. This win lose, zero sum competition between groups can therefore initiate mutually negative feelings and stereotypes between members of different groups. In contrast, cooperatively interdependent relations that result in positive outcomes can reduce bias.

Competition need not be explicit to elicit intergroup bias. In the absence of any direct evidence, people typically presume that members of other groups are competitive and will hinder the attainment of their goals (Fiske & Ruscher, 1993). Moreover, feelings of interdependence among members of one's own social group may be sufficient to produce bias against members of an outgroup. Rabbie and Lodewijkx's (1996) *behavioral interaction model,* for example, argues that both intergroup competition and intragroup cooperation can independently stimulate intergroup bias.

The instrumental model of group conflict (Esses, Dovidio, Jackson, & Armstrong, 2001; Esses, Jackson, & Armstrong, 1998) integrates work on realistic group conflict theory and social dominance theory. This model proposes that resource stress, the threat aroused by the perception that access to a desired good (e.g., wealth or political power) is limited, and awareness of a potentially competitive outgroup produce perceptions of group competition for resources. The combination of resource stress and the potential for competition leads to perceived group competition in the form of zero-sum beliefs that the more the other group obtains, the less is available for one's own group. The response is a strategic attempt to eliminate the competition.

Efforts to remove the other group from competition may include outgroup derogation and discrimination. One may express negative attitudes and attributions about members of the other group in an attempt to convince both one's own group and other groups of the competitor's lack of worth. Attempts to eliminate the competition may also entail negative treatment of the other group and opposition to policies and programs that may benefit that group. Limiting the other group's access to resources also reduces competition. Consistent with the instrumental model of group conflict, individuals in Canada and the United States perceive greater threat from, are more biased against, and are more motivated to exclude immigrant groups that are perceived as zero-sum resource competitors with citizens of the host country (see Esses, Jackson, Dovidio, & Hodson, 2005). In addition to the concrete objective of economic advantage, discrimination can serve less tangible functions. Establishing a superior ingroup position may be associated with the acquisition of intangible resources such as prestige (Blumer, 1958). In fact, symbolic and psychological factors are frequently more important in intergroup bias than are concrete resources.

Social identity and functional relations theories offer complementary explanations of intergroup bias. A large body of work demonstrates the reciprocal and often joint operation of symbolic and realistic threats to group identity in eliciting intergroup bias. Not only do psychological biases produce perceptions of competition and motivate actual competition between groups, competition between groups itself further increases intergroup bias and distrust. When people perceive outgroup members as a threat, they tend to derogate and discriminate against them more directly (Esses et al., 2001). Thus, psychological biases and actual competition often reinforce each other and escalate intergroup biases.

Moreover, according to *integrated threat theory* (Stephan, Renfro, Esses, Stephan, & Martin, 2005; see Stephan & Stephan, 2000), negative stereotypes, symbolic group threat, and realistic group threat all predict discrimination against other groups (e.g., immigrants), and each accounts for a unique portion of this effect. In addition, personal-level biases and collective biases may also have separate and additive influences. That is, personal prejudice and group threat can contribute independently to discrimination against other groups (Bobo, 1999). The independence of these effects points to the importance of considering each of these perspectives for a comprehensive understanding of intergroup bias and reinforces the theoretical distinctions among the hypothesized underlying mechanisms.

RESPONSES TO BIAS: THE TARGET'S PERSPECTIVE

Much of the traditional research on intergroup relations has focused on the expression of intergroup bias and discrimination—the perpetrator's perspective. Recent research has also recognized the importance of understanding people's responses to intergroup discrimination—the target's perspective. When people feel disadvantaged because of their group membership, they typically seek individual mobility, often disidentifying with their group to achieve the personal goal of self-esteem (Tajfel & Turner, 1979).

However, when group membership is un-concealable or group identification is high, targets tend to pursue group-based responses to intergroup discrimination (Ellemers & Barreto, 2001). One group-based response is the strategy of social creativity in which groups emphasize the superior value of their distinctive qualities. Consistent with this strategy, low-status groups show more intergroup bias on qualities that are irrelevant to the status distinction (Mullen et al., 1992), particularly when they view status differences as illegitimate (Bettencourt, Dorr, Charlton, & Hume, 2001). Another group-based response is collective action, or a group's mobilization of coordinated effort to enhance its social standing and access to resources. Collective action is most likely to occur when the salience of group membership is high, people perceive the boundaries between groups as impermeable, group-based inequality is recognized, and the other group is characterized negatively (van Zomeren, Postmes, & Spears, 2008; Wright & Lubensky, 2009).

Nevertheless, many forms of group-based inequality are not fully recognized by members of the targeted group. They are often cloaked by cultural ideologies that legitimatize one group's status over another's. Social dominance theory, for example, argues that under some conditions (such as when they endorse system-justifying ideologies or invest in historical narratives manipulated by dominant groups), both high- and low-status groups tend to defend and reinforce the hierarchical status quo. *System justification theory* (Jost & Hunyady, 2002) explains this phenomenon by positing that people aim to hold favorable attitudes not only about themselves and their ingroups but also about the overarching social system they inhabit. System justification theory thus accounts for the fact that low-status group members often support the societal status quo, often at a cost to themselves and fellow group members (see Jost, Banaji, & Nosek, 2004).

System justification by members of minority groups may seem counterintuitive, but there are several reasons why targets of intergroup bias may not recognize unfair treatment that they personally receive. First, individuals cannot serve as their own control group and test whether they would have received better treatment as a member of a more privileged group (Fiske, 1998). Second, discrimination is easier to detect with aggregated evidence than with single cases because lone incidents are easy to explain away (Crosby, 1984). Third, individuals may deny discrimination to avoid feeling that they are being mistreated or that they do not have control over a situation (Major & Sawyer, 2009). As a result, people are more likely to perceive discrimination against their ingroups on the whole than against themselves as individuals (Crosby, 1984) or to avoid labeling discriminatory experiences as such (Vorauer & Kumhyr, 2001).

Considering the target's perspective on intergroup bias helps to provide a more complete understanding of the interpersonal and intergroup aspects of prejudice, stereotyping, and discrimination. Members of different groups have different needs, motivations, and goals during intergroup interactions, which produce different—and often divergent—perspectives and experiences in intergroup contexts (Demoulin, Leyens, & Dovidio, 2009). For example, Judd, Park, Ryan, Brauer, and Kraus (1995) found that Black students in the United States regarded race as an important and positive part of their identity, whereas White students viewed race-related classes and programs as reinforcements of the racial divide (see also Kaiser & Pratt-Hyatt, 2009).

Examining the target's perspective also provides information about the psychological and physical consequences of exposure to intergroup prejudice and discrimination (see Pascoe & Richman, 2009). For example, discrimination experienced by Black Americans is associated with self-reported ill health, low psychological well-being, and health-related work absences. Studies have also linked perceived discrimination with hypertension, breast cancer, obesity, and substance use (see Williams & Mohammed, 2009, for a review).

Although understanding intergroup relations in terms of the experiences of people who are targets of intergroup bias nicely complements the vast body of traditional literature on how group membership shapes intergroup attitudes and behaviors toward others, intergroup relations fundamentally involve interactions between members of different groups. We consider the unique nature of intergroup interaction in the next section.

INTERGROUP INTERACTION

It is perhaps surprising that relatively little research has directly studied the ways in which members of different groups think, feel, and behave within intergroup interactions. Recently, however, increasing attention has been given to the complex nature of actual interactions (Richeson & Shelton, 2010) and how experiences in these exchanges are shaped by and, in turn, shape intergroup relations more generally (Dovidio, Gaertner, Kawakami, & Hodson, 2002).

In general, this research shows that the earliest stages of intergroup interactions—the anticipation of the interaction and initial contact between members of different groups—differ from those of intragroup interactions in two critical ways: expectations of others and the amount of anxiety experienced. These two elements, separately and in combination, can create important barriers to the formation of positive intergroup relations, leading members of different groups to avoid interacting with one another and creating fragile relations between them in initial encounters.

As noted earlier in the section on social categorization, the mere knowledge that an interaction partner is a member of one's own group or another group arouses differential expectations for and affective reactions toward the individual. In general, people anticipate that outgroup members will behave less positively than ingroup members and will share their attitudes and values less than will ingroup members (Robbins & Krueger, 2005). Moreover, people anticipate that outgroup members will display bias toward their ingroup (Judd, Park, Yzerbyt, Gordijn, & Muller, 2005). As a consequence of these negative expectations, people are less trusting of outgroup than ingroup members (Foddy, Platow, & Yamagishi, 2009) and are vigilant regarding cues of bias from outgroup members (Vorauer, 2006). For example, Shelton and Richeson (2005) found that both Whites and Blacks were personally interested in intergroup interactions but avoided them because they anticipated that their overtures would be rejected by members of the other group. Thus, people not only perceive outgroup members unfavorably, they also have negative expectations about how outgroup members will treat them.

Perceiving others as members of another group, rather than as members of one's own group or as unique individuals, also has a systematic effect on affective responses (see Gaertner & Dovidio, 2000). In part as a result of heightened vigilance and negative expectations (Plant, Butz, & Tartakovsky, 2008), intergroup interactions are characterized by much higher levels of anxiety than are exchanges between members of the same group (Stephan & Stephan, 1985,

2000). Within the United States, interethnic contact, in particular, is often marred by anxiety and distrust (Dovidio et al., 2002; Plant & Butz, 2006), and thus both Whites and Blacks experience heightened anxiety in interracial compared to intraracial interactions but for somewhat different reasons. Whites' anxiety seems to be related to increased cognitive demands associated with not wanting to appear biased (Dovidio & Gaertner, 2004; Richeson & Shelton, 2003; Richeson & Trawalter, 2005). In contrast, Blacks' anxiety seems to be related to vigilance in detecting bias (Vorauer, 2006) and efforts to cope with anticipated prejudice and discrimination (Hyers & Swim, 1998). Feelings of anxiety in anticipation of an interaction, in turn, motivate members of both majority and minority groups to avoid intergroup interaction (Plant, 2004; Plant & Butz, 2006).

When members of different groups do interact, their biases take on a dynamic nature during the exchange. These biases shape individuals' own behaviors as well as their perceptions of their partners' behavior, which can in turn influence their partners' perceptions of them. As a consequence, interracial interactions are not only characterized by a higher level of anxiety than intraracial interactions, but individuals also tend to make more negative attributions to their partners' anxiety during interracial encounters (West, Shelton, & Trail, 2009). In mixed-race interactions, for example, interactants tend to make attributions that support their negative expectations of intergroup relations (Shelton & Richeson, 2005). Whereas both Whites and Blacks attribute nonverbal cues related to high levels of anxiety (e.g., self-touch, inconsistent gaze, closed posture) as mere indications of anxiety when displayed by a person of the same race, these behaviors are also interpreted as unfriendliness when demonstrated by a member of the other race. Thus, both Blacks and Whites tend to conflate cues of anxiety with indications of dislike, but only when the other person is of a different race. Moreover, intergroup interactions are more fragile and easily disrupted than intragroup interactions. Even minor hesitancies and disruptions in an intergroup interaction can lead to reciprocally negative interpretations of the other group member's behaviors (Pearson et al., 2008), thus reinforcing negative group relations more generally.

Interventions that alter people's expectations as they enter intergroup interactions can improve initial contact experiences. For instance, inducing members of different groups to attend to their similarities rather than to their (assumed) dissimilarities produces smoother and more favorable initial interactions between members of different races (Mallett, Wilson, & Gilbert, 2008). In addition, reminding people of personal experiences in which intergroup contact went better than they expected leads individuals to be more relaxed in intergroup interactions and to anticipate more positive responses from members of other groups while producing more satisfying interactions with outgroup members generally and increasing motivation to engage in cross-group contact in the future (Mallett & Wilson, 2010).

IMPROVING INTERGROUP RELATIONS

Because categorization is a basic process that lies at the foundation of intergroup bias, some contemporary work has targeted this process as a starting point for reducing intergroup bias. This work also considers the functional relations among groups. In this section we explore how the forces of categorization can be disarmed or rerouted to promote more positive intergroup attitudes—and potentially to begin to penetrate the barriers to reconciliation among groups with a history of antagonistic relations. One of the most influential strategies to this end involves initiating and structuring intergroup contact.

For over fifty years, *contact theory* (Allport 1954; Williams, 1947; see also Dovidio, Gaertner, & Kawakami, 2003; Pettigrew, 1998) has represented one of psychology's most effective strategies for reducing bias and improving intergroup relations. This framework proposes that simple contact between groups is not sufficient to improve intergroup relations but that it is possible to structure intergroup contact in specific ways to ameliorate prejudice and conflict. In his reformulation of the *contact hypothesis*, Allport (1954) integrated and refined a range of ideas and evidence from different disciplines to identify when contact most effectively reduces intergroup bias. Allport's contact hypothesis included four requisites for contact to be successful in reducing conflict and achieving intergroup harmony: equal status within the contact situation, intergroup cooperation, common goals, and the support of authorities, law, or custom. Since then, two other aspects of contact—opportunities for personal acquaintance between members of different groups (particularly involving non-stereotypic elements) and intergroup friendships—have been identified as important (Pettigrew, 1997, 1998).

Moreover, research on extended contact demonstrates that simply learning that other ingroup members have outgroup friends can improve attitudes toward the outgroup as a whole and reduce intergroup bias (Wright, Aron, McLaughlin-Volpe, & Ropp, 1997). In a laboratory simulation of the Sherif et al. (1961) Robbers Cave studies, two groups of seven participants engaged in a series of competitive tasks (Wright et al., 1997). As expected, competition created conflict and negative intergroup attitudes. However, in the second part of the session, one person from each group participated in friendship-building exercises and then returned to his/her group. For the remaining participants, simply learning that a member of their group had become friends with a member of the other group was sufficient enough to reduce intergroup tension and improve intergroup attitudes.

Since Allport (1954), contact theory has stimulated extensive empirical work. Both laboratory and field research have yielded substantial documentation of improvement in intergroup relations when the six criteria outlined above have been met. In a review of 203 studies from 25 countries involving 90,000 participants, Pettigrew and Tropp (2000) found that 94% of studies supported the contact hypothesis. Pettigrew and Tropp (2006) also provided an extensive meta-analysis of 515 studies involving 713 independent samples conducted in a variety of intergroup contexts that tested the effects of intergroup contact on attitudes. Their findings demonstrate that intergroup contact indeed reduces intergroup prejudice. Furthermore, they found that the beneficial effect of contact was greater when Allport's optimal conditions were present in the contact situation than when they were not (see also Pettigrew & Tropp, 2008).

Although category-based responses are a cognitive "default," people engage in more individuating processes when they are in interdependent relationships with members of other groups or are motivated to form accurate impressions of them (Fiske, 1998, 2000). Moreover, the many social groups to which people belong are often hierarchically organized, with higher-level categories (e.g., nations) more inclusive of lower-level ones (e.g., cities). Modifying either the functional relationship between groups or an interactant's goals, motives, and expectations can alter the level of category inclusiveness that will dominate in a particular context (Brewer, 1988; Fiske et al., 1999). This malleability of social categorization and, consequently, of social identity is important because of its implications for altering the ways that people think about members of other groups and, accordingly, how positively they feel about them.

Researchers have proposed a number of different approaches to structuring group contact in order to reduce bias. Although various models share theoretical assumptions about the importance of social categorization and identity in intergroup relations, they each present different strategies for reducing bias and conflict. Three prominent category-based approaches are *decategorization*, *mutual differentiation* between groups, and *recategorization*. Decategorization refers to influencing people to identify themselves primarily as distinct individuals rather than as members of a group (Brewer & Miller, 1984; Miller, 2002; Wilder, 1986). Mutual intergroup differentiation limits threats to valued social identity (Jetten, Spears, & Postmes, 2004) by maintaining distinct group identities within the context of positive interdependence between groups (Brown & Hewstone, 2005). Recategorization, like decategorization, is designed to alter group boundaries but by redefining, rather than by eliminating, group categorization (Gaertner & Dovidio, 2000, 2009).

The goal of decategorization (Wilder, 1986) is to weaken the salience of group boundaries. Specifically, decategorization interventions encourage people from different groups to regard one another primarily as distinct individuals and to relate to one another interpersonally (i.e., "me" and "you") rather than in a group-based (i.e., "us" and "them") mode. The decategorization strategy of crisscrossing category memberships by forming new subgroups, each composed of members of the original groups (i.e., "we"), changes the pattern of who is "in" and who is "out." Cross-categorization strategies have proven to be effective at reducing biases that occur when people categorize others only as members of an outgroup (Crisp, Ensari, Hewstone, & Miller, 2003; Crisp & Hewstone, 2006) in part by rendering the original categorization less salient. That is, when the original categories are perceived to be less relevant to the current interaction, people tend to see others in a more individualized way rather than primarily as an outgroup member. Decategorization reduces intergroup bias not only by improving attitudes toward others previously seen primarily in terms of their outgroup membership but also by producing less favorable responses to people formerly perceived in terms of their membership in the ingroup (Gaertner, Mann, Murrell, & Dovidio, 1989). Another decategorization strategy is personalized interactions, interactions involving the exchange of information about individuals' unique qualities, which further reduces intergroup bias by undermining the perceived validity of outgroup stereotypes (Brewer & Miller, 1984; Miller, 2002).

Although there are similarities between perceiving others in a decategorized way (i.e., as separate individuals) and having personalized interactions with outgroup members, decategorization and personalization are theoretically distinct concepts. Most notably, decategorization involves perceiving outgroup members (see Wilder, 1986) or members of both groups as individuals and can promote individuated responses even in the absence of interaction or information exchange. For example, receiving information demonstrating variability in the opinions of outgroup members or seeing outgroup members respond as individuals, rather than as a group, renders each member more distinctive, potentially blurring the prior social categorization scheme (Wilder, 1986).

Brewer and Miller (1984; Miller, 2002), however, distinguish the process of *personalization,* which involves receiving self-relevant information about outgroup members, from decategorization. Personalization involves perceiving outgroup members in a more individuated and differentiated way but further focuses on the impact of personally-relevant information. With personalization, an individual's characteristics, rather than his or her group membership, become primarily salient. Personalized impressions can thereby undermine group stereotypes as a source of information about members of the outgroup (Brewer & Miller, 1984; Miller, 2002), producing more positive attitudes toward the group as a whole. Consistent with this reasoning, greater self-disclosure in intergroup contact relates to more positive intergroup attitudes and increased perceptions of the outgroup as heterogeneous (Turner, Hewstone, & Voci, 2007). Nevertheless, Miller (2002) observed that "if personalized information-processing means that information concerning social category membership lacks any salience during the interaction, whatever information and/or affect was acquired cannot generalize to other members of the category... A key point, however, is that in most contact situations ... cues providing information about the category identity of the interacting persons are constantly present" (p. 399). Thus, for personalized contact to prove beneficial and group stereotypes to be weakened, outgroup members' group identities must be somewhat salient, though not primarily so, during the interaction (Brewer & Miller, 1984; Miller, 2002).

Whereas decategorization is designed to degrade group boundaries entirely and personalization attempts to make group membership secondary to interpersonal connection, the *mutual intergroup differentiation model* allows group boundaries to be fully maintained. This alternative framework acknowledges the difficulty of eliminating perceptions of group identity. Rather, the model focuses on changing perceptions of the relationship between groups from competitive to cooperative, all the while emphasizing the positive distinctiveness of each group.

Noting that interventions that threaten the integrity of collective identity can arouse resistance and exacerbate bias, Hewstone and Brown (1986) introduced the mutual intergroup differentiation model. Relative to decategorization strategies, this perspective proposes that maintaining group distinctiveness within a cooperative intergroup relationship will be associated with low levels of intergroup threat and, consequently, with lower levels of intergroup bias. In addition, intergroup boundary salience provides an associative mechanism through which positive changes in outgroup attitudes that occur during contact can generalize to the outgroup as a whole. Because the most recent research has focused on the hypothesis that contact that makes different category memberships salient is most effective for reducing bias, Brown and Hewstone (2005) no longer refer to their approach as the mutual intergroup differentiation model but now label it simply as *intergroup contact theory*.

Intergroup contact theory posits that opportunities for intergroup contact (i.e., quantity of contact) are important because they increase the possibility of forming close friendships with outgroup members (i.e., quality of contact). The salience of a friend's outgroup membership and the perceived typicality of a friend as a member of that group moderate the amount of anxiety experienced with other members of the group and perspective-taking of and empathy for the outgroup as a whole. Lower intergroup anxiety and greater cognitive and affective empathy, in turn, mediate more positive attitudes toward the outgroup. In support of mutual intergroup differentiation/intergroup contact theory, several studies have demonstrated that positive contact produces more generalized reductions in bias toward the outgroup when people focus on the intergroup, rather than the interpersonal, nature of the interaction (Kenworthy, Turner, Hewstone, & Voci, 2005; Pettigrew, 1998).

Brown and Hewstone (2005) further propose that beyond the salience of social categories, the perceived typicality of outgroup members is a critical moderator of the extent to which intergroup contact can reduce bias toward the outgroup as a whole. Consistent with this proposition (see also Rothbart & John, 1985), the more representative or prototypical of his or her group a person is perceived to be, the greater the likelihood that impressions of that person will generalize to and change perceptions of the entire outgroup (Rothbart & Lewis, 1988; Wilder, Simon, & Faith, 1996). Despite the fact that people tend to make stronger generalizations from an individual to a group for stereotype-consistent than stereotype-inconsistent impressions (Johnson, Ashburn-Nardo, Spicer, & Dovidio, 2008), perceived typicality plays an important role in changing group stereotypes.

Whereas decategorization/personalization focuses on tempering social categorization and mutual intergroup differentiation/intergroup contact theory emphasizes the importance of maintaining distinctive social identities, a third approach, the *common ingroup identity model* (Gaertner & Dovidio, 2000,

2009), posits the value of recategorization, the creation of a shared superordinate identity for members of different groups.

Central to the common ingroup identity model is the idea that inducing members of different groups to recategorize themselves as members of the same, all-inclusive ingroup can reduce intergroup bias via cognitive and motivational processes involving ingroup favoritism (Gaertner & Dovidio, 2000, 2009). Recategorization changes the conceptual representations of the different groups from an "us" versus "them" orientation to a more encompassing, superordinate "we" connection. Creating a common ingroup identity redirects the positive beliefs, feelings, and behaviors that are usually reserved for ingroup members and extends them to former outgroup members.

Different types of intergroup interdependence and cognitive, perceptual, linguistic, affective, and environmental factors can either independently or in concert alter individuals' cognitive representations of the aggregate pool of recategorized individuals. Included among the different factors that can increase the perception of a common ingroup identity are the features specified by Allport's (1954) contact hypothesis, such as cooperative interdependence and common fate. In addition, common ingroup identity may be achieved by increasing the salience of existing shared superordinate memberships (e.g., a school, a company, a nation) or categories (e.g., students; Gómez, Dovidio, Huici, Gaertner, & Cuardrado, 2008) or by introducing factors (e.g., common goals or fate; see Gaertner et al., 1999) that are perceived as shared by the original social groups.

Recategorization as a common ingroup can promote intergroup forgiveness and trust. For instance, increasing the salience of Jewish students' "human identity," in contrast to their "Jewish identity," increases their perceptions of similarity with Germans, willingness to forgive Germans for the Holocaust, and interest in associating with German students (Wohl & Branscombe, 2005). A shared superordinate identity also affects interest in and responsiveness to others. People are more accepting of a newcomer's innovation when the newcomer shares a superordinate identity with them than when the newcomer does not (Kane, Argote, & Levine, 2005). In addition, across a range of situations, people are more responsive to the needs of former outgroup members who are currently categorized within a common ingroup (Dovidio et al., 1997; Levine, Prosser, Evans, & Reicher, 2005).

The successful induction of a common ingroup identity does not necessarily eliminate social biases; it may primarily redirect them instead. When recategorization occurs and a superordinate group identity is established, other outgroups at the new level of inclusiveness are likely to be recognized as relevant comparison groups. Because of the need to establish, maintain, or enhance the positive distinctiveness of the new superordinate identity, biases toward these outgroups are likely to arise (Mummendey, Klink, & Brown, 2001). For example, consistent with the common ingroup identity model, East Germans who recategorized West and East Germans within the superordinate identity of "Germans" displayed reduced bias toward West Germans relative to those who continued to categorize on the East-West dimension. However, over time, they also became more biased toward members of other countries (Kessler & Mummendey, 2001). Thus, "recategorization is a 2-edged process: although it reduces conflict at the subgroup level, it may initiate conflict at the common ingroup level" (Kessler & Mummendey, 2001, p. 1099).

The development of a common ingroup identity does not necessarily require each group to forsake its original, less inclusive group identity. Depending on their degree of identification with the different categories and contextual factors that make particular identities salient, individuals may activate two or more of their multiple social identities simultaneously (Roccas & Brewer, 2002) or sequentially (Turner, 1985). As depicted by the dual identity representation of subgroups within one group, people can conceive of two groups (e.g., science and art majors) as distinct units within the context of a superordinate social entity (e.g., university students).

There is evidence that the intergroup benefits of a strong superordinate identity can be achieved for both majority and minority group members when the strength of the subordinate identity is high (Gaertner, Rust, Dovidio, Bachman, & Anastasio, 1996; Huo & Molina 2006; Huo, Smith, Tyler, & Lind, 1996; Smith & Tyler, 1996). These findings are also conceptually consistent with studies that reveal that interethnic attitudes are more favorable when participants are primed with a multicultural, pluralistic ideology that emphasizes the value of a dual identity for increasing harmony, relative to an assimilative ideology, which closely parallels a one-group representation (Richeson & Nussbaum, 2004). Moreover, with a dual identity, the benefits of intergroup contact may more easily generalize to additional outgroup members because the associative link to the original outgroup remains intact, as suggested by mutual intergroup differentiation/intergroup contact theory.

Each of these models has its challenges. However, rather than viewing decategorization, mutual intergroup differentiation, and recategorization as competing perspectives, researchers have recognized that the processes identified in these models may operate in a complementary fashion to reduce intergroup bias in a more general and sustained way (Gaertner & Dovidio, 2000; Hewstone, 1996; Pettigrew, 1998). For example, the favorable impressions of and orientations toward outgroup members elicited by recategorization within a common ingroup identity are not likely to be finely differentiated, at least initially (see Boldry et al., 2007), from the effects of other bias-reduction approaches. Rather, these more elaborate, personalized impressions can quickly develop within the context of a common identity because the newly formed *positivity bias* is likely to encourage a more openly communicative and self-disclosing interaction between former ingroup and outgroup members (see Dovidio et al., 1997). Thus, over time, a common identity can encourage personalization of outgroup members, which further reduces bias through decategorization.

The ongoing nature of the intergroup relationship likely influences how these different processes interrelate. For instance, when relations are highly antagonistic, attempts to form a common ingroup identity through recategorization are likely to be futile and may further increase bias because of identity threat. Under these conditions, decategorization may be the most productive initial step (Pettigrew, 1998). Thus, it is hoped that future research will incorporate these basic principles and processes into a range of different contact situations and explore how the effectiveness of different sequences is determined by the nature of existing intergroup relations.

SUMMARY AND FUTURE DIRECTIONS

In this chapter, we have addressed the psychological processes underlying intergroup relations. Social categorization is a fundamental human process that lies at the heart of these relations and is the foundation of ingroup-outgroup distinctions, which create marked psychological, behavioral, and material disparities between "us" and "them." When individuals' social versus self-identity is activated, they perceive themselves in group-prototypic ways and are motivated by group values and interests. The need to view one's group as positively distinctive from other groups often motivates intergroup competition, bias, and discrimination. Group competition, in turn, increases ingroup identification and solidarity and exacerbates intergroup bias.

Understanding intergroup relations requires more than identifying the cause of bias of one group toward another—it is also important to consider how the targets of bias recognize or respond to unfair treatment. When unfair group-based treatment is apparent and individual mobility is limited, group members—particularly those highly identified with the group—are likely to engage in collective action to improve the group's standing. One main consequence of this action is intergroup conflict. Groups higher in status and power are highly motivated to defend their advantage. However, oftentimes, because this advantage is obscured or legitimized by cultural ideologies or historical narratives, members of disadvantaged groups fail to recognize the unfairness of their disadvantage. Disadvantaged group members may also actively endorse system-justifying ideologies that reinforce the status quo of intergroup relations.

A full appreciation of intergroup relations also requires study of the dynamics between members of different groups during interactions. People enter into intergroup interactions with greater wariness and higher levels of anxiety than they do for intragroup interactions. They are also more likely to misattribute the behaviors of members of other groups in negative ways. Overall, interactions between members of different groups are more fragile and tense than are interactions between members of the same group. Nevertheless, under certain conditions, such as those specified by contact theory, intergroup interaction can not only be quite positive but also critical for improving intergroup attitudes and relations. Frequent and positive intergroup contact is one of the most potent interventions for improving intergroup relations.

A number of theoretical models that attempt to explain why intergroup contact improves intergroup attitudes target categorical representations and the functional relations between groups as central processes for reducing intergroup bias. The three category-based models considered above—decategorization, mutual intergroup differentiation, and recategorization—expand on contact theory and account for the widely-demonstrated beneficial effects of contact through processes of weakening social categorization, recognizing different group memberships within cooperative functional relations, and emphasizing common group membership, respectively. These processes can operate in a complementary fashion over time and successively during different stages of intergroup relationships to promote harmonious intergroup relations.

Despite the vast literature on intergroup relations, both conflictual and cooperative, there are several potentially productive and important directions for future research in this area. We offer two examples. First, despite the importance of intergroup friendships for improving intergroup relations in general (Pettigrew, 1997; Wright et al., 1997), to date there has been limited research examining intergroup friendship formation, specifically the processes that critically shape friendship development across group lines, and how these processes may differ from those underlying intragroup friendship formation. The studies that do exist in this area (see West & Dovidio, 2010, for a review) reveal that interracial dyads in sustained interaction (i.e., college roommates) display more negative trajectories of friendship formation over time than do dyads composed of members of the same racial or ethnic group. However, these effects can be moderated by individual-difference or situational factors. Concerns about appearing prejudiced have a detrimental effect on intergroup roommate relations over time (Shelton, West, & Trail, 2010), while perceptions of different groups belonging to a common superordinate identity promote friendship between cross-race roommate pairs (West, Pearson, Dovidio, Shelton, & Trail, 2009). Future research might productively further consider the types of characteristics, situational influences, and emergent properties of the interactions that shape the ways in which intergroup friendships develop and influence intergroup relations more generally.

Second, future research might further investigate the role of group status and power on group needs and motivations and their influence on intergroup interactions, outcomes, and ultimately relations. In general, groups low in power are motivated to achieve greater power and status, whereas groups high in power are motivated to support the structural status quo, which sustains their advantage. As a consequence, members of low-power groups are motivated during intergroup interactions to be respected and empowered, whereas members of high-power groups are motivated to be liked and accepted (Fiske, Harris, Russell, & Shelton, 2009; Shnabel, Nadler, Ullrich, Dovidio, & Carmi, 2009). Thus, interventions that reduce prejudice and promote intergroup harmony by diverting attention away from group-based inequalities may meet the immediate needs of members of high-power groups to be liked but may not translate to enduring efforts to challenge the *status quo* to create structural social change (see Dovidio, Gaertner, & Saguy, 2009).

Consistent with this perspective, Dixon, Durrheim, and Tredoux (2005, 2007) describe the "principle-implementation gap" in which positive intergroup contact is more likely to improve intergroup attitudes than it is to motivate support for social change. Consequently, Dixon et al. have questioned the traditional focus of social psychological research on intergroup attitudes as the ultimate measure of positive intergroup relations without adequate attention to the impact of attitudes on actual structural change toward equality. Dixon et al. "accept that contact may transform interpersonal attitudes and stereotypes, but caution that it may leave unaltered the ideological beliefs that sustain systems of racial discrimination" (Dixon et al., 2007, p. 868). Thus, future research on intergroup relations needs to go beyond the current emphasis on social attitudes to consider evidence for social action as well.

In conclusion, because people are essentially social animals, group membership and intergroup relations have a substantial effect on people's identities, values, needs, and motivations. Many basic psychological processes converge to make intergroup relations competitive and conflictual, but intergroup conflict is not inevitable nor is it the most desirable outcome for anyone involved. If they are properly understood, the processes that lead to intergroup tensions can be redirected to promote stable and harmonious intergroup relations.

ACKNOWLEDGMENTS

Preparation of this chapter was supported by NSF Grant # BCS-0613218 awarded to the first two authors and Spencer Grant #200900193 awarded to the first author.

REFERENCES

Allport, G. W. (1954). *The nature of prejudice.* Cambridge, MA: Addison-Wesley.

Bettencourt, B. A., Dorr, N., Charlton, K., & Hume, D. L. (2001). Status differences and in-group bias: A meta-analytic examination of the effects of status stability, status legitimacy, and group permeability. *Psychological Bulletin, 127,* 520–542.

Blumer, H. (1958). Race prejudice as a sense of group position. *Pacific Sociological Review, 1,* 3–7.

Bobo, L. D. (1999). Prejudice as group position: Microfoundations of a sociological approach to racism and race relations. *Journal of Social Issues, 55,* 445–472.

Boldry, J. G., Gaertner, L., & Quinn, J. (2007). Measuring the measures: A meta-analytic investigation of the measures of outgroup homogeneity. *Group Processes and Intergroup Relations, 10,* 147–178.

Brewer, M. B. (1988). A dual process model of impression formation. In T. S. Srull & R. S. Wyer (Eds.), *Advances in social cognition: Vol. I. A dual process model of impression formation* (pp. 1–36). Hillsdale, NJ: Erlbaum.

Brewer, M. B. (1991). On the social self: On being the same and different at the same time. *Personality and Social Psychology Bulletin, 17,* 475–482.

Brewer, M. B., & Miller, N. (1984). Beyond the contact hypothesis: Theoretical perspectives on desegregation. In N. Miller & M. B. Brewer (Eds.), *Groups in contact: The psychology of desegregation* (pp. 281–302). Orlando, FL: Academic Press.

Brown, R., & Hewstone, M. (2005). An integrative theory of intergroup contact. In M. P. Zanna (Ed.), *Advances in experimental social psychology* (Vol. 37, pp. 255–343). San Diego, CA: Academic Press.

Campbell, D. T. (1958). Common fate, similarity and other indices of the status of aggregates of persons as social entities. *Behavioral Science, 3,* 14–25.

Campbell, D. T. (1965). Ethnocentric and other altruistic motives. In D. Levine (Ed.), *Nebraska symposium on motivation* (Vol. 13, pp. 283–311). Lincoln, NE: University of Nebraska Press.

Castelli, L., Tomelleri, S., & Zogmaister, C. (2008). Implicit ingroup metafavoritism: Subtle preference for ingroup members displaying ingroup bias. *Personality and Social Psychology Bulletin, 34,* 807–818.

Crisp, R. J., Ensari, N., Hewstone, M., & Miller, N. (2003). A dual-route model of crossed categorization effects. In W. Stroebe & M. Hewstone (Eds.), *European review of social psychology* (Vol. 13, pp. 35–73). Hove, UK: Psychology Press.

Crisp, R. J., & Hewstone, M. (2006) (Eds.). *Multiple social categorization: Processes, models, and applications.* Philadelphia, PA: Psychology Press.

Crosby, F. J. (1984). The denial of personal discrimination. *American Behavioral Scientist, 27,* 371–386.

Demoulin, S., Leyens, J-P, & Dovidio, J. F. (Eds.). (2009). *Intergroup misunderstandings: Impact of divergent social realities.* New York, NY: Psychology Press.

Dixon, J. A., Durrheim, K., & Tredoux, C. (2005). Beyond the optimal strategy: A "reality check" for the contact hypothesis. *American Psychologist, 60,* 697–711.

Dixon, J. A., Durrheim, K., & Tredoux, C. (2007). Intergroup contact and attitudes toward the principle and practice of racial equality. *Psychological Science, 18,* 867–872.

Dovidio, J. F., & Gaertner, S. L. (2004). Aversive racism. In M. P. Zanna (Ed.), *Advances in experimental social psychology* (Vol. 36, pp. 1–51). San Diego, CA: Academic Press.

Dovidio, J. F., & Gaertner, S. L. (2010). Intergroup bias. In S. T. Fiske, D. Gilbert, & G. Lindzey (Eds.), *Handbook of social psychology* (Vol. 2, pp. 1084–1121). New York, NY: Wiley.

Dovidio, J. F., Gaertner, S. L., & Kawakami, K. (2003). The Contact Hypothesis: The past, present, and the future. *Group Processes and Intergroup Relations, 6,* 5–21.

Dovidio, J. F., Gaertner, S. L., & Saguy, T. (2009). Commonality and the complexity of "we": Social attitudes and social change. *Personality and Social Psychology Review, 13,* 3–20.

Dovidio, J. F., Gaertner, S. L., Kawakami, K., & Hodson, G. (2002). Why can't we just get along? Interpersonal biases and interracial distrust. *Cultural Diversity and Ethnic Minority Psychology, 8,* 88–102.

Dovidio, J. F., Gaertner, S. L., Validzic, A., Matoka, K., Johnson, B., & Frazier, S. (1997). Extending the benefits of re-categorization: Evaluations, self-disclosure and helping. *Journal of Experimental Social Psychology, 33,* 401–420.

Ellemers, N., & Barreto, M. (2001). The impact of relative group status: Affective, behavioral, and perceptual consequences. In R. Brown & S. L. Gaertner (Eds.), *Blackwell handbook of social psychology: Intergroup processes* (pp. 324–343). Oxford, UK: Blackwell.

Esses, V. M., Dovidio, J. F., Jackson, L. M., & Armstrong, T. M. (2001). The immigration dilemma: The role of perceived group competition, ethnic prejudice, and national identity. *Journal of Social Issue, 57,* 389–412.

Esses, V. M., Jackson, L. M., & Armstrong, T. L. (1998). Intergroup competition and attitudes toward immigrants and immigration: An instrumental model of group conflict. *Journal of Social Issues, 54,* 699–724.

Esses, V. M., Jackson, L. M., Dovidio, J. F., & Hodson, G. (2005). Instrumental relations among groups: Group competition, conflict, and prejudice. In J. F. Dovidio, P. Glick, & L. A. Rudman (Eds.), *On the nature of prejudice: Fifty years after Allport* (pp. 227–243). Malden, MA: Blackwell.

Fiske, S. T. (1998). Stereotyping, prejudice, and discrimination. In D. T. Gilbert, S. T. Fiske, & G. Lindzey (Eds.), *The handbook of social psychology* (Vol. 2, 4th ed., pp. 357–411). New York, NY: McGraw-Hill.

Fiske, S. T. (2000). Interdependence and the reduction of prejudice. In S. Oskamp (Ed.), *Reducing prejudice and discrimination* (pp. 115–135). Hillsdale, NJ: Erlbaum.

Fiske, S. T., Harris, L. T., Russell, A. M., & Shelton, J. N. (2009). Divergent social realities: Depending on where you sit: Perspectives from the stereotype content model. In S. Demoulin, J. P. Leyens, & J. F. Dovidio (Eds.), *Intergroup misunderstandings: Impact of divergent social realities* (pp. 173–190). Philadelphia, PA: Psychology Press.

Fiske, S. T., Lin, M., & Neuberg, S. L. (1999). The continuum model: Ten years later. In S. Chaiken & Y. Trope (Eds.), *Dual process theories in social psychology* (pp. 231–254). New York, NY: Guilford.

Fiske, S. T., & Ruscher, J. B. (1993). Negative interdependence and prejudice: Whence the affect? In D. M. Mackie & D. L. Hamilton (Eds.), *Affect, cognition, and stereotyping: Interactive processes in group perception* (pp. 239–268). New York, NY: Academic Press.

Fiske, S. T., & Taylor, S. E. (2007). *Social cognition: From brains to culture.* New York, NY: McGraw-Hill.

Foddy, M., Platow, M. J., & Yamagishi, H. (2009). Group-based trust in strangers: The role of stereotypes and expectations. *Psychological Science, 20,* 419–422.

Gaertner, S. L., & Dovidio, J. F. (2000). *Reducing intergroup bias: The Common Ingroup Identity Model.* Philadelphia, PA: Psychology Press.

Gaertner, S. L., & Dovidio, J. F. (2009). A Common Ingroup Identity: A categorization-based approach for reducing intergroup bias. In T. Nelson (Ed.), *Handbook of prejudice* (pp. 489–506). New York NY: Psychology Press.

Gaertner, S. L., Dovidio, J. F., Rust, M. C., Nier, J., Banker, B., Ward, C. M., ... Houlette, M. (1999). Reducing intergroup bias: Elements of intergroup cooperation. *Journal of Personality and Social Psychology, 76,* 388–402.

Gaertner, S. L., Mann, J. A., Murrell, A. J., & Dovidio, J. F. (1989). Reduction of intergroup bias: The benefits of recategorization. *Journal of Personality and Social Psychology, 57,* 239–249.

Gaertner, S. L., Rust, M. C., Dovidio, J. F., Bachman, B. A., & Anastasio, P. A. (1996). The Contact Hypothesis: The role of a common ingroup identity on reducing intergroup bias among majority and minority group members. In J. L. Nye & A. M. Brower (Eds.), *What's social about social cognition?* (pp. 230–360). Newbury Park, CA: Sage.

Gómez, A., Dovidio, J. F., Huici, C., Gaertner, S. L., & Cuardrado, I. (2008). The other side of We: When outgroup members express common identity. *Personality and Social Psychology Bulletin, 34,* 1613–1626.

Gordijn, E. H., Wigboldus, D., & Yzerbyt, V. (2001). Emotional consequences of categorizing victims of negative outgroup behavior as ingroup or outgroup. *Group Processes and Intergroup Relations, 4,* 317–326.

Greenberg, J., Landau, M., Kosloff, S., & Solomon, S. (2009). How are dreams of death transcendence breed prejudice, stereotyping, and conflict: Terror management theory. In T. Nelson (Ed.), *Handbook of prejudice, stereotyping, and discrimination* (pp. 309–332). New York, NY: Psychology Press.

Henderson-King, E. I., & Nisbett, R. E. (1996). Anti-Black prejudice as a function of exposure to the negative behavior of a single Black person. *Journal of Personality and Social Psychology, 71,* 654–664.

Hewstone, M. (1990). The 'ultimate attribution error'? A review of the literature on intergroup causal attribution. *European Journal of Social Psychology, 20,* 311–335.

Hewstone, M. (1996). Contact and categorization: Social psychological interventions to change intergroup relations. In C. N. Macrae, C. Stangor, & M. Hewstone (Eds.), *Stereotypes and stereotyping* (pp. 323–368). New York, NY: Guilford.

Hewstone, M., & Brown, R. J. (1986). Contact is not enough: An intergroup perspective on the "Contact Hypothesis." In M. Hewstone & R. Brown (Eds.), *Contact and conflict in intergroup encounters* (pp. 1–44). Oxford, UK: Basil Blackwell.

Hogg, M. A. (1996). Social identity, self-categorization, and the small group. In E. H. Witte & J. H. Davis (Eds.), *Understanding group behavior: Vol. 2. Small group processes and interpersonal relations. Understanding group behavior* (pp. 227–253). Hillsdale, NJ: Erlbaum.

Hogg, M. A. (2010). Self-categorization theory. In J. M. Levine & M. A. Hogg (Eds.), *Encyclopedia of group processes & intergroup relations* (pp. 728–731). Los Angeles, CA: Sage.

Huo, Y. J., & Molina, L. E. (2006). Is pluralism a viable model of diversity? The benefits and limits of subgroup respect. *Group Processes and Intergroup Relations, 9,* 359–376.

Huo, Y. J., Smith, H. J., Tyler, T. R., & Lind, E. A. (1996). *Superordinate* identification, subgroup identification, and justice concerns: Is separatism the problem; is assimilation the answer? *Psychological Science, 7,* 40–45.

Hyers, L., & Swim, J. (1998). A comparison of the experiences of dominant and minority group members during an intergroup encounter. *Group Processes and Intergroup Relations, 1,* 143–163.

Jetten, J., Schmitt, M. T., Branscombe, N. R., & McKimmie, B. M. (2005). Suppressing the negative effect of devaluation on group identification: The role of intergroup differentiation and intragroup respect. *Journal of Experimental Social Psychology, 41,* 208–215.

Jetten, J., Spears, R., & Postmes, T. (2004). Intergroup distinctiveness and differentiation: A meta-analytic integration. *Journal of Personality and Social Psychology, 86,* 862–879.

Johnson, J. D., Ashburn-Nardo, L., Spicer, V., & Dovidio, J. F. (2008). The role of Blacks' discriminatory expectations in their prosocial orientations toward Whites. *Journal of Experimental Social Psychology, 44,* 1498–1505.

Jost, J. T., Banaji, M., & Nosek, B. A. (2004). A decade of System Justification Theory: Accumulated evidence of conscious and unconscious bolstering of the *status quo. Political Psychology, 25,* 881–919.

Jost, J. T., & Hamilton, D. L. (2005). Stereotypes in our culture. In J. F. Dovidio, P. Glick, & L. A. Rudman (Eds.), *On the nature of prejudice: Fifty years after Allport* (pp. 208–224). Malden, MA: Blackwell.

Jost, J. T., & Hunyady, O. (2002). System justification and the palliative function of ideology. *European Review of Social Psychology, 13,* 111–153.

Judd, C. M., Park, B., Ryan, C. S., Brauer, M., & Kraus, S. (1995). Stereotypes and ethnocentrism: Diverging interethnic perceptions of African American and White American youth. *Journal of Personality and Social Psychology, 69,* 460–481.

Judd, C. M., Park, B., Yzerbyt, V., Gordijn, E. H., & Muller, D. (2005). Attributions of intergroup bias and outgroup homogeneity to ingroup and outgroup others. *European Journal of Social Psychology, 35,* 677–704.

Kane, A. A., Argote, L., & Levine, J. M. (2005). Knowledge transfer between groups via personnel rotation: Effects of social identity and knowledge quality. *Organizational Behavior and Human Decision Processes, 96,* 56–71.

Kaiser, C. R., & Pratt-Hyatt, J. S. (2009). Distributing prejudice unequally: Do Whites direct their prejudice to strongly identified minorities? *Journal of Personality and Social Psychology, 96,* 432–445.

Kenworthy, J. B., Turner, R. N., Hewstone, M., & Voci, A. (2005). Intergroup contact: When does it work, and why? In J. F. Dovidio, P. Glick, & L. A. Rudman (Eds.), *On the nature of prejudice: Fifty years after Allport* (pp. 278–292). Malden, MA: Blackwell.

Kessler, T., & Mummendey, A. (2001). Is there any scapegoat around? Determinants of intergroup conflict at different categorization levels. *Journal of Personality and Social Psychology, 81,* 1090–1102.

Kramer, R. M., & Brewer, M. B. (1984). Effects of group identity on resource utilization in a simulated commons dilemma. *Journal of Personality and Social Psychology, 46,* 1044–1057.

Levine, M., Prosser, A. Evans, D., & Reicher, S. (2005). Identity and emergency intervention: How social group membership and inclusiveness of group boundaries shape helping behavior. *Personality and Social Psychology Bulletin, 31,* 443–453.

Maass, A., Salvi, D., Arcuri, L., & Semin, G. R. (1989). Language use in intergroup contexts: The linguistic intergroup bias. *Journal of Personality and Social Psychology, 57,* 981–993.

Major, B., & Sawyer, P. J. (2009). Attributions to discrimination: Antecedents and consequences. In. T. Nelson (Ed.), *Handbook of prejudice* (pp. 89–110). New York, NY: Psychology Press.

Mallett, R. K., & Wilson, T. D. (2010). Increasing positive intergroup contact. *Journal of Experimental Social Psychology, 46,* 382–387.

Mallett, R. K., Wilson, T. D., & Gilbert, D. T. (2008). Expect the unexpected: Failure to anticipate similarities when predicting the quality of an intergroup interaction. *Journal of Personality and Social Psychology, 94,* 265–277.

McPherson, S., &, Joireman, J. (2009). Death in groups: Mortality salience and the interindividual-intergroup discontinuity effect. *Group Processes & Intergroup Relations, 12,* 419–429.

Miller, N. (2002). Personalization and the promise of Contact Theory. *Journal of Social Issues, 58,* 387–410.

Mullen, B., Brown, R. J., & Smith, C. (1992). Ingroup bias as a function of salience, relevance, and status: An integration. *European Journal of Social Psychology, 22,* 103–122.

Mummendey, A., Klink, A., & Brown, R. (2001). Nationalism and patriotism: National identification and out-group rejection. *British Journal of Social Psychology, 40,* 159–172.

Otten, S., & Wentura, D. (1999). About the impact of automaticity in the minimal group paradigm: Evidence from affective priming tasks. *European Journal of Social Psychology, 29,* 1049–1071.

Paladino, M.-P., & Castelli, L. (2008). On the immediate consequences of ingroup categorization: Activation of approach and avoidance motor behavior toward ingroup and outgroup members. *Personality and Social Psychology Bulletin, 34,* 755–768.

Pascoe, E. A., & Richman, L. S. (2009). Perceived discrimination and health: A meta-analytic review. *Psychological Bulletin, 135,* 531–554.

Pearson, A. R., West, T. V., Dovidio, J. F., Powers, S. R., Buck, R., & Henning, R. (2008). The fragility of intergroup relations. *Psychological Science, 19,* 1272–1279.

Pettigrew, T. F. (1997). Generalized intergroup contact effects on prejudice. *Personality and Social Psychology Bulletin, 23,* 173–185.

Pettigrew, T. F. (1998). Intergroup Contact Theory. *Annual Review of Psychology, 49,* 65–85.

Pettigrew, T. F., & Tropp, L. R. (2000). Does intergroup contact reduce prejudice? Recent meta-analytic findings. In S. Oskamp (Ed.), *Reducing prejudice and discrimination* (pp. 93–114). Hillsdale, NJ: Erlbaum.

Pettigrew, T. F., & Tropp, L. (2006). A meta-analytic test of intergroup contact theory. *Journal of Personality and Social Psychology, 90,* 751–783.

Pettigrew, T. F., & Tropp, L. R. (2008). How does contact reduce prejudice? A meta-analytic test of three mediators. *European Journal of Social Psychology, 38,* 922–934.

Plant, E. A. (2004). Responses to interracial interactions over time. *Personality and Social Psychology Bulletin, 30,* 1458–1471.

Plant, E. A., & Butz, D. A. (2006). The causes and consequences of an avoidance-focus for interracial interactions. *Personality and Social Psychology Bulletin, 32,* 833–846.

Plant, E. A., Butz, D. A., & Tartakovsky, M. (2008). Interethnic interactions: Expectancies, emotions, and behavioral intentions. *Group Processes & Intergroup Relations, 11,* 555–574.

Rabbie, J. M., & Lodewijkx, H. F. M. (1996). A behavioral interaction model: Toward an integrative theoretical framework for studying intra- and intergroup dynamics. In E. H. Witte & J. H. Davis (Eds.), *Understanding group behavior: Vol. 2. Small group processes and interpersonal relations: Understanding group behavior* (pp. 255–294). Mahwah, NJ: Lawrence Erlbaum.

Richeson, J. A., & Nussbaum, R. J. (2004). The impact of multiculturalism versus color-blindness on racial bias. *Journal of Experimental Social Psychology 40,* 417–423.

Richeson, J., & Shelton, J. N. (2003). When prejudice does not pay: Effects of interracial contact on executive function. *Psychological Science, 14,* 287–290.

Richeson, J. A., & Shelton, J. N. (2010). Prejudice in intergroup dyadic interactions. In J. F. Dovidio, M. Hewstone, P. Glick, & V. M. Esses (Eds.), *Handbook of prejudice, stereotyping, and discrimination* (pp. 276–293). London, UK: Sage.

Richeson, J. A., & Trawalter, S. (2005). Why do interracial interactions impair executive function? A resource depletion account. *Journal of Personality and Social Psychology, 88,* 934–947.

Robbins, J. M., & Krueger, J. I. (2005). Social projection to ingroups and outgroups: A review and meta-analysis. *Personality and Social Psychology Review, 9,* 32–47.

Roccas, S., & Brewer, M. (2002). Social identity complexity. *Personality and Social Review, 6,* 88–106.

Rothbart, M., & John, O. P. (1985). Social categorization and behavioral episodes: A cognitive analysis of the effects of intergroup contact. *Journal of Social Issues, 41*(3), 81–104.

Rothbart, M., & Lewis, S. (1988). Inferring category attributes from exemplar attributes: Geometric shapes and social categories. *Journal of Personality and Social Psychology, 55*, 861–872.

Shelton, J. N., & Richeson, J. A. (2005). Intergroup contact and pluralistic ignorance. *Journal of Personality and Social Psychology, 88*, 91–107.

Shelton, J. N., West, T. V., & Trail, T. E. (2010). Concerns with appearing prejudiced: Implications for anxiety during daily interracial interactions. *Group Processes and Intergroup Relations, 13*, 329–344.

Sherif, M. (1966). *Group conflict and cooperation: Their social psychology.* London, UK: Routledge and Kegan Paul.

Sherif, M., Harvey, O. J., White, B. J., Hood, W. R., & Sherif, C. W. (1961). *Intergroup conflict and cooperation: The Robbers Cave experiment.* Norman, OK: University of Oklahoma Book Exchange.

Shnabel, N., Nadler, A., Ullrich, J., Dovidio, J. F., & Carmi, D. (2009). Promoting reconciliation through the satisfaction of the emotional needs of victimized and perpetrating group members: The Needs-Based Model of Reconciliation. *Personality and Social Psychology Bulletin, 35*, 1021–1030.

Shih, M., Pittinsky, T. L., & Ambady, N. (1999). Stereotype susceptibility: Identity salience and shifts in quantitative performance. *Psychological Science, 10*, 80–83.

Sidanius, J., & Pratto, F. (1999). *Social dominance: An intergroup theory of social hierarchy and oppression.* New York, NY: Cambridge University Press.

Smith, H. J., & Tyler, T. R. (1996). Justice and power: when will justice concerns encourage the advantaged to support policies which redistribute economic resources and the disadvantaged to willingly obey the law? *European Journal of Social Psychology 26*, 171–200.

Stephan, W. G., & Stephan, C. W. (1985). Intergroup anxiety. *Journal of Social Issues, 41*, 157–175.

Stephan, W. G., & Stephan C. W. (2000). An integrated threat theory of prejudice. In S. Oskamp (Ed.), *Reducing prejudice and discrimination* (pp. 23–45). Hillsdale, NJ: Erlbaum.

Stephan, W. G., Renfro, C. L., Esses, V. M., Steohan, C. W., & Martin, T. (2005). The effects of feeling threatened on attitudes toward immigrants. *International Journal of Intercultural Relations, 29*, 1–19.

Tajfel, H. (1969). Cognitive aspects of prejudice. *Journal of Social Issues, 25*(4), 79–97.

Tajfel, H., & Turner, J. C. (1979). An integrative theory of intergroup conflict. In W. G. Austin & S. Worchel (Eds.), *The social psychology of intergroup relations* (pp. 33–48). Monterey, CA: Brooks/Cole.

Taylor, D. M., & Moghaddam, F. M. (1994). *Theories of intergroup relations: International social psychological perspectives* (2nd ed.). Westport, CT: Praeger.

Turner, J. C. (1985). Social categorization and the self-concept: A social cognitive theory of group behavior. In E. J. Lawler (Ed.), *Advances in group processes* (Vol. 2, pp. 77–122). Greenwich, CT: JAI Press.

Turner, J. C., Hogg, M. A., Oakes, P. J., Reicher, S. D. , & Wetherell, M. S. (1987). *Rediscovering the social group: A self-categorization theory.* Oxford, UK: Basil Blackwell.

Turner, R. N., Hewstone, M., & Voci, A. (2007). Reducing explicit and implicit outgroup prejudice via direct and extended contact: The mediating role of self-disclosure and intergroup anxiety. *Journal of Personality and Social Psychology, 93*, 369–388.

van Zomeren, M., Postmes, T., & Spears, R. (2008). Toward an integrative social identity model of collective action: A quantitative research synthesis of three socio-psychological perspectives. *Psychological Bulletin, 134,* 504–535.

Verkuyten, M., & Hagendoorn, L. (1998). Prejudice and self-categorization: The variable role of authoritarianism and in-group stereotypes. *Personality and Social Psychology Bulletin, 24,* 99–110.

Voci, A. (2006). The link between identification and in-group favouritism: Effects of threat to social identity and trust-related emotions. *British Journal of Social Psychology, 45,* 265–284.

Vorauer, J. D. (2006). An information search model of evaluative concerns in intergroup interaction. *Psychological Review, 113,* 862–880.

Vorauer, J. D., & Kumhyr, S. M. (2001). Is this about you or me? Self- versus other-directed judgments and feelings in response to intergroup interaction. *Personality and Social Psychology Bulletin, 27,* 706–719.

West, T. V., & Dovidio, J. F. (in press). Intergroup contact across time: From initial contact to friendship. In G. Hodson & M. Hewstone (Eds.), *Advances in intergroup contact.* Malden, MA: Wiley-Blackwell.

West, T. V., Pearson, A. R., Dovidio, J. F., Shelton, J. N., & Trail. T. (2009). Superordinate identity and intergroup roommate friendship development. *Journal of Experimental Social Psychology, 45,* 1266–1272.

West, T. V., Shelton, J. N., & Trail, T. E. (2009). Relational anxiety in interracial interactions. *Psychological Science, 20,* 289–292.

Wilder, D. A. (1986). Social categorization: Implications for creation and reduction of intergroup bias. In L. Berkowitz (Ed.), *Advances in experimental social psychology* (Vol. 19, pp. 291–355). Orlando, FL: Academic Press.

Wilder, D. A., Simon, A. F., & Faith, M. (1996). Enhancing the impact of counterstereotypic information. Dispositional attributions for deviance. *Journal of Personality and Social Psychology, 71,* 276–287.

Wildschut, Y., & Insko, C. A. (2007). Explanations of interindividual-intergroup discontinuity: A review of the evidence. *European Review of Social Psychology, 18,* 175–211.

Williams, D. R., & Mohammed, S. A. (2009). Discrimination and racial disparities in health: Evidence and needed research. *Journal of Behavioral Medicine, 32,* 20–47.

Williams, R. M. Jr. (1947). *The reduction of intergroup tensions.* New York, NY: Social Science Research Council.

Wohl, M. J. A., & Branscombe, N. R. (2005). Forgiveness and collective guilt assignment to historical perpetrator groups depend on level of social category inclusiveness. *Journal of Personality and Social Psychology, 88,* 288–303.

Wright, S. C., Aron, A., McLaughlin-Volpe, T., & Ropp, S. A. (1997). The extended contact effect: Knowledge of cross-group friendships and prejudice. *Journal of Personality and Social Psychology, 73,* 73–90.

Wright, S. C., & Lubensky, M. E. (2009). The struggle for social equality: Collective action versus prejudice reduction. In S. Demoulin, J-P. Leyens, & J. F. Dovidio (Eds.), *Intergroup misunderstandings: Impact of divergent social realities* (pp. 291–310). New York, NY: Psychology Press.

Index